American Writers for Children Before 1900

Dictionary of Literary Biography

Documentary Series

Yearbooks

Dictionary of Literary Biography • Volume Forty-two

American Writers for Children

Before 1900

Edited by
Glenn E. Estes
University of Tennessee

A Bruccoli Clark Book
Gale Research Company • Book Tower • Detroit, Michigan 48226

Manufactured by Edwards Brothers, Inc.
Ann Arbor, Michigan
Printed in the United States of America

Library of Congress Cataloging-in-Publication Data
Main entry under title:

American writers for children before 1900.

(Dictionary of literary biography; v. 42)
"A Bruccoli Clark book."
Includes index.
1. Children's literature, American—History and
criticism. 2. Children's literature, American—Bio-
bibliography. 3. Authors, American—19th century—
Biography—Dictionaries. I. Estes, Glenn E.
II. Series.
PS490.A44 1985   810'.9'9282   85-15990
ISBN 0-8103-1720-6

To

Bette
Todd and Lane

Songs of thankfulness and praise,
Anthems be to you addressed.

with love and gratitude

Contents

Contents

Plan of the Series

. . . Almost the most prodigious asset of a country, and perhaps its most precious possession, is its native literary product—when that product is fine and noble and enduring.

Mark Twain*

The advisory board, the editors, and the publisher of the *Dictionary of Literary Biography* are joined in endorsing Mark Twain's declaration. The literature of a nation provides an inexhaustible resource of permanent worth. It is our expectation that this endeavor will make literature and its creators better understood and more accessible to students and the literate public, while satisfying the standards of teachers and scholars.

To meet these requirements, *literary biography* has been construed in terms of the author's achievement. The most important thing about a writer is his writing. Accordingly, the entries in *DLB* are career biographies, tracing the development of the author's canon and the evolution of his reputation.

The publication plan for *DLB* resulted from two years of preparation. The project was proposed to Bruccoli Clark by Frederick G. Ruffner, president of the Gale Research Company, in November 1975. After specimen entries were prepared and typeset, an advisory board was formed to refine the entry format and develop the series rationale. In meetings held during 1976, the publisher, series editors, and advisory board approved the scheme for a comprehensive biographical dictionary of persons who contributed to North American literature. Editorial work on the first volume began in January 1977, and it was published in 1978.

In order to make *DLB* more than a reference tool and to compile volumes that individually have claim to status as literary history, it was decided to organize volumes by topic or period or genre. Each of these freestanding volumes provides a biographical-bibliographical guide and overview for a particular area of literature. We are convinced that this organization—as opposed to a single alphabet method—constitutes a valuable innovation in the presentation of reference material. The volume plan necessarily requires many decisions for the placement and treatment of authors who might properly be included in two or three volumes. In some instances a major figure will be included in separate volumes, but with different entries emphasizing the aspect of his career appropriate to each volume. Ernest Hemingway, for example, is represented in *American Writers in Paris, 1920-1939* by an entry focusing on his expatriate apprenticeship; he is also in *American Novelists, 1910-1945* with an entry surveying his entire career. Each volume includes a cumulative index of subject authors. The final *DLB* volume will be a comprehensive index to the entire series.

With volume ten in 1982 it was decided to enlarge the scope of *DLB* beyond the literature of the United States. By the end of 1984 fourteen volumes treating British literature had been published, and volumes for Commonwealth and Modern European literature were in progress. The series has been further augmented by the *DLB Yearbooks* (since 1981) which update published entries and add new entries to keep the *DLB* current with contemporary activity. There have also been occasional *DLB Documentary Series* volumes which provide biographical and critical background source materials for figures whose work is judged to have particular interest for students. One of these companion volumes is entirely devoted to Tennessee Williams.

The purpose of *DLB* is not only to provide reliable information in a convenient format but also to place the figures in the larger perspective of literary history and to offer appraisals of their accomplishments by qualified scholars.

We define literature as the *intellectual commerce of a nation:* not merely as belles lettres, but as that ample and complex process by which ideas are generated, shaped, and transmitted. *DLB* entries are not limited to "creative writers" but extend to other figures who in this time and in this way influenced the mind of a people. Thus the series encompasses historians, journalists, publishers, and screenwriters. By this means readers of *DLB* may be aided to perceive literature not as cult scripture in the keeping of cultural high priests, but as at the center of a nation's life.

DLB includes the major writers appropriate to each volume and those standing in the ranks immediately behind them. Scholarly and critical counsel has been sought in deciding which minor figures to include and how full their entries should be. Wherever possible, useful references will be made to figures who do not warrant separate entries.

Each *DLB* volume has a volume editor responsible for planning the volume, selecting the figures for inclusion, and assigning the entries. Volume editors are also responsible for preparing, where appropriate, appendices surveying the major periodicals and literary and intellectual movements for their volumes, as well as lists of further readings. Work on the series as a whole is coordinated at the Bruccoli Clark editorial center in Columbia, South Carolina, where the editorial staff is responsible for the accuracy of the published volumes.

One feature that distinguishes *DLB* is the illustration policy—its concern with the iconography of literature. Just as an author is influenced by his surroundings, so is the reader's understanding of the author enhanced by a knowledge of his environment. Therefore *DLB* volumes include not only drawings, paintings, and photographs of authors, often depicting them at various stages in their careers, but also illustrations of their families and places where they lived. Title pages are regularly reproduced in facsimile along with dust jackets for modern authors. The dust jackets are a special feature of *DLB* because they often document better than anything else the way in which an author's work was launched in its own time. Specimens of the writers' manuscripts are included when feasible.

A supplement to *DLB*—tentatively titled *A Guide, Chronology, and Glossary for American Literature*—will outline the history of literature in North America and trace the influences that shaped it. This volume will provide a framework for the study of American literature by means of chronological tables, literary affiliation charts, glossarial entries, and concise surveys of the major movements. It has been planned to stand on its own as a vade mecum, providing a ready-reference guide to the study of American literature as well as a companion to the *DLB* volumes for American literature.

Samuel Johnson rightly decreed that "The chief glory of every people arises from its authors." The purpose of the *Dictionary of Literary Biography* is to compile literary history in the surest way available to us—by accurate and comprehensive treatment of the lives and work of those who contributed to it.

The *DLB* Advisory Board

*From an unpublished section of Mark Twain's autobiography, copyright © by the Mark Twain Company.

Foreword

A survey of American literature for children before 1900 begins with the seventeenth-century *New England Primer,* a work that spawned a school of thought which dominated children's books for more than one hundred and fifty years. *The New England Primer,* by example, underscored moral and religious instruction as the major purpose in writing for children, and this purpose prevailed until the mid-nineteenth century with few exceptions. In "The Early Record" (*Horn Book Magazine,* June 1971), Elizabeth Nesbitt states that "when an idea or theory reaches a point of absurdity, a reaction sets in, and the pendulum swings, usually to the opposite extreme. The resulting revolt may be partly good or partly bad, or wholly good or wholly bad." In the case of children's books, she adds, the reaction against literature with exclusively moralistic or religious themes "produced books of memorable quality and variety."

Reaction began in Europe as early as 1693 with John Locke's *Some Thoughts Concerning Education.* In 1744 London bookseller and publisher John Newbery, persuaded by Locke's idea that children be brought to pleasure in reading, opened a bookshop for children at 65 St. Paul's Church Yard. The stories he published dealt with the usual moral lessons of his time, but in a lighter, more childlike manner. Newbery covered his books with flowery Dutch papers and added woodcuts for visual enhancement. In addition to his stock of books, he offered balls, pincushions, games, and tops, which were often packaged with books as an enticement to young readers. His marketing devices most clearly reflected his departure from tradition. Rousseau's *Emile* (1762), which promoted the idea of raising children in a natural state removed from the corrupting influences of civilization, provoked another shift in educational thought, but didactic moralism prevailed. Revolution was inevitable, and Nesbitt cogently summarizes the factors that helped eventually to bring it about: "Integrated with the general rebellion against the excesses of the didactic era were several factors of importance: the realization that childhood is a way of life as well as an age of life; that a child is a being in his own right, and not a miniature adult; that as a child, he should not have the preoccupations of adults forced upon him, especially since to a child, most such preoccupations are unimportant and time wasting. And there was a long overdue recognition of the limitless value of the imagination and of the sense of wonder, which are the natural possessions of children until and unless they are atrophied by the unwise neglect or interference of adults."

The break with the tradition of *The New England Primer* was a long, slow process. During the two centuries prior to 1900, the polarity became increasingly clear between writing intended to instruct and writing intended for pleasure and delight. The critical biographies in this volume deal with authors whose works epitomize this dichotomy as well as those whose books sought to bridge the gap.

Benjamin Harris published his *New England Primer* sometime between 1687 and 1690. On the heels of the *Primer,* pirated editions and imitations of John Newbery's books, originally printed in England from 1740, provided a blend of instruction and entertainment for American children, but the underlying purpose of these publications was instruction.

Teaching was, of course, the primary aim of the various textbooks produced in eighteenth- and nineteenth-century America. *A Grammatical Institute of the English Language* (1783-1785), Noah Webster's three-volume speller/grammar/reader, had as its stated purpose "to refine and establish our language, to facilitate the acquisition of grammatical knowledge, and diffuse the principles of virtue and patriotism." Primers and readers by Caleb Bingham were widely used in American schools during the first quarter of the nineteenth century and served as a prelude to the Eclectic Readers of William Holmes McGuffey published in 1836 and 1837. These collections of passages selected from classic English and American literature, with questions to underscore the morals, became standard fare for the classroom. Their impact on the development of American culture and values has often been compared to that of the Bible.

Beginning in 1827 Samuel Griswold Goodrich wrote a series of instructional books under the pseudonym Peter Parley. Goodrich's purpose was to eliminate the British background from American children's books, and the informal, chatty style of the narrator-storyteller Parley led children through a study of history, biography, science, geography, and mythology. Although the simplicity, readability, and attractive design of Goodrich's books represented a break from traditional books of instruction, didacticism remained at the root of the series. Jacob Abbott began to produce his Rollo books in 1835; his first five Franconia stories appeared in 1850. These series, less pious and didactic than most other works of the time, were based on the author's observations and his understanding of the ways in which children's minds operated. Though guarded, Abbott's innovation was noteworthy, and critics have called him the first author to create realistic characters in American children's literature.

By the mid-nineteenth century, domestic novels and adventure stories dominated literature for children. Imaginative writing, long held in low esteem, emerged in works of fiction written to entertain but laced with touches of moral education. Susan Bogert Warner's *Wide, Wide World* (1850), Martha Finley's equally sentimental and lachrymose *Elsie Dinsmore* (1867), Maria Susanna Cummins's *The Lamplighter* (1854), and Augusta Jane Evans Wilson's *St. Elmo* (1867)—all great commercial successes—signaled this new approach to writing for girls. The realistic, sometimes sensational stories by William Taylor Adams (Oliver Optic), Horatio Alger, Jr., and Charles Austin Fosdick (Harry Castlemon) marked the change in writing for boys that continued in the works of James Otis Kaler and Kirk Munroe. Concurrently, the wide acceptance of English translations of the folktales of Jacob and Wilhelm Grimm and the literary fairy tales of Hans Christian Andersen gave evidence that a revolution was in progress which would culminate in the acceptance of imaginative writing for children by the close of the century.

Throughout the nineteenth century periodicals played an important role in the evolution and dissemination of literature for children. *Juvenile Miscellany* (1826-1836), *Youth's Companion* (1827-1929), *Our Young Folks* (1865-1873), *Riverside Magazine for Young People* (1867-1870), and *St. Nicholas* (1873-1940) provided opportunities for writers to test their effectiveness in communicating with children. The editors and associate editors of these periodicals promoted the work of new authors and contributed stories that added to the richness of imaginative writing for children as well as editorials that defended the child's right to read good, creative works. Among those who influenced the development of American literature for children through their editorial work were Sarah Josepha Hale, Louisa May Alcott, Hezekiah Butterworth, Horace E. Scudder, Mary Mapes Dodge, Kirk Munroe, and Frank R. Stockton.

The 1865 publication of Lewis Carroll's British classic *Alice's Adventures in Wonderland*, a book whose main purpose was to delight, marked the decisive break with the past and initiated a new direction in imaginative writing for children. Nesbitt summarizes: "the best writers of children's books all had something to say and they said it surpassingly well. But they did more than this. They permitted children to dance and to dream, to laugh and to cry, to stand in awe before the miracles of nature and before the greatness of man, to be challenged by the mystery of human destiny. In short, they protected and nourished the capacity for wonder inherent in children. This is their greatest gift, the most sustaining bequest any age can bestow upon its children."

Among the late-nineteenth-century books that "protected and nourished the capacity for wonder inherent in children" were Louisa May Alcott's *Little Women* (1868-1869), Frank R. Stockton's *The Bee-Man of Orn and Other Fanciful Tales* (1887), and Howard Pyle's *Otto of the Silver Hand* (1888) and *Men of Iron* (1892). The poetry of Laura E. Richards and Eugene Field and the illustrated volumes by Palmer Cox "permitted children to dance and to dream." Fanciful books by Charles E. Carryl, Frances Hodgson Burnett, and Lucretia Peabody Hale provoked laughter and tears and celebrated the greatness of humankind.

John Cech's *DLB 22, American Writers for Children, 1900-1960* (1983), covers the first six decades of the twentieth century in America, often known as "Childhood's Golden Era." The purpose of this volume, *American Writers for Children Before 1900*, is to trace the development of writing for children that led to this golden era. The writers in this volume are eighteenth- and nineteenth-century American children's authors who set trends or modified and refined the art of writing for children. Several of these writers bridge the nineteenth and twentieth centuries. They are treated here because their works reflect late-nineteenth-century trends which continued to influence writing during the early decades of the twentieth century. Subsequent volumes in the *Dictionary of Literary Biography* series will treat writers for children since 1960 who have continued the energetic and creative pursuits of their predecessors.

—Glenn E. Estes

Acknowledgments

This book was produced by BC Research. Karen L. Rood is senior editor for the *Dictionary of Literary Biography* series. Margaret A. Van Antwerp was the in-house editor.

Art supervisor is Patricia M. Flanagan. Copyediting supervisor is Patricia Coate. Typesetting supervisor is Laura Ingram. The production staff includes Rowena Betts, Kimberly Casey, Tara P. Deal, Kathleen M. Flanagan, Joyce Fowler, Pamela Haynes, Judith K. Ingle, Victoria Jakes, Vickie Lowers, Judith McCray, Jane McPherson, and Joycelyn R. Smith. Jean W. Ross is permissions editor. Joseph Caldwell, photography editor, did photographic copy work for the volume.

Walter W. Ross did the library research with the assistance of the staff at the Thomas Cooper Library of the University of South Carolina: Lynn Barron, Daniel Boice, Sue Collins, Michael Freeman, Gary Geer, Alexander M. Gilchrist, David L. Haggard, Jens Holley, David Lincove, Marcia Martin, Jean Rhyne, Karen Rissling, Paula Swope, and Ellen Tillett.

Special thanks are due Dr. Ruth Baldwin, who permitted access to the Baldwin Library at the University of Florida and gave generously of her time and energy to help assemble illustrative materials for this volume. Valuable assistance was also provided by Sam Gowan, University of Florida Libraries, and Paul Eugen Camp, University of South Florida Library.

This volume was initially developed by Professor John Cech of the University of Florida, who provided the editorial design for a group of *DLB* volumes devoted to American writers for children. *DLB 22, American Writers for Children, 1900-1960,* edited by Professor Cech, was published in 1983; complementary volumes are planned to include American writers for children since 1960. Professor Cech has developed the table of contents for the present volume, *DLB 42,* and assigned entries to the scholars whose work appears here.

The editor expresses his thanks to John Cech for his initial outline of the contents of this volume and his assignments to the contributors; to Marilyn H. Karrenbrock, Assistant Professor, University of Tennessee, for her introduction to Bruccoli Clark Inc. and the opportunity to become involved in this editorial project; and to Susanne King, his graduate assistant, and Lisa Welch, secretary, for their careful attention to every detail that supported the preparation of copy for this volume.

Dictionary of Literary Biography • Volume Forty-two

American Writers for Children Before 1900

Dictionary of Literary Biography

Jacob Abbott
(14 November 1803-31 October 1879)

Carol Gay
Youngstown State University

See also the Abbott entry in *DLB 1, The American Renaissance in New England.*

SELECTED BOOKS: *Conversations on the Bible,* as Erodore (Boston: Massachusetts Sabbath School Union, 1829);

The Young Christian; or, A Familiar Illustration of the Principles of Christian Duty (Boston: Peirce & Parker, 1832; revised and enlarged, New York: American Tract Society, 1832; London: Seeley, 1833);

The Corner-Stone; or, A Familiar Illustration of the Principles of Christian Truth (Boston: Peirce, 1834; London: Seeley, 1834);

The Little Scholar Learning to Talk. A Picture Book for Rollo (Boston: John Allen, 1835); republished as *Rollo Learning to Talk* (Boston: Weeks, Jordan, 1839);

Rollo Learning to Read; or, Easy Stories for Young Children (Boston: John Allen, 1835);

Rollo at Play, or Safe Amusements (Boston: Carter, 1836);

The Way to Do Good; or, The Christian Character Mature (Boston: Peirce, 1836; London: Allan Bell, 1836?; revised and enlarged, New York: Harper, 1852);

Rollo at Work; or, The Way for a Boy to Learn to Be Industrious (Boston: Thomas Webb, 1837);

Hoaryhead; or, Truth Through Fiction (Boston: Crocker & Brewster, 1838; London: Allman, 1851); revised and republished in *Hoaryhead and M'Donner. Very Greatly Improved* (New York: Harper, 1855);

McDonner; or Truth Through Fiction (Boston: Crocker & Brewster, 1839; London: T. Allman, 1839); revised and republished in *Hoary-*

head and M'Donner. Very Greatly Improved* (New York: Harper, 1855);

Rollo at School (Boston: Thomas Webb, 1839);

Rollo's Vacation (Boston: Thomas Webb, 1839);

Rollo's Experiments (Boston: Thomas Webb, circa 1839);

Rollo's Museum (Boston: Weeks, Jordan, 1839);

Rollo's Travels (Boston: Thomas Webb, 1839);

Rollo's Correspondence (Boston: William Crosby, 1840);

The Rollo Code of Morals; or, The Rules of Duty for Children (Boston: Crocker & Brewster, 1841);

The Rollo Philosophy, Part I: Water (Boston: Gould, Kendall & Lincoln, 1842);

The Rollo Philosophy, Part II: Air (Boston: Thomas Webb, circa 1842);

The Rollo Philosophy, Part III: Fire (Boston: Otis, Broaders, 1843);

The Rollo Philosophy, Part IV: Sky (Boston: Otis, Broaders, 1843);

Marco Paul in the City of New York (Boston: Carter, 1843);

Marco Paul on the Erie Canal (Boston: Carter, 1843);

Marco Paul in the Forests of Maine (Boston: Carter, 1843);

Marco Paul in Vermont (Boston: Carter, 1843);

Marco Paul in the City of Boston (Boston: Carter, 1843);

Marco Paul at the Springfield Armory (Boston: Carter, 1843);

The History of Charles the First (New York: Harper, 1848);

The History of Mary, Queen of Scots (New York: Harper, 1848);

The History of Alexander the Great (New York: Harper, 1848);

The History of Julius Caesar (New York: Harper, 1849);

The History of Hannibal the Carthaginian (New York: Harper, 1849);

The History of William the Conqueror (New York: Harper, 1849);

The History of Charles the Second (New York: Harper, 1849);

The History of Elizabeth, Queen of England (New York: Harper, 1849);

The History of King Alfred of England (New York: Harper, 1849);

Malleville: A Franconia Story (New York: Harper, 1850);

Wallace: A Franconia Story (New York: Harper, 1850);

Mary Erskine: A Franconia Story (New York: Harper, 1850);

Mary Bell: A Franconia Story (New York: Harper, 1850);

Beechnut: A Franconia Story (New York: Harper, 1850);

The History of Xerxes the Great (New York: Harper, 1850);

The History of Cyrus the Great (New York: Harper, 1850);

The History of Darius the Great (New York: Harper, 1850);

The History of Cleopatra, Queen of Egypt (New York: Harper, 1851);

Rodolphus: A Franconia Story (New York: Harper, 1852);

Ellen Linn: A Franconia Story (New York: Harper, 1852);

The History of Romulus (New York: Harper, 1852);

The History of Nero (New York: Harper, 1853);

The History of Pyrrhus (London: Cooke, 1853);

Stuyvesant: A Franconia Story (New York: Harper, 1853);

Caroline: A Franconia Story (New York: Harper, 1853);

Agnes: A Franconia Story (New York: Harper, 1853);

Rollo on the Atlantic (Boston: W. J. Reynolds, 1853);

Rollo in Paris (Boston: W. J. Reynolds, 1854);

Rollo in Switzerland (Boston: W. J. Reynolds, 1854);

Rollo in London (Boston: W. J. Reynolds, 1855);

Rollo on the Rhine (Boston: W. J. Reynolds, 1855);

Rollo in Scotland (Boston: W. J. Reynolds, 1856);

Halo Round the Moon (Boston: Sampson, 1857);

Labor Lost (Boston: Phillips, Sampson, 1857);

Rollo's Garden (Boston: Phillips, Sampson, 1857);

Georgie (New York: Sheldon, 1857);

Blueberrying (Boston: Phillips, Sampson, 1857);

Apple Gathering (Boston: Phillips, Sampson, 1857);

Trouble on the Mountain (New York: Sheldon, 1857?);

Rollo in Holland (Boston: Brown, Taggard & Chase, 1857);

The History of King Richard the First (New York: Harper, 1857);

Rollo in Geneva (Boston: Brown, Taggard & Chase, 1857);

The History of King Richard the Second (New York: Harper, 1858);

The History of King Richard the Third (New York: Harper, 1858);

Rollo in Naples (Boston: Brown, Taggard & Chase, 1858);

Rollo in Rome (Boston: Brown, Taggard & Chase, 1858);

The History of Peter the Great (New York: Harper, 1859);

The History of Genghis Khan (New York: Harper, 1860);

Florence and John (New York: Sheldon, 1860);

Grimkie (New York: Sheldon, 1860);

Excursion to the Orkney Islands (New York: Sheldon, 1861);

The History of Margaret of Anjou (New York: Harper, 1861);

The Rocking Horse; or The Rollo and Lucy First Book of Poetry (Philadelphia: Childs, 1863);

Carlo; or The Rollo and Lucy Second Book of Poetry (New York: Sheldon, 1863);

The Canary Bird; or The Rollo and Lucy Third Book of Poetry (New York: Sheldon, 1863);

The English Channel (New York: Sheldon, 1863);

The New Shoes; or, Productive Work by Little Hands (New York: Sheldon, 1863);

The French Flower; or, Be Kind and Obliging to Your Teacher (New York: Sheldon, 1863);

Harlie's Letter; or, How to Learn With Little Teaching (New York: Sheldon, 1863);

Wild Peggie; or, Charity and Discretion (New York: Sheldon, 1863);

The Sea-Shore; or, How to Plan Picnics and Excursions (New York: Sheldon, 1863);

Friskie, the Pony; or, Do No Harm to Harmless Animals (New York: Sheldon, 1863);

The Freshet (New York: Sheldon, 1863);

Rollo in the Woods (New York: Sheldon, 1864);

The Steeple Trip (New York: Sheldon, 1864);

Two Wheel-Barrows (New York: Sheldon, 1864);

Causey Building (New York: Sheldon, 1864);

Visit to the Isle of Wight (New York: Sheldon, 1864);

Florence's Return (New York: Sheldon, 1864);

John Gay; or Work for Boys—Work for Spring (New York: Hurd & Houghton, 1864);

John Gay; or Work for Boys—Work for Summer (New York: Hurd & Houghton, 1864);

Mary Gay; or Work for Girls—Work for Winter (New York: Hurd & Houghton, 1865);

Mary Gay; or Work for Girls—Work for Spring (New York: Hurd & Houghton, 1865);

Mary Gay; or Work for Girls—Work for Summer (New York: Hurd & Houghton, 1865);

Mary Gay; or Work for Girls—Work for Autumn (New York: Hurd & Houghton, 1865);

John Gay; or Work for Boys—Work for Autumn (New York: Hurd & Houghton, 1867);

William Gay; or Play for Boys—Play for Winter (New York: Hurd & Houghton, 1869);

William Gay; or Play for Boys—Play for Spring (New York: Hurd & Houghton, 1869);

William Gay; or Play for Boys—Play for Summer (New York: Hurd & Houghton, 1869);

William Gay; or Play for Boys—Play for Autumn (New York: Hurd & Houghton, 1869);

Juno and Georgie (New York: Dodd, Mead, 1870);

Mary Osborne (New York: Dodd, Mead, 1870);

Juno on a Journey (New York: Dodd, Mead, 1870);

Hubert (New York: Dodd, Mead, 1870);

Gentle Measures in the Management and Training of the Young; or, The Principles on Which a Firm Parental Authority May Be Established and Maintained (New York: Harper, 1871);

August and Elvie (New York: Dodd, Mead, 1871);

Hunter and Tom (New York: Dodd, Mead, 1871);

The Schooner Mary Ann (New York: Dodd, Mead, 1872);

Granville Valley (New York: Dodd, Mead, 1872);

John Gay; or Work for Boys—Work for Winter (New York: Hurd & Houghton, 1876).

Jacob Abbott, teacher, minister, and author, is often unfairly dismissed as a representative of the flock of didactic writers who responded to demands from the American Sunday School Union and the American Tract Society for pious fare for young children. Abbott, the oldest son and second child of Jacob and Betsey Abbot, is remembered primarily as the author of the Rollo series. He was born and spent his childhood with seven brothers and sisters in the Maine town of Hallowell, at the time a bustling Puritan town on the Kennebec River. Abbott's brother John, in his *Reminiscences of Childhood*, recounts the children's early Puritan upbringing, characterized by love and security, rather than by the harshness and rigidity often associated with Puritanism: "We children all knew that both father and mother would rather we would struggle all our days with adversity, and *be Christians*, than to have all the honors of genius, and all the wealth of millionaires lavished upon us, without piety. . . . We loved those Puritan parents with a fervor that could hardly be surpassed." Added insight into Abbott's upbringing and subsequent character and personality can perhaps be gleaned from a remark of one of the townsmen about his father: "Squire Abbot has a remarkable faculty for being happy." All of Squire Abbot's five sons attended Hallowell Academy, graduated from Bowdoin College (Jacob in 1820 at the age of seventeen), studied theology at Andover Seminary, and became teachers and ministers. It was during his years at Bowdoin that Jacob Abbott added a second *t* to the family name.

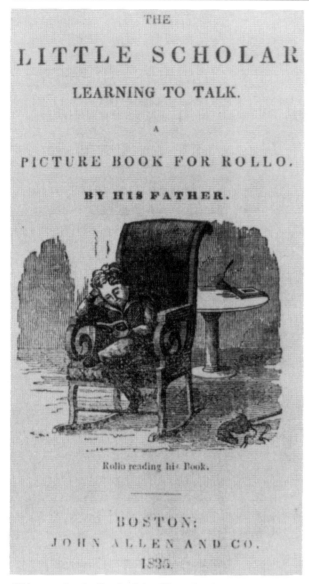

THE

LITTLE SCHOLAR

LEARNING TO TALK.

A

PICTURE BOOK FOR ROLLO.

BY HIS FATHER.

Rollo reading his Book.

BOSTON:

JOHN ALLEN AND CO.

1835.

*Title-page for the first book in Abbott's best-known series (The
Collection of American Literature in the Library of
Pauline and Howard Behrman, 1973). According to Abbott,
the purpose of the Rollo books was "the communication of useful
knowledge; and everything which they contain, except what is
strictly personal, . . . may be depended on as exactly and scrupulously true."*

After completing his theological studies at
Andover in 1824, Abbott began teaching at
Amherst College. In 1925 he was made a professor
of mathematics and natural philosophy at the age
of twenty-two. Although Abbott's first work was
as a teacher, his son Lyman believes there is evidence that Abbott's thoughts turned toward writing
when he was in college, and it is known that he
belonged to a secret literary society while he was

at Andover. His earliest work, *Conversations on the
Bible,* was published in 1829, and fifty years later
when he died in 1879, it is estimated by his bibliographer Carl J. Weber that he had written over
two hundred books, an average of four a year. His
first popular success was *The Young Christian,* first
published in 1832 and in print continuously until
1891. Two years later he produced *The Corner-
Stone,* the second of five volumes in Abbott's Young
Christian series, which was completed in 1839. In
the preface to *The Young Christian* Abbott explains
that the work "is intended as a guide to the young
inquirer in first entering upon his Christian
course." The series comprises works of both fiction
and nonfiction. In 1904 Fletcher Osgood, writing
in the *New England Magazine,* called the combined,
revised edition of *Hoaryhead and M'Donner,* the last
two books in the series, "a masterpiece of American
literature" and called for greater appreciation of
Abbott as a literary artist.

Although he entered the Congregational
ministry in 1826, he was more interested in teaching than in the pulpit in his early years. He
preached occasionally, but soon after marrying
Harriet Vaughan of Hallowell in 1828, he moved
to Boston and founded the Mount Vernon School
with his brother John. After serving as principal
for several years, he decided to return to the pulpit,
and in 1834 he moved to Roxbury as the minister
of the Eliot Congregational Church. Just a year
later, encouraged by the success of the Young
Christian series, he decided to lay aside both teaching and preaching and to embark on a literary career. In 1835 he moved to Farmington, Maine, with
his young family and bought some land directly
across from his father's home. He spent the rest of
his life lovingly cultivating and landscaping it. It
was here at Little Blue that he wrote the famous
Rollo series. In 1843 Harriet Vaughan Abbott died;
a decade later Abbott married Mrs. Mary Dana
Woodbery. Except for joining his brothers at the
Abbott Institution in New York City from 1843 to
1851 and later (1845-1848) at the Mount Vernon
School for girls, he spent most of his time being
both preacher and educator through his writings.

The first of the Rollo series, *The Little Scholar
Learning to Talk. A Picture Book for Rollo* (later entitled *Rollo Learning to Talk*), was published in 1835.
The series continued through twenty-six volumes
plus fifteen Rollo Story Books and Books of Poetry.
In 1945 Professor W. W. Lawrence of Columbia
University called for a deeper appreciation and understanding of Abbott's writing style and educational foresight in his *New England Quarterly* article,

"Rollo and His Uncle George," but no one has followed his lead, and the books that were so extremely popular in the nineteenth century are now little noticed.

There are two things that account for the popularity of the Rollo books, as well as such later series as the Franconia stories: Abbott's attitude toward children and his ability to write in a way that reflected his respect for them. Lyman Abbott discusses both qualities in "Jacob Abbott, Friend of Children," in *Silhouettes of My Contemporaries* (1922): "I have known men as fond of children as my father, but I have never known a man who had for them such respect. In a true sense, it might be said that he treated children as his equals, not through any device or from any scheme, but spontaneously and naturally. This respect which he showed to children inspired them with respect for themselves and for one another. It gave dignity to the children who came under his influence. . . . He did not write books about children for grown people to read. He wrote books for children because he shared their life with them."

Abbott's empathy for the young is easy to recognize in his most successful better series. The narrator of his most popular books has personal charm, calm goodwill, and quiet confidence that captivated nineteenth-century readers and still has appeal among the confused and strident voices that dominate many present-day children's novels. Abbott's narrator's tone is never condescending; instead he expresses quiet amusement and great sympathy for the capabilities of children and their incapabilities.

In the early Rollo books, for instance, when Rollo is five, Abbott portrays children as they really act. In *Rollo at Play* (1836), the lessons to be learned are not based on Rousseau's educational treatise, *Emile* (1762), as they were so laboriously in Thomas Day's *Sanford and Merton* (1783, 1786, 1789) and other popular children's books; they are based on the real experiences of childhood. Abbott's book starts with Rollo trying to make a box with hammer and nails, but soon this project is abandoned because he does not know how to complete the task and no one has time to help him. After spending some time getting his reading lesson out of the way because he had neglected to do it earlier, he is free to go to the woods to search for Jonas, the young farmhand frequently entrusted with his care. Soon, having found Jonas, Rollo is happily building a wigwam while Jonas goes about his work. When Rollo's cousin James comes along, in no time at all there is an argument which the boys attempt to settle by proving which boy is taller. Rollo can stretch his hand higher because he is a bit taller:

> James determined not to be outdone, so he took up a stick, and reached it up in the air as high as he could, and said, "I can reach up as high as *that*."
>
> Then Rollo took up a stone, and tossed it up into the air, saying, "And I can reach as high as that."
>
> Now, when boys throw stones into the air, they ought to consider where they will come down; but unfortunately, Rollo did not in this case, and the stone fell directly upon James's head.

Rollo is no nineteenth-century prig; he is a very real boy, although the reader must accept that Rollo has been raised as a New England Puritan and acts and reacts accordingly. Abbott's portrayal of Rollo continues in this realistic vein in subsequent books, as Rollo grows older and goes across the Atlantic with his parents, his younger brother Thanny, his cousin Jane, and his Uncle George to tour Europe.

Abbott's purpose in the Rollo books is to demonstrate to children not only proper ways of behaving but also how to deal with a variety of situations they will have to face when they are mature enough to assume the duties and responsibilities of American gentlemen and gentlewomen. They are shown not only how to become independent, but also how to handle money, how to order meals in foreign restaurants, how to buy railroad tickets and get about, and they are given instruction in "the customs, usages, and modes of life" of those countries which Rollo visits. As Abbott points out in the preface to *Rollo on the Atlantic* (1853), "The main design of the narrative is, thus, the communication of useful knowledge; and everything which they [the Rollo books] contain, except what is strictly personal, in relation to the actors in the story, may be depended upon as exactly and scrupulously true." Thus, for nineteenth-century readers as well as those of the twentieth, the books offer a delightful and accurate portrayal of customs and practices on both sides of the Atlantic.

Abbott's style and the structure of the Rollo books help account for their success. As Abbott's son Lyman put it, his father "wrote his stories as he might have told them. If shorthand had been in vogue in his time, and one could have taken down any story of my father's as he might have told it to a group of children gathered about his

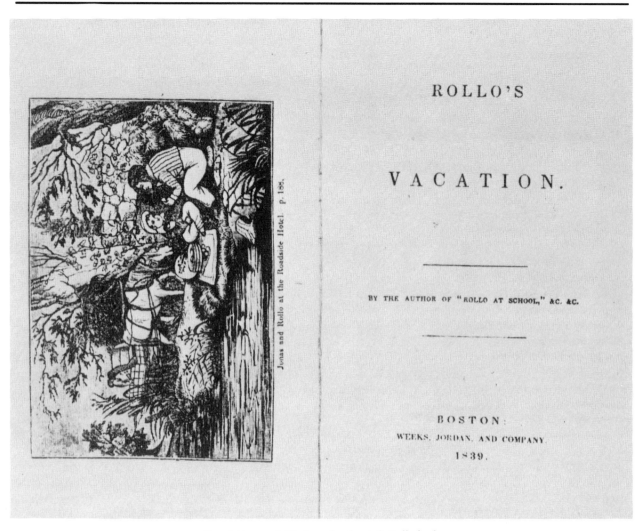

ROLLO'S

VACATION.

BY THE AUTHOR OF "ROLLO AT SCHOOL," &C. &C.

BOSTON:
WEEKS, JORDAN, AND COMPANY.
1839.

Frontispiece and title page for the sixth Rollo book

chair, it would have been essentially the story as it is published from his pen. He did not form a plot beforehand. Each incident led to the next incident; it might be said that each paragraph led to the next paragraph; and when the allotted number of pages was finished, the story came to its end, much as the story-telling would come to an end when the clock struck nine and it was time for the children to go to bed. This method accounts for the artlessness of his narratives. They are natural portrayals of child life to children."

The simple oral quality determines the structure of the tales, in which events of the plot and narrative style are tailored to the age of the child involved in the tale and, therefore, the age of the child who would most likely read the tale. Rollo, when he is five, notices and is concerned with those

details that would preoccupy a five-year-old child. The more mature twelve-year-old Rollo is interested in more sophisticated things, and so Abbott adjusts his narrative accordingly, though Rollo is always guided and controlled to some extent by the attitudes and actions of the cynical and worldly Uncle George, who treats Rollo as an equal, or Mr. Holliday, Rollo's father, wiser and more tolerant than the younger Uncle George, or Jonas, more down-to-earth because he is younger and less experienced than the other two mentors, but still a worthy guide to the young Rollo.

Although these characters are all distinctly drawn, it is in the ten-volume series of Franconia stories that critics and scholars such as John Rowe Townsend, Cornelia Meigs, and W. W. Lawrence believe that Abbott was most successful in deline-

Frontispiece and title page for the fifth "Franconia Story." Beechnut has often been described as Abbott's most autobiographical character (Thomas Cooper Library, University of South Carolina).

ating memorable characters in Phonny, Beechnut, Jonas, and Malleville. It has been said, even, that these were the first realistic, three-dimensional characters to appear in American children's literature. Published from 1850 to 1853, these books, in which Beechnut is the closest to an autobiographical depiction of Abbott, not only demonstrate Abbott's ability with techniques of characterization, they also indicate his desire to entertain his readers even though his purpose is always primarily didactic. At one point, Beechnut asks,

> "Shall I tell you the story just as it was, as a sober matter of fact, or shall I embellish it?"
>
> "I don't know what you mean by embellishing it."

"Why," said Beechnut, "not telling exactly what is true, but inventing something to add to it to make it interesting."

"I want to have it true," said Malleville, "and interesting, too."

"But sometimes," replied Beechnut, "interesting things don't happen; and in such cases, if we should only relate what actually does happen the story would be likely to be dull."

"I think you had better embellish the story a little," said Phonny; "just a little, you know."

In the Franconia stories, then, Abbott, with "just a little" embellishment, recounts the joys of New England child life and the experiences of Beechnut before he arrives in this country from his native Switzerland, a broad enough canvas to both teach and delight his many readers, for this series, too, was extremely popular.

Abbott's Makers of History series was published from 1848 to 1861 and frequently reprinted until the turn of the century. This series, comprised of twenty-two volumes by Jacob Abbott and ten more by his brother John, included biographies of such figures as Charles the First; Mary, Queen of Scots; Alexander the Great; Julius Caesar; Queen Elizabeth I; and Xerxes and was as popular in England as it was in America. Clarence Ghodes in *American Literature in Nineteenth Century England* (1944) says, "it is doubtful whether many British writers of children's books were more popular in England than . . . Abbott." It was to this series that Abraham Lincoln referred in his famous letter to Harper Brothers shortly before he died, "I have read them with the greatest interest. To them I am indebted for about all the historical knowledge I have."

Although most of his life was devoted to writing, Abbott considered himself primarily a teacher. He was the founder of two innovative schools, the Mount Vernon School, which he started in Boston in 1828 with his brother John, and the Abbott Institution in New York, initially called the New Seminary for Young Ladies, which he conducted with his brothers John and Gorham from 1843 until 1851. Both were among the first institutions to offer quality education for young girls, a project Abbott was deeply committed to; he became recognized for his pioneer work in educating young women, and his brother Gorham, founder of the Society for the Diffusion of Useful Knowledge, later served as a consultant when Vassar and Wellesley were founded. In Abbott's schools, young women not only received more advanced academic training than was usually available at the time, but they were also inculcated with the moral values and the child-rearing precepts that infused Abbott's books for young people. The child-rearing theories he developed, with their quiet good sense, helped overthrow the seventeenth-century notion of the child's innate depravity. Abbott's theories, in fact, have a peculiarly modern ring which can be spotted in many twentieth-century "parenting" manuals and child psychology texts.

In *Gentle Measures in the Management and Training of the Young*, published in 1871 and regarded by Abbott as a summary of his life as child, parent, and teacher, he points out, "in respect of moral conduct as well as of mental attainments children know nothing when they come into the world, but have everything to learn either from the in-

structions or from the examples of those around them. . . . The mother is thus to understand that the principle of obedience is not to be expected to come by nature into the heart of her child, but to be implanted by education." This education is to be imparted in an atmosphere of equality and respect, ideally fostered by democracy, where the emphasis is always on encouraging the child to assume greater and greater responsibility and independence. A distinction is drawn between punishment and discipline; the former, retributive in nature, is to be avoided; the latter, preventive in nature, is to be adopted. For instance, in one of the Franconia stories, Beechnut sets up a little test to see if a newcomer, Josie, is well-behaved and mature; he gives her the opportunity to rummage through the drawers of a bureau when she has been told distinctly not to.

> "Why, Beechnut," said Josie, "what did you say I must not open these drawers for? There is nothing in them."
> . . . .
> "Because," said Beechnut, "I have got a number of pictures, and picture-books, and curiosities of various kinds up in my room, which perhaps it would amuse you to see. I let children go up and see them sometimes without me if I am only sure beforehand that they will follow precisely the directions that I give them."

Thus, as Abbott's son points out: "obedience is not a door of admission into a prison; it is a door of exit into liberty; it is an achievement by which one's powers and privileges are increased." Children are encouraged to become increasingly responsible by discovering the logical consequences of their actions. "If a child lied or broke his promises, he was mistrusted. If he was careless or negligent, the things that were given to other children to play with were withheld from him. If he quarreled, he was taken away from his playmates, but made as happy as he could be in solitude." Parent and teacher were admonished to commend often and scold seldom and to assume their full responsibilities in the child's rearing.

These were the tenets that guided Abbott in the classroom and that were illustrated in his many books. He was instrumental, over a long period of years, in helping to dethrone *The New England Primer* as the strongest influence on child-rearing and children's literature. Abbott used the series format in many cases with more literary skill than many of his contemporaries, including Samuel

Griswold Goodrich (Peter Parley), who discovered the series as a valuable vehicle for captivating and educating young readers at the same time. As both educator and author, Jacob Abbott deserves attention.

Bibliography:
Carl J. Weber, *A Bibliography of Jacob Abbott* (Waterville, Maine: Colby College Press, 1948).

Biography:
Edward Abbott, Biographical Sketch of Jacob Abbott in the latter's *The Young Christian: A Memorial Edition* (New York: Harper, 1882).

References:
Lyman Abbott, *Silhouettes of My Contemporaries* (New York: Doubleday, Page, 1922), pp. 332-361;

Lysla I. Abbott, "Jacob Abbott: A Goodly Heritage," *Horn Book Magazine*, 30 (April 1954): 119-131;

William W. Lawrence, "Rollo and His Uncle George," *New England Quarterly*, 18 (September 1945): 291-302;

Emma Huntington Nason, *Old Hallowell on the Kennebec* (Augusta, Maine, 1909);

Fletcher Osgood, "Jacob Abbott, A Neglected New England Author," *New England Magazine* (June 1904): 471-479;

Rollo G. Silver, "Rollo on Rollo," *Colophon: New Graphic Series*, no. 2 (1939).

Papers:
There are collections of Abbott's papers at the Bowdoin College and Colby College libraries.

William Taylor Adams
(Oliver Optic)
(30 July 1822-27 March 1897)

Carol Gay
Youngstown State University

SELECTED BOOKS: *Hatchie, the Guardian Slave; or, The Heiress of Bellevue*, as Warren T. Ashton (Boston: Mussey/Fitte, 1853);

In Doors and Out; or, Views from the Chimney Corner (Boston: Brown, Bazin, 1854); republished with contents rearranged as *Marrying a Beggar; or, The Angel in Disguise* (Boston: Wentworth, Hewes, 1859);

The Boat Club; or, The Bunkers of Rippleton (Boston: Brown, Bazin, 1855; revised and enlarged, Boston: Lee & Shepard, 1896);

All Aboard; or, Life on the Lake (Boston: Brown, Bazin, 1856);

Poor and Proud; or, The Fortunes of Katy Redburn (Boston: Phillips, Sampson, 1856);

Now or Never; or, The Adventures of Bobby Bright (Boston: Brown, Bazin, 1857);

Try Again; or, The Trials and Triumphs of Harry West (Boston: Brown, Taggard, Chase, 1858);

Little by Little; or, The Cruise of the Flyaway (Chicago: Donohue, 1860);

The Birthday Party (Boston: Lee & Shepard, 1863);

Careless Kate (Boston: Lee & Shepard, 1863);

The Christmas Gift (Boston: Lee & Shepard, 1863);

Dolly and I (Boston: Lee & Shepard, 1863);

The Do-Somethings (Boston: Lee & Shepard, 1863);

The Gold Thimble. A Story for Little Folks (Boston: Lee & Shepard, 1863);

The Little Merchant (Boston: Lee & Shepard, 1863);

The Picnic Party (Boston: Lee & Shepard, 1863);

Proud and Lazy (Boston: Lee & Shepard, 1863);

Robinson Crusoe, Jr. (Boston: Lee & Shepard, 1863);

The Sailor Boy; or, Jack Somers in the Navy (Boston: Lee & Shepard, 1863);

The Soldier Boy; or, Tom Somers in the Army (Boston: Lee & Shepard, 1863);

A Spelling Book for Advanced Classes (Boston: Brewer, Tileston, 1863; revised and enlarged, Boston: W. Ware, 1880);

William Taylor Adams

Sports and Pastimes for In-Doors and Out (Boston: G. W. Cottrell, 1863);

The Young Voyagers (Boston: Lee & Shepard, 1863);

Uncle Ben (Boston: Lee & Shepard, 1863);

Rich and Humble; or, The Mission of Bertha Grant (Boston: Lee & Shepard, 1864);

In School and Out; or, The Conquest of Richard Grant (Boston: Lee & Shepard, 1864);

Watch and Wait; or, The Young Fugitives (Boston: Lee & Shepard, 1864);

The Yankee Middy; or, The Adventures of a Naval Officer (Boston: Lee & Shepard, 1865);

Brave Old Salt; A Story of the Great Rebellion (Boston: Lee & Shepard, 1865);

The Young Lieutenant; or, The Adventures of an Army Officer (Boston: Lee & Shepard, 1865);

Fighting Joe; or, The Fortunes of a Staff Officer (Boston: Lee & Shepard, 1866);

Work and Win; or, Noddy Newman on a Cruise (Boston: Lee & Shepard, 1866);

Hope and Have; or, Fanny Grant among the Indians (Boston: Lee & Shepard, 1866);

The Way of the World. A Novel (Boston: Lee & Shepard, 1866); republished as *Three Millions! or,*

The Way of the World (Boston: Lee & Shepard, 1891);

Haste and Waste; or, The Young Pilot of Lake Champlain (Boston: Lee & Shepard, 1867);

Outward Bound; or, Young America Afloat (Boston: Lee & Shepard, 1867);

Breaking Away; or, The Fortunes of a Student (Boston: Lee & Shepard, 1868);

Down the River; or, Buck Bradford and His Tyrants (Boston: Lee & Shepard, 1868);

The Starry Flag; or, The Young Fisherman of Cape Ann (Boston: Lee & Shepard, 1868);

Dikes and Ditches; or, Young America in Holland and Belgium (Boston: Lee & Shepard, 1868);

Freaks of Fortune; or, Half Round the World (Boston: Lee & Shepard, 1868);

Our Standard-bearer; or, The Life of General Ulysses S. Grant (Boston: Lee & Shepard, 1868);

Palace and Cottage; or, Young America in France and Switzerland (Boston: Lee & Shepard, 1868);

Red Cross; or, Young America in England and Wales (Boston: Lee & Shepard, 1868);

Shamrock and Thistle; or, Young America in Ireland and Scotland (Boston: Lee & Shepard, 1868);

Seek and Find; or, The Adventures of a Smart Boy (Boston: Lee & Shepard, 1868);

Bear and Forbear; or, The Young Skipper of Lake Ucayga (Boston: Lee & Shepard, 1869);

Down the Rhine; or, Young America in Germany (Boston: Lee & Shepard, 1869);

Make or Break; or, The Rich Man's Daughter (Boston: Lee & Shepard, 1869);

Through by Daylight; or, The Young Engineer of the Lake Shore Railroad (Boston: Lee & Shepard, 1869);

Brake Up; or, The Young Peacemakers (Boston: Lee & Shepard, 1870);

Lightning Express; or, The Rival Academies (Boston: Lee & Shepard, 1870);

On Time; or, The Young Captain of the Ucayga Steamer (Boston: Lee & Shepard, 1870);

Switch Off; or, The War of the Students (Boston: Lee & Shepard, 1870);

Bivouac and Battle; or, The Struggles of a Soldier (Boston: Lee & Shepard, 1871);

Field and Forest; or, The Fortunes of a Farmer (Boston: Lee & Shepard, 1871);

Plane and Plank; or, The Mishaps of a Mechanic (Boston: Lee & Shepard, 1871);

Desk and Debit; or, The Catastrophes of a Clerk (Boston: Lee & Shepard, 1871);

Up the Baltic; or, Young America in Norway, Sweden and Denmark (Boston: Lee & Shepard, 1871);

Cringle and Cross-tree; or, The Sea Swashes of a Sailor
(Boston: Lee & Shepard, 1872);

Little Bobtail; or, The Wreck of the Penobscot (Boston:
Lee & Shepard, 1872);

Northern Lands; or, Young America in Russia and Prussia (Boston: Lee & Shepard, 1872);

Sea and Shore; or, The Tramps of a Traveller (Boston:
Lee & Shepard, 1872);

*Cross and Crescent; or, Young America in Turkey and
Greece* (Boston: Lee & Shepard, 1873);

Money Maker; or, The Victory of The Basilisk (Boston:
Lee & Shepard, 1874);

The Yacht Club; or, The Young Boat-builder (Boston:
Lee & Shepard, 1874);

*The Coming Wave; or, The Hidden Treasure of High
Rock* (Boston: Lee & Shepard, 1875);

The Dorcas Club; or, Our Girls Afloat (Boston: Lee &
Shepard, 1875);

Ocean-born; or, The Cruise of the Clubs (Boston: Lee
& Shepard, 1875);

Getting an Indorser, and Other Stories (Boston: Lee &
Shepard, 1875);

Sunny Shores; or, Young America in Italy and Austria
(Boston: Lee & Shepard, 1875);

Going West; or, The Perils of a Poor Boy (Boston: Lee
& Shepard, 1876);

The Great Bonanza, by Adams and others (Boston:
Lee & Shepard, 1876);

Living Too Fast; or, The Confessions of a Bank Officer
(Boston: Lee & Shepard, 1876);

Vine and Olive; or, Young America in Spain and Portugal (Boston: Lee & Shepard, 1876);

Just His Luck (Boston: Lee & Shepard, 1877);

Isles of the Sea; or, Young American Homeward Bound
(Boston: Lee & Shepard, 1877);

Out West; or, Roughing It on the Great Lakes (Boston:
Lee & Shepard, 1877);

Going South; or, Yachting on the Atlantic Coast (Boston: Lee & Shepard, 1879);

Lake Breezes; or, The Cruise of the Sylvania (Boston:
Lee & Shepard, 1879);

Down South; or, Yacht Adventures in Florida (Boston:
Lee & Shepard, 1881);

Up the River; or, Yachting on the Mississippi (Boston:
Lee & Shepard, 1882);

All Adrift; or, The Goldwing Club (Boston: Lee &
Shepard, 1883);

Making a Man of Himself; or, Right Makes Might (Boston: Lothrop, 1884);

Snug Harbor; or, The Champlain Mechanics (Boston:
Lee & Shepard, 1884);

Square and Compasses; or, Building the House (Boston:
Lee & Shepard, 1885);

His Own Helper; or, Stout Arm and True Heart (New
York: Street & Smith, 1885);

Stem to Stern; or, Building the Boat (Boston: Lee &
Shepard, 1886);

All Taut; or, Rigging the Boat (Boston: Lee & Shepard, 1887);

Honest Kit Dunstable (Boston: Lothrop, Lee & Shepard, 1887);

Ready About; or, Sailing the Boat (Boston: Lee &
Shepard, 1887);

The Voyage of Life; an Allegory, by Adams and George
M. Baker (Boston: W. H. Baker, 1887);

Nature's Young Nobleman, as Brooks McCormick
(New York: F. A. Munsey, 1888);

Taken by the Enemy (Boston: Lee & Shepard, 1888);

Within the Enemy's Lines (Boston: Lee & Shepard,
1890);

Among the Missing (Boston: Lee & Shepard, 1890);

The Rival Battalions, as Brooks McCormick (New
York: United States Book Company, 1891);

The Young Actor; or, The Solution of a Mystery, as Gayle
Winterton (New York: United States Book
Company, 1891);

On the Blockade (Boston: Lee & Shepard, 1891);

A Missing Million; or, The Adventures of Louis Belgrave
(Boston: Lee & Shepard, 1892);

*A Millionaire at Sixteen; or, The Cruise of the Guardian-
Mother* (Boston: Lee & Shepard, 1892);

Stand by the Union (Boston: Lee & Shepard, 1892);

American Boys Afloat; or, Cruising in the Orient (Boston: Lee & Shepard, 1893);

Fighting for the Right (Boston: Lee & Shepard,
1893);

Strange Sights Abroad; or, A Voyage in European Waters
(Boston: Lee & Shepard, 1893);

A Victorious Union (Boston: Lee & Shepard, 1893);

A Young Knight-Errant; or, Cruising in the West Indies
(Boston: Lee & Shepard, 1893);

Brother Against Brother; or, The War on the Border
(Boston: Lee & Shepard, 1894);

Up and Down the Nile; or, Young Adventurers in Africa
(Boston: Lee & Shepard, 1894);

*The Young Navigators; or, The Foreign Cruise of the
Maud* (Boston: Lee & Shepard, 1894);

Across India; or, Live Boys in the Far East (Boston:
Lee & Shepard, 1895);

Asiatic Breezes; or, Students on the Wing (Boston: Lee
& Shepard, 1895);

Half Round the World; or, Among the Uncivilized (Boston: Lee & Shepard, 1895);

Seek and Find; or, The Adventures of a Small Boy (Boston: Lee & Shepard, 1895);

A Lieutenant at Eighteen (Boston: Lee & Shepard,
1896);

Four Young Explorers; or, Sight-seeing in the Tropics
(Boston: Lee & Shepard, 1896);
At the Front (Boston: Lee & Shepard, 1897);
Pacific Shores; or, Adventures in Eastern Seas (Boston:
Lee & Shepard, 1898);
An Undivided Union, completed by Edward Strate-
meyer (Boston: Lee & Shepard, 1899);
How He Won, as Brooks McCormick (New York:
Street & Smith, 1900);
Building Himself Up; or, The Cruise of the "Fish Hawk"
(Boston: Lothrop, Lee & Shepard, 1910).

William Taylor Adams, the popular Oliver
Optic of the latter half of the nineteenth century,
was born in Medway, Massachusetts, of Captain
Laban Adams, a tavern keeper, and Catherine
Johnson Adams. A descendant of the Adams line
which produced two U.S. presidents, he was an avid
and promising student, whose parents sent him to
Able Whitney's private school in Boston after he
had completed his public schooling. As a boy in
Boston, he spent much time on the docks, talking
to sailors and others who gathered there. When he
was sixteen his family settled in West Roxbury on
a farm, where he started to write. After a few years
of teaching school in Dorchester, Massachusetts, he
traveled widely through the North and South, taking careful and extensive notes (a practice he maintained throughout his writing career). For a short
time he helped his father in the Adams House, a
family-owned tavern and hotel in Boston, before
resuming his teaching career.

The strong interest in education that he exhibited as a student and reaffirmed in his choice
of a vocation never left him. He held teaching and
administrative posts in the Boston schools for
twenty years, and even after he left teaching to
write full-time, he continued to teach Sunday
school and served for fourteen years as a school
board member in Dorchester. As an educator he
was both popular and respected: his first election
to the school board resulted from a vote of 1,150
to 1, that one vote being cast by himself according
to one source. However, his interest in writing was
strong. His first article had been published in the
Social Monitor when he was nineteen, and two temperance tales appeared in the *Washingtonian* in
1845. In 1846 Adams married Sarah Jenkins of
Dorchester, with whom he had two daughters. He
first used the pen name Oliver Optic in 1851, inspired by a character named Doctor Optic who had
appeared in a burlesque playing in Boston. He evidently chose Oliver for the sound of it, creating
the most widely known of the many pseudonyms

he used during his writing career. The others that
have been identified are Irving Brown, Clingham
Hunter, M.D., Gayle Winterton, Brooks Mc-
Cormick, Old Stager, and Warren T. Ashton.

It was *Hatchie, the Guardian Slave; or, The Heiress of Bellevue,* published in 1853 under the Ashton
pen name, that first established Adams as a professional author; he received the sum of $37.50 for
the manuscript. The following year he produced a
collection of stories for young people, *In Doors and
Out; or, Views from the Chimney Corner,* and in 1855,
Brown, Bazin and Company of Boston published
The Boat Club; or, The Bunkers of Rippleton. It was
this book that established him as a major writer for
young people, who eventually became one of the
best-paid writers of his time. (In 1873 he received
$5,000 for two stories published in the *Fireside Com-
panion.*)

The Boat Club pits Frank Sedley, his friend
Charles Hardy, and Tony Weston, son of the impoverished Widow Weston, against Tim Bunker
and his gang of town hoodlums. It sets the pattern
of exciting and dangerous episodes and hard-
fought moral struggles that fill Adams's fast-paced
narratives and brought him both praise and criticism throughout his career, and after. The book
was first of six which became the Boat Club series,
establishing Adams's pattern of having six related
but not continuous narratives in a series. The
Starry Flag series, the Lake Shore series, Young
America Abroad series, the Riverdale Stories, the
Army and Navy Stories, and the Woodville Stories
are his best-known.

After Adams had become popular, a publisher's blurb quoted the *R. I. Schoolmate:* "Boys and
girls have no taste for dry and tame things; they
want something that will stir the blood and warm
the heart. Optic always does this, while at the same
time he improves the taste and elevates the moral
nature. The coming generation of men will never
know how much they are indebted for what is pure
and ennobling to his writings." There is little to
argue with here, except perhaps the phrase "improves the taste." An 1891 reviewer of one of Adams's later books, *On the Blockade* (1891), while
acknowledging the appeal of his early stories to
young readers, concludes, "But what does surprise
the reader, returning with maturer taste to this
writer of his youth, is the execrably stilted quality
of the literary style, which used to pass to the young
mind as the exalted and dignified language of high
official position. This perversion of literary taste is
the gravest fault we have to find with Oliver Optic."

BESSIE'S MISFORTUNE.   Page 4.

THE STARRY FLAG;

OR,

The Young Fisherman of Cape Ann.

BY OLIVER OPTIC.

CHAPTER I.

THE DINGY DORY.

"BUT I must have one more bath before we go, father," said Bessie Watson, as she gazed down into the clear, blue waters of the sea, which surged against the rocks near the hotel on Cape Ann, where she and her parents had been spending a week.

"There is hardly time, Bessie," replied Mr. Watson, as he consulted his watch.

"What time is it, father?"

"Quarter past eight."

"There is time enough then."

"I don't like to have you bathe here, Bessie. It is a dangerous place, and I'm going to Rye Beach almost wholly because you are so fond of the salt water. I have been afraid, every time you went in, that you would slip off that rock."

"There is no danger."

"I think there is."

"The rope will prevent any accident."

"The rope is some protection, but I don't think the place is safe."

"Just one more plunge, pa; I shall feel so much better for the journey!" pleaded Bessie, whose bright eyes and pretty face were so elo-

First page, first issue of Oliver Optic's Magazine: Our Boys and Girls, *founded and edited by Adams until 1875 (Baldwin Library, University of Florida Libraries)*

Engraved title page for an 1871 anthology compiled from
Oliver Optic's Magazine *(Baldwin Library, University of*
Florida Libraries)

Indeed, almost from the beginning Adams was simultaneously praised and derided as an author. The most famous controversy during his lifetime occurred when an author who almost rivaled him in popularity, Louisa May Alcott, attacked him in *Eight Cousins* by having her characters deride the "optical delusions" of a writer known for using slang and concentrating on the sensational more than on the moral. *Eight Cousins* was published at the peak of Adams's popularity in 1875, when his books were selling well enough for him to welcome the controversy. He heightened it by replying in the September 1875 columns of his extremely popular *Oliver Optic's Magazine*, which he had started in 1867, that Alcott should practice what she preached. As Adams put it, she preached "Be honest and you will be rich," but she seemed to practice "Be smart and you will be rich." Alcott, who had been told by Thomas Niles, Jr., of Roberts Brothers just before she wrote *Little Women* to "do something like Oliver Optic," was not pleased.

Adams had resigned from teaching in 1865 at the age of forty-three to continue the writing and editing that had brought him fame. He traveled extensively in Europe, Asia, and Africa and edited the popular *Student and Schoolmate, Oliver Optic's Magazine,* and *Our Little Ones Magazine.* In 1867 he introduced Horatio Alger to the world when Alger's *Ragged Dick* was published as a series in *Student and Schoolmate.* According to one source, in the course of his career Adams produced approximately 126 books that sold over two million copies during his lifetime, a prodigious amount for the times.

Adams's goals as a juvenile writer are perhaps best revealed in the preface to his first important book, *The Boat Club:* "The author of the following story pleads not guilty of being more than half a boy himself; and in writing a book to meet the wants and the tastes of 'Young America,' he has had no difficulty in stepping back over the weary waste of years that separates youth from maturity, and entering fully into the spirit of the scenes he describes. He has endeavored to combine healthy moral lessons with a sufficient amount of exciting interest to render the story attractive to the young; and he hopes he has not mingled these elements of a good juvenile book in disproportionate quantities." His writing motto, "First God, then country, then friends," produced books that pleased some critics and alienated others. In 1879 the American Library Association held its conference in Boston and argued whether or not Adams's works were too sensationalistic to be placed on library shelves. Author and editor Thomas Wentworth Higginson was one of those who defended Adams and his penchant for adventure and melodrama. Twentieth-century commentators have continued the disagreement which persisted throughout Adams's life. John Rowe Townsend observes in *A Sense of Story* (1971), "The invariable combination of bravery with moral uplift resulted in a succession of stereotyped and priggish heroes, occasionally redeemed by the sheer absurdity of their remarks." In contrast, Cornelia Meigs in *A Critical History of Children's Literature* (1953) argues: "Optic's boys were courageous and upright, but though he was consciously a moral writer, he did not allow the moral to interfere with his lively well-told stories, and he was read with enthusiasm by more than one generation of boys and girls."

At his best Adams is able to mingle in proportionate quantities "healthy moral lessons with a sufficient amount of exciting interest." In *The Soldier Boy; or, Tom Somers in the Army* (1863) the de-

Engraved title pages for novels in two of Adams's series

tailed and generally realistic battle scenes sweep the reader quickly past the sentimental passages such as those that describe Tom's last glimpse of his mother's face as he marches off to war and those that recount his self-righteous disdain for people who drink liquor or who do not read the Bible daily. In some works, including those in the Young America Abroad series, in which Adams mingles adventure not only with moral advice, but with geographical and nautical information, there is little to redeem them. They are overly ambitious, heavily didactic, and sentimental. In other works in which his only purpose is to moralize, he is self-righteous and pompous. In, for example, *The Gold Thimble. A Story for Little Folks* (1863) Adams has the rich but extremely moral businessman Mr. Lee trick Mary Long, the gardener's young daughter, into a confession of guilt for stealing a golden thimble

that was carelessly left in her reach. Lee then lectures her mercilessly on how blessed it is to be poverty-stricken and pure.

At times, however, Adams's moral is not so clear-cut. In *Living Too Fast; or, The Confessions of a Bank Officer* (1876), written for young men in their teens and early twenties, Paley Glasswood tells his tale of moral weakness and greed that ends in his covering his frivolous debts by embezzlement. Although he is from the first quite shaky morally, Paley blames most of his troubles on his dominating wife until he overcomes her. By the time Paley sets himself up as the head of the household, it is too late to save himself from financial disaster, and he flees to Europe with Lillian and a large sum of money that is not his. He is eventually caught, but his good friend Tom succeeds not only in covering up the scandal but also in having the charges dismissed. Paley and his wife return from Europe quite rich and quite content, though a bit guilt-ridden: "I do not yet feel like an innocent man; I can never feel so. I shall regret and repent my sin to the end of my life. . . . I still feel that my crime was the legitimate result of LIVING TOO FAST." This last-minute disclaimer from a man who clearly and tangibly profited from his misdeeds is the sort of thing that prompted Adams to preface many of his books with the hope that young readers would emulate only the moral deeds of his characters and that brought upon him charges of sensationalism from some contemporary critics who feared that he emphasized action and adventure more than the moral.

When Adams died in 1897 at the age of seventy-four, he was, along with Jacob Abbott, Samuel Goodrich (Peter Parley), Louisa May Alcott, and Horatio Alger, one of America's most widely read authors.

References:

Jane Bigham and Grayce Scholot, *Fifteen Centuries of Children's Literature: An Annotated Chronology of British and American Novels in Historical Context* (Westport, Conn.: Greenwood Press, 1980);

R. L. Darling, "Authors vs. Critics: Children's Books in the 1870s," *Publishers Weekly*, 192 (16 October 1967): 25-27;

Gene Gleason, "Whatever Happened to Oliver Optic?," *Wilson Library Bulletin*, 49 (May 1975): 647-650;

Albert Johannsen, *House of Beadle and Adams and Its Dime and Nickel Novels: The Story of a Vanished Literature* (Norman: University of Oklahoma Press, 1950).

Papers:

Adams's papers are at Houghton Library, Harvard University.

Louisa May Alcott

Ruth K. MacDonald
New Mexico State University

See also the Alcott entry in *DLB 1, The American Renaissance in New England*.

BIRTH: Germantown, Pennsylvania, 29 November 1832 to Amos Bronson and Abigail May Alcott.

DEATH: Roxbury, Massachusetts, 6 March 1888.

SELECTED BOOKS: *Flower Fables* (Boston: George W. Briggs, 1855);

Hospital Sketches (Boston: James Redpath, 1863); republished in part in *Something to Do* (1873);

The Rose Family. A Fairy Tale (Boston: James Redpath, 1864);

On Picket Duty, and Other Tales (Boston: James Redpath, 1864);

Moods (Boston: A. K. Loring, 1865; revised, Boston: Roberts Brothers, 1882);

Nelly's Hospital (Boston, 1865);

The Mysterious Key, and What It Opened (Boston: Elliott, Thomes & Talbot, 1867);

Morning-Glories, and Other Stories (Boston: Horace B. Fuller, 1868);

Louisa M. Alcott's Proverb Stories (Boston: Loring, 1868); republished in *Something to Do* (1873);

Little Women or, Meg, Jo, Beth and Amy, 2 volumes (Boston: Roberts Brothers, 1868-1869; London: Low, 1868-1869); volume 2 republished as *Little Women Wedded* (London: Low, 1872), *Little Women Married* (London: Routledge, 1873), and *Nice Wives* (London: Weldon, 1875); both volumes republished in one as *Little Women and Good Wives* (London: Nisbet, 1895);

Hospital Sketches and Camp and Fireside Stories (Boston: Roberts Brothers, 1869);

An Old-Fashioned Girl (Boston: Roberts Brothers, 1870; London: Low, 1870);

Will's Wonder Book (Boston: Fuller, 1870);

V.V.: or, Plots and Counterplots, as A. M. Barnard (Boston: Thomes & Talbot, circa 1870);

Little Men: Life at Plumfield with Jo's Boys (London: Low, Son & Marston, 1871; Boston: Roberts Brothers, 1871);

Aunt Jo's Scrap-Bag. My Boys, Etc. (Boston: Roberts Brothers, 1872; London: Low, 1872);

Aunt Jo's Scrap-Bag. Shawl-Straps, Etc. (Boston: Roberts Brothers, 1872; London: Low, 1872);

Something to Do (London: Ward, Lock & Tyler, 1873);

Work: A Story of Experience (1 volume, Boston: Roberts Brothers, 1873; 2 volumes, London: Low, 1873);

Aunt Jo's Scrap-Bag. Cupid and Chow Chow, Etc. (Boston: Roberts Brothers, 1874; London: Low, 1874);

Eight Cousins; or The Aunt-Hill (Boston: Roberts Brothers, 1875; London: Low, 1875);

Silver Pitchers: And Independence, A Centennial Love Story (Boston: Roberts Brothers, 1876; London: Low, 1876);

Rose in Bloom. A Sequel to "Eight Cousins" (Boston: Roberts Brothers, 1876; London: Low, 1876);

A Modern Mephistopheles, anonymous (Boston: Roberts Brothers, 1877; London: Low, 1877);

Aunt Jo's Scrap-Bag. My Girls, Etc. (Boston: Roberts Brothers, 1878);

Under the Lilacs (11 parts, London: Low, Marston, Searle & Rivington, 1878; 1 volume, Boston: Roberts Brothers, 1878);

Aunt Jo's Scrap-Bag. Jimmy's Cruise in the Pinafore, Etc. (Boston: Roberts Brothers, 1879; London: Low, 1879);

Jack and Jill: A Village Story (Boston: Roberts Brothers, 1880; London: Low, 1880);

Aunt Jo's Scrap-Bag. An Old-Fashioned Thanksgiving, Etc. (Boston: Roberts Brothers, 1882; London: Low, 1882);

Spinning-Wheel Stories (Boston: Roberts Brothers, 1884; London: Low, 1884);

Lulu's Library. Vol. I. A Christmas Dream (Boston: Roberts Brothers, 1886; London: Low, 1886);

Jo's Boys, and How They Turned Out. A Sequel to "Little Men" (Boston: Roberts Brothers, 1886; London: Low, 1886);

Lulu's Library. Vol. II. The Frost King (Boston: Roberts Brothers, 1887);

A Garland for Girls (Boston: Roberts Brothers, 1887; London: Blackie, 1887);

A Modern Mephistopheles and A Whisper in the Dark (Boston: Roberts Brothers, 1889; London: Low, 1889);

Louisa May Alcott

Lulu's Library. Vol. III. Recollections (Boston: Roberts Brothers, 1889); republished as *Recollections of My Childhood Days* (London: Low, 1890);

Comic Tragedies Written by "Jo" and "Meg" and Acted by the Little Women (Boston: Roberts Brothers, 1893; London: Low, 1893);

Behind a Mask; The Unknown Thrillers of Louisa May Alcott, edited by Madeleine B. Stern (New York: Morrow, 1975);

Louisa's Wonder Book: An Unknown Alcott Juvenile, edited by Stern (Mount Pleasant, Mich.: Central Michigan University & Clark Historical Library, 1975);

Plots and Counterplots; More Unknown Thrillers of Louisa May Alcott, edited by Stern (New York: Morrow, 1976).

Though she also wrote adult novels, Louisa May Alcott is known primarily for her eight novels for children in the *Little Women* series. Her children's novels are characterized by their glorification of family life, by their wholesomeness and high spirits, and by the lack of the preachiness which was evident in most other children's novels of her time. Though she did not set out to be a children's writer, it is in this field that her greatest achievement was made. Her most popular characters are more than mouthpieces and moral exemplars for the author; they are well-rounded individuals and independent thinkers. In her novels, Alcott criticized many of the current philosophies of education and notions of fashionable behavior. Throughout her works, the ideas of religious faith, sensible eating, learning, and play are dominant themes investigated in a variety of real-life situations. Though her works for children have recently received adverse criticism as compared to her more complex and sometimes sensational adult works, for their time they set a new high standard for excellence in full characterization, both of the attractive and unattractive qualities of children, for the warmth with which she portrayed American family life, for her simple but precise style, and for her New England local color.

Her early life was dominated by the high-minded idealism characteristic of the American transcendentalist movement and by the poverty which necessitated the upheaval of her family as they moved frequently to meet financial exigencies. Born in Germantown, Pennsylvania, on 29 November 1832, Louisa May Alcott was the second of the four daughters of Amos Bronson Alcott, transcendentalist philosopher and educational theorist, and Abigail May, a descendant of one of the leading families of Boston. Bronson Alcott's philosophical flights were outlandish and his educational ideas eccentric. He frequently found himself with no pupils as he tried to establish several different schools, and for most of Louisa's life he failed to support his family by holding a steady job. The most formative event in Louisa Alcott's life was her father's attempt to establish a utopian community called Fruitlands in Harvard, Massachusetts. After the failure of this endeavor, it became apparent that the family would rely no longer on the father and husband for its direction and financial stability; it was at this point, when Louisa Alcott was a mere twelve years old, that she decided to take on the burden of providing for the family. This resolve lasted her whole life.

Though Bronson Alcott was a financial failure, he did provide his daughters with an exceptional, although somewhat erratic education. When

the family lived in Concord, as it did sporadically throughout Louisa Alcott's life, Bronson as well as his daughters were in frequent contact with the leading intellectuals of Boston at the time. Ralph Waldo Emerson was a great friend and near neighbor; the young Louisa May Alcott had free access to his library and read widely there both in the classics and in the masters of English and German philosophy and literature. She later became a tutor to Emerson's daughter Ellen. Though Nathaniel Hawthorne remained aloof from his neighbors in Concord, the Alcott children often met socially with the Hawthorne children, and Alcott knew and read his works. Henry David Thoreau was her botany teacher. The family also had as acquaintances at different times during Alcott's childhood Margaret Fuller, Elizabeth Peabody, William Lloyd Garrison, William Ellery Channing, Lydia Maria Child, James Russell Lowell, and Julia Ward and Samuel Gridley Howe. Though she had almost no formal schooling, Louisa May Alcott was widely read and was familiar with many of the social reform movements of the time. She and her family were avid supporters of women's rights and woman suffrage, abolitionism, temperance, vegetarianism, and dress and educational reform. Many of these causes appear as themes in her novels.

Though her novels are didactic, the most successful of them endure because of the realism with which she portrayed childhood and adolescence. The reputation Alcott garnered as the "Children's Friend" because of the overwhelming popular reception of *Little Women* (published in two volumes in 1868 and 1869) is justly deserved. In this autobiographical novel, Alcott captures the speech patterns and behaviors of children, in this case teenagers, with a reporter's eye for detail. And in Jo March, Alcott's literary recreation of herself, she portrays one of the most enduring and endearing characters in all of children's literature. Jo is ambitious and energetic, loving and charming, awkward and temperamental. Her character is so universally appealing that even boy readers identify with her, though Alcott's expressed intent was to write the novel for girls. The March family is portrayed as a close and loving one and their home a warm nest in which children are nurtured gently before they take flight into the outside world; it is the kind of family that every reader would like for his own. Though as the years progressed Alcott's imitation of her earlier success with Jo and the Marches sometimes became mechanical, there is always the spark of the joy of childhood and the satisfactions of family living that rescue the more

Alcott's parents, Amos Bronson and Abigail May Alcott, the models for the March parents in Little Women

dismal examples. Alcott is also adept as a local colorist; her children's novels are all set in New England, and she captures the pleasures of New England weather and the childhood activities and celebrations that go with the passing seasons with a particularly fine eye. But the local color does not dominate so much that the novels lose their universal appeal.

Alcott's early career as a writer began with her frequent contributions of sentimental short stories and gothic thrillers to such diverse magazines as the *Saturday Evening Gazette, Atlantic Monthly, Frank Leslie's Illustrated Newspaper,* and the *Flag of Our Union.* Though these stories were for adults, Alcott also showed an early predilection to write for children when George Briggs of Boston published her *Flower Fables* (1855), a collection of fairy tales which Alcott had written for Ellen Emerson when Alcott was her tutor. These fairy tales are all heavily didactic. They are concerned with various flowers, animals, fairies of nature, and occasional children, who, through the progress of the short stories, are taught lessons about selflessness, control of temper, gratitude, and the power of love to overcome obstacles and reform the most obdurate sin-

ners. The themes are all ordinary, commonplaces of literature for children at the time, and the collection is altogether undistinguished. Alcott earned thirty-two dollars for the limited edition; it is rarely read now except by Alcott scholars.

Though such writing for children brought in money, it was obvious to Alcott that much more was to be made from the short stories which she could turn out quickly for a profit with which to support her family. Before the Civil War started Alcott's younger sister Elizabeth died and her older sister Anna married and moved away from the family. At the beginning of the war, Alcott found herself lonely and without purpose; she felt keenly the loss of both sisters and realized that it was unlikely that she would marry and find fulfillment in a family of her own, especially given her commitment to the care and financial support of her parents and remaining sister May. But her high ambition was not satisfied with the hack writing she had been doing for profit, and her two adult novels were progressing slowly. The war provided Alcott with the idea of army nursing. Always eager to support a worthy humanitarian cause and never content to stay at home on the sidelines of the action

Fruitlands in Harvard, Massachusetts, the site of Alcott's father's unsuccessful attempt to establish a utopian community in 1843

as women were supposed to, Alcott had had much experience in nursing her sister through her terminal illness. In December 1862, she left to become one of Dorothea Dix's nurses in the U.S. Sanitary Commission at the Union Hotel Hospital in Washington, D.C.

Her nursing experience was crucial in her life in two ways, though she remained in Washington for only about six weeks. First, she contracted typhoid fever, which was the cause of her early departure from the city, and was never well again, due to the effects of mercury poisoning from the treatment prescribed for the fever. For the rest of her life she suffered from spells of nervousness and a variety of aches and pains which plagued her and hampered her writing. For a woman as active as Alcott was, the extended periods of bed rest were a particular trial. Second, she edited and published the letters she wrote to her family from the hospital about the men whom she nursed. *Hospital Sketches*

(1863) was a commercial and popular success, not only because it had an obvious appeal for the readers of the North, but also because of the wry humor and plain, reportorial style in which the book was written. The story collection brought Alcott a modicum of literary fame, enough for her to attempt a serious adult novel, *Moods* (1865), which was not so warmly received. As she left for a European tour, she was disappointed about her writing career.

In 1867, Alcott's career had not progressed much beyond the initial popular and critical success of *Hospital Sketches*. She was still writing her anonymous and pseudonymous gothic thrillers to make money. When her editor, Thomas Niles of Roberts Brothers, approached her about writing a novel for girls, she was not enthused with the suggestion. She had just accepted the editor's position at *Merry's Museum*, a children's monthly magazine. For the January 1868 issue she wrote a short story about a family of four girls who give their Christmas breakfast to a poor German immigrant family. That story later became one of the opening scenes in *Little Women*. Though the novel project did not interest her, she found that the book was easy enough to write. In six weeks' time, from May to July 1868, she completed the first volume. Though the finished manuscript excited neither Alcott nor her editor, when it finally appeared in print in September 1868, it was an overnight success. Prompted by the success of volume one, she began a sequel. It took her another two months to write the second volume, which had the working title, "Good Wives"; when it was published as *Little Women or, Meg, Jo, Beth and Amy, Part Second* in January 1869, it too was a commercial and critical success.

The story of the four teenaged sisters, Meg, Jo, Beth, and Amy, and their growing up into young women succeeded partly because the material was autobiographical and Alcott knew it so well. Though each of the sisters receives equal attention in the novel, it is clear that Jo is the most interesting and best-drawn character, probably because she was Alcott's recreation of herself. Jo's struggles with her temper, her ambition, and her fervent desire to be a boy are well realized in the novel because they are so heartfelt. One identifies with the girl who wishes that she could enjoy the freedom of boys in clothing, manners, and career. One also sympathizes with Jo's attempts to curb her temper and her boyish enthusiasm and with her occasional relapses. Though all four girls have faults which they resolve to conquer at the novel's opening, Jo's are the most difficult and therefore her victory over them the most hard-won.

The faults or "burdens" of the four girls take on a religious cast since they are likened to the symbolic burdens of Christian, the hero of John Bunyan's *The Pilgrim's Progress*. As Christian in Bunyan's allegory must deal with his burden of sin on his journey to heaven, so the girls seek to cast off their burdens in their quest to become "little women." Alcott uses *The Pilgrim's Progress* as a patterning device in the novel. The book begins at Christmastime with each of the girls deciding what her main fault is. In the following year each goes through major changes so that by the next Christmas at the close of the book's first part they are all much improved. Each girl has a chapter devoted to her and her struggles with the title of the chapter taken from an incident in *The Pilgrim's Progress*— "Meg goes to Vanity Fair," "Amy's Valley of Humiliation," "Beth Finds the Palace Beautiful," and "Jo Meets Appolyon." The girls are assured that God will help them on their journey if they will

only appeal to Him. Though Alcott was never a member of a particular religious faith, it is clear that for her, religion was an important part of being a complete woman, and that trust in God was the major emotional support in a woman's life.

It is also important in *Little Women* that a girl learn housewifely accomplishments, such as sewing, cooking, and good manners in society. Though the March sisters show talents which might lead them to careers—Jo as a writer, Meg as an actress, Beth as a pianist, and Amy as an artist—career aspirations by themselves are shown to be inadequate as a complete definition of womanhood. In the novel each girl must learn to keep house and to master the feminine accomplishments of conversation, entertaining, and being pleasant and cheerful even under the most trying circumstances. Mrs. March, known as Marmee, is the model for all the girls to follow. She is a strong woman, the

They all drew to the fire, mother in the big chair, with Beth at her feet; Meg and Amy perched on either arm of the chair, and Jo leaning on the back. — PAGE 12.

Frontispiece by May Alcott for the first volume of Little Women *(Baldwin Library, University of Florida Libraries)*

head of a household, while her husband is away as a Union Army chaplain during the Civil War. She guides her daughters through their troubles with their faults. Throughout the novel she is a reliable source of loving wisdom, strong as a rock and as imperturbable as one. She is the mother that all readers would like to have—always available, always loving, always compassionate. Indeed, she was the model woman for the Victorian period and stands as the emotional center of the book.

The second volume of the book was written at least partly in response to Alcott's readers' demands to see how and whom the March sisters marry. Though it is difficult to ascertain whether Alcott had the sequel to volume one clearly designed when she wrote the first volume, it is clear that her readers' demands changed markedly the direction that the second volume took. Though in real life Alcott's older sister Anna, the model for Meg, had married, neither Alcott nor her younger sister May, the models for Jo and Amy, had marital prospects. Her sister Elizabeth, Beth in the novel, was dead, so that finding a partner for Beth to marry was unthinkable. If Alcott were to continue in her autobiographical vein, it was clear that she would frustrate her readers by not marrying off Jo and Amy, which might hinder the sales of the novel and might endanger future books that she might write. On the other hand, were she to proceed to marry off the March sisters, she would have some strenuous fictionalizing to do.

Alcott would also have to manage her own feelings about marriage. She herself never married; she knew that to marry might not be as desirable as was popularly thought in Victorian America, that there were other ways of leading a satisfying life if a woman were bold enough to try them. She could not consent to marry her own character Jo to the obvious choice in the novel, Laurie, the high-spirited and adventuresome boy next door. Throughout the first half of the novel the two had been fast friends and constant companions; there are even hints that Laurie is interested in Jo romantically. But in the second half of the novel, Jo flatly turns him down. Though some readers may be disappointed that Jo does not choose the most handsome and most eligible bachelor in the novel and may not accept Jo's explanation that she and Laurie "don't agree and we never shall," that "our quick tempers and strong wills would make us very miserable," others may laud Jo's resolution to remain single: "I don't believe I shall ever marry. I'm happy as I am, and love my liberty too well to be in any hurry to give

it up for any mortal man." Laurie, the handsome prince of the story, finally marries Amy, the golden-haired princess; this was Alcott's conciliating gesture to those readers who wanted a typical fairy-tale, happy-ever-after ending.

Writing of her sister Elizabeth's death was particularly painful for Alcott, but at least it gave her an excuse for not marrying Beth to some invented character. And her sister Anna's marriage could simply be transported whole into the fictional world of the novel. But Alcott's sense of her audience's limits told her that her readers would not be willing to accept an unmarried spinster who wrote books for a living as an acceptable ending for Jo. Though Alcott herself had a fulfilling life in just such a role, she was convinced that her public would accept nothing less than marriage as a satisfying happy ending; they were not open-minded enough to accept less traditional possibilities.

What the readers probably did not expect was the kind of character that Alcott finally chose for Jo to marry—Professor Bhaer, the poor German intellectual who is not handsome, young, dashing, or anything else that might have qualified him as a proper romantic hero in a sentimental novel. But Professor Bhaer provides Jo with a married life that suits her. He does not approve of her sensational writing, but he does encourage her intellectually. He also does not expect that she will stay home and take care of him and their children. At the end of the novel the two have established a school, so that both continue to work. They also have two sons, both reincarnations of Jo's energy and high spirits. Though Jo's future does not seem to be the "something splendid" that she aspires to in the first part of the novel, it is more satisfying than the more traditional wifely roles that Amy and Meg take on in their respective marriages.

There are other ways in which Alcott's novel was unconventional for its time. The girls are not perfect models of behavior or of speech. They sometimes utter mild curses and speak in slang. Even though some of her critics attacked *Little Women* and other Alcott novels on this score, Alcott was quick to point out that there was nothing immoral about such language, and that it was more realistic than the pious, perfect little mouthpieces that passed for characters in other children's novels of the time. She avoided the extreme sentimentalism that was characteristic of many deathbed scenes in children's literature when she described Beth March's final moments. Beth utters no parting words, and there is no profusion of tears from those she leaves behind. There is only a simple, heartfelt paragraph which is moving and understated while not resorting to bathos to influence the reader: "As Beth had hoped, the 'tide went out easily,' and in the dark hour before the dawn, on the bosom where she had drawn her first breath, she quietly drew her last, with no farewell but one loving look, one little sigh."

Finally, Alcott presents the first of a long line of imperfect and sometimes outright naughty children in American children's literature. The March sisters are the first in a line of such children which would later include Tom Bailey in *The Story of a Bad Boy* (1870) by Thomas Bailey Aldrich; Katy Carr in *What Katy Did* (1872) by Susan Coolidge; Tom Sawyer (1876) and Huckleberry Finn (1884) in the novels of Mark Twain; and Rebecca Rowena Randall in *Rebecca of Sunnybrook Farm* (1903) by Kate Douglas Wiggin.

Finally, though she may not have been interested in writing the novel to begin with, Alcott was one of the first writers in American children's literature to take seriously the critical questions involved in writing for children. She may seem today to be preaching in *Little Women*, but given the didactic intent of most literature at the time, she showed remarkable restraint. She did not tell, but rather showed, by putting her characters in real-life situations, the dilemmas of deciding what is right action and the thoughts and feelings involved in arriving at a difficult moral choice. Her work was influential in encouraging other writers for children to create real characters and real situations, having them act and speak as real children would.

Though *Little Women* was warmly received by its original readers, the book has not fared so well at the hands of modern critics, who see it as too sweet and sentimental for modern tastes. Martha Saxton in the 1977 biography *Louisa May*, sees *Little Women* as an artistic compromise for Alcott, a retreat into easy moralizing and simplistic characterization after the complexity of her adult novel *Moods* and its lukewarm critical reception. In a 1965 essay entitled "A Masterpiece, and Dreadful" Brigid Brophy criticizes Alcott for being unwilling to analyze characters or to devise situations which might test them and their virtues. In *Women's Fiction* (1978) Nina Baym, while praising Alcott for her artistic accomplishment and her ability to create authentic characters, notes that Alcott took over the themes of adult women's fiction of the time and turned them into a didactic device for girls, simplifying the themes rather than preserving the complexity with which they were illustrated in adult works. David Smith, studying the uses of *The Pilgrim's Progress* in *John Bunyan in America* (1966), levels the same kind of criticism, that Alcott oversimplifies Christian's struggles so that they will fit into the uncomplicated structure and symbol pattern in *Little Women*.

In spite of such criticism, the book endures and continues to be read with pleasure by children and by adults who return to the novel. The reason for the novel's popularity has been identified by Nina Auerbach, whose 1976 article "Austen and Alcott on Matriarchy" points to the warmth and solidarity of the circle of women in the novel and to the nostalgic appeal which makes readers wish for a time when domestic harmony of this order really existed. Though Alcott's own home life was never as placid or as warm as she presents it in the novel, she does create and sustain the atmosphere of emotional and physical sufficiency in the home, where Marmee allows the girls to remain always young and cared for. Readers continue to be enchanted by this never-never land set in New England, and to be lulled and comforted by its emotional richness.

Alcott capitalized on her success in *Little Women* by writing another girls' novel almost immediately. In 1869 *An Old-Fashioned Girl* was published in *Merry's Museum* in two separate parts, the second part again demanded by readers who wanted to know what happened to the characters as they grew up. Book publication followed in 1870. The novel is the story of a poor girl, fourteen-year-old Polly Milton, the old-fashioned girl of the title, who is visiting the rich Shaw family and their three children, six-year-old Maud, fourteen-year-old Fanny, and sixteen-year-old Tom. Though the Shaw family is wealthy and seems to have everything to make them happy, they are not. All the family members are materialistic and self-absorbed; they care little for each other and do nothing to make home life harmonious or comfortable. Mrs. Shaw is a neurasthenic invalid. Mr. Shaw is completely preoccupied by his business dealings. The children are left to their own devices, and their grandmother is ignored by all. Though Polly's own home is never shown in detail, the reader is assured that, in spite of the family's poverty and many children, they are happy, the children well cared for and well behaved.

In the book, Alcott demonstrates the carelessness with which rich people treat other people as well as material goods. She points out how snobby rich people are and how little they realize their complicity in the poverty and social isolation of working women: Fanny's rich friends snub Polly when she decides to make her own living as a music teacher, and women who work, such as seamstresses and servants, are not paid enough money to keep themselves. Alcott points to the silliness of fashionable girls' finishing schools where the girls go not to learn useful accomplishments; rather they attend to show off their clothes, to flirt, and to gossip. Alcott sets Polly as a positive example to the rich people. She is friendly even when the rich girls snub her; she is helpful around the Shaw house and shows the Shaws how happy home life can be if they make the effort to care for each other. She dresses simply and in the style of the young girl she is, instead of as the fashionable young woman Fanny Shaw prinks herself up to be.

In fact, Polly is too good to be true. Alcott does give her one fault, vanity, which makes her envy her rich friends for their finery and many changes of clothes and hats and gloves, but this one fault does not rescue Polly from seeming the perfect domestic little woman. In the book, she is called "sweet P" and "Polly peacemaker." She comes from the same social background as does Jo March but has none of Jo's spirit and ambition; her value in the novel is primarily symbolic. When Polly decides to become an independent working woman and

support herself, she does have the urge to break loose from the severe domestic economy she practices and to spend money extravagantly though she cannot afford it. But it is only here that Polly's character becomes more than just a symbol of "old-fashioned" girlhood based on domestic virtues.

As she shows the joys of poverty in *Little Women*, so in *An Old-Fashioned Girl* Alcott shows the misery of wealth. Though the Shaws try to learn from Polly how to make their house a home, it is not until they lose their fortune that they are properly reformed and learn to be a happy family. The book ends with the traditional marriages, of Fanny to an ardent admirer who loves her even though she is now poor because she has learned to make a proper home for him, and of Polly to Tom Shaw, who has been sobered by the realization that he must work diligently for a living rather than rely on his father's wealth. Alcott uses many of the same formulas she did in *Little Women*, but this time without the vibrancy or vigor that make *Little Women* distinctive. The book did not sell as well as *Little Women* did, although it did well enough: twelve thousand copies were sold by the initial publication date, and Alcott's first royalty check arrived for over $6000.

Having established herself as a wealthy and successful author, Alcott took a prolonged European holiday with her sister May and a mutual friend. While they were in Italy, they heard of the death of Alcott's sister Anna's husband, John Pratt. Though Pratt had arranged his affairs so that his widow and sons would be provided for, Alcott decided to write a book and give the proceeds to them. It was as though providing for her family had become a habit which she practiced even when the situation did not call for it. The result was *Little Men* (1871), a sequel to *Little Women*, the story of the Plumfield School which Professor Bhaer and Mrs. Jo had established at the end of *Little Women*. Alcott wrote the novel while she was in Europe and sent the manuscript to her publishers, Roberts Brothers, in Boston. It was published the day she arrived home and has continued to sell as well as *Little Women*.

Little Men is an educational novel in the manner of *Tom Brown's Schooldays* (1857), and *Tom Brown at Oxford* (1861) by Thomas Hughes. But Alcott's purpose is more than simply to celebrate the joys of school and the high spirits of schoolchildren. She wrote the novel to justify her father's educational methods and ideas. Many of the characters from *Little Women* reappear in *Little Men*—the March sisters and their husbands and off-

Louisa May Alcott

spring, Mr. and Mrs. March—and several children are introduced to demonstrate the effectiveness of Bronson Alcott's theories. The children spend little time in the classroom, though it can be assumed that they do have lessons in traditional subjects such as mathematics, composition, and geography, since the children discourse about these subjects at various points in the novel. Although Bronson Alcott did see that his daughters and the other pupils he taught were grounded in standard academic fare, he felt that other parts of their education were more important. As a consequence, even the most bookish of the children is never allowed to over-indulge for fear he may neglect the other aspects of the educational regime at Plumfield.

Even more important to Bronson Alcott was the education of the child's body and spirit. Louisa May Alcott sees to both of these matters at the fictional Plumfield. The children each receive a garden plot in which they must work; they are encouraged to play cricket, fly kites, go berry-picking, and participate in the household chores, not only to develop their bodies but also to cultivate their senses of responsibility and good sportsmanship. Much of the time is spent romping about Plumfield, since neither Bronson nor Louisa Alcott thought that youthful high spirits should be suppressed; rather they needed to be channeled into healthful, harmless fun. The book opens with a pillow fight at the school. Mrs. Jo has realized early in her career as a teacher that though she might prefer that the boys not sport about this way, such fighting was inevitable; she permits one fifteen-minute pillow fight a week, since everyone is the better for it—the boys for the fun and the release of energy and Mrs. Jo for not having to enforce an unenforceable and unnecessary rule.

But education at Plumfield has a more reflective and meditative side to it. Each Sunday the children attend church and in the afternoon the professor takes them for a nature walk, not only so that they may learn botany but also so that they may observe and appreciate God's handiwork in nature. They say grace at meals and sing hymns in the evenings while the school orchestra plays. Though Alcott does not press any sectarian belief in the book, she does make clear, as she does in *Little Women*, that the proper education of children requires that they understand religious matters.

Bronson and Louisa May Alcott both believed in coeducation, though Bronson was not as ardent a supporter of the cause of educational opportunity for women as was his daughter. In any case, there are girls at the school, both the traditional feminine

domestic kind and the more independent, physically and mentally ambitious kind. Alcott claims in the book that exposing the boys to the girls makes the boys improve their manners, social graces, and standards of cleanliness. They also come to realize that girls can be their physical and educational equals when Nan Harding, one of the girls at the school, competes with them in the classroom and on the playing field, frequently besting them both at games and in schoolwork.

The children are for the most part well behaved and well motivated, but there are times when their desire to please Professor and Mrs. Bhaer is simply not enough to keep them good. Bronson Alcott did not believe in corporal punishment, a revolutionary idea for the time, so he had to devise a number of other ways to chastise his pupils. One, which shows up in *Little Men*, was to have the student strike the teacher as punishment when the student had committed an error. Another was to keep a ledger or an account of each pupil's behavior and to discuss it once a week with the student, rewarding good behavior with praise and a check mark, but punishing misbehavior with a black mark and an expression of the teacher's disappointment. In the case of both punishments, the primary result is guilt on the student's part, which the modern reader may find distasteful. However, guilt can be quite motivating, as Louisa May Alcott knew, and both punishments are shown to work effectively in the novel.

That such mild punishments should succeed so splendidly indicates the major problem in the novel. The children are not well individualized; they are one-dimensional, each having one prevailing fault which they improve upon in the course of the novel. The metaphor which dominates the book is agricultural; the novel begins in the spring with Professor and Mrs. Bhaer planting the seeds of improvement; by the Thanksgiving celebration which closes the book, they reap a bountiful harvest of good deeds from each of the students. There is no really bad child who challenges the educational method, not even Dan Kean, the firebrand "berserker" who smokes, drinks, gambles, and swears. Even he is brought around by being thrown out of the school, the worst punishment available. His longing to return is so great that he promises and delivers reform in order to obtain a second chance at Plumfield.

The atmosphere of the book is tender and sweet; it has long been a favorite both of children and of educational theorists. But the sunny, cheerful surface of the book is not as simple and as harmonious as it seems at first glance. Dan Kean may be reformed, but the bond that results between him and Mrs. Jo is one that Alcott describes in peculiarly sexual terms. Once when she is particularly grateful, Mrs. Jo gives him "a kiss that made Dan entirely hers." When he feels the urge to run away again, Mrs. Jo says, "don't run far, and come back to me soon, for I want you very much." The happiness of the extended family is further called into doubt when Nan Harding tomahawks her dolls and abandons them in a particularly unmotherly way. Mrs. Jo's own five-year-old son Robby makes up a story about "a lady who had a million children, and one nice little boy" who subsequently drowns. It seems that Alcott is indicating here that in spite of her obvious purpose to show that family life and youth in general are happy, there is a darker side to human emotion and the intimacy of families which would destroy such happiness and which will intrude, even when perfect harmony seems to be prevailing. A careful reading of the novel rescues it from the charges of modern critics that the children are too good and the book too simpleminded in its belief that proper education can reform mankind.

After *Little Men*, Alcott did not write another children's novel for four years. In the interim, she rewrote one of the adult novels she had started during the Civil War, a largely autobiographical book entitled *Work: A Story of Experience*, and had it published serially in Henry Ward Beecher's weekly magazine the *Christian Union* and as a single volume with Roberts Brothers in 1873. She also wrote several short stories for children which appeared in magazines such as the *Youth's Companion*, the *Independent*, the *Christian Register*, and *St. Nicholas*. Many of these short stories were collected and republished in the six books of the *Aunt Jo's Scrap-Bag* series (1872-1882), and in other volumes as her career continued. Always one to turn a profit, Alcott realized that she could be paid twice for novels and stories if she sold them to magazines and then had them republished. Her reputation as a writer was well established, and her public was eager to read whatever she wrote, even if it had already appeared elsewhere.

In 1874, Alcott wrote *Eight Cousins* with its sequel, *Rose in Bloom*, clearly in mind. She wrote the former in serial form, to be published in installments in two children's magazines, *Good Things: A Picturesque Magazine for the Young of All Ages* (December 1874-November 1875) and *St. Nicholas* (January-October 1875). Roberts Brothers published the book as *Eight Cousins; or The Aunt-Hill* in

Title page for the first of Alcott's six "scrap-bag" collections (Baldwin Library, University of Florida Libraries). Most of the short stories included in the series first appeared in such magazines as Youth's Companion, Independent, Christian Register, and St. Nicholas.

1875, with a promise in the preface of a sequel, which appeared the next year, although it was not serialized. Both the novels show a technical accomplishment in plotting and characterization which Alcott had not formerly achieved. *Little Men* and *Little Women* are both episodic, devoting individual chapters to single characters. Though *An Old-Fashioned Girl* is concerned with one main character, Polly Milton, Polly's relations with individual members of the Shaw family tend to occupy individual chapters. But Alcott's treatment of Rose Campbell, the central character in *Eight Cousins* and *Rose in Bloom*, shows that she was capable of writing one continuous novel about a single character. Though the story line sometimes becomes episodic when dealing with Rose's seven male cousins, Rose is still the central focus, and it is her progress that dominates the novel.

The two novels taken together comprise a treatise on female education. Rose Campbell is a thirteen-year-old orphaned heiress who comes under the guardianship of her Uncle Alec, a young physician. He takes care of her at their ancestral home, a large house on a hill, near which and in which his many aunts, sisters, and sisters-in-law live; hence the subtitle of *Eight Cousins, The Aunt-Hill*. Rose is surrounded by her many female relatives, each of whom has a different idea about how the young heiress should be brought up. To relieve this female tyranny, Alcott provides Rose with seven male cousins of different ages, all of whom wish to make her one of their set. Uncle Alec is most willing that she should join with them in their games and sports, for Rose has led a rather sheltered life and feels awkward around company, especially boys; she also needs the physical exercise that playing with the boys will provide in order to perk up her spirits and to help her sleep more soundly. In this case, Alcott reverses the rationale for coeducation as she presented it in *Little Men;* whereas in the earlier novel, it was for the improvement of the boys that girls were introduced, in *Eight Cousins* it is decidedly for Rose's benefit that boys should be her companions.

Though it is clear that vigorous physical education is one reason for the presence of the seven male cousins, it is apparent later in the novel that Rose is present to exert her influence on her cousins so that they will refrain from the temptations that beset growing boys—smoking, drinking, and reading unhealthy novels. Though Alcott uses Rose as a vehicle to rail against these errors, it is also clear that these issues point to one of the aspects of female education important to Alcott. Rose's education takes place not only so that she can improve herself, but also so that she may learn to improve her cousins. At one point in *Eight Cousins*, Rose says, "I have discovered what girls are made for. . . . To take care of boys." As independent and strong-minded as Alcott would have her heroines be, she clearly does not have them achieve independence only for their own sakes.

But Alcott does advocate that Rose learn a "trade" so that she can take care of herself should she ever have to, and so that her life will not be an idle one. Part of Alcott's educational regime for Rose is that she learns as her trade housekeeping from her aunts. Her accomplishments in this field are symbolized by her ability to make a wholesome loaf of bread and to sew a shirt with neat buttonholes for her Uncle Alec, both without assistance. These two tasks symbolize in the novel competence in a variety of other household tasks which may be performed easily once these two basic skills are mastered. Alcott's points are two: first, that all women, no matter how wealthy, should be able to earn their own livings, and second, that all women should master the traditional female chores of cooking and sewing, even if they are likely to have servants. Though the first message is decidedly untypical and rather feminist for its time, the second is not. Alcott is again careful not to offend her audience by not being too strident in her ideology about women's work and educational reform.

Alcott also takes up the issue of female dress reform, which was suggested but not examined in depth in *An Old-Fashioned Girl*. Though she does not go as far as to have Rose wear bloomers, assuaging the more fashionable aunts and less daring readers, Alcott does criticize a stylish walking suit as unbecoming, unhealthful with its high boots and open neckline which do not protect the body against inclement weather, and unmanageable and confining because of the tightness of the skirt and the restrictions of the corset. What the aunts propose is that Rose wear a walking suit in which she cannot walk. The suit that Uncle Alec proposes for her is comfortable, warm, attractive in color and design, and decidedly made for moving and playing in. It is eminently sensible and makes Rose look like the schoolgirl she is, rather than a young lady, which as yet she is not. Alcott is not saying that women should look unattractive or that they should wear no ornaments; she does allow Rose to pierce her ears and to enjoy the earrings, although Uncle Alec is disappointed in the girl's vanity about them. But Alcott does indicate that the Victorian way of dressing young girls, and even stylish older women, is unflattering and not conducive to good health.

Rose does study traditional school subjects, but in nontraditional ways. The geography and economy of China are taught by visiting a merchant ship newly arrived from the Orient. Rose learns mathematics by keeping records of the expenditures from her allowance. Uncle Alec points out that this will be particularly important for Rose if she is to manage her own estate when she comes of age. She does study books, but not by doing assigned reading in them; instead she learns while she is reading aloud to one of her cousins who is ill and while she is teaching one of the household servants to read and write. And finally, she learns anatomy and physiology when her physician uncle brings home a real skeleton for her to study. Alcott is posing this curriculum as a much more useful and enjoyable course of study, different from that which girls, or even boys, usually pursued at schools of the time. There is no grinding away at learning useless facts, to the detriment of both health and intellectual progress; nor is there the trivial study typical of finishing schools which might teach a little music and painting and dancing, but nothing of real use in the adult world.

In *Rose in Bloom,* Alcott returns to the Campbell clan of cousins. Her activities in the interim between the composition of *Eight Cousins* and that of *Rose in Bloom* are embodied in the latter book in several ways. Alcott had spent a year attending meetings of women's reform movements, including the Women's Congress in Syracuse in 1875, and had spent the winter holidays in New York, visiting philanthropic institutions, including orphanages and prisons. The novel opens seven years after the close of *Eight Cousins.* Rose and her cousins are now young people considering marriage and a choice of vocation. Rose has just returned from Europe, where her Uncle Alec has taken her to visit philanthropic institutions like those Alcott had observed. Rose has decided to become a professional philanthropist. She converts one of her properties into a lodging house for poor working women. She also adopts an orphan from a workhouse and sponsors outings and picnics for children from a nearby orphanage. Her male cousins find her decidedly strong-minded in her pursuit of these causes, but Rose attributes her resolution to her desire to have a career and be more than a social ornament of a wife and mother: "I believe that it is as much a right and a duty for women to do something with their lives as for men; and we are not going to be satisfied. . . . Would *you* be contented to be told to enjoy yourself for a little while, then marry and do nothing more till you die?" The sermon continues: "We've got minds and souls as well as hearts; ambition and talents, as well as beauty and accomplishments; and we want to live and learn as well as love and be loved. I'm sick of being told that is all a woman is fit for! I won't have any thing to do with love till I prove that I am something besides a housekeeper and baby-tender!" Here is the feminism that Alcott had been experimenting with in her leisure time between books.

In spite of Rose's high-mindedness about a career and philanthropy, in the course of the novel she does marry. Much of the book is devoted to her decision about which of her cousins to choose. At first it seems that she will marry Charlie, but he

proves unsuitable. As an only child, his mother has spoiled him, and he is now unable to concentrate on either studies or a vocation long enough to make a success of himself. He also runs with a bad crowd of other boys and drinks. Though he promises Rose to abstain, one night he breaks his promise. One glass of champagne makes him unable to control his horse; he is thrown and dies of his injuries. Though this may seem like rather drastic punishment for one indulgence in champagne, it is clear that Charlie is unsuitable for Rose because of his irresolution.

After a suitable period of mourning, Rose turns her interest to her bookish cousin Mac. He is the cousin who most resembles her admirable Uncle Alec, for Mac is studying to be a doctor. But even Mac needs improvement, for his manners in social settings are abominable. He does not dress himself neatly, and when he escorts Rose to a ball, he leaves her to her own devices, going off in a corner to talk science with another man rather than dancing with Rose and seeing her home. Rose sends him off to make a success of himself. He does so not only by becoming a worthy physician, but also by writing a volume of poetry which makes him sought after by fashionable society, where he shows off his newly acquired social graces. When he arrives home, he has throughly demonstrated his fitness to be Rose's husband.

At the end of the novel, several other cousins marry, too, but one of the marriages is noteworthy for the social snobbery which is clear in the conduct of the courtship. In *Eight Cousins*, Rose "adopts" as a sister an orphaned servant girl her own age. She sees to it that Phebe has all the educational advantages that she has, especially voice lessons, for Phebe is a natural singer. When Alec, Rose, and Phebe return from Europe, one of Rose's cousins falls in love with Phebe, and she with him, but the family opposes the match because of Phebe's social inferiority. Phebe goes away to a big city where she earns a reputation for herself as a singer in one of the prestigious churches. Both she and cousin Archie prove their love by remaining true to each other during their separation. When Phebe arrives home with sufficient public acclaim to prove her worthiness, then the family consents to the match, but not until then. Though Alcott in other places supports the lot of decent and respectable working women, she will only allow them into the upper class when they prove extraordinarily meritorious, as Phebe does.

Eight Cousins and *Rose in Bloom* are more issue-oriented than any of Alcott's earlier books. She does not hesitate to have her characters preach when she feels strongly about an issue. And though Rose is characterized by many of the high-spirited qualities of children that the girls in *Little Women* have, she too can be preachy and straitlaced, especially when it comes to drinking, smoking, and application to a vocation. The feminism she expresses at the beginning of *Rose in Bloom* seems too bitter for a young girl who has led a privileged and sheltered life; the acerbity is Alcott's, and the didacticism in both novels sometimes overshadows the technical achievements of plot and characterization.

Both Alcott and her mother were ill during the time that the two books were written. By 1877 it became apparent that Abigail Alcott was dying. While Alcott attended her mother's sickbed, Mary Mapes Dodge, the editor of *St. Nicholas,* appealed to her for another children's novel to be serialized in her magazine. *Under the Lilacs* was written in snatches while Alcott nursed her mother. It is the least successful of her juvenile novels. It was published serially from December 1877 to October 1878 in *St. Nicholas.* Her publisher, Roberts Brothers, gave her a $3000 advance on the book's publication in 1878 which Alcott felt she would need for the extra expenses in nursing her mother.

Under the Lilacs is the story of a circus boy and his trained poodle who run away from the circus to find the boy's father. His father had left to find his fortune in the West, promising to return. When he does not and when the boy and the dog are abused by the circus master, they leave. On their way they encounter two young girls and their mother, who take over the care of both boy and dog, giving them a home and the boy schooling to make him respectable. In the process they stifle the boy's fun-loving nature. The best scenes in the book are Alcott's descriptions of the children at their games and the dog doing his tricks. Otherwise, Alcott turns the circus boy into a respectable but boring middle-class schoolboy entirely too quickly. The girls' characters are flatly drawn, and the plot shows little inventiveness. Perhaps Alcott was too involved in caring for her mother to give the novel the attention needed for it to succeed.

At this time Alcott rewrote one of her gothic thrillers to be published in the No-Name series of books published anonymously by famous American authors. Her own publisher, Roberts Brothers, produced the series and wanted a book by their best-known author in disguise. *A Modern Mephistopheles* (1877) is full of gothic horror and evil and might have shocked Alcott's reading public, who expected wholesome juvenile writing. But nothing in the book is really so horrible, and Alcott later consented to have the book republished under her own name.

Just before her mother's death, Alcott and her family moved from their home at Orchard House on the outskirts of Concord to the Thoreau house in Concord village. After her mother's death, Alcott was drawn into the activities of the village children—their sports, dramatic productions, and holiday celebrations. When one of the children died, she was moved to write *Jack and Jill: A Village Story,* which was serialized in *St. Nicholas* from December 1879 to October 1880 and also published by Roberts Brothers in 1880. It is the story of a group of children and uses Alcott's earlier episodic technique of devoting individual chapters to individual children. The book takes place in Harmony Village, the fictional equivalent of Concord, over the course of about a year. Alcott chronicles a Christmas party, the children's dramatic presentation in honor of George Washington's birthday, a May Day celebration, a weekend at a shore resort, and a school exhibition. Her eye for journalistic detail did not fail her, for these are the most interesting incidents in the book. *Jack and Jill* is also the work that succeeds best in capturing the New England setting, which dominates the action and dictates much of the ordering of the celebrations.

Jack and Jill also tells the story of the death of Ed Devlin, the fictional equivalent of a neighboring Concord schoolboy, Ellsworth Devens, to whose memory the book is dedicated. Ed is a good boy, perhaps too angelic in his protection of the younger children from the bullying of the older ones and in his willingness to leave school and go into business in order to support his mother. But Alcott does relieve this portrait of overwhelming goodness by pointing out that Ed is something of a flirt, for he is particularly gallant around girls. In any case, Ed dies of a mysterious fever and all the children attend his funeral. They realize that Ed is sincerely mourned in death because of his goodness in life, and they all resolve to follow his good example in their own lives. Although Ed's death is not described by Alcott, the scene of the funeral is overdone, partly because Alcott does not resist the urge to intrude and preach on the appropriateness of the subject of death in children's books, and partly because Ed was so good. If she had resisted both impulses, she might have written about death with the same sensitivity with which she portrayed Beth's demise in *Little Women.* As it stands in the novel, Ed's death is too sweet and precious to be believed.

Above and opposite page: Manuscript for the preface to the 1889 edition of A Modern Mephistopheles *(Louisa May Alcott, Her Life, Letters and Journals, edited by Ednah Dow Cheney, 1889). As Alcott explains, the first edition, published in 1877 as part of Roberts Brothers' No Name series, "was very successful in preserving its incognito & many persons still insist that it could not have been written by the author of* Little Women.*"*

some years; it is considered
well to add this volume to the
small series of new romances which
one offered not a finished work
by any means but merely attempts
at something graver than
magazine stories or juvenile
side literature,

                                    L. M. Alcott.

LOUISA M. ALCOTT'S STORY-BOOKS.

A CHRISTMAS DREAM.

LULU'S LIBRARY.

A COLLECTION OF STORIES BY "AUNT JO.

With Illustrations by JESSIE McDERMOTT.

3 vols. 16mo. Cloth. Price, $1.00 per volume.

ROBERTS BROTHERS, PUBLISHERS,
BOSTON.

*Publisher's advertisement for the series comprising stories Alcott
had written for her niece Louisa May Nieriker*

Some episodes in *Jack and Jill* are devoted to showing the efficacy of Bronson Alcott's child-rearing principles of "good health, good principles, and a good education." The girls of the village take it upon themselves to reform their male siblings and friends, again by influencing them to be gentlemen in their ladylike presences. The boys, of course, are duly reformed. The boys have a debating team which discusses the idea of coeducation and decides in its favor. They also form an antismoking league to help one another resist the boyish temptation to indulge. What saves *Jack and Jill* from being a slavish imitation of Alcott's earlier books is the portrayal of the children's celebrations. Otherwise, Alcott takes no chances in this novel with inventing new or daring characters and situations or trying out new social ideas.

Alcott continued to be a popular author with children and to write short stories for them; she also kept on with her practice of collecting those short stories for republication in book form. When her younger sister May died from the complications of childbirth and left the guardianship of her baby daughter, Louisa ("Lulu") May Nieriker, to the baby's Aunt Louisa, Alcott started writing stories for the little girl's amusement. The three-volume *Lulu's Library* series (1886-1889) collected these stories and republished some of Alcott's older stories from *Flower Fables*. Alcott also found time to revise her favorite novel, *Moods*, for republication in 1882. Its commercial success no doubt rested on Alcott's fame as a juvenile writer.

Alcott became increasingly ill toward the end of her life. Nannies took over the care of her niece, and Alcott began to settle her financial affairs by adopting her nephew John Sewell Pratt (who took the name John S. P. Alcott) so that there would be no legal problems about the proceeds from her books staying in the family. As early as 1880, Mary Mapes Dodge and Alcott's editor had asked for a

"These were the boys, and they lived together as happily as twelve lads could; studying and playing, working and squabbling, fighting faults and cultivating virtues, in the good old-fashioned way." — PAGE 28.

Engraving of a bas-relief by Walton Rickeison used as the frontispiece for Alcott's 1886 sequel to Little Men *(Baldwin Library, University of Florida Libraries)*

sequel to *Little Men.* Alcott began to write one, but due to ill health, the death of her sister, her grief over the death of her mother, and her father's stroke and deteriorating health, all progress halted. The family moved from Concord to Boston to be nearer to Alcott's doctors. The sequel, *Jo's Boys, and How They Turned Out,* was finally finished and published in 1886 by Roberts Brothers. The pain in which the book was composed is evident from the first chapter, in which the remaining March sisters, Mrs. Jo and Mrs. Meg, mourn the deaths of Beth, Marmee, Meg's husband, and others; it was difficult for Alcott to think about, much less write about, those deaths, and the mental anguish slowed down her progress on the book.

Jo's Boys is set at the Plumfield School, which has been expanded to include Laurence College for both young men and women. The role of the college in the book is to show the success of Bronson Alcott's educational methods as children grow into young adulthood. The many successful careers and marriages pursued and achieved in the novel are indications of the soundness of Bronson Alcott's principles, though it is not always clear from the characterizations that the successes are due solely to the children's educations.

In spite of the educational theme, the novel's main emphasis is on women's rights. Though in other novels Alcott refrained from preaching the feminist gospel and from having her female characters follow it too closely, in *Jo's Boys* she shows no such restraint. She has Mrs. Jo reproach the male students for their condescending attitudes toward their fellow female students; when the women students meet together for a sewing circle, Mrs. Jo reads to them from feminist tracts while they attend to their needlework. Finally, the girls in the novel have successful careers, whereas in *Little Women* they do not. One of the girls in *Jo's Boys,* Nan Harding, becomes a doctor and remains a happy and satisfied spinster. Though there are more conventional "little women" in the book who become happy housewives, they are not as convincingly or as sympathetically drawn as are the career women. The little women seem to be a sop that Alcott throws to readers who might find such strident feminist talk and action distasteful.

At the end of the novel, Alcott ties up the loose ends of the plot, disposing of all the characters so throughly that no sequel would be possible. The exhaustion and relief she felt at finally finishing with the March family are evident at the end when she threatens to destroy Plumfield with an earthquake to prevent clamor from her readers

Alcott in 1887

for yet another sequel. The episodic quality of the book, no doubt resulting at least partly from Alcott's sporadic attempts at writing it over a period of six years, is particularly noticeable. The sharpness of the women's-rights diatribes and the speedy dispatch with which the characters are disposed of and the novel ended underscore Alcott's physical and creative exhaustion. Though it is pleasing to meet the same familiar characters again, *Jo's Boys* is the least satisfactory of the March family stories. No doubt its commercial success and acceptance by the critics owed much to the quality and reputation of its two predecessors.

Alcott's health deteriorated rapidly in early 1888. When on 4 March she was allowed to leave the rest home where she was staying to visit her father on his deathbed, the outing was too much for her both physically and emotionally. Bronson Alcott died that day; early on the morning of 6 March, Louisa May Alcott died in her sleep at the rest home in Roxbury, Massachusetts. The two were eulogized at a joint funeral, and both were buried in the family plot in Sleepy Hollow Cemetery, Concord.

Alcott's reputation as a children's writer was and still is based primarily on her accomplishment in *Little Women*. None of the books that followed reach the same level of technical accomplishment in characterization and structure, and it is this book to which most modern criticism has been directed. The rediscovery of Alcott's adult works inspired by the new interest in nineteenth-century women's fiction has undercut favorable evaluation of the juvenile novels. It is necessary to remember that for her time Alcott showed surprising honesty in her portrayal of authentic human characters with recognizable human feelings. She institutionalized the family story as a staple of American children's fare; she maintained a plain, honest, and yet pleasing style; and even if she did descend into preachiness at times, she did it with a restraint lacking in her contemporaries. Her novels are particularly adept at capturing the high spirits of children at play, and if those children today seem too good to be true, they were much truer to life than other fictional children of the time. Finally, Alcott filled a void in children's literature, for there were no good books for adolescents, especially not for girls. The March sisters, especially Jo, stand as the crowning achievement of Alcott's literary career and as a model for writers of domestic fiction who followed.

Bibliography:

Alma J. Payne, *Louisa May Alcott; A Reference Guide* (Boston: G. K. Hall, 1980).

Biographies:

Ednah Dow Cheney, *Louisa May Alcott, Her Life, Letters and Journals* (Boston: Roberts Brothers, 1889);

Madeleine B. Stern, *Louisa May Alcott* (Norman: University of Oklahoma Press, 1950);

Martha Saxton, *Louisa May: A Modern Biography of Louisa May Alcott* (Boston: Houghton Mifflin, 1977);

Madelon Bedell, *The Alcotts* (New York: Clarkson Potter, 1981).

References:

Nina Auerbach, "Austen and Alcott on Matriarchy: New Women or New Wives?," *Novel*, 10 (Fall-Winter 1976): 6-26;

Nina Baym, *Women's Fiction; A Guide to Novels by and about Women in America, 1820-1870* (Ithaca & London: Cornell University Press, 1978), pp. 296-298;

Brigid Brophy, "A Masterpiece, and Dreadful," *New York Times Book Review*, 10 January 1965, p. 44;

Sarah Elbert, *A Hunger for Home: Louisa May Alcott and Little Women* (Philadelphia: Temple University Press, 1984);

Elizabeth Janeway, "Meg, Jo, Beth, Amy, and Louisa," *New York Times Book Review*, 29 September 1968, pp. 42-46;

Ruth K. MacDonald, *Louisa May Alcott* (Boston: Twayne, 1983);

Joy Marsella, *The Promise of Destiny: Children in the Short Stories of Louisa May Alcott* (Westport, Conn.: Greenwood Press, 1984);

Leona Rostenberg, "Some Anonymous and Pseudonymous Thrillers of Louisa May Alcott," *Papers of the Bibliographical Society of America*, 37, no. 1 (1943): 131-140;

David E. Smith, *John Bunyan in America* (Bloomington & London: Indiana University Press, 1966), pp. 93-102;

Patricia Meyer Spacks, *The Female Imagination* (New York: Knopf, 1975), pp. 95-101;

Madeleine B. Stern, *Critical Essays on Louisa May Alcott* (Boston: G. K. Hall, 1984).

Papers:

The Alcott family papers are in the possession of the Houghton Library at Harvard University.

Isabella Alden
(Pansy)
(3 November 1841-5 August 1930)

J. B. Dobkin
University of South Florida

BOOKS: *Helen Lester* (Cincinnati: American Reform Tract & Book Society, 1865);

Jessie Wells; or, How to Save the Lost (Cincinnati: American Reform Tract & Book Society, 1865);

Bernie's White Chicken (Cincinnati: Western Tract & Book Society, 1867);

Tip Lewis and His Lamp (Boston: Lothrop, 1867);

Ester Ried: Asleep and Awake (Cincinnati: Western Tract & Book Society, 1870);

Docia's Journal; or, God is Love (Philadelphia: J. P. Skelly, 1871);

Three People (Cincinnati: Western Tract & Book Society, 1871);

Julia Ried: Listening and Led (Cincinnati: Western Tract & Book Society, 1872);

The King's Daughter (Boston: Lothrop, 1873);

Wise and Otherwise (Cincinnati: Western Tract & Book Society, 1873);

Household Puzzles (Boston: Lothrop, 1874);

Modern Prophets and Other Sketches, by Pansy and Faye Huntington (Theodosia Maria Foster) (Boston: Lothrop, 1874);

A Christmas Time (Boston: Lothrop, 1875);

Cunning Workmen (Boston: Lothrop, 1875);

Dr. Dean's Way, by Pansy and Huntington (Boston: Lothrop, 1875);

Grandpa's Darlings (Boston: Lothrop, 1875);

Four Girls at Chautauqua (Boston: Lothrop, 1876);

Little Minnie; and Other Stories (Boston: Lothrop, 1876);

Pansy's Picture Book (Boston: Lothrop, 1876);

Pansy's Picture Library, 4 volumes (Boston: Lothrop, 1876);

Pictures From Bobby's Life; and Other Stories (Boston: Lothrop, 1876);

The Randolphs (Boston: Lothrop, 1876);

The Chatauqua Girls at Home (Boston: Lothrop, 1877); republished as *Obeying the Call* (Glasgow: Marr, 1878);

Getting Ahead (Boston: Lothrop, 1877);

The Lesson in Story, 2 volumes (Boston: Lothrop, 1877);

Little People in Picture and Story (Boston: Lothrop, 1877);

Two Boys (Boston: Lothrop, 1877);

From Different Standpoints, by Pansy and Huntington (Boston: Lothrop, 1878);

Little Fishers: And Their Nets (Boston: Lothrop, 1878);

Little Hands (Boston: Lothrop, 1878);

Our Darlings (N.p., 1878);

Links in Rebecca's Life (Boston: Lothrop, 1878);

Pretty Soon (Boston: Lothrop, 1878);

Red Ribbon (Boston: Lothrop, 1878);

Sidney Martin's Christmas (Boston: Lothrop, 1878);

Six Little Girls (Boston: Lothrop, 1878);

Little By Little (Boston: Lothrop, 1879);

Isabella Alden

37

Miss Priscilla Hunter, and My Daughter Susan (Boston: Lothrop, 1879);

My Daughter Susan (Boston: Lothrop, 1879);

Ruth Erskine's Crosses (Boston: Lothrop, 1879);

Divers Women, by Pansy and Mrs. C. M. Livingston (Boston: Lothrop, 1880);

A New Graft on the Family Tree (Boston: Lothrop, 1880);

Next Things and Dorrie's Day (Boston: Lothrop, 1880);

People Who Haven't Time (N.p., 1880);

The Teacher's Helper (Boston: Lothrop, 1880);

That Boy Bob, by Pansy and Huntington (N.p., 1880);

What She Said: And What She Meant (Boston: Lothrop, 1880);

The Hall in the Grove (Boston: Lothrop, 1881);

Mrs. Harry Harper's Awakening (Boston: Lothrop, 1881);

The Pocket Measure (Boston: Lothrop, 1881);

Five Friends (N.p., 1882);

Mary Burton Abroad, and Other Stories, by Pansy, Livingston, Foster, and others (Boston: Lothrop, 1882);

Mrs. Solomon Smith Looking On (Boston: Lothrop, 1882);

Some Young Heroines (Boston: Lothrop, 1882);

Ester Ried Yet Speaking (Boston: Lothrop, 1883);

The Man of the House (Boston: Lothrop, 1883);

Pansy's Home Story Book (Boston: Lothrop, 1883);

Pansy's Scrap Book (Boston: Lothrop, 1883);

Side By Side (Boston: Lothrop, 1883);

Christie's Christmas (Boston: Lothrop, 1884);

An Endless Chain (Boston: Lothrop, 1884);

A Hedge Fence (Boston: Lothrop, 1884);

An Hour With Miss Streator (Boston: Lothrop, 1884);

Interrupted (Boston: Lothrop, 1884);

New Year's Tangles and Other Stories (Boston: Lothrop, 1884);

Pansy's Stories of Child Life, 6 volumes (N.p., 1884-1889);

Gertrude's Diary (Boston: Lothrop, 1885);

In the Woods and Out, and Other Stories (Boston: Lothrop, 1885);

One Commonplace Day (Boston: Lothrop, 1886);

The Browning Boys (Boston: Lothrop, 1886);

Spun From Fact (Boston: Lothrop, 1886);

Stories and Pictures From the Life of Jesus (Boston: Lothrop, 1886?);

Eighty-Seven (Boston: Lothrop, 1887);

A Golden Thought, and Other Stories (Boston: Lothrop, 1887);

At Home Stories (N.p., 1887);

Mother's Boys and Girls (Boston: Lothrop, 1887);

Six O'Clock in the Evening (Boston: Lothrop, 1887);

Sunday Chat (Boston: Lothrop, 1887);

A Dozen of Them (Boston: Lothrop, 1888);

Judge Burnham's Daughters (Boston: Lothrop, 1888);

Monteagle (Boston: Lothrop, 1888);

Pansies for Thoughts, From the Writings of Pansy, compiled by Livingston (Boston: Lothrop, 1888);

Profiles, by Pansy and Livingston (Boston: Lothrop, 1888);

Chrissy's Endeavor (Boston: Lothrop, 1889);

A Sevenfold Trouble (Boston: Lothrop, 1889);

"We Twelve Girls" (Boston: Lothrop, 1889);

Young Folks Worth Knowing (N.p., 1889);

Aunt Hannah And Martha and John, by Pansy and Livingston (Boston: Lothrop, 1890);

The Prince of Peace (Boston: Lothrop, 1890);

An April Walk and Other Stories From The Pansy (Boston: Lothrop, 1890);

Helen the Historian (N.p., 1891);

Her Associate Members (Boston: Lothrop, 1891);

Miss Dee Dunmore Bryant (Boston: Lothrop, 1891);

Glimpses of Girlhood (Boston: Lothrop, 1892);

John Remington Martyr, by Pansy and Livingston (Boston: Lothrop, 1892);

Pansy's Stories of American History (Boston: Lothrop, 1893);

Stephen Mitchell's Journey (Boston: Lothrop, 1893);

Twenty Minutes Late (Boston: Lothrop, 1893);

Worth Having (N.p., 1893);

Stories and Pictures from the New Testament (Boston: Lothrop, 1893);

Only Ten Cents (Boston: Lothrop, 1894);

"Wanted" (Boston: Lothrop, 1894);

Pansy's Boys and Girls Picture Book (Boston: Lothrop, 1895);

What They Couldn't; A Home Story (Boston: Lothrop, 1895);

Making Fate (Boston: Lothrop, 1896);

Their Vacation and Other Stories of Striving and Doing (Boston: Lothrop, 1896);

The Older Brother (N.p., 1897);

Overruled (Boston: Lothrop, 1897);

Sunday Book (Boston: Lothrop, 1897);

Agatha's Unknown Way (New York: Revell, 1898);

As In A Mirror (Boston: Lothrop, 1898);

Reuben's Hindrances (N.p., 1898);

Yesterday, Framed in To-day (Boston: Lothrop, 1898);

By Way of the Wilderness, by Pansy and Livingston (Boston: Lothrop, 1899);

A Modern Sacrifice. The Story of Kissie Gordon's Experiment (Boston: Lothrop, 1899);

Three Times Three; A Story for Young People, and Others (New York: Revell, 1899);

Her Mother's Bible (Boston: Lothrop, 1900);

Missent; or, The Story of a Letter (Boston: Lothrop, 1900);

Pauline (Boston: Lothrop, 1900);

Mag and Margaret; A Story for Girls (Boston: Lothrop, 1901);

Unto The End (Boston: Lothrop, 1902);

Mara (Boston: Lothrop, 1903);

Doris Ferrand's Vocation (Boston: Lothrop, 1904);

David Ransom's Watch (Boston: Lothrop, 1905);

Ester Ried's Namesake (Boston: Lothrop, Lee & Shepard, 1906);

Ruth Erskine's Son (Boston: Lothrop, Lee & Shepard, 1907);

The Browns at Mt. Hermon (Boston: Lothrop, Lee & Shepard, 1908);

Lost on the Trail (Boston: Lothrop, Lee & Shepard, 1911);

The Long Way Home (Boston: Lothrop, Lee & Shepard, 1912);

Four Mothers at Chatauqua (Boston: Lothrop, Lee & Shepard, 1913);

Tony Keating's Surprises (Chicago: Donohue, 1914);

The Fortunate Calamity (Philadelphia & London: Lippincott, 1927);

An Interrupted Night (New York: Burt, 1929);

Memories of Yesterday, edited by Grace Livingston Hill (Philadelphia & London: Lippincott, 1931).

OTHER: *Young Folks Stories of American History and Home Life,* first series, edited by Pansy (Boston: Lothrop, 1884);

Young Folks Stories of Foreign Lands, first series, edited by Pansy (Boston: Lothrop, 1884);

Young Folks Stories of American History and Home Life, second series, edited by Pansy (Boston: Lothrop, 1887);

Young Folks Stories of Foreign Lands, second series, edited by Pansy (Boston: Lothrop, 1887);

Young Folks Stories of American History and Home Life, third series, edited by Pansy (Boston: Lothrop, 1889).

During a career that spanned more than sixty years, Isabella Macdonald Alden, writing as Pansy, composed nearly 150 books which were read by a worldwide public. Her works were so widely appreciated by a popular audience that they were translated into many languages, including Armenian, Bulgarian, Japanese, and Swedish.

Born in Rochester, New York, Isabella Macdonald was the youngest of six children. Her parents were Isaac and Myra Spofford Macdonald. She received her early education from her father, who was an active advocate of the reforms of the day. It was from her father that she received the pet name Pansy. He also encouraged her to keep a daily journal and to write for his criticism stories and reports on sermons that she heard at church. By this means she developed her facility of expression when she was still a child.

Alden, using the pseudonym Pansy, had her first short story printed in a Gloversville, New York, paper when she was only ten years of age. Her formal schooling began at Seneca Collegiate Institute at Ovid, New York, and continued at the Young Ladies Institute at Auburn, New York, where she became a student teacher. Alden's first book was written while at Auburn, inspired by a prize offer from the American Reform Tract and Book Society for the best book setting forth the principles of Christianity for children ten to fourteen years of age. After writing her storybook, which was later published under the title *Helen Lester* (1865), the young author was dissatisfied and buried the manuscript at the bottom of her trunk. It was rescued by a roommate and sent, without the writer's knowledge, to the American Reform Society just three days before the close of the competition. The story won the prize and also a request for more stories for publication.

In writing about her stories, and *Helen Lester* in particular, Alden made her motivation crystal clear. "My very first little story books were written with a single distinct purpose in view, given over to the desire and determination to win souls for Jesus Christ. The longer I wrote and the older I grew, that was my central purpose. I saw the trend away from Christ long ago. I recognized the downward trend not only in girls and boys, but in their mothers and teachers and pastors. I came by degrees to understand that the class of young people to whom I had dedicated my life had made a distinct descent, and that for me to do the same in my writing would be to dishonor Jesus Christ. I determined never to do it. I never have.... It was for that I began to write in the first place. The first real story that I ever wrote was written in answer to a call for the best story that would make plain the way of salvation. My *Helen Lester* was the result. It was then that I dedicated my pen to the direct and continuous effort to win others for Christ and help others to closer fellowship with Him."

In May 1866 she married the Reverend Gustavus R. Alden, a Presbyterian minister and a lineal descendant of John Alden. As she often indicated in her letters, she was never idle. According to her niece, Grace Livingston Hill, "She prepared the

The Aldens at a Chautauqua assembly. Alden and her husband, the Reverend Gustavus R. Alden, are seated in the second row, at left; their son, Raymond Macdonald Alden, is in the back row, at right.

primary lessons for the *Westminster Teacher;* she edited the Presbyterian *Primary Quarterly;* she published a children's magazine entitled *Pansy;* she wrote a serial story every winter for the *Herald and Presbyter;* she taught a Sunday-school class of one hundred children; she married a minister and assisted him in parish work; and she raised a family."

After spending a few years at Almond, New York, the Aldens moved to Utica and then to New Hartford, where on 30 March 1873 their son, Raymond Macdonald Alden, was born. His ill health during his youth caused the family to live for several years in Winter Park, Florida. From Florida, they moved to Pennsylvania and ultimately to Palo Alto, California. From 1873 to 1896 Alden edited the juvenile periodical *Pansy.* Throughout her long and active life she was a devoted church worker. The material for most of her stories was drawn from her experiences as a pastor's wife. "Whenever," as she expressed it, "things went wrong, I went home and wrote a book to make them come out right."

Both Alden's husband and son passed away in 1924. During her lifetime her two most impor-

tant works were considered to be *The Prince of Peace,* a life of Christ, published in 1890, and *Yesterday, Framed in To-day* (1898), a story in which the life of Christ is retold in the framework of modern civilization.

In terms of sales, Alden reached her zenith about 1900 when her books were selling at the rate of 100,000 copies a year. Of all her books, the Ester Ried series (*Ester Ried: Asleep and Awake,* 1870; *Ester Ried Yet Speaking,* 1883; and *Ester Ried's Namesake,* 1906), written from the depths of her personal experience, had the greatest popularity. In 1927 her niece Grace Livingston Hill suggested that she bring the great message of *Ester Ried* up-to-date for the generation of that day. Alden's response came in a letter as follows: "about the story which you want me to write. . . . I am not capable of writing a story suited to the tastes of *present day* young people. They would smoke a cigarette over the first chapter, and toss it aside as a back number. I haven't faith in them, nor in my ability to help them." Alden never lost her religious faith, but her faith in herself and the efficacy of her writings failed her in the final years of her life.

Front cover for an issue of the children's magazine edited by Alden from 1873 to 1896 (Baldwin Library, University of Florida Libraries)

Helen Papashvily, in *All the Happy Endings* (1956), aptly describes the mode of expression that characterizes Alden's fiction, causing many readers to turn away: "So frequently did the clichés of grief appear—the lock of hair, the shoe, the sun's last rays on the fading cheek, the plaintive voice asking, 'Will Papa come home?'—that some later readers found amusement in these bits of sentimentality...."

Alden died on 5 August 1930. One day after carrying her obituary the *New York Times* editorialized about the lack of critical interest in Alden:

> Known to thousands of readers all over the world, Pansy was ignored by the critics who flourished when she was most popular. Her *Chatauqua, Ester Ried,* and *Life of Christ* series were pored over by countless admirers.... People who never read her works must have heard of her, but they disregarded her fascinations.
>
> Now that comic strips are studied seriously as "folk art," ... it is not too much to expect a book about "Pansy" from one of the determined students of American culture.

This book remains unwritten in the history of American literature. Isabella Alden has suffered the fate of all those who survive beyond their own day and attract attention only as anachronisms on the modern scene.

Reference:
Helen Waite Papashvily, *All the Happy Endings* (New York: Harper, 1956), pp. 186-197.

Thomas Bailey Aldrich

(11 November 1836-19 March 1907)

Virginia L. Wolf
University of Wisconsin-Stout

SELECTED BOOKS: *The Bells: A Collection of Chimes* (New York: J. C. Derby/Boston: Phillips, Sampson/Cincinnati: H. W. Derby, 1855);

Daisy's Necklace: And What Came of It. (A Literary Episode.) (New York: Derby & Jackson/Cincinnati: H. W. Derby, 1857);

The Course of True Love Never Did Run Smooth (New York: Rudd & Carleton, 1858);

The Ballad of Babie Bell and Other Poems (New York: Rudd & Carleton, 1859);

Pampinea and Other Poems (New York: Rudd & Carleton, 1861);

Out of His Head, A Romance (New York: Rudd & Carleton, 1862);

Poems (New York: Carleton, 1863);

The Poems of Thomas Bailey Aldrich (Boston: Ticknor & Fields, 1865; revised, Boston: Osgood, 1874; London: Routledge, 1874; revised again, Boston: Houghton Mifflin, 1882; London: Low, 1882; revised again, Boston: Houghton Mifflin, 1885); revised again as volumes one and two of *The Writings of Thomas Bailey Aldrich* (Boston & New York: Houghton Mifflin, 1897);

The Story of a Bad Boy (Boston: Ticknor & Fields, 1869; London: Low, Son & Marston, 1869); republished as *Tom Bailey's Adventures; or, the Story of a Bad Boy* (Boston: Osgood, 1877);

Pansy's Wish: A Christmas Fantasy, With a Moral (Boston: Marion, 1870);

Marjorie Daw, and Other People (Boston: Osgood, 1873; London: Routledge, 1873); enlarged as *Marjorie Daw and Other Tales* (Leipzig: Tauchnitz, 1879) and *Marjorie Daw and Other Stories* (Boston: Houghton Mifflin, 1885; Edinburgh: Douglas, 1894);

Prudence Palfrey. A Novel (London: Routledge, 1874; Boston: Osgood, 1877);

Cloth of Gold and Other Poems (Boston: Osgood, 1874);

Flower and Thorn. Later Poems (Boston: Osgood, 1877; London: Routledge, 1877);

A Midnight Fantasy and The Little Violinist (Boston: Osgood, 1877);

The Queen of Sheba (London: Routledge, 1877; Boston: Osgood, 1877; revised, Edinburgh: Douglas, 1885);

The Stillwater Tragedy (Boston: Houghton Mifflin, 1880; London: Low, 1880);

XXVI Lyrics and XII Sonnets (Boston: Houghton Mifflin, 1881);

Friar Jerome's Beautiful Book (Boston: Houghton Mifflin, 1881);

From Ponkapog to Pesth (Boston: Houghton Mifflin, 1883);

Mercedes, and Later Lyrics (Boston: Houghton Mifflin, 1884); revised in part as *Mercedes, A Drama in Two Acts* (Boston & New York: Houghton Mifflin, 1884);

The Second Son, by Aldrich and M.O.W. Oliphant (Boston & New York: Houghton Mifflin, 1888);

Wyndham Towers (Boston & New York: Houghton Mifflin, 1890);

The Sisters' Tragedy with Other Poems, Lyrical and Dramatic (Boston & New York, 1891; enlarged, London: Macmillan, 1891);

An Old Town by the Sea (Boston & New York: Houghton Mifflin, 1893);

Two Bites at a Cherry With Other Tales (Edinburgh: Douglas, 1893; Boston & New York: Houghton Mifflin, 1894);

Unguarded Gates and Other Poems (Boston & New York: Houghton Mifflin, 1895);

Later Lyrics (Boston & New York: Houghton Mifflin, 1896; London: Lane, 1896);

On Influence of Books (Boston: Hall & Locke, 1901);

A Sea Turn and Other Matters (Boston & New York: Houghton Mifflin, 1902; Edinburgh: Douglas, 1902);

Ponkapog Papers (Boston & New York: Houghton Mifflin, 1903);

Judith of Bethulia, A Tragedy (Boston & New York: Houghton Mifflin, 1904; revised, Boston & New York: Houghton Mifflin, 1905);

42

Pauline Pavlovna, A Drama in One Act (Boston & New York: Houghton Mifflin, 1907?).

Collection: *The Writings of Thomas Bailey Aldrich*, 9 volumes (volumes 1-8, Boston & New York: Houghton Mifflin, 1897; volume 9, Boston & New York: Houghton Mifflin, 1907).

OTHER: *The Young Folks' Library Selections from the Choicest Literature of All Lands*, 20 volumes, edited by Aldrich (Boston: Hall & Locke, 1901-1902).

Thomas Bailey Aldrich is remembered only for his one children's novel, *The Story of a Bad Boy* (1869). He was, however, one of the most respected literary men of his time. Ranked with William Dean Howells and Mark Twain as a novelist and with James Russell Lowell, Henry Wadsworth Longfellow, and John Greenleaf Whittier as a poet, he was also junior literary critic of the *Evening Mirror*, subeditor of *Home Journal*, associate editor of *Saturday Press*, and editor of the *Illustrated News, Every Sat-*

urday, and the *Atlantic Monthly*. He was acquainted with or knew well many artists influential during the late nineteenth century, including the famous Shakespearean actor Edwin Booth, the sculptor Launt Thompson, the painter Bierstadt, Walt Whitman, Longfellow, Lowell, Whittier, Hawthorne, Emerson, Dickens, Howells, and Twain. Although only his minor children's classic survives, Aldrich lived and died at the center of the late-nineteenth-century literary world. But perhaps more interesting than the reasons why most of Aldrich's writing is now forgotten are the reasons why *The Story of a Bad Boy* still lives.

Necessary to solving the riddles of Aldrich's lost reputation and of *The Story of a Bad Boy*'s survival is an understanding of Aldrich's boyhood and heritage. He was born of Elias Taft Aldrich and Sarah Abba Bailey Aldrich in Portsmouth, New

Aldrich as a youth, in military dress

Hampshire (the Rivermouth of *The Story of a Bad Boy*). During his early years his family traveled extensively as his father tried to establish himself in business. They settled in New York in 1841 and then in New Orleans in 1846. At the age of twelve Aldrich returned to Portsmouth to study in the school of Samuel De Merritt in preparation for Harvard. That same year he suffered one of the few tragedies of his life when his father died of cholera on the steamer returning him to New Orleans. Although Aldrich did not live in Portsmouth on a regular basis, except from 1849 to 1852 after his father's death, he clearly considered it his home. He retreated to it again and again for extended vacations throughout his childhood and adult years, and it provided the foundation upon which he built his life and much of his writing. This New England village in the mid-nineteenth century, his grandfather Thomas Darling Bailey (Grandfather Nutter in *The Story of a Bad Boy*), and Portsmouth's other scenes and inhabitants, clearly dear to Aldrich, are the source and substance of his children's novel, an only slightly fictionalized autobiography of Aldrich's experiences from 1849 to 1852. Portsmouth also figures prominently in many of Aldrich's other works, including his short stories "A Rivermouth Romance," "Miss Mehetabel's Son," and "The Friend of My Youth," his novels *Prudence Palfrey* (1874) and *The Queen of Sheba* (1877), and his essay collection *An Old Town by the Sea* (1893). Equally important, Portsmouth, particularly as its values and life-style were embodied by Grandfather Bailey, shaped the young Aldrich in the genteel, conservative tradition of New England Puritanism during what Alexander Cowie, in *The Rise of the American Novel* (1948), calls its "Indian Summer." Indeed, Cowie persuasively suggests that Portsmouth formed the goals, style, felicity, and limitation of Aldrich's life and art.

In 1852, Aldrich, financially unable to attend Harvard to study under Longfellow, left Portsmouth for a position in the counting room of his Uncle Charles Frost's commission house in New York City. After having many poems published in a variety of periodicals, in 1855, the year of the first edition of Whitman's *Leaves of Grass*, Aldrich produced *The Bells: A Collection of Chimes*. Even more important, in that year "The Ballad of Babie Bell" appeared, which brought him immediate fame and allowed him to leave his uncle's business. Aldrich eliminated all the poems in his first volume from all later collections and acknowledged "the obvious crudities" of "The Ballad of Babie Bell" in his later years. But N. P. Willis, editor of the influ-

ential *Home Journal*, printed the poem and thereby introduced Aldrich to New York, later making him junior literary critic on the *Evening Mirror* and eventually sub-editor of. *Home Journal*, a position once held by Edgar Allan Poe. Aldrich's career was launched, and dislike the diversity, squalor, and immorality of New York City as he did, he found himself at the center of its artistic communities. Welcome in the circle of R. H. Stoddard and the genteel, idealistic poets, including Bayard Taylor and E. C. Stedman (followers of Longfellow, Lowell, and Tennyson), Aldrich was also a fellow of the lively bohemians of Pfaff's beer cellar, most notably Walt Whitman and Henry Clapp. Aldrich became the associate editor of Clapp's *Saturday Press* in 1859.

But Aldrich never fully belonged in either circle. His closest friends were Edwin Booth and Launt Thompson, with whom he traveled uneasily back and forth between the two communities. Increasingly, he retreated from the sentimental idealism of the one and the caustic wit of the other to long vacations in Portsmouth. He sought publication in Boston's *Atlantic Monthly* rather than in New York periodicals. In 1859 he produced *The Ballad of Babie Bell and Other Poems*, and in 1860 the *Atlantic* first accepted one of his poems. That year the *Saturday Press* also came to an end.

During the next five years Aldrich worked diligently to establish himself as a writer, relying on journalism to support himself. In 1861, he produced *Pampinea and Other Poems*, and when the Civil War broke out he went to the front as a correspondent for the *New York Tribune*, later creating from this experience two short stories, "Quite So" and "White Feather," and some poems, "Fredericksburg," "Spring in New England," and "The Shaw Memorial Ode." His first collection of short stories, all characterized by the surprise ending, *Out of His Head, A Romance*, appeared in 1862, and he became editor of the *Illustrated News* in 1863. Later that same year, *Poems*, a collection from his first decade as poet, was published and the *Illustrated News* ceased publication. Unemployed again, Aldrich returned to his poetry, met and became engaged to Lilian Woodman, and helped his friend Edwin Booth live through the shame of his brother John's assassination of Lincoln.

The year 1865 was a crucial one for Aldrich, both personally and professionally. He finally persuaded James T. Fields to bring out his collected poems in the Ticknor and Fields Blue and Gold series, one reserved for the most important writers of the day. James Osgood of the same publishing

Fredericksburg

The increasing moonlight drifts across my bed,
And on the churchyard by the road, I know
It falls as white and noiselessly as snow....
'Twas such a night two weary summers fled;
The stars, as now, were waning overhead.
Listen! Again the shrill-lipped bugles blow
Where the swift currents of the river flow
Past Fredericksburg; far off the heavens are
     red.

With sudden conflagration; on yon height,
Linstock in hand, the gunners hold their breath
A signal rocket pierces the dense night,
Flings its spent stars upon the town beneath:
Hark!—the artillery massing on the right,
Hark!—the black squadrons wheeling down to Death!

           Thomas Bailey Aldrich.

Manuscript for one of Aldrich's poems based on his experiences as a correspondent for the New York Tribune *during the Civil War (Ferris Greenslet,* The Life of Thomas Bailey Aldrich, *1908)*

firm asked him to come to Boston to edit *Every Saturday*, a weekly which purported to carry the best foreign literature. On 28 November, feeling financially secure, he married Lilian Woodman.

In 1865 Aldrich also wrote his first pieces for children, a series of monthly articles for *Our Young Folks*, entitled "Among the Studios" and designed to introduce young people to the artists living and working at the famous Studio Building in New York. These pieces are of little interest to anyone but scholars today, most of the artists having long been forgotten. More important to Aldrich's development as a children's writer was his apprenticeship as a poet. Many of his first poems were sentimental in content and diction and contrived in form and rhyme. But Aldrich, with the help of critics such as Oliver Wendell Holmes and Walt Whitman, recognized their flaws and suppressed most of his early poetry, finally keeping in the definitive 1897 collection only eight from the 1859 volume, six from the 1861, twenty from the 1863, and twenty-eight from the 1865 Blue and Gold collection. Furthermore, he grew increasingly meticulous about his language and choice of subject. Although his range of subjects was limited and his themes never profound, during his career in New York he became a fine craftsman of light pieces, able to etch small images with vividness and economy. Readers interested in Aldrich's accomplishment during these years should consider "Hesperides," "Before the Rain," "After the Rain," "A Snowflake," "Frost-Work," "Realism," "Lyrics and Epics," and "Kris Kringle" (a poem for children). In these poems, scene, character, and feeling are genuine and moving. Not written for children, they are, nevertheless, in their apparently artless simplicity and concreteness, poems accessible and appealing to children. During Aldrich's later life, he perfected his craftsmanship, producing fifteen more volumes of poetry in addition to the definitive collection of 1897. The direction of his development was, however, essentially set during his New York years.

In Boston Aldrich found his niche. The rest of his life was singularly happy. He and his wife settled quickly into the genteel, conservative, artistic society of Longfellow, Lowell, Fields, Emerson, Holmes, and Howells. His sense of having arrived is evident in the following comment from a letter to a New York friend:

> There is a finer intellectual atmosphere here than in our city. It is true, a poor literary man could not earn his salt, or more than

Aldrich in 1868. He finished writing The Story of a Bad Boy *on 16 September of that year; his twin sons were born the following day.*

that, out of pure literary labor in Boston: but then he couldn't do it in New York, unless he turned *journalist*. The people of Boston are full-bodied *readers*, appreciative, trained. The humblest man of letters has a position here which he doesn't have in New York. To be known as an able writer is to have the choicest society opened to you. Just as an officer in the Navy (providing he is a gentleman) is the social equal of anybody so a knight of the quill here is supposed necessarily to be a gentleman. In New York—he's a Bohemian! outside of his personal friends he has no standing. I am speaking of a young fellow like myself who hasn't kicked up all the dust he intends to. The luckiest day of my professional life was when I came to Boston to stay. My studies and associates are fitting me for higher ends than I ever before cared to struggle for. . . .

In later years Aldrich indicated his commitment to Boston and its values by saying, "Though I am not genuine Boston, I am Boston-plated."

Aldrich successfully edited *Every Saturday* from 1866 to 1874, years during which Howells was Fields's assistant editor at the *Atlantic Monthly.* Although Aldrich continued to write poetry, this period signals Aldrich's new interest in the short story and novel, an interest that was increasingly to occupy him during the last half of his life. To be sure, he had written fiction before. But between 1866 and 1874 most of Aldrich's writing was prose, and before his death, not counting the nine volumes of *The Writings* (eight in 1897 and one in 1907), he produced twenty-three volumes of prose. This period was critical for Aldrich, leading to his creation of *The Story of a Bad Boy.*

Aldrich's early short stories include "Père Antoine's Date Palm" (1862), "Miss Hepzibah's Lover" (1862), "A Young Desperado" (1867), and "Marjorie Daw" (1873). Characterized by the surprise ending, a concern with romantic love, and some interest in mystery and exotic atmosphere, these stories also realistically create character and scene. Moreover, in their wit and slightly ironic narration, they entertain and amuse even today. "A Young Desperado," in particular, interests the reader tracing the development of *The Story of a Bad Boy.* In tone and characterization, it is a forerunner of Aldrich's classic and an innovation in children's literature. Its realistic protagonist, a mischievous six-and-a-half-year-old boy, believably terrorizes his neighborhood without suffering terrible punishment. He is the first of a tradition of engaging "bad boys" who replaced the pompous little prigs then characteristic of children's stories.

The Story of a Bad Boy was the first full-length book to introduce such a protagonist. Not surprisingly, this work was begun in Portsmouth, where Aldrich usually spent his summers. It was finished on 16 September 1868, in Boston, the day before the birth of his twin sons, and published serially in *Our Young Folks* beginning in January 1869 and in book form both in the United States and in England in late 1869 (though the title pages are dated 1870). By 1893 it was in the thirty-ninth edition, by 1897 the forty-seventh, and today it appears on most lists of children's classics.

Even scholars who do not consider it a literary masterpiece recognize that *The Story of a Bad Boy* was a landmark—in Charles E. Samuels's words, "the first realistic treatment of an American boy" and "an early contribution to the development of Realism." Aldrich himself understood the nature of his innovation, saying in the preface to the 1895 edition that he chose his title because he "wished

OUR YOUNG FOLKS.

An Illustrated Magazine

FOR BOYS AND GIRLS.

VOL. V.　　　　JANUARY, 1869.　　　　No. I.

THE STORY OF A BAD BOY.

CHAPTER I.

IN WHICH I INTRODUCE MYSELF.

HIS is the story of a bad boy. Well, not such a very bad, but a pretty bad boy; and I ought to know, for I am, or rather I was, that boy myself.

Lest the title should mislead the reader, I hasten to assure him here that I have no dark confessions to make. I call my story the story of a bad boy, partly to distinguish myself from those faultless young gentlemen who generally figure in narratives of this kind, and partly because I really was *not* a cherub. I may truthfully say I was an amiable, impulsive lad, blessed with fine digestive powers, and no hypocrite. I didn't want to be an angel and with the angels stand; I didn't think the missionary tracts presented to me by the Rev. Wibird Hawkins were half so nice as Robinson Crusoe; and I didn't send my little pocket-money to the natives of the Feejee Islands, but spent it royally in peppermint-drops and taffy candy. In short, I was a real human boy, such as you may meet anywhere in New England, and no more like the impossible boy in a story-book than a sound orange is like one that has been sucked dry. But let us begin at the beginning.

Entered according to Act of Congress, in the year 1868, by FIELDS, OSGOOD, & CO., in the Clerk's Office of the District Court of the District of Massachusetts.

VOL. V.—NO. I.　　　　　　　1

The first installment in the serial publication of Aldrich's best-known novel (Baldwin Library, University of Florida Libraries)

simply to draw a line at the start between his hero—a natural, actual boy—and that unwholesome and altogether improbable little prig which had hitherto been held up as an example to the young. The poet Wordsworth assisted by Plautus maintains—to the everlasting confusion of Mr. Darwin—that 'the good die first.' Perhaps that explains why the Bad Boy has survived so many good boys in the juvenile literature of the past two decades." But Aldrich did not realize that his novel was to precipitate a long line of bad boys in children's literature and a tradition of the boy in American literature. William Dean Howells perhaps did, calling *The Story of a Bad Boy* "a new thing in American literature" in the *Atlantic Monthly* for January 1879.

The novel's significance as a development in children's and American literature tempts one to focus only on its merits. Most certainly, it is a novel with charm. The story is told by a narrator looking back on the three or so years he spent as a boy in Rivermouth. Its tone, a combination of nostalgia, complacency, and light satire, is enjoyable. The novel is a pleasant, episodic, interesting account of the years spent in this community. Because it is only slightly fictionalized autobiography, it is very close to being nonfiction. Its characters, setting, and action—with the exception of Sailor Ben's fortuitous arrival on his wife's doorstep many years after they lost track of one another—are vividly portrayed and convincingly genuine. As a novel, however, it is a lightweight, lacking depth and fullness because the narrator, the adult Tom, has so thoroughly enjoyed himself as a boy and refuses to take the experience very seriously. The protagonist is essentially a good boy. Tom studies hard and tries fairly successfully to live up to the "manly" code of his peers and his adult world. He frequently gets into scrapes because of insufficient experience, poor judgment, and high spirits, but he is not immoral—only immature. The novel thus flouts the notion that a boy's triumphs and traumas indicate his moral well-being or lack of it. In so doing, it largely ignores the relationship between Tom's experience as a boy and his eventual value as a human being. It only superficially deals with growing up.

Aldrich minimizes the impact of childhood experiences on the personality of an adult and simplistically defines maturity as conformity. The narrator smiles at his boyish mistakes, troubles, and innocence, slighting the complexity implicit in many of his experiences. He even makes light of what were very painful and disturbing events for him as a boy, for example, the separation from his parents, the drowning of his best friend, the death of his father, and the family's loss of financial security. Tom's response to each of these events is quickly passed over. His first crush on an "older" woman is portrayed in more detail than is any less humorous experience. In fact, the book focuses on clever pranks, comic blunders, and other pleasant amusements. Serious scenes are rare and brief. The narrator's determination to keep the novel lighthearted precludes any complicated interest in the process whereby Tom matures. He implies rather pointedly that children will be naughty and will experience pain but that they will have the common sense and decency to accept their responsibilities and to conform to the demands of reality. Thus he ignores the complexity of the internal process Tom experiences, refusing to take childhood seriously.

The novel is, however, less simplistic than the preceding analysis suggests largely because of its narrator. On the one hand, he is smug and complacent, smiling at the boy's foolishness and difficulties. He sympathizes with great reasonableness but always from the perspective of an adult who knows better than the child. Thus, he says: "The burdens of childhood are as hard to bear as the crosses that weigh us down later in life, while the happinesses of childhood are tame compared with those of our maturer years. And even if this were not so, it is rank cruelty to throw shadows over the young hearts by croaking, 'Be merry, for to-morrow you die!' " At the same time he is nostalgic, overidentifying with young Tom and, to some extent, lamenting the loss of his boyish innocence, dreams, and potential. Reflecting on his drowned boyhood friend, he says, "The rest of us have grown up into hard, worldly men, fighting the fight of life; but you are forever young, and gentle, and pure; a part of my childhood that time cannot wither." Throughout the novel, he refers to himself as an "old boy" and, in his obvious delight in his childhood, celebrates being a "bad boy." Because he represses the painful side of childhood, one suspects that he favors youth over adulthood. In any

Aldrich's grandfather Thomas Darling Bailey, the model for Grandfather Nutter in The Story of a Bad Boy

case, the bad boy is the older Tom's hero—the child who could do what he wanted more often than the man—the child who was not yet, like the man, "tamed sufficiently." Indeed, the narrator in celebrating the bad boy is still one himself, pulling one more prank on grown-ups. Outwardly conforming, he is still covertly and in small ways seeking release from his confinement as an adult—longing for the "good old days" when life was simpler, responsibilities lighter, and fun more common than they are for an adult.

The narrator's attitude, in other words, is ambiguous. His nostalgia strongly implies that growing up is definitely not a matter-of-fact, reasonable, easy process and undermines his superior tone as an adult, implying that more was lost, painful, and difficult than the novel clearly reveals. The reader might guess that his father's death, the family's financial crisis, and their consequent change in class constituted losses which importantly affected the boy. The narrator says, "It was hard to give up the long-cherished dream of being a Harvard boy; but I gave it up." The reader learns that he accepts a place in his merchant uncle's business; that his uncle rushes him to New York, worried the youth will become a starving poet; and that Tom does not see Rivermouth again for many years. But how this abrupt and thorough transition into adulthood affected him emotionally, he does not say, identifying this as not "within the scope of these pages." The nostalgia suggests, as those familiar with Aldrich's life have reason to know, that the new life was not fully desirable, but it is impossible to do more than guess at the significance of the boy's experience in Rivermouth.

The community welcomes young Tom Bailey, accepting him as a member of one of the old, established families. Such a welcome, of course, endears Rivermouth to him. But it also suggests that this community is overly concerned with artificial distinctions among its citizens. Here a boy's value is determined on the basis of class, race, sex, age, material possessions, and physical prowess. The narrator can be smug and complacent because the community assures him of his superiority. He displays the self-confidence and self-control of one of his social standing, but so thoroughly has he imbibed Rivermouth's values that he lacks sufficient distance for serious social criticism. Just as he never speaks of his own sacrifices, he never truly censures Rivermouth. Poking fun at the long, dreary Sundays spent with Grandfather Nutter and at the peculiarities of Aunt Abigail's domination of the household, he is only mildly and lovingly satirical.

Apparently, he has never consciously questioned Rivermouth's values. Only nostalgia for himself as a bad boy indicates any need for release from Rivermouth's expectations and confinement.

Finally, the themes of *The Story of a Bad Boy* are neither clear nor evident. Contradictory implications and statements are not resolved. That readers are not allowed to understand Tom's experience is why the novel is best described as a slice of life. Furthermore, because the relationship between Tom and Rivermouth is not fully explored, the novel tends to dissolve into two unrelated parts: a study of its hero and a study of what life was like in a small New England town during the middle of the nineteenth century. Tom is somewhat complex, but he is still largely a type. As a character, he functions to reveal Aldrich's attitude toward boyhood rather than as a unique personality. On the other hand, the world of his boyhood is fully portrayed. His home life with Grandfather Nutter, his education at Temple School, his adventures and escapades—especially the Fourth of July Celebration—with his gang, the Rivermouth Centipedes, and his encounters with the older inhabitants of Rivermouth are concretely and evocatively rendered. As one of the emerging local colorists of the mid-nineteenth century, Aldrich vividly creates a fictional world with a distinct life-style. And, if he does not facilitate understanding of this world or Tom in any complexity, he nevertheless provides an entertaining account of Tom's life during these years spent in Rivermouth.

This is no small accomplishment, especially given the nature of most children's novels in Aldrich's time. Even though the novel is thematically shallow and contradictory, it is to be valued for its vivid details and for its place in the history of realistic novels for children as a forerunner of books less harshly and falsely moralistic than its predecessors. Without *The Story of a Bad Boy* there would probably have been no *Adventures of Huckleberry Finn*, a novel rich in the social criticism and thematic complexity that Aldrich's minor classic lacks but clearly evolved from the tradition Aldrich fathered.

If *The Story of a Bad Boy* is not a masterpiece, it is, nevertheless, Aldrich's best novel and perhaps his best fiction. As critics have often noted, Aldrich could not plot. His other novels, *Daisy's Necklace: And What Came of It* (1857), *Prudence Palfrey* (1874), *The Queen of Sheba* (1877), and *The Stillwater Tragedy* (1880), suffer from Aldrich's inability to proportion and arrange plot elements meaningfully and effectively. He avoided confusion in *The Story of a*

A Rainy Afternoon in the Garret

The Initiation

Illustrations by A. B. Frost for the 1895 edition of The Story of a Bad Boy *(Baldwin Library, University of Florida Libraries)*

Bad Boy, using the simple, episodic structure rather than the complicated subplotting of his adult novels. Fundamentally, however, as his lyrics reveal, Aldrich was a master of the small, sensuous experience and, as his novels reveal, a bungler of large structures. Neither theme nor any other element besides chronology unifies any of his novels, and even chronology provides only an indeterminate framework. Because he ably captured short incidents, Aldrich's short stories are coherent, but they, even more than *The Story of a Bad Boy,* focus on the pleasant, exotic, and entertaining and yield little profundity. In them, too, Aldrich excels only in his evocation of small, concrete, and vivid details.

Thus, *The Story of a Bad Boy* and his lyric poetry, much of which was written prior to 1870, constitute Aldrich's best work. Later in his life he polished his poetry and wrote some excellent lyrics, showing an increasingly careful attention to diction

and syntax. In his fiction he attempted a variety of new endeavors, including consideration of insanity and psychology in *The Queen of Sheba* and of labor problems and social realism in *The Stillwater Tragedy.* But he never learned to plot and never possessed an interest in social issues or the temperament to inquire beyond or to question the values of his own narrow, safe, and comfortable existence. He was mildly interested in the exotic but vehemently repulsed by the sordid or the disorderly. His purism about life and how it should be portrayed in literature correlates with his purism about language. Aldrich was simply incapable of suspending his own viewpoint. Portsmouth and, eventually, Boston endowed him with position and prestige, and he never violated the values these communities upheld. Genteel and conservative, he perceived literature as a gentleman's calling but not as a vehicle for profound truths and certainly not as a purveyor of the unpleasant and degraded exploits of the working class.

Aldrich's later life, principally as editor of the *Atlantic Monthly* (1881-1890) and as author of the critical pieces collected in the *Ponkapog Papers* (1903), clearly proclaims his poise and confidence as a man of letters. As editor, he was very conservative, accepting few innovations and demanding polished language. In his essays he took an essentially classical position toward literature, focusing on the importance of clear and careful craftsmanship in form and of universality, memorability, and imagination in content. He opposed the commonplace in literature and accepted realism only as it implied fidelity to regions and character. Because he believed literature should please and entertain, he rejected the unpleasant, the topical, and the merely factual as unfit for poetry or fiction. Because he upheld tradition, he rejected originality, most notably as it emerged in the irregularities of Walt Whitman's and Emily Dickinson's poetry. Aldrich's longest critical essay, included in *Ponkapog Papers*, is in praise of Robert Herrick, "a great little poet." What he says of Herrick reveals the critical theory from which he operated and describes his own best work as a poet. The essay clearly establishes his distance from romanticism and realism and his respect for classical standards and tradition. In *On Influence of Books* (1901), the introduction he published separately but originally wrote for *The Young Folks' Library Selections from the Choicest Literature of All Lands* (1901-1902), a subscription set of twenty volumes, he espoused essentially the same position while testifying to the importance of literature to civilization.

Aldrich's life after 1890 was mostly a comfortable and happy one of travel, friends, family, and writing. Independently wealthy and internationally famous, he had few worries and few obligations. He moved among his households at 59 Mount Vernon in Boston, at Redman Farm near Ponkapog, Massachusetts, and at The Crags in Tenant's Harbor, Maine. Frequently, the Aldriches went abroad. But this easy life ended in 1901 when Aldrich's son Charles fell victim to tuberculosis. For several years he lingered, undergoing treatment in the Adirondacks. On 6 March 1904 Charles died. His father's grief was enormous; in fact, he never recovered from it. In January of 1907 Aldrich fell suddenly ill and underwent a serious operation. On 19 March 1907 he died at his home in Boston and was buried in Mount Auburn Cemetery.

His death occasioned a host of obituaries and widespread praise of his writing. In 1908 Ferris Greenslet's adulatory biography was published, and there followed positive assessments of Aldrich's poetry by Paul Elmer More and Fred Lewis Pattee—and then silence. The tradition to which Aldrich belonged had gone out of fashion. Realism and naturalism in all genres and experimentation in verse form dominated the early twentieth century, and Aldrich's poetry and fiction were mostly ignored. When they were not, they were harshly criticized. In a 1925 piece published in *American Mercury* C. Hartly Grattan called Aldrich an escapist, condemning even *The Story of a Bad Boy*. Perhaps more damning than the Grattan article was the criticism in the influential Vernon Louis Parrington's *Main Currents in American Thought* (1927). Parrington's liberal bias determined his dismissal of Aldrich as a pseudointellectual and a capitalist who ignored the social problems of his time. In any case, early-twentieth-century criticism effectively destroyed Aldrich's reputation.

Aldrich remains of interest today because he participated in the development of realism in children's literature and invented a character type which would flower in the hands of writers such as Mark Twain and J. D. Salinger. Surely, his contribution is noteworthy. Just as surely, *The Story of a Bad Boy* continues to be delightful reading—if not provocative or significant in its ideas. Although he did not harvest the crop or even tend the field, Aldrich did plant new seed. As sower, if not reaper, Thomas Bailey Aldrich occupies his position in the development of the children's novel. As seed, if not fruit, lives *The Story of a Bad Boy*.

Biographies:

Ferris Greenslet, *The Life of Thomas Bailey Aldrich* (Boston: Houghton Mifflin, 1908);

Charles R. Mangum, "A Critical Biography of Thomas Bailey Aldrich," Ph.D. dissertation, Cornell University, 1950;

Charles E. Samuels, *Thomas Bailey Aldrich* (New York: Twayne, 1965).

References:

Lilian Aldrich, *Crowding Memories* (Boston: Houghton Mifflin, 1920);

Mary Silva Cosgrave, "Life and Times of T. B. Aldrich," *Horn Book Magazine*, 42 (April-August 1966): 223-232, 350-355, 464-473;

Alexander Cowie, *The Rise of the American Novel* (New York: American Book Company, 1948), pp. 579-591;

C. Hartly Grattan, "Thomas Bailey Aldrich," *American Mercury*, 10 (May 1925): 41-45;

William Dean Howells, *Literary Friends and Acquaintances* (New York: Harper, 1900), pp. 64ff.;

Howells, "Mr. Aldrich's Fiction," *Atlantic Monthly*, 46 (November 1880): 695-698;

Howells, "Reviews and Literary Notices," *Atlantic Monthly*, 25 (January 1879): 124;

Paul Elmer More, "Thomas Bailey Aldrich," in his *Shelburne Essays, Seventh Series* (New York: Putnam's, 1910), pp. 138-152;

Vernon Louis Parrington, *Main Currents in American Thought*, volume 3 (New York: Harcourt, Brace, 1927), pp. 54-60;

Fred Lewis Pattee, *A History of American Literature since 1870* (New York: Century, 1917), pp. 126-135;

Bliss Perry, *Park-Street Papers* (Boston: Houghton Mifflin, 1908), pp. 143-170;

William H. Rideing, *The Boyhood of Living Authors* (New York: Crowell, 1887), pp. 16-27.

Papers:

Aldrich's personal library, including many inscribed first editions, is at the Aldrich Memorial Museum, once the Bailey home, in Portsmouth, New Hampshire. Most of his papers are at Houghton Library, Harvard University, and at Olin Library, Cornell University.

Horatio Alger, Jr.

Marilyn H. Karrenbrock
University of Tennessee

BIRTH: Chelsea, Massachusetts, 13 January 1832, to Horatio Alger, Sr., and Olive Augusta Fenno Alger.

EDUCATION: A.B., Harvard University, 1852; graduated Harvard Divinity School, 1860.

DEATH: South Natick, Massachusetts, 18 July 1899.

SELECTED BOOKS: *Bertha's Christmas Vision: An Autumn Sheaf* (Boston: Brown, Bazin, 1856);

Nothing to Do: A Tilt at Our Best Society, anonymous (Boston: French, 1857);

Frank's Campaign; or, What Boys Can Do on the Farm for the Camp (Boston: Loring, 1864); republished as *Frank's Campaign. A Story of the Farm and the Camp* (London: Aldine, 1887);

Paul Prescott's Charge. A Story for Boys (Boston: Loring, 1865); republished as *Paul Prescott the Runaway* (London: Aldine, 1887);

Timothy Crump's Ward; or, The New Years Loan, And What Came of It, anonymous (Boston: Loring, 1866); republished as *Timothy Crump's Ward.*

A Story of American Life (Boston: Loring, 1866);

Helen Ford (Boston: Loring, 1866);

Charlie Codman's Cruise. A Story for Boys (Boston: Loring, 1866); republished as *Bill Sturdy; or, The Cruise of Kidnapped Charlie* (London: Aldine, 1887);

Ragged Dick; or, Street Life in New York With the Boot-Blacks (Boston: Loring, 1868); republished as *Ragged Dick! or, The Early Life of Richard Hunter, ESQ.* (London: Aldine, 1887);

Fame and Fortune; or, The Progress of Richard Hunter (Boston: Loring, 1868);

Mark, the Match Boy; or, Richard Hunter's Ward (Boston: Loring, 1869);

Luck and Pluck; or, John Oakley's Inheritance (Boston: Loring, 1869; London: Aldine, 1887);

Rough and Ready; or, Life Among the New York Newsboys (Boston: Loring, 1869); republished with *Rufus and Rose* (1870) as *Rough and Ready: His Fortunes and Adventures* (London: Aldine, 1887);

Ben, the Luggage Boy; or, Among the Wharves (Boston: Loring, 1870);

Rufus and Rose; or, The Fortunes of Rough and Ready (Boston: Loring, 1870); republished with *Rough and Ready* (1869) as *Rough and Ready: His Fortunes and Adventures* (London: Aldine, 1887);

Sink or Swim; or, Harry Raymond's Resolve (Boston: Loring, 1870); republished as *Paddle Your Own Canoe; or, "Harry Raymond's Resolve"* (London: Aldine, 1887);

Tattered Tom; or, The Story of a Street Arab (Boston: Loring, 1871); republished as *Tattered Tom* (London: Aldine, 1887);

Strong and Steady; or, Paddle Your Own Canoe (Boston: Loring, 1871); republished as *Strong and Steady: A Tale of Self-Help* (London: Aldine, 1887);

Paul, the Peddler; or, The Adventures of a Young Street Merchant (Boston: Loring, 1871); republished as *Plucky Paul* (London: Aldine, 1888);

Phil, the Fiddler; or, The Story of a Young Street Musician (Boston: Loring, 1872);

Strive and Succeed; or, The Progress of Walter Conrad (Boston: Loring, 1872; London: Aldine, 1887);

Slow and Sure; or, From the Street to the Shop (Boston: Loring, 1872);

Try and Trust; or, The Story of a Bound Boy (Boston: Loring, 1873); republished as *Trials and Adventures of Herbert Mason or, Try and Trust* (London: Aldine, 1887);

Bound to Rise; or Harry Walton's Motto (Boston: Loring, 1873); republished as *Bound to Rise; or, Live and Learn* (London: Aldine, 1888);

Julius; or, The Street Boy Out West (Boston: Loring, 1874);

Risen from the Ranks; or, Harry Walton's Success (Boston: Loring, 1874); republished as *Bound to Rise; or, Live and Learn* (London: Aldine, 1888);

Brave and Bold; or, The Fortunes of a Factory Boy (Boston: Loring, 1874); republished as *Brave and Bold or The Fortunes of Robert Rushton* (London: Aldine, 1887);

The Young Outlaw; or, Adrift in the Streets (Boston: Loring, 1875);

Seeking His Fortune, and Other Dialogues, by Alger and O. Augusta Cheney (Boston: Loring, 1875);

Jack's Ward; or, The Boy Guardian (Boston: Loring, 1875; London: Aldine, 1887);

Herbert Carter's Legacy; or, The Inventor's Son (Boston: Loring, 1875); republished as *George Carter's Legacy or The Inventor's Son* (London: Aldine, 1887);

Grand'ther Baldwin's Thanksgiving with Other Ballads and Poems (Boston: Loring, 1875);

Sam's Chance; and How He Improved It (Boston: Loring, 1876); republished as *Sam's Chance and What He Made of It* (London: Aldine, 1887);

Shifting For Himself; or, Gilbert Greyson's Fortunes (Boston: Loring, 1876); republished as *"How His Ship Came Home"* (London: Aldine, 1887);

The New Schoolma'am; or, A Summer in North Sparta, anonymous (Boston: Loring, 1877);

Wait and Hope; or, Ben Bradford's Motto (Boston: Loring, 1877; London: Aldine, 1887);

The Western Boy or, The Road to Success (New York: Carleton/Street & Smith/American News Co., 1878);

The Young Adventurer; or, Tom's Trip Across the Plains (Boston: Loring, 1878); republished as *The Young Adventurer or Tom Nelson in California* (London: Aldine, 1887);

The Telegraph Boy (Boston: Loring, 1879); republished as *The Telegraph Boy; or, Courage Wins* (London: Aldine, 1894);

The Young Miner; or, Tom Nelson in California (Boston: Loring, 1879); republished as *The Young Adventurer or Tom Nelson in California* (London: Aldine, 1887);

Tony, the Hero (New York: Ogilvie, 1880);

The Young Explorer; or, Among the Sierras (Boston: Loring, 1880); republished with *Ben's Nugget* (1882) as *Ben Stanton, The Explorer* (London: Aldine, 1887);

From Canal Boy to President, or The Boyhood and Manhood of James A. Garfield (New York: Anderson, 1881);

From Farm Boy to Senator; Being the History of the Boyhood and Manhood of Daniel Webster (New York: Ogilvie, 1882);

Ben's Nugget; or, A Boy's Search for Fortune. A Story of the Pacific Coast (Philadelphia: Porter & Coates, 1882); republished with *The Young Explorer* (1880) as *Ben Stanton, The Explorer* (London: Aldine, 1887);

The Young Circus Rider; or, The Mystery of Robert Rudd (Philadelphia: Porter & Coates, 1883);

Abraham Lincoln, the Backwoods Boy; or, How a Young Rail-Splitter Became President (New York: Anderson & Allen, 1883);

The Train Boy (New York: Carleton/Street & Smith/New York Weekly, 1883);

Dan, the Detective (New York: Carleton/Street & Smith/New York Weekly, 1884); republished as *Dutiful Dan, the Brave Boy Detective* (London: Aldine, 1895);

Do and Dare; or, A Brave Boy's Fight for Fortune (Philadelphia: Porter & Coates, 1884; London: Aldine, 1887);

Hector's Inheritance; or, The Boys of Smith Institute (Philadelphia: Porter & Coates, 1885); republished as *Never Despair! ("Nil Desperandum!"); or, Courage Against the World* (London: Aldine, 1887);

Helping Himself or Grant Thornton's Ambition (Philadelphia: Porter & Coates, 1886; London: Aldine, 1893);

Joe's Luck; or, A Boy's Adventures in California (New York: Burt, 1887; London: Aldine, 1894);

The Store Boy; or, The Fortunes of Ben Barclay (Philadelphia: Porter & Coates, 1887); republished as *The Fortunes of Ben Barclay, the Store Boy* (London: Aldine, 1896);

Frank Fowler, the Cash Boy (New York: Burt, 1887);

Number 91; or, The Adventures of a New York Telegraph Boy, as Arthur Lee Putnam (New York: Munsey, 1887);

Tom Temple's Career (New York: Burt, 1888; London: Aldine, 1893);

The Young Acrobat of the Great North American Circus (New York: Munsey, 1888); republished as *He Would Be a Mountebank* (London: Aldine, 1888);

Tom Tracy; or, The Trials of a New York Newsboy, as Arthur Lee Putnam (New York: Munsey, 1888);

Tom Thatcher's Fortune (New York: Burt, 1888);

The Merchant's Crime (New York: Lupton, 1888); republished as *Ralph Raymond's Heir* (New York: Lupton, 1892);

The Errand Boy; or, How Phil Brent Won Success (New York: Burt, 1888);

Bob Burton; or, The Young Ranchman of the Missouri (Philadelphia: Porter & Coates, 1888); republished as *The Young Ranchman of the Missouri* (London: Aldine, 1888);

Luke Walton or The Chicago Newsboy (Philadelphia: Porter & Coates, 1889);

$500; or Jacob Marlowe's Secret (New York: United States Book Company, 1890); republished as *Uncle Jacob's Secret or The Boy Who Cleared His Father's Name* (London: Aldine, 1890);

Ned Newton or The Fortunes of a New York Bootblack, as Arthur Lee Putnam (New York: United States Book Company, 1890);

Mark Stanton, as Arthur Lee Putnam (New York: United States Book Company, 1890);

The Erie Train Boy (New York: United States Book Company, 1890); republished as *The Straight Ahead or Life on the Iron Road* (London: Aldine, 1891);

A New York Boy, as Arthur Lee Putnam (New York: United States Book Company, 1890);

Dean Dunham or The Waterford Mystery (New York: United States Book Company, 1890); republished as *Wait Till the Clouds Roll By; or, The Waterford Mystery* (London: Aldine, 1890);

The Odds Against Him or Carl Crawford's Experience (Philadelphia: Penn, 1890; London: Aldine, 1891);

Struggling Upward; or, Luke Larkin's Luck (Philadelphia: Porter & Coates, 1890); republished as *Struggling Upward or A Brave Boy's Purpose* (London: Aldine, 1891);

The Young Boatman of Pine Point (Philadelphia: Penn, 1892);

Digging for Gold A Story of California (Philadelphia: Porter & Coates, 1892);

Facing the World or The Haps and Mishaps of Harry Vane (Philadelphia: Porter & Coates, 1893);

In a New World or Among the Gold-Fields of Australia (Philadelphia: Porter & Coates, 1893); republished as *The Nugget Finders A Tale of the Gold Fields of Australia* (London: Shaw, 1894);

Only an Irish Boy or Andy Burke's Fortunes and Misfortunes (Philadelphia: Porter & Coates, 1894);

Victor Vane, The Young Secretary (Philadelphia: Porter & Coates, 1894);

The Disagreeable Woman. A Social Mystery, as Julian Starr (New York: Dillingham, 1895);

Adrift in the City or Oliver Conrad's Plucky Flight (Philadelphia: Porter & Coates, 1895);

Frank Hunter's Peril (Philadelphia: Coates, 1896);

The Young Salesman (Philadelphia: Coates, 1896);

Frank and Fearless or The Fortunes of Jasper Kent (Philadelphia: Coates, 1897);

Walter Sherwood's Probation (Philadelphia: Coates, 1897);

A Boy's Fortune or The Strange Adventures of Ben Baker (Philadelphia: Coates, 1898);

The Young Bank Messenger (Philadelphia: Coates, 1898);

Mark Mason's Victory The Trials and Triumphs of a Telegraph Boy (New York: Burt, 1899);

Rupert's Ambition (Philadelphia: Coates, 1899);

Jed, the Poorhouse Boy (Philadelphia: Coates, 1900);

A Debt of Honor. The Story of Gerald Lane's Success in the Far West (New York: Burt, 1900);

Out for Business or Robert Frost's Strange Career, completed by Edward Stratemeyer as Arthur M. Winfield (New York: Mershon, 1900);

Falling in with Fortune; or, The Experiences of a Young Secretary, completed by Stratemeyer as Arthur M. Winfield (New York: Mershon, 1900);

Making His Mark (Philadelphia: Penn, 1901);

Ben Bruce. Scenes in the Life of a Bowery Newsboy (New York: Burt, 1901);

Tom Brace Who He Was and How He Fared (New York: Street & Smith, 1901);

Lester's Luck (Philadelphia: Coates, 1901);

Young Captain Jack or The Son of a Soldier, completed by Stratemeyer as Arthur M. Winfield (New York: Mershon, 1901);

Nelson the Newsboy or Afloat in New York, completed by Stratemeyer as Arthur M. Winfield (New York: Mershon, 1901);

Striving for Fortune or Walter Griffith's Trials and Successes (New York: Street & Smith, 1901); republished as *Walter Griffith; or, The Adventures of a Young Street Salesman* (New York: Street & Smith, 1901);

A Rolling Stone or The Adventures of a Wanderer (Chicago: Thompson & Thomas, 1902); republished as *Wren Winter's Triumph; or, The Adventures of a Wanderer* (Chicago: Thompson & Thomas, 1902);

Tom Turner's Legacy The Story of How He Secured It (New York: Burt, 1902);

The World Before Him (Philadelphia: Penn, 1902);

Andy Grant's Pluck (Philadelphia: Coates, 1902);

Bernard Brook's Adventures The Story of a Brave Boy's Trials (New York: Burt, 1903);

Chester Rand; or, a New Path to Fortune (Philadelphia: Coates, 1903);

Forging Ahead (Philadelphia: Penn, 1903);

Adrift in New York; or, Dodger and Florence Braving the World, abridged edition (New York: Street & Smith, 1903); complete edition published as *Adrift in New York; or, Tom and Florence Braving the World* (New York: Street & Smith, 1904);

Finding a Fortune (Philadelphia: Penn, 1904);

Lost at Sea or Robert Roscoe's Strange Cruise, completed by Stratemeyer (Rahway, N.J. & New York: Mershon, 1904);

Jerry, the Backwoods Boy, or The Parkhurst Treasure, completed by Stratemeyer (New York: Mershon, 1904);

The Young Book Agent or, Frank Hardy's Road to Success, completed by Stratemeyer (New York: Stitt, 1905);

Mark Manning's Mission The Story of a Shoe Factory Boy (New York: Burt, 1905);

From Farm to Fortune or, Nat Nason's Strange Experience, completed by Stratemeyer (New York: Stitt, 1905);

Joe the Hotel Boy or Winning Out by Pluck, completed by Stratemeyer (New York: Cupples & Leon, 1906);

The Young Musician (Philadelphia: Penn, 1906);

Randy of the River or The Adventures of a Young Deckhand, completed by Stratemeyer (New York: Chatterton-Peck, 1906);

In Search of Treasure The Story of Guy's Eventful Voyage (New York: Burt, 1907);

Wait and Win The Story of Jack Drummond's Pluck (New York: Burt, 1908);

Ben Logan's Triumph or The Boys of Boxwood Academy, completed by Stratemeyer (New York: Cupples & Leon, 1908);

Robert Coverdale's Struggle or On the Wave of Success (New York: Street & Smith, 1910);

Alger Street: The Poetry of Horatio Alger, Jr., edited by Gilbert K. Westgard II (Boston: Canner, 1964);

Silas Snobden's Office Boy (Garden City: Doubleday, 1973);

Cast Upon the Breakers (Garden City: Doubleday, 1974);

Hugo, the Deformed (Des Plaines, Ill.: Gilbert K. Westgard II, 1978);

Madeline, the Temptress (Gahanna, Ohio: Bob Sawyer, 1981);

The Secret Drawer (Gahanna, Ohio: Bob Sawyer, 1981);

The Cooper's Ward (Gahanna, Ohio: Bob Sawyer, 1981);

Herbert Selden (Gahanna, Ohio: Bob Sawyer, 1981);

Manson, the Miser (Gahanna, Ohio: Bob Sawyer, 1981);

The Gipsy Nurse (Gahanna, Ohio: Bob Sawyer, 1981);

The Discarded Son (Gahanna, Ohio: Bob Sawyer, 1981);

The Mad Heiress (Gahanna, Ohio: Bob Sawyer, 1981);

Marie Bertrand (Gahanna, Ohio: Bob Sawyer, 1981).

OTHER: William Rounseville Alger, *Life of Edwin Forrest, The American Tragedian* (Philadelphia: Lippincott, 1877), includes chapters attributed to Horatio Alger, Jr.

PERIODICAL PUBLICATIONS: "Are My Boys Real?," *Ladies' Home Journal*, 7 (November 1890): 29;

"Writing Stories for Boys," *Writer*, 9 (March 1896): 36-37.

Perhaps the quality which has been most closely identified with the American spirit is success. Success—upward mobility, material prosperity acquired through hard work and shrewd ability—has been for much of our history the quintessential American ideal. And probably no name has so epitomized that ideal as that of Horatio Alger, Jr. Indeed, the American public has endowed it with almost mythological connotations. The common reader "knows" that Alger was a popular and prolific writer whose hackneyed works chronicling the rise of countless poor boys from "rags to riches" were eagerly read by millions. During the twentieth century, patriots and businessmen have praised the Alger hero as the embodiment of the American dream. Alger himself is seen as a living example of this ideal; he has been called "the greatest selling author of all time."

Unfortunately these enthusiasts have often not read Alger's books or at best remember them only dimly from a distant boyhood. Many of the common beliefs about Alger and his books are misconceptions. During his lifetime, his books were neither as popular nor as influential as is commonly supposed. Some writers have estimated that more than one hundred million Alger books were sold, but this is patently ridiculous. He is credited with only one best-seller, and during his own lifetime only about 800,000 of his books were sold. Alger's greatest popularity came after his death. His sales reached their zenith during the first two decades of the twentieth century, when his books were published in cheap editions and when the temper of the country favored their message. Around sixteen or seventeen million books were probably sold altogether, according to Frank Luther Mott's estimate in *Golden Multitudes* (1947).

Studies of Alger are complicated by two formidable problems encountered in any evaluation of his life and work. The first problem is the enormous amount of misinformation which has been published about Alger's life. Many of the well-known "facts" about Alger's life are either unsubstantiated or are outright fabrications. Herbert R. Mayes, author of the first biography (1928), wrote of a repressed boy tyrannized by a puritanical, demanding father who wanted his son to follow in his ministerial footsteps; the boy grew into a pathetic, neurotic man who never fulfilled his desire to write a great novel. His attempts to escape his fate, usually in the arms of a woman, were invariably disastrous. This picture, supposedly taken from Alger's diary, was almost universally accepted for thirty-five years and is still often cited today. John Tebbel's book *From Rags to Riches* (1963) is based almost entirely upon Mayes. In 1972, Mayes admitted that his book was a hoax and the diaries nonexistent; he had written it in an attempt to satirize the debunking biographies so popular at the time. Frank Gruber's biography (1961) is relatively accurate but extremely limited. In 1964, Ralph D. Gardner presented a different picture of Alger. A book collector and unabashed apologist for Alger, his romanticized version portrays a quiet, gentle, sad man. Gardner attempted to research Alger's life, but his documentation, though extensive, is far from clear in its relation to the text; his bias is obvious; and his episodes are so fictionalized that much of the information must be questioned if not discounted. He also accepts some of Mayes's fabrications, such as Alger's supposed stammer as a child, and the portrait of Alger's father as a stern taskmaster who desired his son to become a minister. A major episode in Alger's life, his dismissal

Alger's parents, Olive Augusta Fenno Alger and Horatio Alger, Sr.

from the ministry for homosexuality, was first revealed in 1971 by Richard M. Huber in *The American Idea of Success;* it was not until 1974 that the episode was mentioned by a biographer, Edwin Hoyt, in *Horatio's Boys.* Unfortunately, Hoyt's book relies heavily on Gardner's work and, like it, is poorly substantiated. Only recently has accurate biographical material appeared. The 1985 biography by Gary Scharnhorst with Jack Bales, *The Lost Life of Horatio Alger, Jr.,* is meticulously documented. Because so much misinformation has been published about Alger, it is necessary to address and correct some of the more commonly accepted misconceptions about his life.

The second problem relates to the extent of Alger's work. It is almost impossible to discuss all of his books; there are both too many of them and too few. As Quentin Reynolds says in *The Fiction Factory* (1955), "Alger, according to his biographer, Herbert R. Mayes, wrote 119 books. Actually, he wrote one book and rewrote it 118 times." Although this simplifies the facts (nor is the number exact), it is true that many of Alger's books are very

nearly alike, not only in theme, plot, and style, but also in incident. Readers may often find themselves saying, "Oh, here is the chapter in which: the hero prevents the train from wrecking; the outlaw disguises himself as a stagecoach passenger to learn where the other travelers have hidden their valuables; the villain tries to steal the hero's money while he sleeps; the hero is falsely accused of theft because the stolen property has been planted in his pocket; the hero is offered a job with a traveling show as an actor, singer, violinist, whistler, magician." The list of such overused incidents seems endless. It is also difficult to discuss Alger's books chronologically. His works were often written very quickly and were usually published serially soon after. They might then appear in book form immediately or years later. Two of his books were not published as single volumes until the 1970s; several more appeared in the early 1980s. Furthermore, Alger did not believe in wasting material; many of his adult works were rewritten and published as juveniles. Many of his works were issued as serials several times or as books by several publishers; they were often rewritten and/or seriously cut by Alger or his publisher. Some works had several names; some names were used for two different works. Because of these factors, it is necessary to discuss Alger's work in broad outline, while focusing attention on certain individual books. The books so treated may be either unusual in some respect or representative of many works. Luckily, the very factors which make this approach necessary—the number of books by Alger, the similarities among them, and the difficulties in placing them chronologically—also make it an adequate and useful method for studying his work.

Horatio Alger, Jr., was born on 13 January 1832, in Chelsea, Massachusetts, a community which was later known as North Chelsea and still later became part of Revere. Alger had a fine New England lineage; a Thomas Alger had settled near Taunton, Massachusetts, in 1665, and through his paternal grandmother, Alger was descended from the Pilgrims of Plymouth. His father, a Unitarian minister, was a graduate of Harvard College and Divinity School and a noted writer of biblical commentary. In addition to his ministry, he was postmaster of Chelsea for ten years, served on the town's school committee, taught for a few months, and served one term in the state legislature. Alger's mother was Olive Augusta Fenno, the daughter of a well-known and prosperous businessman of Chelsea. Horatio, Jr., was the eldest of five children.

Although children in that day often started school when very young, Alger was a sickly child and consequently was not pushed in his schooling. He was six before he learned the alphabet, but he made rapid progress, beginning the study of Latin and algebra at age eight. His early education at home was frequently interrupted by his father's business affairs, but he enjoyed reading and became acquainted with a wide variety of books. At the age of ten, he began attending the Chelsea Grammar School where he devoted himself to English studies for a year and a half. It is commonly believed that Alger was called Holy Horatio and was spurned by the other boys of the neighborhood. It is true that Alger was small and that his health was not good as a child; even as an adult he was only five feet, two inches, in height. Mayes claims responsibility for making up Alger's nickname, but it sounds real; it is the kind of name that a small, studious, sickly minister's son might be given.

Horatio Alger, Sr., bought several lots in Chelsea in 1834 and 1836. He fell into debt, and in April 1844 his lands were assigned to Carpenter Staniels, who perhaps was the prototype of the hardhearted squire who forecloses the mortgage in so many of Alger's novels. A few days before the disposal of his land, Reverend Alger had resigned his pulpit, and the family removed in December to Marlborough, Massachusetts, where he assumed the pulpit of the Second Congregational Society. Marlborough was a pleasant town, which the younger Alger was to remember with affection and use as a model for many country towns in his books. Although primarily an agricultural center, it also was noted for the manufacture of shoes in small, unmechanized factories. In later years, many of Alger's heroes worked either on farms or in cobbler shops such as he had seen in his boyhood.

Marlborough claimed one advantage upon which Alger capitalized—it was the site of Gates Academy, a small college-preparatory school run by Obadiah Wheelock Albee, a graduate of Brown University. Alger, like the schoolboy heroes he later wrote about, studied under the academy's elm trees. He completed school in two years and then spent a year reading modern languages before entering Harvard College in 1848, when he was sixteen.

Alger spent four very happy years at Harvard. During his first year he was selected as president's freshman, running errands for the president, receiving free room and a small sum in exchange for his services. Alger was an excellent scholar, graduating eighth in a class of eighty-eight. During his junior year, he took the first Bowdoin prize of forty dollars for an essay on "Athens in the Time of Socrates." He won several awards for Greek composition, was a member of Phi Beta Kappa, gave the English Oration at commencement, and served as class odist.

During his college career, Alger was already evincing an interest in writing. His earliest extant publications are articles on "Cervantes" and "Chivalry" which appeared in the *Pictorial National Library* in 1849. While in college, he wrote James Fenimore Cooper, praising his work and requesting his autograph. Cooper's influence can be seen in some of Alger's books, especially ones set in the West. Alger also called upon Henry Wadsworth Longfellow while in college, an event which he recalled many years later.

Upon graduation from Harvard, Alger apparently felt some indecision about his future career. He lived with his parents for a year, teaching and writing. He then entered Harvard Divinity School in 1853, but withdrew after a few months to become assistant editor of the *Boston Daily Advertiser*. The next summer, Alger began two years of teaching in a boarding school in East Greenwich, Rhode Island. He served as principal of the Deerfield Academy in Massachusetts during the summer of 1856. During the next year, he again tutored and also served as an editorial writer for *True Flag*, a Boston newspaper. An editorial colleague was John Townsend Trowbridge, who later became a children's author and editor. In September 1857, Alger again entered the Divinity School at Cambridge.

During these postcollege years, Alger wrote steadily, producing numerous stories and poems for adults. These were published in various papers and magazines, but only a handful were published in prestigious periodicals such as *Harper's* and *Putnam's*. His first book was *Bertha's Christmas Vision: An Autumn Sheaf*, a collection of these writings published in 1856 by Brown, Bazin and Company. It was followed the next year by *Nothing to Do*, a satirical poem published anonymously by James

Alger upon his graduation from Harvard in 1852

French. Alger occasionally used the pen name of Charles F. Preston. One work first published under that name, *Hugo, the Deformed*, appeared in the *New York Sun* in 1857. It was finally published under Alger's name and in book form in a 1978 limited edition. Nine other novels of the period were published in 1981.

Alger graduated from Divinity School in 1860. In September of that year, he traveled to Europe with two other men, visiting the British Isles, Belgium, the Netherlands, Germany, Switzerland, Italy, and France. He had already written a travel essay about a visit to Quebec, "A Visit to the Falls of Montmorenci," for the *Marlborough Mirror*, and he wrote several such articles about his European travels for the *New York Sun* and other papers. While in Europe he attended (and later wrote about) the funeral of Eugene Scribe, the French playwright.

After returning to the United States in April 1861, Alger preached in Dover, Massachusetts, tutored in Cambridge, and taught in the Nahant, Massachusetts, schools. In 1862, he was offered a pulpit by the Unitarian Society of Alton, Illinois. He declined perhaps because he did not want to be so far from his literary markets. He was drafted by the U.S. Army in 1863, but was exempted because of his small stature and poor eyesight. He continued to write adult stories and poems. *Marie Bertrand*, a novel published in the *New York Weekly* in 1864, was not published as a single volume until 1981.

In 1864 Alger took two momentous steps. He had a juvenile novel published and he accepted an invitation to fill the pulpit of the First Unitarian Church of Brewster, Massachusetts. The latter move was probably made out of necessity. The church was apparently not his first choice for a career, since he had taken twelve years since college to come to it. Certainly he seemed to prefer writing, and continued to do so while in Brewster. But the church was a suitably genteel occupation that provided a steady income.

There is little doubt that Alger would rather have written for adults than for juveniles. Several reasons have been advanced for the change in audience: it was easier to achieve a reputation because there were fewer juvenile authors; it paid better; and his juvenile work was better received. Probably all three reasons are valid. Whatever the reason for changing his audience, Alger contemplated success. The preface of his first juvenile novel states, "Should 'Frank's Campaign' have the good fortune to find favor among the class for whom it is written,

(Baldwin Library, University of Florida Libraries)

Four engraved series title pages from the 1860s and 1870s

it will be followed by other volumes devoted to boy-life."

Frank's Campaign; or, What Boys Can Do on the Farm for the Camp was published by Loring in 1864. Written in three months, it was the first volume of what was later called the Campaign series. The name of the series was obviously chosen to capitalize upon interest in the Civil War, but only the first book dealt with the conflict. The main plot of the book concerns Frank Frost's assumption of the farm work so that his father can enlist in the Union army. Frank's war effort also includes serving as captain of a military company made up of boys in the neighborhood. The Frosts take in a boarder, Henry Morton, whose weekly payment of five dollars helps the family save toward the mortgage held by Squire Haynes. When this unpleasant landlord attempts to foreclose, Morton not only loans Frank the money, but also discloses that he himself had been cheated out of his inheritance by the squire.

Frank's Campaign is in many ways not typical of Alger's later juvenile books. It has more description and depth and is grounded in real events of the Civil War. Several factual accounts of battles and camp life are disguised as letters from Mr. Frost to his family. Frank is supplied with an entire family—father, mother, brother, and two sisters—unlike most Alger heroes who have at best a widowed mother and one dependent younger sibling. Most of Alger's later protagonists are involved in exciting enterprises and often perform feats requiring great bravery, daring, or sagacity. Frank's activities are less spectacular and he performs no heroic feats; he is a much more realistic youth than most of his successors. There are several subplots in which the hero figures only marginally. One of these has to do with Pomp, "a bright little fellow, as black as the ace of spades, and possessing to the full the mercurial temperament of the Southern negro," and his bedeviling of old Mrs. Payson. Alger was no supporter of slavery; he intended this character to be a counterpart of Harriet Beecher Stowe's Topsy. Except for his intelligence, however, Pomp is a stereotype, a mischievous, bright, likable imp. The slapstick episodes concerning him exhibit more humor than is usually found in Alger's books. Alger's first juvenile book does have some elements in common with his later ones. The villainous squire tries to foreclose on the Frost farm, a patron (Morton) is found to pay for Frank's college education, and Alger's characteristic carelessness about details is evident as one character changes names in mid-story.

Alger's second venture of the year, his assumption of the Brewster pulpit, was less successful. His ordination in December 1864 was presided over by Edward Everett Hale, author of *The Man Without a Country* (1865). Alger had probably met Hale when he worked on the *Boston Daily Advertiser*, which was owned by the Hale family. Despite this auspicious beginning, Alger's ministry came to an abrupt end only fifteen months later. In March 1866, he was charged by a committee of his congregation with "a most heinous crime, a crime of no less magnitude than the abominable and revolting crime of unnatural familiarity with *boys*. . . ." Alger admitted that he had been "imprudent," hastily left town, and never thereafter willingly revealed his connection with Brewster. There is some evidence that he contemplated suicide. In the next few weeks, Alger wrote "Friar Anselmo," a poem describing a friar who "committed one sad day a deadly sin," then in horror "besought, with bitter cry, Since life was worthless grown, that he might die." He is rescued from his despair by the appearance of a wounded traveler; in tending to this needy man, Friar Anselmo is called to "a blessed ministry of noble deeds" through which he can expiate his sins. The poem undoubtedly mirrors Alger's disgrace and despair at the time of the Brewster incident. From this time onward, Alger lived primarily in New York and devoted his life to writing for boys, a field to which he later intimated he felt called. His stories, while exciting, were invariably didactic and moralistic, though seldom overtly religious.

The ministerial call had not led Alger to neglect his writing. The Campaign series had proved popular enough for him to write two more volumes. *Paul Prescott's Charge* was published in 1865 and *Charlie Codman's Cruise* in 1866. Both were rewritten versions of earlier adult serials. In spite of their martial titles, neither of the books was about the Civil War. *Paul Prescott's Charge* is the story of a poor orphan whose charge is to repay his father's debt. The book resembles *Frank's Campaign* in its complexity of plot, touches of humor, and leisurely pace. Like Frank, Paul is not thrown upon his own resources. He finds kind adoptive parents who provide a stable home environment until his education is completed. This book, however, is more like Alger's later ones than was the first juvenile. The New York setting, Paul's mercantile career and ultimate advancement because of his fortuitous rescue of a rich businessman's wife, and the liberal use of coincidence to advance the plot are all typical of Alger. This book also exhibits Alger's penchant for aping better writers; the poorhouse scenes are reminiscent of Dickens. Finally, the book is the first juvenile example of one of Alger's chief themes, the poor boy who makes good. Frank Frost does not quite fit the pattern; he is not alone nor destitute enough. But Paul, like other Alger heroes, rises from "rags to respectability."

In the third book of the Campaign series, Charley Codman is the son of an impoverished woman, who lost her fortune when her father was robbed by his clerk. Charlie is kidnapped and taken to sea where he has stirring adventures before returning home to claim his inheritance. *Charlie Codman's Cruise* is the first juvenile book which seems thoroughly typical of Alger's work. It is an example of Alger's second type of plot, the restoration of an impoverished heir to his rightful place. The heir may be lost, disinherited, kidnapped, or cheated out of his inheritance, but this (usually modest) fortune is still available and is restored to the rightful owner when his identity or that of the villain is revealed. (The impoverished heir also figures in *Frank's Campaign* when Morton reveals that he had been cheated out of his inheritance by the Squire, but this is a very minor part of the story.) The plot of *Charlie Codman's Cruise* races along so fast that the reader feels breathless. There are four major villains: the miserly clerk who steals the money, the blackmailing ship's mate who knows the miser's secret, the brutal captain, and a murdering sailor. The coincidences are so numerous, the relationships of all the major characters so tangled, and the author's knowledge of sea life so scant that the story is ludicrous. But it is certainly full of excitement and action.

Alger wrote two other books which were published in 1866. Both were rewritten versions of earlier stories. *Timothy Crump's Ward* is an adult work, published anonymously. There is some question about whether *Helen Ford* should be considered an adult or a juvenile book. At any rate, it is intended for mature girls and young women. The plot is very similar to that of the boys' books. Helen's father is a wronged heir who is disinherited by his father at the instigation of a cheating cousin. Helen, like many Alger heroes, makes her living on the stage. She is a fairy-tale princess, virtuous, happy, and beautiful, almost too good to be true. The minor characters are better rounded than in the boys' books, especially the unscrupulous lawyer Richard Sharp and Margaret Wynne, the forger's wife. Sharp is not Alger's usual thoroughgoing villain; like most people, he is a mixture of good and bad. In his boys' books, Alger's women are usually sweet

nonentities, but Margaret Wynne is angry, suffering, and passionate, a woman of strength and purpose. The book has more description and is more sentimental than Alger's boys' books.

In 1866 one of Alger's stories, "How Johnny Bought a Sewing Machine," was published in *Our Young Folks*, a prestigious juvenile periodical edited by his former colleague John Townsend Trowbridge. At the same time, William Taylor Adams, who as Oliver Optic was a popular author of boys' stories, was editor of *Student and Schoolmate*. He began publishing Alger's stories in 1865. In 1868 Alger's most famous poem, "John Maynard," was published in that periodical. It was frequently anthologized during the late nineteenth century and was a favorite declamation piece for school children of that period. Alger was also writing for other publications, especially adult stories for *Gleason's Literary Companion*.

In 1868, Loring began publication of Alger's new Ragged Dick series, which included six books: *Ragged Dick; or, Street Life in New York With the Boot-Blacks* (1868); *Fame and Fortune; or, The Progress of Richard Hunter* (1868); *Mark, the Match Boy; or, Richard Hunter's Ward* (1869); *Rough and Ready; or, Life Among the New York Newsboys* (1869); *Ben, the Luggage Boy; or, Among the Wharves* (1870); and *Rufus and Rose; or, The Fortunes of Rough and Ready* (1870). The series was suggested by the successful serialization of *Ragged Dick* in *Student and Schoolmate*. Four of the books were serialized in that publication before they appeared in book form; each serial ran for a full year: *Ragged Dick* in 1867, *Fame and Fortune* in 1868, *Rough and Ready* in 1869, and *Rufus and Rose* in 1870. The other two books were not serialized.

Alger is best known for stories of New York street boys who make good, and *Ragged Dick* is the first of his books to exploit this theme. It is the first of three books that tell the story of Ragged Dick, also known as Richard Hunter, Esquire. Dick, a happy-go-lucky bootblack, is imbued with the desire to better himself and rise to a position of respectability. He is one of Alger's most engaging characters. When he first appears, he likes to play tricks, wastes his money on the theater, smokes, and gambles. He is, however, generous to his friends, and he will not lie, steal, or bully younger boys. He is self-reliant, honest, trustworthy, and enterprising. Early in the first book, Dick seizes an opportunity to act as a guide-about-town for Frank Whitney, a visitor to New York. Dick not only points out the city's places of interest, but also its dangers and pitfalls, including crooks and confidence men. Before beginning the tour, Frank gives Dick an old suit. Respectable clothing is often a symbol of a new life in Alger's books. Dick, unwilling to spoil his new clothes, rents a room and stops sleeping in boxes, wagons, and doorways. He opens a bank account, attends Sunday School, and furthers his education with the help of Fosdick, a younger but better-educated boy whom Dick befriends. Dick's chance to rise comes when he saves the life of a boy who falls off a ferryboat. The child's father, Mr. Rockwell, is a prosperous merchant who gives Dick a job as clerk in his establishment.

In the first book, Dick is a lively lad who displays a droll wit. As he advances in life, his speech loses much of its banter and his behavior becomes sober and industrious. At the outset of *Fame and Fortune*, he takes another step upward, moving to a better boardinghouse and receiving a gold watch (also a symbol of new status) and a $1000 reward from Mr. Rockwell, his new employer and patron. During the course of this volume, Dick is framed by a jealous fellow-clerk and is arrested for theft, but the truth is soon discovered. By the end of the book he is on the way to a partnership in Rockwell's firm and marriage with the daughter of another wealthy man who had befriended him when he was a bootblack. In *Mark, the Match Boy*, Dick completes the cycle of "rags to respectability"—he becomes the patron of a young match-seller, Mark Manton. Eventually it is discovered that Mark is the long-lost grandson of a Milwaukee businessman, and he is restored to his rightful place in life.

Rough and Ready and *Rufus and Rose* recount the story of Rufus Rushton, a New York newsboy who rescues his sister Rose when she is kidnapped by their wicked stepfather. Rufus foils a robbery in each book, thus acquiring two prominent patrons. He ends as a partner in a brokerage firm. In *Ben, the Luggage Boy*, Ben Brandon has run away from his stern father and spent six years as a "luggage smasher" who makes a living by carrying luggage for travelers. Ben is a prodigal son who at last returns to the arms of his family.

The Ragged Dick series is the cornerstone upon which Alger's reputation was built. *Ragged Dick* is the book which most closely approximates the archetypal Alger book, the one which readers associate with the author's name. It is also the only book by Alger which Frank Luther Mott is willing to list as a best-seller in *Golden Multitudes:* "But one Alger opus sold about as well as another, and . . . it is hard to get much more than 125,000 copies for a single book; and that is far from enough to make a best seller. . . . However, there were a few, such

as *Ragged Dick, Luck and Pluck, Tattered Tom* and *Phil the Fiddler*, which some veteran booksellers think of as leaders; and we venture to place the first-named of this quartette on our list." Later, Mott lists *Fame and Fortune, Luck and Pluck*, and *Tattered Tom* as "better sellers" which did not quite make the first list.

The Ragged Dick series displays many of the hallmarks associated with Alger's writing. The hero is a robust, intelligent, honest, and hardworking boy in his middle teens. His opportunity for advancement comes through a fortuitous coincidence, but because of his fine character, he thoroughly deserves the reward he gets. Younger boys, such as Mark, the match-seller, are timid, weak, and often sickly; they need the hero's protection. There are snobbish, spoiled self-indulgent boys, exemplified by Roswell Crawford in the three Ragged Dick books, who through pride and dishonesty bring about their own downfall. Each story has wealthy and prominent men who act as patrons for the hero. Although these are stock characters in Alger's books, many of the boys in these books were drawn from real life, including Rough and Ready, whom Alger met at the Newsboys' Lodging House, and Ben, the Luggage Boy. Minor characters in the Ragged Dick series, such as Johnny Nolan, the unambitious bootblack, and Micky Maguire, the street tough, were also modeled on real street boys.

Alger's books have been described as guidebooks to city life, teaching city customs to country boys who aspired to life there. *Ragged Dick*, especially, is touted in this vein; the tour which Dick provides for Frank Whitney is a veritable guide to the sights of New York City. Despite these claims, Alger was no apologist for the city. Many of his books are set in country villages, and the more leisurely, friendly village life is generally portrayed as preferable to the bustling but wicked city. Alger's purpose in the Ragged Dick series was explicit, and it was not to glorify city life. In the preface to *Fame and Fortune* he says: "the author has sought to depict the inner life and represent the feelings and emotions of these little waifs of city life, and hopes thus to excite a deeper and more widespread sympathy in the public mind, as well as to exert a salutary influence upon the class of whom he is writing, by setting before them inspiring examples of what energy, ambition, and an honest purpose may achieve, even in their case."

It is commonly believed that Alger lived much of his life at the Newsboys' Lodging House. Depending on which biographer one reads, Alger is said to have been a good friend of the superintendent, Charles O'Connor, or its founder, Charles Loring Brace. There is no evidence for these claims, however. Alger knew O'Connor, but his personal connection with the Newsboys' House was slight. Alger supported Brace's Children's Aid Society and obviously admired the work of the Newsboys' Lodging House, which was sponsored by the society. Many of the New York City novels mention the Lodging House, and *Mark, the Match Boy* gives a detailed explanation of how it was run. In the preface to *Fame and Fortune*, Alger offers to send a copy of that book and of *Ragged Dick* to "any regularly organized Newsboys' Lodge within the United States," and in the preface to *Rufus and Rose*, he applauds the lodge's work: "Not long since, while on a western journey, the Superintendent of the Lodging House in Park Place found one of his boys filling the position of District Attorney in a western State, another settled as a clergyman, and still others prosperous and even wealthy business men. These facts are full of encouragement for those who are laboring to redeem and elevate the street boy, and train him up to fill a respectable position in society." It is true that Alger was interested in moral reform movements and that he was active in charitable missions among the street boys of New York. He did not smoke or drink and his books discouraged such practices.

Another common belief about Alger, fostered by both the spurious and the romanticized biographies, is that his father was a harsh, stern man who insisted that his son become a minister. There is no proof, however, that Alger did not have a good relationship with his father. He remained on good terms with his family all his life and often spent the summer at their home in South Natick, Massachusetts. Mayes seems to have invented the idea that the senior Alger wished his son to follow in his footsteps. In fact, it is likely that he was pleased with his son's career. Alger dedicated *Fame and Fortune* "To My Father From Whom I Have Never Failed to Receive Literary Sympathy and Encouragement."

Despite the success of the Ragged Dick series, Alger did not depend upon writing alone for his living. About 1869, he began to tutor again. For several years, he tutored the sons of Joseph Seligman, head of an international banking house. Apparently through Seligman's influence, Alger began to have work published in *Young Israel*. Seven of his books were serialized there from 1871 to 1877. Alger continued to tutor for many years. Benjamin Cardozo, who later became a member of the United States Supreme Court, commenced studies with Alger in 1833.

Alger was a prolific writer. Even while he finished the Ragged Dick series, he was beginning another series (Luck and Pluck), contemplating another (Tattered Tom), and writing other books not included in any series. In 1869, in addition to *Mark, the Match Boy* and *Rough and Ready*, there was at least one other book published. *Luck and Pluck; or, John Oakley's Inheritance* was serialized in *Ballou's Monthly Magazine* and published by Loring at the end of the year. An adult work, "Ralph Raymond's Heir; or, The Merchant's Crime," was serialized under the pseudonym Arthur Hamilton in *Gleason's Literary Companion*, but despite the fact that contemporary advertisements note book publication by Gleason that year, no copy of this volume has been located. It was published as *The Merchant's Crime* in 1888 and in 1892 as *Ralph Raymond's Heir.*

Luck and Pluck and *Ralph Raymond's Heir* offer good examples of a recurring figure in Alger's books, the evil stepparent or guardian. Mrs. Oakley in *Luck and Pluck* contrives to steal her stepson's inheritance by hiding her husband's true will. Luckily for John Oakley, his stepmother and her son Ben are not as clever as they are dishonest. Mrs. Oakley ensures the failure of her plan by hesitating to destroy the valid will, and Ben is careless enough to let it be found by one of John's friends. In *Ralph Raymond's Heir*, Paul Morton is both more wicked and more clever than the Oakleys. He not only poisons his friend, Ralph Raymond, but also offers to pay for the murder of Raymond's son. His plan is defeated because his accomplice is weak and inept.

The Luck and Pluck series was published in two parts. In addition to the title volume, the first series included *Sink or Swim; or, Harry Raymond's Resolve* (1870); *Strong and Steady; or, Paddle Your Own Canoe* (1871); and *Strive and Succeed; or, The Progress of Walter Conrad* (1872). The heroes of the Luck and Pluck series are from small rural communities. They often travel far, and while they may live for a time in the city, the stories are not about street life. They are about boys who have been cheated out of their inheritances or poor boys who must rise in the world by their own efforts. In *Sink or Swim*, the hero goes to sea in a story that may have been influenced by Melville, whom Alger admired. *Strong and Steady* and *Strive and Succeed* tell the story of Walter Conrad, who in a manner reminiscent of the heroes of Alger's later Western tales, finds that this supposedly valueless mining stock is worth a fortune.

The last two volumes of the Ragged Dick series and the second volume of the Luck and Pluck series were published in 1870. Alger was already planning another series about street life. In the introduction to *Rufus and Rose,* he said: "Though the six volumes already issued complete his original purpose, the author finds that he has by no means exhausted his subject, and is induced to announce a second series, devoted to still other phases of street life. This will shortly be commenced, under the general name of the 'Tattered Tom Series.'" Like the Luck and Pluck series, the new series has two parts. The first Tattered Tom series includes four books: *Tattered Tom; or, The Story of a Street Arab* (1871); *Paul, the Peddler; or, The Adventures of a Young Street Merchant* (1871); *Phil, the Fiddler; or, The Story of a Young Street Musician* (1872); and *Slow and Sure; or, From the Street to the Shop* (1872).

The books in the Tattered Tom series rank among Alger's most interesting stories. The first volume is Alger's only juvenile book featuring a female protagonist, with the exception of *Helen Ford*, which is for a much older audience. Although Tom is a girl, this is not a "girl's book." Tom, a streetsweeper, is the most engaging of Alger's characters after Ragged Dick. She is no common girl, but one of spunk, intelligence, curiosity, resourcefulness, and courage. Like Dick, she has a sense of humor and is quick at repartee. During the course of the book she fights and defeats two large boys, escapes from a fourth-floor apartment by climbing down a rope ladder and making a ten-foot drop to the ground, and is not frightened at sleeping in a flophouse and literally being penniless. Tom has several more adventures before it is discovered that she is Jane Lindsay, the long-lost heir to a fortune, who was kidnapped by her wicked uncle. The book was well reviewed in *Harper's Magazine*, which reported that Alger "has evidently studied his subject with care, and drawn his portrait from the life. The first part of his story, which contains the street Arab, is by far the best part of the book. No real interest is added to it by the plots and counterplots of the latter chapters, and 'Tattered Tom' is more interesting by far in her original character than when converted into Miss Lindsay." Most readers would probably agree.

Paul, the Peddler is also an atypical Alger book. The portrait of Paul Hoffman is well drawn, and he is unusual because he rises almost entirely by his own efforts. Paul has a patron, but the help he gets is minimal; Mr. Preston asks Mrs. Hoffman, Paul's mother, to sew some shirts for him, and he vouches for Paul's story when Paul is accused of theft. Critics have claimed that while Alger's heroes make good employees, they have very little entrepreneurial spirit. Paul is an exception. The first half of the book is a detailed description of a young merchant in action: selling candy by including a prize in each package, taking over a necktie stand for a sick friend and increasing profits through successful sales techniques, finally buying the stand for himself. As in *Tattered Tom*, the plot changes drastically in the second half, when Paul is swindled by a con artist while attempting to sell a gold ring his mother had found. This section is melodramatic and coincidental, with some touches of humor. Paul's story is continued in *Slow and Sure*. The young merchant gets some help from a new patron, Mr. Talbot, but he still makes his way primarily by his own efforts. At the end of the book, he has purchased his own store. When the Hoffmans' tenement is destroyed by fire, Mr. Talbot engages them as caretakers for his home while he is in Europe. Much of the book is concerned with the attempted robbery of Talbot's house. A new character is introduced, a street boy named Julius, who is the hero of a later book. The two volumes about Paul Hoffman are more realistic and less sensational than many of Alger's books. They were serialized in *Student and Schoolmate* during 1871 and 1872.

In 1872, Alger made a personal contribution to the child welfare movement. His interest was aroused by a particular group of street boys, whom he described as "young Italian musicians, who wander about our streets with harps, violins, or tambourines, playing wherever they can secure an audience." These boys were victims of the padrone system. The padrone bought the services of poor Italian peasant boys from their parents, taught them basic musical skills, and brought them to America. They were expected to wander the city streets, collecting money for the padrone through their performances. Alger gathered information about the system from A. E. Cerqua, superintendent of the Italian School at Five Points in New York, and Mr. G. F. Secchi de Casale, editor of *Eco d'Italia*, an Italian-language newspaper in the city. The result of this research was *Phil, the Fiddler; or, The Story of a Young Street Musician*. Alger's intention in writing the book was to expose the padrone system and to show, as he put it in the preface, "the inhuman treatment which [the boys] receive from the speculators who buy them from their parents in Italy." As Alger explained, the boys were particularly vulnerable because, unlike American-born boys of Italian descent, they "both in dress and

Frontispiece by Laura Caxton for the 1872 Porter & Coates edition of Phil, the Fiddler; or, The Story of a Young Street Musician *(Baldwin Library, University of Florida Libraries)*

Maguire. Pietro has a wet day when he tries to peek into the house; Mrs. Maguire twice empties a dipperful of warm sudsy water on his head, and a cold rain shower completes his discomfort. The padrone comes the next day, but when he pushes his way into the house, Mr. Maguire throws him out the window. The broad humor in these scenes contrasts with Alger's usual sober, earnest tone. The scenes with Giacomo, Phil's smaller and weaker friend who dies from the combined effects of illness and a savage beating by the padrone, are very sentimental. Several of the characters in Alger's earlier books appear here. Phil is befriended by both Ragged Dick and Paul Hoffman.

Alger made a second trip to Europe in 1873, accompanied by his parents, brother, sister, and brother-in-law. They visited Great Britain, France, Switzerland, Italy, Austria, and Germany. In the summer of that year, according to publisher William Ellsworth in *A Golden Age of Authors* (1919), Alger was approached by Frank R. Stockton, assistant editor of *St. Nicholas*, who was seeking stories for the new children's periodical which was to begin publication the next winter. Stockton reported that "Horatio Alger, Jr., finds that his contract with another periodical will not allow him to write for us." This statement refutes the claims of some critics who think that Alger's work was never published in the highly praised *St. Nicholas* because his books placed emphasis on success at the expense of morality (his books are actually very moralistic) and because the quality of his writing was too poor. Alger's *Try and Trust; or, The Story of a Bound Boy* was favorably reviewed in the second issue of the new periodical, which said: "Here is a book for the boys, by a capital writer. . . . Its fresh incidents will delight you and you'll take in good lessons without knowing it."

Try and Trust, which had been serialized under another title in the *New York Weekly* in 1871, was published in 1873 as the first book in the second Luck and Pluck series, which also included *Bound to Rise; or Harry Walton's Motto* (1873); *Risen from the Ranks; or, Harry Walton's Success* (1874); and *Herbert Carter's Legacy; or, The Inventor's Son* (1875). The heroes in this series, like those in the first series, are country boys. *Bound to Rise* and *Risen from the Ranks* are two of Alger's most notable tales. They are modeled upon Benjamin Franklin's *Autobiography*, a book which the hero, Harry Walton, wins as a school prize at the beginning of his career. Harry follows several occupations often found in Alger's books. He gets work in a shoe-pegging shop, then works for a time as helper to a traveling

outward appearance retain their foreign look, while few, even after several years' residence, acquire even a passable knowledge of the English language." The padrone system was broken up within a few years with the passage of child-abuse laws. Whether or not Alger's book helped in bringing about the downfall of the system is questionable, but Alger was apparently convinced that it had played an important part.

The hero of *Phil, the Fiddler* has advantages over the average Italian street boy. He speaks English better than many of the boys, he accepts the hardships of his life philosophically, and ultimately he has the courage to defy the padrone. He runs away to New Jersey, pursued by Pietro, the padrone's bullying nephew. After some difficult days, he is adopted by a doctor who had lost a son about his age. The book has all the liveliness of Alger's street-life books. Soon after running away, Phil takes refuge from Pietro in the home of Bridget

magician and ventriloquist. In *Risen from the Ranks,* Harry imitates his idol Franklin by becoming a printer's devil. Eventually he becomes a writer, editor, and congressman. The two books are earnestly didactic, but their message is obscured by extraneous subplots and careless writing.

The second Tattered Tom series, which began in 1874, consists of *Julius; or, The Street Boy Out West* (1874); *The Young Outlaw; or, Adrift in the Streets* (1875); *Sam's Chance; and How He Improved It* (1876); and *The Telegraph Boy* (1879). None of these books were serialized before book publication. *Julius* shows Alger's continued interest in the work of the Children's Aid Society, which provided a relocation program that helped the street boys find positions in the West, where there were plenty of jobs available for young men with muscles. The West, in those days, was not so far from New York; Julius goes to Wisconsin, where he is adopted by a kind farmer and predictably becomes prosperous. The book is notable chiefly for its picture of the relocation program, but it also includes some vignettes that are common to other of Alger's books. Several of the books written during this period draw on Alger's teaching experience for episodes that gently satirize the educational process. In *Strive and Succeed,* Walter Conrad proves a popular teacher. *Julius,* on the other hand, shows an unsuccessful teacher who is hounded out of the school by his pupils. *Bound to Rise* has a humorous description of a schoolmaster and his class; with the teacher's asides to undisciplined students, the scene is very realistic. *Julius* also has a subplot concerning an Indian who kidnaps a little girl. Alger's later Western books often include Indians who are stereotypical drunken savages. Julius is an early example of one of Alger's stock characters, the adolescent boy who is entrusted with and successfully carries out a mission of great importance or great delicacy.

Sam Barker of *The Young Outlaw* and *Sam's Chance* is for much of his story the antithesis of most Alger heroes. He is lazy and unscrupulous. He lies, steals, cheats, smokes, and gambles. He is also victimized and preyed upon. Not until halfway through the second book does he reform because of the influence of a young woman. Somehow his reformation is too good to be true. Frank Kavanagh of *The Telegraph Boy,* like Sam, is a country boy come to the city. He is a poor boy who makes good, but he spends little time on the streets. Alger was by 1879 turning to other kinds of stories.

The Brave and Bold series also made its debut in 1874. It included *Brave and Bold; or, The Fortunes of a Factory Boy* (1874); *Jack's Ward; or, The Boy Guardian* (1875); *Shifting for Himself; or, Gilbert Greyson's Fortunes* (1876); and *Wait and Hope; or, Ben Bradford's Motto* (1877). *Brave and Bold* had been serialized in the *New York Weekly* in 1872, and *Jack's Ward* is a rewritten version of *Timothy Crump's Ward,* Alger's earlier adult novel. The last two Brave and Bold books were serialized in *Young Israel* in 1876 and 1877. In all four books, Alger continued his turn away from stories of street life. As his sales slipped, the books became more disjointed and melodramatic. Alger's works were receiving mixed reviews. In 1874 *Risen from the Ranks* was given a scathing notice in the *Nation,* which said: "It is to be conceded that naturally clever boys, if they are only young enough or ignorant enough—and of the latter there are countless numbers in country districts—do and will absorb this sort of pabulum; and it goes, if they have nothing to counteract it, an appalling way towards forming mental habits." *St. Nicholas* was more positive, though it entered a caveat: "The book is one that can be honestly commended to young folks, though we do really think that Mr. Alger ought to explain to us how Oscar's father, who begins the story as an India merchant, ends it as a Boston editor." This review continued with criticism of another book: "To *Brave and Bold,* another of Mr. Alger's stories, we cannot award like praise. The story is of the 'sensational' order, while the characters are such as we do not meet in real life—and we are very glad that we don't meet them. The book appears more hurriedly composed than some of the author's other works, and this may account for its deficiencies."

Although Alger was writing primarily for juveniles, he had also continued to produce adult stories. In 1875, Loring published a volume of Alger's poetry, *Grand'ther Baldwin's Thanksgiving.* It was well received, and the author was gratified at receiving letters of commendation from such persons as Henry Wadsworth Longfellow and Edmund Clarence Stedman. Also in 1875 *Seeking His Fortune, and Other Dialogues* was published. For this collection of dialogues by "Horatio Alger, Jr. and O. Augusta Cheney," Alger himself wrote only the title dialogue; the others were written by his sister, Olive Augusta Cheney. In 1877, Alger's *The New Schoolma'am; or, A Summer in North Sparta* was published anonymously. He then wrote "Mabel Parker; or, The Hidden Treasure," but Loring's financial difficulties precluded publication of the book. "Mabel Parker" is the only known unpublished manuscript by Alger. During the same period, Alger probably collaborated in writing a biography of the actor Edwin Forrest. Alger's cousin Reverend William Rounseville Alger had been asked to write the book. *The Life of Edwin Forrest* was published in 1877. It is generally agreed that although Horatio Alger's name does not appear in the book, much of the biographical material bears his style. The book alternates chapters on Forrest's life with others on theater history; the latter chapters were probably written by William Alger. The two cousins were good friends and Horatio Alger was a member of the Church of the Messiah in New York while his cousin was minister there from 1874 to 1878. Alger was also active in the Harvard Club of New York, and composed Odes for the annual dinners from 1869 to 1873.

In an effort to bolster sagging sales, Alger began to travel to gather material about settings other than New York and the Northeast. Alger often wrote about places he knew or had visited. In the early 1870s, several of his heroes visited Niagara Falls, and several books were set in Wisconsin. Alger had certainly seen Niagara Falls, but there is no evidence that he had visited Wisconsin. In 1877, however, Alger traveled to California and in 1878 to Colorado. Although his heroes usually travel West in stagecoaches or wagons, he made the trip more comfortably by rail. The result of these trips was the Pacific series, which included *The Young Adventurer; or, Tom's Trip Across the Plains* (1878); *The Young Miner; or, Tom Nelson in California* (1879); *The Young Explorer; or, Among the Sierras* (1880); and *Ben's Nugget; or, A Boy's Search for Fortune* (1882). The Pacific series was Alger's last for Loring; in fact, only the first three books of the series were published by that firm. Loring went bankrupt in 1881, and *Ben's Nugget* was published by Porter and Coates, a Philadelphia firm. The three Loring books had not been serialized, but *Ben's Nugget* was first published in the *Boston Weekly Globe* in 1882.

Both Tom Nelson, the hero of the first two of the Pacific books, and Ben Stanton, hero of others, travel to the gold fields of California, where they make profitable strikes. Each returns home and pays the wicked squire who is about to foreclose on the family mortgage. Tom returns to San Francisco, but Ben enters a business in New York City. In *The Young Explorer* and *Ben's Nugget*, Alger found another social cause to champion, that of the Chinese immigrants. He hoped, as he put it in the preface to the latter book, that the virtues of Ki Sing, Ben Stanton's servant, "may go far to diminish the prejudice which, justly or unjustly, is now felt toward his countrymen." Alger's picture of

Chinese, like his picture of blacks and of the Irish, is sympathetic but stereotyped. Not all his Chinese characters are virtuous. In *The Young Miner*, one character is robbed by a pair of Chinamen who are amoral but not evil. Alger was at heart an Easterner and an urbanite; his writing profited little from his travels. Not only in these books but also in later ones, the descriptions of the cities—San Francisco, Denver, Omaha, Chicago, St. Louis—are interesting, detailed, and apparently authentic. The West itself, however, serves only as a backdrop for the hero's adventures. Its mountains, valleys, forests, and deserts are unimportant to the story.

Alger wrote three biographies for boys during the early 1880s. Upon the death of President Garfield in 1881, Alger was asked by publisher John R. Anderson to write a biography of the slain leader for quick publication. Alger is said to have written *From Canal Boy to President, or The Boyhood and Manhood of James A. Garfield* (1881) in thirteen days. The book emphasizes those qualities in Garfield which could be instructive for boys: his perseverance, industry, desire for education, and nobility of character. Nothing but good is shown in the president. The book received favorable reviews. According to the *Journal of Education:* "The biography of Garfield presents incidents and reminiscences of a character that tend to stimulate the young men of the republic to emulate his heroic struggles; . . . Mr. Alger presents the story of his life in a most attractive style. . . . Every school and home library should have this record of a life, ripe in experience and noble in character." One can only surmise that this review praises the book for its content, not for its style. Alger includes frequent digressions to tell of other people in similar situations, and extensive quotes from other biographies and from newspaper accounts. Chronological order is not always followed, and the story is highly fictionalized. The book was written for the readers of the day, not for those of the future. Alger seems to assume that everyone will know of Garfield and of his political beliefs. The book was apparently popular enough to encourage Alger's writing of two more biographies: *From Farm Boy to Senator; Being the History of the Boyhood and Manhood of Daniel Webster* (1882) and *Abraham Lincoln, the Backwoods Boy; or, How a Young Rail-Splitter Became President* (1883).

Loring had published thirty-seven of Alger's books from 1864 until 1880. Thirty-two of them were juveniles. Alger wrote his best books during this time. In general, they were more realistic and less sensational than his later books, often amusing and jaunty in tone. Each of the six series published

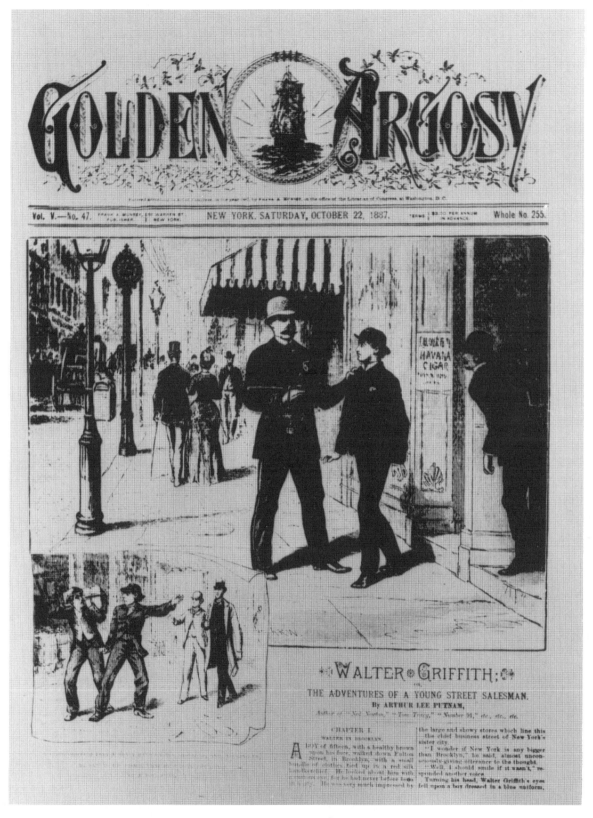

First installment for one of Alger's pseudonymous serials. "Walter Griffith" appeared under Alger's name in 1901 when it was published in book form as Striving for Fortune or Walter Griffith's Trials and Successes *as well as under the title used in* Golden Argosy.

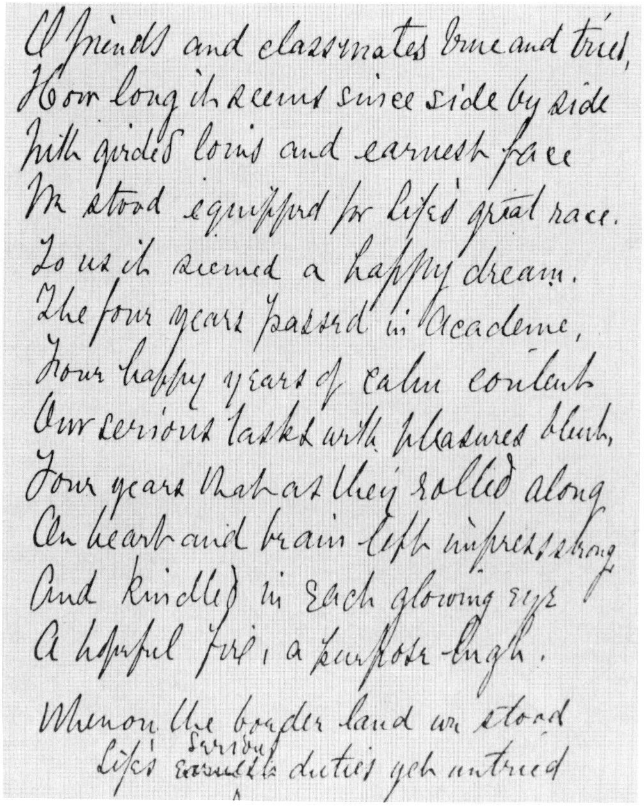

O friends and classmates brave and true,
How long it seems since side by side
With girded loins and earnest face
We stood equipped for life's great race.
To us it seemed a happy dream.
The four years passed in Academe,
Four happy years of calm content
Our serious tasks with pleasures blent,
Four years that as they rolled along
On heart and brain left impress strong
And kindled in each glowing eye
A hopeful fire, a purpose high.

When on the border land we stood
Life's serious duties yet untried

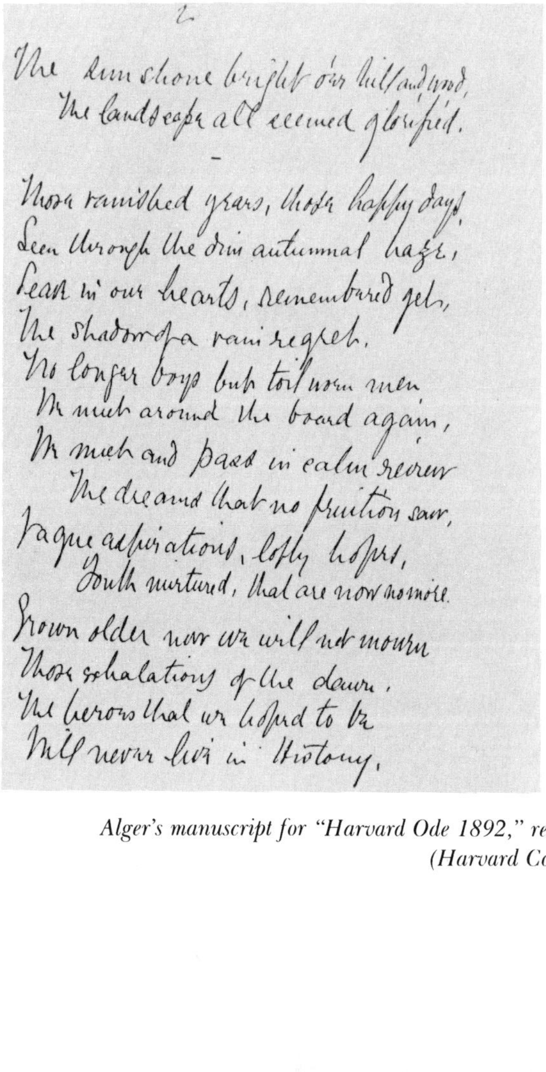

2

The sun shone bright o'er hill and wood,
The landscape all seemed glorified.

—

Those vanished years, those happy days,
Seen through the dim autumnal haze,
Bear in our hearts, remembered yet,
The shadow of a vain regret.
No longer boys but toil worn men
We meet around the board again,
We meet and pass in calm review
The dreams that no fruition saw,
Vague aspirations, lofty hopes,
Youth nurtured, that are now no more.
Grown older now we will not mourn
Those exhalations of the dawn.
The heroes that we hoped to be
Will never live in history.

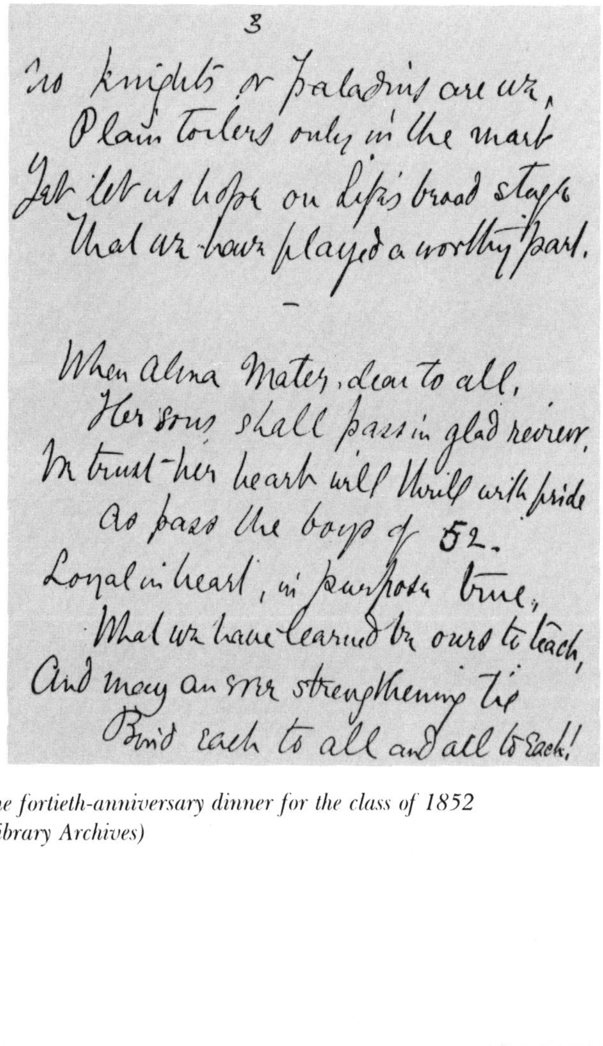

3

No knights or paladins are we,
Plain toilers only in the mart
Yet let us hope on life's broad stage
That we have played a worthy part.

—

When Alma Mater, dear to all,
Her sons shall pass in glad review,
We trust her heart will thrill with pride
As pass the boys of 52.
Loyal in heart, in purpose true,
What we have learned be ours to teach,
And may an ever strengthening tie
Bind each to all and all to each!

Alger's manuscript for "Harvard Ode 1892," read at the fortieth-anniversary dinner for the class of 1852 (Harvard College Library Archives)

by Loring had a theme, and most of the books adhered relatively well to that theme. More than half of the juveniles had been serialized in various periodicals, especially in *Student and Schoolmate* and *Young Israel*. These books were usually published by Loring the same year. For all of these reasons, the books published by Loring present relatively few problems for researchers and bibliographers. This is not true for Alger's other books.

As early as 1871, Alger was writing stories for the *New York Weekly*. This Street and Smith publication wanted fast-paced, sensational stories, and a lot of them. Two years after serialization, Alger's two earliest contributions to the magazine were published by Loring under the titles *Try and Trust* and *Brave and Bold*. Seventeen other stories were published in the *New York Weekly* between 1873 and 1889. Forty stories of the same quality were published in *Golden Argosy* (later *Argosy*) from 1882 to 1894. Because Alger was contributing so many stories to the same periodicals, many of them were serialized under the pseudonym of Arthur Lee Putnam. About a dozen books by Alger were serialized in other periodicals or were published originally as books. The book publications appeared any time from a few months after serialization to thirty years later. One novel, *Cast Upon the Breakers*, was not published as a book until 1974. The Philadelphia firms of Porter and Coates and its successor Henry T. Coates published twenty-six of Alger's books, primarily ones which had appeared in *Golden Argosy*, between 1883 and 1903. Most of these were published only a few years after serialization. Alger's other major publisher was A. L. Burt, whose imprint appeared on thirteen books from 1887 to 1908. Most of the early Burt publications had appeared in *New York Weekly* and were published before Alger's death in 1899; most of the later ones were from *Argosy* and were published after the author's death. More than forty other Alger books were published by various companies. None of these books was particularly well written and few were distinctive in any way. A representative sampling of books written by Alger in the last two decades of his life will illustrate his writing at this time.

The Train Boy was serialized in the *New York Weekly* in 1882 and 1883, and book publication was by G. W. Carleton in 1883. This book is relatively well written, and has two principal plots: Paul Palmer's rise to fortune from a vendor on a train to a mine owner, and the love of Grace Dearborn, a rich young woman, for a struggling artist. Common Alger motifs which appear in the book include a train wreck, during which Paul prevents a robbery,

and a jealous clerk who wanted Paul's position for his own relative. *Do and Dare; or, A Brave Boy's Fight for Fortune* was also serialized in 1882 and 1883. It first appeared in *Golden Argosy* and was published by Porter and Coates in 1884. Herbert Carr is a poor country boy who is hired as a companion to a rich young man with poor health. Herbert accompanies Mr. Melville to Boston, to Chicago, and finally to Colorado. In Boston, Herbert prevents a robbery; in Colorado, he foils a stagecoach holdup, saves Melville from being hanged, and becomes a mine owner. *Do and Dare* was part of the Atlantic series which appeared under the Porter and Coates imprint. Other books in the series are *The Young Circus Rider; or, The Mystery of Robert Rudd* (1883); *Hector's Inheritance; or, The Boys of Smith Institute* (1885); and *Helping Himself or Grant Thornton's Ambition* (1886). Porter and Coates also published the Way to Success series, consisting of *The Store Boy; or, The Fortunes of Ben Barclay* (1887); *Bob Burton; or, The Young Ranchman of the Missouri* (1888); *Luke Walton or The Chicago Newsboy* (1889); and *Struggling Upward; or, Luke Larkin's Luck* (1890).

Several books serialized in the mid-1880s were not published as single volumes until much later. *Frank and Fearless or The Fortunes of Jasper Kent* appeared in the *New York Weekly* in 1885 and was published as a book by Henry T. Coates in 1897. This novel is a variation on the plot of the impoverished heir. Jasper's stepmother shows so much animosity to him after his father's death that he leaves home. He restores a kidnapped child to his parents; the kidnapper turns out to be his stepmother's brother. Jasper is sent on a confidential mission in the West. He is befriended by a beautiful Indian girl who saves him from a robber. He suddenly hears that his stepmother has died in a fire set by her brother. The tale is sensational but relatively coherent, and it is unusual because the chief villain and two rescuers are women. *Mark Manning's Mission The Story of a Shoe Factory Boy* was serialized in the *New York Weekly* in 1886 and published by A. L. Burt in 1905. The plot is a pastiche of many other Alger books. It includes a shoe-factory worker who supports his widowed mother but loses his job, a hermit who is almost robbed of his savings but who is saved by the hero, and a confidential mission during which Mark locates a long-lost grandson who has been supporting a drunken foster mother by selling matches.

At the end of the decade, *$500; or Jacob Marlowe's Secret* was serialized in *Argosy* in 1888 and 1889 before publication as a book by the United States Book Company in 1890. Bert Barton's Uncle

Jacob returns to California and pretends to be a poor man to test his relatives' devotion. During the course of the story, Bert clears his father of a robbery charge. The villains in this tale are less evil than usual, but Alger's careless writing is evident: Mr. Barton's name changes from Simeon to John, and the number of his years in Canada shifts from two to ten. Bert holds several jobs common in Alger's books: he sells berries, works at a shoe factory, and becomes an actor.

Two stories of the period are noteworthy because Alger modeled them upon books by better-known writers, a practice he used more often as his capacity for invention flagged. *Adrift in New York; or, Tom and Florence Braving the World* was serialized in *Norman L. Munro's Family Story Paper* in 1889; an abridged edition, with a slightly different title, was published by Street and Smith in 1903, followed by a complete edition in 1904. The book, which is the story of a kidnapped heir who is raised as a thief, is based upon *Oliver Twist*; the young thief is even named Tom Dodger. *Digging for Gold A Story of California* was serialized in *Argosy* in 1891 and published by Porter and Coates in 1892. Like many of Alger's books, it pays homage to James Fenimore Cooper. Cooper is, in fact, the name of the family with which Grant Colborn travels to California. Although in many ways *Digging for Gold* is typical Alger, it is unusual because the Western setting is well described and vital to the plot. *Digging for Gold* is the first book in the Porter and Coates New World series. The other two books are *Facing the World or The Haps and Mishaps of Harry Vane* (1893) and *In a New World or Among the Gold-Fields of Australia* (1893). Alger's Australian gold fields differ little from his California ones.

During the last two decades of his life, Alger practiced what he had preached in so many books; he became a patron for three poor boys whom he educated and set up in a trade. He found it more difficult to do his charitable works as sales of his books continued to dwindle and his income decreased. He had to write with ever-increasing speed to make enough money, a fact which accounts in part for the poor quality of his writing, although Alger at his best was not really very good. In 1895 G. W. Dillingham published Alger's last adult book, *The Disagreeable Woman. A Social Mystery*, which was written under the pseudonym Julian Starr. In 1896, Alger suffered a nervous breakdown; he wrote very little thereafter. He retired to South Natick, Massachusetts, where he lived with his sister, Olive Augusta Cheney, and her husband, until his death.

In 1898, unable to write due to his breakdown, Alger contacted the young writer Edward Stratemeyer. He suggested that Stratemeyer complete his current book, *Out for Business*. Stratemeyer did so, but the book was not published until after Alger's death on 18 July 1899. Stratemeyer did not

Alger (right) with his brother-in-law Amos P. Cheney (left) and Louis Schick, South Natick, Massachusetts, late 1890s

stop with this book. He completed eleven books which were published under Alger's name, using Alger's manuscripts and plot outlines. One of them, *Jerry, the Backwoods Boy,* is a rewritten version of Alger's unpublished manuscript "Mabel Parker." Several of the books include the notation "completed by Arthur M. Winfield," a favorite Stratemeyer pseudonym. The eleven Stratemeyer completions include *Out for Business or Robert Frost's Strange Career* (1900); *Falling in with Fortune; or, The Experiences of a Young Secretary* (1900); *Young Captain Jack or The Son of a Soldier* (1901); *Nelson the Newsboy or Afloat in New York* (1901); *Lost at Sea or Robert Roscoe's Strange Cruise* (1904); *Jerry, the Backwoods Boy, or The Parkhurst Treasure* (1904); *The Young Book Agent or, Frank Hardy's Road to Success* (1905); *From Farm to Fortune or, Nat Nason's Strange Experience* (1905); *Joe the Hotel Boy or Winning Out by Pluck* (1906); *Randy of the River or The Adventures of a Young Deckhand* (1906); and *Ben Logan's Triumph or The Boys of Boxwood Academy* (1908).

Alger has won a unique place in American literature; he has been enormously influential not for what he wrote but for what people think he wrote. His characters do not, as commonly thought, become rich. Respectability is all they want and all they get. His books are not well written, but they have qualities which appealed to young readers: quick beginnings and transitions; little description (except in the travelogues); much action, excitement, and conversation. The characters visit interesting places and they achieve economic success. Alger wrote cheerful, sprightly books which presented a picture of an America which was innocent but not naive, optimistic, sometimes brash but often kindhearted. It is not a portrait that appeals to today's sophisticated young readers. But if one looks at his books for what they are, rather than demand that they measure up to the standards of great literature, it is easy to see why Alger's books were, a hundred years ago, fun to read.

Bibliographies:
Bob Bennett, *Horatio Alger, Jr.: A Comprehensive Bibliography* (Mt. Pleasant, Mich.: Flying Eagle Publishing, 1980);
Gary Scharnhorst and Jack Bales, *Horatio Alger, Jr.: An Annotated Bibliography of Comment and Criticism* (Metuchen, N.J.: Scarecrow Press, 1981).

Biographies:
Herbert R. Mayes, *Alger: A Biography Without a Hero* (New York: Macy-Masius, 1928);
Frank Gruber, *Horatio Alger, Jr.: A Biography and Bibliography* (West Los Angeles: Grover Jones Press, 1961);
John Tebbel, *From Rags to Riches: Horatio Alger, Jr., and The American Dream* (New York: Macmillan, 1963);
Ralph D. Gardner, *Horatio Alger, or The American Hero Era* (Mendota, Ill.: Wayside Press, 1964);
Edwin P. Hoyt, *Horatio's Boys: The Life and Works of Horatio Alger, Jr.* (Radnor, Pa.: Chilton Book Company, 1974);
Gary Scharnhorst and Jack Bales, *The Lost Life of Horatio Alger, Jr.* (Bloomington: Indiana University Press, 1985).

References:
Jack Bales, "Herbert R. Mayes and Horatio Alger, Jr.; or The Story of a Unique Literary Hoax," *Journal of Popular Culture,* 8 (Fall 1974): 317-319;
William Webster Ellsworth, *A Golden Age of Authors: A Publisher's Recollection* (Boston: Houghton Mifflin, 1919);
"Horatio Alger, Jr.," *Golden Argosy* (17 October 1885): 364;
Frank Luther Mott, *Golden Multitudes: The Story of Best Sellers in the United States* (New York: R. R. Bowker, 1947);
Quentin Reynolds, *The Fiction Factory, or From Pulp Row to Quality Street* (New York: Random House, 1955);
Gary Scharnhorst, *Horatio Alger, Jr.* (Boston: Twayne, 1980).

Papers:
Many of Alger's papers were destroyed after his death. The Alger collection at the Harvard University Archives includes one letter, five student papers, one poem manuscript, and Alger's handwritten biographical entry for the *Class Book* of 1852. The manuscript for his unpublished novel "Mabel Parker; or, The Hidden Treasure" is in the Street and Smith Collection at the Arents Library, Syracuse University.

T. S. Arthur

(6 June 1809-6 March 1885)

J. B. Dobkin
University of South Florida

See also the Arthur entry in *DLB 3, Antebellum Writers in New York and the South.*

SELECTED BOOKS: *The Young Wife's Book; A Manual of Moral, Religious and Domestic Duties* (Philadelphia: Carey, Lea & Blanchard, 1836);

Insubordination: An American Story of Real Life (Baltimore: Knight & Colburn, 1841); republished as *Insubordination; or, The Shoemaker's Daughters* (Philadelphia: Berford, 1844);

The Widow Morrison: A Leaf from the Book of Human Life (Baltimore: Knight & Colburn/New York: Giffing, 1841); republished in *Alice; or, The Victim of One Indiscretion* (1844); republished with *Alice Mellville; or, The Indiscretion* as *Mary Ellis; or, The Runaway Match* (Philadelphia: Anners, 1850);

Six Nights with the Washingtonians. A Series of Original Temperance Tales (Philadelphia: Godey & M'Michael, 1842); republished as *Temperance Tales; or, Six Nights With The Washingtonians* (Philadelphia: Anners, 1849); enlarged as *The Tavern-Keeper's Victims; or, Six Nights with the Washingtonians* (Philadelphia: Leary, Getz, 1860);

Tired of Housekeeping (New York: Appleton, 1842);

Bell Martin; or The Heiress: An American Story of Real Life (Philadelphia: Burgess & Zieber, 1843); revised as *Bell Martin: An American Story of Real Life* (Philadelphia: Anners, 1849);

Fanny Dale; or, The First Year After Marriage (Philadelphia: Berford, 1843); republished as *Fanny Dale; or, A Year After Marriage* (Philadelphia: Berford, 1843); republished as *Fanny Dale; or, A Year After Marriage* (Philadelphia: Anners, 1847);

The Ladies' Fair (Philadelphia: Godey & McMichael, 1843);

The Tailor's Apprentice: A Story of Cruelty and Oppression (Philadelphia: Godey & McMichael, 1843);

The Little Pilgrims: A Sequel To The Tailor's Apprentice (Philadelphia: Godey & McMichael, 1843);

The Story Book (Philadelphia: Godey & McMichael, 1843);

Making A Sensation, and Other Tales (Philadelphia: Godey & McMichael, 1843);

Madeline; or, A Daughter's Love and Other Tales (Philadelphia: Anners, 1843);

The Ruined Family and Other Tales (Philadelphia: Godey & McMichael, 1843); republished as *Temperance Tales* (Philadelphia: Godey & McMichael, 1843);

The Seamstress: A Tale of the Time (Philadelphia: Berford, 1843);

The Stolen Wife: An American Romance (Philadelphia: Berford, 1843);

Sweethearts and Wives; or, Before and After Marriage (New York: Harper, 1843);

The Two Merchants; or Solvent and Insolvent (Philadelphia: Burgess & Zieber, 1843);

The Village Doctors and Other Tales (Philadelphia: Godey & McMichael, 1843);

Alice; or, The Victim of One Indiscretion (New York: Allen, 1844);

Cecilia Howard; or, The Young Lady Who Had Finished Her Education (New York: Allen, 1844);

Family Pride; or, The Palace and the Poor House. A Romance of Real Life (Philadelphia: Berford, 1844);

Hints and Helps for the Home Circle; or, the Mother's Friend, as Mary Elmwood (New York: Allen, 1844);

Hiram Elwood, the Banker; or, "Like Father, Like Son" (New York: Allen, 1844);

The Martyr Wife: A Domestic Romance (New York: Allen, 1844);

Pride or Principle, Which Makes The Lady? (Philadelphia: Berford, 1844);

Prose Fictions. Written For The Illustrations of True Principles, In Their Bearing Upon Every-day Life (Philadelphia: Zieber, 1844);

The Ruined Gamester; or, Two Eras in My Life (Philadelphia: Lindsay & Blakiston, 1844);

The Two Sisters; or, Life's Changes (Philadelphia: Zieber, 1844);

T. S. Arthur

Anna Milner, The Young Lady Who Was Not Punctual, and Other Tales (New York & Philadelphia: Ferrett, 1845);

The Club Room and Other Temperance Tales (Philadelphia: Ferrett, 1845);

The Heiress: A Novel (New York & Philadelphia: Ferrett, 1845);

Lovers and Husbands: A Story of Married Life (New York: Harper, 1845);

The Maiden: A Story For My Young Countrywomen (Philadelphia: Ferrett, 1845);

Married and Single; or, Marriage and Celibacy Contrasted, in a Series of Domestic Pictures (New York: Harper, 1845);

The Two Husbands and Other Tales (Philadelphia: Ferrett, 1845);

The Wife: A Story For My Young Countrywomen (Philadelphia: Anners, 1845);

The Mother (Philadelphia: Ferrett, 1846);

Random Recollections of an Old Doctor (Baltimore: Taylor, 1846);

Advice to Young Ladies on Their Duties and Conduct in Life (Boston: Howe, 1847);

Advice to Young Men on Their Duties and Conduct in Life (Boston: Howe, 1847);

The Beautiful Widow (Philadelphia: Carey & Hart, 1847);

A Christmas Box for the Sons and Daughters of Temperance (Philadelphia: Sloanaker, 1847);

Improving Stories for the Young (Philadelphia: Anners, 1847);

Keeping Up Appearances; or, A Tale for the Rich and Poor (New York: Baker & Scribner, 1847);

Riches Have Wings; or, A Tale for the Rich and Poor (New York: Baker & Scribner, 1847);

The Young Music Teacher and Other Tales (Philadelphia: Anners, 1847);

Stories for My Young Friends (Philadelphia: Gihon, 1848);

Agnes; or, The Possessed. A Revelation of Mesmerism (Philadelphia: Peterson, 1848);

Debtor and Creditor: A Tale of the Times (New York: Baker & Scribner, 1848);

The Lost Children: A Temperance Tale (New York: Oliver, 1848);

Love in a Cottage (Philadelphia: Peterson, 1848);

Lucy Sanford: A Story of the Heart, A Temperance Tale (Philadelphia: Peterson, 1848);

Making Haste to be Rich; or The Temptation and Fall (New York: Baker & Scribner, 1848);

Retiring From Business; or, The Rich Man's Error (New York: Baker & Scribner, 1848);

Rising in the World; or, A Tale for the Rich and Poor (New York: Baker & Scribner, 1848);

Temptations: A Story for the Reformed With Other Tales (New York: Oliver, 1848);

Love in High Life: A Story of the "Upper Ten" (Philadelphia: Peterson, 1849);

Mary Moreton; or, The Broken Promise. A True Story of American Life (Philadelphia: Peterson, 1849);

Our Children: How Shall We Save Them? Also, Keeping It Up, and The Problem, as James Nack (New York: Oliver, 1849);

Sketches of Life and Character (Philadelphia: Bradley, 1849);

Alice Mellville; or, The Indiscretion, published with *Mary Ellis; or, The Runaway Match* (Philadelphia: Anners, 1850);

All for the Best; or, The Old Peppermint Man. A Moral Tale (Boston: Crosby & Nichols, 1850);

The Debtor's Daughter; or, Life and Its Changes (Philadelphia: Peterson, 1850);

The Divorced Wife (Philadelphia: Peterson, 1850);

Golden Grains From Life's Harvest Field (Philadelphia: Bradley, 1850);

Illustrated Temperance Tales (Philadelphia: Bradley, 1850); enlarged as *The Lights and Shadows of Real Life* (Philadelphia: Bradley, 1851);

The Orphan Children: A Tale of Cruelty and Oppression (Philadelphia: Peterson, 1850);

Pride and Prudence; or, The Married Sisters (Philadelphia: Peterson, 1850);

The Two Brides (Philadelphia: Peterson, 1850);

The Young Artist; or, The Dream of Italy (New York: M. W. Dodd, 1850);

Lessons in Life for All Who Will Read Them (Philadelphia: Lippincott, Grambo, 1851);

Off-Hand Sketches, a Little Dashed with Humour (Philadelphia: Lippincott, Grambo, 1851);

Seed-Time and Harvest; or, Whatsoever a Man Soweth, That Shall He Also Reap (Philadelphia: Lippincott, Grambo, 1851);

Stories for Parents (Philadelphia: Lippincott, Grambo, 1851);

Stories For Young Housekeepers (Philadelphia: Lippincott, Grambo, 1851);

The Two Wives; or, Lost and Won (Philadelphia: Lippincott, Grambo, 1851);

The Way to Prosper; or, In Union There is Strength, and Other Tales (Philadelphia: Bradley, 1851);

Woman's Trials; or, Tales and Sketches From the Life Around Us (Philadelphia: Lippincott, Grambo, 1851);

Words for the Wise (Philadelphia: Lippincott, Grambo, 1851);

Cedardale; or, The Peacemakers (Philadelphia: Lippincott, Grambo, 1852);

Haven't-Time and Don't-Be-In-A-Hurry, and Other Stories (Philadelphia: Lippincott, Grambo, 1852);

The History of Georgia, From Its Earliest Settlement to the Present Time, by Arthur and William Henry Carpenter (Philadelphia: Lippincott, Grambo, 1852);

The History of Kentucky, From Its Earliest Settlement to the Present Time, by Arthur and Carpenter (Philadelphia: Lippincott, Grambo, 1852);

The History of Virginia, From Its Earliest Settlement to the Present Time, by Arthur and Carpenter (Philadelphia: Lippincott, Grambo, 1852);

The Last Penny, and Other Stories (Philadelphia: Lippincott, Grambo, 1852);

The Lost Children, and Other Stories (Philadelphia: Lippincott, Grambo, 1852);

Maggy's Baby, and Other Stories (Philadelphia: Lippincott, Grambo, 1852);

Our Little Harry, and Other Poems and Stories (Philadelphia: Lippincott, Grambo, 1852);

Pierre, the Organ-Boy, and Other Stories (Philadelphia: Lippincott, Grambo, 1852);

The Poor Woodcutter, and Other Stories (Philadelphia: Lippincott, Grambo, 1852);

Uncle Ben's New-Year's Gift, and Other Stories (Philadelphia: Lippincott, Grambo, 1852);

Who Are Happiest? And Other Stories (Philadelphia: Lippincott, Grambo, 1852);

Who Is Greatest? And Other Stories (Philadelphia: Lippincott, Grambo, 1852);

The Wounded Boy and Other Stories (Philadelphia: Lippincott, Grambo, 1852);

Confessions of a Housekeeper, as Mrs. John Smith (Philadelphia: Lippincott, Grambo, 1852); enlarged as *Trials and Confessions of an American Housekeeper* (Philadelphia: Lippincott, Grambo, 1854); enlarged edition republished as *Ups and Downs; or, Trials of a Housekeeper* (Philadelphia: Lippincott, 1857) and *Trials and Confessions of a Housekeeper* (Philadelphia: Evans, 1859);

Home Scenes and Home Influence (Philadelphia: Lippincott, Grambo, 1852);

Married Life: Its Shadows and Sunshine (Philadelphia: Lippincott, Grambo, 1852);

The Tried and the Tempted (Philadelphia: Lippincott, Grambo, 1852);

The Ways of Providence; or, "He Doeth All Things Well" (Philadelphia: Lippincott, Grambo, 1852);

The History of New Jersey, From Its Earliest Settlement to the Present Time, by Arthur and Carpenter (Philadelphia: Lippincott, Grambo, 1853);

The History of New York, From Its Earliest Settlement to the Present Time, by Arthur and Carpenter (Philadelphia: Lippincott, Grambo, 1853);

The History of Ohio, From Its Earliest Settlement to the Present Time, by Arthur and Carpenter (Philadelphia: Lippincott, Grambo, 1853);

The History of Vermont, From Its Earliest Settlement to the Present Time, by Arthur and Carpenter (Philadelphia: Lippincott, Grambo, 1853);

The String of Pearls, For Boys and Girls, by Arthur and F. C. Woodworth (Auburn: Derby/Buffalo: Orton & Mulligan, 1853);

Before and After the Election; or, the Political Experiences of Mr. Patrick Murphy (Philadelphia: Bradley, 1853);

Finger Posts on the Way of Life (Philadelphia: Bradley, 1853);

Heart-Histories and Life-Pictures (New York: Charles Scribner, 1853);

Home Lights and Shadows (New York: Charles Scribner, 1853);

The Home Mission (Boston: Crown/Philadelphia: Bradley, 1853);

Iron Rule; or, Tyranny in The Household (Philadelphia: Peterson, 1853);

The Old Astrologer (Philadelphia: Peterson, 1853?);

The Old Man's Bride (New York: Charles Scribner, 1853);

Sparing to Spend; or, The Loftons and Pinkertons (New York: Charles Scribner, 1853);

The Angel of the Household (Philadelphia: Bradley, 1854); enlarged as *The Angel of the Household, and Other Tales* (Philadelphia: Evans, 1858)—adds *The Home Mission* (1853);

The History of Connecticut, From Its Earliest Settlement to the Present Time, by Arthur and Carpenter (Philadelphia: Lippincott, Grambo, 1854);

The History of Pennsylvania, From Its Earliest Settlement to the Present Time, by Arthur and Carpenter (Philadelphia: Lippincott, Grambo, 1854);

The History of Tennessee, From Its Earliest Settlement to the Present Time, by Arthur and Carpenter (Philadelphia: Lippincott, Grambo, 1854);

Ten Nights in a Bar-Room and What I Saw There (Philadelphia: Lippincott, Grambo/Bradley, 1854);

The Good Time Coming (Philadelphia: Bradley, 1855);

Leaves from the Book of Human Life (Boston: Crown, 1855);

Trial and Triumph; or, Firmness in the Household (Philadelphia: Peterson, 1855);

What Can Woman Do? (Boston: Crown/Philadelphia: Bradley, 1856);

The History of Illinois, From Its Earliest Settlement to the Present Time, by Arthur and Carpenter (Philadelphia: Lippincott, Grambo, 1857);

The Withered Heart (Boston: Crown/Philadelphia: Bradley, 1857);

The Little Bound-Boy (Philadelphia: Bradley, 1858);

The Angel and the Demon: A Tale of Modern Spiritualism (Philadelphia: Bradley, 1858);

The Hand But Not the Heart; or, The Life-Trials of Jessie Loring (New York: Derby & Jackson, 1858);

Steps Towards Heaven; or, Religion in Common Life, A Series of Lay Sermons for Converts in the Great Awakening (New York: Derby & Jackson, 1858);

Lizzy Glenn; or, The Trials of a Seamstress (Philadelphia: Peterson, 1859);

The Allen House; or, Twenty Years Ago and Now (Philadelphia: Potter, 1860);

Twenty Years Ago, and Now (Philadelphia: Bradley, 1860);

Growler's Income Tax (New York: Francis & Loutrel, 1864?);

Hidden Wings, and Other Stories (New York: Sheldon, 1864);

Light on Shadowed Paths (New York: Carleton, 1864);

Out in the World: A Novel (New York: Carleton, 1864);

Sunshine at Home, and Other Stories (New York: Sheldon, 1864);

Home-Heroes, Saints, and Martyrs (Philadelphia: Lippincott, 1865);

Nothing But Money: A Novel (New York: Carleton, 1865);

Sowing the Wind, and Other Stories (New York: Sheldon, 1865);

What Came Afterwards: A Novel. Being a Sequel to "Nothing But Money" (New York: Carleton, 1865);

The Lost Bride; or, The Astrologer's Prophecy Fulfilled (Philadelphia: Peterson, 1866);

Our Neighbors in the Corner House: A Novel (New York: Carleton/London: Hotten, 1866);

Blind Nelly's Boy and Other Stories (Philadelphia, 1867);

The Son of My Friend (Philadelphia: T. S. Arthur & Son, 1867);

After the Storm (Philadelphia: Potter, 1868);

After a Shadow, and Other Stories (New York: Sheldon, 1869);

Not Anything for Peace, and Other Stories (New York: Sheldon, 1869);

The Peacemaker, and Other Stories (New York: Sheldon, 1869);

The Seen and the Unseen (Philadelphia: Lippincott, 1869);

Tom Blinn's Temperance Society, and Other Tales (New York: National Temperance Society and Publication House, 1870);

Orange Blossoms, Fresh and Faded (Philadelphia: Stoddart/New York: Gibson/Boston: Maclean, 1871);

The Wonderful Story of Gentle Hand (Philadelphia: Stoddart, 1871);

Three Years in a Man-Trap (Philadelphia: Stoddart, 1872);

Cast Adrift (Philadelphia: Stoddart/New York: Gibson/Boston: Maclean, 1873);

Woman to the Rescue: A Story of the New Crusade (Philadelphia: Stoddart/Cincinnati: Queen City Publishing/Chicago: Goodman/New York: Douglass & Meyers/Boston: George M. Smith/San Francisco: Bancroft, 1874);

Danger; or, Wounded in the House of a Friend (Philadelphia: Stoddart/Chicago: Western Publishing House/Boston: George M. Smith, 1875);

The Bar-Rooms at Brantley; or, The Great Hotel Speculation (Philadelphia: Porter & Coates, 1877);

Grappling With the Monster; or, The Curse and Cure of Strong Drink (New York: Lovell, 1877);

The Latimer Family; or, the Bottle and the Pledge, and Other Temperance Stories (Philadelphia: Peterson, 1877);

Strong Drink. The Curse and the Cure (Philadelphia, Cincinnati, Chicago & Springfield: Hubbard/ St. Louis: Thompson/San Francisco: Bancroft, 1877);

The Wife's Engagement Ring (New York: National Temperance Society, 1877);

The Strike at Tivoli Mills and What Came of It (Philadelphia: Garrigues Brothers, 1879);

Window Curtains (New York: Ogilvie, 1880);

Saved as by Fire: A Story Illustrating How One of Nature's Noblemen Was Saved From the Demon Drink (Philadelphia, Boston, New York, Hartford, Cincinnati, St. Louis, San Francisco, Kansas City & Atlanta: Cottage Library Publishing House, 1881).

OTHER: *The Brilliant; A Gift Book for 1850,* edited by Arthur (New York: Baker & Scribner, 1850);

Friends and Neighbors; or, Two Ways of Living in the World, edited by Arthur (Philadelphia: Peck & Bliss, 1856);

The Mother's Rule; or, The Right Way and the Wrong Way, edited by Arthur (Philadelphia: Peck & Bliss, 1856);

Our Homes: Their Cares and Duties, Joys and Sorrows, edited by Arthur (Philadelphia: Peck & Bliss, 1856);

The True Path, and How to Walk Therein, edited by Arthur (Philadelphia: Peck & Bliss, 1856);

The Wedding Guest: A Friend of the Bride and Bridegroom, edited by Arthur (Philadelphia: Peck & Bliss, 1856);

Words of Cheer for the Tempted, the Toiling, and the Sorrowing, edited by Arthur (Philadelphia: Peck & Bliss, 1856);

Little Gems From The Children's Hour, edited by Arthur with contributions as Uncle Herbert (Chicago: Western Publishing House, 1875);

The Prattler: A Picture and Story Book for Boys and Girls, edited by Arthur as Uncle Herbert (Philadelphia: Lippincott, 1876);

The Budget, Or Picture and Story Book For Boys and Girls, edited by Arthur as Uncle Herbert (Phil-

adelphia: Lippincott/New York: John W. Lovell, 1877);

My Own Book, edited by Arthur as Uncle Herbert (Philadelphia: Lippincott, 1877);

My Pet Book, edited by Arthur as Uncle Herbert (Philadelphia: Lippincott, 1877);

My Primer, edited by Arthur as Uncle Herbert (Philadelphia: Lippincott, 1877);

The Playmate. A Picture and Story Book for Boys and Girls, edited by Arthur as Uncle Herbert (Philadelphia: Lippincott, 1878);

The Boys' and Girls' Treasury. A Picture and Story Book for Young People, edited by Arthur as Uncle Herbert (Philadelphia: Lippincott, 1879);

Lucy Grey And Other Stories for Boys and Girls, edited by Arthur as Uncle Herbert (Philadelphia: Lippincott, 1880);

Pleasant Stories And Pictures, edited by Arthur as Uncle Herbert (Philadelphia, 1880);

Sophy And Prince, and Other Stories For the Young, edited by Arthur as Uncle Herbert (Philadelphia: Lippincott, 1881);

Uncle Herbert's Speaker And Autograph Album Verses, edited by Arthur as Uncle Herbert (Philadelphia: J. A. Ruth, 1886).

Timothy Shay Arthur, author, editor, publisher, devout Christian, temperance crusader, civic leader, and devoted father, was one of the most prolific and influential writers of mid-nineteenth-century America. During the forty years from 1840 to 1880 that form the core of his literary career, Arthur wrote well over two hundred novels and collections of tales and edited or contributed to an array of publications ranging from literary annuals and gift books to periodicals. In the J. W. Bradley catalogue for 1855, he is described as "the most popular of living authors." This sweeping statement is given substance by the fact that during the decade preceding the Civil War he was outsold in American fiction only by Harriet Beecher Stowe's *Uncle Tom's Cabin* (1852). A voluminous writer of moral tales for both children and adults, Arthur is best remembered for his championship of the cause of temperance, an advocacy that made him for decades the literary patron saint of the American temperance movement. It is perhaps fitting that out of his vast literary output, the only one of his works still known outside academic circles is his temperance classic *Ten Nights in a Bar-Room and What I Saw There* (1854).

T. S. Arthur was born on 6 June 1809 near Newburgh in Orange County, New York. His parents, William and Anna Shay Arthur, were of hum-

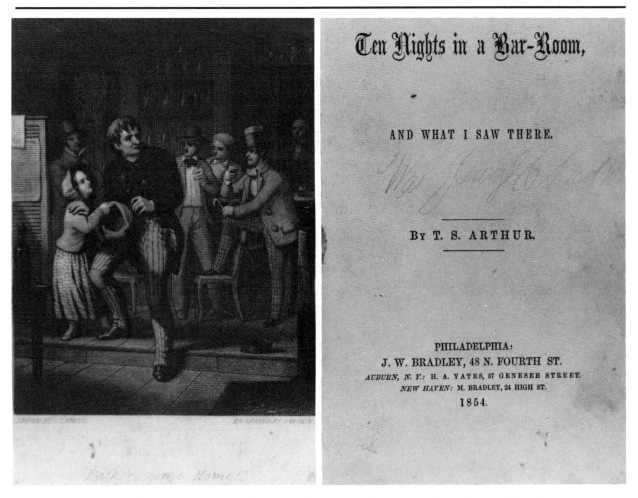

Frontispiece and title page for Arthur's best-known work (University of South Florida Library)

ble circumstances and were hard put to raise their family of one daughter and four sons. Due to poor health, Arthur had little formal education for the first nine years of his life. During these formative years, his instruction consisted of religious precepts, Bible readings, and stories told by his parents about Timothy Shay, Arthur's maternal grandfather, who had been an officer in the American army during the Revolutionary War.

Although young Arthur was enrolled in school following the relocation of his family to Baltimore in 1817, he proved to be a poor scholar. He was removed from school after a short time and apprenticed to a craftsman to learn a trade. Although it is not known exactly which trade Arthur pursued, evidence suggests he was apprenticed to a tailor. The detailed work caused the boy severe eye strain, threatening him with the blindness that was to overtake him in later life.

Although Arthur had been a failure during his brief period of formal schooling, he recognized

his need for knowledge. At age fifteen, he embarked on a program of self-education through reading. With no systematic program or outside direction in his quest for knowledge, he was unable to progress as he had hoped. After a brief and unsuccessful stint at a "mechanic's school," Arthur became a clerk in a Baltimore countinghouse in 1830. In 1833, he became the western agent for the Susquehanna Bridge and Banking Company, traveling to Louisville, Kentucky. After only a few weeks in Louisville, the company went bankrupt, leaving young Arthur with one more failure to his credit and little else.

Arthur returned to Baltimore and shortly thereafter was invited to coedit the *Baltimore Athenaeum and Young Men's Paper*, a weekly literary magazine. Although it lasted only three years, this publication confirmed Arthur's long-held desire to become a writer. On 8 October 1836 he began the *Baltimore Literary Monument*, eventually acclaimed as one of the best magazines of its kind in the city.

With his success as a magazine publisher and writer, Arthur found himself sufficiently well off to permit him to marry. The lady of choice was Eliza Alden, who became his bride in 1836.

In 1837 Arthur acquired the *Baltimore Saturday Visiter,* which counted Edgar Allan Poe among its contributors. Arthur published the *Literary Monument* until 1839 and the *Saturday Visiter* until a year later, when he accepted an editorial appointment with the *Baltimore Merchant.* Through his coverage of the early meetings of the Washington Temperance Society in 1840, Arthur became interested in the temperance movement. In 1842 he produced his first major temperance work, a collection of stories entitled *Six Nights with the Washingtonians. A Series of Original Temperance Tales.* This work established Arthur's reputation as a literary crusader against the evil of strong drink, a theme that pervaded much of his literary output for the remainder of his career.

In April 1841, Arthur left Baltimore for Philadelphia, where he henceforth made his home. There he produced a veritable flood of novels and tales while continuing to contribute to such journals as *Godey's Lady's Book,* the most popular women's magazine of the era. During the 1840s, *Godey's* published sixty of Arthur's tales and sketches. In addition to his prolific literary production, Arthur continued his editorial career. In 1850 he began the most successful of his magazine ventures, a weekly entitled *Arthur's Home Gazette.* In 1853 it became a monthly under the title *Arthur's Home Magazine.* The 1850s mark the apogee of Arthur's career. Four years after the founding of *Arthur's Home Gazette,* he wrote the work that was to bring him enduring fame, *Ten Nights in a Bar-Room and What I Saw There.* The rapidly growing temperance movement made this work an instant best-seller; four years after the novel was published, William W. Pratt adapted it for the stage. Pratt's adaptation of Arthur's temperance fable is still performed, though it is probably received by modern audiences in a less serious view than either Arthur or Pratt intended.

Although best known as an editor and writer of fiction for adults, Arthur was also a productive writer for children. Among his publications for young readers are ten schoolbook state histories written in collaboration with William Henry Carpenter between 1852 and 1854. While these texts are generally considered potboilers and are devoid of original research, some of them apparently filled an educational need of the period and went into many editions. The Georgia volume, for instance, is represented by at least six recorded printings.

Virtually all of Arthur's fictional writings for children offer strong moral lessons, warning of the perils of disobedience, selfishness, sabbath-breaking, and, of course, the perils of drink. By modern standards, the quality of writing in Arthur's juvenile works leaves much to be desired. His characters have little depth and are seldom delineated so that there is more than a single dimension presented. Most of Arthur's short stories for children, the form he most often used, portray a single vice or virtue without confusing side issues. *Maggy's Baby, and Other Stories* (1852) is a typical volume in Arthur's Juvenile Library, his most important and longest-running juvenile series, which began publication with twelve volumes in 1852. Each of the fourteen brief tales comprising *Maggy's Baby* represents a single vice or virtue: charity, disobedience, self-control, evil in man's heart, patience in grief, and so forth. Only rarely is more than a single basic point made in a story. Usually when more than one issue is raised in a tale, one is temperance, or more specifically, the dire fate that befalls the intemperate. As might be expected, in Arthur's juvenile universe good is always rewarded (although the reward is sometimes long in coming), and evil always turns back upon the evildoer. Often good is equated with unquestioning obedience to parents and other authority figures. Obedient children are good and find rewards; disobedient children are bad and come to bad ends; and, of course, go straight to perdition if they drink. On rare occasions, and mostly in his writings after about 1870, Arthur creates a story that could have come from the pen of the brothers Grimm. A fine example is *The Wonderful Story of Gentle Hand* (1871), in which the all-pervading power of love overcomes evil and violence, turning ugliness to beauty.

Arthur's juvenile periodical, the *Children's Hour,* was a major contribution to the literature of youth in the period. It began publication in January 1867 and was absorbed by *St. Nicholas* in 1874 after fifteen volumes had appeared. In many of Arthur's juvenile works he used the pseudonym Uncle Herbert, and children's works published under this name achieved such popularity that after the death of Arthur in 1885 publishers continued to bring out volumes of juvenilia edited by Uncle Herbert— works with which Arthur obviously had no connection. The juvenile prose and verse signed by Arthur with his own name as editor or as Uncle Herbert certainly are no worse than much of that of his era and in rare moments exhibit an acute perception of the mind of Victorian youth. He was

Frontispiece and title page for the bound 1868 issues of Arthur's juvenile magazine (University of South Florida Library)

a product of his day and age, who said in the introduction to his *Advice to Young Ladies on Their Duties and Conduct in Life* (1847), "Although man has the power of abstract thought and the faculty of reasoning in a higher degree than women, yet woman is nonetheless a rational being." What today would be labeled male chauvinism was a basic part of Arthur's outlook, as it was of the world of his day.

Arthur described the *Children's Hour* in an advertising blurb that characterizes much of his juvenile writing extremely well: "A pleasant companion, friend, and counsellor of the little ones; and a helper in the work of storing up things good, and true, and beautiful, in their minds; . . . an attractive illustration of those precepts that lie at the foundation of all right living. It aims to inspire children with reverence for God, . . . to be gentle, forbearing, merciful, just, pure, brave and peaceable." He speaks at length of proper and improper reading in his *Advice to Young Ladies*. It is apparent that he was guided in his writing by the advice that he gave on reading. One arresting sen-

tence states: "A young lady who indulges in much novel reading never becomes a woman of true intelligence." He then states that "all works of fiction, however, are not bad"; "where the author's aim is to give right views of life, and to teach true principles, he may do great good." Arthur recommends a series of authors that "may be read with not only pleasure, but profit, by every young lady." These authors include the best-known of Sunday school writers, including Maria Edgeworth and Mary Howitt.

Arthur always strove to teach and, more important, edify his young readers. He maintained a lifelong religious certitude that he strove to impart to the youth of his day. In addition to his busy career as writer, editor, and publisher, he raised a family of seven children and took an active part in Philadelphia civic affairs. He was deeply interested in Swedenborgian theology and in 1855 was one of twenty selectmen who founded the city's first New Jerusalem Society. Arthur helped establish the Franklin Home for Inebriates in Philadelphia during the late 1870s and served in 1876 as chairman

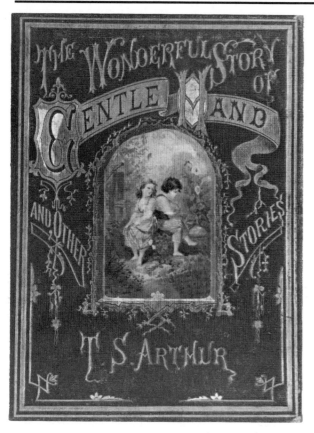

Front cover for Arthur's 1871 fairy tale about the triumph of love, over evil (University of South Florida Library)

of the executive committee for the city's Centennial Exhibition. Through his writings and other activities, Arthur achieved national fame as a temperance champion, authority on marital and family relations, and an advocate of women's rights.

The demands of his many activities eventually exhausted the aging Arthur. As the 1870s drew to a close his health failed and the weakness of his eyes that had troubled him from his youth became increasingly severe. As his world narrowed due to his failing eyesight during the early years of the 1880s, he continued editorial work with the aid of amanuenses. By February 1885, he was unable to leave his home. T. S. Arthur died on 6 March 1885. He was buried in Philadelphia's old Chestnut Street Cemetery.

Biographies:

T. S. Arthur. His Life and Works by One Who Knows Him (Philadelphia: J. M. Stoddart, 1873);

Donald A. Koch, "The Life and Times of Timothy Shay Arthur," Ph.D. dissertation, Western Reserve University, 1954.

References:

Carl Bode, *Anatomy of Popular Culture* (Berkeley: University of California Press, 1959), pp. 119-131;

Warren French, "Timothy Shay Arthur: Pioneer Business Novelist," *American Quarterly*, 10 (Spring 1958): 55-65;

French, "Timothy Shay Arthur's Divorce Fiction," *University of Texas Studies in English*, 33 (1954): 90-96;

Richard R. Gladish, "A Famous New Church Temperance Writer," *New Church Life*, 90 (December 1970): 592-595;

Donald A. Koch, Introduction to Arthur's *Ten Nights in a Bar-Room and What I Saw There* (Cambridge: Harvard University Press, 1964);

D. L. Milliken, "Methods of T. S. Arthur," *Writer*, 1 (1887): 141-142.

John Bennett

(17 May 1865-28 December 1956)

Douglas Street
Texas A & M University

BOOKS: *Master Skylark: A Story of Shakspere's Time* (New York: Century, 1897);

Barnaby Lee (New York: Century, 1902);

The Treasure of Peyre Gaillard (New York: Century, 1906);

Songs Which My Youth Sung (Charleston: Daggett, 1914);

Madame Margot: A Grotesque Legend of Old Charleston (New York: Century, 1921);

The Pigtail of Ah Lee Ben Loo, with Seventeen Other Laughable Tales and 200 Comical Silhouettes (New York & London: Longmans, Green, 1928);

Protest of an Oldtimer (New York: Marchbanks Press, 1930);

Blue Jacket, War Chief of the Shawnees, and His Part in Ohio's History (Chillicothe, Ohio: Ross County Historical Society, 1943);

The Doctor to the Dead: Grotesque Legends and Folk Tales of Old Charleston (New York & Toronto: Rinehart, 1946).

The history of literature is punctuated with the names of men and women who but for creation of a single work would long ago have faded into obscurity. This phenomenon occurs with greater frequency in children's literature, where the success of one inspired tale can earn a writer lasting recognition. Such is the case of the storyteller from Ohio John Bennett, who is remembered for his masterpiece of historical fiction for young people, *Master Skylark* (1897). In discussing Bennett and his contributions to the literary period ranging from 1890 into the 1920s in the revised edition of *A Critical History of Children's Literature* (1969), Elizabeth Nesbitt states that "If this period had produced no other books than those of John Bennett, still it would be a notable one. His books are distinctive and distinguished; so much so that the only possible regret is that there are not more of them."

Master Skylark is easily one of the nineteenth century's premier children's works of historical fiction. Yet though clearly it is this Elizabethan tale which brings forth the Bennett name today, it is not the sole noteworthy creation of this author whose writing career spanned nearly seventy years. *Barnaby Lee*, Bennett's 1902 historical novel about Peter Stuyvesant and New Amsterdam, has been called by many a "classic," its critical acclaim placing it a close second to Bennett's earlier title. The publishing in 1928 of *The Pigtail of Ah Lee Ben Loo*, a collection of poems and stories most of which had appeared in the pages of *St. Nicholas* over a generation before, served to further assure Bennett's literary reputation. Though he died in 1956, Bennett is primarily an author of the turn of the century. All of his important writing for children was first published in *St. Nicholas* during the period from 1890 to 1910.

As a youth John Bennett was intent upon developing the skills of artist and illustrator; his interest in writing came later. He was born on 17 May 1865 to John Briscoe Henry, a merchant, and Eliza Jane Trimble McClintock Bennett of Chillicothe, Ohio. By his own admission, the young Bennett wished to be an illustrator as far back as he could remember. At age four he began drawing, and as he matured his initial scratchings developed into caricatures and cartoons patterned after Thomas Nast, George Cruikshank, and the British cartoonists of the day. School seems to have been a nuisance for the artistically active "Jack" Bennett. While he was intelligent and an avid reader, the school curriculum held little interest for Bennett. He attended public schools in Chillicothe but withdrew after his second year of high school when drawing became far more important than studying. Realizing their son's love for art, in 1882 the Bennetts sent him to art school in Cincinnati to "learn to draw properly," he says. The senior Bennett's failing business forced Jack Bennett to leave art to find employment. The work he chanced upon was newspaper reporting, first as cub reporter for the *Ross County Register* in his hometown, then as reporter and eventually editor of the *Chillicothe Daily News*. Bennett's work on this second paper coupled with word from acquaintances in Cincinnati landed him a position with the *Cincinnati Commercial-Gazette*

John Bennett and Louise Jones DuBose, director of the South Carolina WPA Writers' Project, circa 1938

who was most inventive and ingenious, with my brother Harry a close second."

For Jack Bennett 1891 was the year he first realized his ambitions as both artist and storyteller; the twenty-five year old writer-illustrator submitted two imaginative stories, "Little Peter and the Giant" and the rhymed "The Barber of Sari-Ann," both illustrated with his own silhouettes, to his favorite childhood publication, *St. Nicholas.* Both were accepted, and *St. Nicholas* editor Mary Mapes Dodge asked him for more. Responding that he would send a new story with illustrations in two days, he spent the next forty-eight hours producing "Ye Olde Tyme Tale." Dodge accepted this one too, forwarding Bennett an open invitation to submit all he wrote for children to *St. Nicholas.* Jack (now officially John) Bennett took Dodge's offer. His early work for *St. Nicholas* tends to fit into three general categories. Adventure tales in prose usually exhibited content and style reminiscent of the Arabian Nights as in the humorous "Astonishing Story of the Caliph's Clock" or "The Persian Columbus," or those traditional tales collected and retold by

as a regular contributor to their Saturday and Sunday supplements. It was while writing weekly columns for the *Gazette* that he developed a style of writing more akin to those exhibited by the authors in the literary magazines he admired and less to that of standard journalistic prose. Although illustration was still his love, writing was becoming the key to his livelihood.

Literature had always been a part of Bennett's growing up. His sister Martha Trimble Bennett recalls all the Bennett children as avid readers of juvenile fiction and her parents as enthusiastic supporters of such pastimes. Besides offering an abundance of books to be read, the Bennett household subscribed to several of the best juvenile periodicals of the day; *Little Corporal, Nursery, Youth's Companion,* and, most important, *St. Nicholas* were eagerly awaited and read cover to cover by Jack Bennett and his family. Although he retained his desire to draw, the young Bennett developed a second wish—to write a story for *St. Nicholas.* As a youth Bennett played the role of neighborhood storyteller. Emulating a friend who had once regularly enthralled youths with tales of Irish fairies and Arabian Nights, he sat upon the horse block at the stable and told stories to the others. His sister recalls Jack inventing additional adventures for the characters he had read about in the magazines or inventing more tales from the Arabian Nights. "As I look back," wrote Martha Trimble Bennett in a 1960 article for *Horn Book Magazine,* "it was Jack

"MASTER SHAKSPERE MET THEM WITH OUTSTRETCHED HANDS."

Illustration by Reginald Birch for Master Skylark *(Baldwin Library, University of Florida Libraries)*

such men as the Grimms and Joseph Jacobs. "Little Peter and the Giant," "Hans the Otherwise," and "The Story of the Fool Who Was Willing" all show Bennett's ease in following these fairytale models.

Bennett also contributed narrative verse to *St. Nicholas*. His ballads or metrical romances, many with a decidedly medieval flavor, are patterned closely upon the old metrical broadsides and folk ballads in the vein of "Robyn Hoode" or "The Elfin Knyght" and usually tell the story of a single protagonist. Among Bennett's best medieval parodies are "Ye Olde Tyme Tayle Of Ye Knight, Ye Yeomanne, And Ye Faire Damosel," 170 lines arranged into four "Cantos"; "Ye Very Ancient Ballad of Ye Lily Mayden and Ye Lyttel Taylor-Boye," in 186 lines and five cantos; and "A Jest of Little John," Bennett's 206-line tribute to the exploits of Robin Hood. The ballads were popular among *St. Nicholas* subscribers, and many were included in *The Pigtail of Ah Lee Ben Loo*.

Possibly to combat the weariness of composing these long, elaborate verses, Bennett also con-

tributed jingles and nonsense verse to the magazine. Short, comic, and obviously influenced by the rhymes of Edward Lear and Laura E. Richards, these verses were usually accompanied by Bennett's own illustrations. These offerings were frequently used to fill empty magazine-page space or act as pleasant breaks between long pieces. "The Ingenious Little Old Man," which appeared in the September 1897 issue, is a typical example of Bennett's light verse offerings:

> A little old man of the sea
> Went out in a boat for a sail:
> The water came in
> Almost up to his chin
> And he had nothing with which to bail.
>
> But this little old man of the sea
> Just drew out his jack-knife so stout,
> And a hole with its blade
> In the bottom he made,
> So that all of the water ran out.

Although the prose tales, ballads, and short lyrics kept Bennett's name before the readers of *St. Nicholas* for two decades, it was his major fiction which brought him national recognition.

In the early 1890s, while Bennett contributed to *St. Nicholas*, Martha Trimble Bennett studied at Radcliffe. Whereas John's interest, evident in his many ballads, lay in medieval English lore, Martha grew to love all aspects of Elizabethan culture. She suggested that John write a piece set in the age of Elizabeth, mentioning that it had been a practice at that time to kidnap young boys with notable singing voices for the queen's choir. Bennett conceived the plot line for such a book while he was working as a reporter in Chillicothe, Ohio; *Master Skylark* was to be its title. The first two-thirds of the novel were completed steadily over the next few months, but the last third was a problem. Bennett sent the incomplete manuscript to Dodge at *St. Nicholas*, asking if such a tale would prove acceptable and promising to finish the manuscript eventually. Dodge accepted the unfinished work and suggested he move to New York to hasten its completion. This he did; the book was finally finished, and the first installment of *Master Skylark* was set before the readers in November 1896. *St. Nicholas* carried an episode a month through October of the next year, and the parent Century Company published it in book form in late 1897. Illustrated by Reginald Birch, the "story of Shakspere's time" became an immediate bestseller that quickly went through several printings and is still in print today.

Title page for Bennett's last major children's book (University of Florida Libraries)

Master Skylark begins in Stratford town in 1596, and the events of the novel occur over a year's time. The main character, "Master Skylark," is young Nick Attwood, who is taken by Gaston Carew when his troupe of actors passes through Nick's town. Nick has a haunting singing voice which so enthralls Carew that he forcibly transports Nick to London where, after numerous trials and hardships, the youth sings for the queen. Nick, however, wishes not for fame but only for the familiar confines of his mother's home. A full year and numerous adventures later, with the help of Will Shakespeare and Ben Jonson, Nick is finally reunited with his family as the novel comes to a happy end. Bennett took great pains with his research so that the Elizabethan street scenes and descriptions of village life, as well as the portrayals of Shakespeare and other theater people of the day, are vivid and historically accurate. The story is engrossing; Bennett's plot and character development are meticulous, giving a sense of depth and a reality to the adventure seldom matched in nineteenth-century historical fiction. As a juvenile his-

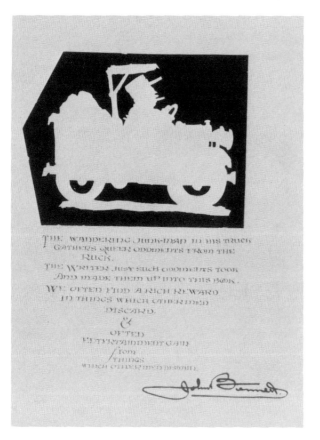

Inscription in The Pigtail of Ah Lee Ben Loo *(Collection of Rowena Betts)*

torical novel of the Shakespearean age, *Master Skylark* has no serious rivals.

Following upon the tremendous success of *Master Skylark* was Bennett's second novel with a historical source of inspiration. *The Story of Barnaby Lee* began serialization in the November 1900 copy of *St. Nicholas* and ran through October of 1901; the Century Company produced it in book form early in 1902 with Clyde De Land's drawings. The historical setting is New Amsterdam, now New York, and the tale involves Peter Stuyvesant and the Dutch settlers who eventually are overrun by the British. The impetus for the novel was Bennett's interest in one of his Dutch ancestors, Gerrit Van Sweringen, who participated in events at New Amsterdam. Like Master Skylark, the character of Barnaby Lee is drawn, and, again, Bennett's talent for making exciting fiction from history is evident. Bennett fills this work with intrigue, with battles and other explosive events that bring to mind the nineteenth-century adventure tales of Mayne Reid and Paul Du Chaillu. Though not as popular with readers as *Skylark*, *Barnaby Lee* received its share of acclaim and remained in print until after the author's death in 1956.

Bennett's last major children's work of note was *The Pigtail of Ah Lee Ben Loo, with Seventeen Other Laughable Tales and 200 Comical Silhouettes.* All but four of the offerings in this collection of verse and short fiction were originally published in *St. Nicholas.* Included are Bennett's first *St. Nicholas* stories together with some from his years as an established contributor to the magazine. The stories and rhymes are enjoyable and entertaining, though not "classics," and the volume contains a liberal selection of Bennett's best silhouette illustrations.

Bennett moved to Charleston, South Carolina, shortly before the turn of the century. There he met and in 1902 married Susan D. A. Smythe; the couple had three children, Jane, John, and Susan. From this time on Bennett wrote little for children, concentrating instead on adult novels and tales of the old Charleston blacks: *The Treasure of Peyre Gaillard* (1906), *Madame Margot: A Grotesque Legend of Old Charleston* (1921), and *The Doctor to the Dead: Grotesque Legends and Folk Tales of Old Charleston* (1946). These books sold well in the first half of the twentieth century.

The creator of *Master Skylark* and *Barnaby Lee* was a gifted writer for children; he wrote so well for them because he respected them and considered them friends. He was such a well-known figure among Charleston children that the children's book room of the Charleston public library was named in his honor. In 1927 the *Saturday Review of Literature* published "I Want An Epitaph" by John Bennett in which the author tells readers how he would like to be remembered:

> I want an epitaph.
> I'm tired of Smith, Brown, and Jones,
> Who say they wish no line above
> Their cast-off bones!

. . . .

> "Of many a life-long friend
> Unforgetful and unforgot:
>   The golden best."
> That much my epitaph should say:
> "For all the rest
> His was the common lot
> And ordinary way."

> Say what you please beyond that line;
> It will not matter.

References:

Martha Trimble Bennett, "Youth in Pleasant Places," *Horn Book Magazine*, 36 (June 1960): 243-245;

"John Bennett, Author of *The Pigtail of Ah Lee Ben Loo*," *Wilson Bulletin for Librarians*, 3 (December 1928): 378;

Elizabeth Nesbitt, "A Rightful Heritage, 1890-1920," in *A Critical History of Children's Literature, Revised Edition*, edited by Cornelia Meigs, Anne Thaxter Eaton, Elizabeth Nesbitt, and Ruth Hill Viguers (New York & Toronto: Macmillan, 1969), pp. 349-363;

Janie M. Smith, "Author and Children in the South," *Horn Book Magazine*, 18 (March 1942): 83-87;

Smith, "John Bennett of Chillicothe," *Horn Book Magazine*, 19 (November 1943): 427-434.

Caleb Bingham

(15 April 1757-6 April 1817)

Paul Eugen Camp
University of South Florida

SELECTED BOOKS: *The Young Lady's Accidence; or, A Short and Easy Introduction to English Grammar . . .* (Boston: Printed by Greenleaf & Freeman, 1785; revised, Boston: Printed by I. Thomas, 1789);

The Child's Companion: Being a Concise Spelling Book . . . (Boston: Printed by Samuel Hall, 1792; revised, Boston: Caleb Bingham, 1819);

The American Preceptor: Being a New Selection of Lessons for Reading and Speaking (Boston: Printed by I. Thomas & E. T. Andrews for the author, 1794); revised as *The American Preceptor Improved; Being a New Selection of Lessons for Reading and Speaking* (Boston: C. Bingham, 1819);

An Astronomical and Geographical Catechism for the Use of Children (Boston: Printed & sold by S. Hall, 1795);

Round Text Copies. Written by Caleb Bingham, Boston, and *Engraved for Him by S. Hall* (Boston: S. Hall, 1795);

The Columbian Orator: Containing a Variety of Original and Selected Pieces; Together with Rules, Calculated to Improve Youth and Others in the Ornamental and Useful Art of Eloquence (Boston: Printed by Manning & Loring for the author, 1797);

Juvenile Letters; Being a Correspondence Between Children, From Eight to Fifteen Years of Age (Boston: Printed by David Carlisle for Caleb Bingham, 1803);

A Birthday Present (Boston: Printed by David Carlisle, 1805);

The Hunters, or The Sufferings of Hugh and Francis in the Wilderness. A True Story (Boston: Printed by Samuel T. Armstrong for Caleb Bingham, 1814).

OTHER: Francois Auguste René, vicomte de Chateaubriand, *Atala; or, The Love and Constancy of Two Savages in the Desert*, translated by Bingham (Boston: Printed by David Carlisle for C. Bingham, 1802);

Jean Lacroze, *A Historical Grammar; or, A Chronological Abridgment of Universal History . . . Translated by Lucy Peacock . . . Revised, Corrected and Greatly Enlarged by Caleb Bingham* (Boston: Printed by David Carlisle for Caleb Bingham, 1802);

An Easy Introduction to the Game of Chess: Chiefly Selected from the Best Writers on the Subject, edited by Bingham as Byan Amateur (Boston: C. Bingham, 1805?).

Caleb Bingham was one of the first American textbook writers of significance. His readers were perhaps the most widely adopted reading texts used in American schools during the first quarter of the nineteenth century. Issued in a multitude of editions by many publishers, some of his textbooks remained in use as late as the 1870s. In many areas of rural America during the first decades of the century Bingham's books were the only juvenile literature available to young readers.

Appropriately for a pioneer writer, Bingham was a son of the frontier. He was born in the settlement of Salisbury in the northwest corner of Connecticut. His parents were Daniel and Hannah Conant Bingham. Young Bingham grew up on the often dangerous frontier of the 1750s and 1760s. After attending the local school, he was prepared for college by the family's minister. Because of his connection with the family of Dartmouth College founder Eleazar Wheelock, Bingham entered Dartmouth in 1779. He stood well in his class, and upon graduation in 1782 was chosen to deliver the valedictory address.

Upon receiving his M.A. from Dartmouth, Bingham was appointed master of the free school for Indians attached to the college. In 1784 he removed to Boston and opened a private school for girls, the first full-time girls' school in the city. While operating this institution he wrote his first textbook, *The Young Lady's Accidence; or, A Short and Easy Introduction to English Grammar . . .* (1785). Bingham's book was the second grammar by an American to attain significant distribution, preceded only by Noah Webster's *A Grammatical Institute of the English Language, Part II*, published in 1784 as a companion to Webster's spelling book (1783), which had appeared as part one. Bingham's grammar easily outdistanced its rival, selling an es-

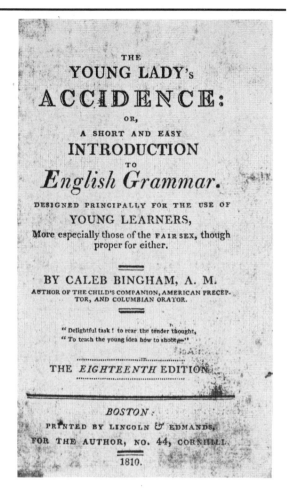

Title page for a nineteenth-century edition of Bingham's first textbook, originally published in 1785 (University of South Florida Library)

timated 100,000 copies in all. A small book of forty-five pages, it was characterized by simplicity and clarity. Though designed for the use of girls, the book was widely used for the instruction of both sexes.

In 1789 Bingham played a significant role in the reorganization of Boston's public schools. Subsequently he was offered an appointment as master of one of the city's newly established reading schools. He accepted the offer, closing his private girls' school to do so.

While teaching in Boston's public schools Bingham continued his career as a writer as well as a user of textbooks. In 1792 his second book appeared. Although it was entitled *The Child's Companion: Being a Concise Spelling Book . . .* , the volume was as much a reader as a speller. It achieved a degree of popularity, but was by far outsold by Webster's immensely successful *American Spelling Book* (1787). Bingham's speller did, however, go through at least eleven editions and remained in use as late as the 1830s.

In 1794 Bingham produced the book for which he is chiefly remembered, *The American Preceptor: Being a New Selection of Lessons for Reading and Speaking*. The *Preceptor* was ideally suited for its time, teaching reading while at the same time inculcating moral virtues. Selection titles such as "On the Duty of Schoolboys" and "Sublimity of the Scriptures" were typical. Most of the *Preceptor*'s one hundred reading selections were, however, interesting and well-written as well as edifying and must have been entertaining for boys and girls whose homes contained little in the way of reading material beyond the Bible and an occasional almanac. Bingham wrote in his introduction to the book that "Although moral essays have not been neglected, yet pleasing and interesting stories, exemplifying moral virtues, were judged best calculated to engage the attention and improve the heart." Bingham was concerned about making his book amusing for young readers as well as instructive. With this in mind he interspersed different kinds of prose and poetry selections throughout the book, hoping through variety to "render it more entertaining to children." *The American Preceptor* was Bingham's most successful text, selling an estimated 640,000 copies overall. It was published in at least seventy editions, some under the title *The American Preceptor Improved*. In 1857 the improved edition was retitled *The Young American's Speaker*. It appeared under this title as late as 1875.

Although best known for his readers, Bingham wrote textbooks in a variety of fields. In 1795, at a time when the teaching of geography was becoming increasingly popular in American schools, Bingham wrote *An Astronomical and Geographical Catechism for the Use of Children*. Patterned on the earlier school geography of Jedidiah Morse, Bingham's text consisted of a set of astronomical and geographical questions and answers to be memorized by students. Among the facts appearing in the book were some rather curious ones, at least to modern eyes. Along with the panthers and bears, Bingham's list of the principal animals inhabiting the American forest includes the "Tyger" and the mammoth. Like Bingham's earlier books, *An Astronomical and Geographical Catechism* achieved considerable popularity, passing through twenty-two editions.

In 1795 Bingham produced the first set of penmanship copy-slips available to American teachers. Published as *Round Text Copies*, they were primarily intended for use in Bingham's own

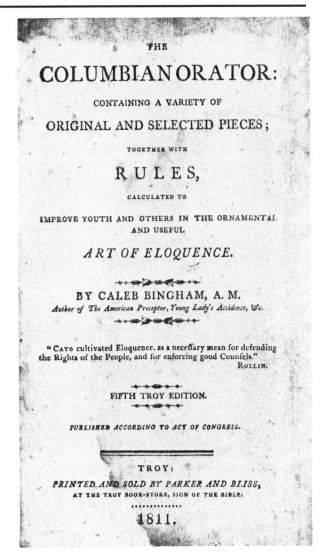

Title page for a nineteenth-century edition of the textbook which Bingham considered a continuation of his American Preceptor *(University of South Florida Library)*

schools and apparently were little used elsewhere. The same year also saw the end of Bingham's career as a teacher. Resigning from the Boston school system, he established himself as a bookseller at 44 Cornhill in Boston.

Although Bingham retired from active teaching, he retained his strong interest in the progress of education. His bookshop was for twenty-one years the favorite meeting place for Boston teachers. Bingham was particularly interested in the establishment of free schools, and his shop became the focal point of the free-school movement in Boston. Bingham's store was also the headquarters of the local Jeffersonian party, in which Bingham was a prominent figure. He ran for public office several times under his party's banner but, due to its local unpopularity, was defeated each time. He was, however, appointed director of the Massachusetts state prison during the governorship of Elbridge Gerry (1810-1812), a post which he occupied for several years. Bingham was also active in the establishment of public libraries. Not only did he help set up local libraries in several New England towns, but he was also a founder of the Boston Society Library (1793), serving as librarian without pay for the first two years of its existence. In 1803 Bingham donated 150 books to his hometown of Salisbury, Connecticut, for the establishment of a public library which was named the Bingham Library for Youth in honor of its benefactor. According to Jesse A. Shera in *Foundations of the Public Library* (1949), Salisbury's 1810 appropriation for the support of the Bingham Library was the first municipal backing of a public library in America.

The end of Bingham's teaching career by no means marked the end of his career as a schoolbook writer. In 1797 the second most successful of his texts, *The Columbian Orator*, was published. As was the case with his earlier *Child's Companion*, *The Columbian Orator* was as much a reading book as anything. It contained a brief introductory section on the techniques of public speaking, followed by eighty-four exercises that comprised the great bulk of the book. The exercises—dialogues, prose, and verse pieces, and extracts from addresses by famous speakers, including George Washington, Cato, and William Pitt—were as suitable for reading as for reciting. In many schools the book filled a dual role as both a reader and an elocution manual. Although Bingham wrote in his introduction that the book was intended as a second part to *The American Preceptor*, the two do not form a graded or progressive series. As with the *Preceptor*, Bingham intentionally eschewed any sort of systematic arrangement of the contents in keeping with his theory that a random mix of exercises was more likely to inspire pupil interest. Although *The Columbian Orator* did not equal the *Preceptor* in overall sales, it was widely accepted and remained in use as late as the 1860s.

Bingham was an extremely well-read, literate man, as might be expected of a professional bookseller. He was an excellent French scholar and translated two books from that language into English. The first was a historical textbook originally written by Jean Lacroze (d. circa 1705). Bingham revised, corrected, and greatly enlarged Lucy Peacock's earlier translation of Lacroze, publishing his revision as *A Historical Grammar; or, A Chronological Abridgment of Universal History* (1802). Bingham also translated Chateaubriand's story *Atala*, which he published as *Atala; or, The Love and Constancy of Two Savages in the Desert* (1802).

Bingham had married Hannah Kemble in 1786. By her he had two daughters, one of whom later collaborated with him without credit in the writing of *Juvenile Letters* (1803), a textbook designed to introduce children to English composition. Although a trailblazer in the field of American textbooks, an early advocate of female education, free schools, and public libraries, as well as a liberal politically, Bingham was a conservative man in his private life. A devout Congregationalist, he remained faithful to the older version of the faith when the churches of Boston adopted Unitarianism. Until the time of his death in 1817, Bingham went about Boston clad in an archaic outfit consisting of a cocked hat, small clothes, white vest and stock, and black silk stockings, complete with silver-buckled shoes. His last known publication was a story entitled *The Hunters, or The Sufferings of Hugh and Francis in the Wilderness*, which appeared in 1814. He died in Boston, survived by his wife, his daughters, and, of course, his textbooks, which continued to enlighten generations of American schoolchildren for decades to come.

References:

Charles Carpenter, *History of American Schoolbooks* (Philadelphia: University of Philadelphia Press, 1963), pp. 61, 67, 160, 181;

William B. Fowle, "Memoir of Caleb Bingham," *American Journal of Education*, 5 (1858): 343;

Clifton Johnson, *Old-Time Schools and School Books* (New York: Dover, 1963);

John A. Nietz, *Old Textbooks* (Pittsburgh: University of Pittsburgh Press, 1961);

Jesse A. Shera, *Foundations of the Public Library* (Chicago: University of Chicago Press, 1949), pp. 158-160;

Elizabeth W. Stone, *American Library Development, 1600-1899* (New York: Wilson, 1977), pp. 140-141.

Noah Brooks

(24 October 1830-16 August 1903)

Douglas Street
Texas A&M University

BOOKS: *The Boy Emigrants* (New York: Scribner, Armstrong, 1877):

The Fairport Nine (New York: Scribners, 1880);

Our Base Ball Club and How It Won the Championship (New York: Dutton, 1884);

Abraham Lincoln: A Biography for Young People (New York & London: Putnam's, 1888); republished as *Abraham Lincoln and the Downfall of American Slavery* (New York & London: Putnam's, 1894); *Abraham Lincoln: His Youth and Early Manhood with a Brief Account of His Later Life* (New York: Putnam's, 1901); and *Abraham Lincoln: The Nation's Leader in the Great Struggle Through Which Was Maintained the Existence of the United States* (New York: Putnam's, 1909);

The Boy Settlers (New York: Scribners, 1891);

Statesmen (New York: Scribners, 1893);

Tales of the Maine Coast (New York: Scribners, 1894);

How the Republic Is Governed (New York: Scribners, 1895);

Washington in Lincoln's Time (New York: Century, 1895);

Short Studies in Party Politics (New York: Scribners, 1895);

The Mediterranean Trip (New York: Scribners, 1895);

The Boys of Fairport (New York: Scribners, 1898);

The Story of Marco Polo (New York: Scribners, 1897);

Henry Knox: A Soldier of the Revolution (New York & London: Putnam's, 1900);

Lem, A New England Village Boy (New York: Scribners, 1901);

First Across the Continent: The Story of the Exploring Expedition of Lewis and Clark (New York: Scribners, 1901).

OTHER: William Cullen Bryant and Sidney Howard Gay, *Scribner's Popular History of the United States*, 5 volumes, revised with additional material by Brooks (New York: Scribners, 1896).

PERIODICAL PUBLICATIONS:

FICTION

"The Cruise of the *Balboa*," *Scribner's Monthly*, 3 (March 1872): 526-537;

"The Waif of Nautilus Island," *Scribner's Monthly*, 4 (May 1872): 65-75;

"By the Sea," *St. Nicholas*, 1 (November 1873): 10-12;

"An Adventure With A Critic," as John Riverside, *St. Nicholas*, 1 (December 1873): 63-64;

"Wrecked at Home," *St. Nicholas*, 1 (March-April 1874): 264-268, 349-353;

"The Coming and the Going of Pete," *St. Nicholas*, 31 (May 1904): 583-586.

NONFICTION

"A Century Ago," *St. Nicholas*, 4 (October 1877): 802-805;

"Personal Reminiscences of Lincoln," *Scribner's Monthly*, 15 (February-March 1878): 561-569, 673-681;

"An Old Town With A History," *Century Magazine*, 24 (September 1882): 695-708;

"A Boy in the White House," *St. Nicholas*, 10 (November 1882): 57-65;

"A Lesson in Patriotism," *St. Nicholas*, 14 (March 1887): 340-341;

"How The Flag Was Saved," *St. Nicholas*, 23 (February 1896): 294-295;

"The Plains Across," *Century Magazine*, 63 (April 1902): 803-820.

While the name of Noah Brooks is rarely heard in today's literary discussions, a century ago he was firmly ensconced in the upper echelon of America's esteemed writers of historical fiction for young people. His boys' adventure stories, which appeared in serial (mostly in the pages of *St. Nicholas* magazine) and in book form throughout the last quarter of the nineteenth century, accorded him both the acclaim and popularity to rank him among America's best children's fiction writers. Whether relating the trials and tribulations of a band of boys emigrating to California in search of gold, or the childhood episodes from a boyhood

Noah Brooks

on the Maine coast, Brooks imbues his characters and situations with a remarkably believable quality. Unlike so many of his peers, Brooks rarely uses his characters to preach for moral goodness. Basing most of his plots and players on actual friends and occurrences, he successfully and continually interweaves fact with fiction to produce stories rich in realistic detail and characterization. His three finest works, *The Boy Emigrants* (1877), *The Fairport Nine* (1880), and *The Boy Settlers* (1891), stand as testimony to his ability to create works that simultaneously capture the reader's imagination and historically precise vignettes of Americana.

Noah Brooks, son of Barker and Margaret Perkins Brooks, was born into an established family in Castine on the shores of Penobscot Bay in Maine. His father was a shipbuilder who had his own yard in a community whose general complexion reflected its nautical history. By age seven Brooks was an orphan in the care of his elder sisters. Brooks spent his elementary years in public school in Castine before transferring to a local private school where he remained until he was eighteen years of age. It was in school in Castine that he developed a strong taste for literature. Among his early favorites were *Peter Parley's Book of the United States*

(1837), *Robinson Crusoe* (1719), *The Swiss Family Robinson* (1813), and above all, the sea adventures of James Fenimore Cooper, which he nearly knew by memory. After graduation in 1847, Brooks left Castine for Boston to train as a landscape painter. Through 1850 he continued his artistic training, yet his interests were being drawn more and more to writing and literature. This new interest spawned several articles and stories for Boston-area newspapers.

Brooks's first break came with the inauguration of the satirical journal, the *Carpet-Bag*, in 1851. For the *Carpet-Bag* he produced several stories and poems, most of a humorous nature. A journey to Kansas Territory in the 1850s interrupted his writing career. This was followed by a trek from Illinois to California and an eventually successful new career as a California newspaperman. When Bret Harte decided California needed a major literary magazine, the *Overland Monthly* was born, with Brooks brought in as an assistant editor. While in California, Brooks met Caroline Fellows, formerly of Massachusetts. They were married in 1856. The outbreak of the Civil War, coupled with the untimely deaths of Brooks's wife and infant daughter, motivated Brooks to leave California for Washington, D.C., where he worked as a special correspondent for the *Sacramento Union* newspaper. In Washington he renewed his acquaintance with Abraham Lincoln. The friendship between the two blossomed and, it was said, Brooks was allowed complete access to the White House.

After the war and the assassination of Lincoln, the year 1871 found Brooks on the staff of the *New York Tribune*. In 1876 he became an editor for the *New York Times*, a position he resigned in 1884 to edit the *Newark Daily Advertiser*. In New York he began contributing pieces to several magazines. "The Cruise of the *Balboa*" was the first in his long line of sea tales and the first of many pieces by Brooks accepted by *Scribner's Monthly*. It is still considered by some Brooks's best piece of writing. When in 1873 the Scribner Company initiated a new children's monthly, *St. Nicholas*, Brooks was chosen to contribute to its inaugural November 1873 issue. With "By the Sea," a semi-autobiographical tale from his Castine boyhood and the first of many such childhood-inspired adventures to grace the pages of *St. Nicholas*, Brooks commenced a literary association with America's finest juvenile periodical which would eventually establish him among that handful of children's writers whom such critics as those with the *Book Buyer* and the *Literary World* recommended as "must" reading for all boys and girls.

In the Brooks canon of juvenile offerings, from the short tales to the major novels, certain concerns and techniques remain constant. The author's strongest fiction emanates from his own past adventures as a boy and as a young adult. He repeatedly lays as his literary foundation a place and time both vivid and fond in his memory upon which he constructs his episodes. The reality of place was always clear in Brooks's mind before he commenced his tales, thus enabling him to concentrate on making his exotic haunts come alive for the reader. In like manner, characterization began most often with memories of friends and antagonists familiar to the author. Brooks's most convincing characters are written remembrances of actual acquaintances, whom Brooks, according to his own frequent admission, recreated but for minor embellishments and changes of name. Vivid and believable, his characters rarely lapse into sentimental caricature or stereotype as is prevalent among his contemporaries.

Although Brooks does not use characters primarily as symbols of moral behavior, his stories are based on a firm value system. Indeed, when one reads sufficiently in Brooks, one realizes that the proper boy hero, while not a Peter Parley à la Samuel Goodrich or a Rollo à la Jacob Abbott, is a good Christian boy, polite and moral, a nondrinker and defender of ladies, and most of all, an American. All of Brooks's heroes embody the vital qualities of the American patriot; Brooks never lets his audience forget that America is a great country and that all of her citizens need to emulate those, both past and present, who have dedicated themselves to maintaining their nation's high ideals.

Brooks's early contributions to *St. Nicholas* quickly established him as one adept at borrowing events from his own past and weaving them into interesting fictional adventures. In his first tales for the publication, "By the Sea" and the 1874 adventure "Wrecked at Home," Brooks fictionalized Castine as the town of Fairport (the name he was to use for all his Castine-based fiction) and patterned the boys rollicking about on the town commons or marooned on "Grampus Rock" offshore on the comrades of his youth. His other early work, two stories of the California gold fields published in *St. Nicholas* under Brooks's California nom de plume John Riverside (he had also regularly, while corresponding for the *Sacramento Union*, signed his columns Castine), showed early success in exploiting what was to be his other staple source of literary

inspiration, his 1859 trek from Illinois to California. Indeed, it was by drawing from his diaries kept during that trip that Brooks was able to fashion his most successful boys' adventure novel, *The Boy Emigrants*.

The Boy Emigrants, published first in serial in *St. Nicholas* from November 1875 through October 1876, established Brooks at the top of the juvenile market. Mary Mapes Dodge, editor of *St. Nicholas*, received such a deluge of letters inquiring about this new author that she printed for readers in the June 1876 issue a sketch of "The Author of 'The Boy Emigrants.' " The story, in which Brooks appears as the former Bostonian dry-goods dealer Montague Perkins Morse, follows the trials and tribulations of Morse and the "Lee County Illinois Boys" as they cross the plains, meet up with Indians, and scale the Sierra Nevada Mountains to find their fortunes in the mining country of the West. Brooks's writing is clear, entertaining, and historically accurate. As the *New York Times* book critic pointed out: "Under the excuse of writing for children, Mr. Brooks can enter into details of the most trifling nature, but details that bring the whole scene vividly before one. His boys are not only thoroughly boys, they not only have that charming mixture of imaginative daring, hasty temper, and lightheartedness which so few writers for children know how to hit but the scenes they pass through are those which thousands of emigrants to California have seen; they undergo the same hardships and enjoy the same pleasures."

The work is fine adventure, yet the good characters in true Brooks fashion prosper, while evil, here in the personification of the evil Bill Bunce, is punished soundly. Before the book may end all our heroes return safely home, to the secure confines of mother, father, and the family. The book sold briskly throughout Brooks's lifetime and remained in print into the 1960s. The format of *The Boy Emigrants* became a standard emulated by other boys' authors of the century.

In 1879 Brooks notified a friend that he had started on another Castine story to be called *The Fairport Nine*: "I shall introduce Castine scenery and incidents, and a mixture of Castine names, but not to make any of the characters recognizable." The first chapter appeared in serial in *St. Nicholas* in May 1880, and the story continued through October. *The Fairport Nine* has as its foundation an intense rivalry between Fairport's two boys' baseball teams, the Fairport Nine, composed of the town's upper-class youths, and the White Bears, rugged brawlers from the south end of town. Two baseball games, one at the beginning of the book and one at the end, frame Brooks's portrayal of growing up in a small Maine town in 1840. When *The Fairport Nine* was published in book form at the close of 1880, Brooks gained the distinction of being America's first author to write a novel about the game of baseball.

The novel focuses not only on the conflicts between the Fairport Nine and the White Bears (both on and off the baseball diamond) but also on the friendship between ten-year-old Billy Hetherington (another fictional recreation of Brooks himself) and the team's star left-fielder, Sam Black. Brooks captures vividly the personalities and lifestyles of these two boys as they share the adventures of a Maine boyhood. What makes these portrayals unique is that Billy is of the town's oldest, most established family and Sam is the son of the town's only black family. Brooks treats Sam, in spite of his color, as an integral member of both the team and the town; he also creates in "Blackie" fiction's first black baseball hero: "Dan Morey was their [White Bears] next striker. He sent a ball straight over to little Blackie, at left field. Blackie was watching the ball as it described a beautiful ascending curve in the air, but his quick eye had also marked the tall thistles on the top of the fort nodding in the wind, which was now rising somewhat. He took a position a little to the right of the place where everybody thought the ball should fall . . . . But the colored member of the Nine knew what he was about. The wind took the ball a little to the north; it then descended with a rush, and dropped directly into his tawny hands; and good Blackie held it like a vice, doubling himself over in his anxiety to grip it. A scream of delight went up from the rampart where the girls waved their sun-bonnets with joy." Although not as tightly composed as *Boy Emigrants*, *The Fairport Nine* was sufficiently successful to spur Brooks on to a second semi-autobiographical baseball adventure. After completing its run in *St. Nicholas*, Brooks's *Our Base Ball Club and How It Won the Championship* was published in 1884.

Whereas plot and characters in *The Fairport Nine* complement each other to create an entertaining adventure, those of *Our Base Ball Club* do not. The scene here is not Maine, but Dixon, Illinois, which Brooks renames Catalpa, and though the main ingredients are drawn again from the author's experience, Brooks is not as comfortable portraying these "all-American boys" as he is their Northeastern cousins. The game of baseball is the primary focus of the novel, for which Albert G. Spalding, sporting equipment manufacturer and

Front cover for Brooks's 1891 novel based on his experiences in Kansas Territory during the mid-1850s (Baldwin Library, University of Florida Libraries)

then president of the Chicago Baseball Club, wrote the introduction. Brooks's boy characters and their female love interests all seem stilted and too good to be true in this, the weakest of Brooks's major novels. Nevertheless the book boasted healthy sales into the 1890s and in tandem with *The Fairport Nine* assured Brooks's position as the father of the baseball adventure novel.

The late 1880s featured a pair of historical pieces by Brooks which appeared regularly in *St. Nicholas*. Brooks put baseball aside and went back to the adventures and settings he knew best. The results appeared in November 1890 when *St. Nicholas* carried the first installment of a new boys' adventure serial, *The Boy Settlers*. Brooks had gone back to the successful formula of *The Boy Emigrants* to produce a story similar in nature, but with its own rugged character. *The Boy Settlers* mirrors Brooks's journals of his 1857 exploits as a settler in eastern Kansas. Again, the subtle blending of fiction and reality works for Brooks as effectively as in the earlier volume. The life on the prairie, the hardships and joys faced by the characters, are portrayed with the attention to detail and historical fact that distinguishes Brooks's writing. When in 1891 Scribners published *The Boy Settlers* in book form, it simultaneously reissued as a companion volume Brooks's earlier success *The Boy Emigrants* in matching binding. Reviewers were unanimous in their praise for the new Brooks novel; its continued success led to reprintings in 1906 and 1924. The reviewer for the *Dial* lauded Brooks's adventures, calling them "excellent reading for boys."

While Brooks was composing *The Boy Settlers*, a second major project shared his thoughts. He was intent upon preparing a biography of his old friend Abraham Lincoln specifically for young readers. This was Brooks's first major attempt at straight history. Although he drew on his memories to reconstruct the years 1862 through 1865, the period in which he was a regular visitor to the White House, the remainder of the book was constructed from secondary sources. *Abraham Lincoln: A Biography for Young People* was finished in 1888 and published by Putnam's three years before *The Boy Settlers* appeared. Although it received favorable reviews, including one by Robert Todd Lincoln who was normally critical of biographies of his father, the book sold poorly.

The publishers had been hoping Brooks's popularity with the young would help the work succeed; it was not the case. Yet they republished the volume with a new title, *Abraham Lincoln and the Downfall of American Slavery*, for a new market. Putnam's took the book, which had been part of their Heroes of the Nations series, from its juvenile market, and under the new title the same biography was sold for adults. As a work for adults it went through several printings before the end of 1908. This same book, while still selling under its 1894 title, was republished in 1901 for the Knickerbocker Literature series as *Abraham Lincoln: His Youth and Early Manhood with a Brief Account of His Later Life*. Finally, in 1909 Putnam's released the Brooks book again, with yet another title: *Abraham Lincoln: The Nation's Leader in the Great Struggle Through Which Was Maintained the Existence of the United States*. Under three different titles and for a period of more than twenty years, the work which from the beginning was created for the pleasure and information of boys and girls captured instead the interest and imagination of their parents. The book today still has merit as a piece of historical writing, though one is tempted to concur with those original critics who thought the piece was eulogistic.

In 1894 Brooks had retired to his boyhood home of Castine, purchasing an old house which he christened The Ark—Noah's Ark. He took an active part in the workings of his old hometown, heading civic activities and giving generously from his own library to the Castine Public Library. Brooks devoted much time during the last ten years of his life to historical writing for adults, most of which appeared in three volumes of nonfiction published in 1895: *Washington in Lincoln's Time*, *Short Studies in Party Politics*, and *The Mediterranean Trip*. Reinspired by memories of the Maine of his youth, he also compiled his short volume of *Tales of the Maine Coast* for publication by Charles Scribner's Sons in June 1894. The book contains seven stories originally published in Scribner's periodicals, including "The Apparition of Jo Murch" and "The Waif of Nautilus Island," two of his best tales from the early years. Though targeted for adult readers, the stories retained the charm and adventure which had earlier captivated the younger audience.

Brooks's last major juvenile effort began serialization in *St. Nicholas* in June 1896. *The Story of Marco Polo* is essentially a collection of historical essays on the life of the explorer. The work was so popular with the *St. Nicholas* readers that upon completion of the serial, the Century Company eagerly published the installments in book form. With this 1897 publication Brooks again moved to the top of the children's authors' popularity list. The critics were unanimous in their approval for this little volume, as were the children whose steady purchases of *The Story of Marco Polo* brought about additional printings in 1899 and 1920. Ten years after the failure of his juvenile biography of Lincoln, Brooks succeeded in using history to capture the child audience that for so many years he had enthralled with his fiction. Brooks also proved that as a writer for children he had few superiors. After *The Story of Marco Polo*, he undertook several major historical and minor fictional projects, yet nothing was of the caliber of his writing for children. After settling in Pasadena, California, for health reasons, Brooks died in August 1903. A steamer brought the body of the writer back home to Castine, where on 26 August Brooks received burial in Castine Cemetery.

If there is one quality for which Noah Brooks can be remembered as a writer of children's books, it is his realistic treatment of characters and settings in his fiction. Brooks's wonderful ability to capture on the page what he saw in real life makes his work as vivid today as when it was written. The accurate portrayals of the true Indians of the plains and of

MARCO POLO'S GALLEY.

Illustration from The Story of Marco Polo, *Brooks's last book for children (Baldwin Library, University of Florida Libraries)*

Sam Black, the only black child in Fairport, exhibit a sensitivity toward other races rarely felt in fiction of the late nineteenth century. Though all but forgotten today, Noah Brooks was a dominating force in boys' adventure fiction, and more than a few twentieth-century children's writers received their first vivid inspirations from the tales and characters of this adventurer from Maine.

References:

"The Author of 'The Boy Emigrants,'" *St. Nicholas,* 3 (June 1876): 524;

Frederick Evans, "Noah Brooks," *Lamp,* 27 (September 1903): 128-132;

Herbert Mitgang, Introduction to his edition of Brooks's *Washington in Lincoln's Time* (New York: Rinehart, 1958), pp. 1-12;

"Noah Brooks," *Book Buyer,* 3 (August 1886): 271-272;

Wayne Calhoun Temple, "Noah Brooks, 1830-1903," Ph.D. dissertation, University of Illinois, 1956.

Frances Hodgson Burnett

Phyllis Bixler
Kansas State University

BIRTH: Manchester, England, 24 November 1849, to Edwin and Eliza Hodgson.

MARRIAGES: 19 September 1873 to Swan Burnett; children: Lionel, Vivian. February 1900 to Stephen Townesend.

DEATH: Plandome, New York, 29 October 1924.

BOOKS: *That Lass o' Lowrie's* (New York: Scribner, Armstrong, 1877; London: Warne, 1877);
"Theo." A Love Story (Philadelphia: Peterson, 1877; revised, New York: Scribners, 1879; London: Ward & Lock, 1877);
Surly Tim and Other Stories (New York: Scribner, Armstrong, 1877; London: Chatto & Windus, 1877);
Dolly: A Love Story, unauthorized edition (Philadelphia: Porter & Coates, 1877; London: Routledge, 1877); authorized edition published as *Vagabondia: A Love Story* (Boston: Osgood, 1884);
Pretty Polly Pemberton. A Love Story, unauthorized edition (Philadelphia: Peterson, 1877; London: Routledge, 1878); authorized edition (New York: Scribners, 1878; London: Chatto & Windus, 1878);
Kathleen. A Love Story, unauthorized edition (Philadelphia: Peterson, 1878; London: Routledge, 1878); authorized edition published as *Kathleen Mavourneen* (New York: Scribners, 1878; London: Chatto & Windus, 1879);
Our Neighbour Opposite (London: Routledge, 1878);
Miss Crespigny. A Love Story, unauthorized edition (Philadelphia: Peterson, 1878; London: Routledge, 1878); authorized edition (New York: Scribners, 1879);
A Quiet Life; and The Tide on the Moaning Bar (Philadelphia: Peterson, 1878); republished as *The Tide on the Moaning Bar* (London: Routledge, 1879);
Lindsay's Luck, authorized edition (New York: Scribners, 1878; London: Routledge, 1879); unauthorized edition (Philadelphia: Peterson, 1879);

Jarl's Daughter; and Other Stories (Philadelphia: Peterson, 1879); republished as *Jarl's Daughter and Other Novelettes* (Philadelphia: Peterson, 1883);
Natalie and Other Stories (London: Warne, 1879);
Haworth's (New York: Scribners, 1879; London: Macmillan, 1879);
Louisiana (New York: Scribners, 1880); republished with *That Lass o'Lowrie's* (London: Macmillan, 1880);
A Fair Barbarian (London: Warne, 1881; Boston: Osgood, 1881);
Esmeralda. A Comedy-Drama Founded on Mrs. Frances Hodgson Burnett's Story of the Same Name, by Burnett and William Gillette (New York, 1881);
Through One Administration (London: Warne, 1883; Boston: Osgood, 1883);
Little Lord Fauntleroy (New York: Scribners, 1886; London: Warne, 1886);
A Woman's Will or Miss Defarge (London: Warne, 1886); republished with John Haberton's *Brueton's Bayou* (Philadelphia: Lippincott, 1888);
Sara Crewe or What Happened at Miss Minchin's (New York: Scribners, 1888; London: Warne, 1888); republished with *Editha's Burglar* (1888);
Sara Crewe; or, What Happened at Miss Minchin's: and Editha's Burglar (London & New York: Warne, 1888); *Editha's Burglar: A Story for Children* republished separately (Boston: Jordan, Marsh, 1888);
The Fortunes of Philippa Fairfax (London: Warne, 1888);
The Pretty Sister of José (New York: Scribners, 1889; London: Blackett, 1889);
Little Saint Elizabeth and Other Stories (London: Warne, 1890?; New York: Scribners, 1890);
Children I Have Known and Giovanni and the Other (London: Osgood, McIlvaine, 1892); republished as *Giovanni and the Other Children Who Have Made Stories* (New York: Scribners, 1892);

The Drury Lane Boys' Club (Washington, D.C.: Moon, 1892);

The One I Knew the Best of All: A Memory in the Mind of a Child (New York: Scribners, 1893; London: Warne, 1893);

Piccino and Other Child Stories (New York: Scribners, 1894); republished as *The Captain's Youngest Piccino and Other Child Stories* (London: Warne, 1894);

Two Little Pilgrims' Progress: A Story of the City Beautiful (New York: Scribners, 1895; London: Warne, 1895);

A Lady of Quality; Being a Most Curious, Hitherto Unknown History, as Related by Mr. Isaac Bickerstaff But Not Presented to the World of Fashion Through the Pages of the Tattler and Now for the First Time

Written Down (New York: Scribners, 1896; London: Warne, 1896);

His Grace of Osmonde; Being the Portions of That Nobleman's Life Omitted in Relation of His Lady's Story Presented to the World of Fashion Under the Title of A Lady of Quality (New York: Scribners, 1897; London: Warne, 1897);

In Connection with The De Willoughby Claim (New York: Scribners, 1899; London: Warne, 1899);

The Making of a Marchioness (New York: Stokes, 1901; London: Smith, Elder, 1901); republished with *The Methods of Lady Walderhurst* as *Emily Fox-Seton* (New York: Stokes, 1909);

The Methods of Lady Walderhurst (New York: Stokes, 1901; London: Smith, Elder, 1902); republished with *The Making of a Marchioness* as *Emily Fox-Seton* (New York: Stokes, 1909);

In the Closed Room (New York: McClure, Phillips, 1904; London: Hodder & Stoughton, 1904);

A Little Princess: Being the Whole Story of Sara Crewe Now Told for the First Time (New York: Scribners, 1905; London: Warne, 1905);

The Dawn of a To-morrow (New York: Scribners, 1906; London: Warne, 1906);

Queen Silver-Bell (New York: Century, 1906); republished as *The Troubles of Queen Silver-Bell* (London: Warne, 1907);

Racketty-Packetty House (New York: Century, 1906; London: Warne, 1907);

The Cozy Lion, as Told by Queen Crosspatch (New York: Century, 1907);

The Shuttle (New York: Stokes, 1907; London: Heinemann, 1907);

The Good Wolf (New York: Moffat, Yard, 1908);

The Spring Cleaning, as Told by Queen Crosspatch (New York: Century, 1908);

The Land of the Blue Flower (New York: Moffat, Yard, 1909; London: Putnam's, 1912);

Barty Crusoe and His Man Saturday (New York: Moffat, Yard, 1909);

The Secret Garden (New York: Stokes, 1911; London: Heinemann, 1911);

My Robin (New York: Stokes, 1912; London: Putnam's, 1912);

T. Tembarom (New York: Century, 1913; London: Hodder & Stoughton, 1913);

The Lost Prince (New York: Century, 1915; London: Hodder & Stoughton, 1915);

The Little Hunchback Zia (New York: Stokes, 1916; London: Heinemann, 1916);

The Way to the House of Santa Claus: A Christmas Story for Very Small Boys in Which Every Little Reader

Is the Hero of a Big Adventure (New York & London: Harper, 1916);

The White People (New York & London: Harper, 1917; London: Heinemann, 1920);

The Head of the House of Coombe (New York: Stokes, 1922; London: Heinemann, 1922);

Robin (New York: Stokes, 1922; London: Heinemann, 1922);

In the Garden (Boston & New York: Medici Society of America, 1925).

PLAY PRODUCTIONS: *That Lass o' Lowrie's*, by Burnett and Julian Magnus, New York, Booth Theater, 28 November 1878;

Esmeralda, by Burnett and William Gillette, New York, Madison Square Theater, 26 October 1881; produced again as *Young Folk's Ways*, London, St. James' Theatre, 29 October 1883;

The Real Little Lord Fauntleroy, London, Terry's Theatre, 14 May 1888; New York, Broadway Theater, 11 December 1888;

Phyllis, adapted from *The Fortunes of Philippa Fairfax*, London, Globe Theatre, 1 July 1889;

Nixie, adapted from *Editha's Burglar* by Burnett and Stephen Townesend, London, Terry's Theatre, 7 April 1890;

The Showman's Daughter, by Burnett and Townesend, London, Royalty Theatre, 6 January 1892;

The First Gentleman of Europe, by Burnett and Constance Fletcher, New York, Lyceum Theater, 25 January 1897;

A Lady of Quality, by Burnett and Townesend, New York, Wallack's Theater, 1 November 1897; London, Comedy Theatre, 8 March 1899;

A Little Unfairy Princess, London, Shaftesbury Theatre, 20 December 1902; produced again as *A Little Princess*, New York, Criterion Theater, 14 January 1903;

The Pretty Sister of José, New York, Empire Theater, 10 November 1903; London, Duke of York's Theatre, 16 November 1903;

That Man and I, adapted from *In Connection with The De Willoughby Claim*, London, Savoy Theatre, 25 January 1904;

Dawn of a Tomorrow, New York, Lyceum Theater, 28 January 1909; London, Garrick Theatre, 13 May 1910;

Racketty-Packetty House, New York, Children's Theater, 23 December 1912.

OTHER: "When He Decides," in *Before He Is Twenty: Five Perplexing Phases of the Boy Question Considered* (New York: Revell, 1894).

PERIODICAL PUBLICATIONS: "A City of Groves and Bowers," *St. Nicholas*, 20 (June 1893): 563-571;

"How Winnie Hatched the Little Rooks," *St. Nicholas*, 34 (November 1906): 3-12;

"The First Knife in the World," *St. Nicholas*, 37 (December 1909): 99-105;

"The Christmas in the Fog," *Good Housekeeping*, 59 (December 1914): 661-671;

"The Woman in the Other Stateroom," *Good Housekeeping*, 60 (March 1915): 357-368;

"The Attic on the House in Long Island," *Good Housekeeping*, 62 (May 1916): 549-559;

"The Passing of the Kings," *Good Housekeeping*, 68 (March 1919): 10-12, 118-128;

"The House in the Dismal Swamp," *Good Housekeeping*, 70 (April 1920): 16-18.

During her own lifetime Frances Hodgson Burnett was best known for *Little Lord Fauntleroy* (1886), the story of a disinherited American boy who charms his irascible English grandfather and wins back his rightful title and fortune. The book's immediate international success and its stage adaptations in England, France, and America made Burnett's innocent child hero prominent in popular culture as well as in children's literature. The curly-headed beauty in dark velvet came to epitomize the sentimental idealization of the child which marked other children's classics of the era such as Lewis Carroll's *Alice's Adventures in Wonderland* (1865) and J. M. Barrie's play *Peter Pan* (1904); and *Little Lord Fauntleroy* has continued to be recognized as a landmark in nineteenth-century children's literature. As some of its early notoriety waned, its genuine literary merits have also been acknowledged. Burnett's book which has most often found its way onto lists of recommended reading for children, however, is *The Secret Garden* (1911). Its mythic plot, rich pastoral imagery, and sensitive portrayal of child character make this book Burnett's masterpiece, and its continuing appeal for readers of all ages has earned it recognition as a classic. *A Little Princess* (1905), a version of the Cinderella tale based on Burnett's earlier story and play, completes the trio of books for which Burnett is most often remembered. In addition, *The Lost Prince* (1915) remains on children's library shelves; though more flawed than the other books, this adventure romance also deserves attention in assessments of Burnett's contribution to children's literature. Finally, as a pastoral evocation of childhood, the autobiographical *The One I Knew the Best of All* (1893) stands up well beside the better-known *The Golden Age* (1895) by Kenneth Grahame.

The circumstances of Burnett's childhood are not unlike the radical changes in fortune or situation which many of her fictional characters later experienced. In the first sixteen years of her life, she went from upper-middle-class comfort to genteel poverty, moving from the British Isles to the United States, from crowded city to rural near-isolation. When she was born in Manchester, England, in 1849, her father, Edwin Hodgson, had a successful business selling household furnishings, and he was able to afford a suburban home for his wife Eliza and their five children. He died in 1853, when Frances was four, however, and Eliza Hodgson had difficulty keeping the business afloat in Manchester's mercurial, textile-based economy. At first, she economized by moving the family into a house in the city, near the factories and tenements over-crowded with mill workers. But eventually, in 1865, after the American Civil War interrupted cotton shipments and the Manchester economy plummeted, she sold the business and took her family to rural New Market, Tennessee, outside Knoxville, where her brother had earlier settled.

Disappointingly, this geographical change brought no improvement in the family's fortune. If anything, meeting life's needs was harder in postwar Tennessee than it had been in Manchester, where at least there were more relatives to help. As might be expected of someone who would later write so appreciatively of nature, sixteen-year-old Frances exulted in the change from a smoky, crowded city to the fresh air and expanse of the Tennessee countryside. That the contrasts in these two ways of living made a deep impression on her is clear in the childhood memoir she later wrote, *The One I Knew the Best of All: A Memory in the Mind of a Child*. She remembered the imprisonment she felt in Manchester when rainy weather often kept her inside the house, and she described the constant smoke and smuts which sullied the environment indoors and out. In addition, although she was fascinated by the mill workers who lived just outside the square of faded gentility where she lived, she was not allowed to play with the workers' children, lest she cease acting and speaking "like a lady." Despite these admonitions, however, Frances loved and became fluent in the Lancashire dialect the children spoke, an interest which would appear in some of her fiction, notably *The Secret Garden*. That book reflects another Manchester experience as well. After long wondering what was behind the locked fence around an abandoned house, young

Frances one day found it open and used her imagination to turn heaps of earth and rubbish with one tiny flower into a garden of roses, violets, and hyacinths. Burnett later commented that she had been an exile in the city; when she moved to the lush thickets, trees, and mountains of Tennessee, she had found her true home.

In addition to these experiences, Burnett's childhood reading provided themes and forms for her later writing. From earliest memory, Frances had an insatiable appetite for stories, searching for them in pictures and her nurse's songs before she could read. Burnett's only formal education was in a school in the home of family friends in Manchester; much of her reading was apparently done in addition to school assignments, a self-educating process she would continue the rest of her life. She was exposed to some children's authors, including Anna Barbauld, Maria Edgeworth, and Samuel Griswold Goodrich, and she was given stories of child saints who died with pious sayings on their lips. Although she was apparently much affected by such moral exempla—later, in her memoir, she claimed that as a child she would have given anything to be considered an example—she did not really like these improving books. She much preferred morals presented through fairy tales, as in Frances Browne's *Granny's Wonderful Chair* (1856), which she memorized before she was six. Later she fed her taste for adventure with books by Sir Walter Scott, Harrison Ainsworth, Mayne Reid, and James Fenimore Cooper as well as with Greek, Roman, and British histories and mythologies. One rainy afternoon when she was seven she discovered a bound volume of *Blackwood's Edinburgh Magazine* and developed a continuing preoccupation with fiction in magazines such as *Young Ladies' Halfpenny Journal*, *Cornhill*, *Temple Bar*, *London Society*, *Godey's Lady's Book*, and *Peterson's*.

According to her memoir, Burnett early enjoyed composing and writing stories as well as reading them. Like the fictional Sara Crewe in *A Little Princess*, Burnett used her doll to act out stories she heard, and she used magazine fiction formulas to compose long stories for her schoolmates. Some of these she wrote down and shared with her mother, sister, and friends; her brothers made her feel there was something presumptuous about this display of talent, and they gave her the derisive label "romantic." Burnett's adult recollection of these childhood attempts at fiction suggests that they were indeed "romantic" and indicative of her lifelong predilection for stories which, like fairy stories, have happy endings. As an adult she continued to use oral methods in her writing process: she would compose a story orally before telling it or, as she was writing, she would try out selected pages by reading them aloud to family, friends, or an editor.

Burnett's childhood practice in composing and writing stories helps account for her early success in publishing magazine fiction. Financial need prompted her to submit her first story. The Hodgsons had come to Tennessee for the protection of Frances's uncle, but his business failed, and her brothers' jobs did not bring home sufficient support. At times the family had barely enough to eat, and Frances increasingly felt the need to help. Projects such as raising geese and establishing a school failed, and so, with the encouragement of her mother and sisters, she sent a story to *Godey's Lady's Book*. She had learned the conventions of British ladies' magazine fiction so well that the editor, Sara Josepha Hale, had to see another story before she was convinced that the first was really written by the person who had sent it from Tennessee. Both stories were published in 1868, when Frances was nineteen, and during the next three years, as she later reported, she contributed stories to almost every popular magazine in America. In 1871, she broke into the prestigious periodicals when *Scribner's Monthly* accepted "Surly Tim," a mining story using Lancashire dialect. In 1873 her first novel, *Dolly* (later titled *Vagabondia*), was serialized in *Peterson's*, though it was not published in book form for four years.

Burnett's personal life expanded with her career. In 1869 the family moved to Knoxville, and by 1872 she had earned enough money with her writing to make a trip to England by way of New York City. In New York, her host was Richard Watson Gilder, the editor with whom she would work during much of a long career with Scribners. During her fifteen months in England, she visited with friends and relatives in Manchester and regularly sent back stories for American periodicals. In 1873 she returned to fulfill her promise to marry Swan Burnett, the son of the doctor in New Market, Tennessee, where the Hodgsons had earlier lived. The couple honeymooned in New York, and Burnett's growing reputation gained her introductions to literary lions such as George MacDonald and Bret Harte.

During the first three years of her marriage Burnett wrote to help support her family. Lionel was born in 1874, and the next year the Burnetts moved to Paris where Swan wanted to develop his specialty in ophthalmology. While there Burnett

Dr. Swan Burnett. His twenty-five-year marriage to Burnett ended with an 1898 divorce.

regularly sent stories back to *Peterson's,* and she finished her second novel, *That Lass o' Lowrie's,* serialized in *Scribner's Monthly* in 1876. That year also, the Burnetts' second son and last child, Vivian, was born, and they returned to New Market, Tennessee, in debt. Swan Burnett moved to Washington, D.C., to set up practice as an eye specialist, and in 1877 the family joined him. During the next five years, when Frances Burnett was in her late twenties and early thirties and her sons were under eight, she wrote four more adult novels. By the time her first major children's book, *Little Lord Fauntleroy,* appeared in 1886, Burnett had earned a reputation as one of the most promising young talents in American adult fiction.

The adult fiction Burnett wrote during this early phase of her long career can be divided roughly into two categories: the fiction she wrote with a concern for what literary critics might say and that aimed at a broader, more popular audience. The stories and novels in the first category are less important for an understanding of her later writing for children, but they represent more substantial achievements in their own right because they are contributions, if minor ones, to the development of British and American realism. *That Lass o' Lowrie's* (1877) and *Haworth's* (1879), as well as stories such as "Surly Tim" which preceded them, were set in Burnett's native England. Because they portray the lives of working-class people and their relationships with their employers, these early realist novels are derivative of the social and political novels written by Benjamin Disraeli, Elizabeth Cleghorn Gaskell, Charlotte Brontë, and Charles Dickens during the 1840s and 1850s. In *That Lass o' Lowrie's*, set in a Lancashire mining town divided by a mine safety controversy, an independent pit girl defies the paternal and social forces which try to limit her development. In *Haworth's*, which focuses on employer rather than worker, Burnett dramatizes the downfall of a self-made industrialist because of his uncontrollable passion for a haughty aristocratic woman.

The most complex and interesting of Burnett's realist works, however, has an American setting. In *Through One Administration*, serialized in 1881 and published in book form in 1883, Burnett dramatizes the social and political intrigue of contemporary life in Washington, D.C.; at the novel's center is a woman celebrated for her social gaiety but unhappy in her marriage. Much of the novel is based on Burnett's personal observations and experience; the Burnetts were prominent in the social life of the capital by now, and there were definite strains within their marriage. *Through One Administration* has Burnett's most fully developed and individualized main character and one of the few unhappy endings in her fiction. The book's poignant exploration of the limited opportunities available to a talented woman invites comparison to novels William Dean Howells and Henry James were producing during the same period, such as *Dr. Breen's Practice* (1881) and *The Portrait of a Lady* (1881).

The second category of fiction by Burnett during this first phase of her career includes three novels and many of the stories which she wrote for popular magazines. The most obvious way in which these works prepared her for later children's writing was in their lighthearted tone and happy endings. In addition, many of their plots turned on the radical changes of fortune or situation which Burnett would depict in *Little Lord Fauntleroy, A Little Princess*, and, to a lesser extent, *The Secret Garden*. In her adult popular fiction, as in these works for children, Burnett had her characters move between social groups or life-styles defined by contrasting economic status, class, culture, or

Burnett's son Lionel, circa 1878. Lionel's death from consumption in 1890 is reflected in several stories collected in Children I Have Known *(1892) and* Piccino and Other Child Stories *(1894).*

nationality. In her first novel, *Dolly*, Burnett describes a group of carefree bohemians in London and their occasional interaction with the wealthier and stolid "Philistines." In *Louisiana* (1880), a New York writer and her brother are charmed by a simple farmer's daughter they meet in a North Carolina mountain resort. And in *A Fair Barbarian* (1881), which some readers saw as an answer to Henry James's *Daisy Miller* (1878), Burnett has a young woman from Nevada win the affections of her relatives in a staid English village. As these brief descriptions suggest, in her early popular fiction for adults as in her later stories for children, she frequently reworked the Cinderella story so often found in formulaic popular fiction—a person from a lower or simpler class in life wins the acceptance of a member of the higher or more sophisticated class. In adult fiction, the charmer is usually a young woman whose reward is marriage. In Burnett's books for children, the winsome one is a child whose reward is being reunited with or finding a family.

From her early popular adult fiction, Burnett took not only her typical themes and plot structure but certain character types as well. The upper or more sophisticated class is usually represented by a haughty and frequently irascible person who must be won over because he or she has some control over the main character's fate. In *Dolly,* for example, the main character becomes the paid companion for a wealthy unmarried woman who also happens to be the aunt of the young man Dolly hopes to marry. The aunt has decided that her nephew is a ne'er-do-well, and Dolly must convince her to smile on the penniless fellow so that they can afford to get married. In similar fashion, little Fauntleroy's fortune lies in the hands of his grandfather who had disinherited Cedric's father because he married an American, and Burnett's "little princess" suffers at the whim of the class-conscious schoolmistress, Miss Minchin. In addition, Little Lord Fauntleroy has much in common with Burnett's earlier coquettes such as Dolly; he has their winsome combination of lighthearted love of fun, earnest sympathy with others, and lack of self-consciousness.

Burnett's other well-known child characters—Sara Crewe in *A Little Princess,* the orphan Mary and hypochondriac Colin in *The Secret Garden*—may sometimes exhibit the charms of Burnett's earlier coquettes; but they also have a temper or the steely defiance of female characters who appear in Burnett's adult fiction. Burnett herself saw this connection when she put into one category the independent pit girl in *That Lass o' Lowrie's,* Bertha Amory in *Through One Administration,* "who laughed and wore tinkling ornaments and brilliant symphonies in red when she was passing through the gates of hell," and "little Sara Crewe when she starved in her garret and was a princess disdaining speech." For the origin of this character type Burnett looked to an experience in her own childhood: "She represents what I have cared for most all my life—from the time I was eight years old and an insensate person in authority struck me across the upper part of my arm with a riding whip, and I lifted the frill of my short sleeve, and after regarding the livid cut on the soft flesh for a moment or so, looked up at the person who had done it and laughed. It was a brief little laugh and I suppose I must have looked like the devil."

Burnett's defiant characters cannot really be called "devils," but it is hardly an overstatement to describe as "saints" her many fictional females who devote themselves to serving others, often helping the main character. In *Dolly,* for example, the her-

oine's tendency toward frivolity is checked by the responsible wisdom of her sober sister; *That Lass o' Lowrie's* has a clergyman's daughter who does quiet charitable acts among the poor and becomes the special patron of Joan Lowrie. A probable literary source for this character type was William M. Thackeray's *Vanity Fair* (1847-1848); Thackeray and Dickens were among Burnett's favorite novelists. Just as some of her coquettes seem good-hearted versions of Thackeray's Becky Sharp, Burnett's self-sacrificing women are sisters of his pale paragon Amelia Sedley. Little Lord Fauntleroy's "Dearest" stands firmly within this tradition; like Amelia Sedley, "Dearest" is a poor widow who yields her son to the care of a grandfather who can give him more opportunities.

To summarize, the adult fiction which Burnett wrote during the first phase of her writing career shows that she had long been preparing herself to write *Little Lord Fauntleroy,* with its fairy tale plot and international theme; even though Burnett would later claim that the winsome lad was based on observations of her son Vivian, Burnett's fictional character had several literary prototypes.

Although Burnett had been composing sto-

Burnett, circa 1880

ries to entertain her own children, it was apparently not until about the time she met Mary Mapes Dodge and Louisa May Alcott at a Boston Papyrus Club dinner in 1879 that she decided to try to have her stories for children published. Three stories appeared in *St. Nicholas*, edited by Dodge, before *Little Lord Fauntleroy* was serialized in that magazine. Two of these were obviously written versions of oral improvisations. "Behind the White Brick," published in 1879, was probably influenced by Lewis Carroll's *Alice* books. While visiting her cross aunt, little Jemima falls asleep, floats up the chimney through the fireplace, and visits some rooms behind a white brick she discovers. Her guides in this fantasy realm are the heroine of a book she had been reading and a saucy version of the baby sister Jemima had been caring for. "The Proud Little Grain of Wheat," published the next year, is a rather silly tale about the grain's transformation until it is made into a cake for Burnett's boys, Lionel and Vivian. Burnett wrote more fantasies during her career, but on the whole she was more successful when she used the folktale tradition less directly, borrowing its themes and motifs to enrich stories having realistic settings.

"Editha's Burglar" (1880), Burnett's third story published in *St. Nicholas* before *Little Lord Fauntleroy*, has a realistic setting, and, especially because of its title character, it most clearly anticipates her famous later work. In this short tale which was later published in book form and turned into the play *Nixie*, seven-year-old Editha asks a burglar to be quiet so that he does not wake her mama, and she brings him her treasures so that he does not take her parents' things. In several ways Editha anticipates Fauntleroy and Burnett's later fictional children—earnest, emotionally mature, imaginative. Often alone, these children associate mainly with adults toward whom they feel emotionally responsible and protective and on whom they have a beneficent effect. Editha's mother, for example, vows to pay more attention to her child and the burglar returns the girl's treasures. Editha and the other exemplary children in Burnett's fictional gallery probably owe something to the moral and religious exempla Burnett read as a child, though Burnett may have been reminded to use this form and character type by George MacDonald's innocent and spiritual child Diamond, in *At the Back of the North Wind* (1871).

Burnett herself apparently believed that the primary model for her exemplary fictional children was her youngest son, Vivian, who was eight in 1885 when *Little Lord Fauntleroy* appeared in *St.*

Nicholas. Her account of "How Fauntleroy Occurred and a Very Real Little Boy Became an Ideal One" (collected in *Piccino and Other Child Stories*, 1894), however, reveals how fiction and fact became inextricably mixed in her creative process, how fictional formulas became a lens through which she apprehended and conceptualized the world. As she herself once put it, "All my life I have made stories, and since I was seven years old I have written them. This has been my way of looking at life as it went by me." The parallels between Vivian and the little lord are many. Vivian called his mother "Dearest," played quietly when she was in bed ill, and humored her love of dressing him in fine clothes. Like Fauntleroy, he was "born without sense of the existence of any barrier between his own innocent heart and any other" and was thus "the young friend of all the world." Like Fauntleroy, Vivian sympathized with the sorrows of others and was always ready to dispense charity. Burnett says that it was his "unconscious, republican mind" that gave her the germ of the story. One day Vivian

Vivian, Burnett's second son and the model for Little Lord Fauntleroy. *This 1885 photograph was sent to Reginald Birch to guide him in preparing the illustrations for Burnett's 1886 best-seller.*

asked her about English dukes and she wondered how he would appear to less republican minds than his own. She asked herself how she could put him into a "close relationship with an English nobleman—irascible, conservative, disagreeable." And the nature and swiftness of her answer, recorded in "How Fauntleroy Occurred," indicates how much she relied on the fictional formulas of which she was already the master: "Eureka! Son of a younger son, separated from ill-tempered noble father because he has married a poor young American beauty. Young father dead, elder brothers dead, boy comes into title! Yes, there it is, and Vivian shall be he. . . . A story like that is easily written."

Little Lord Fauntleroy became a best-seller in English and was soon translated into more than a dozen languages. Burnett's 1888 stage version was popular in England, France, and America—it ran on Broadway four years and was staged by road companies almost as numerous as those producing *Uncle Tom's Cabin* and *Ben-Hur*. By 1893 the book was held by more American libraries than any book except Lew Wallace's *Ben-Hur*, and it spawned products such as Fauntleroy toys, playing cards, chocolate, and the famous dark velvet suits with lace collars, derived especially from Reginald Birch's illustrations for the book. This fashion foisted on unwilling children contributed a great deal to Little Lord Fauntleroy's notoriety, a notoriety which led Burnett to defend her son Vivian as "a perfectly human little thing, not a young cherub," and to aver that her own taste for the "picturesque" had not led her to turn her "manly, robust boys into affected, abnormally self-conscious, little mountebanks."

Little Lord Fauntleroy is still a well known figure. In the twentieth century, film versions—starring Mary Pickford in 1921, Freddy Bartholomew in 1936, Ricky Schroder and Sir Alec Guinness in 1980—have kept him alive in popular culture. And although it does not have the thematic richness or timeless mythic qualities of *The Secret Garden*, *Little Lord Fauntleroy* continues to be a compelling book. In part, it is Burnett's narrative skill that has made the work survive. The length limits imposed by writing for children disciplined her use of detail and kept her attention focused on moving her stories along. In addition, her combination of the exemplum and fairy-tale forms she knew as a child helped give structure to her works. Burnett's adaptation of fairy-tale motifs in a manner sometimes reminiscent of Dickens helps explain not only certain improbabilities in her plots but also her fre-

quent use of typed rather than fully-rounded characters. Thus in her depiction of the little lord Cedric Errol, she emphasizes not so much character development as character revelation, as is especially appropriate to the Cinderella tale which here, as elsewhere in her fiction, is just beneath the surface. Studies of that fairy tale's many variants show that Cinderella is by nature a princess; she is under an enchantment when she is a scullery maid and simply returns to her natural state at the end. Similarly, Cedric Errol's beauty and innocent goodness make it evident that he is "every inch a lord even when the world does not recognize him as such," when, for example, he lives in New York and consorts with a grocery man and a bootblack. Moreover, as is frequently the case with a fairy-tale hero, Cedric must pass a series of tests to prove his worth: he must not allow himself to be "bought" by his grandfather's wealth; he must accept with grace his separation from his mother; he must face the threat of an impostor heir with equanimity. Passing all these tests and eventually transforming a selfish old man into an affectionate grandfather and respon-

Illustration by Reginald Birch for Little Lord Fauntleroy
(Baldwin Library, University of Florida Libraries)

sible landlord, Little Lord Fauntleroy is the personification of heroic innocence. Burnett's book survives not as a realistic novel of child life but as a symbolic statement about the testing and power of virtue.

Little Lord Fauntleroy and its phenomenal success came at a crucial time in Burnett's life and career. During the three years before she wrote the book, she had often been ill and unable to write. In part, she was simply tired from over a decade of productivity during which she had also tried to fulfill her responsibilities as mother of two small sons and wife of a prominent doctor. In addition to her career and family responsibilities, she had tried to fill the gaps in her education by following a reading course a friend at the Congressional Library had given her. And although as Washington socialites the Burnetts showed happy faces to the world, their marital problems continued.

One result of *Little Lord Fauntleroy*'s success, therefore, was financial independence which allowed Burnett an informal separation from her husband. In 1887 she took her boys and a Boston friend, Kitty Hall, to England, where they enjoyed the pageantry of Queen Victoria's Jubilee. Her money and fame as Little Lord Fauntleroy's creator allowed her to live out some of her earlier romantic dreams. From this point on, she spent much of her time in Europe—London, rural England, Paris, Florence, and Rome—while Swan Burnett lived in their Washington, D.C., home. Sometimes accompanied by her boys, she met socially with royalty, persons of title, a prime minister, writers, artists, and theater people. She enjoyed playing the role of lady bountiful, giving lavish gifts to her children, her English friends and relatives, and various charities.

The success of her play based on *Little Lord Fauntleroy* also persuaded her to continue the theatrical career she had begun earlier. In 1878 a dramatized version of *That Lass o' Lowrie's* by Burnett and Julian Magnus had been produced on Broadway. In 1881 *Esmeralda,* by Burnett and William Gillette, had a successful run in New York, though its 1883 London opening as *Young Folk's Ways* was unfavorably reviewed by Henry James. During the 1890s, however, she had more success on the London boards than did that other American expatriot, with whom she had now become acquainted. *Phyllis* (adapted from her *Fortunes of Philippa Fairfax,* 1888) played at the Globe Theatre in 1889. With London doctor and aspiring actor Stephen Townesend she collaborated on *Nixie* (1890), *The Showman's Daughter* (1892), and *A Lady of Quality* (1897).

Vera Beringer and Alfred Bishop in the London production of The Real Little Lord Fauntleroy, *which opened at Terry's Theatre in May 1888*

With Constance Fletcher she wrote *The First Gentleman of Europe* (1897).

Besides encouraging her to continue her theatrical career, *Little Lord Fauntleroy* affected the nature of her subsequent fiction. In 1887 and 1888, *St. Nicholas* published "Sara Crewe," a preliminary sketch for the later Cinderella tale, *A Little Princess.* "Little Saint Elizabeth," which the same magazine published in 1888 and 1889, testified to her continuing fascination with the exempla she read as a child, though in her childhood memoir she was critical of their possible effects on the reader. Orphaned as a baby, Elizabeth grew up with her ascetic aunt in Normandy before coming, at age eleven, to live with her worldly bachelor uncle in New York. Influenced by reading saints' legends and tales of martyrs, she tries to continue her self-denying and charitable ways, but her uncle proves unsympathetic. One day she tries unsuccessfully to sell her jewels for money to give to the poor and then walks alone into a poverty-stricken area of the city. She gives her coat to a poor woman and walks shivering until her uncle and his friend, a doctor, find her. The doctor nurses her through her subsequent illness, and with his help she finds ways to dispense charity while becoming more accustomed to her uncle's wealth. Through the narrator, Burnett points out how asceticism can distort the innocent goodness of children: "though she lost none of her sweet sympathy for those who suffered," Little Saint Elizabeth "learned to live a more natural and childlike life, and to find that there were in the world innocent, natural pleasures which should be enjoyed."

Burnett's continued interest in writing for and about children was caused not only by her interest in children's literary forms such as the fairy tale and exemplum but also by events in her own life. In the spring of 1890, she came home from Italy to be at the bedside of her oldest son, Lionel, who was ill. American doctors said that the fifteen-year-old's consumption was incurable, and so she spent almost nine months taking him to sanatoriums in Europe, hoping for a cure. The way she dealt with Lionel's illness and death demonstrated the penchant she always had for dramatizing her fictional ideals in her own life and for creating fictions to make life's vicissitudes more bearable—a theme she would pick up in *A Little Princess*. Imitating the selfless devotion of Fauntleroy's "Dearest," she concentrated on making her invalid son as comfortable as possible, and she created around him the fiction that he was not seriously ill but rather a traveling prince whose every wish was to be granted. In a letter she wrote to a cousin after Lionel died, she thanked God for her success in hiding her own suffering to play her role: "I never allowed him to know that I was *really* anxious about him. I never let him know that he had consumption or that he was in danger—and when he died he passed away so softly and quickly that I know he wakened in the other world without knowing how he had left this one."

Just as her observations of Vivian as a child had prompted her to write *Little Lord Fauntleroy*, the death of Lionel and her subsequent trip to Italy to recover from her grief elicited a spate of stories about children who die and children from the Italian peasant or other working classes. "Giovanni and the Other," collected with similar tales in *Children I Have Known and Giovanni and the Other* (1892), contains a rather indulgent self-portrait. An English woman grieving for her dead son becomes interested in a young peasant boy who comes to sing for money outside her hotel in a town on the Italian Riviera. In memory of her dead son, Leo, she provides him with money so that he will not have to

Stephen Townesend, Burnett's collaborator on the plays Nixie *(1890),* The Showman's Daughter *(1892), and* A Lady of Quality *(1897). Townesend became Burnett's second husband in 1900.*

ruin his voice with excessive singing. "The Other" is a boy who did thus ruin his voice. When he dies, the English lady tries to console his peasant mother. The two mothers find that their common suffering creates a bond that crosses class lines, and the English lady sees to it that the peasant need not suffer more from poverty. Giovanni eventually becomes a celebrated tenor, and the English lady shares his glory when he sings for the queen.

The title story in another collection, *Piccino and Other Child Stories* (1894), similarly portrays an English tourist on the Riviera who becomes interested in a peasant child. In this case, the wealthy English lady is portrayed less sympathetically. To alleviate her boredom, she pays a peasant woman to "borrow" her beautiful six-year-old boy. She bathes him, dresses him elaborately like an English child, and parades him before her guests. The child is understandably perturbed by this treatment and flees back home. But the lady is not upset: "She had found it too tiresome an amusement to undertake the management of the lovely little wild animal, to whom civilization only represented horror and dismay," and she regards him as only an "amusing" anecdote to relate to her friends back in London.

Through her portrayal of the wealthy lady in this story, Burnett implies a gentle criticism of the superior attitude English tourists often adopted toward the Italian peasantry; but she shares with them the romantic view that the peasants, especially their children, are picturesque. This attitude is evident in a sketch in *Children I Have Known and Giovanni and the Other*, "The Pretty Roman Beggar." In "The Little Faun," in the same volume, Burnett similarly describes a seamstress's son in Washington, D.C., who plays happily outside wearing only his shirt. These portraits of beautiful children of the poor are balanced by sketches about wealthy and royal children, "Illustrissimo Signor Bébé" and "Eight Little Princes." *Piccino and Other Child Stories* and *Children I Have Known and Giovanni and the Other* thus reflect social class as a determinant of human fate and welfare, an interest she demonstrated elsewhere in her fiction. As usual, to ameliorate inequities, Burnett prescribes individual acts of charity rather than broad social change, as is evident by the mother's comments to her son, who has been impressed by Edward Bellamy's *Looking Backward* in "The Boy Who Became a Socialist" (collected in *Children I Have Known and Giovanni and the Other*). Burnett practiced what she preached. Partly in Lionel's memory, but also because she was moved by the plight of the poor children in London, she organized financial support for a children's charity hospital there; she also established a library for children near Drury Lane, as described in "The Drury Lane Boys' Club" (1892), an essay published first in *Scribner's Magazine* and then by Vivian Burnett, who printed a limited edition on a machine he had at home.

Burnett's grief over Lionel's death not only guided her choice of charities but also accounts for the many stories she wrote at the time dealing with dead or dying children. In addition to the title story, *Children I Have Known and Giovanni and the Other* contains a sketch about a girl who died at Pompeii and one about a consumptive girl who shows tourists the tombs of Shelley and Keats. *Piccino and Other Child Stories* includes the story of a beautiful boy who is trampled by a horse while trying to retrieve his sister from the clutches of a seducer and perhaps the worst of Burnett's sentimental tales, a story narrated by a kitten who cannot understand why her little playmate Betty "falls asleep" under a rose bush and never comes out to play again.

These two collections of sketches and stories about children are of interest mainly for their amplification of themes found elsewhere in Burnett's

fiction and for the ways in which they reflect her international life-style and her continued preoccupation with Lionel's death. However, her autobiography, *The One I Knew the Best of All: A Memory in the Mind of a Child*, published between the two collections, maintains an appeal in its own right. Burnett's memoir is a portrait of the artist as a child, an account of how she "spent her early years in unconscious training, which later enabled her to make an honest livelihood" with her writing. Much of the memoir is devoted to descriptions of her childhood reading, her early love of composing and writing stories. Ending at the point when she sells her first story, the memoir also contains Burnett's fullest exploration of pastoral themes before *The Secret Garden*. As she explored her earliest memories and her most formative childhood experiences, Burnett was no doubt conscious of the great Romantic poem of childhood, William Wordsworth's *The Prelude*, published in 1850.

Perhaps most obviously, Burnett follows Wordsworth by suggesting that a rural rather than

Illustration by Charles Robinson for The Secret Garden

urban environment is best for the natural development of the child. She emphasizes the imprisonment she often felt in Manchester and the freedom she enjoyed when the family moved to Tennessee. Like Wordsworth, Burnett suggests that the child has a special affinity with nature: she felt at home in the Tennessee thickets because "dim, far-off beautiful ages before, she had been a little Faun or Dryad" herself; in the thicket she talked to flowers and the squirrels regarded her as "another kind of little animal." Also as in Wordsworth's *Prelude,* Burnett has Nature act as the child's tutor. Nature aids in disciplining the young person. "The First Crime of her Infancy"—a peccadillo by adult standards—is magnified for the child by its setting in "the Back Garden of Eden," an estate garden where she loved to play. In her exaggerated sense of guilt, the child fears her presence will blight the gooseberries and shrivel the currents.

Nature also teaches the child Burnett lessons about love, death, and immortality. In a passage reminiscent of Walt Whitman's "Out of the Cradle Endlessly Rocking" (1860), Burnett describes the inchoate longings she felt watching a pair of doves who become separated. Birds provide images of death and immortality as well as of love. She recalls lying on the ground watching the clouds and feeling that her soul was a bird that had broken loose from her body and hovered above it, attached by a slender cord. If the chain broke, the child speculated that "Nobody would know that I had only died because I was so happy that my soul broke the chain." As in the poems by Whitman and Wordsworth, Nature also educates the imagination of the budding writer. In describing the stories she wrote in Manchester, Burnett emphasizes their artificiality, their reliance on fictional conventions. In the Tennessee woods, however, she ceased "'to pretend' in the old way" because there were "real things enough." She "began to deal with emotions . . . and forests and Autumn leaves assisted." In Manchester "she had imagined—in the forests she began to feel."

Some of the most moving passages in the memoir, however, are Burnett's explorations of her mind as a very young child. She describes poignantly her frustrations when her insufficient ability to use language kept her from expressing clearly to adults her desires and her sense of injury when they misunderstood or underestimated her. In a similar vein, she describes the pain caused by thoughtless grown-ups when they made jokes at the trusting child's expense. For example, a wry park policeman told her that he would have to arrest her for trespassing, and the child was horrified lest her small body slip through the huge gaps in the park bench's supporting back. In another episode, little Burnett and a friend equally infatuated with babies took seriously a woman's joking promise to give them her baby, and they generously made excuses for her when she did not meet them with the baby as prearranged.

Burnett also portrays effectively her childhood perception of death. Her treatment of this subject is far less morbid and sentimental than in the stories she was producing during the same period, no doubt because her feelings about these deaths were "recollected in tranquility" rather than, as with her grief over Lionel's death, exorcized through her writing. Her father's death, when she was four, elicited little immediate interest and apparently stocked her memory with few details. At age four, death was a "mystery of which there was so little explanation that it was not terrible"; it was "an idea too vague to grasp." When she was several years older and death touched two of her schoolmates, she was ready to study the dead bodies and ask herself questions about the causes and meaning of this "Strange Thing." For its evocation of a child's view of the world as well as for its use of pastoral themes she would return to in *The Secret Garden, The One I Knew the Best of All* commands a place among her works which continue to deserve reading in the twentieth century.

Burnett's memoir was sure to find an audience in the 1890s among the many who would be curious about the childhood of one who by now was famous as a writer about childhood. Her thoughts on a boy's career choices, "When He Decides," were published with essays by four other writers in *Before He Is Twenty: Five Perplexing Phases of the Boy Question Considered* (1894). *Two Little Pilgrims' Progress: A Story of the City Beautiful* (1895) resulted from a commission to describe the 1893 Chicago Columbian Exposition in a story for children. Describing a trek to the Exposition by two rural orphans, the book pays homage to American ingenuity and technological achievement. Also in an educational vein, Burnett and Senator Henry Cabot Lodge wrote essays describing Washington, D.C., for the young readers of *St. Nicholas* in 1893. Burnett describes Washington as a child would see it. From a second-story nursery window, this "City of Groves and Bowers" looks more like a forest than a city, though the carriages with lovely ladies on the street might well suggest "Cinderella's ball to the small watcher at the window."

Although Burnett was famous on both sides of the Atlantic and was having no difficulty finding publishers for her work, her decade of writing mainly for or about children caused critics to wonder when she would write an adult work that fulfilled the promise she had shown earlier in *That Lass o' Lowrie's* and *Through One Administration*. *A Lady of Quality*, published in 1896, did not satisfy their expectations. In the novel Burnett portrays a strong-willed girl who is reared as a boy and then later accidentally kills her former lover, hides his body, marries, and lives happily thereafter. Some readers were shocked at this story from the creator of *Little Lord Fauntleroy*, but the book became a bestseller. The critics found the novel lacking in substance, and when she quickly answered requests for a stage version and wrote a companion volume, *His Grace of Osmonde* (1897), to appear when *A Lady of Quality* opened in New York, the critics decided she was no longer interested in doing serious literary work. When in 1899 she did produce a work drawing from her earlier, American realist tradition, *In Connection with The De Willoughby Claim*, many of the critics had turned their attention elsewhere. It is probable that Burnett decided to repay them in kind. By now she knew what her audience liked, and before she died in 1924, she turned out four more best-sellers about fashionable British and American life, *The Shuttle* (1907), *T. Tembarom* (1913), *The Head of the House of Coombe* (1922), and *Robin* (1922).

In addition to ignoring the critics of her writing, Burnett also tried not to be hurt by the increasing criticism of her flamboyant, international lifestyle. *Little Lord Fauntleroy* had brought her notoriety as well as fame; her love of wearing fancy clothes reinforced the popular image of Fauntleroy as a fop. Gossip magazines criticized her unusual domestic arrangement, and when she and Swan were divorced by mutual consent in 1898, her relationship with her theatrical collaborator Stephen Townesend was cited as the cause, even though her separation from her husband had preceded her friendship with Townesend. She married Townesend in 1900, and newspapers hinted that she had bartered her wealth and fame for his youth; he was ten years her junior. The marriage proved unhappy, and after 1902 she and Townesend lived separately until he died in 1914. During these years she probably needed to repeat often to herself the sentiments which had concluded *The Two Little Pilgrims' Progress*: "There are beautiful things in the world, there are men and women and children with brave and gentle hearts. . . . There are birds in the sky and flowers in the woods, and Spring comes every year. And these are the fairy stories."

By this definition, most of what Burnett wrote during the final phase of her career as a children's writer could be called fairy stories. Those which are justifiably most famous, notably *A Little Princess*, are fairy stories with real-world settings. Others, however, continue the tradition of literary fairy tale and fantasy Burnett had begun in "Behind the White Brick" and "The Proud Little Grain of Wheat." "The Story of Prince Fairyfoot" (serialized in 1886 and 1887) almost immediately followed *Little Lord Fauntleroy* in *St. Nicholas* and contained some of the same themes. Like Fauntleroy, Prince Fairyfoot is different from those around him—he has tiny feet in a kingdom whose citizens are proud of their huge feet; and like Fauntleroy, Prince Fairyfoot visits other countries—the land of the fairies and a kingdom of people with small feet, whose princess he marries. The tale's light tone with its suggestion of a moral invites comparison with George MacDonald's "The Light Princess" (1864), but it was based on Burnett's recollection of a tale in Frances Browne's *Granny's Wonderful Chair*, which she had owned as a child but lost.

Like Browne's stories, Burnett's fairy tales and fantasies are didactic, often clumsily so. In "The Quite True Story of an Old Hawthorne Tree," collected in *Children I Have Known* and *Giovanni and the Other*, a tree begins its life happily in the country but is gradually surrounded by the growing city of London; the tree is very sad until a rector makes it the center of a people's garden. In part because the tree itself narrates the story, the tale is sentimental, which is the usual result when Burnett adopts a nonhuman point of view, such as that of a plant, bird, or animal. A similar gracelessness in using fantasy conventions recurs in a series of tales she published in *St. Nicholas* from 1906 through 1909. All were narrated by a fairy, Queen Crosspatch. The first story, "The Troubles of Queen Silver Bell" (1906), explains that Queen Silver Bell became Queen Crosspatch because people are ceasing to believe in fairies; if this continues, the fairies will fade and die. Burnett likely borrowed this theme from J. M. Barrie's play *Peter Pan*, which was popular at the time. Much as Peter Pan asks children in the audience who believe in fairies to clap so that Tinker Bell will not die, Queen Crosspatch decides to write stories to help children believe in fairies so that fairyland will not disappear.

The resulting tales are an odd assortment. In "How Winnie Hatched the Little Rooks" (1906),

Queen Crosspatch makes a girl tiny enough to sit on a nest of eggs abandoned by the mother bird; there are some rather absurd scenes in which the little girl and the father bird play husband and wife. "Racketty-Packetty House" (1906-1907), dramatized in 1912 by the Children's Theater in New York, is more successful. The story grew out of Burnett's fondness for elaborate dollhouses which she kept in her home to share with children who visited her. The tale depicts a happy-go-lucky family of Victorian dolls who watch the high-society antics of a new set of dolls which their owner prefers. A similar sociability is demonstrated by the title character in "The Cozy Lion" (1907), who learns not to eat children so that he can play with them. In "The Spring Cleaning" (1908-1909), Queen Crosspatch and her fairies hasten the coming of spring so that a little girl can invite her friends to a primrose party.

Similar in nature and quality are two short books by Burnett published at about the same time as the Queen Crosspatch series. In *The Good Wolf* (1908), a poor boy, Barty, is taken by the wolf to a feast held by animals. In *Barty Crusoe and His Man Saturday* (1909), Barty has just read *Robinson Crusoe*, and the good wolf takes him to a desert island where a monkey, Saturday, helps him deal with the Polite Pirates and the Impolite Pirates. Both books are didactic and episodic, showing their origin in the tales Burnett had told her boys to keep them quiet while she curled their hair. Narrative frames explain that the tales were told to little Tim by his mother. The frame to *Barty Crusoe and His Man Saturday* also explains that what Tim likes best about the tale is the paratactic structure typical of oral tales: "that sudden way it had of beginning all over again with something new when you felt quite mournful because you thought it had come to an end."

The narrative frames in the two Barty books indicate Burnett's constant awareness of the audience for her stories. *The Way to the House of Santa Claus: A Christmas Story for Very Small Boys in Which Every Little Reader Is the Hero of a Big Adventure* (1916) allows spaces in the text so that the reader's name can be written where the hero's name would be mentioned. The story has a cumulative form, as a succession of animals guide him on the stages of his journey to Santa Claus's house. This is Burnett's only picture book, although most of her stories and books were illustrated. After the *St. Nicholas* illustrator Reginald Birch gave visible form to Little Lord Fauntleroy, he created line drawings for many of Burnett's books, especially those published by Scribners. *The Way to the House of Santa Claus* gives no indication of who did the bold full-page pictures which accompany each page of the text.

Unity of purpose and clarity of form make *The Land of the Blue Flower* (1909) Burnett's best fairy tale or fantasy effort. The reason, perhaps, is that here she was exploring themes which genuinely engaged her, while in the other tales she often seemed to be writing down for a child audience. Published just two years before *The Secret Garden*, this tale anticipates themes in that book. A prince from the plains is educated on a mountain. His life is Edenic. He tends a garden once owned by a young queen but then left to grow wild. Named Amor, the prince learns to love the natural elements and all creatures as his brothers. When he experiences anger his teacher tells him, "If you put into your mind a beautiful thought it will take the place of the evil one." He returns to the plains to become king and finds only dissension and gloom among his subjects. He makes a law that every person must plant and tend a blue flower, and this shared interest in growing things transforms the kingdom into one governed by love. Like her early writing for children, this best of her literary fairy tales demonstrates that fantasy did not engage Burnett's best talents. Although like *The Secret Garden*, *The Land of the Blue Flower* stresses the healing effect of good thoughts and gardening, its message is more simplistic and obvious; and its images are not nearly so evocative.

Before writing *The Secret Garden* (1911), however, Burnett used themes from her literary fairy tales and fantasies to enrich *A Little Princess* (1905), which joins that pastoral classic and *Little Lord Fauntleroy* to form the triad of her best works for children. Sara Crewe, the heroine of *A Little Princess*, follows the tradition of child paragons Burnett had begun in the 1880s with "Editha's Burglar," *Little Lord Fauntleroy*, and "Little Saint Elizabeth." And even more explicitly than *Little Lord Fauntleroy*, *A Little Princess* is the Cinderella tale in a realistic setting. Sara undergoes a pattern of enchantment and disenchantment parallel to Cinderella's. When she arrives at Miss Minchin's Select Seminary for Young Ladies in London, Sara is recognized as a princess by all because of her fine clothes and regal bearing. But word arrives that her father has died penniless, and Sara is treated as a servant by the "wicked stepmother," Miss Minchin, and some of the older "stepsisters" in the school. Her real identity is finally discovered by the recluse next door, and he restores to her the vast fortune which her father mistakenly thought he had lost.

Like little Cedric Errol, Sara Crewe must prove her innate nobility when the world does not recognize it: she must maintain the charitable nature and even temper of a princess while she is being treated as a beggar. Even more than in *Little Lord Fauntleroy*, however, Burnett makes recognition of the child's true nature a test for others in the story. Because she judges by external appearances only, Miss Minchin fails this test. She thinks that Sara can be turned from a princess into a beggar by simply exchanging her pink silk party dress for a tight black frock. Miss Minchin lacks the imagination to see the fairy-tale magic at work in Sara's life; in this book, as in *The Secret Garden*, Burnett uses magic as a metaphor for the ability to see with the imagination. It is Sara's ability to imagine her attic room a banquet hall and to see herself as a princess in a fairy tale that gives her the power to endure her hardships. And when the recluse next door has Sara's room transformed as she imagined it and then restores her lost fortune, Sara's story is a fairy tale come true. Previewing similar themes in *The Secret Garden*, Burnett thus dramatizes her belief in the power of the imagination to effect external as well as internal change. The contrasting points of view of Sara and Miss Minchin, the use of fairy-tale magic as a metaphor for the imagination make *A Little Princess* more complex and symbolically richer than *Little Lord Fauntleroy*.

To see how Burnett had developed her skill and self-awareness as a writer since the 1880s, one need only look at the earlier versions of Sara's story. The earliest form was a story entitled "Sara Crewe," serialized in *St. Nicholas* in 1887-1888, and published in book form in the United States in 1888. In this short version Sara is not the paragon she is in *A Little Princess;* at the beginning of the story, in fact, she more resembles Mary Lennox at the start of *The Secret Garden*— thin, not pretty, spoiled, and saucy. Sara decides to be well-mannered and even tempered because she does not want to be like Miss Minchin, whom she despises. As in the book, she does use her imagination to help her act like a princess, and in the end she recognizes that she is living in a fairy story; but these themes are suggested rather than developed. Also, only one of the other schoolgirls, Ermengarde, is individualized. The second version of the story was a play which opened in London in 1902 as *A Little Unfairy Princess* and in New York in 1903 as *A Little Princess*. Probably to make the play more appealing for its intended audience of children, Burnett developed more of Sara's classmates, especially the jealous Lavinia and the toddler Lottie. These expanded

Frances Hodgson Burnett (The Huntington Library, San Marino, California)

roles plus the condensation necessary for the stage may have prompted Burnett to abandon the attempt to portray a change in Sara. She is presented as temperamentally a princess when the first curtain rises. The fact that Burnett maintained this idealistic portrayal of Sara in the book *A Little Princess*, however, suggests that if she had not earlier been aware that her popular tales were often fairy tales with realistic settings, she was conscious of it now. This hypothesis is supported by *The Making of a Marchioness*, published in 1901; in this light romance for adults, Burnett makes explicit comparisons of the idealized main character to Cinderella.

In addition to these developments in her writing, features of Burnett's life affected preoccupations in her fiction. Burnett, like the fictional Sara Crewe, was living out some of the romantic fantasies she had had when she was a genteel beggar. From 1898 through 1907, Burnett leased Maytham, a country estate in Kent, and she enjoyed playing the role of lady of the manor as she became acquainted with the villagers in neighboring Rolvenden. In part to escape the curious and often hostile press, she began to live a more retiring life. She enjoyed gardening, and often, wearing white dress and large hat, she sat in her favorite rose garden to write. It was here that she changed "Sara Crewe" into *A Little Princess*. And while the seeds for *The Secret Garden* had been planted during her childhood, as her memoir shows, the rose garden at Maytham encouraged their growth in her imagination. The bird who shows Mary how to get into the locked garden had its original in a robin Burnett befriended at Maytham, as explained in *My Robin* (1912).

A likely conscious or unconscious literary source for *The Secret Garden* is Charlotte Brontë's *Jane Eyre* (1847), as Burnett's biographer Ann Thwaite conjectures in noting some of the similarities between the two books. Like *Jane Eyre, The Secret Garden* is set in the Yorkshire moors rather than in Burnett's native Lancashire, the provincial setting for much of Burnett's early adult fiction. Like Jane Eyre, Mary Lennox is an ill-tempered orphan who lives first with relatives and is taunted by her cousins. Both orphans travel to the moors where they find a mansion with a secret resident connected to the absent owner's unhappy past—both books have gothic overtones. While Jane Eyre discovers a hidden mad wife, however, Mary Lennox finds a hypochondriac cousin, Colin. She befriends him, and their shared enjoyment of the secret garden brings physical and psychological healing to both.

Burnett borrows from her own earlier work as well as from *Jane Eyre*. Like Sara in *A Little Princess*, Mary and Colin describe the changes in their lives as caused by magic. In part, this magic is the power of the mind to heal the body; but this magic is portrayed as Nature's magic as well. The sun which shines on them as they work in the long-neglected garden helps them gain strength as their pruning and planting help restore the garden. All of this healing they eventually share with Colin's father. At the end of the book he experiences psychological healing when he finds that his son has gained health through the garden his dead wife had once loved. This return of a misanthropic adult to the human community parallels the changes in Little Lord Fauntleroy's grandfather. In *The Secret Garden*, however, Burnett deviates from her earlier focus on the child as the source of redemption. This is a richer book than its predecessors largely because she makes Nature the ultimate source of this power; she is thus able to draw on the ancient pastoral tradition to give mythic resonance to her fairy-tale themes.

Like pastoral writers before her, Burnett uses the seasonal cycle, expecially the new life of spring after the death of winter, to provide a mythic metaphor for human rebirth and to give structure to her book. Mary arrives at Misselthwaite during a late-winter rain storm; it is spring when she and Colin begin working in the garden; during the summer the children and the garden fully recover; and this harvest of health is ready for Colin's father when he returns in the fall. The children are introduced to the miracles of nature by those persons pastoral writers often depict as being closest to the earth, the rural folk. Mary befriends Ben Weatherstaff, the gardener, who eventually shares the children's garden secret. They are helped also by the Pan-like Dickon, a child of the moors, and by his mother, who has the aura of the archetypical earth mother. And like many of its pastoral predecessors, *The Secret Garden* is a lyrical book, since the members of the garden community are constantly describing nature's beauty in paeans of joy. Many of these are in folk dialect, which Burnett never used to better effect.

Finally, the book is unified by Burnett's use of the garden, which is the symbolic as well as dramatic center of the story. The garden represents that which is sick or dead in the past, the illness of the children as well as Colin's dead mother. It had been her garden, and Colin's father had locked it up when she died, shortly after Colin was born. But the garden also represents redemptive forces in the present and future, since Burnett identifies it with the children as well as Colin's mother. Like Mary, the garden is a neglected "orphan." And like Colin, the garden has been avoided by his father because he did not want to be reminded of his dead wife. The children, like the garden, are gifts from the past which Colin's father must accept if he is to live joyfully in the present and future. Since Burnett has invested the secret garden with so much symbolic meaning, the reunion which takes place there has much more resonance than those which concluded her earlier works. By offering a credible portrayal of changes within child as well as adult characters and by amplifying these changes through the use of pastoral images and themes, Burnett created a work which deserves its status as a juvenile masterpiece.

While its use of the ancient pastoral tradition has contributed in large part to *The Secret Garden*'s survival as a classic, many of its contemporary readers regarded it in the light of more recent religious and philosophical trends. According to Burnett's son Vivian, *The Secret Garden* as well as *The Dawn of a To-morrow,* a book for adults published in 1906, were generally regarded as Christian Science books. Evidence for this reading of *The Secret Garden* can be found in the children's self-healing and in several pages in which Burnett relates bodily health to one's state of mind: one of the "wonderful" discoveries of "the last [nineteenth] century was that thoughts—just mere thoughts—are as powerful as electric batteries—as good for one as sunlight is, or as bad for one as poison. To let a sad thought or a bad one get into your mind is as dangerous as letting a scarlet fever germ get into your body." As some of the other books Burnett wrote during the last phase of her career demonstrate, she was influenced by the New Thought movement, Christian Science, and Theosophy, which came into prominence during the second half of the nineteenth century.

According to Vivian Burnett, his mother always had a strong religious sense and read the Bible regularly, though she was neither orthodox nor a regular churchgoer. During her early years in Washington, she took treatments from a mind healer for her nervous prostration; she read works by Mary Baker Eddy and attended Christian Science meetings, though she never enrolled as a member. Congruent with the tenets of this group are not only Burnett's emphasis on the power of the mind but also the general belief in the power of goodness and the possibility of happiness for everyone, shown in much of Burnett's fiction. At about the same time that she became interested in mind-healing, she came in contact with Theosophy and Spiritualism and attended some séances. She developed a belief in a happy afterlife which later consoled her after Lionel's death. These beliefs were expressed most explicitly in several works of short fiction and a longer children's book published between 1904 and 1917.

Burnett's belief in an afterlife was expressed in two short books which dramatize communication between the living and the dead. The more effective of these is *In the Closed Room* (1904), which portrays yet another of Burnett's idealized children, though now with a heavenly aura. Seven-year-old Judith is a dreamy child who plays wordlessly with a girl she sees in a locked room upstairs in the house where her parents are caretakers. The story incorporates some of Burnett's pastoral themes. Just outside the room is a roof garden, and eventually Judith and her friend step into the garden and disappear along a green path. Judith's body is discovered in the room by her mother and the wealthy owner of the house.

The owner recognizes that the room has been rearranged as her own daughter, recently dead, would have done it, and she concludes that her daughter had returned to tell her that she is not far away. Through its portrayal of an ethereal child with only a tenuous hold on earth, *In the Closed Room* invites comparison to George MacDonald's *At the Back of the North Wind,* but it also recalls the stories about dead or dying children Burnett wrote shortly after Lionel's death. It is more effective and less morbid than these, however, because it is told with greater restraint and emphasizes the dead children's joy rather than the mothers' grief.

The White People (1917) is dedicated to Lionel and may contain a fictional tribute to MacDonald, whom Burnett had met on her 1873 honeymoon in New York. Set in MacDonald's native Scotland, the short novel is narrated by a young woman who, since her solitary childhood in a Highland castle, has occasionally seen pale "white people" nobody else sees. Much of the story depicts the narrator's growing friendship with a writer she had long admired. Like MacDonald, the writer is a world-renowned Scotchman who writes essays, poems, and marvelous stories. He shares with the narrator a sense of the living reality of the ancient legends which she had derived from reading manuscripts and old books in the castle library. (An ancient library figures prominently in several of MacDonald's fantasies, such as *Phantastes,* 1858.) And *The White People* offers assurances similar to those in some of MacDonald's fantasies, including "The Golden Key" (1867), which depicts the soul's progress after death. In Burnett's story, the writer, his mother, and the narrator become intimate friends, and since the writer has a fatal disease, the narrator's ability to see the dead helps them overcome the fear of death. In the final scene the writer dies, and the narrator says that she has frequently seen him since, smiling at her. Like *In the Closed Room,* *The White People* contains some evocative scenes, but it is flawed by the fact that in the interest of narrative suspense Burnett has the narrator understand the nature of "the white people" much later than the reader does. What was probably intended to be the narrator's humble reluctance to recognize that she has a special gift has instead the effect of seeming an incredible dullness in deriving the fairly evident conclusion. Burnett's extraordinary fictional characters are more effective when she describes them from the outside, in third person.

In some ways more interesting as an exploration of the powers of the mind is a short story Burnett published in a 1909 issue of *St. Nicholas,*

"The First Knife in the World." Like the narrator in *The White People*, Angus Farquhar grew up in a Scotch castle, was steeped in romances and local legends, and is regarded as a seer because of his gift of second sight. Visiting the British Museum with his cousins, he declares a piece of flint on display to be the first knife in the world. He goes into a trance and tells how a prehistoric boy simultaneously discovered how to make the knife and how to talk. When he used the knife to kill a wolf about to attack a baby, the boy began to walk erect and chant: "I am Man. I made that which was not in the world before. I save as well as kill. I am Man." Burnett thus continues the exploration of early mental processes she had begun in her memoir, which she had subtitled *A Memory in the Mind of a Child*. In her step-by-step dramatization of the interrelated roles of the body, the physical world, and language in the development of human consciousness and by stressing the role of *making* in that process, she suggests the elemental nature of the artistic impulse and the power for good or ill in what it creates. *The Little Hunchback Zia* (1916), a slight, rather sentimental story, is the only one of Burnett's explorations into the supernatural which is specifically Christian. Twelve-year-old Zia is a hunchback and leper who has beautiful eyes which reflect the sin of evil persons who gaze into them. Cast out by the beggar who cared for him, Zia goes to Bethlehem, where he beholds Mary, Joseph, and the baby Jesus, who touches him and makes him look like a king's son.

A quasi-religious kingly aura also surrounds the main characters of *The Lost Prince* (1915), which continues Burnett's exploration into the powers of the mind. This last of her longer books for children, like many of her earlier ones, grew out of her experiences and preoccupations at the time. A patriotic story, this adventure romance reflects her concern for the war that was ravaging European countries she had come to love during her years of living abroad. She had become an American citizen in 1905 and built herself a beautiful home on Long Island in 1909; in 1914, a month before the Austrian Archduke Ferdinand was assassinated in Sarajevo, she made her last trip from Europe to the United States. Though separated by the Atlantic, she followed the war closely and lent her support by entertaining and collecting books for sailors in Bermuda, where she spent winters, and by carrying on extensive correspondence with soldiers at the front and her friends in England. The specific inspiration for *The Lost Prince*, however, had come in 1913 in Vienna when she had been struck by the

resemblance of a Van Dyck portrait of a Bavarian prince to her dead son Lionel. Her musings about the prince's personality were augmented by an interest in Serbian history she developed after a conversation with a Balkan princess.

The role of Serbian nationalism in precipitating world war in 1914 is reflected in Burnett's portrayal of Samavia in *The Lost Prince*. The larger neighbors of the small, mountainous Samavia fear that its political chaos will spread, and leaders in various European capitals have become allies of a secret Samavian society dedicated to putting a responsible leader on its throne. To these political themes, Burnett added the mythic plot of the return of an exiled king. Five hundred years before the story opens, the Samavians had tried to replace a vicious king with his virtuous son. Civil war broke out, but there is a Samavian legend that the good prince—who was strong and handsome "as a young Viking god"—escaped unharmed and that his descendants have been living secretly in exile until the time is right for his return.

Burnett's narrative focuses not so much on the lost prince who returns to Samavia as king at the end of the story but on his twelve-year-old son, Marco. Once again there is civil war in Samavia, and Marco and his street urchin friend, "Rat," travel as beggars to various European capitals to tell sympathizers that the secret society of Samavian nationalists—The Forgers of the Sword—is ready to take the throne for the lost prince. In her portrayal of the children's journey against the background of the adults' military plan, Burnett anticipates the double plot of J. R. R. Tolkien's *The Lord of the Rings* (1954-1955). Like Tolkien's two hobbits, Burnett's children succeed in their journey because they are small and can escape notice—the fact that Rat is crippled and walks with a crutch emphasizes the heroism of the small and lowly. And Burnett's portrayal of Loristan, Marco's father, anticipates Tolkien's returning king in the ability to inspire followers; Loristan's supporters behave to him as to a god.

As a worldly-wise and sometimes comic sidekick for his more idealistic friend, Rat plays a role similar to that of Don Quixote's Sancho or Frodo's Sam. But he also recalls Mark Twain's Tom Sawyer in his love for imaginative games. When Marco meets him in the streets of London, he is drilling a squad of street boys, and they form a secret society to help Samavia. During these games Rat devises a plan for Marco and him to carry the secret sign to Samavian sympathizers. As Tom Sawyer's outlaw games result in his encountering a real outlaw, Rat's

Burnett and her granddaughter Verity at Burnett's home in Plandome, Long Island

game plan is adopted by Loristan, who says, "Perhaps only boyhood . . . could have dared imagine it." Probably a more direct influence on Burnett, however, was Rudyard Kipling's *Kim* (1901), which similarly portrays a disguised young prince traveling and playing "The Great Game" of spying among the natives in India. Moreover, as Kim encounters Oriental mysticism when he becomes the student of a lama, Burnett's Loristan learns from a Himalayan Buddhist that the human mind is part of "The Thought That Created the World" and can learn to tap the power of that great Thought. When he becomes king, he will teach others that power's laws of light, order, love, and peace. He has helped Marco train his mind to control his body in times of crisis, and several events show that the power is aiding Marco in his mission. *The Lost Prince* thus demonstrates Burnett's continued theosophical speculations even as it echoes her portrayal of a prince's education in *The Land of the Blue Flower*.

The Lost Prince has not received as much appreciative attention as Burnett's other long works for children, *Little Lord Fauntleroy*, *A Little Princess*, and *The Secret Garden*. One reason, perhaps, is the portrayal of intense nationalism in *The Lost Prince*.

Loristan's leadership has a strong religious aura, not only in his ideas of power but also in the unquestioning devotion of his followers. These royalist and military values are combined with aristocratic assumptions which were present but less obvious in early works such as *Little Lord Fauntleroy*. Rat's heroic potential is explained in part by the fact that his father had been a gentleman, and the obeisance of Loristan's servant, Lazarus, is not qualified as it is by the acerbic temper and wry humor of the gardener Ben Weatherstaff in *The Secret Garden*. Finally, *The Lost Prince* is often repetitious, and Burnett has the same problem depicting Marco's self-awareness she had with the narrator of *The White People*. To have Marco's recognition of his identity dramatically coincide with his change in fortune, Burnett does not let Marco realize until the very end, at the crowning ceremony, that his father is the lost prince, despite the transparency of this conclusion much earlier. Though somewhat flawed in execution and dated in its awe of royalty and the aristocracy, *The Lost Prince* demonstrates that Burnett had not lost her mythic imagination nor her ability to involve readers in the adventures of her child characters.

Contemporary reviews of *The Lost Prince* typified the way in which Burnett was viewed by the critics when she died in 1924. The *New York Times* stated that the book showed Burnett's continuing ability to tell an engrossing story but could also be regarded as "superficial, sentimental, conventional and other such things." Remembering mainly Burnett's best-selling romances for adults published during the twentieth century, critics who were by now reading James Joyce, Virginia Woolf, Ernest Hemingway, and F. Scott Fitzgerald often dismissed Burnett as a relic of Victorianism. Often forgotten in obituary surveys of her career were early adult works such as *That Lass o' Lowrie's* and *Through One Administration,* which had been praised for their thoughtful studies of social life. The popular and influential *Little Lord Fauntleroy* was usually stressed as the book for which she would be remembered.

The knowledge that she had never lost an appreciative audience for her adult and children's books, however, probably helped Burnett overlook the frequent condescension of the critics. In addition, she enjoyed a comfortable personal life at Plandome, her estate on Long Island. She often had her family and friends around her. Vivian had married in 1914 and soon presented her with two granddaughters; she was able to continue a more personal version of her lifelong enjoyment of children. Finally, on the grounds of her estate, she was able to indulge her love of gardening. It is appropriate that, as the author of *The Secret Garden,* her last days were spent revising an essay describing the joys of gardening. Published posthumously in 1925, *In the Garden* has a recurring sentence which stands as a fitting epitaph for Burnett: "As long as one has a garden one has a future; and as long as one has a future one is alive."

Biographies:

Vivian Burnett, *The Romantick Lady (Frances Hodgson Burnett): The Life Story of an Imagination* (New York: Scribners, 1927);

Constance Buel Burnett, *Happily Ever After: A Portrait of Frances Hodgson Burnett* (New York: Vanguard, 1969);

Ann Thwaite, *Waiting for the Party: The Life of Frances Hodgson Burnett 1849-1924* (New York: Scribners, 1974).

References:

Phyllis Bixler, *Frances Hodgson Burnett* (Boston: G. K. Hall, 1984);

Bixler, "*Little Lord Fauntleroy:* Continuity and Change in Popular Entertainment," in *Children's Novels and the Movies,* edited by Douglas Street (New York: Ungar, 1983), pp. 69-80;

Bixler, "The Oral-Formulaic Training of a Popular Fiction Writer: Frances Hodgson Burnett," *Journal of Popular Culture,* 15 (Spring 1982): 42-52;

Madelon S. Gohlke, "Rereading *The Secret Garden,*" *College English,* 41 (April 1980): 894-902;

Elizabeth Lennox Keyser, " 'Quite Contrary': Frances Hodgson Burnett's *The Secret Garden,*" *Children's Literature,* 11 (1983): 1-13;

Phyllis Bixler Koppes, "Tradition and the Individual Talent of Frances Hodgson Burnett: A Generic Analysis of *Little Lord Fauntleroy, A Little Princess,* and *The Secret Garden,*" *Children's Literature: An International Journal,* 7 (1978): 191-207;

Marghanita Laski, *Mrs. Ewing, Mrs. Molesworth and Mrs. Hodgson Burnett* (New York: Oxford University Press, 1951);

Francis J. Molson, "Frances Hodgson Burnett (1848-1924)," *American Literary Realism,* 8 (Winter 1975): 35-41;

Molson, "*Two Little Pilgrims' Progress:* The 1893 Chicago Columbian Exposition as Celestial City," *Markham Review,* 7 (Spring 1978): 55-59;

Robert Lee White, "Little Lord Fauntleroy as Hero," in *Challenges in American Culture,* edited by Ray B. Browne, Larry N. Landrum, and William Bottorff (Bowling Green: Bowling Green University Popular Press, 1970), pp. 209-216.

Papers:

The Scribner Archives at the Princeton University Library has a large collection of Burnett's professional correspondence.

Hezekiah Butterworth

(22 December 1839-5 September 1905)

Mark Irwin West

University of North Carolina at Charlotte

SELECTED BOOKS: *The Story of the Hymns: or, Hymns that Have a History* (New York: American Tract Society, 1875);

Zigzag Journeys in Europe. Vacation Rambles in Historic Lands (Boston: Estes & Lauriat, 1880);

The Story of the Notable Prayers of Christian History (Boston: Lothrop, 1880);

Young Folks' History of Boston (Boston: Estes & Lauriat, 1881); republished as *Popular History of Boston* (Boston: Estes & Lauriat, 1894);

Zigzag Journeys in Classic Lands; or, Tommy Toby's Trip to Mount Parnassus (Boston: Estes & Lauriat, 1881);

Zigzag Journeys in the Orient. The Adriatic to the Baltic. A Journey of the Zigzag Club from Vienna to the Golden Horn, the Euxine, Moscow, and St. Petersburg (Boston: Estes & Lauriat, 1882);

Zigzag Journeys in the Occident. The Atlantic to the Pacific. A Summer Trip of the Zigzag Club from Boston to the Golden Gate (Boston: Estes & Lauriat, 1883); republished as *Zigzag Journeys in the Western States of America* (London: Dean & Song);

Up From the Cape. A Plea for Republican Simplicity, anonymous (Boston: Estes & Lauriat, 1883);

The Great Composers (Boston: Lothrop, 1884; revised and enlarged, Boston: Lothrop, 1894);

Zigzag Journeys in Northern Lands. The Rhine to the Arctic. A Summer Trip of the Zigzag Club through Holland, Germany, Denmark, Norway, and Sweden (Boston: Estes & Lauriat, 1884);

Poems for Christmas, Easter, and New Year's (Boston: Estes & Lauriat, 1885);

Zigzag Journeys in Acadia and New France. A Summer's Journey of the Zigzag Club through the Historic Fields of the Early French Settlements of America (Boston: Estes & Lauriat, 1885);

Zigzag Journeys in the Levant, with a Talmudist Storyteller. A Spring Trip of the Zigzag Club through Egypt and the Holy Land (Boston: Estes & Lauriat, 1886);

Ballads and Stories for Readings with Musical Accompaniments for Public Entertainments, Church Socials, School, and the Family Circle (Cincinnati:

Hezekiah Butterworth

John Church/Chicago: Root, 1886);

Songs of History. Poems and Ballads upon Important Episodes in American History (Boston: New England Publishing, 1887; London: Murray, 1887);

A Zigzag Journey in the Sunny South; or, Wonder Tales of Early American History (Boston: Estes & Lauriat, 1887);

Zigzag Journeys in India; or, The Antipodes of the Far East. A Collection of the Zenänä Tales (Boston: Estes & Lauriat, 1887);

Zigzag Journeys in the Antipodes (Boston: Estes & Lauriat, 1888); republished as *Cruising in the Indian Seas* (New York: Sully, 1894);

Zigzag Journeys in the British Isles; or, Vacation Rambles in Historic Lands (Boston: Estes & Lauriat, 1889);

The Story of the Tunes (New York: American Tract Society, 1890);

The Log School-House on the Columbia. A Tale of the Pioneers of the Great Northwest (New York: Appleton, 1890);

Zigzag Journeys in the Great Northwest; or, A Trip to the American Switzerland (Boston: Estes & Lauriat, 1890);

Zigzag Journeys in Australia; or, A Visit to the Ocean World (Boston: Estes & Lauriat, 1891);

The Christmas Book (Boston: Lothrop, 1891);

In the Boyhood of Lincoln. A Tale of the Tunker Schoolmaster and the Times of Black Hawk (New York: Appleton, 1892);

Little Arthur's History of Rome, from the Golden Age to Constantine (New York: Crowell, 1892);

Zigzag Journeys on the Mississippi, from Chicago to the Islands of the Discovery (Boston: Estes & Lauriat, 1892);

The Boys of Greenway Court. A Tale of the Early Days of Washington (New York: Appleton, 1893);

Zigzag Journeys on the Mediterranean (Boston: Estes & Lauriat, 1893);

The Parson's Miracle, and My Grandmother's Christmas Candle; Christmas in America (Boston: Estes & Lauriat, 1894);

The Patriot Schoolmaster; or, The Adventures of the two Boston Cannons, the "Adams" and "Hancock." A Tale of the Minute Men and the Sons of Liberty (New York: Appleton, 1894);

Zigzag Journeys in the White City, with Visits to the Neighboring Metropolis (Boston: Estes & Lauriat, 1894);

In Old New England. The Romance of a Colonial Fireside (New York: Appleton, 1895);

The Knight of Liberty. A Tale of the Fortunes of Lafayette (New York: Appleton, 1895);

Zigzag Journeys Around the World (Boston: Estes & Lauriat, 1895);

The Wampum Belt; or, "The Fairest Page of History." A Tale of William Penn's Treaty with the Indians (New York: Appleton, 1896);

Over the Andes; or, Our Boys in New South America (Boston: Wilde, 1897);

True to his Home. A Tale of the Boyhood of Franklin (New York: Appleton, 1897);

In the Days of Massasoit. A Tale of Roger Williams (Philadelphia: American Baptist Publication Society, 1897);

The Pilot of the Mayflower. A Tale of the Children of the Pilgrim Republic (New York: Appleton, 1898);

South America. A Popular Illustrated History of the Struggle for Liberty in the Andean Republics and Cuba (New York: Doubleday & McClure, 1898);

In the Land of the Condor. A Story of Tarapaca (Philadelphia: American Baptist Publication Society, 1898);

Lost in Nicaragua; or, Among the Coffee Farms and Banana Lands in the Countries of the Great Canal (Boston & Chicago: Wilde, 1898);

The Story of Magellan and the Discovery of the Philippines (New York: Appleton, 1899);

The Bordentown Story-tellers; or, Little Lady Lucy and the Merry Berry Pickers (Boston: Bradley, 1899);

The Treasure Ship: A Tale of Sir William Phipps, the Regicides, and the Inter Charter Period in Massachusetts (New York: Appleton, 1899);

Traveller Tales of South Africa, or Stories Which Picture Recent History (Boston: Estes, 1900);

Jack's Carrier Pigeons. A Tale of the Times of Father Taylor's Mariners' Home (Boston: Bradley, 1900);

In the Days of Jefferson (New York: Appleton, 1900);

In the Days of Audubon. A Tale of the "Protector of Birds" (New York: Appleton, 1901);

Little Sky-High; or, The Surprise Doings of Washee-Washee-Wang (New York: Crowell, 1901);

Traveller Tales of China; or, The Story-telling Hongs (Boston: Estes, 1901);

Traveller Tales of the Pan-American Countries (Boston: Estes, 1902);

A New England Miracle; or, Seekers After Truth. A Tale of the Days of King Philip (Philadelphia: American Baptist Publication Society, 1903);

Brother Jonathan (New York: Appleton, 1903);

Little Metacomet; or, The Indian Playmate (New York: Crowell, 1904);

The Young McKinley; or, School-days in Ohio. A Tale of Old Times on the Western Reserve (New York: Appleton, 1905);

A Heroine of the Wilderness. The Story of Lincoln's Mother (Philadelphia: Winston, 1906).

OTHER: *Sunday School Concert Book*, edited by Butterworth (Boston: Young, 1872);

Young Folks' History of America, edited by Butterworth (Boston: Estes & Lauriat, 1881); republished as *Popular History of America* (Boston: Estes & Lauriat, 1894); revised and enlarged as *The Story of America* (New York & Akron: Werner, 1898).

Hezekiah Butterworth was among the nineteenth century's prolific authors for children. He produced scores of books, contributed many articles to magazines, and served as assistant editor of the *Youth's Companion* for twenty-four years. He is best remembered for the *Zigzag Journeys,* a series of travel books, but he also wrote numerous biographies and histories. While some critics charged that his writing read like pages from an encyclopedia, librarians, parents, and teachers commended his books for their wholesomeness.

Hezekiah Butterworth grew up on a farm in Warren, Rhode Island. The land had been in the Butterworth family for generations, and his parents, Gardiner M. and Susan Ritchie Butterworth, were quite content working the farm and raising their six children. Farm life, however, had little appeal for the young Butterworth. He preferred to listen to his aunt's ghost stories instead of doing his chores, and he dreamed of becoming a writer. As a young man, he began selling stories to religious magazines. This source of income enabled him to move to Providence and enroll in a few courses at Brown University. He soon left Providence and took up residence in Boston where he

thought his opportunities would be greater. He continued to write, and a series of articles he had published on self-education attracted the attention of Daniel Sharp Ford, the editor of *Youth's Companion.* In 1870 Ford offered Butterworth a position with the magazine, and before long he became its assistant editor. While Butterworth's editorial duties consumed much of his energy, he still found time to work on other projects. In 1875 his first major book, *The Story of the Hymns,* was published. For this book, he was given the George Wood Gold Medal, an annual prize awarded by the American Tract Society.

In 1880 Dana Estes of Estes and Lauriat, a Boston publishing firm, approached Butterworth with a proposal. She had recently read *Voyages en Zigzag* (1844) by Rodolphe Toepffer, a French schoolteacher. In his book, Toepffer described the adventures of a teacher who had taken a class of boys on a journey through Switzerland. She felt that Toepffer's book could serve as a model for a new series of children's travel books, and she asked Butterworth if he would be willing to take on the project. He agreed and began working on the first

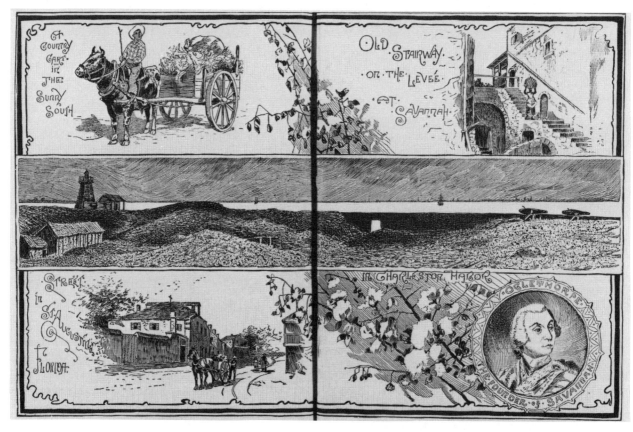

Endpapers for A Zigzag Journey in the Sunny South, *the eighth volume in Butterworth's travel series inspired by Rodolphe Toepffer's* Voyages en Zigzag *(Baldwin Library, University of Florida Libraries)*

volume, *Zigzag Journeys in Europe* (1880), the next day. Actually, Butterworth had never been to Europe when he wrote his first Zigzag book. He simply walked a few blocks to the Boston Public Library where he researched European history, geography, and folklore. Not surprisingly, when the book was published, some reviewers discovered several errors, including Butterworth's reference to Henry VIII's chapel as Westminster Abbey. Nevertheless, the book sold well, and Butterworth was soon able to afford to take lengthy trips to Europe, Cuba, and South America. He made extensive use of his travel experiences in several later volumes of the *Zigzag Journeys.*

The main character in the Zigzag books is Master Lewis, the principal of a private school located near Boston. In each book, Master Lewis takes a group of approximately six boys on a journey during the school's summer vacation. The specific boys who accompany Master Lewis generally are different in each book, although a few boys, such as Tommy Toby, Herman Reed, and Willie Clifton figure in several volumes. The books usually begin with the boys visiting the library and reading about the places they are about to visit. By the time Butterworth had finished the final volume of the series, Master Lewis and his students had toured Europe, Russia, India, Canada, Australia, America, and the Middle East. For the most part, Butterworth did not dwell on the adventures of the travelers; instead, he filled the Zigzag books with history and folklore. On the slightest pretext, Master Lewis or one of the boys would sing a ballad, tell a legend, or expound upon the history of the particular region in which they happened to be. The colorful folklore included in each volume partially accounted for the books' popularity with children. Young readers also enjoyed the many lavish illustrations.

In addition to his travel books, Butterworth wrote over a dozen biographies for children. For the most part, the people he chose to write about were patriotic figures, but he also produced books on religious leaders and people in whom he had a personal interest, such as John James Audubon and Sarah Lincoln, Abraham Lincoln's stepmother. He frequently focused on the childhood of his subjects. Many of his biographies contained fictional elements, and he tended to idealize and romanticize his subjects' lives. *In the Boyhood of Lincoln*, published in 1892, was his most popular biography. The tension between white settlers and Native Americans serves as the backdrop to this partially fictional account of Abraham Lincoln's youth. But-

terworth used this and other books to condemn the settlers' brutal treatment of Native Americans.

Butterworth also wrote several children's history books. His histories of Boston, South America, and the United States all had a textbook flavor to them, and they were often used in schools. However, his best-selling history books were those which included a story line along with the historical information. *The Log School-House on the Columbia* (1890), the most popular of Butterworth's histories, dealt with the pioneers who settled Oregon and Washington. The book revolved around the experiences of a schoolmaster and a heroic Indian chief.

Butterworth dedicated his life to literary pursuits. He usually wrote during the early morning hours, worked at the offices of the *Youth's Companion* for most of the day, and either wrote or entertained in the evening. Since he never married, he essentially had no family life. He did, however, become involved with several organizations. He was vice-president of the American Peace Society and

Title page for Butterworth's most popular juvenile biography (Baldwin Library, University of Florida Libraries)

served as president of the New England Anti-Cigarette League. His income was sizable, but because he gave large sums of money to friends, relatives, and various causes, his financial condition fluctuated dramatically. In fact, he was sometimes forced to lecture in order to meet his expenses. He suffered from diabetes and was often in poor health during his later years. He died in his brother's home in Warren, Rhode Island, in 1905. A few decades after his death, Butterworth's books were all out of print, and his name had faded into obscurity. While his writing was certainly wholesome and instructive, it lacked the artistry and originality of lasting literature. Still as one of the best-selling children's authors of the 1880s and 1890s, he remains an important figure in the history of nineteenth-century children's literature.

References:

Ralph Davol, "Hezekiah Butterworth: A Sketch of his Personality," *New England Magazine*, 33 (January 1906): 507-517;

Virginia Haviland, "The Travelogue Storybook of the Nineteenth Century," in *The Hewins Lectures 1947-1962*, edited by Siri Andrews (Boston: Horn Book, 1963), pp. 34-38.

Charles E. Carryl
(30 December 1841-3 July 1920)

Douglas Street
Texas A & M University

BOOKS: *The Stock Exchange Primer* (New York: Sears & Cole, 1882);

Davy And The Goblin, Or What Followed Reading "Alice's Adventures In Wonderland" (Boston: Ticknor, 1885);

The Admiral's Caravan (New York: Century, 1892);

Stories of the Sea (New York: Scribners, 1893);

The River Syndicate and Other Stories (New York & London: Harper, 1899);

Charades by an Idle Man (Boston: Little, Brown, 1911);

A Capital Ship; or The Walloping Window-blind (New York: Whittlesey House, 1963; London: Bodley Head, 1964).

The period in American literary history from 1880 to the turn of the twentieth century was a landmark era for children's literature. Nowhere was this more visible than in the realm of fiction for children. *St. Nicholas* and other influential children's periodicals presented wondrous new worlds and showcased many talented authors to eager juvenile readers. Among the authors whose works appeared in the pages of *St. Nicholas*, few could match the appeal of the slightly built stockbroker from New York, Charles Edward Carryl. Though forgotten by the young of today, Carryl, at the end of the last century, was hailed as the American Lewis Carroll, his nonsense classic *Davy And The Goblin* (1885), the *Alice In Wonderland* of America. The title was apt in that Carryl frankly acknowledged influence from the British Carroll, yet the work, though similar to the English one in its nonsensical nature, proved an original children's fantasy. Carryl's *Davy And The Goblin* expanded the realm of possibility in American fantasy for children when it first appeared in serial in 1884. Here was a complete piece of fiction in the Carrollian mode, yet not a copy, created by an American for an American public. Carryl's adeptness at wordplay and at creating memorable plots and characters is noteworthy.

Charles Edward Carryl wrote for his children and for himself; by trade he was a businessman and stockbroker who used his writing as a diversion. His interest in the business world came early, fostered partly by the work of his father, Nathan Taylor Carryl. The elder Carryl and his wife sent their son Charles, born in New York on 30 December 1841, to day school in the city while the family business prospered. Nathan Carryl earned enough money to enroll his son in the Irving Institute at Tarrytown, where he remained until the summer before his sixteenth birthday in 1857. The year closed with the young Carryl progressing rapidly up the business ladder, working as an officer and director of various railroad companies until 1872. In 1874 he landed a seat on the New York Stock Exchange, which he held for the next thirty-four years. From the 1850s through the 1870s the bulk of Carryl's writings were of the stock transfer-business memorandum variety.

In 1869 Carryl married Mary Wetmore, and the first of their two children was born four years later. The stockbroker turned family man, and with the influence of such imaginative children as his Guy (Guy Wetmore Carryl later became a notable writer on his own) and Constance, Carryl's storytelling soon began. Though the beginnings of Carryl's literary career were inauspicious—his first published work was the 1882 *Stock Exchange Primer*—he was soon thoroughly ensconced in a nonsense fantasy world that would, when it was introduced in *St. Nicholas*, elicit overwhelming approval from child readers.

The December 1884 issue of *St. Nicholas* brought before the youthful reading public the beginning of a tale destined to become one of the century's most widely praised. *Davy And The Goblin,*

Charles E. Carryl

Or What Followed Reading "Alice's Adventures in Wonderland" was written by Carryl for his son, Guy, to whom the work is dedicated. In the dedication the author laments:

> Dear little boy, upon these pages find
> The tangled fancies of thy father's mind,
> Born of the hours when thou, a little child,
> Throned on his knee in breathless rapture smiled,
> Hearing entranced the marvels that were told
> Of fay and goblin in the days of old.
> Would that the glamour of those cloudless days
> Might cheer thee still, what time the toilsome maze
> Of riper years hath banished fairy lore—
> And blithesome youth hath fled to come no more!

Though Guy was eleven, no longer "a little child," the author received great satisfaction in taking the little child within him and within all readers along with Davy and his Goblin mate on a "Believing Voyage" to meet a host of fantastic characters, including Mary Farina, the Cockalorum, the Hole-keeper, and the giant Badorful. After its successful serialization Ticknor published the novel in book form in autumn 1885.

The novel starts with a snowstorm raging outside one dreary Christmas Eve when Davy is eight. Davy curls up in a cozy chair by the fire and begins to read again of Alice's adventures in Wonderland. As the warmth of the fire and the smells of dinner cooking seem to relax him, he suddenly "discovered a little man perched upon that identical knob of the andiron, and smiling at him with all his might." This is the reader's introduction to the Goblin who will shortly take Davy to meet all manner of people and things. They climb aboard the long Dutch clock and sail out the window into a new Wonderland.

The plot line, loosely joined in many parts, is organized around the concept of the "Believing Voyage." Chapter one introduces the Goblin; chapter two elaborates "The Beginning of the Believing Voyage," and the final chapter, fourteen, brings readers to "The End of the Believing Voyage." This concept of Carryl's is directly tied to his lamentations in the dedication over the banishment of faerie and "blithesome youth" that has fled "to come no more!" In *Davy And The Goblin* one of Carryl's themes is that age does not matter when it comes to believing in wonders and wondrous beings. Carryl also pays homage to the greats of child lore by reintroducing Davy to Robinson Crusoe, Jack of the Beanstalk, Robin Hood, Sinbad, and others in comical situations. Davy is amazed when the Goblin informs him that they are at the house of Sinbad the Sailor:

> Davy looked around and saw an old man coming toward them across the lawn. He was dressed in a Turkish costume, and wore a large turban and red morocco slippers turned up at the toes like skates; and his white beard was so long that at every fourth step he trod upon it and fell flat on his face. . . .
>
> "This here Turk is the most reckless old story-teller that ever was born," said the Goblin, pointing with his thumb over his shoulder at Sinbad. "You can't believe half he tells you."
>
> "I'd like to hear one of his stories, for all that," said Davy.

Incidents of this sort always lead to rollicking adventures in which characters relate their life stories in prose or recite nonsense lyrics rivaling those of Lewis Carroll. In Carrollian fashion, *Davy And The Goblin* draws to a close with the hero stating his case before the Queen and her fairy court, growing in size to dwarf the courtly congregation, and disappearing from wonderland to find "himself curled up in the big easy-chair, with his dear old grandmother bending over him, and saying gently, 'Davy! Davy! Come and have some dinner, my dear!' "

In *Davy And The Goblin*, as in his later important work, *The Admiral's Caravan* (1892), Carryl's use of nonsense is noteworthy. It is undeniable that his creations were influenced by the nonsense stories of Lewis Carroll, yet Carryl was not merely an imitator. *Davy And The Goblin* and *The Admiral's Caravan* employ a technique of blending nonsense and reality that in modern terms might be considered cinematic. Unlike the more tightly structured Alice books, Carryl's works seem at times to melt from one scene into another as quickly as a camera's lens fades from one scene into focusing on another. The following passage is typical:

> "Don't you go with them!" shouted Davy, made really desperate by the Hole-keeper's danger. "They're nothing but a lot of molasses candy!"
>
> At this the king gave a frightful shriek, and, aiming a furious blow at Davy with his wand, rolled off the platform into the midst of the struggling crowd. The wand broke into a hundred pieces, and the air was instantly filled with a choking odor of pepper-

mint; then everything was wrapped in darkness, and Davy felt himself being whirled along, heels over head, through the air. Then there came a confused sound of bells and voices and he found himself running rapidly down a long street with the Goblin at his side.

Carryl's second children's novel, *The Admiral's Caravan*, ran in serial in *St. Nicholas* from November 1891 through May 1892, before Century published it in book form later in 1892. Although *Davy And The Goblin* was written for his children, Carryl composed this work to please himself. Though *The Admiral's Caravan* was popular with admirers of *Davy And The Goblin*, it eventually faded quietly into the back shelves of bookstores while *Davy* continued to sell respectably into the 1940s. Yet in some ways *The Admiral's Caravan* is the more intriguing of the two.

The plot focuses on Dorothy and her adventures commencing on Christmas Eve (this one snowless) with the statues in the lane who come alive and lead her on a nonsensical journey through another of Carryl's wonderlands. Her first adventure begins at the Ferry To Nowhere, where she encounters the Ferryman, a great stork who relates to her a verse "Ferry Tale" before she floats down the river on a sideboard and into the Tree-top Country. Dorothy also has adventures in Bob Scarlet's Garden (Bob is a larger than normal Robin Redbreast), the Toy Shop, and the Sizing Tower before "the Caravan comes home."

In *The Admiral's Caravan* nonsense takes precedence over action. There are instances in this story in which nonsense and wordplay seem to serve the author's whim, having little impact on the plot itself. Taken singly these passages afford the reader moments of amusement within the novel. Dorothy, for instance, comes across "a charming little cottage with vines trained about the latticed windows, and with a sign over the door, reading, THE OUTSIDE INN." As she pushes open the cottage door to investigate, she finds "there was no inside to the house, and she came out into the field again on the other side of the door." This wall was papered and curtained nicely "but there was a notice pasted up beside the door, reading—THE INN-SIDE OUT as if the rest of the house had gone out for a walk, and might be expected back at any time." It is precisely because of incongruities such as these that Carryl's stories were enjoyed. The absurdity of *The Admiral's Caravan* gave readers a distinctive entertainment, one eclipsed only

OR, WHAT FOLLOWED READING "ALICE'S ADVENTURES IN WONDERLAND."

BY CHARLES CARRYL.

CHAPTER I.

HOW THE GOBLIN CAME.

IT happened one Christmas eve, when Davy was about eight years old, and this is the way it came about.

That particular Christmas eve was a snowy one and a blowy one, and one generally to be remembered. In the city, where Davy lived, the storm played all manner of pranks, swooping down upon unwary old gentlemen and turning their umbrellas wrong side out, and sometimes blowing their hats quite out of sight. And in the country, where Davy had come to pass Christmas with his dear old grandmother, things were not much better; but here people were very wise about the weather, and staid indoors, huddled around great blazing wood fires; and the storm, finding no live game, buried up the roads and the fences, and such small-fry of houses as could readily be put out of sight, and howled and roared over the fields and through the trees in a fashion not to be forgotten.

Davy, being of the opinion that a snow-storm was a thing not to be wasted, had been out with his sled, trying to have a little fun with the weather; but presently, discovering that this particular storm was not friendly to little boys, he had retreated into the house, and having put his hat and his high shoes and his mittens by the kitchen fire to dry, he began to find his time hang heavily on his hands. He had wandered idly all over the house, and had tried how cold his nose could be made by holding it against the window-panes, and, I am sorry to say, had even been sliding down the balusters and teasing the cat; and at last, as evening was coming on, had curled himself up in the big easy-chair facing the fire, and had begun to read once more about the marvelous things that happened to little Alice in Wonderland. Then, as it grew darker, he laid aside the book and sat watching the blazing logs and listening to the solemn ticking of the high Dutch clock against the wall.

Then there stole in at the door a delicious odor of dinner cooking down-stairs—an odor so suggestive of roast chickens and baked potatoes and gravy and pie as to make any little boy's mouth

From the first installment in the serial publication of the fantasy Carryl wrote for his son, Guy
(St. Nicholas *magazine, December 1884*)

"THE ADMIRAL, MAKING A DESPERATE ATTEMPT TO GET A VIEW OF HIS LEGS THROUGH HIS SPY-GLASS."

Illustration by Reginald Birch for The Admiral's Caravan
(Baldwin Library, University of Florida Libraries)

by Carryl's earlier work. Judging from responses

of readers printed in *St. Nicholas* magazine after the novel's serialization, nineteenth-century America had rarely experienced such inventiveness from a native-born novelist.

At the time of his death in 1920, the works of Carryl were still in print and widely read. If Carryl is to be remembered for any one contribution to American children's literature, it should be that he, more than any other American children's fantasist of the past century, found a key to successful nonsense fantasy so long thought the exclusive property of the British. He did justice to the title given him of "America's Lewis Carroll," for to the children of turn-of-the-century America, *Davy And The Goblin* remained, as Earnest Calkins remembers, "the authentic 'Alice in Wonderland of America.'"

References:

Brian Attebery, *The Fantasy Tradition in American Literature* (Bloomington: Indiana University Press, 1980);

Earnest Elmo Calkins, "St. Nicholas," *Saturday Review of Literature,* 22 (4 May 1940): 7-14;

Alice M. Jordan, *From Rollo to Tom Sawyer And Other Papers* (Boston: Horn Book, 1948);

Mary Jane Roggenbuck, "*St. Nicholas Magazine:* A Study of the Impact and Historical Influence of the Editorship of Mary Mapes Dodge," unpublished dissertation, University of Michigan (Library Science), 1976.

Rebecca Sophia Clarke
(Sophie May)
(22 February 1833-16 August 1906)

Carol A. Doll
University of South Carolina

BOOKS: *Little Prudy* (Boston: Lee & Shepard, 1864);

Little Prudy's Sister Susy (Boston: Lee & Shepard, 1864);

Little Prudy's Captain Horace (Boston: Lee & Shepard, 1864);

Little Prudy's Cousin Grace (Boston: Lee & Shepard, 1864);

Little Prudy's Fairy Book (Boston: Lee & Shepard, 1865);

Little Prudy's Dotty Dimple (Boston: Lee & Shepard, 1865);

Dotty Dimple at Her Grandmother's (Boston: Lee & Shepard, 1868);

Dotty Dimple at Home (Boston: Lee & Shepard, 1868);

Dotty Dimple Out West (Boston: Lee & Shepard, 1869);

Dotty Dimple at Play (Boston: Lee & Shepard, 1869);

Dotty Dimple at School (Boston: Lee & Shepard, 1869);

Dotty Dimple's Flyaway (Boston: Lee & Shepard, 1869);

Little Folks Astray (Boston: Lee & Shepard, 1870);

Prudy Keeping House (Boston: Lee & Shepard, 1870);

Aunt Madge's Story (Boston: Lee & Shepard, 1871);

The Doctor's Daughter (Boston: Lee & Shepard, 1871);

Little Grandmother (Boston: Lee & Shepard, 1872);

Little Grandfather (Boston: Lee & Shepard, 1873);

Miss Thistledown (Boston: Lee & Shepard, 1873);

Our Helen (Boston: Lee & Shepard, 1874);

The Asbury Twins (Boston: Lee & Shepard, 1875);

Flaxie Frizzle (Boston: Lee & Shepard, 1876);

Doctor Papa (Boston: Lee & Shepard, 1877);

Quinnebasset Girls (Boston: Lee & Shepard, 1877);

Little Pitchers (Boston: Lee & Shepard, 1878);

Drone's Honey (Boston: Lee & Shepard, 1878); republished as *Her Friend's Lover* (Boston: Lee & Shepard, 1893);

The Twin Cousins (Boston: Lee & Shepard, 1880);

Janet, a Poor Heiress (Boston: Lee & Shepard, 1882);

Kittyleen (Boston: Lee & Shepard, 1884);

Flaxie Growing Up (Boston: Lee & Shepard, 1884);

The Campion Diamonds (Boston: Lee & Shepard, 1887);

The Old Quinnebasset (Boston: Lee & Shepard, 1891);

Wee Lucy, Little Prudy's "Wee Croodlin' Doo" (Boston: Lee & Shepard, 1894);

Jimmy Boy (Boston: Lee & Shepard, 1895);

Kyzie Dunlee, "A Golden Girl" (Boston: Lee & Shepard, 1895);

Pauline Wyman (Boston: Lee & Shepard, 1898);

Wee Lucy's Secret (Boston: Lee & Shepard, 1899);

Jimmy, Lucy, and All (Boston: Lee & Shepard, 1900);

Lucy in Fairyland (Boston: Lee & Shepard, 1901);

Joy Bells: A Quinnebasset Story (Boston: Lee & Shepard, 1903).

OTHER: *The Horn of Plenty of Home Poems and Home Pictures,* preface by Clarke (Boston: Gill, 1876);

"Joe," in *Plucky Boys,* Business Boys Library, volume 3 (Boston: Lothrop, 1884);

"A Christmas Breeze," in *A Christmas Breeze and Other Stories for Young Folks* (Boston: Lothrop, 1886).

PERIODICAL PUBLICATIONS: "How I Happened to Marry," *Harper's New Monthly Magazine,* 34 (April 1867): 656-660;

"King's Cup and Cake," *Atlantic Monthly,* 63 (April 1889): 544-549.

Rebecca Sophia Clarke was one of the first authors of the nineteenth century to abandon the moralistic, gloomy style favored by children's authors of that era. In her works the moral and religious elements are more subdued and her children break out of the rigid good-and-evil dichotomy of the earlier writers. Clarke's fictional children misbehave, fight, argue, are punished, and, in general, act more like real children than characters of other authors.

Born in Norridgewock, Maine, on 22 February 1833, Rebecca Clarke came from a well-established family which traced its lineage to pioneer settlers of the Massachusetts Colony and soldiers who fought in the Revolutionary War. She was one of four daughters of Asa and Sophia Bates Clarke. Rebecca Clarke was educated in Norridgewock's public schools and privately tutored in Latin and Greek. A journal she kept as a child details daily events of attending school, church services, and evening lectures. The entry for Thursday, 22 February 1844 states: "It is my birthday today. I am eleven years old and my father has given me a 25-cent piece. I am much pleased with it." She also writes on several occasions of having a "pleasant time" at school. Overall, the journal projects the image of a happy, bright, active girl. As a child Clarke also enjoyed sewing small paper books and writing stories to fill them. She had a talent for rhyming, which her mother discouraged, but she continued to write stories for her own amusement as she grew older.

Rebecca Clarke is reported to have been a beautiful woman, with black curly hair and deep blue eyes. More important, several sources indicate she was a friendly, outgoing, generous, well-liked person, sincerely interested in her town and the people around her. All information about Clarke in the rather limited biographical material available is unfailingly positive, especially when quoting her fellow townspeople or surviving relatives.

She wanted to be a teacher and did not intend to pursue a career as a writer. In 1851 she joined an older married sister in Evansville, Indiana, and taught school. She is reported to have been a successful teacher, although increasing deafness soon forced her to retire from teaching and return to Maine.

She and her sister Sarah, who wrote children's books using the pseudonym Penn Shirley, lived together in a large brick house with stately columns and a spiral staircase, on a large lot on the bank of the Kennebec River in Norridgewock. Together they presented the town with a brick building for a public library, which is still in use today.

When she was twenty-eight, Clarke began seriously to consider writing as a career when a friend asked her to write for his Memphis, Tennessee, newspaper. When she decided to write, Clarke selected a pseudonym. She chose Sophie because it was her middle name, and as she tried to come up with a last name she thought, "I may write and I may not." So she became Sophie May.

Once she started, Clarke wrote several short stories for the *Little Pilgrim* and the *Congregationalist*. Some of these were collected and published as a book, *Little Prudy*, in 1864. Prudy Parlin, at the start of the book, is three years old. *Little Prudy* describes the summer adventures she has with her sister Susy, cousins Grace and Horace, and several aunts, uncles, other relatives, and friends. Their adventures are continued in *Little Prudy's Sister Susy, Little Prudy's Captain Horace, Little Prudy's Cousin Grace, Little Prudy's Fairy Book,* and *Little Prudy's Dotty Dimple.* Together these six volumes comprise the Little Prudy series.

The series records in meticulous detail the daily life of Prudy and her relatives and friends as they go from one adventure to the next. Prudy, Susy, and Grace trespass while picking strawberries and flee in terror from Mr. Judkins. Susy and her

PRUDY'S IRONING — Page 147

Frontispiece for Little Prudy's Cousin Grace, *the fourth book of six in Clarke's first series (Baldwin Library, University of Florida Libraries)*

friends form a club called the Ruby Seal and vow to never marry. Cousin Harry and Susy's friend Mahla die of illnesses. Prudy gets sick, but recovers. Aunt Madge gets married.

The stories are told with humor and in a light style. In *Little Prudy's Dotty Dimple,* Prudy's sister, nicknamed Dotty Dimple, is born. The new addition to the household disrupts life:

> Mrs. Parlin did not approve of cradles, and the nurse had a fashion of rolling the baby in a blanket and laying her down in all sorts of places. One day little Prudy flung herself into the big rocking chair, not noticing the small bundle which lay there.
>
> It was feared at first that the baby was crushed to death; but when she was heard to cry, Mrs. Parlin said, "We have great cause for thankfulness. So far as I can judge, it is only her *nose* which is broken!"
>
> But the doctor pronounced the baby's bones as sound as ever.
>
> "It is only little Miss Prudy whose nose is out of joint," added he.
>
> Prudy ran to look in the glass, but could not see anything the matter with her nose, or anything that looked like "a joint." But after this she was as careful as a child of her heedless age can be not to injure her tender sister. She never again saw a silk handkerchief without shaking it to make sure there was not a baby under it.

The religious tone common in children's books of the era is not lacking in Clarke's books, but it is not overpowering and all pervasive. In *Little Prudy,* for example, Mrs. Parlin discovers three-year-old Prudy on the highest beam of a house under construction. "Her trembling lips moved a little, but it was in prayer; she knew that only God could save the precious one." Jingling keys attract Prudy's attention and she quickly climbs down to join in a promised snack of crimson jellies and fruitcake.

Clarke's fictional children talk, think, and imagine like real children. They misuse or mispronounce words: "condemned" milk, "smashed" potatoes, and "Sabber" school. Prudy explains the moon by saying, "It's a silver ball as big as a house, and there's a man lives there, and I've seen him making up faces."

Susy forbids Prudy to go into their mother's room after Dotty Dimple is born because Prudy is crying so hard. " 'Poh!' replied three-year-old Prudy, twinkling off the tears; 'Yes, I can neither.

I won't go *crying* in! I didn't hurt me velly bad. I'm weller now!' "

In *North America Review* (January 1866) T. W. Higginson reviewed *Little Prudy* enthusiastically: "Genius comes in with 'Little Prudy.' Compared with her all other book-children are cold creations of literature only; she alone is the real thing. All the quaintness of childhood, its originality, its tenderness, and its teasing,—its infinite, unconscious drollery, the serious earnestness of its fun, the fun of its seriousness, the natural religion of its plays, and the delicious oddity of its prayers,—all these waited for dear little Prudy to embody them.... the rare gift of delineating childhood is hers [Sophie May's]; and may the line of Little Prudy go on to the end of the earth." The majority of other contemporary reviews also approved of Clarke's work. For example, the critic for the *Nation* (12 December 1867) wrote: "We have heretofore had occasion to praise the author of the Little Prudy Stories; we can praise her again as the author of 'Dotty Dimple.' Miss May succeeds in making her

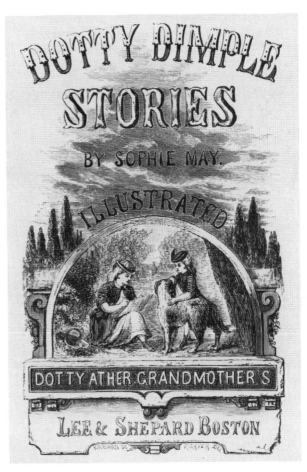

Engraved title page for one of Clarke's books about Little Prudy's sister (Baldwin Library, University of Florida Libraries)

children talk like children, and often carries on their conversation with no little humor."

Little Prudy's Dotty Dimple introduced the title character of Clarke's next series of six books, published between 1868 and 1870. Whereas Prudy is a normal child who tries to be good, Dotty Dimple is more imaginative and mischievous and sometimes deliberately misbehaves. As a toddler, Dotty Dimple coerces Little Prudy into taking her to Sunday school. There Dotty Dimple hears the Bible verse "Thy word is a lamp unto my feet, and a light unto my path." This inspires a rather unexpected chain of events:

> [Dotty] had brought from the kitchen a "Tom Thumb lamp" and a bunch of matches.
>
> Without a word she seated herself on the floor, behind her sister, and drew off her shoes and stockings. She looked for a moment at her little pink toes, then rubbed the whole bunch of matches on the carpet, saying to herself, "A lamp to my feet."
>
> But, somehow, the lamp would not light itself. Dotty did not know how to turn back the chimney, and, though there was certainly blaze enough in the matches, it did not catch the wick. It leaped forward and caught the skirt of Prudy's dress.
>
> "You're burnin' afire! You're burnin' afire," shouted Dotty, dancing around her sister. Prudy now felt the heat, and screamed too, bringing her mother and [her sister] Norah to the spot at once. The flames were soon smothered in a rug, and so Prudy's life was mercifully saved.
>
> It was sometime before any one understood what Dotty had been trying to do with a light.
>
> "I was just only a-puttin' a lamp to my feet," sobbed she. "I learned it to Sabber school."
>
> But the little one's rare tears were soon dried by a romp with [her dog] Zip out of doors.

Nor is Dotty averse to some adventuring. In *Dotty Dimple Out West*, Dotty and her relatives visit a coal mine. There Horace and Dotty go to "sniggle for eels." After a lengthy wait, Horace hooks an eel: "Dotty gave a little start of disgust but had the presence of mind not to scream at sight of the ugly creature, because she had heard Horace say girls always did scream at eels." On the way home Dotty and Horace discuss the event:

"Did you notice," asked Dotty, "how I acted? I never screamed at that eel once."

"You're a lady, Dotty. I don't know but you might be trusted to go trouting. I never dared take Prudy, she is troubled so with palpitation of the tongue."

In *Dotty Dimple at School* Dotty's major battle is to avoid whispering. The first day at school Dotty sits next to Sarah "Tate" Penny. From that time on the two great friends spend a good deal of time visiting each day. One day Dotty makes a real effort not to talk. After an unsuccessful beginning she renews her resolve not to whisper, shaking her head "no" while Tate continues to talk:

> The more Tate talked, the more she shook it; and while it was going like a tree in the wind, and she was bending on her friend a feebly furious scowl, Miss Parker drew near.
>
> "Why, Dotty, I am astonished," said she, with marked displeasure; "what makes you behave so strangely today? You keep jerking your neck as if you meant to break it off. . . ."

After further mishaps and incidents over the course of the book, Dotty and her teacher come to understand each other better. Miss Parker realizes her own inattention in the classroom enables Dotty and Tate to whisper together, and Dotty learns how to better control her tongue.

Contemporary critics continued to praise Clarke's work. In June 1869, the *Catholic World* reviewed *Dotty Dimple at School* with praise: "for children's stories, [Clarke's books] are almost perfect. They teach important lessons without making the children feel that they are taught them, or giving them an inclination to skip over those parts. If the little folks get hold of these books, they will be certain to read them, and ever after count Miss Dotty Dimple and dear Little Prudy among their very best friends."

Clarke's only praise did not come from reviewers. The 15 July 1871 issue of the *American Literary Gazette and Publishers' Circular* identifies Clarke as the author of "the brightest, sprightliest child-literature in print. They are books that grown people as well as children enjoy, and their popularity is indicated by the fact that their sale has reached three hundred thousand copies."

The last title of the Dotty Dimple series centers on Katie "Flyaway" Clifford, younger sister of the Parlins' Indiana cousins Horace and Grace, and serves as introduction to Little Prudy's Flyaway series of six titles published between 1870 and 1873. "Her hair was soft and flying like cornsilk, and when the wind took it you would think it meant to blow it off like a dandelion top. She was so light and breezy and so little for her age that her father said 'they must put a cent in her pocket to keep her from flying away'; so, after that, the family began to call her *Flyaway*." In addition to the title character, this series features the Parlins and Cliffords in continuing adventures as the children grow older.

Little Prudy's Flyaway series does include two "historical" titles—*Little Grandmother* (1872) and *Little Grandfather* (1873). These books tell of the childhood experiences of Grandma and Grandpa Parlin, Prudy and Dotty's grandparents. Except for the change in setting, the style and types of incidents are similar to Clarke's more contemporary works.

Although new titles continued to receive praise, a few reviewers were totally negative about Clarke's work. *Scribner's Monthly* (February 1871) described *Little Folks Astray* of Little Prudy's Flyaway series as "mere negation. It is an insipid, insipidly told."

Clarke's fourth series, published from 1876 to 1884, stars Flaxie Frizzle and does not feature the Parlins and Cliffords from earlier titles. Nevertheless, the same style is used to portray daily life of Flaxie Frizzle and people connected with her:

> Her name was Mary Gray, but they called her Flaxie Frizzle. She had light curly hair and a curly nose; that is, her nose curled up at the end a wee bit, just enough to make it look cunning. Her cheeks were rosy red, and she was so fat that when Mr. Snow, the postmaster, saw her, he said, "How d'ye do, Mother Bunch?"
>
> What kind of child was she? Well, I don't want to tell, but I suppose I shall have to. She wasn't gentle and timid and sweet, like you little darlings,—O, not like you; and Mrs. Prim, who went to the house a great deal visiting, said she was "dreadful." But somehow her father loved her, and her Aunt Jane loved her, and so did her sister and her brother, and everybody else that ever saw her and heard her speak. Even Mrs. Prim loved her, though Mrs. Prim said she "ran wild"; and I suppose that was true.
>
> She might have been a better child if the whole household had not petted her, and I laughed at all she said and did. There was no one to control her, for when she was two years old, just learning to talk and say, "I's

Engraved title page for Clarke's 1871 book in the series devoted to Little Prudy's cousin Katie "Flyaway" Clifford (Baldwin Library, University of Florida Libraries)

two-uz-*ould*," her dear mamma was called away to heaven.

Having set the stage in Flaxie Frizzle, Clarke narrates the events that occur in Flaxie's life through early adolescence in *Flaxie Growing Up* (1884). This series follows essentially the same pattern as the earlier works.

By 1884 Lee and Shepard had published twenty-eight different Rebecca Clarke titles. J. C. Derby identified Clarke as author of "the most popular juvenile books published in this country at the present time." In spite of the fact that Clarke continued to receive many highly favorable reviews, some contemporary critics were not entirely pleased. A review of *Little Pitchers* (1878) in the Flaxie Frizzle series appeared in the January 1879 issue of *Atlantic Monthly.* "We say very properly that these are . . . stories about children for parents to read and laugh over. . . . We do not think . . . that children or grown people find the ungrammatical nonsense in print so very charming; but for all that these little Yankee children and their Western kinsfolk are a sunny, happy-go-lucky set, and we cannot frown on their delinquencies very seriously."

Clarke's next and last series of six volumes for "little folks" returned to the familiar character of Little Prudy. In this series, published between 1894 and 1901, the featured characters are Prudy's children, Kyzie Dunlee, Jimmy, and Wee Lucy. In her usual style, Clarke recounts the daily activities of the children, with Prudy providing the help and guidance her own mother gave in earlier works. In August 1901, Caroline M. Hewins wrote for *Library Journal,* "In one list the 'Dotty Dimple' and 'Flaxie Frizzle' books are recommended for the third-grade reader. Children who are in this grade cannot read the ungrammatical baby-talk easily, and if they could it would demoralize their English."

In addition to these five series for "little folks," Clarke wrote six books for teenage girls between 1871 and 1891. Referred to as the Quinnebasset or the Maidenhood series, these books are chronicles of the daily life and travels of young girls and their friends. They were well received, but never rivaled popularity of Clarke's works for children. She also wrote several adult novels, including *Drone's Honey* (1878), *The Campion Diamonds* (1887), and *Pauline Wyman* (1898).

Rebecca Clarke died at home on 16 August 1906, when she was seventy-three years old. She had been afflicted with a "nervous trouble" for two years. Hemorrhages were given as the cause of death.

Twentieth-century critics are not usually as lavishly laudatory of Clarke's work as were contemporary critics. In *From Rollo to Tom Sawyer and Other Papers* (1942), Alice M. Jordon summarizes quite nicely: "Sophie May was not given to overmuch moralizing and she made a real effort to bestow individuality upon her children—Prudy, Dotty Dimple, Flaxie Frizzle, and Flyaway—all pet names. The incidents in the uneventful lives of the Parlin children are those commonly found in books for little girls, accidents and misunderstandings, mischievous pranks and willful disobedience, the marriage of a favorite aunt, a visit to New York. It is hard now to grasp the reason for the widespread affection for these books until we contrast the children in them with the children of earlier stories. Then it becomes evident that Sophie May made an effort to get away from the type of impossibly exemplary children, and attempted to give personality to her children and draw them as they are, in good moods and in bad."

Perhaps Clarke's greatest skill was her ability to portray children realistically. Her writing reflects her knowledge and enjoyment of children. And there is evidence of her ability and how she came by it in the available biographical material. One Maine resident describes her memory of Rebecca Clarke's books: "I recall my grandmother's tone as she interrupted the reading (which she enjoyed as much as did the little girls) to remark 'Now isn't that just like children.' I wondered, sometimes, why she should sound surprised. I know, now, that the children in the rare children's books of her childhood were not in the least like the real article for our Sophie May was one of the pioneers in writing books about real children." Henrietta Wood of Clarke's hometown wrote, "The characters in her books were largely taken from her nieces and nephews, though she listened to the prattle of any child she chanced to meet and reproduced the quaint and funny sayings, making real children of them. She did more than any other writer of her day to change the style from the stiff, proper, always perfect children of the earlier period to the loving, rollicking, teasing, but always dear and lovable ones of real life."

Evidence of Clarke's fondness for and understanding of children is also apparent in this reminiscence by her niece, Elizabeth Morse, who was the model for Little Prudy. Remembering her aunt fondly, Morse said, "It was sixty years ago that I spent the summer at Norridgewock, so my recollections of the visit are rather hazy. We all adored Aunt Becca, who told us the most delightful stories, and our housekeeping in the seat in the willow tree was a constant joy. This, with paper dolls, croquet, picnics in the pine woods and jumping on the hay in the barn, filled the happy but uneventful days."

Richard Darling remarked, "Rebecca Clarke (Sophie May), too, was a writer in the realistic vein who, though surely not the genius Thomas Wentworth Higginson declared her to be, was by no means to be despised. If some of her stories seem to be more about children than for them, there is no denying that the children are real. Her greatest fault may well have been that she wrote too much, so that her books showed evidence of haste. Yet, they were extremely popular."

References:

George L. Austin, "Lee and Shepard," *Bay State*

DLB 42

Palmer Cox

Monthly, 2 (March 1885): 309-316;

Richard L. Darling, *The Rise of Children's Book Reviewing in America, 1865-1881* (New York: Bowker Company, 1968);

J. C. Derby, *Fifty Years Among Authors, Books and Publishers* (New York: Carleton, 1884), pp. 524-525;

Caroline M. Hewins, "Book Reviews, Book Lists, and Articles on Children's Reading: Are They of Practical Value to the Children's Librarian?," *Library Journal*, 26 (August 1901): 57-62;

Alice M. Jordan, *From Rollo to Tom Sawyer and Other Papers* (Boston: Horn Book, 1942), pp. 35-37;

"Lee and Shepard, Boston," *American Literary Gazette and Publishers' Circular*, 17 (15 July 1871): 149-151;

The Maine Writers' Research Club, *Just Maine Folks* (Lewiston: Journal Printshop, 1924), pp. 143-150;

Annie Russell Marble, *Pen Names and Personalities* (New York: Appleton, 1930), p. 169;

"Sophie May (Rebecca Clarke, 1833-1906)," *Maine Library Bulletin* (January 1929): 97-101;

Gertrude E. Upton, "Best Reading for the Young," *Public Libraries*, 6 (February 1901): 88-101;

Henrietta Danforth Wood, *Early Days of Norridgewock* (Skowhegan, Maine: Skowhegan Press, 1941), pp. 84-87.

Palmer Cox

(28 April 1840-24 July 1924)

Charlotte Spivack
University of Massachusetts

BOOKS: *Squibs of California; or, Every-day Life Illustrated* (Hartford, Conn.: Mutual Publishing, 1874); republished as *Comic Yarns in Verse, Prose and Picture* (Philadelphia: Hubbard, 1889);

Hans von Pelter's Trip to Gotham, in Pen and Pencil (New York: Art Printing, 1876);

How Columbus Found America, in Pen and Pencil (New York: Art Printing, 1877);

That Stanley! (New York: Art Printing, 1878);

The Brownies, Their Book (New York: Century, 1887; London: Unwin, 1887);

Queer People with Paws and Claws, and Their Kweer Kapers (Philadelphia: Hubbard, 1888; London & Sydney: Griffith, Farran, Okedon & Welsh, 1889);

Queer People with Wings and Stings, and Their Kweer Kapers (Philadelphia: Hubbard, 1888; London & Sydney: Griffith, Farran, Okedon & Welsh, 1889);

Queer People Such as Goblins, Giants, Merry-Men and Monarchs and Their Kweer Kapers (Philadelphia: Hubbard, 1889);

Another Brownie Book (New York: Century, 1890; London: Unwin, 1890);

The Brownies at Home (New York: Century, 1893; London: Unwin, 1893);

The Brownies Around the World (New York: Century, 1894; London: Unwin, 1894);

The Brownies in Fairyland: A Cantata in Two Acts, lyrics and music by Malcolm Douglas (New York: Harms, 1894; enlarged, New York & London: Century, 1925);

The Brownies Through the Union (New York: Century, 1895; London: Unwin, 1895);

Brownie Year Book (New York: McLoughlin, 1895);

Frontier Humor, Some Rather Ludicrous Experiences That Befell Myself and My Acquaintances Among Frontier Characters Before I Made the Acquaintance of My Esteemed Friends "The Brownies" (Philadelphia: Hubbard, 1895);

The Brownies Abroad (New York: Century, 1899; London: Unwin, 1899);

The Brownies in the Philippines (New York: Century, 1904; London: Unwin, 1904);

Brownie Clown of Brownie Town (New York: Century, 1908);

The Brownies' Latest Adventures (New York: Century, 1910; London: Unwin, 1910);

The Brownies Many More Nights (New York: Century, 1913);

The Brownies and Prince Florimel; or, Brownieland, Fairyland, and Demonland (New York: Century, 1918);

Bugaboo Bill, the Giant (New York: Farrar, Straus & Giroux, 1971).

PLAY PRODUCTION: *Palmer Cox's Brownies*, New York, Fourteenth Street Theater, 12 November 1894, 100 performances.

OTHER: *The Palmer Cox Brownie Primer*, text by Mary C. Judd, graded and edited by Montrose J. Moses (New York: Century, 1906)—includes illustrations by Cox and selections from his Brownie books.

PERIODICAL PUBLICATION: "The Origin of the Brownies," *Ladies' Home Journal*, 9 (November 1892).

Known to young readers all over the world as creator of the Brownies, Palmer Cox was one of the most popular American writers for children in the last two decades of the nineteenth century. A professional illustrator as well as a writer, he com-

Palmer Cox

bined his talents to produce thirteen books about the Brownies, his own delightful adaptation of the traditional figures from folklore. He sketched them all with spindly legs, tapered feet, round paunches, and no necks, but in a variety of postures and garments and with highly individualized facial expressions. He told their lively adventures in lilting tetrameter rhymed couplets, fun to hear and easy to recite. He thus made them at once pictorially and verbally memorable to his youthful audience.

Cox, the son of Michael and Sarah Miller Cox, was born in Canada. During his childhood in Granby, a small community settled by Scotch immigrants, he listened to folktales about the mischievous sprites called Brownies, who lived in the Grampian mountains of Scotland. As a child he displayed a distinct talent for drawing and decorated his school books and his bedroom walls with sketches of Brownies. After completing his schooling at the Granby Academy, he left for San Francisco, where he worked for a railroad and as a ship carpenter while trying to begin a career in journalism. Although he drew political cartoons for the local newspapers and had a collection of short pieces about life in California published in 1874, he felt dissatisfied with his achievements and moved to New York City. The turning point in his career occurred there when he contributed a poem, "The Wasp and the Bee," to *St. Nicholas*, the most prestigious children's journal of its time. Then aged forty, Palmer Cox began the career that would continue the rest of his long life, that of writing widely and almost exclusively for children.

The Brownies first appeared in print in 1880 in a series of pictures drawn by Cox to illustrate a poem on the alphabet by Arthur Gilman. Each letter of the alphabet is held by a different Brownie. The first poem written and illustrated by Cox himself about his Brownies was "The Brownies' Ride," published in *St. Nicholas* in 1883. Since he wanted to write a continuing series of poems for the magazine, he decided to develop further adventures of the Brownies. Over the next thirty years these illustrated verse narratives would expand not only as a standard feature of both *St. Nicholas* and the *Ladies' Home Journal* but also into thirteen published volumes, beginning in 1887 with *The Brownies, Their Book* and ending in 1918 with a book based on a stage adaptation of their adventures.

Although Cox's little figures were drawn from the folktales he had heard in his youth, he modified their nature and adapted them to the nineteenth-century American scene. He drastically diminished the supernatural element in their tradition, retaining only such incidental features as their need to disappear from human haunts at the break of day. They also use their mystic art to replace what they take and repair what they break, but the art also requires industry for its effectiveness. They cannot work miracles. Cox also made his Brownies more gregarious and more inclined to travel than their counterparts in folklore who tended to remain singly by the hearthside of an adopted family. Whereas folklore creatures were also occasionally given to malicious mischief, Cox's Brownies are entirely good-natured and wholly without malice.

Each of the published story collections began with a foreword describing the Brownies' habits: "BROWNIES, like fairies and goblins, are imaginary little sprites, who are supposed to delight in harmless pranks and helpful deeds. They work and sport while weary households sleep, and never allow themselves to be seen by mortal eyes." In per-

THE BROWNIES' RIDE.

By Palmer Cox.

ONE night a cunning brownie band
Was roaming through a farmer's land,
And while the rogues went prying round,
The farmer's mare at rest they found;

And peeping through the stable-door,
They saw the harness that she wore:
The whip was hanging on the wall,
Old Mag was grinding in the stall;

Opening illustration and verse of Cox's first published work about the Brownies from St. Nicholas *magazine, February 1883 (Baldwin Library, University of Florida Libraries)*

sonality they are an appealing blend of sound morality and spirited fun. They enjoy being helpful and neither expect nor want any reward for their assistance. Their motto is "Do good for goodness' sake always, / Not for reward on earth, or praise." Their world is filled with exuberant play and laughter and is devoid of violence and suffering. It was Cox's belief, expressed in a 1916 interview with Joyce Kilmer, that there should be no death or pain in children's literature: "The children will find pain and suffering enough as they go on throughout life. The Brownies, you know, never give pain, nor do they ever suffer real pain. They are often in danger, but they always escape. I think that every story or poem for children should leave a pleasant impression on its reader's mind, should even make him want to commit it to memory."

Cox also individualized his Brownies and engaged them in activities of contemporary interest. Distinctive in appearance and behavior, individual Brownies included the Dude, the Irishman, the Chinaman, the policeman, the cowboy, and others. The Dude was especially popular. Based on a well-known American type, he was fashionably dressed with silk top hat, swallow-tailed coat, monocle, and walking stick. Brownie adventures were often based on recent events and discoveries. Brownies were among the first to ride bicycles, drive automobiles, and fly airplanes. As early as 1893 they were building their own airship. They visited the newly constructed Brooklyn Bridge and the Columbian Exposition in Chicago. Shortly after the annexation of the Philippines, they traveled to those islands. Among their number on that trip was a "rough rider" Brownie modeled on Theodore Roosevelt, hero of the Philippine campaign and an ardent fan of Cox's Brownies.

In the twenty-four stories contained in *The Brownies, Their Book* (1887) the lively sprites take part in a variety of activities of interest to children. They play tennis and baseball, ride horseback, ice-skate and roller-skate, bicycle and toboggan, visit a circus and a menagerie, and even move a beehive. The *New York Times* reviewer was delighted with their escapades: "long live the American elfkinship, the Palmer Cox Brownie." *Another Brownie Book* followed in 1890, with a special section for older children called "Brownies in the Academy," in which readers learn about such scientific subjects as phrenology and stereopticons. The third book in the series, *The Brownies at Home* (1893), collects a series of poems Cox had written for the *Ladies' Home Journal.* Together they form a seasonal narrative that includes each month of the year, moving from the January sleigh ride and the February valentines on to the December story of choosing a Christmas tree.

The next few books in the series find the Brownies traveling. In *The Brownies Around the World* (1894) they cross the Atlantic ocean on a raft to visit several European countries as well as parts of the Orient and the polar regions. With a full chapter for each country visited, this book has much of historical and literary interest about places such as London Bridge and the dungeon prison of Chillon. In *The Brownies Through the Union* (1895) each chapter is devoted to the story of one state. *The Brownies Abroad* (1899) continues the travel adventures, this time organized into episodes rather than focused on countries. *The Brownies in the Philippines* (1904) concentrates on the islands where the Brownies have exciting encounters with tigers, flying fish, and an army of ants. Cox did research abroad in order to gather accurate material for each of these travel books.

The last three books in the series are more explicitly didactic in purpose than the earlier ones. The Brownies are at home again in *Brownie Clown of Brownie Town* (1908), *The Brownies' Latest Adventures* (1910), and *The Brownies Many More Nights* (1913), and their many good deeds now seem more important than their sense of sheer merriment. Cox's last published story concerning the Brownies appeared in *St. Nicholas* in 1914 and was called "The Brownies and the Railroad."

The Brownies also made their mark on the American theatrical scene. Cox wrote a cantata, *The Brownies in Fairyland* (1894), which was produced successfully by children's groups and published in pamphlet and later book form. He also wrote a play in three acts, *Palmer Cox's Brownies*, which opened in 1894 at Fourteenth Street Theater in New York. Billed as a musical extravaganza, it ran for a hundred consecutive performances, then went on tour for five years, playing in Canada and in England as well as in major cities all over the United States. The plot concerns the marriage of the Queen of Fairies to the adopted son of the King of the Brownies. The obvious obstacle of an all-human cast did not diminish the effectiveness of stage presentation, which was enormously enhanced by a flying ballet and other acrobatic feats. Praised by reviewers, the play was later published

CONTENTS.

Cox's table of contents for The Brownies, Their Book *(Baldwin Library, University of Florida Libraries)*

as *The Brownies and Prince Florimel; or, Brownieland, Fairyland, and Demonland* (1918).

Although Cox is primarily remembered for his Brownie books, he did write other stories for children. In the 1880s he produced a series of three "queer people" books designed to teach children about the world of nonhuman creatures: *Queer People with Paws and Claws* (1888), *Queer People with Wings and Stings* (1888), and *Queer People Such as Goblins, Giants, Merry-Men and Monarchs and Their Kweer Kapers* (1889). In addition to the Brownie stories he wrote several short pieces for *St. Nicholas*, and in *Harper's Young People* several illustrated poems, mostly about animals, appeared. One of the stories appearing in an 1880 issue of *St. Nicholas* was *Bugaboo Bill, the Giant,* which was published in book form in 1971 with illustrations by William Curtis Holdsworth.

In one book, Cox played the pedagogue. *The Palmer Cox Brownie Primer* (1906) is a child's how-to-read book, with carefully graded selections from Cox's books, text by Mary C. Judd, and a vocabulary with a pronunciation key. It was enthusiastically received as an educationally sound enterprise. A second edition appeared in 1907 and it was reprinted more than fifteen times through 1930.

In one sense Palmer Cox was the Walt Disney of the nineteenth century. In anticipation of twentieth-century techniques of commercial art, he used the Brownie figures in pamphlets advertising over forty different commercial articles. The cheerful sprites helped to sell cups and spoons, carpets and wallpaper, stationery and jewelry, crackers and biscuits. Their catchy couplets extolled the virtues of Ivory soap, Pond's extract, and Jersey coffee. Cox was thus a pioneer in taking subjects from one area, children's art, and introducing them into other forms.

Cox was remarkably successful for his time. His Brownie books sold over a million copies during his lifetime, and his popularity continued after his death. The year 1929 produced more royalties than had any of the four years immediately preceding his death. Some of his books were republished in the 1960s, in attractive Dover editions.

When he retired as a wealthy man to his hometown of Granby, Canada, Cox built a medieval-style Brownie castle with seventeen rooms, six stairways, and a four-storied octagonal tower with battlements. A special window for Brownies was featured at the foot of one staircase, and a Brownie flag flew from the tower. Children from all over the world wrote letters to him, and many visited him at the castle. A friendly man, he always liked

Front cover for one of the three "Queer People" books Cox produced in the late 1880s (Baldwin Library, University of Florida Libraries)

the company of children and delighted in their visits. He was described by a contemporary as "affable, hearty, and sympathetic, a lover of children, and fond of out-of-door sports." On his eighty-first birthday, he was honored with a public concert, complete with a Brownie band in costume. He died at Brownie Castle on 24 July 1924. On his tombstone a fitting tribute summarizes his achievement: "In creating the Brownies, he bestowed a priceless heritage on childhood."

Cox's enormous success was reflected in the many obituaries which honored him at his death. The *New York Times* item read: "It is doubtful whether any fashion in children's literature has ever swept the country so completely as Brownies took possession of American childhood in the early eighties. The imagination of the Canadian-born Scotchman opened up a new continent of faery into which the young entered by the millions. . . . And for all Palmer Cox's resolve that there should be no pain or crime in his pictures and metric chronicles, he managed to convey a deeper suggestion of reality than we supply today for a childhood that must not be 'sheltered.' " *Current Opinion* noted that "He opened up a new world to the imagination," and the *Nation* commented that the Brownies had become "a living part of contemporary life."

What were the reasons for this sweeping success? First and foremost was Cox's skill in matching words and pictures. Either the drawings or the verse narratives by themselves might have been amusing but not impressive. Together they vivify each other in an unforgettable way. The narratives are always direct, straightforward, and fast-paced, and the drawings are sharply focused and beautifully clear in spite of their intricate detail.

The tone of Cox's stories is highly appealing. They abound in cheerfulness and optimism. Dangers and mistakes do not alter the conviction that things will turn out all right. At the same time the reader is not led to believe that success and happiness come easily. The Brownies work hard and accept their responsibilities. They remain happy more because of their profound integrity than in spite of it. They also balance the relationship between individual and group in a way satisfying to both. Theirs is a working democracy.

It is also easy for the child reader to identify with the Brownies. They are childlike in their exuberance and playful curiosity. Like children in their eagerness to explore and to experiment, they typically leap before they look into their next adventure. At the same time they are adult in their ready acceptance of responsibility for their actions. Although grown-up in their unimpeachable integrity, they never seem stuffy and never degenerate into complacent self-esteem. Neither idealized nor caricatured, they capture a universal childlike component in human nature.

The Brownie stories are never interrupted by intrusive moralizing. An underlying ethic of behavior is always quietly implicit in the Brownies' joyful way of life, but a consistently humorous tone dominates. Morality is to be learned, but through example rather than precept. Cox wanted his stories to be enjoyable rather than morally edifying. They succeeded in being both.

To be successful is not necessarily to be influential, and it might seem at first as if Palmer Cox's long and overwhelmingly successful career was an isolated triumph in the history of children's literature. To a certain extent this is true, for he did create a unique world that produced no direct imitations. On the other hand, Cox has had an indirect long-range influence on writing for children. Although he was essentially a nineteenth-century writer, the twentieth century is in many ways his heir and beneficiary.

Cox helped to free children's literature from the hold of didacticism on nineteenth-century taste. He also helped to establish the legitimate role of fantasy in American children's literature. The Brownie world is a fantasy world although it is represented in a realistic way. The style is not at all dreamlike or impressionistic. Nor is the fantasy explained away: there is no waking up at the end. The Brownies simply exist in their own right, and readers accept their existence because the author has made them so lifelike in such an entertaining way. In this sense the Brownies are a logical antecedent of the hobbits.

Cox's work has provoked comparison with other nineteenth-century writers, including Joel Chandler Harris, James M. Barrie, and Lewis Carroll. The twentieth-century writers with whom he best bears comparison are the fantasists. His verse narratives somewhat resemble those of Theodore Giesel (Dr. Seuss), who shares Cox's comic tone, recitable verse, unobtrusive educational content, and strange fanciful creatures. Cox's portrayal of a sustained fantasy world suggests other contemporary counterparts in the works of Frank Baum and Mary Norton. The father of the Brownies is thus also a precursor of modern fantasy writing for children.

References:

Roger W. Cummins, *Humorous but Wholesome: A History of Palmer Cox and the Brownies* (Watkins Glen, N.Y.: Century House, 1973);

Joyce Kilmer, "Palmer Cox of Brownie Castle Comes to Town," *New York Times Magazine*, 16 January 1916, pp. 19-20.

Christopher Pearse Cranch

(8 March 1813-20 January 1892)

David L. Greene
Piedmont College

See also the Cranch entry in *DLB 1, The American Renaissance in New England.*

SELECTED BOOKS: *Poems* (Philadelphia: Carey & Hart, 1844);

The Last of the Huggermuggers: A Giant Story (Boston: Phillips, Sampson, 1856); republished in *Giant Hunting; or, Little Jacket's Adventures* (Boston: Mayhew & Baker, 1860);

Kobboltozo: A Sequel to The Last of the Huggermuggers (Boston: Phillips, Sampson, 1857); republished with *The Last of the Huggermuggers* in *Giant Hunting; or, Little Jacket's Adventures* (1860);

Satan: A Libretto (Boston: Roberts Brothers, 1874);

The Bird and the Bell, with Other Poems (Boston: Osgood, 1875);

Ariel and Caliban, with Other Poems (Boston & New York: Houghton Mifflin, 1887).

TRANSLATION: *The Aeneid of Virgil Translated into English Blank Verse by Christopher Pearse Cranch* (Boston: Osgood, 1872).

Christopher Pearse Cranch's two Huggermugger or Little Jacket books are milestones in the development of nondidactic literature for children and of American fantasy. Although they are known today only to specialists, both books remain highly readable, and the second, *Kobboltozo,* is by almost any standard a work of considerable merit.

Cranch was born in the District of Columbia, the youngest son of William Cranch, a prominent jurist, and Anna Greenleaf Cranch. After graduating from Columbian College in Washington, he was trained at Harvard as a Unitarian minister and served churches in New England, the Midwest, and the South. By 1840 he had moved to Boston, where he was sympathetic to transcendentalism and became a friend of Ralph Waldo Emerson; in 1856, he supplied a memorial tribute to Margaret Fuller for a collection of some of her fugitive works. In Boston, he came to know most of the prominent writers. He gave up the ministry and turned to

landscape painting, for which he had considerable aptitude, although his greatest talent was in humorous drawing. Painting remained his profession, but Cranch became best known to the public for his writing. In addition to writing the Huggermugger books, he contributed competent poems to periodicals and anthologies and produced three collections of verse.

In 1843 Cranch married Elizabeth de Windt. In 1853 he took his family to Paris, where they began a ten-year residence. It was there that he wrote the two Huggermugger books. The first, *The Last of the Huggermuggers* (1856), was written during the winter of 1854-1855. That its author did not consider it of great significance is indicated by his comments in a letter of 10 August 1855 to an American acquaintance: "Last winter I wrote a child's story called 'The Last of the Huggermuggers,' about a good giant, which, if it is ever published, will, I think, amuse you and your children. I illustrated it and drew the designs on wood for the engraver.... I should like you to see it. It is amusing, with some pathos at the end."

Cranch's "child's story" was published, with his illustrations, in 1856 by the Boston firm of Phillips, Sampson, a publishing house whose associations with Boston writers culminated with its establishment of the *Atlantic Monthly* the next year.

The Last of the Huggermuggers tells of the wreck of an American ship on an island off the eastern coast of Africa, an island peopled by giants and "dwarves" who are in fact human-sized and small only when compared with the giants. The central figure, a New England boy named Jackie Cable, or Little Jacket, goes through several ludicrous adventures all based on the fact that everything on the island is proportioned for giants. Eventually, he and the other shipwrecked sailors are rescued by another American ship. On board is Zebedee Nabbum, a shrewd Yankee who tries to convince Mr. and Mrs. Huggermugger, the last of the giants, to come to America to be exhibited. Because of an ancient curse unleashed on the giants by the jealous dwarf Kobboltozo, Mrs. Huggermugger dies; her husband agrees to come to America with Nabbum and Jackie, but he does not survive the voyage.

The Last of the Huggermuggers seems improvised throughout; it is, in fact, the sort of story that an imaginative father might evolve for his children over a week or two of bedtimes. Despite this structural looseness, parodistic elements provide the book with some degree of unity. Nabbum, for example, represents Yankee acquisitiveness, and his plans to make a fortune exhibiting the giant explicitly imitate the successes of P. T. Barnum, a Connecticut Yankee from Bridgeport. Other elements of the book, especially the description of the flora and fauna on the island, mock mid-nineteenth-century scholarly and scientific works. More important, the entire book is a burlesque of the moralistic and highly didactic travel books written for young readers during the first half of the nineteenth century, works that—in sheer volume at least—were among the most influential available for children during this period.

In burlesquing serious books of travel, *The Last of the Huggermuggers* is part of a tradition that goes back much further than does children's lit-

C. P. Cranch

erature. This tradition, that of the fantastic travel book, is found as early as *The Odyssey* and continues through Sir John Mandeville (d. 1372) and the tales of anthropophagi and other wonders to which Shakespeare alludes in *Othello*, to one of the strong influences on Cranch's work, Jonathan Swift's *Gulliver's Travels* (1726). Certainly the benevolent Mr. and Mrs. Huggermugger owe much to Swift's land of giants, Brobdingnag, and the dwarf Kobboltozo, whose malice and envy lead him to unleash the curse that brings about the giants' destruction, represents a central Swiftian theme, the potential viciousness of mankind. Cranch's satire, however, is Horatian rather than Juvenalian; *The Last of the Huggermuggers* is protected by its tolerant and usually lighthearted tone from the bitterness that dominates *Gulliver's Travels*.

Cranch considered some of his readers to be his own contemporaries, especially that small circle of writers that lived in or near Boston. His asides on such matters as the New England character were directed toward adults, though they were not beyond the understanding of intelligent young readers. Fortunately, *The Last of the Huggermuggers* lacks the condescension of much children's literature—the works of Andrew Lang and A. A. Milne come immediately to mind—written with at least one eye on adult readers.

The almost complete lack of didacticism in the two Huggermugger books was a harbinger of later work for children by such authors as Louisa May Alcott, Frank R. Stockton, and, to a lesser degree, Mary Mapes Dodge. Although Cranch avoids didacticism, he does include sentimentality in *The Last of the Huggermuggers*, with the death of Mrs. Huggermugger, her husband's mourning, and his own death on shipboard. That most work for adults, in a period when Lydia Howard Sigourney, the Sweet Singer of Hartford, outsold the transcendentalists, was much more sentimental than Cranch's does not justify his descent into facile emotionalism.

Cranch's friend W. W. Story was well aware that *The Last of the Huggermuggers* seemed improvised and that it fell into easy sentimentality. On 18 April 1856, he wrote Cranch:

> I have promised on your behalf to Phillips, Sampson & Co. that you will write them another story with illustrations of about the length of "Huggermugger," and send it to them in July. So bestir your stumps.
>
> Now I am going to advise you. Take it kindly, for it is so meant. Your "Hugger-

Illustration for an 1869 edition of Cranch's The Last of the
Huggermuggers *(Baldwin Library, University of
Florida Libraries)*

mugger" was a considerable success in certain quarters, but your friends did not think
it up to your mark. . . . You must invent a
new story, and tell it in a livelier and sharper
way. Make the sentences tingle. Don't get lazy
over it, and think it will do itself. . . . I pray
you on my knees, oh! Cranch, wake up to
this and do it well. Put as much *fun* as possible
into it. Be *gay!*. . .Don't begin till you have
settled all your plot in your mind; and if you
can, let it hold a double story, an internal one
and an external one, as Andersen's do, so
that the wiseacres shall like it as well as the
children. . . . Your "Huggermugger" is a little too lachrymose and it isn't *new* enough.
Still it has had success. . . .

In his sequel, Cranch ignored Story's advice
to add more humor, and *Kobboltozo* (1857) is no-
ticeably less amusing than its predecessor, but in
other important respects, he accepted his friend's
suggestions. The plot of *Kobboltozo* was clearly de-

veloped before the book was written, and there is
little in the book that is at all sentimental. More
important, Cranch made its themes deeper and
broader. He took the dwarves he had introduced
in *The Last of the Huggermuggers,* and by making
their resemblance to mankind more explicit, he emphasized, without didacticism, man's potential for
self-degradation.

Kobboltozo describes the return of Jackie Cable
and Zebedee Nabbum to the Huggermuggers' island, not out of the desire of financial gain that
prevailed in *The Last of the Huggermuggers* but out
of curiosity about what had happened on the island
since they had left. The first part of the story is
dominated by a sense of loss because the giants are
dead. The book then moves to the mystery of what
has happened to the dwarves, who have abandoned
their village on the island and disappeared. One
dwarf, the tailor Stitchkin, appears and reveals
what happened. After Mr. Huggermugger had left
the island with Jackie, Nabbum, and the sailors,
Kobboltozo and a dwarf named Hammawhaxo began to search for the secret of becoming a giant.
The two entered a long underground passage that
led them to the gnomes, visited the cave of a long-
dead witch, and received an obscure prophecy
from the Mer-King before Hammawhaxo's wife revealed the quest to other dwarves. The results of
this revelation were predictable: "Bloody battles
sometimes took place among them [the dwarves].
Sometimes the waves would wash them away and
drown them. Some fell sick, or died from exposure
to the hot sun or the damp night air. . . . Some of
them took a fancy, as Kobboltozo did, that the
giants' food was to be found in caves, or by bur-
rowing in the earth. Many of them went under
ground, and never returned. In fine, all was dis-
order, strife, and disunion. And, in the mean time,
their houses, and shops, and gardens were totally
neglected. . . ."

Finally, the chastened dwarves come to their
senses and begin the task of establishing a new community elsewhere. Kobboltozo, however, is driven
to madness by his futile wish to be as great as a
giant; he grows smaller and smaller but believes,
after eating thousands of oysters, that he is growing
larger and soon will be able to enslave the world.

Except at the beginning of the book, when
Cranch says that he has been severely criticized for
publishing *The Last of the Huggermuggers* in advance
of an elaborate scientific description of the island,
there is little room for parody in *Kobboltozo.* The
tone is almost always somber, though, as in *The Last
of the Huggermuggers,* there is no Swiftian bitterness.

In their quest, the dwarves follow an illusory ideal based upon self-aggrandizement. Because of its very nature, such a quest must have some quality of the heroic even though it is perverted by unenlightened self-interest; it is a quest that, despite its uselessness, could not have been undertaken by Swift's physically degraded Yahoos. Cranch expects his readers to see themselves not only in the dwarves' vain desires but also in their ability ultimately to abandon illusions and to return to an integrated community life. The parallel with views of repentance held by religious liberals is plain.

The Last of the Huggermuggers and *Kobboltozo* were written early in the movement to give literary value to children's literature. They significantly influenced later authors, especially Frank R. Stockton and Howard Pyle, and possibly L. Frank Baum as well. Contemporary comment indicates that they were popular, and *Kobboltozo* is still considered a work of substantial literary merit.

References:

F. DeWolfe Miller, *Christopher Pearse Cranch and His Caricatures of New England Transcendentalism* (Cambridge: Harvard University Press, 1951);

Leonora Cranch Scott, *The Life and Letters of Christopher Pearse Cranch* (Boston: Houghton Mifflin, 1917).

Maria Susanna Cummins
(9 April 1827-1 October 1866)

Carol Gay
Youngstown State University

BOOKS: *The Lamplighter,* anonymous (Boston: Jewett, 1854; London: Routledge, 1854);

Mabel Vaughan (Boston: Jewett, 1857; London: Low, 1857);

El Fureidis (Boston: Ticknor & Fields, 1860; London: Low, 1860);

Haunted Hearts (Boston: Tilton, 1864; London Low, 1868).

Maria Susanna Cummins is known for one book which made publishing history when it appeared in 1854. That book is *The Lamplighter.* Cummins was one of the most successful of the women authors, along with Mary Jane Holmes and Susan Bogert Warner, whose works of domestic fiction dominated the book-buying patterns of mid-nineteenth-century American girls and women.

Born in Salem, Massachusetts, of Judge David Cummins and Mehitable Cave Cummins, she was dominated by her intelligent and successful father, who evidently encouraged her to read widely and to develop her mind. He sent her to Mrs. Charles Sedgwick's Young Ladies School in Lenox, Massachusetts, where she not only met other bright young ladies but doubtless also came into contact with one of the most respected of American novelists of that time, Mrs. Sedgwick's sister-in-law Catharine Sedgwick, whose *A New England Tale* (1822) and *Hope Leslie* (1827) were held in high esteem. Catharine Sedgwick, considered in America and in Europe a respected peer of James Fenimore Cooper and Washington Irving, presented a strong role model to the young women who attended the school in Lenox; she frequently read them passages from her books and visited in their classroom.

It seems likely that after Cummins returned home from Lenox and resumed the quiet, uneventful life she was to lead until her death, she published pieces anonymously in some of the New England periodicals that flourished at the time; however, none of her early work has been identified. In March 1854, when Cummins was twenty-six, *The Lamplighter* was anonymously published. It is not known how long it took her to write the book, nor are her reasons for writing it clear, although one source says *The Lamplighter* was intended to amuse a sick niece. Certainly it was not need of money that served as the impetus, since Cummins continued to live a comfortable and secure life with her affluent father.

As soon as the book came out, her publishers, John P. Jewett and Company, knew it was a best-seller, for within twenty days, 20,000 copies had been sold. At the end of two months this figure had doubled, and within a year of publication, *The Lamplighter* had reached the 70,000 mark. It had been published in England, translated into French and German, and it sold well in Europe.

The year 1854 also saw the publication of Thoreau's *Walden,* followed in 1855 by Whitman's *Leaves of Grass,* although both of these sold few copies and were ignored, on the whole, by critics. Hawthorne, struggling to raise a family, chafed over the abominable taste of the American reader in a famous 1855 letter to his Boston publisher William Ticknor, in which his wrath is focused on Cummins: "America is now wholly given over to a d--d mob of scribbling women, and I should have no chance of success while the public taste is occupied with their trash—and should be ashamed of myself if I did succeed. What is the mystery of these innumerable editions of the 'Lamplighter,' and other books neither better nor worse?—Worse they could not be, and better they need not be, when they sell by the 100,000." Although Hawthorne later tempered this harsh judgment of Cummins and commented that she had more merit than many of her sister authors, there is no denying that the so-called domestic novel, which appealed to a large American audience, primarily of women and young girls, from about 1850 to 1870, was an interesting sociological and literary phenomenon.

What was the "mystery" behind the success of domestic novels and the ardent response which they evoked from their readers? On the surface, the answer seems obvious, and in the preface to an edition of Cummins's second novel, *Mabel Vaughan,* the successful English novelist Elizabeth Cleghorn Gaskell stated it with clarity and grace: "These American novels unconsciously reveal all the little household secrets; we see the meals as they are put on the table, we learn the dresses which those who sit down to them wear; . . . we hear their kindly discourses, we enter into their home struggles, and we rejoice when they gain the victory."

The accurate reflection of real women's joys, pain, and triumphs that fills the pages of these very long novels undoubtedly explains much of their appeal. *Mabel Vaughan* was published in 1857, and like Cummins's earlier novel, it was well received. The novel, with the preface by Gaskell, was published in the Tauchnitz Library of British and American Authors in 1857. With *The Lamplighter* part of the series since 1854, Cummins had earned international recognition.

From the beginning, however, the domestic

Spine from an 1854 edition of Cummins's phenomenal best-seller (Baldwin Library, University of Florida Libraries). With this edition there were fifty-four thousand copies of the book in print.

novel received no critical respect. "Women's fiction," in the terms of one feminist critic, was either ignored or treated condescendingly under the denigrating rubric "the sentiment novel"—a form described time and again as overly pious, unashamedly moralistic, maudlin, romanticized, suffused with bathos, preoccupied with insignificant themes, events, and details. To a certain degree *The Lamplighter* fits this description, but it has only been since the advent of such feminist critics as Helen Waite Papashvily and Nina Baym that Cummins's novel and others of its kind have been scrutinized to ascertain the full significance of their literary force and cultural impact.

The Lamplighter opens on the streets of·Boston, where eight-year-old Gerty, the abused ward of Nan Grant, is brutalized by her surroundings and neglect. One of the most shockingly graphic scenes in a genre that frequently reveled in description of the harsh and lurid occurs when Gerty, given a kitten by lamplighter Trueman Flint, is forced to watch as the animal—the only "gleam of joy" on "a desolate little heart"—is discovered by Nan Grant and thrown into a pail of boiling water to drown in torture. Eventually Trueman Flint takes the girl in, allowing her to escape the clutches of Nan Grant, and Gerty begins her arduous struggle, physical and moral, to overcome her self and the world. When Flint is dying with Gerty as his nurse, she is nurtured by a neighbor, Mrs. Sullivan, and her son Willie, who help to guide her and to inculcate the moral and physical submissiveness necessary for her to survive. After Flint dies, Gerty moves to the home of Emily Graham, a young blind woman with a harsh father and a cruel housekeeper. Emily becomes Gerty's mentor in a world that Cummins depicts as cruel and unjust. "I begin to think everyone has trouble," says Gerty at one point, and Emily answers:

> "It is the lot of humanity, Gertrude, and we must not expect it to be otherwise."
> "Then who can be happy, Miss Emily?"
> "Those only, my child, who have learned submission; those who, in the severest difficulties, see the hand of a loving Father, and obedient to his will, kiss the chastening rod."
> "It is very hard, Miss Emily."
> "It is hard, my child, and therefore few in this world can rightly be called happy; but if, even in the midst of our distress, we can look to God in faith and love, we may, when the world is dark around, experience a peace that is a foretaste of heaven."

Gerty learns the lesson and in the process performs some almost superhuman displays of charity and goodwill: she insists that her most bitter and vengeful enemy be rescued from a fast-sinking boat first; she nurses the cruel Nan Grant on her deathbed; she gives up her fiancé (Willie) to someone she believes he loves better; and she becomes "at last a wonder to those who knew the temperament she had to contend with." That temperament is a feisty one; even more, it is one quickly aroused to fury, seen when Gerty throws a stone through a window or picks up a stick and heaves it at Nan Grant, striking her on the head and causing blood to flow.

This spirit and strength in Gerty are appealing qualities of *The Lamplighter* that many of the other heroines of the domestic novel do not share. According to Nina Baym in *Woman's Fiction: A Guide to Novels By and About Women in America, 1820-1870* (1978), Gerty's fortitude is part of the book's distinction and literary and cultural significance. Distinctly feminine in outlook and subject matter, the domestic novel frequently does more than simply mirror and propagate the nineteenth century's ideals of piety, submissiveness, and purity for its young women. As Helen Waite Papashvily comments in *All the Happy Endings* (1956), few realized "that these pretty tales reflected and encouraged a pattern of feminine behavior so quietly ruthless, so subtly vicious that by comparison the ladies at Seneca appear angels of innocence; these books were rather a witches' broth, a lethal draught brewed by women and used by women to destroy their common enemy, man."

Cummins would certainly not have described any of her books in these terms; indeed, it seems likely that she would have been shocked and disturbed to see them thus classified. But as Baym points out, Cummins's lessons of submission as shown, for instance, in the exchange between Gerty and Emily, are learned with such strength and power that they deny "that women are submissive by nature," asserting instead that "submission is the means by·which a woman can overcome or at least check her chief adversary, God." Baym is convinced that Cummins's purpose is "to persuade woman that she is responsible for saving herself and equal to the demand." Baym points out that in all her relations with men, Gerty is the one in control, as she nurses Flint, as she deals with Mr. Graham, as she greets her long-lost father (Emily's former sweetheart!), and as she finally accepts her fiancé, Willie. Gerty has a "force of character" that allows her to go beyond "all her mentors." "She is her own woman, and requires no parent [or husband] to provide identity." In *Mabel Vaughan,* Cummins attacks the materialism of American society by depicting her wealthy heroine Mabel without moral values until she is forced by economic reversals to make a new life for herself and her family on the Midwestern plains. The novel suggests that unless women subvert the economic system which tends to make their position in the home merely ornamental and to destroy their power of creating, educating, and protecting a family, all is lost. Baym concludes that "*Mabel Vaughan*'s ideal is the United States as a matriarchy."

Two books followed the phenomenally successful *Lamplighter* and the respected *Mabel Vaughan*. *El Fureidis*, published in 1860, and *Haunted Hearts*, which appeared in 1864, were ignored by critics and readers alike and sold very few copies even though their heroines, according to Baym, present an interesting contrast. *El Fureidis* tells the tale of Havilah, a child of nature, raised in exotic Palestine, where, free from the constraints of Western culture, she is allowed to follow her passions. Quite an opposite story is told in *Haunted Hearts,* in which the heroine, with one thoughtless act, destroys her life and that of her lover and is redeemed only after years of suffering. As Baym puts it, the former book "recognizes that passion in itself is not impure" but has no chance of being expressed in Western civilization, and the latter sets forth the more conventional theme that in such a perverse civilization a woman is given "no power except to injure, and no moral destiny other than silent suffering."

There is no indication that the international renown that *The Lamplighter* showered on its author ever disturbed the quiet, even tenor of Cummins's life. Marion Harland, a sister author and an acquaintance of Cummins at the time *The Lamplighter* was published, comments in her autobiography that Cummins remained "incredibly unspoiled" even though, "In 1855, no other woman writer was so prominently before the reading public. *The Lamplighter* was in every home, and gossip of the

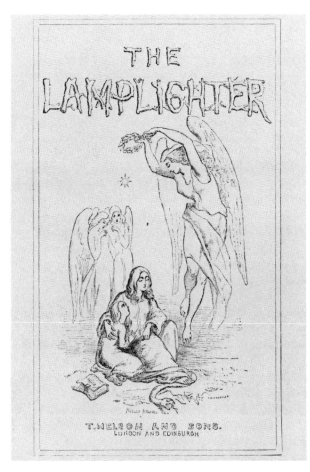 

Title page and frontispiece from two of the many British editions of The Lamplighter *(Baldwin Library, University of Florida Libraries)*

personality of the author was seized upon greedily by press and readers." The most noteworthy events that are recorded in the few brief biographical sketches of Cummins are her move from Salem to Dorchester, Massachusetts, where she spent most of her adult life in a colonial house on Bowdoin Street, and the fact that while in Dorchester she joined the First Unitarian Church and taught Sunday school. Early in the year 1866, two years after *Haunted Hearts*, she became ill, and on 1 October 1866, she died at the age of thirty-nine of what one source describes as an "abdominal disease."

Literary critics and social historians will probably never know the full impact of Cummins on the minds of the young people who read *The Lamplighter* through the years or even what the complex nature of that impact was. However, the fact that there was an edition of her work in in 1927, another in 1968, and still another in 1969 indicates that *The Lamplighter*, in some ways the epitome of an important literary genre, is assured a stable place in the history of literature.

References:

Nina Baym, *Woman's Fiction: A Guide to Novels By and About Women in America, 1820-1870* (Ithaca: Cornell University Press, 1978);

Marion Harland, *Marion Harland's Autobiography* (New York: Harper, 1910);

Jane Manthorne, "The Lachrymose Ladies," *Horn Book Magazine*, 43 (June 1967; August 1967; October 1967): 375-384; 501-513; 622-631;

Helen Waite Papashvily, *All the Happy Endings* (New York: Harper, 1956).

Mary Mapes Dodge

Marilyn H. Karrenbrock
University of Tennessee

BIRTH: New York, New York, 26 January 1831?, to James Jay Mapes and Sophia Furman Mapes.

MARRIAGE: 13 September 1851, to William Dodge; children: James Mapes and Harrington Mapes.

DEATH: Onteora, New York, 21 August 1905.

SELECTED BOOKS: *The Irvington Stories* (New York: James O'Kane, 1864; enlarged, New York: Allison, 1898);

Hans Brinker; or, The Silver Skates. A Story of Life in Holland (New York: James O'Kane, 1865); republished as *The Silver Skates* (London: Low, 1867);

A Few Friends and How They Amused Themselves: A Tale in Nine Chapters Containing Descriptions of Twenty Pastimes and Games, and a Fancy-dress Party (Philadelphia: Lippincott, 1868);

Rhymes and Jingles (New York: Scribner, Armstrong, 1874; enlarged, New York: Scribners, 1904; London: Gay & Bird, 1904);

Theophilus and Others (New York: Scribner, Armstrong, 1876; London: Low, 1876);

Along the Way (New York: Scribners, 1879);

Donald and Dorothy (London: Warne, 1882?; Boston: Roberts Brothers, 1883);

The Land of Pluck: Stories and Sketches for Young Folk (New York: Century, 1894; London: Unwin, 1894);

When Life Is Young: A Collection of Verse for Boys and Girls (New York: Century, 1894; London: Unwin, 1894);

Poems and Verses (New York: Century, 1904).

OTHER: *Baby Days: A Selection of Songs, Stories, and Pictures, for Very Little Folks*, compiled by Dodge (New York: Scribners, 1877); revised as *A New Baby World: Stories, Rhymes, and Pictures for Little Folks* (New York: Century, 1897);

The Children's Book of Recitations, compiled by Dodge (New York: DeWitt, 1898).

PERIODICAL PUBLICATION: "Children's Magazines," *Scribner's Monthly*, 6 (July 1873): 352-354.

Mary Mapes Dodge is no longer widely known, but when she died in 1905, her name had been associated for forty years with quality in children's literature. She is best known today as the author of an enduring classic, *Hans Brinker; or, The Silver Skates.* During her lifetime, however, she was equally well known as the editor of *St. Nicholas; Scribner's Illustrated Magazine for Girls and Boys.* She was its first editor and for thirty-two years guided this periodical which has been acclaimed as the finest children's magazine of all time.

Mary Elizabeth Mapes, known as Lizzie, was the second of five surviving children of James Jay Mapes and his wife, Sophia Furman Mapes. There is some question about her exact birthdate. All sources agree that she was born on 26 January; the year, however, is variously given as 1830, 1831, and 1838. Catherine Morris Wright, who wrote a 1979 biography authorized by Dodge's descendants, gives the date as 1830, apparently because of a poem entitled "1905 Seventy-five" which Dodge wrote in her last year. Most sources state that she was born in 1831, and this is probably the correct date. In the *St. Nicholas* tribute at her death, William Fayal Clarke, who was not only her assistant editor but also a member of her household for twenty years, gave her birth year as 1831. At the same time, Jeannette Gilder of *Critic,* who had known Dodge for forty years, gave her age at death as seventy-four, which would place her birth in 1831.

Lizzie Mapes's parents were members of prominent New York families. Her paternal grandfather, General Jonas Mapes, was a Revolutionary War veteran and was commander of the military forces in and around New York City during the War of 1812. He was a personal friend of the Marquis de Lafayette. General Mapes was also an importer and merchant tailor. Garrit Furman, her maternal grandfather, was a judge, owner of a large estate at Maspeth, Long Island, and co-owner of a farmers' market in New York City. The two men were close friends and neighbors. Lizzie Mapes was named for her grandmothers, Mary Eton Furman and Elizabeth Tylee Mapes.

James Jay Mapes began his career as a merchant in the family firm, but he was a maverick who had no talent for business. He was a many-sided genius—an inventor, agriculturist, chemist, artist, and editor. During Lizzie Mapes's early years, he invented a process for refining sugar, and he later became a consulting chemist and an expert witness in patent cases. He was for a time professor of chemistry and natural philosophy at the National

Mary Mapes Dodge

Academy of Design in New York, edited the *American Repertory of Arts, Sciences, and Manufactures,* and served as member, officer, and editor of several learned societies and institutes. He was not well paid for his various endeavors, and his financial situation was often precarious.

Nevertheless, childhood was a happy time for the Mapes children. Both parents were loving and devoted to their offspring. The children were educated at home by tutors and governesses. Because James Mapes believed that children instinctively appreciated good literature, he provided his family with the works he considered the best in the English language. The children also studied French, Latin, music, and drawing. Life in the Mapes household was itself a liberal education. Frequent guests included leading literary and scientific figures of the time. Among them were Horace Greeley, William Cullen Bryant, and John Ericsson, the noted nautical engineer who during the Civil War built the first armored turret ship, the *Monitor.* As a child, Lizzie Mapes was an avid reader, exhibited interest in music and art, and from an early age marked family occasions with what she later termed her own "poetical effusions."

About 1846 James Mapes embarked on a course which he had long anticipated. Anxious to demonstrate scientific methods of agriculture and the effect of chemical fertilizers on worn-out soil, he purchased a run-down farm at Waverly, New Jersey, near Newark. In 1847, the Mapes family moved to Mapleridge, a large, comfortable, but shabby farmhouse. Mapes was as usual in monetary difficulties. The purchase was apparently financed by a friend from New York, a lawyer named William Dodge. It is not clear whether Dodge had already met Lizzie Mapes when he loaned the money for the farm to her father. It was certainly not long after the loan was arranged that they met, and although Dodge was fifteen years older than Lizzie Mapes, the relationship quickly ripened. They were married on 13 September 1851.

Little information about the Dodge marriage is available. Certainly no account suggests that it was unsuccessful, and many of Lizzie Dodge's adult stories, often autobiographical in tone, describe a happy marital life. William Dodge brought his wife to his family home in New York City, where three generations were living together. Soon this ex-

Dodge as a young woman

tended family included another generation with the births of the Dodge's two sons, James ("Jamie") Mapes Dodge on 20 June 1852 and Harrington ("Harry") Mapes Dodge on 15 November 1855. Lizzie Dodge was probably living the comfortable life of a well-to-do wife and mother in a large, urban clan. This placid surface was abruptly shattered in 1858. Exactly what happened is unknown; most accounts simply state that William Dodge died suddenly. Apparently he left home on the evening of 28 October and never returned. He was in a state of depression brought on by the critical illness of his son Jamie and by financial difficulties precipitated by loans made to his father-in-law. Burial records say that he was a victim of drowning. There is no mention of suicide, but in view of the silence surrounding his death, the possibility cannot be ignored. It was the first tragedy of Mary Mapes Dodge's life, and she never spoke of it. Since she seems to have been devoted to both her father and her husband, it was undoubtedly traumatic for her. William Dodge was buried on 11 November, and Lizzie Dodge, with her sons, soon returned to her family and Mapleridge, their home at Waverly.

Dodge devoted herself to her sons. Living in the midst of a large family, with her parents and three sisters close at hand, it would have been easy to let others take much of the responsibility for the children. Instead, she looked for a place where she could take part in her sons' activities. She appropriated the attic of an old building near Mapleridge, turning it into a pleasant retreat which came to be known as "The Den." Many visitors described it in later years, mentioning a Franklin stove; ivy-covered windows; rag rugs; cast-off furniture; decorations of moss, leaves, and flowers; pictures; books; and a sloping ceiling which sported a panorama of the Rhine. Here Dodge talked and read to her sons and took part in their many hobbies—skating, swimming, walking, collecting nature specimens, kite-flying, music, printing. The Den also had another purpose; she used its large desk as a place to write.

Dodge had always been especially close to her father. In 1850, he had founded a periodical called *Working Farmer*. It is possible that she had helped with this venture before her marriage. Upon her return to Mapleridge after William Dodge's death, James Mapes attempted to divert her mind from her troubles by urging her to become involved in writing for the publication. In 1861 he purchased the *United States Journal,* adding it to the original publication with his daughter as editor of the new section. Like many editors of the time, Dodge did much of the writing for the *Working Farmer* and *United States Journal,* using several pseudonyms and sets of initials to suggest different authors. Her writing was so well received that she began sending stories to other publications. In 1863 she began contributing adult stories to *Harper's New Monthly Magazine.* An income, however small, was very useful to a young widow with two sons and a loving but improvident father.

James Mapes soon conceived an even happier plan for his daughter. He was referred by William L. Allison, the publisher of the *Working Farmer,* to James O'Kane, a publisher and bookseller in New York who wanted to produce a book for boys. Mapes suggested to his daughter that she write a juvenile book which would include a series of stories, perhaps with a military theme, since the Civil War was then in progress. Dodge, who was undoubtedly telling stories to her sons at the time, was happy to comply. The result was *The Irvington Stories,* published by O'Kane in November 1864. It is ironic that this book, conceived to capitalize on the Civil War, was published in the same month that Dodge's sister, Sophie Tolles, lost her husband, who was wounded in battle and died only a few days after the death of their infant son.

Dodge was fortunate in having *The Irvington Stories* reviewed in the prestigious *North American Review,* which said of them, "very pleasant little stories, . . just enough improbability in them; . . . what is gracious and lovely in childhood is appealed to indirectly, and with something of motherly tenderness in the tone. . . ." The eight selections are extremely varied and in many ways not typical of Dodge's later work. She is noted for her preference for realism, action, and gentle humor, but four of these stories have elements of fantasy, the action is subdued, and humor is rare. Although Dodge later disavowed excessive didacticism in children's magazines, almost all *The Irvington Stories* are didactic and moralistic. Some seem better suited for adults than children. "The Heart of the Hills: A Christmas Story," a religious fantasy about the rehabilitation of a confirmed recluse through the love and understanding of a child (who later proves to be his long-lost granddaughter), had already been published in *Harper's* with the title "A Visit from the Christ Child." "Capt. George, the Drummer Boy. A Story of the Rebellion" is the military story her father had urged her to write; it is a straightforward tale of camp life

Dodge's father, James Jay Mapes

which promotes duty, loyalty, and courage. "Po-No-Kah: An Indian Tale" tells of white children captured by savage Indians. It is replete with stereotypes but has more action than the other stories. "Brave Robby and the Skeleton," one of the less didactic tales, is a ghost story marred by an arch and condescending tone. Dodge considered it the weakest of the stories, and it was replaced by other tales in later editions.

The Irvington Stories was not a best-seller, but it proved sufficiently popular for Dodge to begin work on another book. She had long wanted to write a story about Holland. Her interest in that country had begun when she read John Lothrop Motley's *Rise of the Dutch Republic,* published in 1856. Although she had never been to Holland, she had been collecting material about it for years. Realizing the need for firsthand information, she enlisted the aid of the Scharffs, Dutch friends whose family had emigrated to Newark from Amsterdam. From them she learned details of Dutch life and locales which she wove into the story; at night she read her work to her sons. Her efforts were justified, for the book which she produced was *Hans Brinker; or, The Silver Skates* (1865).

Hans Brinker had been intended for serial publication, but it was too long, so Dodge submitted the book to O'Kane. The publisher was unenthusiastic, but the success of *The Irvington Stories* had been great enough that he agreed to publish the new book. It appeared in December 1865, with illustrations by F. O. C. Darley, who had illustrated *The Irvington Stories*, and Thomas Nast. During the next fifteen years, it received more reviews than any other children's book in America. The early reviews were excellent. The *Nation* called it a "charming tale, alive with incident and action, adorned rather than freighted with useful facts, and moral without moralization." Both the *Independent*, which reported, "It is by no means an ordinary book," and the *Atlantic Monthly*, which praised it as "a charming domestic story," thought that it would be popular with adults as well as young people. At the time sales of at least 300,000 copies were required to make a best-seller; only two books published in 1865 achieved this coveted status, *Hans Brinker* and the American edition of Charles Dickens's *Our Mutual Friend*. By comparison with later sales, the initial success of Dodge's book was mild; it obtained its greatest popularity when republished by Scribners in the next decade.

Hans Brinker had all the ingredients necessary to attract children of the nineteenth century. It is written with verve; the style is natural, and Dodge includes plenty of conversation. The action is fast-moving; there is mystery, romance, pathos, humor, which culminate in the exciting skating match whose prize is the coveted silver skates. In the introduction, Dodge says that almost all the main incidents, including the account of Raff Brinker's problems, are true stories. The numerous subplots provide something for every reader. One of the book's most notable features is the long skating trip to Amsterdam, which gives the author an excuse to introduce many details about Dutch customs and history. The most famous of these, the story of the boy who saved Holland by sticking his finger in the dike, was Dodge's own invention. Dodge's use of Dutch words and phrases varies inconsistently between modern and older spellings; the foreign expressions are not always accurately translated; and some spellings and usages are more typical of German than of Dutch. Moral teachings are not often intrusive, although Dodge cannot resist pointing to a few obvious ones in the final disposition of her characters.

Underlying *Hans Brinker* is Dodge's philosophy of children's literature which came to fruition in her editorship of *St. Nicholas*. As Dodge's friend Lucia Gilbert Runkle wrote: "She believed that their literature should stimulate and quicken children intellectually, but discourage emotional precocity. . . . [She wrote for] simple, natural, real children, whose interests are external to themselves." In *Hans Brinker*, the chief conflicts are certainly external. Raff Brinker's amnesia, the reaction of family members to his violent state, the poverty-stricken straits to which the Brinkers are reduced, the flight of Dr. Boekman's son because of the death of a patient to whom the youth had given the wrong medicine—all provide opportunities to explore the dark side of the psyche. Dodge, however, did not choose to do so. Perhaps she could not. She met her own emotional tragedies with a deep-seated reserve that did not allow penetration beneath the surface of her grief.

One of these emotional crises occurred less than a month after *Hans Brinker* was published. James Jay Mapes, Dodge's beloved father, died in January 1866. He left her a legacy of debts and financial problems but also a rich heritage of literary skills. When he died, she was well on her way to success in the literary world.

Several months after James Mapes's death, his old friend Robert Dale Owen, the author, diplomat, and social reformer, came to pay his respects to the Mapes family. Dodge soon became his friend, and he was delighted to sponsor her in New York literary circles. During the next years Dodge made and renewed many friendships with persons of note. Among her new friends was Lucia Gilbert Calhoun, later Lucia Gilbert Runkle, who was on the editorial staff of the *New York Tribune*. Another new friend was Horace E. Scudder, newly elected editor of the *Riverside Magazine for Young People*. Although published for only four years (1867-1870), the *Riverside Magazine* is second only to *St. Nicholas* in its reputation as a quality periodical for children. Scudder immediately enlisted Dodge as a contributor. Her first effort for him, "The Funny Land of Pluck," another story of Holland, was published in May and June 1867.

The Mapes family had often amused themselves and entertained friends with parlor games. Dodge is attributed with the invention of two card games, *The Protean Cards* and *The Stratford Game*. She wrote for Scudder an article reviewing toys and games, including her own, which were suitable for Christmas gifts. In the article, she describes *The Stratford Game* as the creation of "a little boy ten years of age." The boy was almost certainly her son Harry. Dodge's interest in games culminated in an adult book, *A Few Friends and How They Amused*

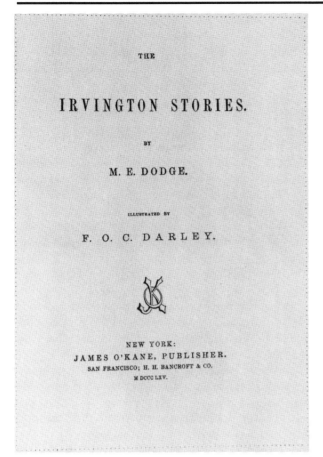

Title page and illustration by Darley, for Dodge's first book, a collection of stories with military themes conceived to capitalize on the Civil War. Although the title page is dated 1865, The Irvington Stories *was actually published in November 1864.*

Themselves, incorporating a love story with descriptions of twenty "pastimes and intellectual games which persons of culture may enjoy." Owen, who like her father took an active role in promoting her work, recommended the book to Lippincott in Philadelphia, who published it in November 1868.

Dodge entered another phase of her career that year when she accepted the position of associate editor for a new weekly periodical, *Hearth and Home*. The editors were Donald Grant Mitchell (who used the pen name Ik Marvel) and Harriet Beecher Stowe, but Dodge did much of the actual writing and editing. Her contribution began with the first issue in December 1868 and continued until 1873. During these years her salary and responsibilities, which included the home and juvenile departments, increased steadily, but so did her family obligations. Forced to spend the week in New York, she returned each weekend to Harry and her mother and sisters in Waverly.

Besides paying for the upkeep for Mapleridge, she was at the time providing for Jamie

Dodge's college education. Like his grandfather, he had scientific and mechanical interests. Dodge, who was knowledgeable in perhaps as many fields as her father, had encouraged her son's interests. According to Lucia Gilbert Runkle, "When the elder [son], a born inventor, began to care for the things of his craft, it was she who was ready to explain to him the crystallization of iron, the effect of heat and cold, the laws of statics and dynamics." Jamie entered Cornell in 1868. Dodge had fostered both her sons' interests in the printing press, and Jamie earned some of his college expenses through printing. However, he was expelled from Cornell in 1871 for "over-preoccupation with his printing press." He graduated from Rutgers in 1872, just as his mother was considering her last and most important career change.

During her tenure at *Hearth and Home*, Dodge was also writing steadily for the *Riverside Magazine* (until its demise in 1870) and for adult periodicals such as *Scribner's Monthly* and *Atlantic Monthly*. Her most famous adult sketch, "Mrs. Maloney on the

Frontispiece by F. O. C. Darley for the third edition of Hans Brinker; or, The Silver Skates *(Baldwin Library, University of Florida Libraries)*

Chinese Question," was published in 1871. Written in only a few hours when *Scribner's Monthly* needed a quick filler, it is a humorous anecdote in Irish dialect, which today would be considered demeaning to both ethnic groups. In the nineteenth century it was much admired and became a favorite selection of the well-known actress Charlotte Cushman who used it as a dramatic reading in the early 1870s.

It was also during the early 1870s that Mary Elizabeth Dodge began to use the name of Mary Mapes Dodge. The new designation was adopted to avoid confusion with several other authors named Mary Dodge. (One of these, Mary Abigail Dodge, better known by her pseudonym of Gail Hamilton, had been one of the original editors of the children's periodical *Our Young Folks*, which was soon to merge with *St. Nicholas.*)

In 1872 a new opportunity presented itself. Josiah Holland and Roswell Smith, who with Charles Scribner had founded *Scribner's Monthly*, were considering adding a children's periodical to the Scribner line. Smith asked Dodge to write out her thoughts about such a publication. "Children's Magazines," her reply which has become famous as the statement of principle upon which *St. Nicholas* was founded, was published anonymously in *Scribner's Monthly* in July 1873. "The child's magazine," she said, "needs to be stronger, truer, bolder, more uncompromising than the [adult's]. . . . Let there be no sermonizing either, no wearisome spinning out of facts, no rattling of the dry bones of history. A child's magazine is its pleasure ground." She did not wholly disdain didacticism: "Doubtless a great deal of instruction and good moral teaching may be inculcated in the pages of a magazine; but it must be by hints dropped incidentally here and there; by a few, brisk, hearty statements of the difference between right and wrong. . . . Harsh, cruel facts—if they must come, and sometimes it is important that they should—must march forward boldly, say what they have to say, and go."

Smith soon asked Dodge to found and edit a periodical such as she had described. She had been offered the editorship of *Hearth and Home* and was also contemplating a return to full-time writing. The offer was too good to turn down, however, both financially and personally. Her critical ability and her talents for detail, organization, and persuasion marked her as a born editor, and her overwhelming concern for her own sons spilled over into an abiding interest in all children. She agreed to found the periodical, leaving *Hearth and Home* in March 1873.

Dodge asked Frank R. Stockton, who had worked closely with her at *Hearth and Home*, to be assistant editor of the new periodical. The first order of business was to choose a name for the journal. It was Dodge herself who chose *St. Nicholas;* she had always been fascinated by and often written about the patron saint of New Amsterdam. In the lead editorial of the first issue, Dodge wrote, "Is he not the boys' and girls' own Saint, the especial friend of young Americans? That he is. And isn't he the acknowledged patron saint of New York—one of America's greatest cities—dear to old hearts as well as young? Didn't his image stand at the prow of the first emigrant ship that ever sailed into New York Bay, and wasn't the very first church the New Yorkers built named after him? Didn't he come over with the Dutch, ever so long ago and take up his abode here? Certainly. And, what is more, isn't he the kindest, best, and jolliest old dear that ever was known? Certainly again."

Front cover for the 1885 Scribners edition of Dodge's best-known work and decorative title page for a British edition published in 1892 (Baldwin Library, University of Florida Libraries)

With the name chosen and the first issue underway, the busy editor was finally able to take a well-deserved vacation. She had begun to gain weight and was physically and mentally exhausted. Leaving Jamie settled in a new job following his graduation and the capable and trustworthy Stockton in charge of *St. Nicholas*, Dodge and Harry sailed from New York in May 1873 on a long-awaited trip to Europe. Although the visit to Britain was occasionally marred by her ill health, Dodge was able to accomplish her objectives. She went sight-seeing; visited Sampson Low, who had published the first English edition of *Hans Brinker* in 1867; met many literary contemporaries, including George MacDonald, the Rosettis, and Lewis Carroll; and made personal contact with writers, publishers, and editors who could help her in her quest for material for *St. Nicholas*. After leaving England, she visited the Netherlands, where she wrote a preface for a new edition of *Hans Brinker* which Scribner was planning to publish the next year. It was during this visit that an incident often cited in

memoirs and biographies of Dodge occurred. *Hans Brinker* was recommended to Harry Dodge by a bookseller, who praised it as the best juvenile story about Dutch life. The first Dutch edition had appeared in 1867, adapted by well-known children's writer Pieter Jacob Andriessen. In the introduction to his 1870 edition, Andriessen stated that he had made many changes so that the story might conform to Dutch life as his readers knew it; of Dodge's work there was "little more left than a skeleton." It is doubtful that Dodge knew this, as she was very pleased with the book's reception in the land which it celebrated.

By the time that Dodge returned to New York in the fall, the Panic of 1873 had begun. Holland, Smith, and Scribner took advantage of the economic situation by buying out a financially hard-pressed rival periodical, *Our Young Folks*. It ceased publication in October 1873, and the first issue of *St. Nicholas*, originally scheduled to appear in January 1874, was advanced to November 1873 to take advantage of the situation.

The following list of objectives guiding the editorial policy of *St. Nicholas* was purportedly written by Dodge:

> To give clean, genuine fun to children of all ages
> To give them examples of the finest types of boyhood and girlhood
> To inspire them with an appreciation of fine pictorial art
> To cultivate the imagination in profitable directions
> To foster a love of country, home, nature, truth, beauty, and sincerity
> To prepare boys and girls for life as it is
> To stimulate their ambitions—but along normally progressive lines
> To keep pace with a fast-moving world in all its activities
> To give reading matter which every parent may pass to his children unhesitatingly

Although this list is ambitious, the policy set forth prevailed from the first issue of *St. Nicholas*. It is not surprising that the magazine was an immediate and resounding success. The first issue opened with a poem by Dodge's old friend William Cullen Bryant. Among the authors represented were Noah Brooks, Olive Thorne (Miller), Rebecca Harding Davis, Lucretia P. Hale, Lucy Larcom, Donald G. Mitchell, and Celia Thaxter. Features included the "Little Folks Page"; a foreign-language story in German (alternating with French in other issues) "so that readers who are studying those languages may have a chance to do a little translating out of school"; and "The Riddle Box" with sophisticated verbal and pictorial puzzles.

One of the reasons for the popularity of *St. Nicholas* was the way in which Dodge involved the readers. Scientific activities were popular. In the early years of the magazine, "Bird Defenders" were solicited and their names published. In 1880 the Agassiz Association, named for scientist Louis Agassiz, was formed; it encouraged budding scientists to exchange information and scientific specimens. Children were also encouraged to write. "The Letter Box" began in the fifth issue (March 1874). When children were asked to translate foreign-language stories, write stories from a series of pictures, or submit answers to puzzles, they were assured that the best efforts would be published. Dodge was not above cheating a little, though. In March 1874 a French story by "J. S. S." (Joel S. Stacy, one of Dodge's favorite pseudonyms) was offered, with the promise that the best translation

would be published in the May issue. The winner was "Nellie Brinkley," and the translation, "Borrowing Trouble," was published as promised, complete with corrections for the few minor mistakes supposedly made by Brinkley. Twenty years later, "Borrowing Trouble" (in English) was included in *The Land of Pluck*, a collection of Dodge's stories.

Another important feature of *St. Nicholas* was illustration. In her *Scribner's Monthly* article on children's periodicals Dodge had written: "A child's periodical must be pictorially illustrated, of course, and the pictures must have the greatest variety consistent with simplicity, beauty and unity. They should be heartily conceived and well executed; and they must be suggestive, attractive and epigrammatic. If it be only the picture of a cat, it must be so like a cat that it will do its own purring, and not sit, a dead, stuffed thing, requiring the editor to purr for it." *St. Nicholas* became as well known for its illustrations as for its stories. Dodge sought the best illustrators she could find and was equally concerned with the quality of the printing. Among the illustrators who contributed to *St. Nicholas* in later years were Reginald Birch, George Wharton Edwards, Oliver Herford, Joseph Pennell, Arthur Rackham, Frederic Remington, and N. C. Wyeth. Howard Pyle, when he began to write for *Scribner's Monthly*, was encouraged to send stories to *St. Nicholas* as well. Dodge soon discovered his gift for art as well as literature, and *St. Nicholas* was the first periodical to publish his illustrations.

Although the first issue contained works by several respected writers, half of the contributions were by Stockton and Dodge, who used their own names as well as pseudonyms and also wrote unsigned entries such as "Jack-in-the-Pulpit," Dodge's popular column of advice and information. As the fame of *St. Nicholas* grew, it became unnecessary for the editors to do so much of the writing. Established authors were soon clamoring to be included. John Townsend Trowbridge, editor of the defunct *Our Young Folks*, appeared as an author in the third issue of *St. Nicholas* (January 1874). The demise of *Our Young Folks* was so sudden that the last issue was in press before Trowbridge knew of the sale. Nevertheless, for the third *St. Nicholas*, he wrote a letter to readers of *Our Young Folks*, giving his blessing to the new periodical.

In its first decade *St. Nicholas* published Louisa May Alcott's *Eight Cousins* and *Jack and Jill*, *The Boy Emigrants* by Noah Brooks, Edward Eggleston's *The Hoosier School-boy*, Lucretia Peabody Hale's Peterkin stories, Jack Hazard stories by John Townsend Trowbridge, and works by Thomas Bailey Aldrich,

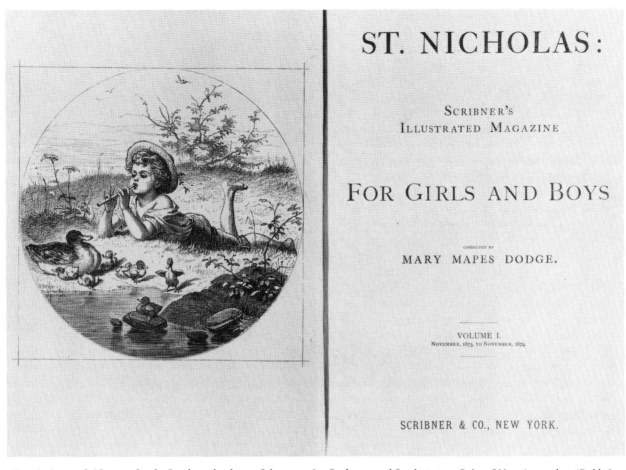

Frontispiece and title page for the first bound volume of the magazine Dodge named for the patron Saint of New Amsterdam (Baldwin Library, University of Florida Libraries)

Hezekiah Butterworth, Sarah Chauncy Woolsey (Susan Coolidge), Bret Harte, Helen Hunt Jackson, Sarah Orne Jewett, Horace E. Scudder, Bayard Taylor, Charles Dudley Warner, and Kate Douglas Wiggin. William Cullen Bryant, Henry Wadsworth Longfellow, John Greenleaf Whittier, and Alfred Tennyson contributed poems. Many of these authors continued to write for *St. Nicholas.*

During the early years of *St. Nicholas,* Dodge was at the pinnacle of her success. She was in her early forties, attractive and popular. Her work was absorbing, and she had gathered about her a set of friends, many of them writers and editors like herself. She became well known for the weekly receptions given at her home. Home was now New York City; the happy family life in Waverly had ended by 1874. Charles Mapes, Dodge's only brother, had married and left even before James Mapes's death in 1866. The youngest sister, Kate, had married and moved to California in 1871. Now Dodge took quarters in a boardinghouse, the first

of a long series of New York rooms and apartments in which she spent much of the rest of her life. Her sons were with her; her mother and sister Sophie also boarded in New York. The oldest sister, Louise, was dying of consumption in South Carolina, where she had gone for the milder climate. Louise's death in June 1876 may have been the inspiration for Dodge's best-known poem, "The Two Mysteries," which appeared in *Scribner's Monthly* in October 1876. In later years, Dodge was several times thanked for the comfort it had brought to those bereaved by the death of a loved one.

The 1870s were also marked by steady recognition of Dodge's work. Hard on the heels of *St. Nicholas's* auspicious debut, *Hans Brinker* was revived in an edition published by Scribners in 1874. The next year it was published in a French edition translated by P. J. Stahl. This edition, which also included a French translation of *Little Women,* won the Montyon prize of 1500 francs, given by the

French Academy for the book which each year rendered the greatest service to humanity. An Italian edition of *Hans Brinker* was published in 1876.

Scribners published four other books by Dodge before the end of the decade. *Rhymes and Jingles* appeared in 1874. The poems were collected from her writings for the *Working Farmer, Hearth and Home,* and the early volumes of *St. Nicholas.* The book was favorably received and was republished in various editions for nearly sixty years. *Harper's New Monthly Magazine* commented that it was "full of queer, quaint fancies, abounding with humor, but without much sentiment or pathos." "Full of comical wise nonsense and the most felicitous absurdities of language" was the verdict of the *Nation.* Many of the poems are glimpses of nature, pretty elves and fairies, and amusing children. What sounded fresh to a nineteenth-century reader often seems overly sweet to the modern ear. At their best, these poems for young children are short, with bouncing rhythm or gay, sing-song lilt that makes them appropriately resemble Mother Goose verse.

Baby Days: A Selection of Songs, Stories, and Pictures, for Very Little Folks (1877) was a collection taken from the "Little Folks" columns of *St. Nicholas* edited by Dodge. It was profusely illustrated with 300 pictures. Music for several songs by Dodge was included. It was a delightful, fun-filled volume for the young child and beginning reader. Even today it has a nostalgic charm.

Dodge's other two Scribners books were published for adults. *Theophilus and Others* (1876) contains stories, essays, and sketches which range from the mildly humorous to the frankly sentimental. Most are about the daily life and family concerns of happy wives. *Along the Way* (1879) is a poetry collection, including some verses first published in *Rhymes and Jingles.* The poems are chiefly on nature, romance, and death. Rhyme, meter, and sentiment seem cloying today.

A minor crisis in Dodge's professional life arose in 1877, when Frank Stockton resigned his post as assistant editor of *St. Nicholas* because of poor health and the press of other writing. Dodge and Stockton had worked so well together that she despaired of finding another assistant who was so attuned to her own ideas. She need not have worried, because the position was soon ably filled by a young man recently come to Scribners' firm, William Fayal Clarke. Almost the same age as her younger son, Clarke became a close friend to both Jamie and Harry Dodge and soon moved into the Dodges' boardinghouse. He remained with *St.*

Nicholas for fifty years, and he was part of Dodge's household for almost twenty.

In 1878 Dodge visited her sister Kate in San Francisco. Dodge's health had been poor, and it seemed an ideal way to rest. Work never stopped completely for Dodge, however. Among the persons she met in San Francisco was a woman whose first story in *St. Nicholas* was signed Katherine D. Smith but who achieved fame after marriage as Kate Douglas Wiggin. A highlight of the California trip was a party given for Dodge by her sister and attended by children who brought flowers and banners to the editor of their beloved *St. Nicholas.* On the way home, Dodge visited fellow author and friend Helen Hunt Jackson in Colorado.

Jamie Dodge's marriage to Josephine Kern in September 1879 and the birth of the first Dodge grandchild, Kern, in July 1880 were bright spots in the years 1879 to 1881, which otherwise were as dark as any in Dodge's life. She fell while on vacation in the Adirondacks and broke one of her teeth off below the gum, which caused her much suffering. Estate troubles loomed large. As a widow and legal owner of the Waverly property, which had been purchased with William Dodge's money, she had signed papers in her father's behalf which left her deep in debt. Now a legal judgment resulted in the loss of the Waverly property and a great deal of money as well. But the most serious problem was the poor health of her younger son.

Harry Dodge, plagued by poor health and a nervous temperament, had never been able to use his artistic and musical talents with success. A job in Scribners' art department ended when his eyes became inflamed. Other attempts at employment were equally unsuccessful. He nursed his mother after her fall, but this chore left him highly nervous and unwell. In September 1879, the month of his brother's wedding, Harry Dodge developed typhoid, which so broke his health that he never recovered. During the next year or so, relapses alternated with limited recoveries. He died unexpectedly on 2 February 1881 of "congestion of the brain." Dodge was left to carry on, sustained by her family, Fayal Clarke, and her work.

In 1881 Roswell Smith bought out both Josiah Holland and Charles Scribner to form the Century Company, which assumed publication of *St. Nicholas.* In the December 1881 issue of *St. Nicholas,* Dodge's novel *Donald and Dorothy* began serialization. It completed its run in October 1882 and should have been published in book form the next month in time for Christmas sales. The English edition was published by Warne in December 1882, but unfortunately the American edition was not published for another year. Dodge was making excessive demands which Charles Scribner was unwilling to meet. She wanted a contract, covering not only new books but also the ones already published, which would allow her to take her works to another publisher after a few years. As Scribner pointed out, if he gave her this privilege, other authors would expect the same treatment. No publisher could afford such a system. Dodge, beset by personal and financial problems, perhaps felt that Scribner had not sufficiently promoted her books. Except for *Hans Brinker*, none had done exceptionally well. The result of this power struggle with Scribner was that Mrs. Dodge took *Donald and Dorothy* to Roberts Brothers, who published the books of her friend Louisa May Alcott. The firm was delighted to publish such a book in the Alcott tradition and brought it out in November 1883.

Except for *Hans Brinker*, it is Dodge's only novel-length work. It never attracted the attention of her earlier classic. *Donald and Dorothy* is primarily a mystery. Three babies boarded ship; only two were rescued from a shipwreck. Is Dorothy really Donald's twin, or is she his cousin Delia instead? Interspersed with the mystery and its resolution are incidents of childhood pleasure as the children frolic with their friends. There is a "house picnic" (Dodge, who never hesitated to reuse old material, included here some games first described in *A Few Friends*), a shooting match which ends in a rescue from a mad dog, a mock boat race in which a practical joke is turned upon the perpetrators. The passages which show the children's daily activities are reminiscent of Alcott's works; there are especially parallels in incident and tone with *Eight Cousins*, which had been serialized in *St. Nicholas* in 1875. Like Rose Campbell in Alcott's book, Donald and Dorothy are raised by a bachelor uncle whom they adore. Just as Rose adopted her maid Phebe, Dorothy champions poor but industrious Charity Danby. Dorothy, like Rose, learns to cook and sew; each girl pleases her uncle by baking and mending for him. Each has a bedroom filled with treasures; Dorothy calls hers the "cosey corner," which is the name of the mountain farm which Rose visits. The sermon preached by one of the Dove boys during this visit is echoed by the one which Fandy Danby directs to his brothers and sisters in *Donald and Dorothy*.

Although Donald spends the last quarter of the book in Europe, Dodge does not delineate geography and customs as she did in *Hans Brinker*. He is there to learn who Dorothy is, and that is

what he does. The portrayal of Donald's and Dorothy's attachment to one another is excessively sentimental. The mystery, though trite and its solution rife with coincidence, is well plotted. There are no dangling ends, no details left unexplained. The style is natural and easy. The book falls far behind *Hans Brinker*, but it is better reading than any of Dodge's short works.

During the years following Harry's death, Dodge was often in poor health. She was aging and so were others; deaths among friends became more common. Her mother died in 1884, Helen Hunt Jackson in 1885, Louisa May Alcott in 1888. An especially tragic death for the Mapes family was the accidental drowning of her brother Charley's son Bert in 1891. Good things happened, too. Jamie and Josephine Dodge presented her with two more grandchildren, Fayelle (named for Clarke) in 1885, and Charles Lorimer (Karl) in 1891. In 1888 her sister Kate made a long-desired visit from California.

Perhaps the best thing that happened in these years came about almost by chance. In 1886 Dodge, overworked and ill, made a trip to Europe for rest. In London she met Candace Wheeler, who was promoting a colony at Onteora Park in the Catskills, where writers and artists could relax in a lovely locale. In 1888 Dodge purchased Yarrow, one of the Onteora cottages. She spent her summers there for the rest of her life. More and more she could leave the routine of *St. Nicholas* to Fayal Clarke, finding at Onteora the peace that eluded her in the city.

In the second decade of *St. Nicholas*, new contributors included John Kendrick Bangs, Charles E. Carryl, Richard Harding Davis, Edward Everett Hale, Joel Chandler Harris, William Dean Howells, Tudor Jenks, Joaquin Miller, Mayne Reid, Edmund Clarence Stedman, and Palmer Cox. Laura E. Richards, who had contributed a few poems during the first decade, now sent stories as well. Thomas Nelson Page's *Two Little Confederates* appeared in the magazine, and John Burroughs contributed articles on nature. One of the most popular stories published in *St. Nicholas* began in November 1885: Frances Hodgson Burnett's *Little Lord Fauntleroy*. It took readers by storm, and during the 1888-1889 season the dramatic version captivated theatergoers as well. Elsie Leslie Lyde, the young actress who played Fauntleroy in the New York production, became a favorite of Dodge and an article about her was published in *St. Nicholas*.

In 1893 Dodge acquired a new author, one who had grown up reading *St. Nicholas* and who would become one of its most famous contributors. He was Rudyard Kipling, and his first story for *St. Nicholas* was "The Potted Princess." The second story, "Collar-Wallah and the Poison-Stick," was illustrated by Reginald Birch, the Englishman who had made such a hit with his illustrations for *Little Lord Fauntleroy*, although reportedly Kipling did not think his pictures were accurate representations of India. Kipling became best known to *St. Nicholas* readers for the stories which later appeared in the Jungle Books: "Rikki-Tikki-Tavi," "Toomai of the Elephants," "Mowgli's Brothers," and "Tiger! Tiger!" The first three Just So stories were also originally published in *St. Nicholas*.

Another major author publishing in *St. Nicholas* at this period was Mark Twain. The serialization of *Tom Sawyer Abroad* began in the first issue of the third decade (November 1893). The Cle-

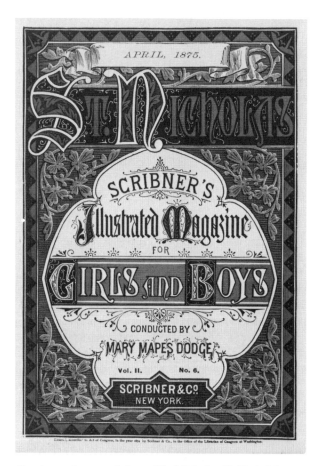

Front cover for an early issue of St. Nicholas *(Baldwin Library, University of Florida Libraries). Among the contributions are Frank R. Stockton's fairy tale "Cinderella," the fourth install-ment of Louisa May Alcott's* Eight Cousins, *a poem entitled "Colorado Snow-Birds" by Helen Hunt Jackson, and one of Lucretia Peabody Hale's Peterkin Tales.*

mens family were neighbors of Dodge in Onteora and became friends. She was especially close to Susy Clemens, Mark Twain's daughter. In 1896, Dodge earned the gratitude of the Clemens family for her kindness to Susy in the months before the girl's tragic death from meningitis.

Dodge's next two books were published in 1894 by the Century Company. *The Land of Pluck* is a collection of short works, mostly culled from the pages of *St. Nicholas*. The title work is a series of sketches about Holland which in essence dated back to the *Riverside Magazine*. They had also been published in *St. Nicholas* but were greatly expanded for *The Land of Pluck*. They include description and history of the country, its customs, costumes, food, sights, and oddities. The volume also included a story set in Holland, "Daydreams on the Dike." The stories in the second half of the book were chiefly taken from the early years of *St. Nicholas*, where they were often published under pseudonyms. They are extremely varied; there are fairy tales, dreams, frontier stories, realistic stories, and informational essays. Some of the stories are humorous, such as "The Law That Could Not Be Broken" (the law of gravity) and "A Garret Adventure," in which neighborhood children try to build a skating pond in an attic. Some are touching; in "Grandmother" (based on a story published in the first issue of *St. Nicholas*), two girls learn to see the importance of their grandmother's contribution to the family circle. Still others are surprisingly harrowing stories to have come from Dodge's pen. "Only a Rose" tells of a small girl who misbehaves when her older sisters should have been watching her; the older girls feel great remorse when their little sister has an almost fatal fall while being punished. In "Limpety Jack," a practical joke played on a retarded man almost leads to the drowning of the son of one of the jokers. There are stories which are didactic and some which are sentimental. Some are more suited to adults than children. The collection shows the variety of Dodge's writing, its virtues and its faults.

The other book published in 1894 was a book of verses, *When Life Is Young*. It opens with what is today one of her better known poems, "The Minuet," which perhaps celebrates the occasion when her Grandmother Mapes danced with the Marquis de Lafayette. Some of the poems made their first appearance in the volume, some were reprinted from *Along the Way*, and some were first found in *St. Nicholas*. Generally they are for older children than those who delighted in *Rhymes and Jingles;* most of the poems are longer than those of the earlier book, although some are reminiscent of the nursery songs. Some are about nature and the fairy world, but most are about children and their growth. They are filled with delightful language and funny names: Aramantha Mehitabel Brown, a poet named Mr. Tennyson Tinkleton Tupper von Burns, an artist called Corregio Delmonico del Michael Angelina. The book never achieved the popularity of *Rhymes and Jingles*, however.

In 1894 *St. Nicholas* had just entered its third decade. In the years just before the new century, it continued its tradition of excellence, but Dodge, although she never gave up her interest or her control, was leaving more of the work to Fayal Clarke and other staff members. One of the highpoints of the third decade was John Bennett's *Master Skylark;* another was *Jack Ballister's Fortunes* by Howard Pyle. Theodore Roosevelt, who had written on buffalo hunting in the previous decade, wrote a series of "Hero Tales from American History" in 1895; in 1900 he contributed "What We Can Expect of the American Boy." Another special acquisition was "Letters to Young Friends" by Robert Louis Stevenson. Dodge had met and become friends with Stevenson several years before, but he had never written a story for her. After his death, his stepson sent Dodge a series of letters which Stevenson had written from Samoa to young friends in Scotland. Gelett Burgess's characters the Goops appeared in *St. Nicholas* during this period, and another new contributor was G. A. Henty. One of the most popular of *St. Nicholas* departments was begun by Albert Bigelow Paine in 1899. This was the St. Nicholas League, which encouraged young contributors under the age of eighteen to submit stories, poems, puzzles, drawings, and photographs for publication. Gold and silver badges were given for the best contributions. The League's Honor Roll virtually became a Who's Who of persons who were famous during the first half of the twentieth century. Among its members were Faith Baldwin, Ralph Henry Barbour, Norman Bel Geddes, Robert Benchley, Stephen Vincent Benét, Bennett Cerf, Henry Steele Commager, Babette Deutsch, Rachel Field, F. Scott Fitzgerald, Ring Lardner, Edna St. Vincent Millay, Sterling North, Alan Seegar, Cornelia Otis Skinner, Deems Taylor, Eudora Welty, Margaret Widdemer, Edmund Wilson, and Elinor Wylie.

In the 1890s several new editions of Dodge's books were brought out. In 1896 Scribners published the New Amsterdam Edition of *Hans Brinker*, with illustrations by Allen B. Doggett, who had been sent to Holland especially to make the pic-

tures. It was a handsome edition that proved very popular. In 1897 the Century Company published *A New Baby World*, compiled from *St. Nicholas* but with some changes from the earlier *Baby Days*. In 1898 another book compiled by Mrs. Dodge, *The Children's Book of Recitations*, was published by the DeWitt Publishing Company. In the same year, a new edition of her first book, *The Irvington Stories*, appeared under the imprint of the William L. Allison Company. It contained the original illustrations, but only five of the original stories were retained, and several new ones were added. The Allison Company had once been the publisher of the *Working Farmer*, and it was Allison who had recommended that Dodge take the book to her first publisher, James O'Kane. Allison had also published an edition of *Hans Brinker* in 1869, before the book was taken over by Scribner.

For many years, Dodge's health had not been good, and in 1898, as often before, she was tired and lacking in strength. In July of that year, while at Onteora, Fayal Clarke had an emergency appendectomy from which his recovery was very slow. When he was able to return to New York, he took his own apartment. For the first time in twenty years, Dodge would be without his companionship at home. At the moment, however, she had more immediate concerns. Nursing Clarke had proved very taxing, and she was finally ordered by her doctor and the Century Company to take a trip to Europe to recuperate. She sailed in December for Naples, accompanied by her friend Ida Medairy, who had accompanied her on her last trip to Europe in 1886. John Kendrick Bangs and his wife sailed on the same ship, and the four remained together in Naples for several weeks. Dodge and Ida Medairy then traveled to Egypt, where they saw the pyramids and journeyed up the Nile. Not until they returned to Italy did they learn that during their sojourn in Egypt, Dodge's sister Sophie had died. It was too late to hurry home; they continued to Rome, Florence, and Genoa before returning to New York in May.

Dodge's life was gradually drawing to a close. In 1904, Scribners published an enlarged edition of *Rhymes and Jingles* with illustrations by Sarah Stilwell. The same year, the Century Company published *Poems and Verses;* about two-thirds of the poems originally appeared in *Along the Way*, Dodge's earlier book of adult poetry. *St. Nicholas* was publishing such tales as L. Frank Baum's *Queen Zixi of Ix* and Howard Pyles's *The Story of King Arthur and His Knights*. A debt was paid in 1902 when Jack

London wrote *The Cruise of the Dazzler* for *St. Nicholas*. In 1884, London, a young wharf rat on the docks of San Francisco, read by chance a story in *St. Nicholas* that caused him to reform his life, join the California Fish Patrol, and eventually become a writer.

Dodge's health was deteriorating rapidly, but two weddings brightened her last years. In 1903 the Dodge family was startled when Fayal Clarke announced his engagement to Dodge's nurse, Katherine Strickland. The marriage took place in June, but not as expected; Clarke became ill and they were married at the side of his hospital bed. In November 1904, Kern Dodge, Jamie's oldest son, was married to Helen Green, with his grandmother in attendance.

Mrs. Dodge went as usual to Onteora in the summer of 1905. She died there of cancer on 21 August. Two days later the children of Onteora, dressed in white and carrying flowers, accompanied her coffin to the church, which was decorated with a large cross made of yarrow blossoms. Dodge's poem "The Two Mysteries" was read at the service. She was buried the next day in Evergreen Cemetery, Elizabeth, New Jersey.

The influence of Mary Mapes Dodge on literature for children was unequalled in the late nineteenth century. Through the pages of *St. Nicholas*, she offered some of the best literature ever available for children; a surprising amount of what she published is still read today. At her death, William Fayal Clarke called her "the recognized leader in juvenile literature for almost a third of a century, . . . universally honored by the children of America and even of the world. . . . Two generations of girls and boys have known her work and learned to love [her]." In its heyday *St. Nicholas* had a circulation of about 70,000, but this was by no means the limit of its readership. Children who were not fortunate enough to subscribe to *St. Nicholas* borrowed the copies from their luckier friends. Issues were reread over the years or passed down to younger siblings. The annual volumes, bound in red and gold, were issued in time for Christmas and were a favorite present to give or to receive. After Dodge's death, Clarke continued as editor until 1927. After his retirement and the sale of the magazine by the Century Company in 1930, it rapidly deteriorated and ceased publication in 1940. A brief revival in 1943 lasted for only three issues. So passed the magazine of which Sarah S. McEnery said in 1905, "So far is it above other children's magazines that its position is unique; in-

deed measured by its own standards, it is at this time the only magazine for children in the English tongue."

Great as was its influence, *St. Nicholas* was not Dodge's only achievement. Although most of her books were quickly forgotten, her amusing jingles lasted for years. One book, though, has endured. As Catherine Morris Wright says, it is *Hans Brinker* that "keep[s] the name of Mary Mapes Dodge fresh and recognized, year after year—decade following decade. Who reads *St. Nicholas* now? No one. Only oldsters who devoured it avidly in a far-away childhood have ever heard of it. But in every public library, on household shelves in America, England, France, Holland, the name of Mary Mapes Dodge can be read from the spine of a familiar-looking, well-worn volume, a classic more than a century old, beloved and used." Although Wright exaggerates a bit, two editions of *Hans Brinker* remain in print in the United States today. It has played an important part in the history of children's literature. It was the forerunner of many books set in foreign lands, and it established a high standard indeed. It remains one of the earliest American books for children which is still read today.

Whatever her reputation in the future, Dodge was loved and appreciated in her own time. Any writer or editor would be proud to receive the tribute paid to Mary Mapes Dodge by William Fayal Clarke: "It is given to few to exercise so far-reaching an influence upon young minds, and thus upon the future of the nation. She left the world not only happier, but better than she found it."

References:

William Fayal Clarke, "In Memory of Mary Mapes Dodge," *St. Nicholas*, 32 (October 1905): 1059-1071;

Alice B. Howard, *Mary Mapes Dodge of St. Nicholas* (New York: Messner, 1943);

Sarah S. McEnery, "Mary Mapes Dodge: An Intimate Tribute," *Critic*, 47 (October 1905): 310-312;

Lucia Gilbert Runkle, "Mary Mapes Dodge," in *Our Famous Women: An Authorized Record of the Lives and Deeds of Distinguished American Women of Our Times* (Hartford, Conn.: A. D. Worthington, 1886);

Catherine Morris Wright, *Lady of the Silver Skates: The Life and Correspondence of Mary Mapes Dodge* (Jamestown, R.I.: Clingstone Press, 1979).

Edward S. Ellis

(11 April 1840-20 June 1916)

Paul Eugen Camp
University of South Florida

SELECTED BOOKS: *Seth Jones; or, The Captives of the Frontier* (New York: Beadle, 1860; London: Beadle, 1861); revised as *Seth Jones of New Hampshire* (New York: Dillingham, 1907);

The Life and Times of Christopher Carson, the Rocky Mountain Scout and Guide (New York & London: Beadle, 1861);

Irona; or, Life on the Southwest Border (New York: Beadle, 1861; London: Beadle, 1863?);

Oonomoo, the Huron (New York: Beadle, 1862; London: Beadle, 1864);

The Hunters; or, Life on the Mountain and Prairie, as Latham C. Carleton (New York: Beadle, 1863);

Kent, the Ranger; or, The Fugitives of the Border (New York: Beadle, 1863); republished as *The Ranger* (London: Beadle, 1864);

Squatty Dick; or, The Short-Legged Hunter, as Captain Latham C. Carleton (New York: Munro, 1863);

The Lion-Hearted Hunter; or, The Captives of the Wyandottes. A Tale of the Mahoning, as Captain Latham C. Carleton (New York: Munro, 1864);

Peleg Smith; or, Adventures in the Tropics, as Boynton Belknap (New York: Beadle, 1866);

Kit Carson, the Scout, as J. H. Randolph (New York: Beadle, 1868);

Burt Bunker, the Trapper. A Tale of the North-West Hunting-Grounds, as Charles E. LaSalle (New York: Beadle & Adams, 1870);

The Huge Hunter; or, The Steam Man of the Prairies (New York: Beadle & Adams, 1870);

Old Zip; or, The Cabin in the Air. A Story of the Sioux Country, as Bruin Adams (New York: Beadle & Adams, 1871);

The Scalp King; or, The Squaw Wife of the White Avenger, as Ned Hunter (New York: Frank Starr, 1872);

Wolf-Fang Fritz; or, The Mad-Grisly Slayer, as Captain Marcy Hunter (New York: Dewitt, 1873); republished as *Oregon Sol; or, Nick Whiffles's Boy Spy* (New York: Beadle & Adams, 1878);

The Young Spy; or, Nick Whiffles Among the Modocs.

A Romance of the North-West, as Captain J. F. C. Adams (New York: Beadle & Adams, 1873);

Old Grizzly, the Bear Tamer, as Captain Bruin Adams (New York: Beadle & Adams, 1874);

Tahle, the Trailer; or, The Block-House, as Seelin Robins (New York: Beadle & Adams, 1875);

A Comedy of Cupid; or, Faint Heart Never Won Fair Lady, as Oswald A. Gwynne (Philadelphia: W. P. Kildare, 1879);

Jack's Horseshoe; or, What the "Waugroo Bitters" Did (New York: National Temperance Society, 1883);

Ned in the Block-House. A Tale of Early Days in the West (Philadelphia: Porter & Coates, 1883);

The Eclectic Primary History of the United States (New York: American Book Company, 1884);

Ned in the Woods. A Tale of Early Days in the West (Philadelphia: Porter & Coates, 1884);

Ned on the River (Philadelphia: Porter & Coates, 1884);

The Lost Trail (Philadelphia: Porter & Coates, 1885);

Camp-Fire and Wigwam (Philadelphia: Porter & Coates, 1885);

The Continental Primary Physiology; or, Good Health for Boys and Girls (New York: D. Van Winkle, 1885); republished as *Ellis's Primary Physiology* (New York: Taintor, 1889);

Down the Mississippi (Philadelphia: Porter & Coates, 1886);

Footprints in the Forest (Philadelphia: Porter & Coates, 1886);

Lost in the Wilds (New York: Cassell, 1886);

Standard Complete Arithmetic, Combining Oral and Written Exercises (St. Louis: Standard School Book Co., 1886);

Up the Tapajos; or, Adventure in Brazil (New York: Cassell, 1886); republished as *The Rubber Hunters; or Adventures in Brazil* (London: Cassell, 1886);

The Youths' History of the United States from the Discovery of America by the Northmen to the Present Time, 4 volumes (New York: Cassell, 1886-1887; London: Cassell, 1887);

University of South Florida Library

The Camp in the Mountains (Philadelphia: Porter & Coates, 1887);

The Heart of Oak Detective, or, Zigzag's Full Hand, as E. A. St. Mox (New York: Beadle & Adams, 1887);

The Hunters of the Ozark (Philadelphia: Porter & Coates, 1887);

The Last War Trail (Philadelphia: Porter & Coates, 1887);

On the Trail of Geronimo; or, In the Apache Country, as Lieutenant R. H. Jayne (New York: Lovell, 1887); republished as *In the Apache Country; or, On the Trail of Geronimo* (New York: Hurst, 1910);

Wyoming (Philadelphia: Porter & Coates, 1888);

Adrift in the Wilds; or, The Adventures of Two Shipwrecked Boys (New York: Burt, 1889);

The Boy Hunters of Kentucky (London: Cassell, 1889);

Elementary Arithmetic, Combining Oral and Written Exercises (Indianapolis: Indiana School Book, 1889);

The Land of Mystery, as Lieutenant R. H. Jayne (New York: Lovell, 1889);

Red Feather. A Tale of the American Frontier (London: Cassell, 1889); republished as *The Story of Red Feather. A Tale of the American Frontier* (New York: Cassell, 1909);

The Star of India (New York: American News Company, 1889);

Storm Mountain (Philadelphia: Porter & Coates, 1889);

The White Mustang. A Tale of the Lone Star State, as Lieutenant R. H. Jayne (New York: Lovell, 1889);

A Young Hero; or, Fighting to Win (New York: Burt, 1889);

Hands Up! or, The Great Bank Burglary, as J. G. Bethune (New York: United States Book Company, 1890);

Lost in Samoa. A Tale of Adventure in the Navigator Islands (London: Cassell, 1890; New York: Cassell, 1891);

On the Trail of the Moose (Philadelphia: Porter & Coates, 1890);

Perils of the Jungle, as Lieutenant R. H. Jayne (New York: Lovell, 1890);

Tad; or, "Getting Even" With Him (London: Cassell, 1890);

The Cabin in the Clearing. A Tale of the Frontier (Philadelphia: Porter & Coates, 1891);

Through Forest and Fire (Philadelphia: Porter & Coates, 1891);

Complete School History of the United States (Philadelphia: Porter & Coates, 1892; revised, Chicago: Werner, 1894);

From the Throttle to the President's Chair. A Story of American Railway Life (New York: Cassell, 1892); republished as *Bob Lovell's Career. A Story of American Railway Life* (London: Cassell, 1892); republished as *The Boys' and Girls' Story Book* (New York: Mershon, 1898);

Through Apache Land, as Lieutenant R. H. Jayne (St. Paul, Minn.: Price-McGill, 1893); republished as *Ned in the Mountains; or, Through Apache Land* (Chicago: Thompson & Thomas, 1908);

Across Texas (Philadelphia: Porter & Coates, 1893);

The Campers Out; or, the Right Path and the Wrong (Philadelphia: Penn, 1893);

The Wilderness Fugitives (St. Paul: Price-McGill, 1893);

Lena Wingo the Mohawk. A Sequel to "The Wilderness Fugitives" (St. Paul: Price-McGill, 1893);

Lost in the Wilderness, as Lieutenant R. H. Jayne (St. Paul: Price-McGill, 1893);

The River Fugitives (St. Paul: Price-McGill, 1893);

The Third Man, as J. G. Bethune (New York: Cassell, 1893);

Among the Esquimaux; or, Adventures Under the Arctic Circle (Philadelphia: Penn, 1894);

Brave Tom; or, The Battle That Won (New York: Merriam, 1894);

The Cave in the Mountain, as Lieutenant R. H. Jayne (New York: Merriam, 1894); republished as *Lone Wolf Cave. The Adventures of Two Boys in the Rocky Mountains* (Chicago: Thompson & Thomas, 1908);

The Great Cattle Trail (Philadelphia: Porter & Coates, 1894);

Common Errors in Writing and Speaking; What They Are and How to Avoid Them (New York: Woolfall, 1894);

Honest Ned (New York: Merriam, 1894);

In the Pecos Country, as Lieutenant R. H. Jayne (New York: Merriam, 1894);

The Path in the Ravine (Philadelphia: Porter & Coates, 1894);

Righting the Wrong (New York: Merriam, 1894);

Comrades True; or, Perseverance Versus Genius (Philadelphia: Penn, 1895);

Jack Midwood; or, Bread Cast Upon the Waters (New York: Merriam, 1895);

The Young Conductor; or, Winning His Way (New York: Merriam, 1895);

The Young Ranchers; or, Fighting the Sioux (Philadelphia: Coates, 1895);

The Young Scout. The Story of a West Point Lieutenant (New York: Burt, 1895);

Arthur Helmuth of the H. & N.C. Railway, as Lieutenant R. H. Jayne (New York: American Publishers Corporation, 1896);

Check Number 2134: A Sequel to Arthur Helmuth, as Lieutenant R. H. Jayne (New York: American Publishers Corporation, 1896);

Four Boys; or, The Story of a Forest Fire (New York: Merriam, 1896);

The Golden Ridge, as Captain R. M. Hawthorne (New York: American Publishers Corporation, 1896);

The Golden Rock, as Lieutenant R. H. Jayne (New York: American Publishers Corporation, 1896);

Shod with Silence. A Tale of the Frontier (Philadelphia: Coates, 1896);

The Phantom of the River. A Sequel to "Shod With Silence" (Philadelphia: Coates, 1896);

Uncrowning A King. A Tale of King Philip's War (New York: New Amsterdam Book Company, 1896); republished as *The Last Struggle. A Story of King Philip's War* (London: Cassell, 1908);

In the Days of the Pioneers. A Sequel to "The Phantom of the River" (Philadelphia: Coates, 1897);

Lives of the Presidents of the United States. Designed for Study and Supplementary Reading (Chicago: Flanagan, 1897);

Pontiac, Chief of the Ottawas. A Tale of the Siege of Detroit, as Colonel H. R. Gordon (New York: Dutton, 1897);

A Strange Craft and its Wonderful Voyage (Philadelphia: Coates, 1897);

True To His Trust (Philadelphia: Penn, 1897);

The Eye of the Sun (New York: Rand, McNally, 1897);

Ashtray in the Forest (London: Cassell, 1898);

Captured by Indians. A Tale of the American Frontier (London: Cassell, 1898);

Cowmen and Rustlers. A Story of the Wyoming Cattle Ranges in 1892 (Philadelphia: Coates, 1898);

The Daughter of the Chieftain. The Story of an Indian Girl (London: Cassell, 1898);

Klondike Nuggets and How Two Boys Secured Them (New York: Doubleday & McClure, 1898); enlarged as *The Young Gold Seekers of the Klondike* (Philadelphia: Penn, 1899);

Lost in the Rockies. A Story of Adventure in the Rocky Mountains (New York: Burt, 1898);

The Secret of Coffin Island (Philadelphia: Coates, 1898);

Tecumseh, Chief of the Shawanoes. A Tale of the War of 1812, as Colonel H. R. Gordon (New York: E. P. Dutton, 1898); republished as *Scouts and Comrades; or, Tecumseh, Chief of the Shawanoes. A Tale of the War of 1812* (London: Cassell, 1898);

Two Boys in Wyoming. A Tale of Adventure (Philadelphia: Coates, 1898);

Wolf-Ear the Indian. A Story of the Great Uprising of 1890-91 (London: Cassell, 1898);

Young People's History of Our Country (Boston: Lee & Shepard, 1898);

Dorsey the Young Inventor (New York: Fords, Howard & Hulbert, 1899);

Iron Heart, War Chief of the Iroquois (Philadelphia: Coates, 1899);

A Jaunt Through Java. The Story of a Journey to the Sacred Mountain By Two American Boys (New York: Burt, 1899);

The Land of Wonders (New York: Mershon, 1899);

Osceola, Chief of the Seminoles, as Colonel H. R. Gordon (New York: Dutton, 1899); republished as *In Red Indian Trails; or, Osceola, Chief of the Seminoles* (London: Cassell, 1899);

Through Jungle and Wilderness (New York: Mershon, 1899);

Blazing Arrow. A Tale of the Frontier (Philadelphia: Coates, 1900);

The Boy Patriot. A Story of Jack the Young Friend of Washington (New York: Burt, 1900);

Red Jacket, the Last of the Senecas, as Colonel H. R. Gordon (New York: Dutton, 1900);

Red Plume (New York: Mershon, 1900);

A Waif of the Mountains (New York: Mershon, 1900);

Our Jim; or, The Power of Example (Boston: Estes, 1901);

Red Eagle. A Tale of the Frontier (Philadelphia: Coates, 1901); republished as *The Chieftain and the Scout. A Tale of the Frontier* (London: Cassell, 1901);

The Story of the Greatest Nations, From the Dawn of History to the Twentieth Century; A Comprehensive History, Founded Upon the Leading Authorities, Including a Complete Chronology of the World, and A Pronouncing Vocabulary of Each Nation, by Ellis and Charles F. Horne, 9 volumes (New York: Niglutsch, 1901-1903);

Young People's History of England (Philadelphia: Altemus, 1901);

Young People's History of France (Philadelphia: Altemus, 1901);

Young People's History of Germany (Philadelphia: Altemus, 1901);

Bear Cavern (London: Cassell, 1902);

Jim and Joe, Two Brave Boys (Philadelphia: Coates, 1902);

Logan the Mingo. A Story of the Frontier, as Colonel H. R. Gordon (New York: Dutton, 1902);

Lucky Ned (G. F. S.) (Boston: Estes, 1902);

An American King. A Story of King Philip's War (Philadelphia: Coates, 1903);

The Jungle Fugitives. A Tale of Life and Adventure in India, Including Also Many Stories of American Adventure, Enterprise and Daring (New York: Hurst, 1903);

Limber Lew, the Circus Boy! or, The Battle of Life (Philadelphia: Coates, 1903);

Old Ironsides, The Hero of Tripoli and 1812 and Other Tales and Adventures on Sea and Land (New York: Hurst, 1903);

True Blue. A Story of Luck and Pluck (Boston: Estes, 1903);

The Cromwell of Virginia. A Tale of Bacon's Rebellion (Philadelphia: Coates, 1904);

Patriot and Tory (Boston: Estes, 1904);

Teddy and Towser. A Story of Early Days in California, as Seward D. Lisle (Philadelphia: Coates, 1904);

The Telegraph Messenger Boy; or, The Straight Road to Success (New York: Mershon, 1904);

Up the Forked River; or, Adventures in South America, as Seward D. Lisle (Philadelphia: Coates, 1904);

Deerfoot in the Forest (Philadelphia: Winston, 1905; London: Cassell, 1906);

Deerfoot on the Prairies (Philadelphia: Winston, 1905; London: Cassell, 1906);

Deerfoot in the Mountains (Philadelphia: Winston, 1905; London: Cassell, 1906);

Plucky Jo (Boston: Estes, 1905);

The Lost River (London: Cassell, 1905);

River and Forest (London: Cassell, 1905);

The Young People's Imitation of Christ, Based on the Work of Thomas à Kempis (Philadelphia: Griffith & Rowland, 1905);

Black Partridge; or The Fall of Fort Dearborn, as Colonel H. R. Gordon (New York: Dutton, 1906);

The Cruise of the Firefly, by Ellis and William Pendleton Chipman (Philadelphia: Winston, 1906);

From Low to High Gear (Boston: Estes, 1906);

From the Ranch to the White House; Life of Theodore Roosevelt, Author, Legislator, Field Sportsman, Soldier, Reformer and Executive (New York: Hurst, 1906);

A Hunt on Snow-Shoes (Philadelphia: Winston, 1906);

A Princess of the Woods (London: Cassell, 1906); republished as *Pocahontas, A Princess of the Woods* (New York: McLoughlin Brothers, 1908);

Brave Billy (Philadelphia: Winston, 1907);

Fighting to Win. The Story of a New York Boy (New York: Burt, 1907);

The Forest Messengers (Philadelphia: Winston, 1907);

River and Jungle (Philadelphia: Winston, 1907);

The Hunt of the White Elephant. A Sequel to "River and Jungle" (Philadelphia: Winston, 1907);

The Lost Dragon (Boston: Estes, 1907);

The Mountain Star (Philadelphia: Winston, 1907);

Plucky Dick; or, Sowing and Reaping (Philadelphia: Winston, 1907);

The Queen of the Clouds (Philadelphia: Winston, 1907);

Tam; or, Holding the Fort (Philadelphia: Winston, 1907);

Fire, Snow and Water; or, Life in the Lone Land (Philadelphia: Winston, 1908);

Off the Reservation; or, Caught in an Apache Raid (Philadelphia: Winston, 1908);

The P. Q. & G.; or, "As the Twig is Bent the Tree's Inclined" (Boston: Estes, 1908);

The Phantom Auto (Philadelphia: Winston, 1908);

The Round-Up; or, Geronimo's Last Raid (Philadelphia: Winston, 1908);

Trailing Geronimo; or, Campaigning with Crook (Philadelphia: Winston, 1908);

The Young Pioneers; or, Better to be Born Plucky than Rich (New York: Burt, 1908);

Alden the Pony Express Rider; or, Racing for Life (Philadelphia: Winston, 1909); republished as *The Pony Express Rider* (London: Cassell, 1919);

Alden Among the Indians; or, The Search for the Missing Pony Express Rider (Philadelphia: Winston, 1909); republished as *Lost Among the Redmen* (London: Cassell, 1919);

Lost in the Rockies (London: Cassell, 1909);

Unlucky Tib (Boston: Estes, 1909);

Upside Down. An Automobile Story for Boys (Philadelphia: Winston, 1909);

Bill Biddon, Trapper; or, Life in the North-West (New York: Hurst, 1910);

Captain of the Camp; or, Ben the Young Boss (Philadelphia: Winston, 1910);

Catamount Camp (Philadelphia: Winston, 1910);

The Forest Spy. A Tale of the War of 1812 (New York: Hurst, 1910);

The Forest Angel. A Romance of Kentucky Rangers' Life (New York: Hurst, 1910);

Nathan Todd; or, The Fate of the Sioux' Captive (New York: Hurst, 1910);

Work and Win. The Story of a Country Boy's Success (New York: Burt, 1910);

The Flying Boys in the Sky (Philadelphia: Winston, 1911); republished as *The Dragon of the Sky* (London: Cassell, 1915);

The Flying Boys to the Rescue (Philadelphia: Winston, 1911);

A Grandfather's Historic Stories of our Country From Its Discovery to the Present Time, 10 volumes (New York: Hartley-Thomas, 1911);

The Lost Trail (New York: Hurst, 1911);

The Ranger; or, The Fugitives of the Border (New York: Hurst, 1911);

The Hunter's Cabin. An Episode of the Early Settlements of Southern Ohio (New York: Hurst, 1911);

Adrift on the Pacific. A Boys' Story of the Sea and its Peril (New York: Burt, 1912);

Fighting Phil (Philadelphia: Winston, 1912);

The Launch Boys' Adventures in Northern Waters (Philadelphia: Winston, 1912);

The Launch Boys' Cruise in the Deerfoot (Philadelphia: Winston, 1912); republished as *Cruise of the Deerfoot* (London: Cassell, 1915);

The Riflemen of the Miami (New York: Hurst, 1912);

The Worst Boy (New York: American Tract Society, 1912);

The Boy Patrol Around the Council Fire (Philadelphia: Winston, 1913);

The Boy Patrol on Guard (Philadelphia: Winston, 1913);

Remember the Alamo (Philadelphia: Winston, 1914); republished as *Redskin and Scout* (London: Cassell, 1915);

The Three Arrows (Philadelphia: Winston, 1914).

OTHER: *The Youth's Dictionary of Mythology for Boys and Girls*, edited by Ellis (New York: Woolfall, 1895); republished as *1000 Mythological Characters Briefly Described* (New York: Hinds & Noble, 1899);

The Youth's Plutarch's Lives for Boys and Girls, edited by Ellis (New York: Woolfall, 1895).

Edward Sylvester Ellis began his half-century literary career in 1860 with a tale of Indian fighting on the post-Revolutionary American frontier; by the time he ceased to write, his subjects included aeroplanes and motorcars. In between, he had been one of the most prolific and widely read writers of American boys' books of all time and done much to create the romantic myth of the American West.

Since Ellis was perhaps the most extensive user of pseudonyms in American literary history, it is virtually impossible to tell how many works he actually wrote. Ellis scholar Denis R. Rogers estimates that he wrote at least 467 major works during his active writing years from 1860 to 1915. Additionally, Rogers credits Ellis with a monumental total of from 523 to more than 650 minor works such as sketches, articles, and poems. Of this vast output the bulk consists of works for children, though Ellis also turned out adult books as well. Of the popularity of Ellis's books for children, Albert Johannsen wrote, "His juvenile stories had an enormous sale, ranking with those of William T. Adams and Horatio Alger."

Ellis began life in the town of Geneva, in Ashtabula County, Ohio. He was the son of Sylvester and Mary Alberty Ellis. In 1846, the family removed to New Jersey where, with brief interruptions, he was to reside for the remainder of his life. Active in the Methodist Church, Ellis in later life frequently used religious elements in his plots and titles. In his teens, Ellis attended the State Normal School of New Jersey at Trenton. He became a teacher upon graduation. It was while teaching at Red Bank, New Jersey, in 1860 that the nineteen-year-old Ellis wrote *Seth Jones; or, The Captives of the Frontier*, the work that launched his career as a novelist.

Seth Jones is a Fenimore Cooperish tale of the frontier immediately following the American Revolution. It is replete with captures, escapes, rescues, dialect humor, and all the other paraphernalia that became associated with the early dime novel. The hero, an aged, dialect-speaking frontiersman of peculiar appearance and habits, sets out to rescue a fair damsel carried off by hostile Indians. Successful at the end of the novel, the eccentric Seth is revealed as none other than the young, handsome Eugene Morton, long lost lover of the kidnapped girl's attractive aunt. A secondary hero gets the girl, Morton gets the aunt, and virtue triumphs over savagery.

Ellis submitted his manuscript to the New York offices of Irwin P. Beadle & Company, pioneer publisher of the dime novels that would shortly flood the nation with cheap fiction. Realizing the potential of the story Beadle accepted it, paying the unknown young author $75.00 for publication rights. Released after a saturation advertising campaign that plastered New York billboards, barns, and newspaper columns with curiosity-stimulating advance notices, *Seth Jones* sold an estimated 60,000 copies during the first week at a time when sales of 20,000 made a novel a bestseller. The story of how the unknown young teacher struck it rich with his very first book entered the realm of literary folklore, to be retold in books and articles down through the years.

In point of fact, Ellis had been writing in a small way for some time before *Seth Jones* catapulted him to fame. His first known publication was a poem entitled "The Wanderer," which had appeared in *Ballou's Dollar Monthly* for September 1857. He had even sold a full-length story prior to *Seth Jones.* Entitled "Dick Flinton; or, Life on the Border," it had been serialized in the *New York Dispatch* beginning on 5 March 1859. With some characters' names changed, this story was later published as a dime novel by Beadle as *Kent, the Ranger* (1863). It was, however, the phenomenal success of *Seth Jones* that determined young Ellis to begin a serious writing career.

From the virtual standing start of *Seth Jones,* Ellis suddenly found himself one of the best known popular novelists in the nation. Beadle contracted with him for four novels annually, and Ellis commenced a five-year stint of writing dime novels for the country's premier dime novel house. During the years from 1860 to 1865 that he wrote for Beadle, he by no means restricted his burgeoning output to a single firm. Out of the 354 known numbers of the Ten Cent Novels series published by Beadle's

leading rival, George Munro & Company, nearly a third were written by Edward S. Ellis. As it was undesirable to have too many works by a single author, many of Ellis's publications starting as early as 1862 appeared under pseudonyms.

In an era notable for the use of pseudonyms, Ellis excelled. Ellis bibliographer Denis R. Rogers has identified no less than ninety-eight names associated with him in the course of his career. Thirty-four have been definitely confirmed as Ellis pseudonyms. These are: Captain "Bruin" Adams; Captain J. F. C. Adams; Boynton Belknap, M.D.; J. G. Bethune; J. H. Bethune; Henry R. Brisbane; Mahlon A. Brown; Captain Latham C. Carleton; The Ex-Reporter; Frank Faulkner; Colonel H. R. Gordon; Oscar A. Gwynne; Oswald A. Gwynne; Captain R. M. Hawthorne; Lieutenant R. H. Jayne; Charles A. LaSalle; George E. Hunter; Our New Contributor (in the *New York Fireside Companion*); Robin Playfellow; Boynton Randolph, M.D.; Geoffrey Randolph; Lieutenant J. H. Randolph; Rollo Robins, Jr.; Seelin Robins; Emerson Rodman; E. A. St. Mox; Egbert S. Thomas; A U.S. Detective (in *Saturday Night* and the *Hearthstone*); Nick Wilson.

Perhaps the best known of Ellis's pseudonyms was Lieutenant R. H. Jayne, which he first used in 1874. Ellis was fond of using names with military titles attached, as they added a touch of verisimilitude to his tales of adventure. The most interesting of his many noms de plume, however, was Captain J. F. C. Adams, also known as Bruin Adams, who for decades was believed to be a real person. "Adams" wrote Western tales of hunting and trapping and was purported to be the nephew of James Capen Adams (1807-1860), the famous Grizzly Adams. By comparing the texts of the Adams stories of the 1870s with later works which appeared with different titles under Ellis's name, Albert Johannsen has conclusively proven that Adams was in fact Edward S. Ellis.

When Irwin Beadle left his dime novel firm in 1865, Ellis went with him. On 7 October of that year, Ellis contracted to write exclusively for the American Novels series to be published by the newly formed firm known as Irwin P. Beadle. Ellis remained a contributor to Beadle's new publishing house until December 1868, a year after Irwin Beadle himself had left the firm. Ellis then returned to the original Beadle & Company, where he remained a mainstay of the Beadle writers' stable until 1874. After the number 308 of Beadle's Dime Novels was published on 19 May 1874, he dissolved his association with Beadle and thereafter wrote very little for the firm. This was not readily ap-

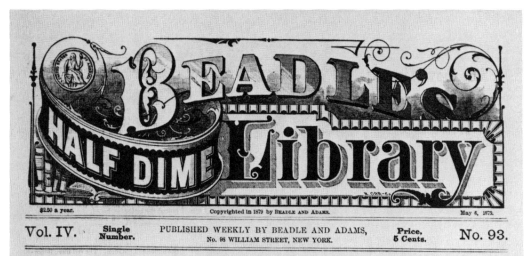

Front cover for one of Ellis's tales published in Beadle and Adams's weekly series for boys (University of South Florida Library)

parent to the reading public, as Beadle continued for many years to republish Ellis's earlier works, often under altered titles and author credits.

Ellis's early novels were not only well received by the public but also got favorable notice from many reviewers. William Everett wrote in his "Critical Notices" in the *North American Review* for July 1864 that "Mr. Ellis's 'Seth Jones' and 'Trail Hunters' are good, very good. Mr. Ellis's novels are favorites, and deserve to be. He shows variety and originality in his characters; and his Indians are human beings, and not fancy pieces." Although Ellis never visited the frontier and committed such faux pas as having Indians and pioneers alike propel canoes with oars (complete with muffled oarlocks), he began rather early in his career to strive for factual and historical accuracy. In speaking of Ellis's stories of the early 1870s, Denis Rogers said "Certainly the proven Ellis tales of the period show an accuracy of detail as to fauna, flora and geography and an attention to an intelligible plot which is conspicuously absent from the five Marcy Hunter tales."

On a personal as well as a professional basis, the 1860s were significant years for Ellis. On 25 December 1862 Ellis married Anne M. Deane. By this marriage he had one son, Wilmot Edward, later a U.S. Army officer and instructor at West Point, and three daughters, Miriam, Lillian, and Helen. Unfortunately the marriage proved unsuccessful, ending in divorce in 1887, the same year Ellis was awarded an honorary Master of Arts degree by Princeton College.

Seth Jones and most of Ellis's other early works were not written specifically with juvenile readers in mind, but the colorful, action-packed, adventure stories were avidly devoured by young American readers satiated with the "improving" juvenile literature of the day. Realizing his talent for children's literature, from around 1872 Ellis turned more and more toward the writing of stories intended for young people. As was the case with Edgar Rice Burroughs's Tarzan books at a much later date, many of Ellis's stories originally written for the adult market were subsequently republished as juveniles.

Like *Seth Jones*, most of Ellis's early output was in the form of frontier epics along the lines of Cooper's Leatherstocking Tales, though Ellis omitted the often tedious descriptive passages found in Cooper. As the American frontier moved westward, so did the scenes of Ellis's Western tales, though he continued to write "leatherstocking" titles. While his forte was the Western adventure

story, Ellis was a versatile writer who handled successfully such diverse novel subgenres as detective stories and love stories. He has, in fact, a good claim to being among the first American science-fiction writers. His 1870 dime novel *The Huge Hunter; or, The Steam Man of the Prairie 5* was a Western built around a boy inventor who had created a steam-powered robot capable of hauling a wagon rickshaw-fashion. As Denis Rogers wrote, "it is difficult to be emphatic that anything was outside the scope of such a prolific and versatile writer."

While producing his multitude of novels, Ellis found time to contribute extensively to weekly story papers, newspapers, and other periodical publications. Items from his pen appeared under his own name and under his many pseudonyms in such popular juvenile periodicals as *Banner Weekly, Boys' Holiday, Family Story Paper, Fireside Companion, Frank Leslie's Boys' and Girls' Weekly, Golden Days, Golden Argosy, Good News, New York Weekly,* and *Saturday Night.* In a letter to *New York Ledger* publisher Robert Bonner in 1881, Ellis stated that in the twelve years between 1869 and 1881 he had written more than forty serials for periodical publishers Davis & Everson alone. Many of Ellis's stories were first published as serials in periodicals, then as dime novels, and finally as clothbound books. Ellis also on several occasions tried his hand at editing juvenile periodicals. He was associate editor for *Golden Days* in 1878 and 1879 and edited *Boys' Holiday* in 1890 and 1891. It was while on the staff of *Golden Days* that he met his second wife, the writer Clara Spaulding Brown, a fellow staff member whom he married twenty-one years later on 20 November 1900.

After 1883 the bulk of Ellis's nonperiodical output appeared in the form of clothbound books rather than in the paperbound dime novel format of his earlier days. The Philadelphia firm of Porter and Coates became his most important publisher, a role that was fulfilled in turn by its successors Henry T. Coates and Company and the J. C. Winston Company. In Britain, where Ellis's novels had been popular since the 1861 appearance of *Seth Jones* as part of Beadle's American Library, the most important of his publishers was the London firm of Cassell and Company, Limited. Although these firms published most of Ellis's books, in the course of more than a half a century of writing his works appeared under the imprints of more than 279 American and foreign publishers.

The 1880s saw Ellis branch out from fiction into the fields of historical and educational writing. His *The Eclectic Primary History of the United States*

Covers for four dime novels by Ellis (University of South Florida Library)

(1884) was his first foray into the textbook field. It enjoyed considerable popularity and encouraged Ellis to pursue the writing of school books. Between 1884 and 1889 he wrote a total of ten school texts, including four arithmetics, four histories of America, a physiology text, and an English grammar. As a textbook writer Ellis was best known for his American histories, which were considered to be accurate, scholarly, and free of regional or political bias. In writing history Ellis was, however, a devoted American nationalist where international relations were concerned. He once wrote of the United States that "The record of no people can approach it in magnificence of achievement as regards art, science, education, literature, invention, and all that makes for true progress." Ellis's history texts were entertainingly written and well illustrated, giving them great appeal to students used to drab school books. "I regret very much," Albert Johannsen once wrote, "that I did not have a book like Ellis' 'Youth's History of the United States' when I was a boy, in place of a history that was simply a mass of names and dates of battles, as are, I am afraid, many of the modern school histories."

Ellis was eminently qualified to write school books. Although *Seth Jones* and subsequent novels had brought Ellis a flourishing career as a writer of popular fiction, he did not give up teaching. While actively cranking out stories he continued through the 1860s and 1870s to teach in New Jersey's public schools, becoming vice-principal of a school in Patterson and principal of the largest grammar school in Trenton. Ultimately, he became Trenton's city superintendent of education and served a term on the New Jersey State Board of Education. Not until the mid-1880s did he finally resign from teaching to devote himself to full-time writing. In addition to giving him outstanding credentials as a writer of school books, his long and intimate acquaintance with boys and girls in the classroom explains his remarkable understanding of the reading tastes and interests of America's youngsters.

Early in the 1880s Ellis created his most popular character, the Indian Deerfoot, the Shawanoe. Deerfoot was "one of the handsomest and ablest warriors who ever trod the forest, skillful beyond compare with bow and arrow, later with the rifle, and a friend of the white man." Deerfoot was featured in twelve novels, which appeared in four series over the period from 1883 to 1905. Each of the series consisted of three books, the whole comprising a saga tracing the life of Deerfoot from his untamed pagan youth in the 1780s to his death as a mature Christian. The character of Deerfoot was progressively developed in each book of the first nine volumes, giving him a depth contrasting strongly with the one-dimensional "redskins" inhabiting most juvenile Westerns of the period.

Deerfoot made his entrance in *Ned in the Block-House* (1883), the first volume of the Boy Pioneer series. A tale about an attack on a frontier fort by Indians in 1788, *Ned in the Block-House* became Ellis's most successful book, appearing in fifty-eight editions, including those published in Danish, Dutch, Finnish, and Swedish. In this and the succeeding books of the series Deerfoot's companions are two boys, one white, the title character, boy frontiersman Ned Preston, and his black friend Wildblossom. *Ned in the Woods* (1884), a story of hunting in Kentucky enlivened by the presence of horse thieves and hostile Wyandottes, was the next Deerfoot story, followed by *Ned on the River* (1884), in which Deerfoot outwits the young Tecumseh on the Ohio River to save a flatboat crew.

The first Deerfoot trilogy was followed by the Log Cabin series, in which Deerfoot's two young friends are an American and a German boy. In the first volume of the series, *The Lost Trail* (1885), Deerfoot saves the boys from an Indian band in the Mississippi country during the 1790s. In *Camp-Fire and Wigwam* (1885), Deerfoot's youthful companions are looking for a lost horse when they are captured by a band of Sauks. Though Deerfoot manages to rescue the American boy, he is forced to leave the German behind until the next book, *Footprints in the Forest* (1886). In this final volume of the series, he saves the young German from some Pawnees to whom the Sauks had transferred him.

The next three Deerfoot novels, The Deerfoot series, were intended by Ellis to conclude a nine-volume whole. Deerfoot's young sidekicks this time are American and Irish. In *The Hunters of the Ozark* (1887), the two boys join a trapping party in Missouri. They are captured by Winnebagoes but delivered by the gallant Deerfoot. The story, like those of the preceeding series, is set in the 1790s. *The Camp in the Mountains* (1887) carries on where the previous volume leaves off, with the resourceful Deerfoot again saving his white friends from their Indian foes. The final volume of the series, *The Last War Trail* (1887) has Deerfoot leading an expedition to rescue captives carried off from a frontier settlement by Winnebagoes. Although the expedition succeeds in delivering the captives, Deerfoot's wife and child are accidentally killed, and the incomparable Deerfoot dies of grief.

A creation as popular as Deerfoot is, however, not easily disposed of, as Arthur Conan Doyle discovered when he tried to kill off Sherlock Holmes. Ellis's public was not pleased with the death of so sympathetic a character. In 1905 Ellis bowed to popular demand and resurrected his Indian hero in The New Deerfoot series. Unfortunately, the three books of the new series lack the sureness of touch and appeal of the original nine volumes. The stories are placed in time between the events of the Log Cabin series and those of the Deerfoot series. The first book, *Deerfoot in the Forest* (1905) shows the noble red man rescuing teenage twins from hostiles. In the second, *Deerfoot on the Prairies* (1905), Ellis's hero journeys from Ohio to the Pacific coast, while in the final tale, *Deerfoot in the Mountains* (1905), Deerfoot converts a Blackfoot chief to Christianity, apparently by bludgeoning him into submission with religious platitudes. Denis Rogers summed up the final New Deerfoot story with the comment, "In the final tale, 'Deerfoot in the Mountains,' Ellis' normally sure touch deserts him altogether, when he places undue emphasis on militant Christianity and degenerates to mere preaching at his young readers; moreover there is an epilogue more suitable to a book on spiritualism than to a boys' adventure yarn."

In the 1890s and into the early twentieth century Ellis turned out several nonfiction books for children, including *The Youth's Dictionary of Mythology for Boys and Girls* (1895), *Young People's History of Our Country* (1898), and *The Young People's Imitation of Christ* (1905). In Ellis's own opinion, the crowning achievement of his career as a writer was *A Grandfather's Historic Stories of our Country From Its Discovery to the Present Time* (1911). Sold through an intensive nationwide subscription campaign, this ten-volume illustrated history of America is written in the style of Samuel Goodrich's earlier Peter Parley books. Unfortunately, the public did not share Ellis's enthusiasm for the work, and it was a financial failure. Residing at Upper Montclair, New Jersey, Ellis continued to write books for children and adults until at least as late as 1915. He died on 20 June 1916 while vacationing at Cliff Island, Casco Bay, Maine.

The 1926 volume of *The National Cyclopedia of American Biography* in its entry on Edward S. Ellis said of his books, "They are clean, wholesome and instructive, usually with a background of real history, and while abounding in such incidents as delight young readers, are manly and moral in their teachings." Though his works are not great literature, Ellis deserves a prominent niche in the his-tory of American writing for children if for no reason other than the sheer volume and popularity of his juvenile output. His work is, for its period, well written, well plotted and usually—within the often fantastical limits of individual stories—believable. Ellis's major characters are generally well delineated, in some cases with considerable perception. The best of his creations are endowed with human qualities that appealed vividly to his young readers. Most important of all, his stories both reflected and shaped the America he lived in, a nation in transition from a frontier to a modern urbanized society. Ellis was a storyteller who for almost half a century was able with almost instinctive precision to turn out the kind of literature young Americans wanted and in quantities seldom equaled by any writer of his day or our own.

References:

John Levi Cutler, "Gilbert Patten and His Frank Merriwell Saga," *Maine Bulletin*, 36 (May 1934): 20-21;

Albert Johannsen, *The House of Beadle and Adams* (Norman: University of Oklahoma Press, 1950), I: pp. 31-37; II: pp. 93-100;

J. Edward Leithead, "Now They're Collector's Items #1, Edward S. Ellis and Harry Castlemon," *Dime Novel Round-Up*, no. 405 (15 June 1966): 58-60; no. 406 (15 July 1966): 66-69;

Mary Noel, *Villains Galore . . . The Heyday of the Popular Story Weekly* (New York: Macmillan, 1954), pp. 118, 121, 173, 178, 181, 185, 223-224;

Edmund Pearson, *Dime Novels; or, Following an Old Trail in Popular Literature* (Boston: Little, Brown, 1929), pp. 33-34, 46, 84-85, 91, 98, 100-103, 132, 259;

Denis R. Rogers, "The Detective Stories of Edward S. Ellis," *Dime Novel Round-Up*, no. 558 (December 1982): 94-101; no. 559 (February 1983): 2-10, 23-24;

Rogers, "The Edward S. Ellis Stories Published by the Mershon Complex," *Dime Novel Round-Up*, no. 490 (15 July 1973): 70-76; no. 491 (15 August 1973): 86-92; no. 492 (15 September 1973): 104-110;

Rogers, "Ellis for Beginners," *Dime Novel Round-Up*, no. 529 (February 1978): 2-20;

Rogers, "Ellis' Ten War Chief Tales," *Dime Novel Round-Up*, no. 539 (October 1979): 74-76;

Rogers, "The Lovell Complex," *Dime Novel Round-Up*, no. 527 (October 1977): 98-115;

Rogers, "Oddities of Dime Novel Days," *Dime Novel Round-Up*, no. 526 (August 1977): 85-88.

Rogers, "The Pseudonyms of Edward S. Ellis," *Dime Novel Round-Up*, no. 266 (15 November 1954): 82-83; no. 267 (15 December 1954): 90-94; no. 268 (15 January 1955): 2-4; no. 307 (15 April 1958): 25-28; no. 315 (15 December 1958): 148-150; no. 318 (15 March 1959): 22-25; no. 319 (15 April 1959): 30-32, 35-37; no. 320 (15 May 1959): 42, 45; no. 330 (15 March 1960): 18-30; no. 334 (15 July 1960): 58-62; no. 336 (15 September 1960): 74-78; no. 363 (15 December 1962): 108-109;

Rogers, "A Statistical Alphabet of Edward S. Ellis,"

Dime Novel Round-Up, no. 446 (15 November 1969): 117-118;

Rogers, "A Survey of the Probable Publication Pattern of the Books by Edward S. Ellis Issued Under the Imprints of A. L. Burt and the A. L. Burt Company, New York," *Dime Novel Round-Up*, no. 524 (April 1977): 26-43;

Rogers with J. Edward Leithead, "A Publication Pattern of Edward S. Ellis," *Dime Novel Round-Up*, no. 481 (15 October 1972): 96-106.

Eugene Field

(2? September 1850-4 November 1895)

Norma Bagnall
Missouri Western State College

See also the Field entry in *DLB 23, American Newspaper Journalists, 1873-1900*.

SELECTED BOOKS: *The Tribune Primer* (Denver: Tribune Publishing Company, 1881);

Culture's Garland: Being Memoranda of the Gradual Rise of Literature, Art, Music and Society in Chicago, and Other Western Ganglia (Boston: Ticknor, 1887);

A Little Book of Profitable Tales (Chicago: Wilson, 1889; London: Osgood, McIlvaine, 1891);

A Little Book of Western Verse (Chicago: Wilson, 1889; enlarged, New York: Scribners, 1890; London: Osgood, McIlvaine, 1891);

Echoes from the Sabine Farm, by Field and Roswell M. Field (New Rochelle: Wilson, 1891; revised, Chicago: McClurg, 1893);

With Trumpet and Drum (New York: Scribners, 1892);

Second Book of Verse (Chicago: Stone, 1892);

The Holy-Cross and Other Tales (Cambridge & Chicago: Stone & Kimball, 1893; enlarged, New York: Scribners, 1896);

Love-Songs of Childhood (New York: Scribners, 1894);

The Love Affairs of a Bibliomaniac (New York: Scribners, 1896; London: Scribners/Lane, 1896);

The House: An Episode in the Lives of Reuben Baker,

Astronomer, and of His Wife Alice (New York: Scribners, 1896);

Songs and Other Verse (New York: Scribners, 1896);

Second Book of Tales (New York: Scribners, 1896);

Sharps and Flats, 2 volumes, collated by Slason Thompson (New York: Scribners, 1900);

A Little Book of Tribune Verse: A Number of Hitherto Uncollected Poems, Grave and Gay, edited by Joseph G. Brown (Denver: Tandy, Wheeler, 1901);

Nonsense for Old and Young (Boston: Dickerman, 1901);

The Stars: A Slumber Story (New York: New Amsterdam Book Company, 1901);

Hoosier Lyrics, edited by Charles Walter Brown (Chicago: Donohue, 1905).

Eugene Field was a popular humorist and newspaperman often called the "Poet of Childhood." Born in St. Louis, Missouri, to Roswell M. and Frances Reed Field, both of New England ancestry, Field claimed two birthdates—2 and 3 September 1850—in later years so that if friends forgot him on the first day, they could remember him on the second. His father was an attorney and attained some fame after successfully defending Dred Scott, fugitive slave, in Scott's first trial. Field's mother died when he was six, and he and his younger brother Roswell were sent to Amherst, Massachusetts, to be cared for by their paternal cousin Mary Field French until their maturity.

Field began college at Williams in 1868, after barely passing the entrance exams; he left New England the following spring because of the serious illness and subsequent death of his father in St. Louis. In the fall of 1869 he entered Knox College at Galesburg, Illinois; the following fall he enrolled as a junior at the University of Missouri at Columbia. In all of these attempts at higher learning Field was better known for his wit and conviviality than for his seriousness as a student, and he never graduated from college. In 1871 he collected his share of the inheritance from his father's estate, and he spent six months and his inheritance in Europe.

In 1873 Field married Julia Sutherland Com-

Eugene Field (from the George H. Yenowine Collection and published in Eugene Field, Verse and Prose, *edited by Henry H. Harper, 1917)*

stock, then sixteen, of St. Joseph, Missouri, and they had eight children, five of whom reached maturity. Field worked as a journalist on several Missouri newspapers during the next eight years: the *St. Louis Evening Journal, St. Joseph Gazette, St. Louis Times-Journal,* and the *Kansas City Times.* In 1881 he moved his family to Denver where he wrote for the *Denver Tribune.* In 1883 Field received an offer to move to Chicago, where he wrote a column entitled "Sharps and Flats" for the *Chicago Morning News* until his death in 1895 of heart failure.

Virtually all of Field's writings first appeared in one of his newspaper columns. *The Tribune Primer* (1881) is made up of selections from the *Denver Tribune* and modeled after *The New England Primer.* Field's *Primer* is a parody of the earlier one and directed at an audience considerably older than the subheadings suggest. The whimsical, often sardonic, humor in *The Tribune Primer*—for example, suggesting that children pat the wasp, eat a wormy apple, or put mud in baby's ears—seems indicative of Field's early attitude toward children. He had the reputation of making faces at, or otherwise teasing, small children when he thought he was unobserved by adults. Slason Thompson, Field's early biographer, suggests that Field did not like children, but Charles Dennis, writing later, believes that Field had an attitude of one child to another; Dennis further argues that Field went through a "sweetening process" which made his later works gentler and more sentimental than this early, satiric work.

Field found much to be satiric about in his early days in Denver, and as managing editor of the *Denver Tribune* and writer of a column, "Odds and Ends," he managed to poke fun at the climate, the muddy roads, the frontier language, and other aspects of Denver life he found hypocritical. *Nonsense for Old and Young* (1901) contains humorous sketches from the *Denver Tribune* not included in *The Tribune Primer.*

Field had a large following of readers by 1883, the year he was lured to Chicago to write his own column for the *Chicago Morning News* at a salary of fifty dollars a week. Once established in the city, Field found that the salary, munificent by Denver's standards, was only reasonable in Chicago. He saw much in Chicago that begged for reform, particularly the emphasis on making money. *Culture's Garland* (1887) is made up of selected satirical essays from Field's column "Sharps and Flats." Chiding Chicagoans for their materialism and calling their city "Porkopolis," Field found, not surprisingly, that the local residents did not appreciate

First page of an undated letter from Field explaining when and under what circumstances he wrote some of his best-known poems and stories, including "Wynken, Blynken and Nod" and "Little Boy Blue" (from the George H. Yenowine Collection and published in Eugene Field, Verse and Prose, edited by Henry H. Harper, 1917)

being on the acid end of his pen. Perhaps he redeemed himself later with his often quoted reply to British novelist Mrs. Humphry Ward in London. She asked him, "Do you not find the social atmosphere of Chicago exceedingly crude, furnishing one with little intellectual companionship?" Field replied, "Really Mrs. Ward, . . . I do not consider myself competent to give an opinion . . . up to the time Barnum captured me and took me to Chicago to be civilized I had always lived in a tree in the wilds of Missouri."

In addition to satiric essays, Field was also writing stories and verse of a sentimental nature. It was in 1888 with the publication of "Little Boy Blue" in *America,* a weekly journal, that Field won immediate and long-lasting fame. The same issue of *America* carried a poem by James Russell Lowell, "St. Michael the Weigher," and it was a great satisfaction to Field that his "Little Boy Blue" was more popular than the offering of an established poet. Field's poem is about toys waiting on the shelf for their little owner who has toddled off to bed

Engraving of Field with children used as the frontispiece to Poems of Childhood *(1896), volume four of* The Writings in Prose and Verse of Eugene Field *(Baldwin Library, University of Florida Libraries)*

and died in his sleep. While on lecture tours, Field was almost invariably asked first to read this poem. He followed his success of "Little Boy Blue" with a tremendous outpouring of poetry. He not only wanted his poetry well received, but he also wanted to write much of it, and he did. *A Little Book of Western Verse* was published in an edition of 250 subscription copies in 1889, followed by *Second Book of Verse* in 1892. During this period Field also produced two volumes specifically about childhood: *With Trumpet and Drum* (1892) and *Love-Songs of Childhood* (1894). *With Trumpet and Drum* includes "The Sugar Plum Tree," "Wynken, Blynken and Nod," "Little Boy Blue," and a selection of lullabies and folk songs of different lands. Field had studied books of children's writers from many lands, and he collected legends and folktales. *Love-Songs of Childhood* includes "The Duel" (or "The Gingham Dog and the Calico Cat") and "The Rock-a-By Lady." Much of his childhood verse had been published in the *Chicago Morning News* or in periodicals such as *Youth's Companion* and *Ladies' Home Journal.* This verse established Field's reputation as the "poet laureate" of children; it was well received during his lifetime, and some of it was included in readers for much of the early part of the twentieth century.

Throughout his career, Field was well regarded by his fellow journalists, and he had a wide circle of friends. His love of pranks and flippant sense of humor, which caused him trouble in his school days, made him popular as an adult, for the pranks were without intent to harm and were the basis of much fun. Some of his privately printed ribald humor, *Little Willie* and "Only a Boy," for example, was intended for male audiences only; there was a major attempt by Anthony Comstock, representing the Society for the Suppression of Vice, to ban this part of Field's work; Comstock felt that it would tarnish Field's reputation as the "poet of childhood."

With his brother Roswell, Field produced *Echoes from the Sabine Farm* (1891), a modern and loose translation of Horace. At the time of his death, he was working on *The House* (1896), autobiographical in nature, about the problems of a family moving into a new house (his own Sabine Farm, which the Fields bought and moved into the year before his death). *The Love Affairs of a Bibliomaniac* (1896), also published just after Field's death, is about his constant search for lovely books. Field treasured beautiful books and had a library lined with rare and unusual volumes. He liked making nice books himself and frequently worked dili-

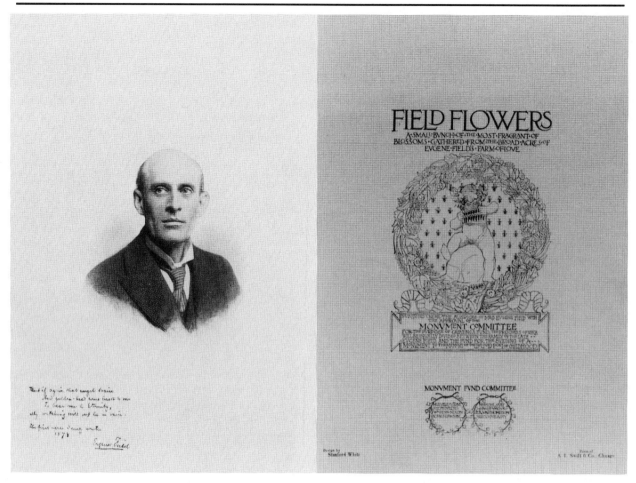

Frontispiece and title page for an 1896 souvenir collection of poems. Proceeds from subscription sales were used to erect the monument The Rock-a-By Lady from Hush-a-By Street *which stands in Chicago's Lincoln Park.*

gently with various colored inks decorating the first letter of a poem; he would then finish the verse in compact script so as not to waste any strokes of the pen.

Memorials to Field include the preservation of the Field home in Denver for many years as a branch library and the Eugene Field House in St. Louis. This latter was formally dedicated in 1902 by Mark Twain as Field's birthplace. It was not the place of his birth, as Roswell Field interrupted ceremonies to say, but Twain was undaunted and insisted that it was the formal and official recognition which mattered; the Eugene Field House in St. Louis remains a memorial open to visitors today. Monuments commemorating Field's work are "The Rock-a-By Lady from Hush-a-By Street" in Lincoln Park, Chicago, and "Wynken, Blynken and Nod" in Washington Park, Denver. Schools in many American cities were named for Field shortly after his death, and in Missouri "Eugene Field Days"

were observed annually across the state to honor the anniversary of the date of Field's death. Early in the twentieth century grade-school readers frequently included one of Field's childhood poems.

Considered from the 1980s, Field's "poems of childhood" appear to be about childhood rather than for children. That is, they deal with childhood nostalgically, and children have not lived long enough to be nostalgic about much of anything, certainly not about their own childhood. However, adaptations of some of Field's work into film and drama in the 1960s and inclusion of one or more of his poems in current poetry anthologies for children are indications that Field's verse for children continues to be read and that many still remember him as the "Poet of Childhood."

References:

Ida Comstock Below, *Eugene Field in His Home* (New York: Dutton, 1898);

Robert Conrow, *Field Days: The Life, Times, & Reputation of Eugene Field* (New York: Scribners, 1974);

Charles H. Dennis, *Eugene Field's Creative Years* (Garden City: Doubleday, 1924);

Slason Thompson, *Eugene Field: A Study in Heredity and Contradictions*, 2 volumes (New York: Scribners, 1901).

Papers:

There are collections of Field's papers at Brown University, the Library of Congress, the Lilly Library of Indiana University, the Missouri Historical Society, the New York Public Library, Lockwood Memorial Library at the State University of New York at Buffalo, the University of Illinois at Chicago Circle, Washington University in St. Louis, and the Beinecke Rare Book and Manuscript Library of Yale University.

Martha Finley
(Martha Farquharson)
(26 April 1828-30 January 1909)

M. Sarah Smedman
University of North Carolina at Charlotte

BOOKS: *Ella Clinton, or By Their Fruits Ye Shall Know Them* (Philadelphia: Presbyterian Board of Publication, 1856);

Aunt Ruth (Philadelphia, 1857);

Marion Harvie, A Tale of Persecution in the Seventeenth Century (Philadelphia: Presbyterian Board of Publication, 1857);

Annandale, a Story of the Times of the Covenanters (Philadelphia: Presbyterian Board of Publication, 1858);

Lame Letty (Philadelphia, 1859);

Try; Better Do It, Than Wish It Done (Philadelphia: Presbyterian Board of Publication, 1863);

Little Joe Carter, the Cripple; or Learning to Forgive (Philadelphia: Presbyterian Board of Publication, 1864);

Mysie's Work, and How She Did It (Philadelphia: Presbyterian Board of Publication, 1864);

Willie Elton, the Little Boy Who Loved Jesus (Philadelphia, 1864);

Black Steve, or The Strange Warning (Philadelphia: Presbyterian Publication Committee/New York: A. D. F. Randolph, 1865);

Brookside Farm-house, from January to December (Philadelphia: Presbyterian Publication Committee, 1865);

Hugo and Franz (Philadelphia, 1865);

Robert and Daisy (Philadelphia, 1865);

Allan's Fault (Philadelphia: Presbyterian Board of Publication, 1866);

Elsie Dinsmore (New York: Dodd, Mead, 1867; London: King, 1873);

Holidays at Roselands: with Some After Scenes of Elsie's Life (New York: Dodd, Mead, 1868; London: King, 1873);

Casella; or, The Children of the Valleys (New York: Dodd, Mead, 1868);

Anna Hand, the Meddlesome Girl (Philadelphia, 1868);

Grandma Foster's Sunbeam (Philadelphia, 1868);

Little Patience (Philadelphia, 1868);

Little Dick Positive (Philadelphia, 1868);

Loitering Linus (Philadelphia, 1868);

Maud's Two Homes (Philadelphia, 1868);

Milly; or the Little Girl Who Tried to Help Others and Do Them Good (Philadelphia, 1868);

The Shannons, or, From Darkness to Light (Philadelphia: Presbyterian Publications Committee, 1868);

Stupid Sally, the Poor-house Girl (Philadelphia, 1868);

Amy and Her Kitten (Philadelphia, 1870);

Betty Page (Philadelphia, 1870);

The Broken Basket (Philadelphia, 1870);

Jamie by the Lake (Philadelphia, 1870);

Rufus the Unready (Philadelphia, 1870);

The White Dress (Philadelphia, 1870);

Martha Finley

An Old Fashioned Boy (Philadelphia: Evans, Stoddart, 1871);

Lilian; or Did She Do Right? (Philadelphia: Evans, 1871);

Wanted—a Pedigree (New York: Dodd, Mead, 1871);

Contented Jim (Philadelphia: Presbyterian Board of Publication, 1872);

Elsie's Girlhood (New York: Dodd, Mead, 1872; London: King, 1873);

Honest Jim (Philadelphia: Presbyterian Board of Publication, 1872);

How Jim Did It (Philadelphia: Presbyterian Board of Publication, 1872);

Noll in the Country (Philadelphia: Presbyterian Board of Publication, 1872);

Noll the Beggar Boy (Philadelphia: Presbyterian Board of Publication, 1872);

The Twin Babies (Philadelphia: Presbyterian Board of Publication, 1872);

Our Fred; or, Seminary Life at Thurston (New York: Dodd, Mead, 1874);

Elsie's Womanhood (New York: Dodd, Mead, 1875; London: Routledge, 1889);

The Peddler of LaGrave (Philadelphia: Presbyterian Board of Publication, 1875);

Aunt Hetty's Fowls; or, Harry at the Farm (Philadelphia: Presbyterian Board of Publication, 1876);

Elsie's Motherhood (New York: Dodd, Mead, 1876; London: Routledge, 1889);

Harry and His Chickens (Philadelphia: Presbyterian Board of Publication, 1876);

Harry and Cousins (Philadelphia: Presbyterian Board of Publication, 1876);

Harry at Aunt Jane's (Philadelphia: Presbyterian Board of Publication, 1876);

Harry's Christmas in the City (Philadelphia: Presbyterian Board of Publication, 1876);

Harry's Fourth of July (Philadelphia: Presbyterian Board of Publication, 1876);

Harry's Grandma and the Stories She Told Him (Philadelphia: Presbyterian Board of Publication, 1876);

Harry's Little Sister (Philadelphia: Presbyterian Board of Publication, 1876);

Harry's Ride with Papa (Philadelphia: Presbyterian Board of Publication, 1876);

Harry's Walks with Grandma (Philadelphia: Presbyterian Board of Publication, 1876);

The Pewit's Nest (Philadelphia: Presbyterian Board of Publication, 1876);

Rosa and Robbie (Philadelphia: Presbyterian Board of Publication, 1876);

Elsie's Children (New York: Dodd, Mead, 1877; London: Routledge, 1889);

Mildred Keith (New York: Dodd, Mead, 1878; London: Routledge, 1890);

Mildred at Roselands (New York: Dodd, Mead, 1879; London: Routledge, 1890);

Signing the Contract, and What It Cost (New York: Dodd, Mead, 1879);

Elsie's Widowhood (New York: Dodd, Mead, 1880; London: Routledge, 1889);

Mildred and Elsie (New York: Dodd, Mead, 1881; London: Routledge, 1890);

Grandmother Elsie (New York: Dodd, Mead, 1882; London: Routledge, 1889);

Mildred's Married Life, and a Winter with Elsie Dinsmore (New York: Dodd, Mead, 1882; London: Routledge, 1890);

Elsie's New Relations (New York: Dodd, Mead, 1883; London: Routledge, 1889);

Mildred at Home (New York: Dodd, Mead, 1884; London: Routledge, 1890);

Elsie at Nantucket (New York: Dodd, Mead, 1884; London: Routledge, 1889);

The Two Elsies (New York: Dodd, Mead, 1885; London: Routledge, 1889);

Mildred's Boys and Girls (New York: Dodd, Mead, 1886; London: Routledge, 1890);

Elsie's Kith and Kin (New York: Dodd, Mead, 1886; London: Routledge, 1889);

The Thorn in the Nest (New York: Dodd, Mead, 1886);

Elsie's Friends at Woodburn (New York: Dodd, Mead, 1887; London: Routledge, 1889);

Christmas with Grandma Elsie (New York: Dodd, Mead, 1888; London: Routledge, 1888);

Elsie and the Raymonds (New York: Dodd, Mead, 1889; London: Routledge, 1890);

Elsie Yachting with the Raymonds (New York: Dodd, Mead, 1890; London: Routledge, 1890);

Elsie's Vacation and After Events (New York: Dodd, Mead, 1891; London: Routledge, 1891);

Elsie at Viamede (New York: Dodd, Mead, 1892; London: Stevens, 1892);

Elsie at Ion (New York: Dodd, Mead, 1893; London: Routledge, 1893);

The Tragedy of Wild River Valley (New York: Dodd, Mead, 1893);

Elsie at the World's Fair (New York: Dodd, Mead, 1894; London: Routledge, 1895);

Mildred's New Daughter (New York: Dodd, Mead, 1894; London: Stevens, 1894);

Elsie's Journey on Inland Waters (New York: Dodd, Mead, 1895; London: Stevens, 1895);

Elsie at Home (New York: Dodd, Mead, 1897);

Elsie on the Hudson (New York: Dodd, Mead, 1898);

Twiddledetwit, a Fairytale (New York: Dodd, Mead, 1898);

Elsie in the South (New York: Dodd, Mead, 1899);

Elsie's Young Folks in Peace and War (New York: Dodd, Mead, 1900; London: Routledge, 1900);

Elsie's Winter Trip (New York: Dodd, Mead, 1902);

Elsie and Her Loved Ones (New York: Dodd, Mead, 1903);

Elsie and Her Namesakes (New York: Dodd, Mead, 1905; London: Stevens & Brown, 1905).

Practically a pariah among historians and critics of children's literature, Martha Finley was popular with readers. Though reviewers ignored her, for more than three generations her *Elsie Dinsmore* outsold every other juvenile book with the exception of *Little Women*, and, according to one source, the sad-eyed, humble but resolute Elsie "attained more widespread interest and affection" than any other character in juvenile fiction except Huckleberry Finn. Although she is remembered only for

the Elsie books, Finley wrote prodigiously, about one hundred books in all, the first of which was a Sunday school story published by the Presbyterian Board of Publication. Most of her writing, which included many Sunday school stories by the end of her career, was for children. The few adult novels she attempted never attracted much of an audience. By contrast, the twenty-eight volumes of her Elsie Dinsmore series, one of the first American series for girls featuring a continuing cast of characters, were great popular successes in both the United States and England. For thirty-eight years, each successive volume left in its wake an importunate clamor for another, a demand which more than once altered the author's publicized plans to bring the series to a close.

Today it is difficult to comprehend the public's insatiable appetite, not so much for the themes that Finley hammered at nor the incidents through which she walked set after set of supporting characters but for the labored and lugubrious style in which she recorded the performance of the same trite gestures and unnatural conversations. The Elsie books follow in the tradition of the stories of pietistic children born with an instinct for good and evil as delimited by the Puritan code, children who not only fight off temptations but also enlighten and urge to salvation their elders, thereby appeasing an angry God, eluding Satan, and earning their rewards in heaven when they die holy and dramatic deaths sometime between the ages of two and twelve. Finley tempered the pattern. Elsie, as she herself announced early on, was not quite perfect. Her God was not wrathful but gentle, comforting, the loving father of the New Testament and the bridegroom of the Song of Solomon. Both were incarnated in her earthly father, whom she dreaded displeasing because she so reverenced him. Elsie actually did pass briefly beyond the boundaries of the living in the second volume of the series, but miraculously she rose again to live a long life, and a happy one, though it was filled with trials that tested her mettle, proving her virtue unassailable and endearing her to millions of devoted fans.

Martha Finley herself was a private person who lived a quiet life, apparently dividing her energies among her writing, her many friends, and her church activities. Of Scots-Irish descent, she was born on 26 April 1828 of first cousins, Dr. James Brown Finley and Maria Theresa Brown Finley, in Chillicothe, Ohio. Her mother having died when Finley was very young, her father moved to Philadelphia, where he remarried. Finley grew up

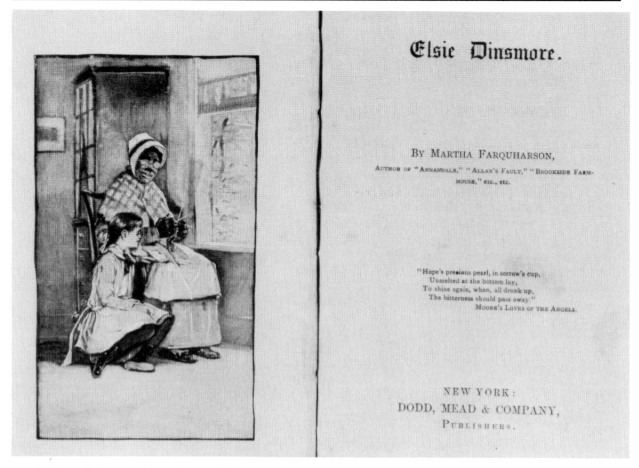

Frontispiece and title page for the first novel about Elsie (Baldwin Library, University of Florida Libraries). In the preface to one of the later Elsie books Finley described her character as a "companion and friend" to readers and "a useful example particularly in her filial love and obedience."

among a brood that eventually numbered fourteen. When Finley was eight, her father moved his family to the pioneer territory of South Bend, Indiana, a journey she faithfully described in *Mildred Keith* (1878). Finley was educated in private schools in Philadelphia and South Bend, the quality of her later literary work suggesting that, like Elsie, "Though not a remarkably precocious child in other respects, she seemed to have very clear and correct views on almost every subject connected with her duty to God and her neighbor."

For a short time, from 1851 to 1853, Finley taught school in Indiana and then in Phoenixville, Pennsylvania, before she returned to Philadelphia soon after her father's death. There, at age twenty-six, she unspectacularly launched her career as a writer. Her early writings, stories, and books for the children's departments of various Sunday schools were published anonymously. Because these were successful, her publisher persuaded her

to sign her works, though for many years she used the pseudonym Martha Farquharson because her family objected to the public parading of her own name. She chose Farquharson because it was the name of her clan, the Gaelic equivalent of Finley. Between 1856 and 1875, she wrote some thirty-five ephemeral Sunday school books, typical of which are: *Marion Harvie, A Tale of Persecution in the Seventeenth Century* (1857); *Little Joe Carter, the Cripple; or Learning to Forgive* (1864); *Grandma Foster's Sunbeam* (1868); *Rufus the Unready* (1870); and *Lilian; or Did She Do Right?* (1871).

In 1867 *Elsie Dinsmore* was published. Finley conceived the character Elsie when she was bedridden with a back ailment and financially dependent upon her stepbrother. The inspiration for Elsie, she said, came in answer to her prayer for "something which would yield her an income . . . and with no intention of ever being continued in sequels." During the Philadelphia years she also tested, but found wanting, her talent for adult novels with *Wanted—a Pedigree*, published in 1871. In that same year, desirous of "setting forth the faults and foibles" of the typical boy of the period, as several other writers had done for the girl, Finley produced *An Old Fashioned Boy*. Its hero, Fred Landon, is a touchstone of filial obedience, Christian fellowship, and patriotism against which the antics of his school fellows are measured. So steady were the sales of this episodic, comparatively fast-paced narrative of school and domestic life that the publishers encouraged a sequel, though Finley's original plans had not included one. In 1874, *Our Fred* took Fred to Thurston Seminary and his family from a hops farm in Wisconsin back to New York.

In 1876, with failing and frail health, Finley visited Elkton, Maryland, where her stepmother had moved with the family. She liked it so well she settled there, buying a house not unlike the homes she gave many of her characters, with verandas overlooking the Elk River and beautiful grounds. During her Maryland years Finley continued to write the Elsie books and completed several other adult novels. In 1878, with the publication of *Mildred Keith*, she started a companion series to Elsie Dinsmore, with a new set of characters, cousins of the Dinsmores, who interact with them through visits of the families back and forth. The Mildred series, consisting of six titles published between 1878 and 1886 with a seventh tacked on in 1894, never enjoyed the same success as the Elsie books.

After years of debilitating ill health, Finley died at the age of eighty on 30 January 1909. As little notice was taken of Finley's death as of her life. Simple obituaries appeared in the local newspapers.

Finley's famous Elsie Dinsmore series, like most family sagas, is what Henry James would call a "loose baggy monster." When the demure, determined little girl with limpid hazel eyes and golden-brown curls was born, Finley had no idea that she would grow to grandmotherhood and become the benevolent, eternally youthful matriarch of a large clan. The author had created Elsie to be a sacrificial lamb and savior, ardently desirous of winning the love and conversion to Christianity of Horace Dinsmore, the father she had never seen. The path to those goals was trouble-ridden and tearful, but it had an end, beyond which Finley had not projected any future for Elsie. The manuscript she took to Dodd, Mead, destined to become one of the most profitable of all American publications, was far too long to appear as a single volume. Dodd suggested that the first part be published as *Elsie*

Dinsmore and the second as a sequel. The story was divided in half with no consideration for its structure, and *Holidays at Roselands*, published in 1868, picked up where *Elsie Dinsmore* had abruptly stopped. Although initial response to the books was favorable but not enthusiastic, within a few years the volumes had inflamed the public's fancy. To satisfy the ensuing demand, Finley, between 1872 and 1877, produced four additional Elsie books, taking her in *Elsie's Girlhood* (1872) through those "years in which her character was developing, and mind and body were growing and strengthening for the real work and battle in life."

Finley's purpose for Elsie's existence, as she avowed in *Elsie's Girlhood*, was to provide readers with "a companion and friend," "a useful example particularly in her filial love and obedience." Though Elsie grew physically taller, morally she was the same sweet, staunch beauty, her greatest conquest having been won by the end of the second volume, in which her father's conversion is achieved. Not even Finley could have actually believed that Elsie's "real work and battle" began when she married Edward Travilla, her father's best friend and eighteen years her senior, and bore him eight children without losing for a moment her complacent and sentimental composure. At the end of *Elsie's Children*, Finley again proposed laying Elsie to rest. "With this volume, bringing the Story of Elsie down to the present time," she wrote in the preface, "the series closes." Again the voracious friends and admirers of Elsie demanded more, and in 1880 Finley responded, this time with *Elsie's Widowhood*, reluctantly bestowing such sorrows upon her "favorite child" only to please what she termed an "autocratic" public who "made the title."

Though not originally planned as a whole, the first six volumes of the series do have a thematic and structural unity, revolving about the relationship between Elsie and her father. Each succeeding book, comments Janet Elder Brown in "The Saga of Elsie Dinsmore" (1945), "like a wing on a house, added systematically to what had gone before." Each book picks up where the preceding stopped and progresses to a point which logically could have concluded the series. In *Elsie's Widowhood*, however, Finley introduces new characters, apparently looking ahead to sequels without any foreseeable end. Elsie's daughter Violet marries a domineering but kindly widower very much like Horace Dinsmore. Captain Levis Raymond has three children, and in his relationship with his headstrong daughter Lulu, the Horace-Elsie, father-daughter love struggle is reincarnated. The next several books are composed

Frontispiece for the first British edition of Elsie Dinsmore
(Baldwin Library, University of Florida Libraries)

of events loosely linked by the finally successful attempt of Raymond to bring to heel, through the discipline of love, his intractable daughter. Their story is concluded, predictably, when Lulu, as reluctant to leave her father as Elsie was hers, marries.

The following fifteen volumes, beginning with *Christmas with Grandma Elsie* (1888) and ending with *Elsie and Her Namesakes* (1905), are virtually plotless. New characters are introduced, frequently to marry into the family and perpetuate it. The Dinsmores, the Travillas, and the Raymonds travel up, down, and across the United States, often by yacht. They carry on lengthy, if not learned, theological disputations on such subjects as the nature of Satan. They read to each other seemingly interminable, often irrelevant disquisitions taken with little alteration from such sources as George Ban-

croft's and Benson J. Lossing's histories of the American Revolution and the War of 1812 and from a *Harper's* article on the life of a West Point cadet. Tediously, characters reaffirm one another with wisdom from the Bible, which they quote incessantly. Horace grows more flaccid; Elsie retains her beauty; the descendants increase and multiply. The final volume gives no hint that it was destined to be the last. Presumably Elsie was to go on as long as Finley was able to write.

In the middle volumes, from *Grandmother Elsie* (1882) through *Elsie's Friends at Woodburn* (1887), Finley focuses her attention on Lulu and Captain Raymond, relegating Elsie to a less prominent place. Lulu, a livelier, more self-willed child than Elsie, resents her stepmother and in a jealous rage goes so far as to kick her infant half-sister down the stair. Her father, as stern a disciplinarian and as fond a parent as his predecessor, resigns from the navy to undertake personally her reform. The clash of wills that ensues is more invigorating, less morbid, than that between Elsie and Horace, perhaps because, as Janet Brown suggests, Finley had come to terms with her own relationship with her father and been able to put greater distance between herself and Lulu. Perhaps it is because Finley, having expressed the conventional, submissive side of her personality, is tentatively giving voice to her anger. For whatever reason, she writes with more objectivity, less sentimentality, about Lulu than about Elsie. However, many of the scenes between Lulu and her father are almost word-for-word reenactments of earlier ones.

Finley was not a great writer, probably not even a reader of much else than the Bible, for its precepts. She was impervious to the beauties of King James prose; nonetheless, she was a powerful writer who produced several, if not a whole series, of those proverbial good bad books. Her enormous popularity resulted largely from a workable formula of flaws whose chemistry appealed to a particular people at a favorable time. The world of the Elsie books is a soap-opera-like composite of fantasy and realism, an imitation fairy-tale world, peopled by wealthy white folks and contented, servile blacks. The setting for the Elsie stories is based on exaggerated tales returning Union soldiers told of the sumptuous elegance of the pre-Civil War South. Characters live on palatial, well-ordered estates with elegantly furnished, airy apartments, manicured lawns rolling through avenues of trees to a distant river, spit-and-polished horses and carriages. They wear the latest fashions and opulent jewels. They dine lavishly but always remind each other that they are only custodians of the wealth entrusted to them. They are generous, bestowing upon one another munificent gifts; to their loyal black dependents, they are kind, if condescending, dispensing tokens of tobacco and bandannas at Christmas and other feasts. Custodians they are, but also adherents of the creed that God's reward to those who rank Him first is a plethora of material goods. The people in Finley's world live as one imagines princes and princesses do: grownups do not work; children study but then they play with wondrous toys; everyone reads; they stroll and ride horses; they have breakfast in sun-filled morning rooms after devoted servants have dressed them and their hair; they go to holiday house parties with their friends; they travel abroad and stay in magnificent hotels; after romantic courtships they marry happily, move onto their own estates, and raise closely knit families with an occasional black sheep to provide suffering and excitement. In the Elsie books Finley repeats the same generalized scenes over and over again, creating through repetition with some variation what can become an intensely felt, powerfully enveloping, almost surrealistic world. Rarely does she introduce contemporary historic events into her novels. Finley's experience and imagination were limited. She was incapable of particularizing her fictional worlds through local color and specific detail unless she was writing from experience, as she was in the autobiographical *Mildred Keith*.

Making the male protagonist of her Elsie stories a father rather than a lover or husband provided Finley not only her dominant motif but also a channel for her primary theme: woman is by nature fragile, subservient, and ornamental and as such deserves to be elevated to a pedestal. Finley intended Elsie to be a model of loving obedience and filial duty even to a parent who alternately tyrannized and pampered her. Her upbringing prepared her to be a dutiful wife. Frequently, as in *Elsie's Widowhood*, grown women in Finley's fiction manifest their innate dependence on a man: "it was the love of a stronger nature than her own that she craved, a staff to lean upon, a guiding, protecting love, a support such as is the strong, stately oak to the delicate clinging vine." Against the preponderance of similar passages, Finley now and then timidly intimates dissatisfaction with that status. On one occasion Elsie's stepmother explains to her that the desire for a husband is "part of a woman's curse."

Interknit with the theme that woman is the docile appendage of man is a corollary endorsed

Frontispiece for Mildred Keith, *Finley's autobiographical novel based on her family's move to South Bend, Indiana (Baldwin Library, University of Florida Libraries)*

repeatedly by word and deed in Finley's novels: the primacy of unselfishness. To sacrifice one's own needs to the welfare of others is the key to felicity—this is the first guide to living well, for boys and girls, men and women alike. Selfish people are portrayed always as vicious, and inevitably they get their comeuppance.

Selfish characters appear in minor vignettes, a form at which Finley is unexpectedly skilled. Not all the characters who flash briefly but memorably across a page or two are wicked; toward some Finley is ambivalent. Dynamic, diverting characters, who pop up here and there sounding notes of fun, offer persuasive evidence of Finley's belief that Christianity need not be long-faced, not always grave and sober. The most poignant vignettes are conceivably self-portraits of aspects of the author herself. Finley has a predilection for rendering redeeming idiosyncrasies of otherwise stereotypical old maids, and her sketches of the chronically ill catch the quiet desperation beneath their resignation.

Skillful at sketching character types to which she adds an original stroke, Finley is not adept at creating authentic protagonists. She lacks insight into the depths of human nature. She does not explore or analyze motives. Her major characters, if they are interpreted as attempts at realistic portrayals, appear flat and irritatingly self-satisfied. However, as ideal types in a quasi romance, in keeping with the quasi-fairy-tale world in which they live, they achieve a credibility through almost ritual repetition of predictable gestures and utterances. The cumulative impact effects a kind of fascination-aversion for the things Finley's characters say and do, things we ourselves conceivably might, if our situations were altered and we acted unswervingly in accord with a few fundamental principles to which we voiced adherence. That ambivalent attraction to Finley's major characters constitutes a measure of the power of the Elsie books. Finley herself was conscious that Elsie and her dear ones are liable to charges of priggishness and saccharinity. Frequently, minor characters mouth such criticism.

Although dialogue is Finley's principal vehicle of narration, she is as heavy-handed at transcribing characters' speech as she is in suggesting their motivation. With few intrusions by the author either to inform or to interpret, characters deliver themselves of formal, set pieces, uncommonly articulate, rather than speaking in natural tones. Finley apparently worked from the premise that the language of fiction is invented, not recorded, speech.

Not only the Elsie series but all of Finley's fiction is imbued with vulgar, pernicious attitudes. Two of the most offensive to modern readers pander to contemporary popular conceptions: the subordination of women and the equation of blacks with servile, simpleminded, pious "chilluns" who require supervision and protection from benevolent white masters, to whom, as a consequence, they willingly return loyal affection. Also prevalent is a snobbish conviction that wealth breeds a gentility and refined spirituality which augment personal and social worth. The poorer whites, few in the Elsie series, more numerous in the Mildred and Fred Landon books, may be upright and well-intentioned, but they are not fit for the friendship of the cultivated. The latter, though they are not overtly rude to their inferiors, may among themselves acknowledge, even ridicule, the unworthiness of the poor. Finley applies a weak corrective for such snobbery in mild rebukes from minor characters,

but the gentle reminders serve only to affirm the superiority of the wealthy white Protestant.

If Finley is a social snob, she is also a religious bigot, her hatred, especially of Catholicism and Mormonism, inspiring vituperative passages whose sensationalism becomes absurd. *Casella; or, The Children of the Valleys* (1868) is an inflammatory chronicle for children of the horrors of the Catholic persecution of the Waldensians, which Finley thought, despite its imagined characters, hardly deserved to be called fiction: "it has been throughout my earnest endeavor to make it a true picture of life in the valleys at that period, and of the Christian patience and heroism and the forgiving, forbearing spirit of those dear people of God." Finley's accumulation of atrocities and acrimonious banalities trivializes a historical tragedy and becomes excruciatingly tiresome. Like Elsie, Finley had obviously read something "on the subject of Popery and papal institutions; . . . she had pored over histories of the terrible tortures of the Inquisition, and stories of martyrs and captive nuns, until she had imbibed an intense horror and dread of everything connected with that form of error and superstition." Whenever Catholics appear, they are treated as deluded and depraved. For reasons of her own, Finley believed Mormonism closely resembled Catholicism, once called by Captain Raymond "Satan's masterpiece"; therefore, it too had to be a false religion. "Both pander to men's lusts . . . both train children to forsake their parents; both teach lying and murder, when by such crimes they are expected to advance the cause of their Church," explains Raymond to a Mormon acquaintance whose conversion he has undertaken. Angered by what she called a wanton and wicked attack on creeds which had provided hope to multitudes, in an 1896 article for *Scribner's Magazine* Agnes Repplier caustically expressed her wish that Finley and other "pious women . . . would learn at least to express themselves—especially when their words are intended for little children to read—with some approach to decency and propriety."

Finley's artistic flaws have evoked not only censure but also satire from her critics. Josie Turner's *Elsie Dinsmore On the Loose* (1930) parodies Finley's bombast, her exaggeration of situation, and her excessive sentimentality. Like the model, the imitation is melodramatic, milks sentiment, and never explores, just reiterates. However, the Elsie books have too much substance to be dismissed as merely silly and do have such reputable champions as G. B. Stern, who when she craved "really tough stuff," returned to Elsie, whose moral fiber offers "tough neurotic realism."

The dominant motif of the Elsie books, the relationship between daughter and father, has evoked most of what substantive criticism the series has received. Psychological critics have pointed out that Finley, who never married, created subconsciously in her fiction the ideal lover who eluded her in real life. Because it would have been indecorous to give Elsie a lover who fondled her indiscriminately in public, she gave her a father whose affection combined with a protective instinct so possessive that he controlled every detail of her life. Recent assertions that the books' great appeal depended on readers' subconscious attraction to the theme of veiled incest is, like Repplier's or Turner's, an exaggerated response to only one dimension of the Elsie series. It is quite reasonable to suppose that the young Martha Finley, one among many half-siblings of a stepmother and a busy physician father, longed for more of her father's attention, that Elsie's longing embodied Finley's own, and that child-readers empathized. But that longing was not necessarily sexual. Just as reasonable as the Freudian interpretation is the supposition that the blatant sexual overtones went unnoticed, even subconsciously by Elsie's young fans. Because the typical reader of the Elsie books was an immature, young girl, who had herself unquestionably been right in real situations yet made to knuckle under by adults, she admired and wished she dared emulate Elsie's courage in standing up to authority. And she cheered the Highest Authority for bearing her up on His wings. A few concomitant sufferings only satisfyingly proved the preciousness of Elsie's mettle. Whatever else the Elsie books are, they are a conscious effort to make real for children the image of God as father-protector and heart's love. What better image of that intangible relationship for an age which sanctified the family than a fleshly father's and daughter's mutual, sometimes intransigent, love.

Whatever the secret of Elsie's appeal, her success was phenomenal. According to the publisher, *Elsie Dinsmore* was their best-seller in 1868, and in 1939, it was one among only eighteen of their titles that had survived for fifty years. In the seventy-odd years between 1867 and 1939 the novel sold more than five million copies. Conjecturing that at an average of five readers per copy, personal and library, the book had twenty-five million readers, its public constituted "nothing more nor less than a civilization." The influence on public opinion of the beautiful, hazel-eyed paragon is staggering to contemplate, and as Chesterton says of bad literature, "may tell us of the mind of many [women]." Today, *Elsie Dinsmore* is no longer sold, as Edward Dodd said it still was in 1939, over "book counters in Middletown, U.S.A.," but her story is available in expensive reprints in two series, whose titles offer their own comment: Popular Culture in America and Classics of Children's Literature.

References:

Janet Elder Brown, "The Saga of Elsie Dinsmore," *University of Buffalo Studies*, 17 (July 1945): 75-129;

Edward M. Dodd, Jr., *The First Hundred Years* (New York: Dodd, Mead, 1939);

Amy H. Dowe, "Elsie Finds a Modern Champion," *Publishers Weekly*, 122 (31 December 1932): 2384-2387;

Jacqueline Jackson and Phillip Kendall, "What Makes a Bad Book Good: *Elsie Dinsmore*," *Children's Literature*, 7 (1978): 45-67;

Honoré Willsie Morrow, "My Favorite Character in Fiction, Elsie Dinsmore," *Bookman*, 62 (January 1926): 546-547;

Barbara Parry, Preface to Finley's *Elsie Dinsmore* (New York & London: Garland, 1977);

Agnes Repplier, "Little Pharisees in Fiction," *Scribner's Magazine*, 20 (December 1896): 718-724;

G. B. Stern, "Onward and Upward with the Arts—Elsie Reread," *New Yorker*, 12 (14 March 1936): 52-55;

Ruth Suckow, "Elsie Dinsmore: a Study in Perfection; or How Fundamentalism Came to the South," *Bookman*, 66 (October 1927): 126-133;

Florence Wilson, "The Author of the Elsie Books," *Ladies' Home Journal*, 10 (April 1893): 3.

Charles Austin Fosdick
(Harry Castlemon)
(16 September 1842-22 August 1915)

Ken Donelson
Arizona State University

BOOKS: *Frank, the Young Naturalist* (Philadelphia: Porter & Coates/Cincinnati: Carroll, 1864);

No Moss; or, The Career of a Rolling Stone (Philadelphia: Porter & Coates/Cincinnati: Carroll, 1864);

Frank on a Gunboat (Philadelphia: Porter & Coates/Cincinnati: Carroll, 1864);

Frank in the Woods (Philadelphia: Porter & Coates, 1865);

Frank Before Vicksburg (Cincinnati: Carroll, 1865);

Frank Among the Rancheros (Philadelphia: Porter & Coates, 1865);

Frank on the Lower Mississippi (Cincinnati: Carroll, 1867);

Go-ahead; or, The Fisher-boy's Motto (Philadelphia: Porter & Coates/Cincinnati: Carroll, 1867);

Frank on the Prairie (Philadelphia: Porter & Coates/Cincinnati: Carroll, 1867);

Tom Newcomb; or, The Boy of Bad Habits (Cincinnati: Carroll, 1868);

Frank at Don Carlos' Ranch (Philadelphia: Porter & Coates, 1868);

Frank in the Mountains (Cincinnati: Carroll, 1871);

The Sportsman's Club in the Saddle (Philadelphia: Porter & Coates/Cincinnati: Carroll, 1873);

The Sportsman's Club Afloat (Philadelphia: Porter & Coates/Cincinnati: Carroll, 1874);

The Sportsman's Club Among the Trappers (Philadelphia: Porter & Coates/Cincinnati: Carroll, 1874);

Snowed Up; or, The Sportsman's Club in the Mountains (Philadelphia: Porter & Coates, 1876);

Frank Nelson in the Forecastle; or, The Sportsman's Club Among the Whalers (Philadelphia: Porter & Coates/Cincinnati: Carroll, 1876);

The Boy Traders; or, The Sportsman's Club Among the Boers (Philadelphia: Porter & Coates/Cincinnati: Carroll, 1877);

The Buried Treasure: or, Old Jordan's "Haunt" (Philadelphia: Porter & Coates, 1877);

The Boy Trapper (Philadelphia: Porter & Coates, 1878);

The Mail Carrier (Philadelphia: Porter & Coates, 1879);

George in Camp; or, Life on the Plains (Philadelphia: Porter & Coates, 1879);

George at the Fort; or, Life Among the Soldiers (Philadelphia: Porter & Coates, 1881);

George at the Wheel; or, Life in the Pilot-house (Philadelphia: Porter & Coates, 1881);

Don Gordon's Shooting-box (Philadelphia: Porter & Coates, 1883);

The Rod and Gun Club (Philadelphia: Porter & Coates, 1883);

The Young Wild-fowlers (Philadelphia: Porter & Coates, 1885);

Joe Wayring at Home; or, The Adventures of a Flyrod

Charles Austin Fosdick

(Philadelphia: Porter & Coates, 1886);

Julian Mortimer: A Brave Boy's Struggle for Home and Fortune (New York: Burt, 1887);

Our Fellows; or, Skirmishes with the Swamp Dragons (Philadelphia: Porter & Coates, 1887);

Snagged and Sunk; or, The Adventures of a Canvas Canoe (Philadelphia: Porter & Coates, 1888);

The Steel Horse; or, The Rambles of a Bicycle (Philadelphia: Porter & Coates, 1888);

True to His Colors (Philadelphia: Porter & Coates, 1889);

Rodney the Partisan (Philadelphia: Porter & Coates, 1890);

Marcy, the Blockade-runner (Philadelphia: Porter & Coates, 1891);

Marcy, the Refugee (Philadelphia: Porter & Coates, 1892);

Rodney the Overseer (Philadelphia: Porter & Coates, 1892);

Two Ways of Becoming a Hunter (Philadelphia: Porter & Coates, 1892);

The Camp in the Foot-hills (Philadelphia: Porter & Coates, 1893);

Sailor Jack, the Trader (Philadelphia: Porter & Coates, 1893);

Oscar in Africa (Philadelphia: Porter & Coates, 1894);

Elaim Storm, the Wolfer; or, The Lost Nugget (Philadelphia: Porter & Coates, 1895);

The House-boat Boys (Philadelphia: Coates, 1895);

The Missing Pocket-book; or, Tom Mason's Luck (Philadelphia: Coates, 1895);

The Mystery of Lost River Canyon (Philadelphia: Coates, 1896);

The Young Game-warden (Philadelphia: Coates, 1896);

A Rebellion in Dixie (Philadelphia: Coates, 1897);

A Sailor in Spite of Himself (Philadelphia: Coates, 1897);

The Ten Ton Cutter (Philadelphia: Coates, 1897);

The Pony Express Rider (Philadelphia: Coates, 1898);

The White Beaver (Philadelphia: Coates, 1899);

Carl the Trailer (Philadelphia: Porter & Coates, 1900);

The First Capture; or, Hauling Down the Flag of England (New York: Saalfield, 1900);

Winged Arrow's Medicine; or, The Massacre at Fort Phil Kearney (Akron: Saalfield, 1900);

Floating Treasure (Philadelphia: Coates, 1901);

White Horse Fred; or, Julian Among the Outlaws (Philadelphia: Coates, 1901);

The Haunted Mine (Philadelphia: Coates, 1902);

A Struggle for a Fortune (New York: Saalfield, 1902).

PERIODICAL PUBLICATION: "How to Write Stories for Boys," *Writer*, 9 (January 1896): 4-5.

Charles Austin Fosdick, who wrote under the pseudonym Harry Castlemon, was a prolific author of boys' books rivaling in popularity and sales both Horatio Alger, Jr., and William Taylor Adams (Oliver Optic). *The National Union Catalog, Pre-1956 Imprints* lists nearly sixty Castlemon novels from 1864 to 1902, and although the number of printings per book dropped dramatically for his last ten or so books, other works ran through thirty printings or more. His first series of books, the six-volume Gunboat series, helped to establish the popularity of series books with a common hero and often several secondary characters that appeared in a number of volumes. His titles consistently announced adventure and thrills, and series titles such as Roughing It, Rod and Gun, and The Pony Express made his works favorite reading of many boys.

Fosdick, the son of John Spencer and Eunice Andrews Fosdick, was born in Randolph, New York. Early in his life, his educator father moved the family to Buffalo, where Fosdick attended Buffalo Central High School for a short time before enlisting in the U.S. Navy as a landsman in 1862. During his stay in high school, he was influenced by an English teacher who asked him once to write about "What a Man Would See If He Went to Greenland." Fosdick wrote later that within ten minutes he had filled his slate with words. After reading the compositions to the class, the teacher announced, "Some of you will make your living by writing one of these days." Fosdick never forgot those words. "That gave me something to ponder upon," he reflected in "How to Write Stories for Boys," an 1896 article for the *Writer*. "I did not say so out loud, but I knew that my composition was as good as the best of them." He wrote some of his first novel, *Frank, the Young Naturalist* (1864), during high school.

When the Civil War broke out, Fosdick enlisted as a landsman in the Mississippi River Squadron. He served on a gunboat patrolling the river and was present at the siege of Vicksburg. While *Frank, the Young Naturalist* had come out of his boyhood experiences, Fosdick's naval life provided details for the next book, *Frank on a Gunboat* (1864), and several books that followed. As he told Edgar G. Alcorn in an 1893 interview for the *Writer*, "Almost everything that happened to Frank Nelson and Archie Winters, as narrated in the *Gunboat Se-*

ries, really did take place. Of some of the scenes I was an eye-witness, and others were told to me by those who took part in them."

After completing *Frank on a Gunboat,* Fosdick asked Admiral David B. Potter to read the book, and Potter advised him to submit the novel for publication. Fosdick sent the manuscript to Cincinnati publisher R. W. Carroll, who accepted the book and published it and *Frank, the Young Naturalist* as the first two of six novels in the Gunboat series. Fosdick's career was underway.

After the war, Fosdick became a clerk in Villa Ridge, Illinois, near Cairo. He married Sarah Stoddard and began to devote most of his spare time to writing boys' books. His novels are uniformly

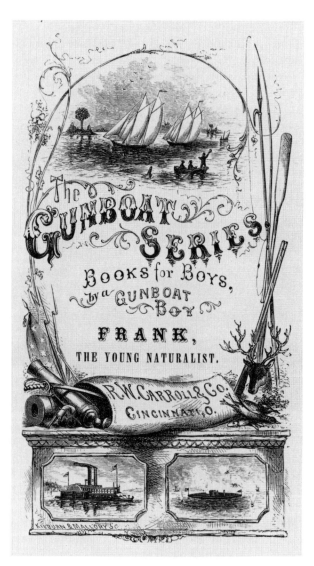

Engraved title page for a later edition of Fosdick's first book, based on his boyhood experiences (Baldwin Library, University of Florida Libraries)

filled with thrills and chills. They are moralistic but not in the vein earlier established by Samuel Griswold Goodrich (Peter Parley) and Jacob Abbott's Rollo books. Neither is the moralism as heavy-handed as that of Fosdick's contemporary Horatio Alger, Jr. The portrayal of manliness accompanied by manly virtues was Fosdick's aim. But he never forgot, as he put it, that "Boys don't like fine writing. What they want is adventure, and the more of it you can get into 250 pages of manuscript, the better fellow you are." A few of Fosdick's early books tell boys about the Civil War, but many later ones are set in the mysterious wild West, a place Fosdick never visited.

Fosdick's successful formula for his books was simple. Take a lively and likable boy, set him in a place that would appeal to young readers with its potential for excitement, and give the boy a chance to do things all boys secretly wanted to do—hunt, fish, find secret passages, chase bears and panthers, escape from Indians, sail the seas, anything that took readers away from mundane life. While Fosdick never attacked formal education, his heroes made do without much schooling and sometimes they seemed to benefit because they learned in places other than classrooms. In one of the later books, *Carl the Trailer* (1900), the hero is described: "He despised school and everything connected with it, and longed for horses, guns, and excitement." That was not Carl's sole virtue, but it would be enough for boys to want to know him better.

Because his formula made each book like the previous ones, Fosdick's best work comes early in his career. *Frank, the Young Naturalist,* first in the Gunboat series, shows young Frank killing animals and preserving and mounting them. Although Frank is a bit of a prig by twentieth-century standards and his perfection might have repelled a few contemporary readers—he rises early to study and work and he is an exemplary student and gentleman—his love of sailing and his prowess at hunting make him an embodiment of boy readers' wishes and dreams.

The duality of goodness and excitement is well illustrated in a later book, *Frank at Don Carlos' Ranch* (1868). Frank and his cousin Archie visit their uncle's California ranch. When the uncle must leave, the boys are left in charge with two specific chores: shoot a mean grizzly bear and catch some horse thieves. Adventures follow, each one more thrilling than the last. But as the thrills unfold and as they become more incredible, Fosdick steps in to instruct. Separated from Frank, Archie stands before an oil painting. Something catches his eye;

Series title for the 1878 edition of Fosdick's The Boy Trapper *published by John C. Winston (Baldwin Library, University of Florida Libraries)*

he leans forward to touch a wooden button which opens a mysterious door:

> "Now I'd like to know what this means," thought he, pressing the knob harder than before. "This thing must be attached to a spring, because it comes back when I let go of it. Well—by—gracious!"
>
> It was very seldom indeed that Archie used any slang words, but sometimes, when he was greatly excited or astonished, he did like other boys—forgot all the good resolutions he had made regarding this bad habit.

But if moralistic episodes intrude occasionally, ad-

venture rarely lets up. *Frank in the Mountains* (1871) has exciting encounters with Indians, *The Boy Traders; or, The Sportsman's Club Among the Boers* (1877) features battles and an escape from a cyclone, and *The Buried Treasure; or, Old Jordan's "Haunt"* (1877) centers on a barrel containing $80,000.

Popular as Fosdick was during the last thirty years of the nineteenth century, his reputation had waned by 1900. But his message as Jacob Blanck described it, "Success lies in application, and in doing what you can well, and with tenacity of purpose," was carried on by later, equally popular writers for boys, including H. Irving Hancock, Gilbert Patten, Percy Keese Fitzhugh, and Edward Stratemeyer.

Along with William Taylor Adams, Fosdick established the series format for boys' books, an idea taken to its limits by Edward Stratemeyer and the Stratemeyer Syndicate. Because Fosdick's books were in series and because they were filled with improbable and often sensational adventures with sometimes priggish and unbelievable heroes, librarians and teachers were quick to attack him. The *Library Journal* from its first volume through the 1890s made him the whipping boy for all the evils and ills of boys' books, often unfairly so. Educators mentioning Fosdick could be counted on to use words like *low, unwholesome,* or *coarse.* Librarians rarely ceased worrying about him and his pernicious influence. But he never claimed to write for adults. He wrote for thousands of boys who read him and delighted in his adventures.

References:

Edgar G. Alcorn, "Are the Characters of Juvenile Fiction Real?," *Writer,* 6 (August 1893): 153-157;

Jacob Blanck, *Harry Castlemon, Boys' Own Author: An Appreciation and Bibliography* (New York: Bowker, 1941);

"The Inventor of the Boy-Thriller," *Literary Digest,* 15 (11 September 1915): 558-560;

Maurice Owen, "Harry Castlemon (Charles A. Fosdick): Chronology of Books," *The Boys' Book Collector,* 1 (Spring 1970): 75-78;

Samuel Scoville, Jr., "Rescue, Robbery, and Escapes," *Forum,* 74 (July 1925): 83-91.

Samuel Griswold Goodrich
(Peter Parley)
(19 August 1793-9 May 1860)

Ruth K. MacDonald
New Mexico State University

See also the Goodrich entry in *DLB 1, The American Renaissance in New England.*

Bibliographical Note: Goodrich never clearly distinguished between the books he wrote, those he commissioned, and those he edited. His Peter Parley was so popular that many books have been falsely attributed to Goodrich. Because it is impossible to compile a comprehensive bibliography of his works, this list includes only works for which Goodrich's authorship can be established with some certainty. In England numerous pirated editions were published. According to Goodrich in *Recollections of a Lifetime* (1856), many of these were "counterfeits, every means being used to pass them off upon the public as by the original author of Parley's tales." British "counterfeits" cited by Goodrich are omitted from this list.

SELECTED BOOKS: *The Child's Arithmetic, Being an Easy and Cheap Introduction to Daboll's, Pike's, White's, and Other Arithmetics* (Hartford: S. G. Goodrich, 1818);

Blair's Outlines of Chronology, Ancient and Modern, Embracing Its Antiquities (Boston: S. G. Goodrich, 1825);

The Tales of Peter Parley about America (Boston: S. G. Goodrich, 1827);

The Child's Botany (Boston: S. G. Goodrich, 1828);

Tales of Peter Parley about Europe (Boston: S. G. Goodrich, 1828; London: Tegg, 1834);

A Geographical View of the United States. Embracing Their Extent and Boundaries, Government, Courts and Laws (New York: W. Reed, 1829);

Peter Parley's Method of Telling about Geography to Children (Hartford: H. & F. J. Huntington, 1829);

Stories about Captain John Smith, of Virginia; for the Instruction and Amusement of Children (Hartford: H. & F. J. Huntington, 1829);

A System of School Geography, Chiefly Derived from Malte-Brun, and Arranged According to the In-ductive Plan of Instruction (Boston: Carter & Hendee, 1830);

Atlas, Designed to Illustrate the Malte-Brun School Geography (Boston: Carter & Hendee, 1830);

Peter Parley's Tales about Asia (Boston: Gray & Bowen, 1830; London: Allman, 1839);

Peter Parley's Tales of Animals; Containing Descriptions of Three Hundred Quadrupeds, Birds, Fishes, Reptiles, and Insects (Boston: Carter & Hendee, 1830; London: Tegg, 1832);

Peter Parley's Winter Evening Tales (Boston: Carter & Hendee, 1830);

Tales of Peter Parley about Africa (Boston: Gray & Bowen, 1830);

The Child's Book of American Geography (Boston: Waitt & Dow, 1831);

The First Book of History. For Children and Youth (Boston: Richardson, Lord & Holbrook, 1831);

Peter Parley's Tales about the Islands in the Pacific Ocean (Boston: Gray & Bowen, 1831);

Peter Parley's Tales about the Sun, Moon, and Stars (Boston: Gray & Bowen and Carter & Hendee, 1831; London: Tegg, 1836);

Peter Parley's Tales of the Sea (Boston: Gray & Bowen, 1831);

Peter Parley's Tales about South America (Baltimore: Jewett, 1832);

Peter Parley's Method of Telling about the History of the World to Children (Hartford: F. J. Huntington, 1832);

Peter Parley's Tales about Ancient and Modern Greece (New York: Collins & Hannay, 1832);

A System of Universal Geography, Popular and Scientific, Comprising a Physical, Political, and Statistical Account of the World and Its Various Divisions (Boston: Carter & Hendee, 1832);

The Second Book of History, Including the Modern History of Europe, Africa, and Asia (Boston: Carter & Hendee, 1832);

Peter Parley's Tales about the State and City of New York (New York: Pendleton & Hill, 1832);

Peter Parley's Tales about Great Britain, including En-

gland, Wales, Scotland, and Ireland (Baltimore: Jewett, 1832);

Peter Parley's Method of Teaching Arithmetic to Children (Boston: Carter & Hendee, 1833);

Peter Parley's Tales about Ancient Rome, with Some Account of Modern Italy (Boston: Carter & Hendee, 1833);

The Every Day Book for Youth (Boston: Carter & Hendee, 1834);

Peter Parley's Short Stories for Long Nights (Boston: Allen & Ticknor, 1834);

The Third Book of History, Containing Ancient History in Connection with Ancient Geography (Boston: Carter & Hendee, 1834);

The Benefits of Industry. An Address Delivered Before the Inhabitants of Jamaica Plain, July 4, 1835 (Boston: Ticknor, 1835);

The Story of Captain Riley and His Adventures in Africa (New York: Peaslee, 1835);

The Story of La Peyrouse (New York: Peaslee, 1835);

Bible Gazetteer, Containing Descriptions of Places Men-

tioned in the Old and New Testament (Boston: Otis, Broaders, 1836);

The Outcast, and Other Poems (Boston: Russell, Shattuck & Williams, 1836);

Peter Parley's Bible Dictionary (Philadelphia: Tower, 1836);

Peter Parley's Dictionary of the Animal Kingdom (New York: Hunt, 1836);

Peter Parley's Dictionary of Astronomy (New York: Hunt, 1836);

A Present from Peter Parley to All His Little Friends (Philadelphia: Pomeroy, 1836);

Peter Parley's Arithmetic (Boston: Hendee, 1837);

Peter Parley's Method of Telling about the Geography of the Bible (Boston: American Stationers' Company, 1837);

Fireside Education (New York: Colman, 1838; London: Smith, 1839);

Five Letters to My Neighbor Smith, Touching the Fifteen Gallon Jug (Boston: Weeks, Jordan, 1838);

Peter Parley's Cyclopedia of Botany (Boston: Otis, Broaders, 1838);

The First Reader for Schools (Boston: Otis, Broaders, 1839);

The Second Reader for Schools (Louisville: Morton & Griswold, 1839);

The Third Reader for the Use of Schools (Boston: Otis, Broaders, 1839);

The Fourth Reader for the Use of Schools (Boston: Otis, Broaders, 1839);

Peter Parley's Farewell (New York: Colman, 1840);

Peter Parley's Wonders of the Earth, Sea, and Sky (New York: Colman, 1840);

A Pictorial Geography of the World, Comprising a System of Universal Geography, 10 parts (Boston: Otis, Broaders/New York: Tanner & Disturnell, 1840);

Sketches from a Student's Window (Boston: Ticknor, 1841);

The Story of Alexander Selkirk (Philadelphia: Anners, 1841);

A Pictorial Natural History; Embracing a View of the Mineral, Vegetable, and Animal Kingdoms (Boston: Munroe, 1842);

The Young American; or, Book of Government and Law (New York: W. Robinson, 1842);

Make the Best of It; or, Cheerful Cherry, and Other Tales (New York: Wiley & Putnam, 1843); republished as *Cheerful Cherry; or, Make the Best of It* (London: Darton & Clarke, 1843?);

A Tale of Adventure; or, The Siberian Sable-hunter (New York: Wiley & Putnam, 1843); republished as *Persevere and Prosper; or, The Siberian Sable-hunter* (London: Darton, 1843);

What to Do and How to Do It (New York: Wiley & Putnam, 1844);

Fairy Land, and Other Sketches for Youth (Boston: Munroe, 1844);

Peter Parley's Little Leaves for Little Readers (Boston: Munroe, 1844);

Wit Bought; or, The Life and Adventures of Robert Merry (New York: Wiley & Putnam, 1844; London: Cassell, Petter & Galpin, 1844);

Dick Boldhero; or, A Tale of Adventure in South America (Philadelphia: Sorin & Ball, 1845; London: Darton, 1846);

A Home in the Sea; or, The Adventures of Philip Brusque; Designed to Show the Nature and Necessity of Good (Philadelphia: Sorin & Ball, 1845);

A Tale of the Revolution, and Other Sketches (Philadelphia: Sorin & Ball, 1845);

The Truth-Finder; or, The Story of Inquisitive Jack (Philadelphia: Sorin & Ball, 1845);

A National Geography, for Schools (New York: Huntington & Savage, 1845);

Right Is Might, and Other Sketches (Philadelphia: Sorin & Ball, 1846);

Tales of Sea and Land (Philadelphia: Sorin & Ball, 1846);

A Primer of Geography (New York: Huntington & Savage, 1850);

Take Care of Number One; or, The Adventures of Jacob Karl (New York: Huntington & Savage, 1850);

A Comprehensive Geography and History, Ancient and Modern (New York: Huntington & Savage, 1850);

Poems (New York: Putnam's, 1851);

Faggots for the Fireside; or, Fact and Fancy (New York: Appleton, 1855; London: Griffin, 1855);

The Wanderers by Sea and Land, with other Tales (New York: Appleton, 1855; London: Darton, 1858);

A Winter Wreath of Summer Flowers (New York: Appleton, 1855; London: Trübner, 1855);

The Balloon Travels of Robert Merry and His Young Friends over Various Countries in Europe (New York: J. C. Derby/Boston: Phillips, Sampson, 1855; London: Blackwood, 1857);

The Travels, Voyages, and Adventures of Gilbert Go-Ahead in Foreign Parts (New York: Derby, 1856);

Recollections of a Lifetime; or, Men and Things I Have Seen: In a Series of Familiar Letters to a Friend, Historical, Biographical, Anecdotal, and Descriptive, 2 volumes (New York & Auburn: Miller, Orton & Mulligan, 1856);

Illustrated Natural History of the Animal Kingdom, 2 volumes (New York: Derby & Jackson, 1859).

OTHER: *Parley's Cabinet Library*, 20 volumes, edited by Goodrich (Boston: Bradbury, Soden, 1843-1845).

Samuel Griswold Goodrich was an author and editor of children's books in the nineteenth century, the most popular and successful of which appeared under his pseudonym, Peter Parley. Goodrich was the only children's author of his time to make his living entirely by writing children's books; by his own estimate, seven million of his books were in print in 1857 and three hundred thousand were printed annually. Though not original for their time nor literarily noteworthy, his books met the need of the early American republic for stories and textbooks which were authentically American, produced by American authors, illustrated by American engravers, with American settings and topics relevant to American ways of life.

Born in Ridgefield, Connecticut, to Samuel, a Congregational minister, and Elizabeth Ely Goodrich, Goodrich was educated at local schools but showed no propensity for study. At the age of fifteen, his parents removed him from the village schoolmaster's school and apprenticed him as a clerk to his brother-in-law, a merchant. Thus began Goodrich's business career. Though he later taught himself through home study in most of the subjects known at the time, he never received any formal advanced education. He served in the army briefly during the War of 1812 but saw no combat. Returning to Hartford in 1814, he turned his hand to several projects but settled on publishing, in partnership with his friend George Sheldon. During this time he published a few toybooks, but nothing which would indicate his later success as a children's writer. In 1818, he married Adeline Gratia Bradley.

After his wife's untimely death in 1822, he decided to spend a year in England. There he met the prolific British writer Hannah More, whose series of pamphlets, *Cheap Repository Tracts*, with their insistence on realism and moral teaching, inspired him to write American stories in the same mode for American children. His own experiences with fairy tales in his youth had impressed him with their monstrosity and horrific qualities, as well as a sense that fairy tales were essentially lies that were told to children at an impressionable age. Goodrich was also eager to fill an American demand for informative schoolbooks and truthful stories without the

PETER PARLEY TELLING STORIES.

PETER PARLEY'S TALES.

Here is a picture of the world: 'tis round
And cover'd over with mountains hills & seas;
Millions of people on its face are found
And vessels sail around it as they please.

REVISED EDITION.

Frontispiece and engraved title page for a retitled edition of The Tales of Peter Parley about America, *which incorporates revisions made by Goodrich to adapt his book for use in schools (Baldwin Library, University of Florida Libraries)*

British biases that imported works for children so frequently exhibited.

After his return to Hartford in 1824, he again tried publishing; he also remarried. Mary Booth, an Englishwoman, was the mother of his six children. In 1826 he moved to Boston, and there, in 1827, he published the first of his Peter Parley tales, *The Tales of Peter Parley about America,* under his own imprint. Though the book was not an immediate success, it slowly attracted much favorable attention from critics and was successful enough so that Goodrich wrote a series of such books in the years immediately following: *Tales of Peter Parley about Europe* (1828), *Peter Parley's Tales about Asia* (1830), *Tales of Peter Parley about Africa* (1830), *Peter Parley's Tales about the Islands in the Pacific Ocean* (1831), *Peter Parley's Tales about the Sun, Moon, and Stars* (1831), and so on. The books' focal point is the title character, Peter Parley, an elderly, gouty old man who is well known as a storyteller among the local children. Parley tells them stories about his own adventures and those of various acquaintances and gives them facts about geography, his-

tory, social customs, and national characters. Goodrich rewrote the first edition of the America tales to include chapter divisions and questions about the contents on the bottom of the pages to accommodate the book's usage in schools and by those who might wish to educate their children at home, as well as those children who might teach themselves, as Goodrich did. All subsequent books followed the form of this revision. The books were illustrated with many steel engravings which, although not distinguished in artistry, were lively, clear representations of the relevant subject matter. Goodrich later said that he chose for his books "things capable of sensible representation," which made the process of illustration much easier.

By far the greatest attraction of the Parley books is the narrator himself. Parley can be a lively narrator of high adventure and a source of chatty conversation and exotic detail; he can also be boringly exact and simplistically general about the attitudes and habits of people of other countries. His American parochialism is justified in the name of patriotism, but Goodrich shows no impulse to have

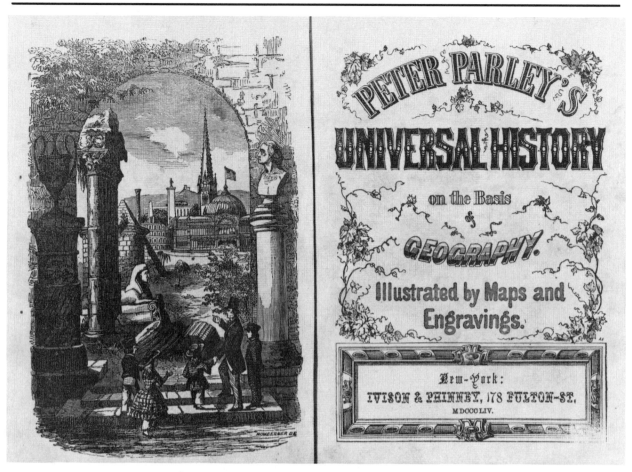

*Frontispiece and title page for a later edition of the best-known Goodrich geography (Baldwin Library, University of Florida Libraries).
Originally published in 1837,* Peter Parley's Universal History on the Basis of Geography *was ghostwritten for Goodrich
by Nathaniel and Elizabeth Hawthorne.*

Parley explain or investigate the social conditions or morality of any other country beyond his initial judgment of it. Occasionally Parley's information is wrong; but his word goes unquestioned in the stories, which are mostly thinly disguised story lines dependent on overblown vocabulary and contrived coincidences provided to present factual or ethical matters for children.

This pervasive insistence on realism and factuality is characteristic of the Goodrich books; he wrote in the tradition of the Rousseauists, following Hannah More, Letitia Barbauld, Thomas Day, and Maria Edgeworth, and rarely gave in to flights of fancy in his works. Rather, he presented the facts about various aspects of the world in as tantalizing a mode as possible, given his emphasis on the useful and truthful, in order to induce children to read and learn rather than forcing them to it. He also stayed away from the gory aspects of history, and though bloodshed and the casualties of battle were clearly presented in his sections on history, they are usually described in an inoffensive way. Goodrich was also careful in his descriptions to use only the simplest vocabulary so that children would clearly understand what was being said. Above all was Goodrich's design to teach the useful and present the virtuous for emulation, motives typical of, although not always so unfailingly striven for, by most writers for children at the time.

By his own estimate in his autobiography, *Recollections of a Lifetime* (1856), Goodrich went on to write or edit a total of 170 volumes, 116 of which bore the name Peter Parley. Among these were a series of textbooks, similar to, but not modeled after, McGuffey's Eclectic Readers; they featured excerpts from some of the most notable authors of the day, including Washington Irving, Lydia Huntley Sigourney, and Henry Wadsworth Longfellow. They sold well in the East, whereas the McGuffey readers sold in the West, and at a later period. The Goodrich readers featured a graduated vocabulary list and the questions that were typical of the Parley

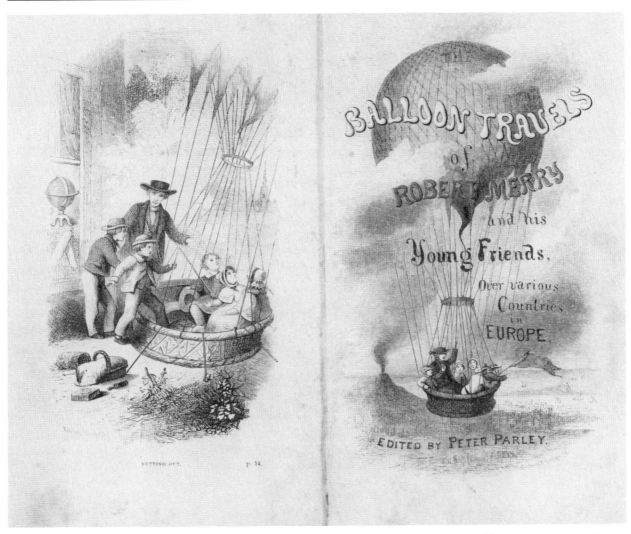

Frontispiece and engraved title page for Goodrich's 1855 book of educational adventure tales whose title character resembles Peter Parley (Baldwin Library, University of Florida Libraries)

tales. Goodrich also wrote or edited several text-books on other areas of knowledge; his most innovative contributions were in geography where he used many maps, especially globe maps instead of maps of single countries or areas outside of a global context, a typical device in other geographies of the time. The best known of the Goodrich geographies was written by Nathaniel and Elizabeth Hawthorne. *Peter Parley's Universal History on the Basis of Geography* (1837) was one of the most popular textbooks that Goodrich edited and was only one of several works that Hawthorne ghostwrote for Goodrich which were subsequently paid for, as Hawthorne thought, inadequately. The volume is also noteworthy in the Goodrich canon for the goriness of detail that Goodrich might elsewhere have edited out.

Goodrich also wrote or edited several adventure books with a thinly disguised educational bent. The most noteworthy of these is *The Balloon Travels of Robert Merry and His Young Friends over Various Countries in Europe* (1855). Like the Parley tales, the book features a title character who is a wise, elderly storyteller with a wealth of information on almost any subject. Merry takes a group of children on a balloon trip all over the world. Like Parley, Merry is particularly good at engaging children's attention; the dialogues between him and the children are particularly sprightly, ebullient, and authentically colloquial. Also like Parley, Merry is also preachy and relentlessly didactic once the initial pleasantries have been exchanged. He will hold forth for paragraphs on the morals and governments of foreign countries and on agriculture, his-

Price.—For 1 dozen of either No. 50 cents.—For a single copy 6 1-4 cents. For one year (a volume of 416 pages,
I dollar.—Payment always *in advance.*

PARLEY'S

MAGAZINE

NO. 3.

APRIL 13, 1833.

PUBLISHED EVERY OTHER WEEK.

BOSTON:
LILLY, WAIT, AND COMPANY.

PORTLAND:
COLMAN, HOLDEN, AND CO.

Sold by the principal Booksellers in the U States.

A. HARTWELL DEL. ET SC.

*By a decision of the General Post Office, the postage of this Magazine is three fourths of one
cent if under 100 miles, and only one cent and a quarter each number for any greater distance.
For terms see next page. All orders post-paid promptly answered.*

*Front cover for an early issue of the magazine which Goodrich
eventually merged with his other juvenile periodical,* Merry's
Museum *(Baldwin Library, University of
Florida Libraries)*

tory, and geography. *Merry's Museum,* a magazine
for children which Goodrich edited from 1841 to
1850, was a similar informative publication full of
Merry's stories for children. He also started *Parley's
Magazine* for children in 1833, merged it with *Merry's
Museum* in the 1840s, and continued to edit it
until 1850.

As the years passed and the number of Parley
books continued to grow, Goodrich began to borrow from earlier books for later ones and to press
on producing more books in the series without inspiration. The twenty volumes in *Parley's Cabinet
Library* (1843-1845) borrowed heavily, both in text
and illustration, from the early Parley books.
Though not clearly intended for children, the series was inevitably read by juvenile audiences lured
to it by the name of Parley. Finally, Goodrich said
that the constant production of those books required drudgery rather than creativity.

After having established himself as a writer
and editor of note, Goodrich dabbled in politics.
In 1837 and 1838 he served as state representative
to the Massachusetts legislature from Roxbury, the
suburb of Boston where he had built a large family
mansion. In 1851, at the request of Millard Fill-
more, Goodrich also served as American consul in
Paris; a medal was struck in his honor when he
retired to private citizenship in 1853. In 1854 he
returned to Southbury, Connecticut, near the place
of his birth, where he died on 9 May 1860.

Goodrich's success was more dependent on
his skill as a businessman than as an artist or editor.
His books are sometimes haphazardly put together,
and by modern standards they are dull; none are
read by children now. His greatest accomplishment
was creating the original character of Peter Parley
and making child readers love him; he traded on
their affection for him by featuring him or using
his name on subsequent books, thereby increasing
sales. Goodrich's insistence on realism, on the truth
as he perceived it, was not approved by everyone.
There were those who criticized him for his pronouncements on and avoidance of fantasy, especially Felix Summerly, alias Henry Cole, and
Michael Angelo Titmarsh, presumably a pseudonym for William Thackeray. But these were British critics, and Goodrich's goal was always to
dissociate his kind of literature as much as possible
from the English and Continental fare produced
for children. That the American public favored
Goodrich's point of view is evident from their purchases of his books. The obvious superiority of the
American nation in Goodrich's books for children
appealed to a republic which felt a need for truly
American books to insure the future vitality of the
country, and his relentless reworkings of the same
themes and events in book after book simply fed
the American reading public's appetite for realistic,
moral, informative books for children. His publishing strategy opened the American book trade
to more imaginative and truly literary works for
children later in the century.

References:

Helen S. Canfield, "Peter Parley," *Horn Book Mag-
    azine,* 46 (April, June, August 1970): 135-141,
    274-282, 412-418;

F. J. Harvey Darton, "Peter Parley and the Battle
    of the Children's Books," *Cornhill Magazine,*
    73 (Summer 1932): 542-558;

Alice M. Jordan, "Peter Parley," *Horn Book Magazine*, 10 (January-February 1934): 96-101;

Daniel Roselle, *Samuel Griswold Goodrich, Creator of*

Peter Parley; A Study of His Life and Work (Albany: State University of New York Press, 1968).

Edward Everett Hale
(3 April 1822-10 June 1909)

Carol Billman

See also the Hale entry in *DLB 1, The American Renaissance in New England.*

SELECTED BOOKS: *How to Conquer Texas* (Boston: Redding, 1845);

Margaret Percival in America, by Hale and Lucretia Peabody Hale, as A. B. (Boston: Phillips, Sampson, 1850);

Letters on Irish Emigration (Boston: Phillips, Sampson, 1852);

Kanzas and Nebraska (Boston: Phillips, Sampson, 1854);

Elements of Christian Doctrine and Its Development (Boston: Walker, Wise, 1860);

Ninety Days' Worth of France (Boston: Walker, Wise, 1861);

The Man Without a Country, anonymous (Boston: Ticknor & Fields, 1865);

If, Yes, and Perhaps (Boston: Ticknor & Fields, 1868); republished as *The Man Without a Country, and Other Tales* (Boston: Ticknor & Fields, 1868);

The Ingham Papers (Boston: Fields, Osgood, 1869);

Sybaris and Other Homes (Boston: Fields, Osgood, 1869);

How to Do It (Boston: Osgood, 1871);

Ten Times One Is Ten: The Possible Reformation, as Colonel Frederic Ingham (Boston: Roberts Brothers, 1871; revised and enlarged, Boston: Roberts Brothers, 1883);

His Level Best and Other Stories (Boston: Roberts Brothers, 1872);

Six of One by Half a Dozen of the Other. An Every Day Novel, by Hale, Lucretia Peabody Hale, Harriet Beecher Stowe, and others (Boston: Roberts Brothers, 1872);

Christmas Eve and Christmas Day. Ten Christmas Stories (Boston: Roberts Brothers, 1873);

In His Name (Boston: Proprietors of Old and New, 1873);

Ups and Downs: An Every-day Novel (Boston: Roberts Brothers, 1873; London: Low, 1873);

The Good Time Coming; or Our New Crusade (Boston: Roberts Brothers, 1875); republished as *Our New Crusade: A Temperance Story* (Boston: Roberts Brothers, 1894);

G.T.T., or The Wonderful Adventures of a Pullman (Boston: Roberts Brothers, 1877);

Philip Nolan's Friends: A Story of the Change of Western Empire (New York: Scribner, Armstrong, 1877);

The Wolf at the Door, anonymous (Boston: Roberts Brothers, 1877);

Back to Back: A Story of Today (New York: Harper, 1878);

Mrs. Merriam's Scholars: A Story of the "Original Ten" (Boston: Roberts Brothers, 1878);

What Career? Ten Papers on the Choice of a Vocation and the Use of Time (Boston: Roberts Brothers, 1878);

From Thanksgiving to Fast (Boston: Ellis, 1879);

Stories of the War, Told by Soldiers (Boston: Roberts Brothers, 1879);

Crusoe in New York, and Other Tales (Boston: Roberts Brothers, 1880);

The Kingdom of God, and Twenty Other Sermons (Boston: Roberts Brothers, 1880);

The Life in Common, and Twenty Other Sermons (Boston: Roberts Brothers, 1880);

Stories of the Sea, Told by Sailors (Boston: Roberts Brothers, 1880);

A Family Flight through France, Germany, Norway, and Switzerland, by Hale and Susan Hale (Boston: Lothrop, 1881);

June to May: The Sermons of a Year (Boston: Roberts Brothers, 1881);

Edward Everett Hale, 1902

Stories of Adventure, Told by Adventurers (Boston: Roberts Brothers, 1881);

A Family Flight Over Egypt and Syria, by Hale and Susan Hale (Boston: Lothrop, 1882);

Our Christmas in a Palace, A Traveller's Story (New York: Funk & Wagnalls, 1883);

Seven Spanish Cities, and the Way to Them (Boston: Roberts Brothers, 1883);

Stories of Discovery, as Told by Discoverers (Boston: Roberts Brothers, 1883);

A Family Flight Through Spain, by Hale and Susan Hale (Boston: Lothrop, 1884);

A Family Flight Around Home, by Hale and Susan Hale (Boston: Lothrop, 1884);

Christmas in Narragansett (New York: Funk & Wagnalls, 1884);

The Fortunes of Rachel (New York: Funk & Wagnalls, 1884);

Boys' Heroes (Boston: Lothrop, 1885);

Stories of Invention, Told by Inventors and Their Friends (Boston: Roberts Brothers, 1885; London: Nelson, 1887);

A Family Flight Through Mexico, by Hale and Susan Hale (Boston: Lothrop, 1886);

Spain, by Hale and Susan Hale (New York: Put-

nam's, 1886); republished as *The Story of Spain* (New York: Putnam's, 1887);

History of the United States (New York: Chautauqua Press, 1887);

Franklin in France, from Original Documents, by Hale and Edward E. Hale, Jr., 2 volumes (Boston: Roberts Brothers, 1887, 1888);

How They Lived in Hampton. A Study of Practical Christianity Applied in the Manufacture of Woollens (Boston: J. S. Smith, 1888);

The Life of George Washington, Studied Anew (New York: Putnam's, 1888);

Mr. Tangier's Vacations; A Novel (Boston: Roberts Brothers, 1888);

My Friend the Boss: A Story of Today (Boston: J. S. Smith, 1888);

Four and Five: A Story of a Lend-a-Hand Club (Boston & London: Roberts Brothers, 1891);

The Story of Massachusetts (Boston: Lothrop, 1891);

The Life of Christopher Columbus; From His Own Letters and Journals and Other Documents of the Time (Chicago: Howe, 1891); republished as *The Story of Columbus, As He Told It Himself* (Boston: J. S. Smith, 1893);

The New Harry and Lucy: A Story of Boston in the Summer of 1891, by Hale and Lucretia Peabody Hale (Boston: Roberts Brothers, 1892);

East and West: A Story of New-born Ohio (New York: Cassell, 1892); republished as *The New Ohio: A Story of East and West* (London: Cassell, 1892);

Every-day Sermons (Boston: J. S. Smith, 1892);

Sybil Knox; or Home Again; A Story of To-day (New York & London: Cassell, 1892);

A New England Boyhood (New York: Cassell, 1893);

Sermons of the Winter (Boston: J. S. Smith, 1893);

If Jesus Came to Boston (Boston: J. S. Smith, 1895);

Studies in American Colonial Life (Meadville, Penn.: Chautauqua Press, 1895);

Susan's Escort, and Others (New York & London: Harper, 1895);

Historic Boston and Its Neighborhood (New York: Appleton, 1898);

James Russell Lowell and His Friends (Boston: Houghton Mifflin, 1899);

Memories of a Hundred Years, 2 volumes (New York: Macmillan, 1902; revised and enlarged, New York: Macmillan, 1904);

"We the People"; A Series of Papers on Topics of To-day (New York: Dodd, Mead, 1903);

Prayers in the Senate (Boston: Little, Brown, 1904);

The Foundations of the Republic (New York: Pott, 1906);

Tarry At Home Travels (New York: Macmillan, 1906).

Collection: *The Works of Edward Everett Hale,* 10 volumes (Boston: Little, Brown, 1898-1900).

Edward Everett Hale was a Unitarian minister from a well-respected New England family. His father, Nathan Hale, was the editor of Boston's primary newspaper, the *Daily Advertiser;* his great-uncle, also Nathan Hale, the Revolutionary War patriot whose words "I only regret that I have but one life to lose for my country" are well known to American school children. His mother, Sarah Preston Everett, was from a family of notable Unitarian clergymen; his wife, Emily Perkins, the granddaughter of Lyman Beecher and niece of Henry Ward Beecher and Harriet Beecher Stowe. Among Edward Everett Hale's childhood and adult acquaintances, friends, and parishioners were such nationally prominent New Englanders as Daniel Webster, Henry Clay, John Quincy Adams, Henry Wadsworth Longfellow, James Russell Lowell, and William Dean Howells. Hale was not, however, only a regionalist in his experience and concerns nor merely a local colorist in his writings. Among the

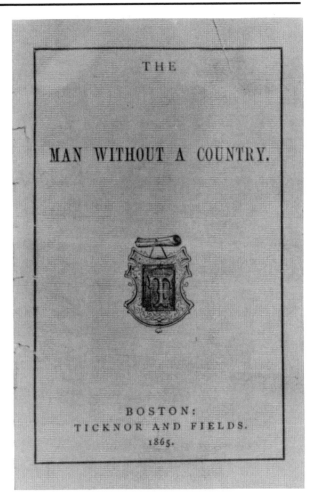

Front cover for the first separate publication of Hale's best-known work, which had been serialized two years earlier in the Atlantic Monthly (The Collection of American Literature in the Library of Pauline and Howard Behrman, *1973)*

causes he championed were the admission of Texas to the Union in 1845 and the Emigrant Aid Society dedicated to keeping slavery out of Kansas. These interests resulted in two written works, the pamphlet *How to Conquer Texas* (1845) and *Kanzas and Nebraska* (1854). Hale was also active in the founding of the Unitarian Church of America. Though he served the United Church of Worcester, Massachusetts, for ten years and the South Congregational Church of Boston for forty-three years, his last five years of work and life were spent as chaplain of the United States Senate. He died in Boston on 10 June 1909.

Edward Everett Hale's writing is inclusive and reflects his involvement in matters of public concern during his long life. This written work has been called by one biographer a "bibliographical puzzle," on account of all the pseudonymous, anon-

Hale with his sister Susan circa 1855. In the 1880s Edward Everett and Susan Hale collaborated on a series of travel books describing "family flights" in the U.S. and abroad.

ymous, original, and reprint material it comprises. In addition to sermons, Hale wrote history, biography, journalistic essays, moral and ethical tracts, short fiction and novels; and his literary works range from Utopian romances (*Sybaris and Other Homes*, 1869) to historical novellas (*In His Name*, 1873). The immediate popularity of *The Man Without a Country* (1865) made him known throughout America as a man of letters rather than a Unitarian minister and made his fictional exile, Philip Nolan, the legendary equal of contemporary characters such as Uncle Tom and Simon Legree, Tom Sawyer and Huck Finn. It is interesting to note that *The Man Without a Country* first appeared in serial form in the *Atlantic Monthly* (1863), a magazine Hale contributed to regularly and that nearly thirty years later published his *A New England Boyhood* (1893). Both of these, Hale's major works, appeared as books after their successes in the magazine.

The Man Without a Country and *A New England Boyhood*, while not expressly written for or read by the young, indicate the concerns that occupy Hale in his work for children and adolescents. The former suggests a patriotic purpose in writing fiction, for the story of the young army officer convicted of treason and then granted his wish never to see his country again makes clear the author's sentiments against the idea of secession, which was still current in 1863. The moral quality of Hale's literary work is also represented in this story of a sympathetic man who deserves the retribution he receives and even gains strength from his suffering. The work was scrupulously researched by the author, who read histories and newspaper accounts of the Aaron Burr conspiracy, which the fictional Nolan fell in with, as well as U.S. Navy Department records to make authentic the section of the work set at sea. Ironically, the name of the protagonist, a choice Hale thought was of his own making, turned out to be that of a Texas hero. In an unsuccessful effort to set the historical record straight, Hale wrote a sequel, *Philip Nolan's Friends* (1877).

A New England Boyhood (1893), written at the suggestion of Horace E. Scudder, was intended as a counterpart to Lucy Larcom's *A New England Girlhood* (1889). It is, in fact, part of a subgenre, the childhood memoir, that flourished in late nineteenth- and early twentieth-century America—and included William Dean Howells's *A Boy's Town* (1890), Charles Dudley Warner's *Being a Boy* (1877), John Muir's *The Story of My Boyhood and Youth* (1913). That Larcom's and Howells's work directly influenced Hale is evident from the second

chapter of his memoir; after studying those accounts, Hale tells readers, he determined not to tell his story chronologically. Organized instead into nine chapters on such subjects as "Out of Doors," "Life at Home," and "Social Relations," the book records Hale's untroubled boyhood in Boston through his years at Harvard, to which he was admitted at the age of thirteen.

In *A New England Boyhood*, Hale devotes considerable space to school life and to his education at home through reading books, many of which were sent to his father for review in the *Boston Daily Advertiser*. *Robinson Crusoe* was among those works he favored, as was a volume of Sir Walter Scott's minor poems, but so, too, was *The Treasury of Knowledge*, which included Jeremy Belknap's *American Biography*. In an often-quoted passage from the memoir, Hale describes a *Life of William Tell* he won as a school prize at the age of five. He includes, "by way of showing what was then thought fit reading for boys," the first sentence of this biography: "Friends of liberty, magnanimous hearts, sons of sensibility, ye who know how to die for your independence and live only for your brethern, lend an ear to my accounts. Come! hear how one single man, born in an uncivilized clime, in the midst of a people curbed beneath the rods of an oppressor, by his individual courage, raised this people so abased, and gave it a new being."

Hale's writing most often read by young Americans seems a natural extension of the author's life and of the interests he demonstrated in his two major works. In 1871 he produced *How to Do It*, a book of moral advice that originally appeared as articles in *Our Young Folks* and the *Youth's Companion*. (Hale also wrote moral counsel for adults *What Career?*, published in 1878). This work is punctuated, in capital letters, with such injuctions as: "DO NOT TALK ABOUT YOUR OWN AFFAIRS," "CONFESS IGNORANCE," and "NEVER UNDERRATE YOUR INTERLOCUTOR." While plainly didactic and obviously an early part of the American tradition of self-help literature, this book of advice is far more pointed in its urging and less generally moralistic than the contemporary lessons found, for example, in Horatio Alger's fiction.

Hale's important work expressly for young readers followed in the 1880s and was historical in subject matter. Not surprisingly, given his familiarity with historians of his day—he knew from childhood George Bancroft and later reviewed volumes of that scholar's *History of the United States*—Hale himself produced an elementary *History of the*

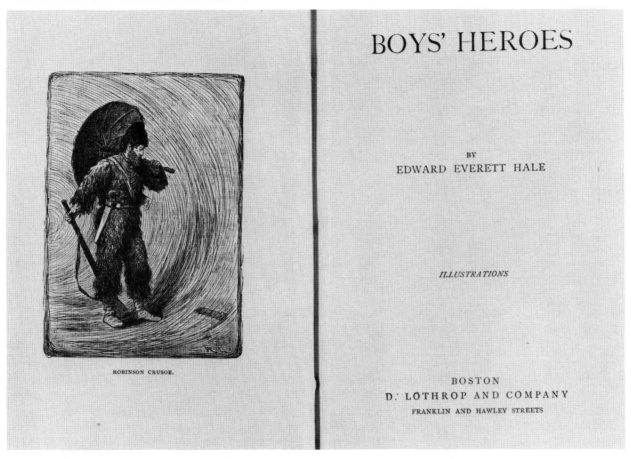

BOYS' HEROES

BY
EDWARD EVERETT HALE

ILLUSTRATIONS

BOSTON
D. LOTHROP AND COMPANY
FRANKLIN AND HAWLEY STREETS

ROBINSON CRUSOE.

Frontispiece and title page for an 1886 edition of Hale's collection of sketches about famous fictional and historical men (Baldwin Library, University of Florida Libraries)

United States, published by the Chautauqua Press in 1887. He acknowledges that this is an introductory history in the preface and goes on to refer readers to Bancroft and to the study of primary sources, such as documents pertaining to the history of the neighborhoods in which they live. This history ends appropriately, since it has charted the *progress* of the American nation, with the "era of good feeling" after the war of 1812: "As soon as the war was over, the immense and rapid advance of the United States in every victory of peace and in all the lines of national life began. Parties disappeared from politics. What was called an era of good feeling began. The nation knew it was a nation. The people began to see—what more and more it knows—that its success depends on an upright and honorable public opinion, an intelligent enterprise, its refusal to entrust power to any class, and on open lines of promotion."

Hale also produced biographical writing popular with the young: the collection of sketches *Boys' Heroes* (1885); a book-length biography of George

Washington, *The Life of George Washington, Studied Anew* (1888), which was published by G. P. Putnam's in a series called the Boys' and Girls' Library of American Biography; and a similar *The Life of Christopher Columbus* (1891). *Boys' Heroes* is a collection of twelve stories about fictional and factual men from Hannibal and King Arthur to Robinson Crusoe, Israel Putnam, and Napoleon the First. Hale subscribes to Thomas Carlyle's edict that the lives of "great men, taken up in any way, are profitable company." His subjects are portrayed as "great" and heroic figures and as profitable, illustrative company for young nineteenth-century readers. About Richard the Lionhearted, for example, Hale speculates: "I think that the reason that boys of our time and country are so much interested in Richard is that he is so well described in *Ivanhoe* and in the *Talisman.* Then we are all interested in the Crusades." What the author read and liked as a boy (Scott, Defoe, and others) surely informed his choice and treatment of these heroes of history and literature, as did his strong opinions

Hale at work

regarding how past events should be interpreted—
for example, the anarchy of the Crusades, the savagery of the Turks in Jerusalem.

Hale's book-length works on Washington and
Columbus are two of three long biographical studies he undertook; the other, the two-volume *Franklin in France* (1887-1888) written in collaboration
with his son is generally considered the most accomplished of the three. *The Life of George Washington, Studied Anew* is the best known of the
biographies for young readers. In its preface, Hale
claims that a new treatment of Washington is in
order "after a careful study of his own memoranda." Later he speaks disparagingly of a habit
"of deifying" the first president, thereby separating
himself from the Mason Locke Weems school of
biography that children in the nineteenth century
were brought up on. Hale, using Washington's private correspondence, focuses on what Victorian librarian Caroline Hewins summed up as "the life
and the progress of the nation [rather] than details
of his battles." This "life-and-times" approach,

however, does not undermine Washington's character or accomplishments; indeed, Hale says that
enthusiasm for Washington is greater when the human side of the man is studied. The biographer
presents his subject as an exemplary moral figure.
Washington's "Rules for Conduct" written in a
notebook during his youth—"sleep not when others speak," "turn not your back to others," "use no
reproachful language"—offer advice on morals
and manners not unlike that found in Hale's own
How to Do It. In conclusion, the author judges
Washington's life without qualification: "Men agree
to honor Washington because in his life they think
they have a demonstration that right is might."

Clergyman, reformer, philanthropist, journalist, educator, creative writer—Edward Everett
Hale was a man of such diverse activity that it is
difficult to capture him in a single, clear image.
Hale provided a model to his countrymen in both
his conduct and his writing. He transmitted and
mirrored almost all the important social and cultural ideas of his day. Upon Hale's death, William

Dean Howells characterized him: "In all the vast range of his work he was always an artist in his ethics and a moralist in his art."

Biographies:
Edward Everett Hale, Jr., *The Life and Letters of Edward Everett Hale* (Boston: Little, Brown, 1917);
Jean Holloway, *Edward Everett Hale: A Biography* (Austin: University of Texas Press, 1956).

Reference:
John R. Adams, *Edward Everett Hale* (Boston: Twayne, 1977).

Papers:
The Edward Everett Hale Papers are at the State University of New York, Albany.

Lucretia Peabody Hale
(2 September 1820-12 June 1900)

Carol Gay
Youngstown State University

SELECTED BOOKS: *Margaret Percival in America,* by Hale and Edward Everett Hale, as A. B. (Boston: Phillips, Sampson, 1850);
Struggle for Life (Boston: Walker, Wise, 1861);
The Lord's Supper and its Observance (Boston: Walker, Fuller, 1866);
The Service of Sorrow (Boston: American Unitarian Association, 1867);
Six of One by Half a Dozen of the Other. An Every Day Novel, by Hale, Edward Everett Hale, Harriet Beecher Stowe, and others (Boston: Roberts Brothers, 1872);
The Peterkin Papers (Boston: Osgood, 1880);
The Last of the Peterkins, With Others of Their Kin (Boston: Roberts Brothers, 1886);
An Uncloseted Skeleton, by Hale and Edward Lassetter Bynner (Boston: Ticknor, 1888);
Fagots for the Fireside (Boston: Ticknor, 1889; enlarged, Boston: Houghton Mifflin, 1894);
Sunday-School Stories for Little Children on the Golden Texts of the International Lessons of 1869, by Hale and Mrs. Bernard Whitman (Boston: Roberts Brothers, 1889);
Stories for Children. Containing Simple Lessons in Morals. A Supplementary Reader for Schools, or for Use at Home (Boston & New York: Leach, Shewell & Sanborn, 1892);
The New Harry and Lucy: A Story of Boston in the Summer of 1891, by Hale and Edward Everett Hale (Boston: Roberts Brothers, 1892).

Lucretia Peabody Hale was the first American writer to introduce American children to the delightful, slightly mad world of nonsense when six stories outlining the adventures of the Peterkin family began to appear in *Our Young Folks* in 1868. Hale was born into a large and distinguished family. Her father, Nathan, was a descendant of the famous Revolutionary War hero, and her mother, Sarah Preston Everett, the sister of the respected orator and divinity scholar Edward Everett. Eleven children were born to the Hales, seven surviving to form a family that was noted for its closeness and its humor and congeniality through the years. The four older children—Sarah, Nathan, Jr., Lucretia, and Edward—were separated by at least seven years from the younger ones—Alexander, Charles, and Susan—and formed their own little group within the family. Their adventures on the Boston Common, the secrets and enterprises hatched in the attic retreat of their Tremont Street home (where the Parker House now stands), the everyday round of early Boston childhood activities are recounted in Edward Everett Hale's *A New England Boyhood* (1893) and reflected in a slightly topsy-turvy manner in Lucretia Peabody Hale's *The Peterkin Papers* (1880) and *The Last of the Peterkins, With Others of Their Kin* (1886).

Six years before Lucretia Hale's birth, her father had bought the *Boston Daily Advertiser,* which he guided for almost forty years, developing it with the help of his family into a prominent and influential newspaper. Sarah Hale and her children often helped correct copy and contributed pieces to the paper when there was space to be filled. Nathan Hale's second love, the railroad, also involved all the members of the family, and he was instrumental in bringing the railroad into Massachusetts and to Boston, becoming the president of the Boston and Worcester Railroad (the B & W) when it went into operation in 1834. The strong bonds of the large and congenial family, involvement in the everyday workings of the *Advertiser,* watching with pride and excitement as their father slowly but surely convinced others of the efficacy of railroad travel by showing them the model railroad which stood in their living room—all of these experiences formed Lucretia Hale's outlook and skills. The family seemed to have had an extraordinary talent for getting on with one another, and as the children grew older, they maintained the close relationship that they had developed as children. Mrs. Hale, when asked what rule she followed to raise such a large and successful family, answered, "Dear child, the rule is to get along as well as you can."

Lucretia Peabody Hale

The Hale family shared years of comfort and affluence when many of the most influential members of Boston's society, including the historian George Bancroft and Senator Daniel Webster, were frequent callers at their home, described by one of Edward Everett Hale's biographers as "an intellectual three-ring circus." However, they shared bad times as well, gaining strength from each other. In the 1850s Alexander drowned, Sarah died, a magazine which Charles had started failed, and their father was forced after forty years to sell the *Advertiser* due to a long series of financial setbacks, which culminated in the family's having to leave Boston for a smaller home in Brookline.

Writing was second nature to this family, as was a respect and love for education. The older children were sent to Miss Susan Whitney's Dame School. Lucretia Hale joined Sarah and Nathan there when she was four, and Edward begged to be taken along when he was three. Lucretia Hale then studied with Miss Elizabeth Peabody, who was gaining a reputation for innovative educational techniques and was soon to join Bronson Alcott in his famed Temple School venture. At Miss Peabody's Hale met Margaret Harding. Together they attended the George B. Emerson School for Young Ladies in Boston where they were joined by Susan Inches Lyman. The three became lifetime friends, and both Harding and Lyman were instrumental in Hale's creation of the Peterkins.

Lucretia Hale's first novel, *Margaret Percival in America* (1850), was written with her brother Edward as was her last novel, *The New Harry and Lucy* (1892), a delightful take-off on Maria Edgeworth's *Harry and Lucy* tales that they had pored over in their attic retreat as children. It was at the end of the 1850s, when the family fortunes were rapidly worsening, that she started to write in earnest in order to work toward becoming self-supporting. She produced stories that were published in the *Atlantic Monthly,* manuals on needlework, reading texts, and a good deal of hackwork.

Hale began telling the tales of the Peterkins around 1861 to her brother Edward's children and the children of her former school friends Margaret Harding White and Susan Inches Lyman Lesley. A sick, five-year-old Meg Lesley provided the first audience for these tales, in which the wise "Lady from Philadelphia" is modeled on Meg's mother, Susan. The Peterkin stories did not appear in print until 1868 when John Trowbridge was looking for something for *Our Young Folks* magazine without the heavy-handed didacticism and religiosity of many children's stories at the time. *Our Young Folks* was

Hale's parents, Nathan and Sarah Preston Everett Hale

superseded by *St. Nicholas,* in which several Peterkin episodes also appeared.

All those who have enjoyed Hale's creations undoubtedly have their own cherished Peterkin adventure. The Peterkins are faced with problems of all kinds that require resolution. The first published episode deals with "The Lady Who Put Salt in Her Coffee"; in other stories they contend with a piano placed by movers with the keyboard toward a wall and an outside window, a Christmas tree that is too tall to fit in a room, and the more weighty problem of trying to become wise. Usually all of the family joins together to try to solve the problem, from Mr. and Mrs. Peterkin to Agamemnon, who "had been to college," Elizabeth Eliza, Solomon John, and the little boys, who are never named but are carefully and unforgettably distinguished by their ever-present india rubber boots. They do everything quite methodically, though it is Agamemnon who, as the most educated, is the most logical and given to trust in encyclopedias and manuals of learning. The Peterkins, however, usually involve themselves in such webs of logic and attempts to adhere to tradition that at each step the problem becomes even more perplexing until the thread can only be cut by the common sense wis-

dom of the Lady from Philadelphia.

The Peterkin episodes are based on Hale's own family foibles and those of her friends. Agamemnon, for instance, is Edward Everett Hale, who became one of the most respected ministers in Boston, prolific as a writer and a speaker and known as a promoter of good causes in the liberal tradition of mid-nineteenth-century educated Boston citizens. Edward Everett Hale is best known today for *The Man Without a Country,* first published in the *Atlantic Monthly* in 1863, and like Agamemnon, from early childhood he had a great love of encyclopedic knowledge. Through Agamemnon and the other Peterkins, Lucretia Peabody Hale makes fun of mid-century New England, primarily Boston, by turning it upside down, in a nonsense vein reminiscent of Lewis Carroll's mockery of Victorian England's penchant for pomposity and dependence on book learning and convention in *Alice in Wonderland.*

After her father's death in 1863 and her mother's in 1865, Hale went to Egypt in 1867 with her youngest sister, Susan, to visit Charles, who was serving as the American consul-general there. It was this trip that gave her material for the last volume of Peterkin stories. After Hale returned

Illustration for Hale's 1886 book, The Last of the Peterkins, With Others of Their Kin *(Baldwin Library, University of Florida Libraries)*

Front cover for Lucretia Hale's 1892 collaboration with her brother Edward Everett Hale (Baldwin Library, University of Florida Libraries)

from the Egyptian trip, she settled in Boston, spending months at a time with either family or friends, but at the same time maintaining her independence and continuing with her writing. In 1872 she again collaborated with her brother Edward, with Harriet Beecher Stowe, to whom she was related through marriage, and with three other close friends on *Six of One by Half a Dozen of the Other,* "An Every Day Novel" which grew out of the intellectual bonhomie of the circle she moved in. Although there is no indication that she was a strong feminist, she was the first woman to be elected to the Boston School committee, after a long and noisy battle which extended from the city council of Boston to the state legislature of Massachusetts, where her brother Charles voted to keep women off the school committee. Edward, who along with Charles also held rather conventional views, opposed her when she wanted to take up residence in a settlement house to live with and help the poor. So she compromised by maintaining

her own apartment and being as self-supporting as possible.

In 1886 *The Last of the Peterkins* was published. As Hale grew old, her eyesight failed and an operation to check the growing blindness affected her mind and left her totally incapacitated. She had never married and died in a mental institution, after having been cared for by Edward and his family. Lucretia Peabody Hale is buried at Mount Auburn, the Cambridge resting place of so many of New England's distinguished writers and intellectuals.

References:

Edward Everett Hale, *A New England Boyhood* (New York: Cassell, 1893);

Madelyn C. Wankmiller, "Lucretia Peabody Hale and *The Peterkin Papers,*" *Hornbook Magazine,* 34 (April 1958): 95-103;

Eliza Orne White, "Lucretia P. Hale," *Hornbook Magazine*, 16 (September-October 1940): 317-322.

Papers:
The Hale family papers are in the Sophia Smith Collection, Smith College Library.

Sarah Josepha Hale

(24 October 1788-30 April 1879)

M. Sarah Smedman
University of North Carolina at Charlotte

See also the Hale entry in *DLB 1, The American Renaissance in New England.*

SELECTED BOOKS: *The Genius of Oblivion; and Other Original Poems* (Concord, N.H.: Jacob A. Moore, 1823);

Northwood: A Tale of New England, 2 volumes (Boston: Bowles & Dearborn, 1827); republished as *Sidney Romelee: A Tale of New England* (London: Newman, 1827);

Sketches of American Character (Boston: Putnam & Hunt/Carter & Hendee, 1829);

Conversations on the Burman Mission (Boston: Printed by T. R. Martin for the Massachusetts Sabbath School, 1830);

Poems for Our Children (Boston: Marsh, Capen & Lyon, 1830);

The School Song Book (Boston: Allen & Ticknor, 1834); republished as *My Little Song Book* (Boston: Allen & Ticknor, 1841);

Traits of American Life (Philadelphia: Carey & Hart, 1835);

The Good Housekeeper; or, The Way to Live Well and to Be Well While We Live (Boston: Weeks, Jordan, 1839);

Keeping House and House Keeping (New York: Harper, 1845);

Alice Ray: A Romance in Rhyme (Philadelphia: Printed by A. Scott, 1845);

"Boarding Out." A Tale of Domestic Life (New York: Harper, 1846);

Three Hours; or, The Vigil of Love: and Other Poems (Philadelphia: Carey & Hart, 1848);

Harry Guy, the Widow's Son. A Story of the Sea (Boston: Mussey, 1848);

Woman's Record; or, Sketches of All Distinguished Women, From "The Beginning" Till A.D. 1850 (New York: Harper, 1853; London: Low,

1863; revised and enlarged, New York: Harper, 1855; revised and enlarged again, New York: Harper, 1870);

Liberia; or, Mr. Peyton's Experiments (New York: Harper, 1853);

Manners; or, Happy Homes and Good Society All the Year Round (Boston: Tilton, 1868);

Love; or, Woman's Destiny. A Poem in Two Parts: With Other Poems (Philadelphia: Duffield Ashmead, 1870).

OTHER: *Flora's Interpreter: or, The American Book of Flowers and Sentiments*, edited with contributions by Hale (Boston: Marsh, Capen & Lyon, 1830); republished as *Flora's Interpreter, and Fortuna Flora* (Boston: Mussey, 1849; revised and enlarged, Boston: Sanborn, Carter & Bazin/Portland: Sanborn & Carter, 1856; revised again, Boston: Chase, Nichols & Hill, 1860);

John Mason Good, *Good's Book of Nature*, abridgment and adaptation attributed to Hale (Boston: Allen & Ticknor, 1834);

The Ladies' Wreath; a Selection from the Female Poetic Writers of England and America, edited with contributions by Hale (Boston: Marsh, Capen & Lyon, 1837; enlarged, Boston: Marsh, Capen, Lyon & Webb, 1839);

Jane Taylor, *The Pleasures of Taste, and Other Stories*, preface and "Sketch of Miss Jane Taylor" by Hale (Boston: Marsh, Capen, Lyon & Webb, 1840);

John Aikin, *The Juvenile Budget Opened*, introductory materials and "Biographical Sketch of John Aiken [sic]" by Hale (Boston: Marsh, Capen, Lyon & Webb, 1840);

Anna Letitia Barbauld, *Things by Their Right Names, and Other Stories, Fables, and Moral Pieces, in*

Sarah Josepha Hale, portrait used as the frontispiece for the 1870 edition of Woman's Record *(Baldwin Library, University of Florida Libraries)*

Prose and Verse, preface and "Sketch of Mrs. Barbauld" by Hale (Boston: Marsh, Capen, Lyon & Webb, 1840);

The Countries of Europe, and the Manners and Customs of Its Various Nations. In Easy and Entertaining Verse for Children, edited by Hale (New York: Edward Dunigan, circa 1842);

Gift to Young Friends; or the Guide to Good, edited by Hale (New York: Edward Dunigan, circa 1842);

Good Little Boy's Book, edited by Hale (New York: Edward Dunigan, circa 1842);

Good Little Girl's Book, edited by Hale (New York: Dunigan, circa 1842);

Happy Changes; or Pride and Its Consequences, edited by Hale (New York: Edward Dunigan, circa 1842);

Short Tales in Short Words, edited by Hale (New York: Edward Dunigan, circa 1842);

Spring Flowers, or the Poetical Bouquet, edited by Hale (New York: Edward Dunigan, circa 1842);

The Three Baskets; or How Henry, Richard, and Charles Were Occupied While Papa Was Away, edited by Hale (New York: Edward Dunigan, circa 1842);

Uncle Buncle's True and Instructive Stories, about An-

imals, Insects, and Plants, edited by Hale (New York: Edward Dunigan, circa 1842);

The Wise Boys, edited by Hale (New York: Edward Dunigan, circa 1842);

The Opal; A Pure Gift for the Holy Days. MDCCCXLV, edited with contributions by Hale (New York: Riker, 1845);

The Opal: A Pure Gift for the Holy Days. MDCCCXLVIII, edited with contributions by Hale (New York: Riker, 1848);

The Opal: A Pure Gift for All Seasons, edited with contributions by Hale (New York: Riker, 1849);

Mary Hughs, *Aunt Mary's New Stories for Young People*, edited by Hale (Boston: Munroe, 1849);

The Crocus: A Fresh Flower for the Holidays, edited by Hale (New York: Edward Dunigan, 1849);

The Poets' Offering: For 1850, edited by Hale (Philadelphia: Grigg, Elliot, 1850); republished as *A Complete Dictionary of Poetical Quotations* (Philadelphia: Lippincott, Grambo, 1850) and *The Poets' Offering: For 1851* (Philadelphia: Lippincott, Grambo, 1851);

The Ladies' New Book of Cookery: A Practical System for Private Families in Town and Country, edited by Hale (New York: Long, 1852); republished as *Modern Household Cookery* (London: Nelson, 1863); enlarged as *Mrs. Hale's New Cookbook* (Philadelphia: Peterson, 1857);

The New Household Receipt-Book, edited by Hale (New York: Long, 1852); enlarged as *Mrs. Hale's Receipts for the Million* (Philadelphia: Peterson, 1857);

The White Veil: A Bridal Gift, edited with contributions by Hale (Philadelphia: Butler, 1854);

The Bible Reading-Book: Containing Such Portions of the History, Biography, Poetry, Prophecy, Precepts, and Parables, of the Old and New Testaments, As Form a Connected Narrative, in the Exact Words of the Scripture, edited by Hale (Philadelphia: Lippincott, Grambo, 1854);

The Letters of Madame de Sévigné, to Her Daughter and Friends, edited by Hale (New York: Mason Brothers, 1856; revised, Boston: Roberts Brothers, 1869);

The Letters of Lady Mary Wortley Montagu, edited by Hale (New York: Mason Brothers, 1856; revised, Boston: Roberts Brothers, 1869).

A fascinating, capable, and prolific author and, for fifty years, editor of her day's most successful magazine, Sarah Josepha Hale influenced immeasurably American middle-class mores. Sensitive to the contemporary social currents, astute in her assessment of the status quo, compassionate in the directives she set forth, and diplomatic in pursuing her goals, she molded the course of education, charitable enterprise, and woman's position in American life. The literature she wrote for children was an integral dimension of her intent to improve their education and of a piece with the objectives of her other literary works: to teach truth and to build character while imparting pleasure through story and verse. Ironically, while the most famous of her poems, "Mary's Lamb" ("Mary Had a Little Lamb"), lives on as traditional nursery lore, its author's name has been all but forgotten, most people crediting the lilting lines to Mother Goose.

Sarah Josepha Buell Hale was born on 24 October 1788, in what was then the wilderness of Newport, New Hampshire, the third of four children of Captain Gordon Buell, a Revolutionary soldier, and Martha Whittlesey Buell, also of a distinguished New England family. Hale attributed her love of learning and her confidence in woman's acumen to her early teaching by her mother, whom she described as having had "uncommon advantages of education for a female of her times," and "possessed [of] a mind clear as rock-water, and a most happy talent of communicating knowledge." Her mother's method of teaching her children "serious truth" while charming them with stories, songs, and legends, Hale accounts a major influence in making her the woman she became.

Subsequently studying Latin, philosophy, English, and classical literature with her brother Horatio, then a student at Dartmouth and later a highly esteemed New York judge, Hale acquired the equivalent of a college degree, a rare possession for a woman of her day. She put her talents to use in a Newport private school. From her eighteenth to her twenty-fifth year, at a time when women were considered unfit for the classroom, Hale proved herself an innovative and gifted teacher, emphasizing writing, reading, and mathematics, even introducing Latin in the elementary grades.

In 1813, she married David Hale, a promising young lawyer, with whom she continued to study for two hours daily, "from eight o'clock in the evening till ten," such subjects as French, botany, geology, and literature. She credited her husband with guiding the progression of her prose style from the verbose and grandiloquent to one more terse and idiomatic. When, after nine years of a halcyon marriage, she was suddenly left a widow with five children, she tried first a millinery business with her sister-in-law, but the venture was unsuccessful.

Although Hale had had some poetry published before her marriage, only after her husband's death did she think seriously of becoming an author, turning to literature as one of the few employments in which a woman of her rather frail health and specific talents could, as she said, "engage with any hope of profit." Her first book, *The Genius of Oblivion; and Other Original Poems,* published in 1823 with the aid of her husband's Masonic friends, was representative of the popular tastes and styles of the day: wordy, sentimental, moralistic. Still, some of the poems display her fluent rhythms, her ease in rhyming, and a characteristic theme—woman's natural role in the home, influencing public affairs through the exertion of her spiritual and moral superiority on her husband and children. In 1826 her poem "Hymn to Charity" attracted attention when it was awarded the gold medal and a twenty-dollar prize as the best poem submitted in a competition sponsored by the *Boston Spectator and Ladies' Album.*

In 1827 Hale's *Northwood,* the first American novel by a woman, was published. The story contrasted life in the North and the South, though the description of the Northern characters and life was much more natural and vivid. Almost without precedent for an American work, the book was also published in England, where it appeared under the title *Sidney Romelee: A Tale of New England* (1827). *Northwood* was deservedly popular for its realistic detail, straightforward prose, and perspicacious recognition that the tension rising among the states was as much a result of economic conditions as of moral conflict over slavery. In 1852 it was republished with the subtitle *Life North and South: Showing the True Character of Both. Northwood's* success had to have been heady for its author, who recorded how thrilled she had been when, as a child, she read Ann Radcliffe's *The Mysteries of Udolpho* (1794), "the most fascinating [novel] I had ever read, . . . [and it was] written by a *woman.* How happy it made me!" In 1827 Hale's literary prestige earned her the invitation from Reverend John L. Blake to move to Boston to take charge of the *Ladies' Magazine,* which was designated as "the first magazine edited by a woman for women . . . either in the Old World or the New." Beginning in January 1828, and for the next nine years, with unrivaled success she edited that magazine, establishing the policy then virtually unthinkable of printing only original works by American writers.

In 1836, looking for an editor for his *Lady's Book* who would please the readers' tastes, Louis A. Godey bought the *Ladies' Magazine* to secure Hale's services. Taking charge of *Godey's Lady's Book* on 1 January 1837, Hale edited it for four years from Boston, while continuing to provide a home for her youngest son until he had graduated from Harvard. In 1841 she moved to Philadelphia, where she lived for the rest of her life, imprinting her mark on the entire country through the *Lady's Book* until she resigned at the age of eighty-nine in December 1877. She died quietly, with no preceding illness, sixteen months later, on 30 April 1879.

Under the energetic and imaginative editorship of Hale, *Godey's Lady's Book* flourished, reaching by 1861 a circulation of 61,000, twice that of any competitor, and by 1865, 150,000. Dedicated to woman's improvement and proudly described by its publisher as "the mirror of woman's mind," *Godey's Lady's Book* understood the limitations of its convention-bound public but was also alive to the changing consciousness of women. Each issue contained hand-colored and black-and-white fashion plates and other engravings, sewing and handwork patterns, recipes, house plans, columns devoted to other domestic and child-rearing concerns, the words and music for a song, fiction, poetry, and essays. Hale continued her former policy of giving the magazine an American flavor by printing only new material by American authors, the best and the most popular writers of the day. Because, according to its editorial policy, *Godey's Lady's Book* abstained from politics and economics as subjects inappropriate for women, it did not enter into the controversy between the States; thus, an acknowledged power bypassed its opportunity to influence action.

Always fiercely patriotic and an advocate of human rights, especially of equal education for women, Hale used her editor's chair as a platform from which to campaign enthusiastically and patiently for the causes to which she was committed and to effect reforms today taken for granted in American life. However, her sound judgment and journalistic sense restrained her from turning the magazines she edited into organs for reform. In 1832 she undertook the first magazine solicitation for money to complete construction of the Bunker Hill Monument, halted because of lack of funds. Ten years later she organized the trend-setting women's national fair at Quincy Market in Boston, which netted $30,000, more than enough to complete the monument, thus succeeding where the Men's Committee had failed. One of her most telling arguments in behalf of the monument, as it was to be later for the restoration of Mount Vernon, had been the urgency of preserving the heritage

of the United States for its children. In 1833 she organized and was elected president of the Seaman's Aid Society, which gave employment to and improved wages and working conditions for impoverished sailors' wives. Outgrowths of the foundation of that society included her successful fight for legal retention of property rights for women, the establishment of sailors' homes, a trade school for girls, and the first day nursery. In the 1840s, Hale began her campaign to have Thanksgiving declared a national holiday, an effort which succeeded only after she had written numerous editorials and corresponded personally with five presidents. She persuaded twenty-two states to celebrate it, publishing the roster of their names in *Godey's Lady's Book*, before Abraham Lincoln finally issued a National Thanksgiving Proclamation on 3 October 1863, the first since George Washington's in 1789.

By her personal iteration, Hale's earliest ambition was "to promote the reputation of my own sex" and the primary and constant theme of her work was to improve woman's education and increase her usefulness. She was an early champion of an elementary education for girls equal to that for boys; of the necessity of physical education for girls; of creating environmental conditions conducive to healthy physical and psychic growth; of schools for the training of teachers and nurses. She was the first advocate of women teachers in public schools and women administrators and faculty in colleges for their sex. She promoted the elevation of housekeeping to a profession, coining the phrase "domestic science." It was she who was responsible for the establishment of the first Female Medical College of Philadelphia in 1850, of the Ladies' Medical Missionary Society in 1851, and the education and dispatch of the first women medical missionaries. As a friend and collaborator of Matthew Vassar, she advised in the organization and curriculum development of Vassar, the first college for women. One of the proudest and happiest moments of Hale's life came on 1 February 1867, when after thundering editorials and pleading correspondence with Matthew Vassar, the New York State Legislature was persuaded to authorize the change in name from Vassar Female College to Vassar College. The vulgarism *female*, Hale pointed out, degraded woman from her "position as a rational being," reducing her to the level of animals: "Females, indeed! They might have been sheep!," labeled as they were by "the animal term for gender." After heated agitation, the word was removed from the facade of the main college building by replacing the stone on which it was carved with a blank one, which remains in place to this day.

Toward her many accomplishments Hale worked unflaggingly, compelled by her paradoxical convictions: that woman had the right to an education equal to man's; that she had the stronger mental influence on her own sex; that her nature was morally and spiritually more sensitive, essentially less selfish; and that her role was to affect political and economic affairs through her obedient service to and gentle influence over man in the domestic sphere. In her work for women's rights, she divorced herself from the militant feminists of her day and appealed ingratiatingly to masculine pride and interests, insisting that advances for women should always accrue only with the consent of their husbands and fathers.

Although the editing of *Godey's Lady's Book* was Hale's most distinctive contribution to American culture, she produced many successful volumes of poetry, prose, and plays and contributed voluminously to gift books and periodicals other than her own. Particularly noteworthy in her prodigious bibliography is *Woman's Record* (1853), a universal biographical dictionary with over 2500 sketches of notable women. Entries varied in the amount and specificity of information, frequently providing valuable details about her contemporaries. Selections from the works of "authoresses" were included. *Woman's Record* was divided into four eras from the creation until 1850 and supplemented by two revised editions that brought the material up to 1868. Closely bound up with the primary ambition of her life, *Woman's Record* is the only work she mentioned by title in the summation she gave of her literary life in her farewell editorial in *Godey's Lady's Book:* "My object . . . was to illustrate the great truth that woman's mission is to educate and ameliorate humanity: as man's mission is to subdue Nature, and the world of inanimate matter. . . . I have aimed to render it the most thorough and trustworthy of feminine biographies."

Two collections particularly gratifying to Hale were *The Ladies' Wreath* (1837) and *The Poets' Offering: For 1850. The Ladies' Wreath,* her compilation of the works of English and American women poets, she believed would disprove the theory of a "true feminine style" and exhibit that, though woman's range of subject was more limited than man's, in her treatment of material "the delicate shades of genius are as varied and distinctly marked in the one sex as the bold outlines are in the other." The book, credited by the *North American Review* "as the first effort to gather enough poetry by women to

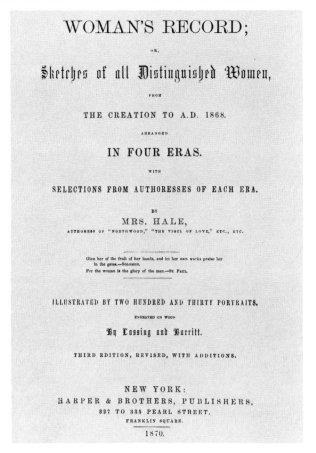

Title page for the second revised edition of Hale's biographical dictionary (Baldwin Library, University of Florida Libraries). "My object," she wrote, "was to illustrate the great truth that woman's mission is to educate and ameliorate humanity. . . ."

make an anthology," included biographical and critical introductions which were incisive if somewhat lavish in their praise. *The Poets' Offering,* republished with the more appropriate title *A Complete Dictionary of Poetical Quotations* (1850), contained 600 double-column octavo pages of selections from the best British and American poets since Spenser, arranged under a host of subjects. It was the most complete work of its kind.

Typical of Hale's short fiction are *Sketches of American Character* (1829) and *Traits of American Life* (1835), collections of her previously published stories of representative characters, for example, "The Soldier of the Revolution," "The Village Schoolmistress," and "The Catholic Convert." For the most part these tales are preachy and trite, with artificial dialogue and Hale's authorial commentary. More dramatic novelettes in the same vein include *Keeping House and House Keeping* (1845) and *"Boarding Out." A Tale of Domestic Life* (1846), both

Decorative title page for the anthology described in Hale's preface as "a Gift-book on a new plan. The contents are of more value than the cover. . . . because in this volume will be found the most perfect gems of genius the English language has preserved since the days of Spenser."

designed to instruct young women in household management and to convince them of the importance of diligent fulfillment of their domestic roles. Much of Hale's poetry, that published under the early pseudonym Cornelia and anonymously as well as under her own name, has never been collected, but such volumes as *Alice Ray: A Romance in Rhyme* (1845) and *Three Hours; or, The Vigil of Love: and Other Poems* (1848) reveal her to be caught up in the sentimental and religious currents of Victorianism.

So reliable a barometer of nineteenth-century popular American culture as Sarah Hale was predictably immersed in the gift-book mania of the 1830s, 1840s, and 1850s. Between 1827 and 1855, she contributed signed and unsigned stories and poems to at least eighteen of those beautifully

bound collections of literature and engravings. She edited two, *The Opal* for three of its appearances (1845, 1848, 1849) and *The Crocus* (1849), "a new flower for our friends," for young people. The last stanza of the title poem phrased the lesson to be learned from "so simple a flower": "Patient to-day, through the gloomiest hour,/We come out the brighter tomorrow."

Hale's books for children were but one manifestation of her desire to ensure them a healthy, happy, holy, and useful life. When she moved to Boston, she founded and directed in her home the first Infant's School, or kindergarten, in order to control the quality of her youngest son William's education. Having gained firsthand knowledge of child psychology from her experience as an elementary schoolteacher and as the mother of five, her theories concerning the child's need for individual development before being absorbed into a larger, more strictly disciplined classroom were realistic but radical for her time. Her lifelong interest in kindergartens was intensified by her friendship with Elizabeth Peabody, who introduced the Froebel system into the United States.

Although it is not a simple matter to distinguish between literature for adults and that for juveniles during Hale's day, when children's earliest reading was likely to be the Bible, *The Pilgrim's Progress*, Milton, Shakespeare, and Pope, she sometimes made such a distinction. Among those books for the very young are *Poems for Our Children, The School Song Book,* and the Little Boy's and Girl's Library, a series of ten volumes edited by Hale and published about 1842. Of most lasting significance among Hale's literature for children are her poems, several of which have become classics. Her first volume of children's poetry, a twenty-four-page paperbound book entitled *Poems for Our Children* (1830), was written in response to a request from Lowell Mason, the American composer responsible for the addition of music to the public school curriculum. Mason asked for verses appealing and comprehensible to children for which he could write the melodies; the songs would serve to teach music as well as wholesome precepts in the schools. He included, and thereby helped to popularize, eight of Hale's fifteen simple, catchy, moral pieces in his successful *Juvenile Lyre* (1832). Three of these are among America's best-known children's poems: "Prayer," a paraphrase of the Our Father; "Birds," later retitled "The Bird's Nest," by William Holmes McGuffey; and "Mary's Lamb." Subsequently, these were appropriated with no credit to the author by virtually every nineteenth-century juvenile poetry anthology and by McGuffey's first and second Eclectic Readers (1836). The 1857 edition of McGuffey's *Second Eclectic Reader,* later published by Henry Ford, offered "The Bird's Nest" as lesson five and "Mary's Lamb" as lesson forty-seven, still without acknowledging the author. Another famous Hale poem, "It Snows," first published in the January 1837 *Godey's Lady's Book,* was included in McGuffey's *Fifth Eclectic Reader* (1844), this time attributed to its author. These poems were memorized by generations of Americans and thus, as Hale's biographer Ruth Finley says, "slipped into the language uncredited, easy prey to theft of ideas, verbal plagiarisms, and even bodily apparition."

During the last years of her life, "bodily apparitions" did haunt Sarah Hale in the form of rival claimants to the identity of the original Mary and to authorship of "Mary's Lamb." In 1879 the most serious of these challenges occurred, involving Mary Sawyer Tyler, then working as a matron in a Somerville, Massachusetts, mental institution, who claimed that she was the model for Mary, and John Roulstone, who, by Tyler's account, had years earlier presented her with the first twelve lines of "Mary's Lamb." According to Tyler, a woman by the name of Hale later added twelve more lines.

Four days before her death, with characteristic quiet dignity, Hale dictated a letter to her daughter, defending her authorship in reply to an inquiry from the children's periodical *Wide Awake.* Ten years later in a letter written to the *Boston Transcript,* her son Horatio described the circumstances of his mother's childhood that had inspired the poem.

Later proponents of Tyler's version stressed the fact that Hale's grandchildren had said their grandmother had told them the poem did not rise out of any personal experience. However, Hale's claim to authorship, verified by both external and internal evidence, is widely accepted today. "Mary's Lamb" had been published under her name in *Poems for Children* and, either just prior to or shortly after the appearance of that book, in the September-October 1830 issue of *Juvenile Miscellany,* a magazine for children. In response to critics who have argued for two different authors on the basis that the poem is internally inconsistent, the first part telling a story and the last teaching a lesson, Ruth Finley has aptly contended in *The Lady of Godey's* (1931) that structurally the poem falls into three stanzas of eight lines each, the first two narrating an incident, the last drawing the moral embodied in the story. To arrange the poem in quatrains— as was done for purposes of layout by McGuffey,

among others—and to divide it after twelve lines is to violate its thematic and structural unity. The components of story with moral and its balladlike qualities are typical of the poems in Hale's volume and achieve the intent she stated in the preface to *Poems for Our Children:* "Dear Children, I wrote this book to please and instruct you. . . . I intended . . . to furnish you with a few pretty songs and poems which would teach you truth and goodness." Despite the evidence, the controversy over the authorship continued in newspapers and journals for decades. It has unfortunately been perpetuated by the plaque supporting Roulstone's authorship that Henry Ford had mounted near the Sterling Redstone School when he restored it as the Little Red Schoolhouse and moved it to Sudbury, Massachusetts, near the Wayside Inn, in 1926.

At the close of her preface to *Poems for Our Children,* Hale suggested that if the book were well received, she would write a second part. A second, larger volume of verse, *The School Song Book,* appeared in 1834 and was republished in 1841 under the title *My Little Song Book.* This volume includes favorites from the first, "Mary's Lamb" among them, as well as many new poems.

In March of 1830, Hale produced *Flora's Interpreter,* a different kind of gift book, which became immensely popular and profitable. A poetical-botanical book, it listed flowers alphabetically by common name, then, following Linnaeus's classification, gave the scientific name of each, its order, class, and species, and finally a poem illustrating its significance in "the language of flowers." Most of the poetry was selected from British poets—Chaucer, Shakespeare, Pope, Burns, Keats—but Whittier and Bryant, as well as an "anonymous" poet—Hale—were included. In the 1849 edition, Hale added *Fortuna Flora,* a lengthy section in which readers could ascertain their "condition, character, and probable success in life" by studying the influence of their flowers, thereby discerning "warnings or encouragements, according to the tenor of life pursued." Flowers were assigned to each month and day and to the four temperaments; then the meaning of each flower was interpreted.

In her introduction to this edition, Hale expressed her feminine concern for teaching the young the modes of knowing with the heart as well as the head. The book, she says, is an effort "to stimulate the young to the observance of the hidden meanings which may lie concealed in the flower volumes of nature," so that they feel that " 'Wisdom is with the heart.' " The method the book

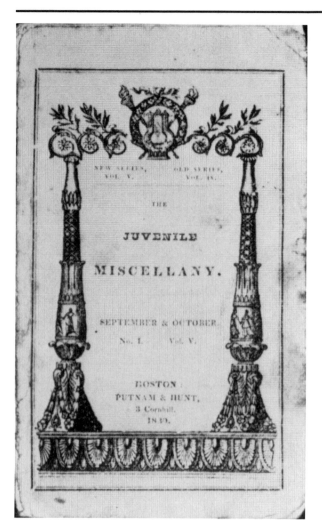

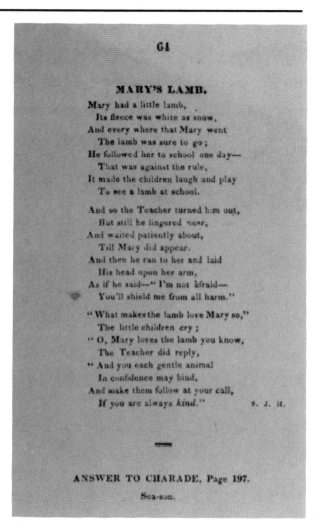

64

MARY'S LAMB.

Mary had a little lamb,
    Its fleece was white as snow,
And every where that Mary went
    The lamb was sure to go;
He followed her to school one day—
    That was against the rule,
It made the children laugh and play
    To see a lamb at school.

And so the Teacher turned him out,
    But still he lingered near,
And waited patiently about,
    Till Mary did appear.
And then he ran to her and laid
    His head upon her arm,
As if he said—" I'm not afraid—
    You'll shield me from all harm."

"What makes the lamb love Mary so,"
    The little children cry;
"O, Mary loves the lamb you know,
    The Teacher did reply,
" And you each gentle animal
    In confidence may bind,
And make them follow at your call,
    If you are always *kind*."   s. j. h.

ANSWER TO CHARADE, Page 197.
Sea-son.

Front cover of the first magazine to publish "Mary's Lamb" and the poem as it appeared there, signed with Hale's initials

employs is characteristic of Hale, connecting knowledge with amusement to help "the young learn these lessons easier, and remember them longer." From sales figures it appears that the signs of the flowers enchanted the young, and the not so young, of Hale's day as the signs of the zodiac have fascinated people of other ages. Godey announced that by 1850 the book had sold more than 40,000 copies; it was still in print at least through the 1860s and was regularly reviewed among giftbooks as late as 1871. Several of the many editions of *Flora's Interpreter* contained substantial revisions and additions. One story has it that among Hale's personal effects was a copy with an 1870 imprint having handwritten notes in the margins, as though she had planned but never completed yet another revision.

In addition to writing her original works, Hale edited the works of several other authors for

an audience of American children. Although her name does not appear on the juvenile version of *Good's Book of Nature* (1834), the adaptation has been attributed to her. She had recently been introduced to the textbook field through her cooperation with Lowell Mason, and certain stylistic qualities in this edition of John Mason Good's book are characteristic of her. In 1840 Hale edited three volumes for the School Library Juvenile series sponsored by the Massachusetts Board of Education: Jane Taylor's *The Pleasures of Taste*, John Aikin's *The Juvenile Budget Opened*, and Anna Letitia Barbauld's *Things by Their Right Names*. For each of the volumes, Hale wrote biographical sketches and glossed a few British terms not familiar to American children. In the early 1840s, probably in 1842, Hale edited a ten-volume series of "juveniles," republished about 1860 as *The Little Boy's and Girl's Library*. Bound in printed paper wrappers, the

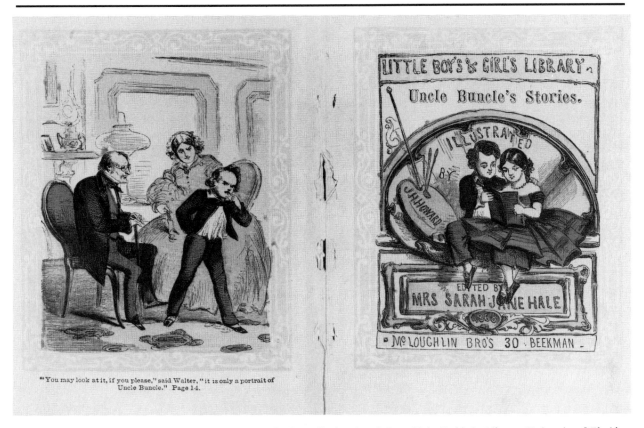

Frontispiece and title page for a juvenile volume mistakenly credited to Sarah Jane Hale (Baldwin Library, University of Florida Libraries). Hale edited a series of ten children's books which were published in the early 1840s. When McLoughlin Bros. republished the series as the Little Boy's and Girl's Library, about 1860, Hale's name was given incorrectly on all the title pages, an error which, according to the Bibliography of American Literature, *"has caused much confusion."*

books were published simultaneously in two formats, with uncolored illustrations and with illustrations colored by hand. Reviews called the books "beautiful" and "highly popular," commenting that "their endorsement by the well-known editor offers [a very] strong guarantee for their internal excellence." Of undetermined authorship, some pieces signed with the untraced pseudonym Thomas Lovechild, the series comprises prose and verse, moral tales about places, plants, and animals, wise and naughty boys and girls. Because the publisher moved sometime in 1843 or 1844, the history of the printing of these books is difficult to trace; nonetheless, the *Bibliography of American Literature* cautiously suggests that each of the ten volumes went into two or more printings. In 1849 Hale produced an edition of Mary Hughs's popular tales entitled *Aunt Mary's New Stories for Young People.* Hale's last work for the young child was *The Bible Reading-Book* (1854), an arrangement of selections from the Old and New Testaments.

For a brief time when she was in Boston, Hale

was also involved in the editorial management of a children's magazine. In September 1826, Putnam and Hunt, soon to be the publishers of the *Ladies' Magazine*, launched the *Juvenile Miscellany* under the editorship of Lydia Marie Child. A pioneer in the field of children's magazines, *Juvenile Miscellany* was instructive and highly moralistic. It numbered among its regular features natural history, biography, and fiction, including short, easy pieces in French and German. In the September 1834 issue, Child announced that she was relinquishing her interest in the magazine to a friend. That friend was Sarah J. Hale, although her name did not appear on the title page until September 1835. Hale managed to keep the *Juvenile Miscellany* afloat until the spring of 1836, when it sank under economic pressures.

Dedicated to "Young People Particularly" but directed toward a wider audience, *Manners; or, Happy Homes and Good Society All the Year Round* (1868) is a collection of articles Hale had written the previous year for a family newspaper, the *Home*

Weekly. The articles, Hale explained in the preface to the single volume, were written for the paper's "Home Circle," whose purpose "was to include the etiquette of social observances and the philosophy of home happiness." The book exhibits Hale's concurrence in the eighteenth-century philosophy of happiness that self-love and social are the same and her commitment to the observance of exterior forms of courtesy, not as artificial covers cloaking and choking natural instincts but as integral expressions of sensitive feelings for others. She had early learned, she said, "to distrust the abstract and ideal as guides in the duties of life." Her precepts are utilitarian and tolerant. The book includes sections on parties and "A Plea for Dancing," along with guides for domestic etiquette and hints for dress, foreign travel, and letter writing. In "Happy Sundays for Children" she asserts that linking "Sunday and sadness in the brain of a child" does not benefit the young but rather stems from a "mistaken sense of duty on the part of rightly-meaning parents" seeking to observe the day of rest. In an early chapter Hale demonstrates her reverence for language

as the highest human faculty by urging the cultivated to use diction and grammar with precision and propriety. In a later chapter, "Mistakes in Language," she utters one of her last vehement, yet witty, diatribes against the barbarous use of *female.*

Hale enjoyed a notable literary reputation in her own time. Although advanced in many of her ideas, her conventional morality, Biblical spirituality, and pleasant, sentimental style appealed to a populace whose tastes she catered to and whose responses she knew how to manipulate. In her will Hale appointed her children literary executors of all the manuscripts and papers she had meticulously preserved, hoping they would be published in a collected edition, but, as Isabelle Webb Entrikin remarked in *Sarah Josepha Hale and Godey's Lady's Book* (1946), "she had gone out of style and no complete edition was ever called for or undertaken." In her own lifetime, however, her writings were included in five anthologies of American prose or poetry, most notably those edited by Thomas B. Read and Rufus Wilmot Griswold. Ironically, the titles of four of those anthologies included the word *female.* Hale's personality and her journalistic efforts did exert an enduring force, leaving her indelible imprint on the ethos of an era. Today she is remembered chiefly for what she did toward the recognition and development of woman's intellectual capacities. Ever a powerful impetus behind her commitment to the development of woman's mind was her conviction that the formation of children, and therefore the health and happiness of the race, was her proud and privileged responsibility.

Hale at the age of eighty-five

Bibliography:

"Sarah J. Hale," *Bibliography of American Literature*, compiled by Jacob Blanck, volume 3 (New Haven & London: Yale University Press, 1959), pp. 319-340.

References:

Isabelle Webb Entrikin, *Sarah Josepha Hale and Godey's Lady's Book* (Philadelphia: University of Pennsylvania, 1946);

Ruth E. Finley, *The Lady of Godey's: Sarah Josepha Hale* (Philadelphia: Lippincott, 1931);

Norma R. Fryatt, *Sarah Josepha Hale: The Life and Times of a Nineteenth-Century Career Woman* (New York: Hawthorn Books, 1975);

George Bancroft Griffith, "Author of 'Mary's Little Lamb,'" *Granite State Magazine*, 1 (May 1906): 210-214;

Richard Walden Hale, " 'Mary Had a Little Lamb,'

and Its Author," *Century Magazine,* 67 (March 1904): 738-742;

Joseph Kastner, "The Tale Behind Mary's Little Lamb," *New York Times Magazine,* 13 April 1980, pp. 116-119;

Lawrence Martin, "The Genesis of Godey's Lady's Book," *New England Quarterly,* 1 (January 1928): 41-70;

Fred Lewis Pattee, *The Feminine Fifties* (New York: Appleton-Century, 1940);

Lucy E. Sanford, "Mrs. Sarah J. Hale," *Granite Monthly,* 3 (March 1880): 208-211;

The Story of Mary and Her Little Lamb: as told by Mary and Her Neighbors and Friends (Dearborn: Mr. and Mrs. Henry Ford, 1928);

Ralph Thompson, *American Literary Annuals & Gift Books, 1825-1865* (New York: Wilson, 1936);

E. A. Warren, "The True Story of Mary and Her Little Lamb," *National Magazine,* 6 (June 1897): 251-255.

Benjamin Harris

(birthdate unknown-circa 1720)

Edward J. Jennerich
Virginia Intermont College

SELECTED BOOKS: *The Protestant Tutor: instructing children to spel and read English and grounding them in the true Protestant Religion and discovering the errors and deceits of the Papists* (London: Printed for Benjamin Harris, 1679);

Triumphs of Justice over Unjust Judges (London: Printed for Benjamin Harris, 1681);

The New England Primer (Boston: Printed by R. Pierce for Benjamin Harris, 1687-1690?; enlarged, Boston: Printed by R. Pierce for, and sold by Benjamin Harris, 1691);

Boston Almanack for the Year of Our Lord God 1692, attributed to Harris (Boston: Printed by Benjamin Harris & John Allen, 1692);

The Holy Bible in Verse, attributed to Harris (London: Printed & sold by Benj. Harris, Senior, 1698; Boston: John Allen?, 1724).

Benjamin Harris, a printer, journalist, author, and bookseller, was the most widely read author of children's books in seventeenth- and eighteenth- century America. His *New England Primer* served the dual purpose of teaching Puritan children to read as well as providing their religious instruction. Few books have influenced as many children for as long a period of time as has *The New England Primer,* with its reign of over 150 years as the fundamental reading material for children.

Little is known of Harris's life beyond what

he published or wrote. He was a staunch, outspoken Anabaptist who possessed in large measure that sect's aversion to the Roman Catholic faith. Harris was a product of the volatile, intolerant period during which he lived. His frequent conflicts with the law were the result of the religious transitions in Restoration England, the lack of freedom of the press, and an unfortunate discernment in the way Harris expressed his beliefs.

The first record of Harris is as a London printer who began his career with a religious book, *War with the Devil* (1673). In 1679, in collaboration with an anonymous writer (purportedly Charles Blount), Harris printed a pamphlet entitled *An Appeal From the Country to the City* which was a seditious, stinging attack on Roman Catholicism and that religion's adherents. This attack was followed shortly by the publication of a Whig newspaper, *Domestick Intelligence; or News both from City and Country,* which first appeared on 7 July 1679. This endeavor was soon suppressed for containing false information about Roman Catholics and also Quakers.

Response to Harris's injudicious attacks was soon forthcoming. He was brought to trial in 1679 for libel in *An Appeal From the Country to the City*. In early 1680 he was convicted, sentenced to the pillory, and ordered to pay a fine of £500. His wife accompanied him to the pillory, and her efforts (though they made her the butt of several ribald pamphlets and ballads) and a largely sympathetic crowd of supporters saved him from serious injury and bolstered his already strong convictions. The matter of the fine was a more serious obstacle, and Harris was imprisoned in King's Bench Prison for nonpayment.

Harris's ardor was undiminished, and with the help of friends he secured an illegal release from prison. Soon after leaving jail in December 1680, he published a pamphlet in his defense entitled *Triumphs of Justice over Unjust Judges* (1681). The effect of this publication was the rearrest and imprisonment of Harris for two additional years.

In addition to producing these seditious attacks, Harris was busy in other ways to stem the spread and influence of Roman Catholicism. In 1679 he compiled and printed *The Protestant Tutor: instructing children to spel and read English and grounding them in the true Protestant Religion and discovering the errors and deceits of the Papists*. This was a catechism designed to instruct children in the "true Protestant Religion" (that is, Harris's) and to prepare children to defend themselves against the perceived evils of Roman Catholicism. The book received some favorable attention, but it was so severe in approach that it was shunned by most professed Anabaptists.

Harris finally secured his release from prison and decided that, with the succession of Catholic James II to the English throne, he would be wise to leave the country for a more receptive environment. He sailed for Boston in 1686.

He established himself in Boston, and it was here that, despite a sojourn of only eight years in the city, he made his greatest contribution to the history of literature for children. Upon his arrival, Harris opened a book and "Coffee, Tee and Chucaletto Shop," which eventually became so popular that local women, denied entrance to the taverns, gathered there. The favorable religious climate of Puritan Boston and several profitable partnerships combined to make Harris one of the wealthiest printers of his time. He printed John Tully's *An Almanack for the Year of Our Lord 1687* and subsequent almanacs by Tully in 1693 and 1695; the *Boston Almanack for the Year of Our Lord God 1692*,

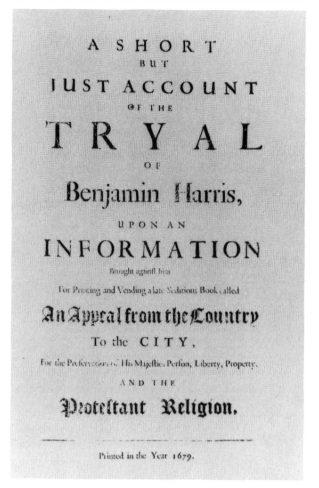

A SHORT BUT JUST ACCOUNT OF THE TRYAL OF Benjamin Harris, UPON AN INFORMATION Brought against him For Printing and Vending a late Seditious Book called An Appeal from the Country To the CITY, For the Preservation of His Majestie, Person, Liberty, Property, AND THE Proteſtant Religion.

Printed in the Year 1679.

Cover for a pamphlet reporting details of Harris's trial as the printer of a libelous attack on Roman Catholics (John Carter Brown Library, Brown University)

signed H. B., has been attributed to Harris.

With the accession of the Protestant William and Mary of Orange to the English throne in 1688 the political climate encouraged Harris to resume his religious printing. *The Plain Case Stated of Old— But Especially of New England in an Address to His Highness the Prince of Orange* (1688), a broadside attributed to Harris, was a declaration in support of the new monarchs that included a series of familiar and popular denigrations of Roman Catholics. No doubt Harris, remembering his treatment under the Catholic Charles II, was not averse to making a profit while attempting to ingratiate himself with the new monarchs, should he decide to return to England.

Harris's return to religious printing led him to revise his *Protestant Tutor*. The result was a text whose title as well as its content was designed to be popular with his Puritan audience. *The New England*

THE
Saint turn'd Curtezan:

OR,

A New PLOT difcover'd by a precious Zealot, of an Affault and
Battery defign'd upon the Body of a Sanctify'd Sifter, &c.

Who in her Husband's abfence, with a Brother
Did often ufe to comfort one another;
Till wide-mouth'd Crop, who is an old Italian,
Took his Mare napping, and furpriz'd her Stallion:
Who 'ftead of Entertainment from his Miftris,
Did meet a Cudgelling not match'd in Hift'ries.

To the Tune of the *Quakers Ballad* : or, *All in the Land of Effex.*

ALL in the Zealous City,
  Near the *Exchange* fo Royal,
    In dead of Night
    Appear'd fuch a Sprite,
Wou'd make a Saint difloyal.
  Help Care, Vile, Smith, *and* Curtis,
    Each pious Covenanter,
      Now alas what hope
      Of converting the Pope,
    When a Sifter turns a Ranter?

A precious Goofe-quill Brother,
  Joyn'd with a Holy Sifter,
    In place of Mate
    To propagate
The Holy Seed, he kifs'd her.
  Help, &c.

About the time of Midnight,
  When th'Saints are Caterwauling,
    The Youngfter came
    To cherifh the Dame,
While the Cuckold was a ftroleing.
  Help, &c.

For while her Factious Gaol-bird,
  That Type of Reformation,
    Lay clofe by the heels,
    The flippery Eels
Lay in clofe Copulation.
  Help Care, Vile, Smith, *and* Curtis,
    Each pious Covenanter,
      What hopes have we got
      To defeat the Sham-Plot,
    If a Sifter turns a Ranter?

But as the Devil wou'd have it,
  The Devil of Luft and Malice,
    That night he broke Gaol,
    And boggl'd her Tail;
She wifh'd him at the Gallows.
  Help Care, Vile, Smith, *and* Curtis,
    Each zealous Covenanter,
      What hopes have we got
      To defeat the Sham-Plot,
    If a Sifter turns a Ranter?

For at the ufual hour,
  In comes the Clerk oth' *Quorum*
    Where to fpoil the Plot,
    The Devil had got
Poffeffion long before him.
  Help, &c.

My faireft *Helen* open,
  Here's thy own loving *Paris*
    Get away from my door,
    You Son of a whore,
For here's th'old Cuckold *H——is.*
  Help, &c.

Then damn the Factious Lubber,
  To fpoil our Recreation:
    Quoth *H——is,* what's there?
    'Tis nothing, my Dear,
But the Spirit of Revelation.
  Help Care, Vile, Smith, *and* Curtis,
    Each zealous Covenanter,
      Who wou'd credit Ben. T——k,
      Tho' he fwore on a Book,
    That a Saint fhould turn a Ranter?

                    O.d

One of several broadsides ridiculing Harris's wife for supporting him during the 1679 libel trial (British Library)

Primer, published between 1687 and 1690 (the exact publication date is unknown), was an immediate best-seller. This volume, sometimes referred to as the Little Bible of New England, enjoyed an unprecedented and seldom equaled popularity. Subsequent editions were published for the next two hundred years, and it has been estimated that between six and eight million copies were sold. It was even translated into an American Indian language. The earliest extant edition of the *Primer* is dated 1727.

The New England Primer differed from Harris's earlier tracts in that the *Primer* was a more restrained volume and did not contain any vitriolic attacks on the papists. Since it was designed as a schoolbook for children, it was more subtle in its attempts at indoctrination. *The New England Primer*'s avowed purpose was to teach children spelling, the true Protestant religion, and the follies and dangers of espousing Catholicism. To this end, the *Primer* contained proverbs; pages of letters of the alphabet printed in various forms; easy syllables; words of one, two, three, four, and five syllables; the Lord's Prayer; the Creed; an illustrated alphabet; a rhymed alphabet; animal pictures with rhymes; Isaac Watts's "Cradle Hymn"; rhymed admonitions and prayers; the complete text of a poem purportedly about the martyrdom of John Rogers by burning at the stake; a catechism of questions and answers; and the poem "A Dialogue between Christ, Youth and the Devil."

The tone of *The New England Primer* is, without question, didactic and clearly representative of its author's convictions and its audience's fundamentalist viewpoint. A constant theme throughout is the need for eternal salvation. Given the uncertainties of seventeenth-century life, children were constantly reminded of the real possibility of an early death and the need to prepare for such an eventuality. Children were brought up on the principle that they were not born to live but born to die. Original sin and human shortcomings were discussed in detail and children were admonished to respect and conform to established religious and social norms, that is, to preserve the status quo.

While the concept of teaching reading and religious instruction had antecedents as far back as the fifteenth-century in the *Enschede Abecedarium*, no prior or subsequent book written specifically for children had a greater impact than *The New England Primer*. It served for generation upon generation as the tool whereby young minds and manners were developed. While it is true that other

writers for children were more prolific, none was more influential than Benjamin Harris.

Harris's zeal led him to other endeavors and problems. As he had in England, Harris began publication of a newspaper. On 25 September 1690 his *Publick Occurrences Both Foreign and Domestick* became the first newspaper in America and Harris the first American journalist. Old habits die hard, and, not surprisingly Harris's fervor overshadowed his judgment. *Publick Occurrences* contained several noteworthy but misguided references to the French monarchy and Boston's Narragansett Indian allies. The publication was seized after this one issue since Harris apparently overlooked the fact that he needed a license, issued by the governor, in order to publish a newspaper.

Harris's local reputation and political allies probably saved him from further harassment, and his place in Bostonian society appears not to have been tarnished. Indeed in 1692 and 1693 he was appointed official printer to the governor and Council of Massachusetts, a prestigious but financially unrewarding position.

Believing that London might be more receptive to his presence now that William and Mary were firmly enthroned, Harris decided to return there in 1695. He resumed his newspaper publishing in London with the short-lived *Intelligence Domestick and Foreign* (1695). His longest-running venture, *London Slip of News, both Foreign and Domestick*, began publication on 6 June 1699; after the first issue it was retitled the *London Post* and ran until 1705. Harris is also believed to have published another book for children, *The Holy Bible in Verse* (1698), which went into at least five subsequent editions. Little is known about Harris after the *London Post* ceased publication and his death, like his birth, has been lost to history.

References:

Daniel A. Cohen, "The Origin and Development of the *New England Primer*," *Children's Literature*, 5 (1976): 52-57;

Sandford Fleming, *Children and Puritanism* (New Haven: Yale University Press, 1933), pp. 80-81;

Paul L. Ford, ed., *The New England Primer: A History of Its Origin and Development with a Reprint of the Unique Copy of the Earliest Known Edition* (New York: Teacher's College, Columbia University, 1962);

Mary Lystad, *From Dr. Mather to Dr. Seuss* (Boston: G. K. Hall, 1980), pp. 39-44;

Frank Monaghan, "Benjamin Harris: Printer,

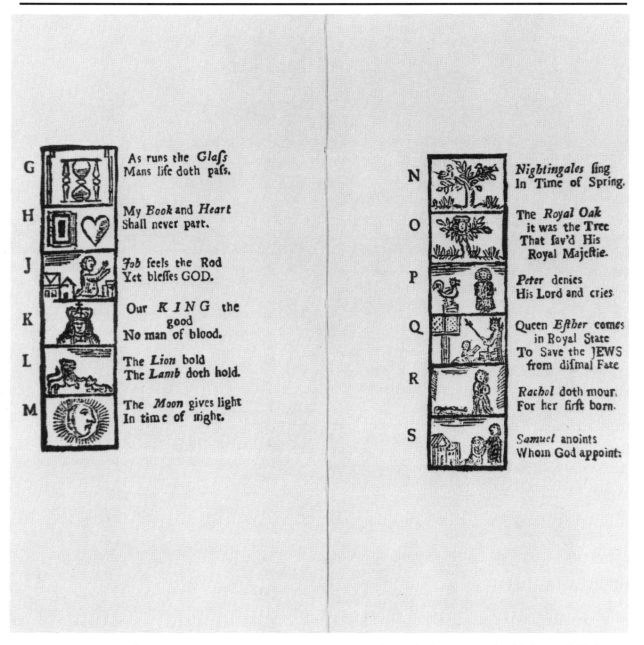

Pages of the illustrated alphabet from the unique copy of the earliest extant edition of The New England Primer, *1727 (Lenox Library, New York Public Library)*

Bookseller, and the First American Journalist," *Colophon*, part 12 (1932);

Madeline Pecora, "The Authorship of 'The Plain Case Stated,'" *Seventeenth Century News*, 30 (Summer 1972): 44-47;

John Tebbel, "Benjamin Harris," in *Boston Printers,*

Publishers, and Booksellers: 1640-1800, edited by Benjamin Franklin V (Boston: G. K. Hall, 1980), pp. 277-280;

Isaiah Thomas, *The History of Printing in America* (New York: Weathervane Books, 1970), pp. 88-90.

Joel Chandler Harris

Hugh T. Keenan
Georgia State University

See also the Harris entries in *DLB 11, American Humorists, 1800-1950,* and *DLB 23, American Newspaper Journalists, 1873-1900.*

BIRTH: Eatonton, Georgia, 9 December 1848, to Mary Harris.

MARRIAGE: 21 April 1873 to Esther LaRose; children: Julian LaRose, Lucien, Evan Howell, Evelyn, Mary Esther, Lillian, Linton, Mildred, Joel Chandler, Jr.

AWARDS: Litt.D., Emory College, 1902; elected member of the American Academy of Arts and Letters, 1905.

DEATH: Atlanta, Georgia, 3 July 1908.

BOOKS: *Uncle Remus: His Songs and His Sayings* (New York: Appleton, 1880); republished as *Uncle Remus and His Legends of the Old Plantation* (London: David Bogue, 1881; revised edition, New York: Appleton, 1895; London: Osgood, 1895);

Nights with Uncle Remus: Myths and Legends of the Old Plantation (Boston: Osgood, 1883; London: Routledge, 1884);

Mingo and Other Sketches in Black and White (Boston: Osgood, 1884; Edinburgh: Douglas, 1884; London: Hamilton Adams, 1884);

Free Joe and Other Georgian Sketches (New York: Scribners, 1887; London: Routledge, 1888);

Daddy Jake The Runaway and Short Stories Told After Dark (New York: Century, 1889; London: Unwin, 1889);

Balaam and His Master and Other Sketches and Stories (Boston & New York: Houghton Mifflin, 1891; London: Osgood, McIlvaine, 1891);

A Plantation Printer: The Adventures of a Georgia Boy During the War (London: Osgood, McIlvaine, 1892); also published as *On the Plantation: A Story of a Georgia Boy's Adventures During the War* (New York: Appleton, 1892);

Uncle Remus and His Friends (Boston & New York: Houghton Mifflin, 1892; London: Osgood, McIlvaine, 1893);

Little Mr. Thimblefinger and His Queer Country: What the Children Saw and Heard There (Boston & New York: Houghton Mifflin, 1894; London: Osgood, McIlvaine, 1894);

Mr. Rabbit at Home: A Sequel to Little Mr. Thimblefinger and His Queer Country (Boston & New York: Houghton Mifflin, 1895; London: Osgood, 1895);

The Story of Aaron (So Named) The Son of Ben Ali (Boston & New York: Houghton Mifflin, 1896; London: Osgood, 1896);

Stories of Georgia (New York, Cincinnati & Chicago: American Book, 1896);

Sister Jane: Her Friends and Acquaintances (Boston & New York: Houghton Mifflin, 1896; London: Constable, 1897);

Aaron in the Wildwoods (Boston & New York: Houghton Mifflin, 1897; London: Harper, 1897);

Tales of the Home Folks in Peace and War (Boston & New York: Houghton Mifflin, 1898; London: Unwin, 1898);

Plantation Pageants (Boston & New York: Houghton Mifflin, 1899; London: Constable, 1899);

The Chronicles of Aunt Minervy Ann (New York: Scribners, 1899; London: Dent, 1899);

On the Wing of Occasions (New York: Doubleday, Page, 1900; London: Murray, 1900);

The Making of a Statesman and Other Stories (New York: McClure, Phillips, 1902; London: Isbister, 1902);

Gabriel Tolliver: A Story of Reconstruction (New York: McClure, Phillips, 1902);

Wally Wanderoon and His Story-Telling Machine (New York: McClure, Phillips, 1903; London: Richards, 1904);

A Little Union Scout (New York: McClure, Phillips, 1904; London: Duckworth, 1905);

The Tar-Baby and Other Rhymes of Uncle Remus (New York: Appleton, 1904);

Told by Uncle Remus: New Stories of the Old Plantation (New York: McClure, Phillips, 1905; London: Hodder & Stoughton, 1906);

Joel Chandler Harris at forty-three, portrait used as the frontispiece for On the Plantation: A Story of a Georgia Boy's Adventures During the War, *1892 (Baldwin Library, University of Florida Libraries)*

Uncle Remus and Brer Rabbit (New York: Stokes, 1907);

The Bishop and the Boogerman (New York: Doubleday, Page, 1909); also published as *The Bishop and the Bogie-Man* (London: Murray, 1909);

The Shadow Between His Shoulder-Blades (Boston: Small, Maynard, 1909);

Uncle Remus and the Little Boy (Boston: Small, Maynard, 1910; London: Richards, 1912);

Uncle Remus Returns (Boston & New York: Houghton Mifflin, 1918);

The Witch Wolf: An Uncle Remus Story (Cambridge, Mass.: Bacon & Brown, 1921);

Joel Chandler Harris: Editor and Essayist, edited by Julia Collier Harris (Chapel Hill: University of North Carolina Press, 1931);

Qua: A Romance of the Revolution, edited by Thomas H. English (Atlanta: The Library, Emory University, 1946);

Seven Tales of Uncle Remus, edited by English (Atlanta: The Library, Emory University, 1948);

The Complete Tales of Uncle Remus, compiled by Richard Chase (Boston: Houghton Mifflin, 1955).

OTHER: F. R. Goulding, *The Young Marooners,* introduction by Harris (New York: Dodd, Mead, 1887);

Irwin Russell, *Poems,* introduction by Harris (New York: Century, 1887);

Life of Henry W. Grady, edited with a biographical sketch by Harris (New York: Cassell, 1890);

F. L. Stanton, *Songs of a Day,* introduction by Harris (Atlanta: Foote & Davies, 1893);

Stanton, *Songs of the Soil,* introduction by Harris (New York: Appleton, 1894);

Jennie T. Clarke, *Songs of the South,* introduction by Harris (New York: Doubleday, Page, 1896);

Eugene Field, *The House, an Episode in the Lives of Reuben Baker, Astronomer, and of His Wife Alice,* introduction by Harris (New York: Scribners, 1896);

Howard Weeden, *Bandanna Ballads,* introduction by Harris (New York: Doubleday & McClure, 1899);

Rudolph Eickemeyer, Jr., *Down South: Pictures,* introduction by Harris (New York: Russell, 1900);

The Book of Fun and Frolic, volume 2 of *The Young Folks' Library Selections from the Choicest Literature of All Lands,* introduction by Harris (Boston: Hall & Locke, 1901); republished as *The Merry Maker* (Boston: Hall & Locke, 1902);

A. B. Frost, *A Book of Drawings,* introduction by Harris (New York: Collier, 1904);

American Wit and Humor, 5 volumes, introduction by Harris (New York: Review of Reviews Company, 1907).

TRANSLATION: *Evening Tales Done into English from the French of Frédéric Ortoli* (New York: Scribners, 1893; London: Low, 1894).

In 1882, according to Mark Twain, a group of children who were invited to the New Orleans home of George Washington Cable to meet the newly famous author of "Brer Rabbit and the Tar-Baby" were doubly disappointed. Not only was Joel Chandler Harris too shy to read his tale to this small admiring public but also he was of the wrong race. When the children were introduced, they exclaimed in disappointment, " 'Why, he's white!' " Not only these New Orleans children but also his adult audiences persisted in identifying this shy Georgia author with his relaxed voluble narrator Uncle Remus. At last Harris acceded to his public and retreated almost completely behind that mask or persona. He never addressed any public gathering in his life, and he became Uncle Remus to the world.

The implications of this anecdote explain in part the decline in popularity of Harris's stories for children, especially the Uncle Remus ones. His stories in dialect demanded that adults, white for the most part, had to read them aloud to their children, but increasingly as the twentieth century progressed fewer and fewer adults have been willing to read Negro dialect stories to their children because of heightened sensitivity to the portrayal of blacks in literature. More scholars wrote about the white man behind the black mask of Uncle Remus than they did about the tales as African folklore preserved and transmitted to a wider audience. By the late 1940s and especially the 1950s, blacks and those whites sympathetic to the Civil Rights Movement had disavowed the tales, the teller, and the author. Ironically, the one-volume edition of all the Uncle Remus tales as compiled by Richard Chase appeared in 1955, the same year that Rosa Parks, a Negro seamstress, refused to give up her seat on a Montgomery, Alabama, city bus.

A decade earlier the stories had been sentimentalized and popularized in the movie *Song of the South*. Released by Walt Disney in 1946, this saccharine, postwar propagandist film romanticized the Old South legend, perhaps for the final time. The film is a very thin, romantic adaptation. It shows not only that Uncle Remus tales can make a real boy out of the girlish Johnny, played by Bobby Driscoll, but also that the values of the old plantation can reunite Johnny's separated parents. The movie was a vast success. It flattered Southern ideas of the glorious life on the plantation and reflected Northern popular ideas of the real South: a confection, standard from 1890 to the 1930s, blended, as Earl F. Bargainner put it in 1975, of "somewhat incongruous elements drawn from Stephen Collins Foster's songs, *Uncle Tom's Cabin, In Ole Virginia*, and the Uncle Remus stories." The movie included singing by both the animals and the plantation hands, moral and amusing tales from Uncle Remus, and a clear contrast of the wealth of the white plantation owners against the poverty of the black field hands and the poor white Faver family. Disney, in a sentimental equalitarian gesture, had Uncle Remus promote the childhood romance of Johnny and little Ginny Faver, some-

thing Harris's Uncle Remus would never have condoned.

By 1958 Walt Disney had withdrawn *Song of the South* from circulation as its objectionable racial biases could not be edited out. Harris's books were removed as well from public-library shelves and taken out of classrooms. The 1950s stand in sharp contrast to the author's extreme popularity in the last two decades of the nineteenth century and the first two of the twentieth century. During this period, his books appeared in numerous authorized and pirated editions; the notice that a book was "By the author of Uncle Remus" guaranteed sales. Along with Booker T. Washington, Harris was accounted one of the two experts in the nation on the Negro. And while Harris continued to be a shy man, he enjoyed the acclaim and friendship of important figures in business, politics, and literature. Andrew Carnegie visited him at his home in the West End section of Atlanta. In 1905 President Theodore Roosevelt and his wife commanded his presence at Roosevelt's speaking engagement in Atlanta. They subsequently invited him to a private dinner at the White House in November 1907. And in print Roosevelt praised the good humor and wholesomeness of the Uncle Remus tales and commended Harris for improving race relations. Harris also enjoyed the company of and correspondence with Mark Twain, George Washington Cable, James Whitcomb Riley, and Don Marquis, among others. Marquis was an associate on the *Atlanta Constitution* and later an associate editor of the *Uncle Remus Magazine*, which Harris and his son Julian established in 1907 to provide wholesome literature for the entire family and to encourage business development and investment in the South.

Harris came a long way from his beginnings as an illegitimate poor boy born in the wealthy cotton planter's town of Eatonton, Georgia. He was born on 9 December 1848 to Mary Harris; his father, an Irish laborer, deserted after the child's birth. Harris started work at thirteen on the only plantation newspaper ever published in the South, Joseph Addison Turner's quixotic enterprise the *Countryman*. Turner modeled his paper on such publications as Joseph Addison's *Spectator* and Oliver Goldsmith's *Bee*, both of eighteenth-century England. Harris lived on the plantation Turnwold and wrote small squibs for the paper under the tutelage of Turner while performing the chores of the printer's devil and reading widely in Turner's private library of about 1000 volumes.

Harris worked for Turner from 1862 to 1866.

Harris in the late 1860s

The aftermath of the Civil War put an end to the *Countryman* and the way of life Harris was to romanticize and popularize throughout the rest of his life. He then advanced in positions on a series of small-town newspapers in Macon, Forsyth, and Savannah, Georgia (1866-1876), while planning to be a great belletristic writer with less success. In 1876, to escape the yellow fever epidemic in Savannah, he came to Atlanta with his wife, Esther LaRose Harris, and two small sons. He took a temporary job writing for the *Atlanta Constitution* at twenty-five dollars per week and rapidly rose to be associate editor. He found happiness as the father of an increasing family and in the professional prestige of being an editorial writer for the *Constitution* and a coworker with Henry W. Grady in the latter's program to create a "New South" by attracting industry and business to the region.

The success of a few dialect sketches, the first written in 1876 for the *Constitution*, led to the publication of a humorous book in 1880. The collection of sketches featuring a character called Uncle Remus who criticized city ways and romanticized pre-Civil War days on a plantation in Putnam County became a best-seller and made Harris a household

name for the entire United States. Reviews of *Uncle Remus: His Songs and His Sayings* appeared in the *New York Times, Nation, Scribner's Magazine, Dial, Godey's Lady's Book, Harper's New Monthly Magazine,* the *Spectator,* in the London periodicals *Literary World* and *Punch,* and in lesser publications. They raved about Uncle Remus, the tales, and the dialect of the stories. In later years, Harris referred to himself modestly and diffidently as "an accidental author" and "a cornfield journalist," but this unexpected success came after he had tried earnestly to be a poet after the fashion of Poe and a novelist in the sentimental tradition while continuing to work as a journalist.

The competition, aggressiveness, and voraciousness behind the necessary social veneer of the antebellum and postwar periods of Southern history; the reunion of North and South through intermarriages and joint business ventures; the mutual dependence of white and black in Southern life; the keen observation of how the weak continually outsmarted the powerful; the concern for a humorous rather than a witty view of life; a nostalgic view of the good-neighbor relationships of the past; an orientation toward rural rather than city life; the continuing search for an informing, nurturing father figure; an emphasis on the heroic view of life while depicting warm, wholesome extended families—these are some of the concerns of Harris's fiction in general, and they are found as well in his stories for children.

In technique of writing, Harris remained somewhat limited. Although at Turnwold he supplemented his primary education by extensive reading in Turner's private library, from his childhood his favorite novel remained Oliver Goldsmith's episodic *Vicar of Wakefield* (1766). Writing for newspapers did force him to compress his expression of ideas, though he never really mastered the form of the novel or the longer story. Harris excelled in character delineation through speech in his brief sketches or tales as well as in longer works.

In many ways *Uncle Remus: His Songs and His Sayings* remains both his best work and typical of the scope and limitations of his subsequent literary effort. A three-part miscellany, it contains: thirty-four Uncle Remus tales taken from the *Atlanta Constitution;* ten plantation or church songs plus a sentimental love story of a wounded Yankee soldier and the sister of a plantation owner; and a series of Uncle Remus sketches wherein the old Negro criticizes Atlanta and city blacks. The collection was offered to a general audience in the catalogue of humor books published by D. Appleton and Company. Characteristically, in his introduction Harris warns the reader "that however humorous it may be in effect, its intention is perfectly serious; and, even if it were otherwise, it seems to me that a volume written wholly in dialect must have its solemn, not to say melancholy features." The remainder of his introduction stresses the relation of his stories to the emerging scholarly study of folklore, a study that Harris had taken up with great enthusiasm. As it was, the book aimed at a mixed audience of adults and children. Only the first section, the tales, directly appealed to the young. Although the collection is flawed, it introduced Harris's best-known character, Uncle Remus; his best-known story, that of the tar-baby; his characteristic setting, the benevolent plantation; and the conflict of society versus the individual.

As R. Bruce Bickley observes in *Joel Chandler Harris* (1978), "Harris's fame would be secure today had he written no other volumes after *Uncle Remus: His Songs and His Sayings* (1880). Later collections of Remus stories reveal more fully elaborated portraits of Uncle Remus and the little boy, an expanded cast of storytellers, and more sophisticated sequencing and structuring of tales.... Despite these later developments, the three things in Harris that popular readers and critics alike have most frequently praised—his portrait of the old plantation South; one of the world's most enduring characters, Uncle Remus; and Brer Rabbit, the archetypal trickster—are fully realized in Harris's first book." This book sold ten thousand copies in four months and made Harris an accepted interpreter of the Negro to the world. There were a number of cheap reprints published in the U.S and abroad, most of them unauthorized. Mark Twain wrote the author that the stories were alligator pears or "avocados," palatable only for their dressing; the teller Uncle Remus and the little boy were more important. Harris mildly disagreed; for him the stories were more significant, and history has borne him out.

In *Uncle Remus: His Songs and His Sayings* Harris put the slave cabin ahead of the plantation hall. The setting is the leaky cabin of Uncle Remus, where the old Negro tells thirty-four stories to the little boy, son of the yankee soldier and plantation lady whose romantic story is told in the second section. In Uncle Remus's stories animals steal food from one another, lie, cheat, trick, and occasionally maim or kill each other while observing the rules of sociality speaking as neighbors when they meet, taking meals together, starting communal

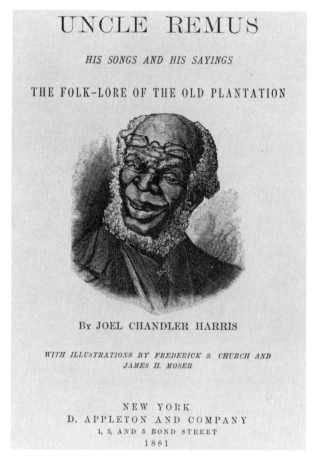

Title page for Harris's first book, a miscellany of sketches and songs that became an immediate best-seller (Baldwin Library, University of Florida Libraries). Although the title page bears the date 1881, the collection had been published by the end of the previous year.

projects, and going together to court "Miss Meadows and the gals." Power, food, and sex are the important topics of the book, as the title of the first sketch, "Uncle Remus Initiates the Little Boy," suggests. The major characters are Brer Rabbit, Brer Fox, Brer Bear, Brer Wolf, and Old Man Tarrypin. In *Uncle Remus* the rabbit is responsible for the killing of his three enemies, fox, wolf, and bear. The wolf is scalded to death; the bear is stung to death. Brer Rabbit gets the fox killed by Mister Man and then carries the head to the fox's family for their dinner. The violent endings of many of the Uncle Remus tales recall those in Grimm's *Fairy Tales*, a work which Harris had read as a teenager when he began his creative writing. He also read the *Arabian Nights* during this period, and it is possible that he used one of its characteristic structural devices, the interrupted or the continued story, as one of Uncle Remus's techniques for keeping the little boy's attention. He introduces this technique with the tar-baby story. Remus concludes the second storytelling session with the rabbit trapped by the tar figure set by the fox and sends the little boy home. The next day Remus tells an entirely different story about the possum. And only at the request of the little boy on the third day, does he conclude the tar-baby's story with the rabbit's escape.

"The Wonderful Tar-Baby Story" fascinated Harris and his audience alike. He gave them three different versions of it: one in prose in *Uncle Remus*, another translated from a French folk tale (1893), and, finally, the last in verse (1904). A brief look at this familiar tale reveals the propagandistic slant and the multiple meanings of many of the tales. After Harris first read a version of the story by William Owens in *Lippincott's Magazine* of December 1877, he became alerted to the possibilities of such folkloric materials. But instead of the racist, sexist version found in Owens's article in *Lippincott's*, Harris has the rabbit trapped because the tar

figure violates social expectations—an exchange of greetings. In subsequent Harris stories the fox and the rabbit continue to make and break social contracts; as here, each time the rabbit escapes by outsmarting the enemy.

The result is a series of stories that flatter the little boy who identifies with the rabbit. The tar-baby story, like many others, flattered audiences in both the North and the South. On the one hand, Northerners were impressed by the warm, human, familylike relationships possible between blacks and whites as evidenced by Uncle Remus and the little boy. They were encouraged to see the black man as the instructor of the New South. On the other hand, Southerners could identify with the paternalism of the little boy, who brings food to the old man as he visits him almost daily. This kind of noblesse oblige flattered the aristocratic pretensions of the middle-class New South. And blacks could regard the story as a capsule history of black-white relations, wherein the black man constantly had to use guile to get around the white one. At

Harris on the steps of The Sign of the Wren's Nest, the home in suburban Atlanta which the Harris family rented in 1881 and purchased in 1883 (Emory University Library)

the same time the more political Southerner could see the story as propounding, as Jesse Bier put it in *The Rise and Fall of American Humor* (1968), "a cynical ethic of success at any cost, placing the rabbit (the wily, unreconstructed south) against the fox (the predatory north) allowing Brer Rabbit any means to the end of survival." As an allegory, the tale shows the rabbit (South) escaping the entanglement of the tar-baby (the Negro Question) by deluding the North into letting the South handle its own race relations.

The relationship between Uncle Remus and the little boy is more complicated than popular sentiment has ever admitted. Remus is a father figure, a teacher, an upholder of social mores, an antisocial critic, a manipulator, and a trickster by turns. He cautions the little boy against associating with the Faver children, tattling on his own siblings, being cruel to the farmyard animals, destructive to property, and an irritation to others. He also asserts his rights as storyteller, manipulating the little boy's response. After he deliberately frightens the boy with a series of witch and ghost stories, he walks him home. On the other hand, he shows how the excessive trickery and overconfidence of the animals are punished. Others of his tales which give a non-biblical theory of creation and explanation for the creation of different races contradict the cultural traditions and explanations of the little boy's family. Truly, this first volume marks an initiation for the little boy. In revealing Southern culture to the rest of the nation which took to it with enthusiasm, it initiated them as well. Brer Rabbit's exploits became a watchword.

By the time *Uncle Remus* was published Harris had four children—three boys and a girl. Their Whitehall Street cottage was too small for them and Harris's mother, who lived with the family. Harris first rented (1881) and then bought (1883) a house on five and a quarter acres in West End, near Atlanta. He later named it The Sign of the Wren's Nest for a pair of birds which nested in the mailbox. Harris left his home and family infrequently. He did all of his creative writing there and also produced many of his editorials for the *Constitution*.

In correspondence with Mark Twain, Harris had asked the more famous author's advice about the best way to capitalize on the Uncle Remus materials. Twain suggested that the next effort be a subscription book and that Harris be chary of publishing tales in the newspapers, only releasing enough to keep the appetite of the public whetted for more. Harris ignored Twain's sage advice.

In *Nights with Uncle Remus: Myths and Legends of the Old Plantation* (1883), Harris included seventy tales and a concluding sketch, "The Night Before Christmas," more than double the number in the first collection. Though the illustrations by Frederick Church were acclaimed at the time, now they seem uninspired and derivative: the animals look like drowned rats; the female figures are copies of Charles Dana Gibson's models. Harris used a much more complicated frame for these tales and provided an even more impressive introduction about the tales as folklore. It seemed the journalist was threatening to become a scholar. The book also covers a clear time span, from fall to Christmas. There are more narrators. Daddy Jack, a Gullah Negro visiting from a coastal plantation; 'Tildy, a house servant with whom Jack becomes enamored; and Aunt Tempy the cook join Uncle Remus as narrators in the latter part of the book. These storytellers compete for the attention of the little boy and vie in telling versions of the same tale, Harris's way of dramatizing the folklore scholar's knowledge of variants. After describing his method of verifying the tales by investigation in the field, Harris quotes at length a French version of an Uncle Remus tale in the first collection. He also takes himself seriously as a reporter of dialect. In the middle of *Nights with Uncle Remus* he gives the reader an introduction to the Gullah dialect of Daddy Jack and includes a short glossary of Gullah. Unfortunately for the reader seeking only amusement, Daddy Jack's Gullah is very difficult to understand. Harris was not to repeat this comparison of dialects.

Nights with Uncle Remus is directed also toward the joint adult-children audience. But in this volume Harris does not give any humorous sketches of life in Atlanta or any plantation proverbs or songs. Some of the tales are not based on Harris's own knowledge. Having begun to exhaust his stock of stories, he had already begun his practice of soliciting and later paying for outlines or synopses of Anglo-African tales which he could expand as Uncle Remus tales. He said he always verified the existence of these stories in Middle Georgia. Harris became so expert that Walter H. Page said in 1881 that he could turn Emerson's essays into Negro dialect. He was on his way to becoming a showman.

The opening of *Nights with Uncle Remus* is more sober than that of its predecessor, perhaps because a baby son, Evan Howell, had died in May 1878; Harris's daughter Mary Esther had died in 1882. By the end of 1883 though, another daughter, Lillian, and a son, Linton, had joined the family. The collection opens in the somber, rainy fall season with Remus housebound in his cabin. In fact, the first fifteen stories had been originally published in *Scribner's Monthly* (June-August 1881) under the running title "A Rainy Day with Uncle Remus." The little boy and 'Tildy bring dinner to Remus. Remus responds by telling stories. In general, the stories in this larger collection are both less violent and less memorable, lacking the novelty of the first volume's tales. The pattern of food exchanged for stories continues through the tenth tale. Some of the stories are etiological, explaining the origins of things in nature; some are trickster stories about Brer Rabbit. The twelfth tale has Brer Rabbit use a ruse similar to that in the tar-baby story to escape. The sixteenth tale echoes Aesop's fable of the fox and the grapes.

With the sixteenth tale the setting changes. The little boy falls sick and Remus goes to the big house to sit with him and tell him stories sixteen through eighteen. The nineteenth tale, one of the memorable ones, is the classic one of the rabbit tricking the other animals into fishing for the moon in the millpond. In number twenty-one, Remus helps the little boy escape parental punishment; the two of them exchange meals and then Remus tells how the Bear lost his tail.

Number twenty-four gives an introduction to the Gullah dialect, and Daddy Jack enters the scene. Several of Daddy Jack's violent stories are more suitable for adults, and the language would be impossible for a child to understand on his own. The report of Daddy Jack's courtship of 'Tildy results in Aunt Tempy's being sent along as a chaperone for the little boy. Then one tale told by Daddy Jack scares the little boy so badly that Remus has to walk him home. Soon Daddy Jack, 'Tildy, Uncle Remus, and Aunt Tempy are competing as storytellers; numbers thirty-one and thirty-two; thirty-nine, forty, and forty-one; forty-seven and fifty, fifty-five and fifty-six are versions of the same stories. Daddy Jack tells nine in all; Aunt Tempy tells six; and 'Tildy tells four. Remus tells the rest. One of 'Tildy's is the golden-arm ghost story suggested to Harris by Mark Twain. Several stories have the wolf tricked by the rabbit into selling his family for food or devouring his kin. The result is the portrayal of a world more threatening to the child.

Uncle Remus too seems more cynical and critical. He tells the little boy that getting money is important, not how one gets it (number fifty-two) and that the stories he tells are not just for amusement (number fifty-six). But the mood lightens with tale number sixty-three as preparations are made for Christmas and the marriage of Jack and 'Tildy. Tale number sixty-eight, which has the fox copy

the rabbit's deception in the fifth tale, recalls the beginning of the book. And the final sketch, "The Night Before Christmas," brings together various elements of the book. Jack and 'Tildy are married. At the festivities, Remus acts as the choral leader of the plantations hands as they sing songs. Harris includes several stanzas, "My Honey, My Love," a love song of farewell. The little boy falls asleep and Remus carries him home to "the big house." And the author in turn wishes his reader "Good Night."

Harris never attempted so much with another collection. Later books give fewer tales, though Harris repeated some of the stories from *Nights with Uncle Remus* and reused some of the devices, especially that of telling tales to an invalid child and that of a competition among narrators. Later books lacked the naturalness of *Nights with Uncle Remus*, which went through twenty-three printings and sold 24,890 copies. In 1904 it was republished by Houghton Mifflin, selling 81,563 copies. It remains in print today.

Capitalizing on this success and desiring to expand into adult fiction, Harris produced two collections of long short stories or novellas for adults: *Mingo and Other Sketches in Black and White* (1884) and *Free Joe and Other Georgian Sketches* (1887), in which thwarted romance figures prominently. Though both were less successful than the Uncle Remus material, *Mingo and Other Sketches* did have eight printings and sold 3,038 copies.

With *Daddy Jake The Runaway and Short Stories Told After Dark* (1889) Harris returned to a book for a family audience. The cover was elaborately stamped and colored, depicting Brer Rabbit and other characters. The title story is a novella in three chapters about Lucien and Lillian (named after Harris's own children), Gaston, ages nine and six, and their search for Daddy Jake, who becomes a runaway in 1863 after being struck by a new overseer. It is the first story by Harris to feature children as protagonists. The children float down the Oconee River and are rescued by Jake and other runaways hiding in Hudson's canebrake. One of them, Crazy Sue, tells a Brer Rabbit story to the children, and at the end of the novella, Jake returns with the children to the sentimentalized, romanticized plantation. Lucien and Lillian foreshadow Buster John and Sweetest Susan of the Mr. Thimblefinger series.

The title novella is followed by thirteen Uncle Remus tales that show some important changes in content and in the relationship between Remus and the little boy. The little boy is more skeptical and questions Remus more closely about minor points,

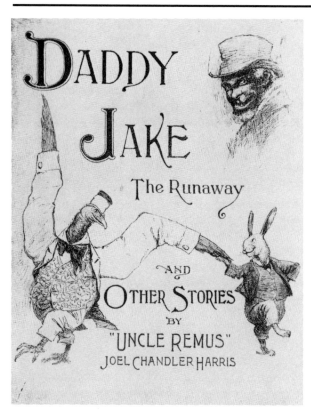

Front cover for the collection whose title novella features Harris's first child protagonists, named Lucien and Lillian for two of his own youngsters

and Remus's testy disposition confirms his "dictatorial, overbearing, and quarrelsome" character as sketched in the tale entitled "How the Birds Talk." The tales are more brief than the previous ones; the framework is skimpy, though the pattern of food exchanged for stories continues. There are four stories about witches: one male and three female ones. Brer Rabbit appears in only three tales. The best story in the volume is probably "How the Terrapin Was Taught to Fly," a story about Brer Buzzard and one which Harris later repeated. The publisher, the Century Company, issued *Daddy Jake* as a companion volume to Kipling's *Jungle Books*, probably to stimulate sales. Harris, however, seemed to be tiring of Uncle Remus and resentful of having to continue the series. This book sold 11,000 copies in its three printings.

Harris's last child, named Joel Chandler, Jr., was born in 1888 and was chronically ill. Harris was much affected by the death of an older son, Linton, the next year. And on 30 March 1891, Harris's mother, who had lived with the family since 1877, died. He became increasingly reclusive. After 1890 he went to the *Constitution* office only in the morn-

ings and returned home to do his work for the paper and his own creative writing. Curious visitors had become a nuisance in the newspaper's offices. At home his wife, Esther, shielded him from strangers. In the company of his children or sitting on the wide veranda of his front porch, he wrote. He produced twelve volumes from 1891 to 1899, including what he intended to be his last series of Uncle Remus tales, published first in the *Constitution* (1892).

During this period, besides writing a volume that became a state school-history text (*Stories of Georgia*, 1896) and a fictionalized biography (*On the Plantation*, published in England as *A Plantation Printer*, 1892), Harris produced a translation of Frédéric Ortoli's *Les Contes de la veillée*, a collection of French folktales, in 1893. Probably Harris's wife did the major work for the volume, entitled *Evening Tales*, while her husband polished the language. It is interesting that the first story is a French version of the tar-baby story in which the rabbit's enemy is the goat, not the fox. Harris's volume included fifteen of the twenty-one tales in his source. One, "A Child of the Roses," is a version of the *King Lear* story, Harris's favorite tragedy. At least two of these translations, "Teenchy Duck" and "Mr. Snail and Brother Wolf," were later used by Harris in *Uncle Remus and the Little Boy*. "Brother Tiger and Daddy Sheep" presents a motif that Harris employed several times with different animals, that of an animal having his head cut off to be in fashion.

Although Harris's earlier works had been written for a single audience of adults and children, or, as he often put it, for children from twelve to seventy, beginning in 1891 he divided his energies evenly between the two groups. His books of the period for adults included *Balaam and His Master* (1891), a collection of six short stories; *Sister Jane* (1896), another of Harris's attempts at a novel and indebted to Hawthorne's *Scarlet Letter*; and *Tales of the Home Folks in Peace and War* (1898), notable for a new character, Billy Sanders, whom one critic described as "the embodiment of middle Georgia democracy." In later children's stories Harris returned to Billy Sanders, who "eventually became his spokesman on current events, political issues, and politicians." In *The Chronicles of Aunt Minervy Ann* (1899), Harris created a vigorous, forthright Negro woman who tells eight tales to the narrator, a newspaperman from Atlanta.

During this period, 1891-1899, Harris wrote six books especially for children: *Uncle Remus and His Friends* (1892); *Little Mr. Thimblefinger and His Queer Country* (1894); *Mr. Rabbit at Home* (1895);

The Story of Aaron (So Named) The Son of Ben Ali
(1896); *Aaron in the Wildwoods* (1897); and *Plantation
Pageants* (1899). These books are overly sentimental and occasionally scolding in tone; in them Harris
writes down to his audience. During this period,
Harris's works were enhanced by the illustrations
of Arthur Burdett Frost, whom he had met in 1886.
Frost, who was influenced by John Tenniel's drawings for the Alice in Wonderland books, had the
ability to draw animals that were realistic and yet
equally believable when dressed in clothes and acting like humans. Twelve illustrations by Frost add
to the 1892 collection of *Uncle Remus and His
Friends*. His drawings graced the fifteenth-anniver-
sary edition of the first Uncle Remus book published in 1895. In appreciation Harris dedicated
the revised, anniversary edition to him.

In the introduction to *Uncle Remus and His
Friends* (1892), Harris apologizes for returning to
similar stories. He says of his sources: "some of
them are discoveries, many are verifications of stories that have been sent to me by friends, and other

are the odds and ends and fragments from my
notebooks which I have been able [since 1884] to
verify and complete." Harris depended on his children and the household servants, especially the
cook, for verification. He apologizes for his earlier
introductions, which pretended a deep knowledge
of folklore, and satirizes the scientific pretensions
of that study—an important shift for one who had
been a charter member of the American Folklore
Society in 1888 and who had bought and studied
many books on the subject besides corresponding
with folklorists in the U.S. and abroad. He declares
that his own interest is restricted to the stories
themselves and their revelations of human nature,
and he announces that this will be his last such
collection of Uncle Remus tales.

In structure, *Uncle Remus and His Friends* repeats the collection of 1880. There are three sections: twenty-four tales told to the little boy; sixteen
songs and ballads; twenty-one sketches of Uncle
Remus in town and his misadventures there. Most
of the first tales are about animals. Some are intended for entertainment; some explain the origins
of things; some are admonitory, warning the boy
against bluffing, cruelty, talking "biggety," taking
the values and actions of the "creeturs" for models.

Although Harris continues to be competent
at writing dialect, in this collection he apologizes
for it. In the introduction, he recognizes the public's objection to dialect as difficult to read, and he
concludes, "this is a tremendous apology to make
for the humble speech of Uncle Remus, yet it has
delayed for a moment the announcement that the
old man will bother the public no more with his
whimsical stories." This is a promise he did not
keep. The tales in *Uncle Remus and His Friends* are
not among Harris's best, but the book found an
eager audience; it had forty printings and sold 56,-
866 copies.

In 1894 Harris produced *Little Mr. Thimblefinger and His Queer Country*, the first of a series of
six books designed for children and with children
as the main characters. Uncle Remus disappears
from the scene as a narrator, but the setting remains a Middle Georgia plantation. Five books of
the series were published between 1891 and 1899;
the sixth, *Wally Wanderoon and His Story-Telling Machine*, did not appear until 1903. All focus on two
little white children, Sweetest Susan (aged seven)
and her brother Buster John (aged eight), and their
black nurse/companion Drusilla (aged twelve). Together they have varied adventures in which Susan
and John are eager and trusting but Drusilla is
hesitant and skeptical. Guided by Mr. Thimblefin-

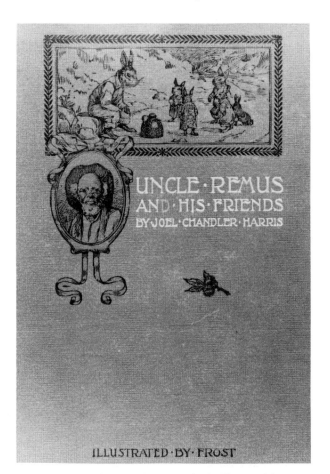

*Front cover for the first of Harris's books illustrated by A. B.
Frost (Baldwin Library, University of Florida Libraries)*

Harris in 1894 at the offices of the Atlanta Constitution

ger who is four inches high, the three children are led to a magic other world beneath a spring on the plantation. There they meet Mrs. Meadows (supposedly married to Brer Rabbit) and Brer Rabbit (now called Mr. Rabbit), who is much older and human-sized. The children are entertained by stories told by the two of them. Their stories, which are interrupted by inferior verses, are either revisions of classical myths, as in "Valentine and Geraldine," or German folktales, as in "The Strawberry Girl," or Uncle Remus tales taken out of dialect, as in "How Brother Bear's Hair Was Combed" (later included in its original dialect form in the posthumously published collection *Seven Tales of Uncle Remus*, 1948). *Little Mr. Thimblefinger* includes several witch stories and English folktales as well.

Two grotesque and aged narrators join Mrs. Meadow and Mr. Rabbit: Chickamy Crany Crow and Tickle-My-Toes, a "queer-looking girl" and a "very queer-looking boy." Their presence, however, does not redeem the book. In Harris's generally artificial scheme, the cruelty and trickery in the tales told by Mr. Rabbit seem pointless. The Rabbit even indulges in rather cheap humor, pretending to mistake Drusilla for the Tar-Baby. Though Harris claimed not to have read Lewis Car-

roll's Alice books, he has Mrs. Meadows create Looking-Glass children to play with John, Susan, and Drusilla. The last story told is a Horatio Alger type—a poor boy gets rich by rescuing the son of a rich man. All these details are evidence of a weakened imagination on the part of Harris. He chose to develop or try out various kinds of artificial fancy, abandoning his true strength, the realistic description of characters and places he knew as a boy. The tales are mostly weak and derivative. Mrs. Meadows and Mr. Rabbit are crotchety narrators. The two white children are as sugary sweet as their names indicate, and the tales they are told lack the purpose, conviction, and realism of the Uncle Remus material. But *Little Mr. Thimblefinger* went through twenty-five printings and sold 20,035 copies. A 1923 reprint sold even more: 75,000 copies in six printings.

Harris had obviously planned the whole series of six books, for when the children leave the magic world under the spring, they are told to look up Uncle Aaron on the plantation and pass on a secret sign to him, so that he will teach them the language of the animals. Thus, this book seems to declare Harris's farewell both to the realm of Uncle Remus and Brer Rabbit and Mr. Thimblefinger.

The sequel, however, is *Mr. Rabbit at Home* (1895), originally titled *Little Mr. Thimblefinger and His Queer Country—The Children's Second Visit* when the first fifteen chapters were published in the Sunday supplement of the *Atlanta Constitution* (2 December 1894 through 10 March 1895). In the sequel Buster John, Sweetest Susan, and a very reluctant Drusilla are guided by Mr. Thimblefinger back to the magic land under the spring. They renew acquaintance with Mrs. Meadows, Mr. Rabbit, Chickamy Crany Crow, and Tickle-My-Toes. This time Harris tries once more the device of a storytelling contest, which he had introduced in the 1883 Uncle Remus book. Here it is much less successful. There are twenty-four tales, told by Mr. Rabbit, Mr. Thimblefinger, and Mrs. Meadows. The children are restless and critical. The Rabbit finds Mr. Thimblefinger's stories dull. In fact, the narrators get into an extended querulous debate about the stories and the best way of telling a story. The controversy seems a reflection of Harris's increased disillusionment with the science of folklore and a consciousness of his flagging creativity. In *Mr. Rabbit at Home* Harris also reuses Uncle Remus's technique of the interrupted story and includes many tales reworked from other sources. "The King of the Clinkers" uses a kind of Trojan horse; "A Mountain of Gold" retells the King Midas

Grandfather's reminiscences of the Mexican War.

WALLY WANDEROON

AND HIS STORY-TELLING MACHINE

BY JOEL CHANDLER HARRIS

AUTHOR OF UNCLE REMUS, GABRIEL TOLLIVER
THE MAKING OF A STATESMAN, ETC.

ILLUSTRATED BY KARL MOSELEY

NEW YORK
McCLURE, PHILLIPS & CO.
MCMIII

Frontispiece and title page for Harris's sixth and final book about the adventures of two white children, Sweetest Susan and Buster John, and their black companion, Drusilla

story; and four stories—"How Brother Lion Lost His Wool," "Brother Lion Has a Spell of Sickness," "The Fate of the Diddypawn," and "The Rabbit and the Moon"—are Uncle Remus tales shorn of their dialect. (The first appears in its original form in the 1907 collection; dialect versions of the remaining three are included in the 1910 collection *Uncle Remus and the Little Boy*.) The critical discussion among the narrators and the generally poor quality of the stories indicate Harris had exhausted this method of development and his supply of old materials. *Mr. Rabbit at Home* was less popular with Harris's public. It sold 14,562 copies in twenty printings, and a 1923 reprint sold only 3,000 copies.

The Story of Aaron (So Named) The Son of Ben Ali (1896), which continues the Sweetest Susan and Buster John series, is a decided improvement. Harris abandons Mr. Thimblefinger, Mrs. Meadows, Mr. Rabbit, and their quirky world underneath the spring. Again the setting is one familiar to Harris,

a plantation in Middle Georgia before the Civil War.

Sweetest Susan, Buster John, and Drusilla meet Aaron, an Arab slave (a figure of historical validity), and they pass on the sign of recognition from Mr. Thimblefinger. Aaron then teaches them how to understand the language of the farm animals. Each animal in turn tells part of the story of Aaron—how he ran away from a bad master on a neighboring plantation; how he became the devoted servant of Little Crotchet, the crippled son of Major Abercrombie; how he rescued members of the family when the Abercrombie house was set on fire by the son of Aaron's legal owner, Mr. Gossett; and finally how he was bought by Major Abercrombie and given a good home.

Much of the story is sentimental, such as the devotion of the slaves for Crotchet whom they adore and call "Little Marster," the romance that develops between Rachel Abercrombie and her poor but noble suitor David Wyche (who later be-

Harris in his fifties (photograph by Frances B. Johnston)

come the parents of Susan and John), and the sparing of the plantation by General Sherman. But the character of Aaron has dignity and conviction. His language, unlike Uncle Remus's, differs very little from that of the whites. As an Arab, he is set apart from both the whites and blacks, making it easier to accept his power to communicate with the animals.

There is one human who adds to what the animals tell of the story of Aaron. This is Free Polly, as independent as her name and much like Minervy Ann in Harris's 1899 adult book. Like Remus, she has to be well fed by the children before she tells her part of the story. But Aaron was not Uncle Remus, and the public bought only 8,622 copies of his story's twelve printings. A 1922 republication sold 7,500 copies in two printings.

The sequel to this book, *Aaron in the Wildwoods* (1897), is little more than a repetition of the same story. Harris gives the excuse that the animals in the first version were not really interested in telling the story in full, so this time Aaron himself fills in many of the missing details. The Brindle Steer is added to the animal narrators of the first book.

Aaron explains that Mr. Thimblefinger, Mrs. Meadows, and Mr. Rabbit gave him the power to talk to animals. And Harris gives a strange, unconvincing, and inappropriate apology for slavery as a means of civilizing and Christianizing the African, propagandist material that seems lifted from his essays. The book sold 8,697 copies in thirteen printings. A 1923 republication sold 2,500 copies.

With *Plantation Pageants* (1899), Harris continues the adventures of the Abercrombie children. There are fourteen episodic chapters. The book is framed by Aunt Minervy Ann who announces at the beginning that she is moving to town with Major Perdue and his family; at the end she has her farewell dinner at the Abercrombie plantation. In between, Harris seems to be trying out and discarding several unsuccessful devices. He has the children enter a large bubble which gives them a different view of the world as they meet the Queen of Dreams and her court of dreams and are finally frightened by a Nightmare. Harris uses Aunt Minervy Ann, the forthright and independent Negro woman of his adult book published the same year, in the role of Uncle Remus. She tells two Brer Rabbit tales, one at the beginning and another at the end of the book.

In the middle, Harris employs characters and situations from previous books. There is a three-year-old orphan child, Billy Biscuit, who is rescued from the village idiot, Roby Ransom. The child is adopted by the old maid Miss Elvivy and her brother, Mr. Bobbs. Joe Maxwell (the protagonist from Harris's fictionalized autobiography *On The Plantation*) joins Drusilla, Aaron, Uncle Fountain, Big Sal, Johnny, the White-Haired Master (Colonel Abercrombie), Major Perdue, and his family. The time of the story is just after Sherman's march to the sea. The death of Little Crotchet is referred to, and it turns out that Mr. Barlow Bobbs knows Mr. Thimblefinger as well. At the end of the book, there is a realistic description of a fox hunt similar to that in *On The Plantation*, except that Aaron talks to and tries to warn the fox, Scarface. At the end, Harris recognizes the rather incoherent nature of the narrative: "The story was ended, and so is this book. Aunt Minervy Ann's time was up, and so is mine. Glancing back over its pages, it seems to be but a patchwork of memories and fancies, a confused dream of old times. Perhaps some youngster tiring of better things, may take it up and follow it to this point, and then close it wondering as to the fate of Billy Biscuit. But his story would make another book, and we cannot have two books in one." Mercifully, Harris spared the reader from this other book about Billy Biscuit. *Plantation Pageants* sold only 5,326 copies in five printings.

In 1900 Harris achieved a long-held desire. He retired from the *Atlanta Constitution* on 5 September 1900 to devote his full time to creative writing. He had signed a contract with McClure, Phillips Company which gave him a fixed annual salary in return for rights to his literary output. Though he wrote several works during this period, none is very notable. He was ill-suited to the kind of work in demand. His specialty was the local-color story, not the sentimental novel. The current fiction, according to Harris, was marked by "its mood of pessimism, futility, and defeat." Harris persevered in his "dogged optimism." In the words of biographer Paul M. Cousins, when Harris looked at his own region, "he saw evidence that its people were becoming more and more enamored of industrialism to the neglect of those qualities in the old agrarian society which he felt were worth preserving in the new civilization." The New South that he and Henry Grady had helped to bring about was not entirely to his liking.

Harris continued to write in his own old-fashioned way and to champion the optimism he thought essential to life. His later books sold, but not as well as earlier ones. During the period from his retirement until his death on 3 July 1908, he busied himself with four adult novels, two collections of short stories for adults, the editorship of a new magazine, and five books for children. *Gabriel Tolliver*, a novel about Reconstruction days, was published in 1902. The mixed reviews noted the absence of an Uncle Remus figure. *Qua*, a romantic historical novel about an actual African prince made a slave during the Revolutionary period, was abandoned, and though Harris never completed the book a fragment was published by the Emory University Library in 1946. A Civil War novel, *The Shadow Between His Shoulder-Blades*, was serialized in the *Saturday Evening Post* in late 1907 and published posthumously as a book in 1909. *A Little Union Scout* (1904) depended on the well-worn convention of a woman Union spy disguised as a man who falls in love with a Confederate. Harris's short-story collections from the period are *On the Wing of Occasions* (1900), five tales of the Confederate secret service, about which Harris knew little, and *The Making of a Statesman and Other Stories* (1902), four stories originally published in the *Saturday Evening Post* (1900-1901), best characterized by Cousins as "pleasant but mediocre narratives."

The first of his five books for children during this period is *Wally Wanderoon* (1903), the sixth and final volume of the Sweetest Susan and Buster John series. It was published by McClure, Phillips, who retained the rights to publish Harris's books although he gave up their annual contract that year. In this book, as in *Little Mr. Thimblefinger and His Queer Country*, the children who are on their way to visit Billy Biscuit meet and subsequently become acquainted with the title character. Wally Wanderoon, who stands for Harris, is searching for "The Good Old Times we used to have." He finds traces in a story here and there. He has a storytelling machine but it has grown cranky and wants to analyze the stories. The machine and the little fat man inside it stand for the analytical side of himself that Harris is rejecting. Wally and the machine quarrel until it produces the required old-fashioned, once-upon-a-time stories, with no folklore parallels, no introductions, no moral messages.

In execution, this is a very peculiar children's book, interesting more for the author's dramatizing of his own varied approaches to his materials. The eight stories themselves seem to comprise a sampler: they include a fairy tale, a folktale, and a classical myth, among other types. But the running criticism of the stories told by the machine and Wally proves tedious. After the machine and the man inside have produced three tales and Wally one, Drusilla tells four stories of various kinds, all in dialect. She proves not only the most vocal critic of the other stories but also the most accomplished storyteller. At the end of the book, Sweetest Susan and Buster John say politely but without enthusiasm that they like the stories of the machine. But Drusilla says she finds him too long-winded. Wally leaves the children "to find a better story-teller than the one you have heard or else find a remedy for his scientific foolishness, which is a disease hard to cure." Clearly the book proves that Harris needed a black mask like that of Drusilla through which to speak.

Three of the final four books for children show Harris returning to the character of Uncle Remus and his tales, though much of this material is reworked from earlier volumes. And each book has a smaller number of tales than the early ones. The three books are *The Tar-Baby and Other Rhymes of Uncle Remus* (1904), *Told by Uncle Remus* (1905), and *Uncle Remus and Brer Rabbit* (1907). The fourth book, *The Bishop and the Boogerman* (1909), is another strange hybrid of a children's and an adults' book.

The Tar-Baby and Other Rhymes of Uncle Remus displays a consciousness of the new market for illustrated children's books. There are nine full-page color illustrations by A. B. Frost and E. W. Kemble, and each page has a border of six animals featured in the tales, three at the top and three at the bottom. But in structure this book is a miniature of the 1880 collection. Not only does it versify the tar-baby story but also it includes all ten of the plantation and church songs found in the second section of the earlier book. It adds to these "A Howdy Song," a lullaby to a little boy.

The first part of *The Tar-Baby and Other Rhymes* consists of fifteen poems, six of them lyrics and the other versified narratives in stanzas of six, seven, eight, nine, or ten lines and in couplets or with alternately rhymed lines. Narrative and lyric poems alternate. According to Harris, with the exception of the tar-baby tale and "How Brer Tarrypin Learned to Fly," the stories are new ones. And he claims the rhymed version of the tar-baby story preserves "the genuine version," a judgment that is hard to accept. The four-beat line and the rhyme are hardly primitive; regular iambic tetrameter couplets do not convincingly reproduce Afro-American rhythm. The plot of the story is closer to the African original, but the fox has become bombastic. And when "Brer Rabbit, he grin like a Chessy-cat," the influence of Lewis Carroll peeks through.

The story about the tarrypin is a versification of a story in *Daddy Jake the Runaway*. And five of the new stories are repeated in prose in the 1905 collection: "De 'Gater and de Rabbit Gizzard," "The Hard-Headed Woman," "Why the Frog Has No Tail," "Why the Buzzard's Head is Bald," and "Brer Rabbit's Gigglin-Place." Evidently Harris was running out of material.

The 1904 poems lack the little boy and the old plantation setting. As Harris admitted privately, he had a "suspicion" that "the new Remus stuff" was not "quite up to the old mark." But he was still able to market his material; before being organized into a book, these versified legends had appeared in the *Saturday Evening Post* (1903-1904, 1905). McClure, Phillips Company, however, waived its rights of publication. D. Appleton and Company brought the book out in a holiday edition. And at that time, his editor at Appleton wrote that Harris's first book, *Uncle Remus: His Songs and His Sayings* (1880), continued to sell 4,000 copies a year after twenty years.

The 1905 collection, *Told by Uncle Remus*, is notable principally for providing the basis of Walt Disney's movie *Song of the South*. The opening section explains why Uncle Remus had ceased to tell his stories: the white family had moved to Atlanta and the little boy had grown up. But now the family is moving back to the Putnam county plantation. The little boy, now grown up into a man, has married and has a son named Johnny. Remus is happy to leave Atlanta or " 'Lantamatantarum." But this new little boy puzzles Remus because he does not believe in Santa Claus and "he was a beautiful child, too beautiful for a boy. He had large dreamy eyes, and the quaintest little ways that ever was seen; and he was polite and thoughtful of others. He was very choice in the use of words, and talked as if he had picked his language out of a book. . . . This little boy was not like the other little boy. He was more like a girl in his refinement. . . ." Remus has an antagonist in the boy's mother: "All the boyishness had been taken out of him by that mysterious course of discipline that some mothers know how to apply. He seemed to belong to a different age— to a different time; just how or why, it would be impossible to say." Miss Sally, the boy's grandmother, and Uncle Remus conspire to make a real boy out of him through Remus's storytelling sessions.

As in previous collections, the little boy and Uncle Remus establish their friendship through the sharing of food sent from the big house. Remus tells sixteen tales, mainly about Brer Rabbit, trying out various kinds of stories to get the boy's interest. But the boy is disturbed by the cruelty of the rabbit who gets the wolf to scald his own child to death and the fox to be stung by hornets. When the little boy tells Remus the story of Cinderella, the old man is polite but not impressed by the "purty tale." He replies that one cannot depend on fairy godmothers in this world but must shift for oneself as the animals do.

Uncle Remus also has to counter the mother's prejudice against dialect, as she is "a great stickler for accuracy of speech. She was very precise in the use of English and could not abide the simple dialect in which the stories had been related to the little boy's father." Nevertheless, the boy listens to the stories and improves "in health and strength every day he remained on the plantation." At the end of the book, the boy has gotten so rowdy that Remus tells him the tale of "The Hard-Headed Woman" as a warning.

In this book many of the concerns of Remus are those of Harris about city life, materialism, the advantages of rural experiences, the passing of the local-color story, and the feeling of being out of date. But Harris perseveres in his ways and has Remus tell two stories about animals that have their heads cut off just to be in fashion.

*1907 photograph of Harris, his wife, Esther, and two
of their grandchildren*

Uncle Remus and Brer Rabbit (1907), like *The
Tar-Baby and Other Rhymes*, is an expensive picture
book for children. There are only eleven tales, six
in prose and five in verse. There is no introduction,
no reference to time and setting. But the cover
features a large colored illustration of Uncle Remus, the little boy in a sailor suit, and Brer Rabbit.
The first tale and the last story are laid out in cartoon fashion, with two large colored pictures to
each page and the text below. Tales two through
ten have a single large colored picture on each page
with the text below in large type. As R. Bruce Bickley says, the book "is more a footnote to the Remus
tradition than a significant addition, but the animal
cartoons anticipate the comic strips and the movie
cartoons that soon took a permanent place in
American popular culture." Three of the stories in
Uncle Remus and Brer Rabbit are new: "The Creeturs
Go to the Barbecue," "Brer Rabbit's Frolic," and
"Brer Rabbit Treats the Creeturs to a Race." The
rest are either similar to previous tales or versifi-
cations of them. All of the stories feature Brer Rabbit, but except for the first two there is no
connection among them beyond the rabbit's ability
to get the best of the other animals.

All these stories had been published serially
in *Uncle Remus's Magazine* during 1907. Harris came
out of retirement to be the editor of this publication, organized by his son Julian and others. Its
ideals were lofty, according to the prospectus of
1906, which cited among its aims to "preach a
Cheerful Philosophy and practice a seasonable tol-
eration in all matters where opinions and beliefs
are likely to clash." It was to promote "neighbor-
knowledge" between the North and the South, to
introduce Southern literature to the rest of the nation, and to encourage industrial and business development. Above all, it was to "enter the homes
of its friends clean, sweet, and wholesome." Harris
had wanted to call the magazine "The Optimist,"
but the others persuaded him to capitalize on the
name Uncle Remus. The first issue appeared in
June 1907. Ironically, Harris was to end his career
as he began it, as a journalist and as the editor of
as quixotic an enterprise as the *Countryman*, published by his first mentor, Joseph Addison Turner.
Harris wrote book reviews under the name of Anne
Macfarland, headed the children's department,
and contributed Uncle Remus stories or other stories for children. As in *Wally Wanderoon*, he promised to hold on to "the good old times" but also to
welcome the new.

*The Bishop and the Boogerman: Being the Story
of a Little Truly-Girl, Who Grew Up; Her Mysterious
Companion; Her Crabbed Old Uncle; the Whish-Whish
Woods; A Very Civil Engineer*, and *Mr. Billy Sanders,
the Sage of Shady Dale* appeared as a serial in this
magazine, starting with the first issue. It was published as a book posthumously in 1909. The lengthy
title of this five-part work is indicative of its contents
and the self-indulgence of the author-editor. The
story is set in Shady Dale. It opens in 1868 and
leaps to 1885 in part five, the final section, enabling
the author to contrast Reconstruction with Recovery. The book tries to be both children's story and
romantic novel. The early portion of the book concerns the childhood of Adelaide, the orphaned
niece of Jonas Whipple, who, like Silas Marner, has
his life humanized by the presence of the niece,
whose dead mother is named Cordelia like Lear's
daughter. Section five is the same sort of story of
regional reconciliation through romance and marriage that Harris had told many times before in
books for adults.

Other characters in the story are Mr. Billy
Sanders, the bishop of the title who knows everyone
in the town and their histories and reveals all. The
Boogerman is the Negro Randall, whom Adelaide
captures in the Whish-Whish Woods (the few rows

Front cover for the July 1908 issue of Harris's magazine. Uncle Remus's Magazine *began publication in June 1907 and merged with Bobbs-Merrill's* Home Magazine *in May 1908. The July 1908 issue was the last edited by Harris.*

of corn in Jonas's garden). Adelaide is responsible for Randall's being cleared of charges of assault brought by Mr. Tuttle, once a plantation overseer and now a Radical ordinary and the villain of the story. And in part five John Somers, a civil engineer for the planned railroad, rediscovers his roots in the town and falls in love with Adelaide, a sweet and bright but unspoiled lady of seventeen.

Into this work Harris put all of the popular ideas that he had entertained in previous books, short stories, essays, and editorials. It shows the New South on its economic feet. It shows that the freed Negro like Randall can through thrift and hard work become both a preacher and a wealthy man. It shows the Old South (that of Jonas) yielding to the New (John Somers) as the railroad crosses Jonas's land, but the Southern traditions are continued in the marriage of the young couple. And the Radical politician Mr. Tuttle is revealed to be a scoundrel, abusing both white and black. In *The Bishop and the Boogerman* all the characters are flat,

stereotyped, and sentimental. Whipple's cook Lucindy and her son Randall Holden are no more realistic than the whites.

The remaining posthumously published Uncle Remus books consist mainly of stories that originally appeared in magazines and were later collected by others. They add very little to the substance of the canon. *Uncle Remus and the Little Boy* (1910) continues in the tradition of lavishly illustrated books for the children's market. It has fifty-three colored and black-and-white illustrations by J. M. Conde. It consists of seven prose sections in Uncle Remus's dialect which alternate with six poems in dialect. Uncle Remus receives a letter from the little boy in the latter part of the book. This reveals that the little boy is on his way to California for his health and that he is acting like a real boy. In "The Story of Teenchy-Tiny Duck," the boy has returned, with his weak lungs much better. Now he is just as mischievous as his father was when he sat at Remus's knee and heard the animals' tales. Thus, this book concludes the relationship of the second little boy and Uncle Remus which had begun in the 1905 collection.

Most of the poems and tales in *Uncle Remus and the Little Boy* are rewrites of earlier published material. "The Story of the Doodang" takes its title from a story, "The Doo-Dang," which Harris published in Turner's *Countryman* of 21 April 1863. The later story is the same as "The Fate of the Diddypawn" in *Mr. Rabbit at Home*. "The Story of Teenchy-Tiny Duck" comes from Harris's 1893 translation of Ortoli. In the final story, "The Story of Brer Fox and Little Mr. Cricket," Uncle Remus speaks for the later view of Harris: "when you git so you can't b'lieve tales, it's time fer yo' pa fer ter put you in some sto' whar you kin l'arn all about swindlin' yo neighbors." The earlier Remus would never have said this.

Uncle Remus Returns (1918) consists of stories originally published in the *Metropolitan Magazine* (1905-1906) and collected by Harris's wife. His daughter-in-law and biographer Julia Collier Harris wrote the introduction. There are six Uncle Remus tales, five of which feature Brer Rabbit, and five sketches about the Old Negro in Atlanta. The little boy, the same child who is in the 1905 collection, is a reasonable, practical, modern youngster who has been denied both Santa Claus and fairy tales. The book had ten printings and sold 15,993 copies.

The Witch Wolf (1921) is "Uncle Remus's Wonder Story" republished as a children's booklet from *Daddy Jake The Runaway*. In this humorous ghost story, a witch wolf must first change herself into a beautiful young woman and marry the man she desires before she can eat him up. The cows she is sent to milk expose her transformation and the man escapes.

The final collection is *Seven Tales of Uncle Remus* (1948), edited by Thomas H. English while he was curator of the Harris Collection at Emory University. Five of the stories first appeared in *Dixie* (1889-1892), an Atlanta publication. Four of these were told later, without dialect, in *Little Mr. Thimblefinger and His Queer Country*. The remaining two tales, both written in dialect, were found in manuscript; according to English, one was taken out of dialect and included in *Mr. Rabbit at Home*.

Harris's use of the same materials in dialect and standard English proves that, contrary to his statements, he was not the simple recorder of folklore that he claimed. He used the materials in the way they best suited his needs. The two dialect stories in *Seven Tales of Uncle Remus* are interesting. "Brother Rabbit's Barbecue" shows a spiteful Uncle Remus. When Miss Sally calls him down, Uncle Remus gets back by telling that her son is getting dirty playing in the road with the "white trash" Stallins children. Remus gets him cleaned up and to make amends tells him a story of how Brer Rabbit stole food at the barbecue and was exposed by the bear. Perhaps Harris thought this frame and tale would reflect too badly on Remus. The other story, "Why Brother Rabbit Doesn't Go To See Aunt Nancy," is his only tale in which the West African spider god Anansi is identified. English, however, speculates that Harris got this tale and two others from a Jamaican source. English's collection of seven tales brings the final count of so-called Uncle Remus tales to 184 in Richard Chase's edition of the *Complete Tales* (1955); Uncle Remus is the narrator of most, but not all, of them. Crazy Sue, Daddy Jack, Aunt Tempy, and 'Tildy have a minor share in the telling.

Time has proven that the Uncle Remus stories are the ones that have lasted. There have been no new editions or republications of five of the six Sweetest Susan and Buster John books since the 1920s; only *Plantation Pageants* was republished in the 1930s. *The Bishop and the Boogerman* was even less successful than these volumes and the least popular of Harris's books. But his first book, *Uncle Remus: His Songs and His Sayings*, and the second, *Nights with Uncle Remus*, as well as *The Complete Tales of Uncle Remus* remain in print. In 1947, it was estimated that *Uncle Remus: His Songs and Sayings* had sold 500,000 copies.

Most popular today are the many editions shorn of both the dialect and the Negro narrator and the books based on Walt Disney's *Song of the South,* which was re-released to large audiences in 1972. In the twentieth century Harris's Uncle Remus tales continue to be important as a resource collection while scholars continue to argue about their folkloric authenticity. Some editions of the tales in standard English for children to read to themselves are quite attractive, for example, *Brer Rabbit and His Tricks*, retold in couplets by Ennis Rees and illustrated by Edward Gorey (1967). Editions such as these continue a tradition begun in the nineteenth century of retelling tales in standard English. For example, in *Books for the Bairns* (volume six, 1896), edited by W. T. Stead, the tar-baby story was retold for an English audience for whom the American Negro dialect would have been a serious obstruction.

It is to Joel Chandler Harris's credit that he created a complex and unforgettable narrator in Uncle Remus, gave worldwide popularity to the tar-baby story, and passed on a collection of stories as significant for children as *Grimm's Fairy Tales*. And though Harris drew selectively on Afro-American folklore and omitted, as one commentator put it, "the sometimes comic and often powerful sexual overtones" of much of it, he told the types of stories most popular with children: animal tales and those of the supernatural. Given these accomplishments, readers can forgive his sentimentality, his apologies for slavery, and the flawed children's books of his later career. They can accept his tales as literature and not folklore, and they may realize that he says more about the naturalistic view of the world and the art of survival than is apparent on the surface.

Bibliographies:

"Joel Chandler Harris," in *Bibliography of American Literature*, edited by Jacob Blanck, volume 3 (New Haven & London: Yale University Press, 1959), pp. 154-162;

Arlin Turner, "Joel Chandler Harris (1848-1908)," *American Literary Realism,* 1 (Summer 1968): 18-23;

C. A. Ray, comp., "Joel Chandler Harris," in *Bibliographical Guide to the Study of Southern Literature*, edited by Louis D. Rubin (Baton Rouge: Louisiana State University Press, 1969), pp. 212-214;

William Bradley Strickland, "Joel Chandler Harris: A Bibliographical Study," Ph.D. dissertation, University of Georgia, 1976;

Strickland, "A Check List of the Periodical Contributions of Joel Chandler Harris (1848-1908)," *American Literary Realism,* 9 (Summer 1976): 207-229;

Strickland and R. Bruce Bickley, "A Checklist of the Periodical Contributions of Joel Chandler Harris: Part 2," *American Literary Realism,* 11 (Spring 1978): 139-140;

Bickley, *Joel Chandler Harris: A Reference Guide* (Boston: G. K. Hall, 1978).

Biographies:

Ivy L. Lee, ed., *"Uncle Remus:" Joel Chandler Harris as Seen and Remembered by a Few of His Friends* (N.p.: Privately printed, 1908);

Julia Collier Harris, *The Life and Letters of Joel Chandler Harris* (Boston & New York: Houghton Mifflin, 1918);

Robert Lemuel Wiggins, *The Life of Joel Chandler Harris* (Nashville: Publishing House, Methodist Episcopal Church, South, 1918);

Paul M. Cousins, *Joel Chandler Harris: A Biography* (Baton Rouge: Louisiana State University Press, 1968).

References:

Florence E. Baer, *Sources and Analogues of the Uncle Remus Tales* (Helsinki: Suomalainen Tiedeakatemia, Academia Scientiarum Fennica, 1980);

R. Bruce Bickley, Jr., *Joel Chandler Harris* (Boston: Twayne, 1978);

Jesse Bier, *The Rise and Fall of American Humor* (New York: Holt, Rinehart & Winston, 1968);

Stella Brewer Brookes, *Joel Chandler Harris—Folklorist* (Athens: University of Georgia Press, 1950);

Margaret Taylor Burroughs, "Uncle Remus for Today's Children," *Elementary English,* 30 (December 1953): 485-492;

Beverly R. David, "Visions of the South: Joel Chandler Harris and His Illustrators," *American Literary Realism,* 9 (Summer 1976): 189-206;

Robert B. Downs, "Black Folktales: Joel Chandler Harris's *Uncle Remus: His Songs and Sayings,*" *Books That Changed The South* (Chapel Hill: University of North Carolina Press, 1977);

Thomas H. English, "In Memory of Uncle Remus," *Southern Literary Messenger,* 2 (February 1940): 77-83;

Lucinda Hardwick MacKethan, *The Dream of Arcady: Place and Time in Southern Literature* (Baton Rouge: Louisiana State University Press, 1980), pp. 61-85;

William F. Mugleston, "The Perils of Southern Publishing: A History of *Uncle Remus's Magazine,*" *Journalism Quarterly,* 52 (Autumn 1975): 515-521, 608;

Louis D. Rubin, Jr., "Uncle Remus and the Ubiquitous Rabbit," *Southern Review,* new series 10 (October 1974): 784-804;

John Stafford, "Patterns of Meaning in *Nights with Uncle Remus,*" *American Literature,* 18 (May 1946): 89-108;

John Tumlin, Introduction to *Uncle Remus: Tales by Joel Chandler Harris* (Savannah: Beehive Press, 1974);

David A. Walton, "Joel Chandler Harris as Folklorist: A Reassessment," *Keystone Folklore Quarterly,* 11 (Spring 1966): 21-26.

Papers:

The Joel Chandler Harris Memorial Collection located in the Special Collections Department of the Robert W. Woodruff Library for Advanced Studies, Emory University, is the principal collection, consisting of manuscripts, first editions, correspondence, articles, and family photographs.

Helen Hunt Jackson

(15 October 1830-12 August 1885)

Taimi M. Ranta
Illinois State University

SELECTED BOOKS: *Verses,* as H. H. (Boston: Fields, Osgood, 1870; enlarged, Boston: Roberts Brothers, 1874);

Bits of Travel, as H. H. (Boston: Osgood, 1872);

Bits of Talk About Home Matters, as H. H. (Boston: Roberts Brothers, 1873; London: Low, 1873);

Saxe Holm's Stories, as Saxe Holm (New York: Scribner, Armstrong, 1874);

The Story of Boon, as H. H. (Boston: Roberts Brothers, 1874);

Bits of Talk, in Verse and Prose, for Young Folks, as H. H. (Boston: Roberts Brothers, 1876);

Mercy Philbrick's Choice, anonymous (Boston: Roberts Brothers, 1876; London: Low, 1876);

Hetty's Strange History, anonymous (Boston: Roberts Brothers, 1877);

Bits of Travel at Home, as H. H. (Boston: Roberts Brothers, 1878);

Nelly's Silver Mine: A Story of Colorado Life, as H. H. (Boston: Roberts Brothers, 1878);

Saxe Holm's Stories, second series, as Saxe Holm (New York: Scribners, 1878);

Letters from a Cat: Published by Her Mistress for the Benefit of All Cats and the Amusement of Little Children, as H. H. (Boston: Roberts Brothers, 1879);

A Century of Dishonor: A Sketch of the United States Government's Dealings with Some of the Indian Tribes, as H. H. (New York: Harper, 1881; London: Chatto & Windus, 1881); enlarged edition (Boston: Roberts Brothers, 1885)— includes *Report on the Condition and Needs of the Mission Indians of California* (1883);

Mammy Tittleback and Her Family: A True Story of Seventeen Cats, as H. H. (Boston: Roberts Brothers, 1881);

Report on the Condition and Needs of the Mission Indians of California, by Jackson and Abbot Kinney (Washington, D.C.: Government Printing Office, 1883);

Ramona: A Story, as H. H. (Boston: Roberts Brothers, 1884; London: Macmillan, 1884);

The Hunter Cats of Connorloa (Boston: Roberts Brothers, 1884);

Zeph: A Posthumous Story (Boston: Roberts Brothers, 1885; Edinburgh: Douglas, 1886);

Sonnets and Lyrics (Boston: Roberts Brothers, 1886);

Glimpses of Three Coasts (Boston: Roberts Brothers, 1886);

Between Whiles (Boston: Roberts Brothers, 1887);

Pansy Billings and Popsy, as H. H. (Boston: Lothrop, 1898).

TRANSLATION: Jean Pierre Claris de Florian, *Bathmendi: A Persian Tale* (Boston: Loring, 1867).

Helen Maria Fiske Hunt Jackson, a versatile and prolific writer, was popular with a large and devoted reading public, praised by most contemporary critics, and acclaimed by such key literary figures as Ralph Waldo Emerson and Emily Dickinson. For two decades she wrote verse, essays, travel sketches, editorials, book reviews, short stories, novels, and literature for children. Adverse to publicity and seemingly intent on bewildering her readers, she signed little of her work with her own full name. Sometimes she used pseudonyms, such as Saxe Holm, Marah, and Rip Van Winkle. More often, she signed only H. H. Many of her book reviews were unsigned, and only some have been identified.

Fifty years after Jackson's death, Ruth Odell pointed out in her 1939 biography that Jackson's place in American literature was due, not to her poems, as predicted by her contemporaries, but to *A Century of Dishonor* (1881) and *Ramona* (1884). Nearly ninety years after Jackson's death, John R. and Elizabeth S. Byers indicated, in the introduction to their comprehensive critical bibliography of secondary comment on her, that she is remembered for one novel, *Ramona,* and one cause, that of the Indian. Evelyn I. Banning, in her 1973 biography, echoes this view. However, Jackson's cat stories, her book about "Colorado life" *Nelly's Silver Mine* (1878), her many contributions to magazines for children and young people, and her much-anthologized and often-memorized poetry have helped earn her a secure place among nineteenth-

century authors of juvenile literature.

Helen Hunt Jackson was born into an academic environment in Amherst, Massachusetts, on 15 October 1830. She was brought up in a stern, restraining atmosphere of learning, religion, and decorum. Her father, Nathan Welby Fiske, was a serious young clergyman and a professor of Latin and Greek at Amherst College, a stronghold of orthodox Calvinism, and her mother, Deborah Vinal Fiske, was a pious, educated Bostonian. At age nine, Helen Fiske catalogued the books in her personal library, including *The Pastor's Child, The Child's Book of Repentance, Scripture Animals, The Reformation*, and other solemn titles. As a child, Helen Fiske was impulsive, often recalcitrant, with a strong will of her own, not "tractable and easily managed," as her mother once wrote. She remained a unique combination of rebel and conformist throughout her life.

There were four children in the Fiske family, two boys who died in infancy and Helen and Anne. After the Fiske parents died when Helen was a teenager, she was raised by an aunt. After schooling in Charlestown, Pittsfield, and Falmouth, Helen Fiske's rather random education continued at the well-known Ipswich Female Academy, where

Henry Home's 1762 volume *Elements of Criticism* seemed to make quite an impression on her, because she later quoted it frequently. In New York City, she attended the school of John and Jacob Abbott (the latter wrote the then-popular Rollo books). Emily Dickinson had been an early neighbor and schoolmate in Amherst, and the two women were lifelong friends and admirers of each other's poetry.

In 1852 Helen Fiske married Lieutenant Edward Bisell Hunt, eventually a major in an army corps of engineers, and lived the transitory life of a military household. Her husband was a man of no small scientific accomplishment and through him Helen Hunt met many important men in the military and in science. The Hunts had two sons; one died in infancy and the other not long after her husband was killed in 1863 while experimenting with an invention he called a "sea miner."

Before her husband's death, Helen Hunt had led an active life, but as Thomas Wentworth Higginson pointed out in his *Contemporaries* (1899), she gave no particular indication of wanting to become a writer. Until she went to live in Newport, Rhode Island, in 1866, she had little contact with persons in the literary world. In Newport, Higginson, one of the founders of the Town and Country Club, held meetings which attracted writers who lived in the town or were visiting there. Helen Hunt became one of Higginson's protégées and made the acquaintance of such writers as George Bancroft, James Parton, the Reverend Charles T. Brooks, and Katherine P. Wormeley. These contacts brought a new interest to a life she considered prematurely ended and led her to a profitable way of making a living. Her writing was to support her and her wide travels in America and abroad, where she gathered much of her material firsthand.

In the stimulating Newport atmosphere, she began to study literary styles and methods and to exchange criticism with friends. With the encouragement of Higginson, she began contributing poems and prose pieces to periodicals, often to the *New York Evening Post, New York Independent, Hearth and Home, Atlantic Monthly*, and *Scribner's Monthly*. For the *New York Independent* alone, she wrote hundreds of book reviews, poems, and articles. In the 1870s and 1880s, most of the day's leading magazines published her work.

Verses, her first volume of poetry, was published in 1870. *Scribner's* and *Atlantic Monthly* carried glowing reviews. The reviewer for the latter magazine noted that there was a "freshness of imagination and an intensity of feeling unsurpassed by a woman since Elizabeth Barrett Browning." Emerson, a man who understood the principles of poetry that had roots in a love for the land, was one of the first to see Hunt's special gift. In his journal (13 July 1868), Emerson wrote that her verse had the "merit of originality, elegance, and compassion." He thought so much of her poetry that he included five examples from the enlarged edition of *Verses* (1874) in the second edition of his anthology *Parnassus* (1875). In the preface Emerson wrote, "The poems of a lady who contents herself with the initials H. H. in her book published in Boston (1874) have rare merit of thought and expression, and will reward the reader for the careful attention which they require."

At the time of Helen Hunt Jackson's death in 1885, her longtime mentor Higginson rated her poetry at the top of her contribution to American literature, as did most critics of the day. A century later, her poetry is generally considered dated, her handling of the major themes of life, love, death, and nature frequently too devout and sentimental.

After several years in Newport and an extended European trip, Helen Hunt traveled through the West with her close friend Sarah Chauncy Woolsey, whose books for young people were published under the pseudonym Susan Coolidge. In 1873 Hunt fell ill and went to Colorado for her health. There she met William Sharpless Jackson, a Pennsylvania Friend, financier, and railroad promoter, whom she married in 1875, making Colorado Springs her home for the last decade of her life. In 1874 and 1878, she produced two volumes of short stories, *Saxe Holm's Stories*, first and second series. Although she never acknowledged the authorship of these, a multitude of clues help attribute them to her and they are today generally accepted as her work. Her two novels published anonymously in Roberts Brothers' No Name series, *Mercy Philbrick's Choice* and *Hetty's Strange History*, with their New England settings and strong women characters, appeared in 1876 and 1877. In Odell's opinion these four books are "formless, over-intense, sentimental, and artificial." In them there is "nothing to offend the moral scruples of the most rigid idealist."

Commentaries on her life, her personal letters, and her considerable literary output attest to the fact that Helen Hunt Jackson loved children. The loss of her second child was her greatest grief, out of which came her first published poems in 1865. At the homes of friends, she often entertained the children with her stories of adventure and mischief. Her book-length work and the first

Jackson's second husband, William Sharpless Jackson, with whom she settled permanently in Colorado in 1875

of several works for children was *Bathmendi: A Persian Tale,* a translation from the French Jean Pierre Claris de Florian published in 1867.

Jackson was one of many authors, especially women, who responded to the growing demand for juvenile literature with her poems and stories for young people. In spite of her formal upbringing, there was always something of the rebel in Jackson. In many of the stories she sent to Mary Mapes Dodge of *St. Nicholas* and Horace E. Scudder of *Riverside Magazine for Young People* she delighted young readers with her own childhood pranks and escapades. Jackson also contributed to *Our Young Folks, Wide Awake,* and *Youth's Companion. Bits of Talk, in Verse and Prose, for Young Folks,* a volume of her collected pieces for children, was published in 1876.

The style of *Bits of Talk, in Verse and Prose, for Young Folks* is clear and simple. Its content and organization, alternating selections of poetry and prose, show the influence of Jacob Abbott, whose school the author had attended. The poems often point to morals and the prose selections include animal stories, fairy tales, travel talk, and advice on good behavior. The tone of the prose is conversational and Jackson's touches of humor often leaven the didacticism. Jaekson's desire to improve people and situations surfaces in this work and in her earlier *Bits of Talk About Home Matters* (1873), a collection of forty editorials from the *New York Independent* on more humane child care and the general conduct of life.

In 1878 Jackson's novel for children *Nelly's Silver Mine* was published. Walking and riding in the canyons and mountains, Jackson had become familiar with the country around Colorado Springs. She gained further insights on jaunts with her husband, especially after Colorado's admission into the Union in 1876, when areas earlier closed to tourists were opened. *Nelly's Silver Mine* gave her opportunity to incorporate her impressions into a realistic adventure story about the March family who came from the East to settle in the mining country of Colorado. Reviewers commended the book as a relief from stories which presented the barbaric side of frontier life. In Jackson's work emphasis is on family life and the natural beauty of the new state. Praising the book, a reviewer for the *New York Tribune* wrote, "Its vivid portraiture of Colorado life and its truth to child nature give it a charm which the most experienced cannot fail to feel."

Possibly as a form of rebellion against her own strict Calvinistic upbringing, the author made Nelly the daughter of a minister, as she did several of the girl characters in the Saxe Holm stories. Perhaps like Jackson herself, Nelly has, as Odell observed, a "contemptuous sort of pity" for her father. Nelly, however, is also unselfish, thoughtful,

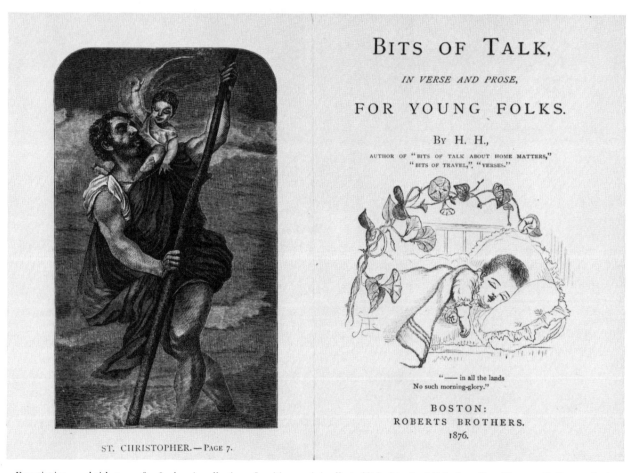

ST. CHRISTOPHER. — PAGE 7.

BITS OF TALK,

IN VERSE AND PROSE,

FOR YOUNG FOLKS.

BY H. H.,

AUTHOR OF "BITS OF TALK ABOUT HOME MATTERS,"
"BITS OF TRAVEL", "VERSES."

"—— in all the lands
No such morning-glory."

BOSTON:
ROBERTS BROTHERS.
1876.

Frontispiece and title page for Jackson's collection of writings originally published in St. Nicholas, Our Young Folks, *and other juvenile magazines (Baldwin Library, University of Florida Libraries)*

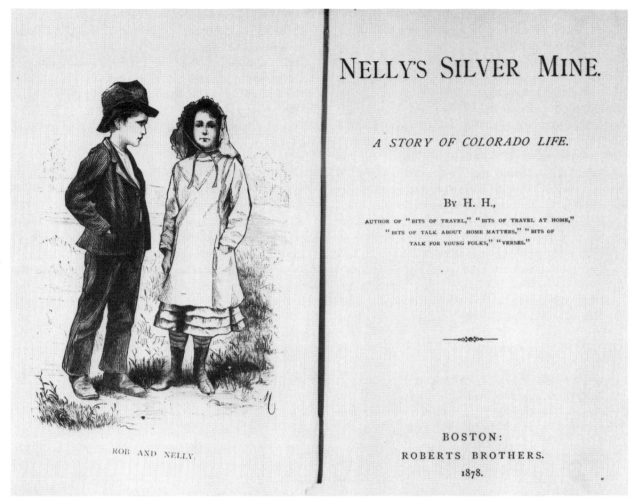

ROB AND NELLY.

NELLY'S SILVER MINE.

A STORY OF COLORADO LIFE.

By H. H.,

AUTHOR OF "BITS OF TRAVEL," "BITS OF TRAVEL AT HOME,"
"BITS OF TALK ABOUT HOME MATTERS," "BITS OF
TALK FOR YOUNG FOLKS," "VERSES."

BOSTON:
ROBERTS BROTHERS.
1878.

Frontispiece and title page for Jackson's novel about a family of Easterners who settle in the mining country of Colorado (Baldwin Library, University of Florida Libraries)

and resourceful as she matures from twelve to fifteen over the course of the novel, and she is one of Jackson's strong female characters. *Atlantic Monthly* reported in 1878 that Jackson "has done better than reward the patient little Nelly with material wealth; she has shown the expansion of a gentle character, and the reader discovers at the end that a pretty moral lies in the title,—a moral which is not obtruded but pervades the book as a delicate perfume."

The beginnings of Jackson's fascination with the West can be perceived in *Nelly's Silver Mine.* She appears in the novel as Mrs. Williams, one of several characters who has come to Colorado for the rehabilitating effects of its climate. The book contains passages of sociological and historical interest, foremost among them Jackson's description of the wonderment that Nelly and her twin brother Rob experience riding on one of the first railroad pas-

senger cars. Although the *New York Tribune* called *Nelly's Silver Mine* "a true classic for the nursery and the school room," the novel has not endured; it is now read as a historical curiosity.

Jackson's poetry has been anthologized frequently and school texts have often included her verses. Some of her best-known poems she specifically wrote for children and published in juvenile magazines and others came from her collected verse for adults. In verse she celebrated every month of the year and commemorated holidays, including New Year's Day, Decoration Day, Thanksgiving, and Christmas. In addition she wrote on many aspects of nature. Even in the 1920s and 1930s, American school children were memorizing and reciting poems such as "September" and "October's Bright Blue Weather." *The Brewton Index to Poetry* listed eleven poems by her and one about her in 1942, three by her in 1957, and two in 1965. The *Index to Poetry for Children and Young People* included two of Jackson's poems in 1972, one in 1978 ("September").

The first of Jackson's three cat stories, *Letters from a Cat: Published by Her Mistress for the Benefit of All Cats and the Amusement of Little Children* (1879), contains the story of Pussy's life and some letters she supposedly wrote to little Helen Fiske. The letters included in the volume were actually written by Jackson's mother, who sent them to the child as she traveled to Boston and Weston with her father during the summer of 1836. In each missive, Pussy relates the happenings of the day that affect her, including suffering a fall, injuring her nose trying to jump at a robin through a clean window, attending a tea party given by Judge Dickinson's elderly cat and being escorted by another cat named Caesar, and accidentally falling into a barrel of soft soap. Each letter is charming and the book, which had many years of popularity, remains entertaining today.

Of *Mammy Tittleback and Her Family: A True Story of Seventeen Cats* (1881) *Century Magazine* reported that the "younger brood of readers will light on a wonderfully real and jolly tale of a cat and her family." Jackson and her second husband spent Christmas Day of 1880 with his family in Pennsylvania in the house she recreated in this story. The preface, at the back of the book to be read last, discloses how Jackson heard Mammy's story in bits and pieces from different family members. Beginning with the "Genealogical Tree of Mammy Tittleback's Family," the little large-print book describes how Mammy spends her days in typical family-pet activities.

The Hunter Cats of Connorloa (1884) is about George Connor, a California man whose seventeen cats are trained to destroy rabbits and gophers and retrieve linnets that are ruining his orchards. The model for Connor is Abbot Kinney of Los Angeles, with whom the author officially investigated the conditions of California's Mission Indians; the setting for the book is his Kinneyloa property. The cat story is not the only, or even the primary focus in this work. Jackson first gives an account of Kinney's wide travels and includes an entirely fictitious subplot about his adoption of an orphaned niece and nephew and an account of how the California missions were settled. The cat story ends abruptly, and Jackson spends over forty pages on her Indian crusade, which includes a piteous account of an elderly Indian couple forced to leave the home in which they had lived all their lives. The children, Rea and Jusy, are deeply moved by the incident,

and Jusy, hearing his uncle explain the government's stance, vows to be an officer for the American president when he grows up and tell him about the injustices Indians have suffered. The *Critic* reviewer commended Jackson for letting "our children know the wrongs to be righted by the country they were to love and honor most."

Jackson's children's books were so popular that thirteen years after her death Roberts Brothers republished her three stories about felines in *Cat Stories* (1898). The same year, Lothrop published *Pansy Billings and Popsy*, a book containing two stories that had appeared in the magazine *Wide Awake*. The first story "Pansy Billings" is about a poor little eight-year-old girl whose father has died and whose mother takes in washing and raises chickens. Crotchety old Archie McCloud, the florist, is so impressed by Pansy's exemplary character that he befriends her and teaches her to raise pansies and other flowers to supplement her family's sparse income. When Archie dies he bequeaths his entire estate to Pansy, and she at seventeen is a "florist and proprietor, in her own right, of a prosperous business and a good home," which she shares with her family. Jackson ends her story with the observation that it had all come "from a little girl's affectionate good will, good cheer, honesty, and industry,—qualities which never fail, in the long run, to win."

The second story in the book, "Popsy," is about a Tennessee girl and her poor tobacco-farming family. The first part of the tale takes place in Tennessee and the second involves the long journey to Missouri, where the family decides to move for better farming opportunities. Resourceful, thoughtful Popsy reminds the reader of Nelly in *Nelly's Silver Mine* and of Pansy in "Pansy Billings." In Tennessee, she raises flax, painstakingly prepares the thread, and weaves eleven large tablecloths and fourteen towels. Uncle Eli buys her a special trunk for them, which goes on the long journey to Missouri. There Popsy's project is to transplant and cultivate a hundred wild gooseberry bushes. The moral lesson of how hard work pays off runs throughout the story.

The last five years of Jackson's life were devoted to a crusade on behalf of the American Indians. During her Western period she had become increasingly aware of the Indians' plight. This interest climaxed when she heard Ponca chieftain Standing Bear and Susette "Bright Eyes" La Flesche lecture in Boston in 1879 on the suffering of many dispossessed Plains Indians. As Odell notes, Jackson's was a "sudden and consuming interest." For the first time she identified herself with a national reform movement, not having written for the causes of black-white equality, temperance, and suffrage. Before this she had alluded only casually to Indians. In *Bits of Travel at Home* (1878) she described the Indians encountered on her first trip to California as picturesque, and she exclaimed over Indian names. Now, however, she started writing letters and articles on behalf of the Indians.

Jackson became determined to write a nonfiction book that would expose the government's maltreatment of its wards and plead for America to correct its record. Her campaign to arouse public opinion culminated in the publication in 1881 of *A Century of Dishonor*, a document of some four hundred fifty pages whose major thesis is that the Indian policy of the United States defied the basic principles of justice.

Jackson, who had resolved to do an exhaustive study, did extensive research in New York City's Astor Library, investigating materials relating to the U.S. Indian policy from the Revolutionary period. Her book begins with an introduction in which she challenges the 1880 Congress "to cover itself in a lustre of glory" and "to redeem the name of the United States from the stain of a century of dishonor." She presents her case in emotional narratives of the history of seven tribes, the Cheyennes, Cherokees, Delawares, Nez Perces, Poncas, Sioux, and Winnebagoes, and on the massacres of Indians by whites. The lengthy appendix includes Jackson's newspaper correspondence with Secretary of Interior Carl Schurz and other officials, Ponca case developments, Indian character testimonials, accounts of outrages committed by whites, excerpts from Indian Bureau reports, treaty digests, and Indian statistics.

The 1880 Congress was apparently not interested in covering "itself with a lustre of glory" and paid no attention to the volume, although Jackson sent copies to members at her own expense. Theodore Roosevelt, who considered himself an authority on the West, caustically criticized the volume. However, the powerful Indian Rights Association was formed within a year of its publication. President Chester Arthur appointed Jackson a commissioner of Indian Affairs in 1882, assigned to visit and report on the condition of California's Mission Indians, and the Dawes Act was passed in 1887, largely due to the campaign in behalf of the Indians in which Jackson and other prominent people were involved.

Jackson herself believed that *A Century of Dishonor* was her best work, but Odell believes that "In point of content it is, but in that of style it is her weakest" because there is "evidence of hurried writing, without the necessary revision." Although after her death the book went out of print, over the years students of the American Indian have considered it "one of the soundest and most exhaustive works" on Indian rights. Eighty years after its publication, when there was a pronounced increase in interest in civil rights, Harper republished the volume, minus the appendix, as a Torchbook in their American Perspectives series (1965).

Realizing that neither *A Century of Dishonor* nor the government report she and Abbot Kinney, who was also an Indian commissioner, prepared on the California Mission Indians as having the desired effect, Jackson continued her plea for justice for the Indians with the publication in 1884 of *Ramona*. In *Ramona*, which cast the deplorable circumstances of the Indian in fiction, Jackson's intent was to arouse further public indignation and bring about social change. Working toward this goal she produced her magnum opus: a romantic novel set against the background of the passing of the old Spanish patriarchal life in California.

Throughout *Ramona* Jackson's poetic vision and her eye for the beauty of the landscape can be seen in passages such as this one: "And the delicious, languid, semi-tropic summer came hovering over the valley. The apricots turned golden, the peaches glowed, the grapes filled and hardened like opaque emeralds being thick under the canopied vines. The garden was a shade brown, and the roses had all fallen; but there were lillies, and orange blossoms; and poppies, and carnations and geraniums in the pots, and musk,—oh, yes, ever and always musk." As she wrote to Thomas Bailey Aldrich, "What I wanted to do, was to draw a picture so winning and alluring in the beginning of this story, that the reader would become thoroughly interested in the characters before he dreamed of what was before him:—and would have swallowed a big dose of the Indian question, without knowing it."

Ramona, half-Indian, half-white, is one of nineteenth-century America's most memorable female characters. One of the finest scenes in the novel occurs when Ramona meets Father Salvierderra in the mustard patch early in the story: "Ramona's beauty was of the sort to be best enhanced by the waving gold which now framed her face. She had just enough olive tint in her complexion to underlie and enrich her skin without making it swarthy. Her hair was like her Indian mother's, heavy and black, but her eyes were her father's,

Illustrations by Henry Sandham for a later edition of Ramona. *Sandham had traveled with Jackson and Abbot Kinney on their tour of Mission Indian settlements in California.*

steel blue. Only those who came very near to Ramona, knew, however, that her eyes were blue for the heavy black eyebrows and long black lashes so shaded and shadowed them that they looked black as the night. . . . She had looked to the devout old monk, as she sprang through the cloud of golden flowers, the sun falling on her bared head, her cheeks flushed, her eyes shining, more like an apparition of an angel or saint than like the flesh-and-blood maiden whom he had carried in his arms when she was a babe."

Ramona's beauty goes beyond the physical. She embodies the best qualities of the two races that she represents. She is thoughtful, generous, loving, noble, and pious. She sees that the tired

sheep shearers are fed when the callous Juan Con would have let them go hungry. She protects the frightened maid Margarita from the wrath of Señora Gonzaga Moreno by mending in secret the torn altar cloth.

Señora Gonzaga Moreno is Jackson's catalyst in the novel *Ramona*. Robbed of her husband's best grazing land after his death when the boundaries of her ranch are pushed back by the United States Land Commission, Señora Moreno never again feels safe and secure in her valley, which is the envy of other land owners. She is the foster mother of Ramona, but her feelings for the girl are negative. Because Ramona falls in love with and eventually marries the Indian Alessandro, she is disinherited by the proud señora and gives up her comfortable life for one of dire poverty among the displaced Indians. Señora Moreno is unable to appreciate the irony of her rejection of her foster child: it is bigotry that has robbed her of her best land because she is a Mexican-American, as her own prejudice against Indians condemns her foster daughter to a life of hardship and grief.

Jackson has two main themes in *Ramona*. The first is miscegenation and the second is pride that cannot accept a person for what he or she is rather than as a representative of a particular racial or ethnic group. The hero and heroine of *Ramona* are fictitious, but Jackson maintained that every incident relating to the Indian experience is true. In the novel three civilizations meet at a crossroads, two fading from the scene and the third taking over.

In 1886 Albion W. Tourgée wrote in the *North American Review* that *Ramona* is "unquestionably the best novel yet produced by an American woman. It is doubtful whether in clearness of conception, depth of coloring, purity of tone, individuality and pleasing contrast of characters, and intensity of emotion it is excelled by any American writer." It was ranked with *Uncle Tom's Cabin* as one of the two great ethical novels of the nineteenth century. Jackson thought of herself as an "Indian Harriet Beecher Stowe" and wrote to a friend that "If I can do one-hundredth part for the Indian as Mrs. Stowe did for the Negro, I will be thankful."

In 1941 Allan Nevins, commenting on Jackson's two Indian books, stated that they "are sentimental in that they present only one aspect of a complex and difficult problem and thereby oversimplify and distort it" and that they "offer no constructive remedy for the difficult problem they expose." However, he added, "But it is no real condemnation to say they are sentimental. That is merely a statement of their limitations"; "American history owes much to our long line of sentimental books."

In 1965, comparing the success of *Ramona* with that of *A Century of Dishonor*, Andrew F. Rolle noted that "the superiority of imaginative literature over non-fiction in arousing the public is obvious." As he pointed out, *Ramona* "quickly became famous far beyond its original didactic intentions." The book's continued popularity has been more as a romantic novel than as a work concerned with a problem. *Ramona*, though written for adults, was read by many young people in the 1880s and 1890s. Over the years, the novel has had more than three hundred printings and has been produced several times as a motion picture, staged as a play, and presented as a pageant.

A Century of Dishonor and *Ramona* crowned Jackson's literary output and were, in her own words just before her death, "the only things I have done of which I am glad now." "I am leaving this earth with no regret except that I have not accomplished more work; especially that it was so late in the day when I began to write in earnest." Higginson reported that in one of her last letters she mentioned that she had intended to write a children's book on the same theme as *Ramona*, but that it probably was well she did not because she doubted she could have made it "so telling a stroke."

Soon after *Ramona* was published, a fall in her Colorado Springs home resulted in a compound fracture of the hip that crippled her for the rest of her life. Plagued by illness, she went to California to recuperate, but her health never returned and she died in San Francisco of cancer on 12 August 1885 at age fifty-four. Eulogies in prose and poetry were published in newspapers and magazines across the United States, praising her dynamic personality and her work. Emily Dickinson wrote: "Helen of Troy will die, but Helen of Colorado, never."

According to Odell, it was Hamilton Wright Mabie's appraisal at the time of Jackson's death that proved in time to be the most insightful. His comment had been, "What a difference separates her earlier from her latest work! It is this noble growth which one recalls with fullest satisfaction." Jackson's contributions to nineteenth-century American literature deserve attention for several reasons. Although late twentieth-century readers may not find her writing "graceful, colorful or brilliant in tone" as her contemporary readers did, hers was a decorous style, marked by propriety and good taste, which pleased the publishers, the public, and critics of her day. Much of her work provides a keen index to the concerns of her times and is interesting from a twentieth-century viewpoint for its historical significance.

Jackson was a prolific writer when the attitude of many people was hostile toward "ink-stained women" and when a woman who was identified as a writer invited disrespect. She developed strong, independent female characters who grappled with difficult problems. She contributed to the school of local color as well. Her writings in prose and poetry covered New England, the West, and foreign lands, acquainting many readers with places inaccessible to them in real life.

As a crusader for the Indian cause and defender of human rights, she informed and awakened many to thought and action. The cause she promoted was controversial, comparable in the 1980s to the problem of the Mexican alien in California and the Southwest. Her outstanding book, read by adults and young people to this day, is *Ramona*, for which she deservedly will be remembered beyond the twentieth century. As Allan Nevins concluded in the *American Scholar*, "In looking back on a long, sad history of error and oppression marking our relationship with the Indian from the days of the Pequot War, we can point to her volume(s) as eloquent evidence that at one period in our history a large body of Americans began to care, a large body began to be ashamed. And if her writings lacked constructive qualities they were not devoid of vision."

Bibliography:

John R. Byers, Jr., and Elizabeth S. Byers, "Helen Hunt Jackson (1830-1885): Critical Bibliography of Secondary Comment," *American Literary Realism, 1870-1910*, 6 (Summer 1973): 197-241.

Biographies:

Ruth Odell, *Helen Hunt Jackson (H. H.)* (New York: Appleton-Century, 1939);

Evelyn I. Banning, *Helen Hunt Jackson* (New York: Vanguard, 1973).

References:

John R. Byers, Jr., "Helen Hunt Jackson (1830-1885)," *American Literary Realism, 1870-1910*, 2 (Summer 1969): 143-148;

Frank J. Dobie, "Helen Hunt Jackson and *Ramona*," *Southwest Review*, 44 (Spring 1959): 93-98;

A. A. Hamblen, "*Ramona:* A Story of Passion," *Western Review*, 8, no. 1 (1971): 21-25;

Thomas Wentworth Higginson, "Helen Jackson ('H. H.')" in his *Contemporaries* (Boston & New York: Houghton Mifflin, 1899), pp. 142-167;

Wayne R. Kime, "Helen Hunt Jackson," *American Literary Realism, 1870-1910*, 8 (Autumn 1975): 291-292;

Carey McWilliams, "Southern California: Ersatz Mythology," *Common Ground*, 6 (Winter 1946): 29-38;

Allan Nevins, "Helen Hunt Jackson: Sentimentalist vs. Realist," *American Scholar*, 10 (Summer 1941): 269-285;

Louise Pound, "Biographical Accuracy and 'H. H.,' " *American Literature*, 2 (January 1931): 418-421;

Andrew F. Rolle, "Introduction to Jackson's *A Century of Dishonor*" (New York: Harper & Row, 1965), pp. vii-xxii;

M. W. Shinn, "The Verse and Prose of 'H. H.,' " *Overland Monthly*, second series, 6 (September 1885): 315-323.

Papers:

The Huntington Library in San Marino, California, the James Library in Amherst, Massachusetts, the public libraries of Pasadena and New York, and Sterling Memorial Library of Yale University have collections of manuscripts and letters.

Annie Fellows Johnston

(15 May 1863-5 October 1931)

Marilyn Kaye
St. John's University

BOOKS: *Big Brother* (Boston: Knight, 1894);

Joel: A Boy of Galilee (Boston: Roberts Brothers, 1895; London: Arnold, 1895);

The Little Colonel (Boston: Page, 1895; London: Jarrold, 1897);

In League with Israel; A Tale of the Chattanooga Conference (Cincinnati: Curtis & Jennings/New York: Eaton & Mains, 1896);

Ole Mammy's Torment (Boston: Page, 1897);

The Gate of the Giant Scissors (Boston: Page, 1898; London: Jarrold, 1900);

Two Little Knights of Kentucky (Boston: Page, 1898);

The Little Colonel's House Party (Boston: Page, 1900; London: Jarrold, 1901);

The Story of Dago (Boston: Page, 1900; London: Jarrold, 1902);

The Little Colonel's Holidays (Boston: Page, 1901; London: Jarrold, 1903);

The Little Colonel's Hero (Boston: Page, 1902; London: Jarrold, 1903);

Asa Holmes; or, At the Crossroads (Boston: Page, 1902);

Cicely, and Other Stories (Boston: Page, 1903);

Flip's "Islands of Providence" (Boston: Page, 1903);

The Little Colonel at Boarding-school (Boston: Page, 1903);

Aunt 'Liza's Hero, and Other Stories (Boston: Page, 1904);

In the Desert of Waiting: The Legend of Camel-back Mountain (Boston: Page, 1904);

The Little Colonel in Arizona (Boston: Page, 1904; London: Seeley, 1906);

The Quilt that Jack Built (Boston: Page, 1904);

The Little Colonel's Christmas Vacation (Boston: Page, 1905);

The Little Colonel: Maid of Honor (Boston: Page, 1906);

Mildred's Inheritance; Just Her Way; Ann's Own Way (Boston: Page, 1906);

The Legend of the Bleeding-heart (Boston: Page, 1907);

The Little Colonel's Knight Comes Riding (Boston: Page, 1907);

Mary Ware, the Little Colonel's Chum (Boston: Page, 1908); republished as *The Little Colonel's Chum, Mary Ware* (Boston: Page, 1919);

The Little Colonel's Good Times Book (Boston: Page, 1909; London: Jarrold, 1936);

Mary Ware in Texas (Boston: Page, 1910);

Travelers Five Along Life's Highway (Boston: Page, 1911);

Mary Ware's Promised Land (Boston: Page, 1912);

Miss Santa Claus of the Pullman (New York: Century, 1913);

Georgina of the Rainbows (New York: Britton Publishing, 1916);

Georgina's Service Stars (New York: Britton Publishing, 1918);

The Little Man in Motley (Boston: Page, 1918);

The Story of the Red Cross as told to the Little Colonel (Boston: Page, 1918);

It Was the Road to Jericho (New York: Britton Publishing, 1919);

The Road of the Loving Heart (Boston: Page, 1922);

The Land of the Little Colonel; Reminiscence and Autobiography (Boston: Page, 1929);

For Pierre's Sake, and Other Stories (Boston: Page, 1934).

Annie Fellows Johnston is primarily known for her Little Colonel stories, an enormously popular series which sold in the range of two million copies in her lifetime. Johnston was born in Evansville, Indiana. Following the death of her father, Albion Fellows, she grew up with her mother and two sisters on a farm in the Indiana countryside. In her autobiography, *The Land of the Little Colonel* (1929), she notes an early desire to become a writer, and in her late adolescence she had several poems published, one of which appeared in *Harper's Weekly*. She studied at the University of Iowa for one year and in 1888 married William Johnston, a widower with three children. After three years of marriage, William Johnston died. Faced with the prospect of raising three stepchildren, Johnston began to write seriously. She wrote several short stories for *Youth's Companion;* many of these were later gathered into collections or published in the Cozy

251

Johnston, early 1880s

Corner series. She also wrote and had published two longer works for children. During this period, Johnston visited Kentucky, where she discovered a leisurely, gracious world which had changed little since the days before the Civil War. While in Kentucky, she met an old Confederate colonel and his pretty, imperious granddaughter; these acquaintances became the inspiration for the Little Colonel series.

The first book, published in 1895, begins the saga of Lloyd Sherman, the Little Colonel of the title. It is much shorter than the works which followed; the story is simple and direct, and there are only a few characters. Set in the fictional town of Lloydsboro, Kentucky, the plot concerns the role of five-year-old Lloyd in reuniting her estranged mother and grandfather. The latter had disowned his daughter when she married a Northerner. (The 1935 Shirley Temple film *The Little Colonel* was loosely based on the plot of this story.) Though melodramatic in tone, and embodying various outmoded attitudes and prejudices, the story retains a certain charm in its simplicity.

The second book of the series, *The Little Colonel's House Party* (1900), was published five years

later and established the pattern followed by the remainder of the books in the series. Plots revolve around less dramatic, more common occurrences than those in the first book and deal with the young people's daily adventures and experiences. In *The Little Colonel's House Party*, Lloyd is eleven years old and described as "such an attractive little bunch of mischief," famous for her "lordly manner . . . hot temper . . . imperious ways." One does get glimpses of Lloyd's renowned temper and her lordly manner is a constant position, but rarely does one see Lloyd involved in any mischief. In the first book, when she is five, she does perform an occasional mischievous act; but by the time she is eleven Lloyd is also noted for her "delicate, flower-like beauty . . . dainty ways . . . little schoolgirl accomplishments." These so-called accomplishments are difficult to ascertain. The one talent she possesses throughout the series is harp playing, a habit encouraged by her grandfather, the colonel, because it reminds him of his late wife. Her schoolgirl role is also limited. Although two of the books take place mostly in a school environment and there are occasional references to school throughout the books, there is little mention of any actual schoolwork or career ambition for Lloyd. When she does attempt to study diligently, in *The Little Colonel's Christmas Vacation* (1905), she becomes seriously ill as a result of overworking.

Beauty and aura of nobility appear to be Lloyd's major attributes. In *The Little Colonel at Boarding-school* (1903), a young invalid girl through an elaborate series of events comes into possession of a photograph of Lloyd, whom she does not know. For some unknown reason, looking at the picture of the "Princess" (another of Lloyd's nicknames) gives her strength, and she eventually recovers. In a way, this episode offers a clue to the reason behind Lloyd's appeal to readers: she is accepted and adored simply by reason of her existence; she does not have to do or say anything notable, she has no real responsibilities or acts to perform in order to reap praise. The author was aware of Lloyd's limitations, but they become insignificant in the light of what Lloyd is. As Johnston put it in *The Little Colonel's Hero* (1902), Lloyd "knows that she can never be a Joan of Arc or a Clara Barton, and her name will never be written in America's hall of fame, but with the sweet ambition in her heart to make life a little lovelier for everyone she touches, she is growing up into a veritable Princess Winsome." It may have occurred to Johnston that young readers might envy a life like this. Lloyd serves neither as a standard of behavior

*Hattie Cochran, the model for the Little Colonel, and
Annie Fellows Johnston*

nor as a goal to which the reader might aspire; she is a fairy-tale character, created to please and titillate the reader's imagination.

If Lloyd represents the unattainable, idealized version of young girlhood, providing vicarious pleasures for her readers, her friend Betty can perhaps be seen as the author's interpretation of what a girl should strive for. Betty is introduced in *The Little Colonel's House Party* as a poor orphan whose mother was a school friend of Mrs. Sherman, Lloyd's mother. Brought from a foster home for a visit to Locusts, the Sherman home, she later becomes a permanent resident and grows up with Lloyd.

Betty is portrayed as having an instinctive sense of conscience which always causes her to act in appropriate ways. Throughout the series the other girls look to her for guidance. She is virtuous but rarely moralizes, nor does she consciously set herself up as an example to her friends. Although her perpetual integrity occasionally defies credibility, as a character she is saved by a spontaneous and affectionate personality and a strong intelligence. She has talent and ambition—she wants to

be a writer—and her striving toward her goal makes her a growing and developing character.

Betty serves as the author's voice for unobtrusively explaining values and morals. In *The Little Colonel's Holidays* (1901), she says to a restless Lloyd, "Patience isn't just sitting all day without fidgeting. It's putting up with whatever happens to you, without making fuss about it." Betty is the embodiment of the premise that all good things come to one who behaves well, works diligently and does not complain. In Dorothea Mann's 1931 tribute to Johnston in *Publishers Weekly*, Mann notes that Johnston based the character of Betty on her own two sisters and that she always felt that Betty was her most realistic character.

Adults tend to stay in the background in the Little Colonel's world. With the exception of the first book in which the major problem centers around adults, parents are portrayed as supportive characters who hover on the periphery of childhood's world. They are almost always wise and strong. If, as happens on occasion, they become inattentive or unconsciously neglectful, they soon discover their errors and correct themselves accordingly. Frequently consulted by the major characters, they come into the picture offering wise and sound guidance and then quietly retreat from the mainstream of events.

Childhood in the Little Colonel's world is a glorious time, a time which is to be treasured and prolonged. Lloyd is reluctant to leave her childhood behind. In the 1904 book *The Little Colonel in Arizona* (she is in her early teens at this point), she says to her father, "Seems to me I'd be contented always, just to be you'ah deah little daughter." (Curiously, Lloyd is the only character Johnston attempts to portray with a Southern accent.)

Her reluctance is understandable, for Lloyd is doomed to enter an adult world which has little to offer to women. For most young women, traditional roles await; and while occasionally a woman is portrayed as having a hobby, such as photography, most of the adult women are preoccupied with motherhood and the running of a household. In one story, however, Lloyd's parents criticize the husband of a friend who refuses to allow his wife any responsibility or social freedom. This criticism could reflect Johnston's own views, which may have been more liberal than the common social attitudes. Betty's career plans are encouraged, as are the ambitions of the young Mary Ware in later books. But for Lloyd, the social order will prevail, and she is aware of this fact. In *The Little Colonel at Boardingschool*, she says to a friend, "We're growing up so

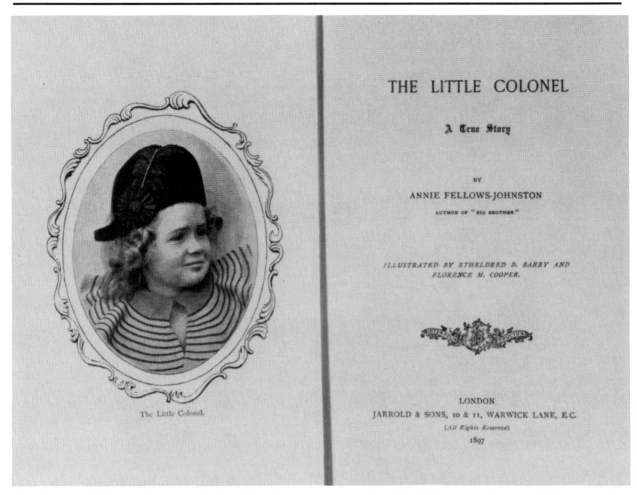

THE LITTLE COLONEL

A True Story

BY

ANNIE FELLOWS-JOHNSTON

AUTHOR OF "BIG BROTHER"

ILLUSTRATED BY ETHELDRED B. BARRY AND
FLORENCE M. COOPER.

LONDON
JARROLD & SONS, 10 & 11, WARWICK LANE, E.C.
[All Rights Reserved]
1897

The Little Colonel.

Frontispiece and title page for the first British edition of the book that introduced Lloyd Sherman and her grandfather to juvenile readers (Baldwin Library, University of Florida Libraries)

fast that if we don't have some fun soon, it will be too late. In only a few moah yeahs I'll be through school, and then I'll have to be a debutante and settle down to be propah and young ladified."

Young men, too, have restrictive ideals which society has set for them. Honor and integrity are attributes which every young man must consistently display. They are not allowed the occasional lapses which girls might have; silly coyness or petty rivalry must remain foreign to them. From their youngest days, the importance of the noble life is impressed upon them. In *The Little Colonel at Boarding-school*, it is recalled that when Lloyd's friend Malcolm was a young boy, he was referred to as "a winning little Knight of Kentucky," who wore a small pin as the badge of that knighthood, a badge which stood for "wearing the white flower of a blameless life." As a young man, he ceases to wear the badge; Lloyd believes he has forsaken this "blameless" way of life and discards any romantic inclinations she has be-

gun to have toward him. In order to marry, a man has to prove himself worthy of the woman he loves, a fact that is emphasized repeatedly to the girls once they reach mid-adolescence. As one adult warns the girls, "In olden times a man didn't come whining to a maiden and say, 'I long to be a knight, but I am too weak to do battle unaided. Be my ladye fair and help me win my spurs.' No, she would have laughed him to scorn. He won his spurs first, and only after he had proved himself worthy and received his accolade, did she give him her hand."

The values of these "olden times" are impressed upon the girls as having contemporary validity; they must hold themselves dear and critically examine any young man who dares to approach. The girls have before them the example of a willful and reckless friend, Ida Shane, who falls in love with a careless boy of poor reputation. They elope in a frenzy of adolescent passion. Years later, Ida is discovered in poverty and ill-health; her husband is an alcoholic. The pressure is on the young man to meet certain standards of behavior in order to win his "ladye fair"; and the pressure is on the girl to keep herself pure and to withhold her hand until she finds her true prince. In *The Little Colonel at Boarding-school* Johnston illustrates this notion with the tale of "Hildegarde"—a fairy-type story in which a young woman named Hildegarde weaves a mantle for her future husband, who can only be a true prince; the mantle must be of a certain length to fit a prince, and she measures it with a yardstick. Lloyd and her friends are fascinated with this story, and Lloyd asks her father to give her a symbolic yardstick by which she can measure her true prince. Her father sums up the standards for young men when he tells her: "The prince who comes asking for you must have, first, a clean life. There must be no wild oats sowed through its past for my little girl to help reap, for no man ever gathers such a harvest alone. Next, he must be honourable in every way which that good old word implies. The man who is that will not ask anything clandestine, nor will he ask to take you from a comfortable home before he is able to provide one for you himself. Then . . . he must be strong. Strong in character, in purpose and endeavour." Women in the Little Colonel's world are born on high pedestals, and men have to achieve moral perfection before they can approach them.

Romance in general is discouraged for young people until they are considered old enough to make critical judgments. Perhaps this strict injunction against male/female relationships of a romantic nature is partially responsible for the strangely intense relationships between girls which carry strong overtones of sexuality. Lloyd and her schoolmates constantly develop crushes on each other, giving each other flowers and gifts and becoming jealous and depressed if the special friend's attention strays. As they begin to awaken sexually, forbidden to express any budding passions toward boys, their attention is easily diverted to an attractive school chum.

Later, the girls are permitted to flirt as long as they are careful not to make any commitments. References to Hildegarde and her yardstick abound in the books after *The Little Colonel at Boarding-school*, and in *The Little Colonel's Knight Comes Riding* (1907), Lloyd recognizes the one young man who measures up to her yardstick. But there are indications of changing social mores. As she begins to think about marriage seriously in this last book of the series, Lloyd expresses herself on the subject: "Out heah in the country I'd grown up believing that it's a kind, honest old world. I'd seen only its good side. I took my conception of married life from mothah and Papa Jack, Doctah Shelby and Aunt Alicia. . . . They made me think that marriage is a great strong sanctuary, built on a rock that no storm can hurt and no trouble move. But this wintah I found that that kind of marriage has grown out of fashion. It's something to jest about, and it's a mattah of scandal and divorce and unhappiness." Even the sanctified world of the Little Colonel is susceptible to occasional intrusions of realism, but usually, only through word of mouth.

Distinct attitudes toward race and class prevail throughout the series. The Shermans are one of the "first families" of Lloydsboro, and Lloyd's aristocratic breeding is frequently noted. In *The Little Colonel at Boarding-school*, speaking of a girl she dislikes, Lloyd suggests that the girl is "common": "The blue blood of an old patrician family, proud of its traditions and proud of its generations of gentle breeding was coursing hotly through the Little Colonel's veins as she spoke." While good breeding does not preclude all indiscretion—the wild boy Ida Shane ran off with was of good family—breeding does seem to represent certain obligations in regard to personal behavior, and it is considered particularly shameful when someone of a good family drifts from the approved code of behavior.

Betty, too, is a symbol of the power of high birth. Although she is introduced in *The Little Colonel's House Party* as a poor orphan, it is made clear that her mother had been of a certain social class; and although misfortune has reduced her to impoverished circumstances, she retains a certain gentility which her ragged clothes cannot hide. When she visits the Locusts, "in some vague, sweet way Betty felt that she had come back to her own and had been welcomed home." She can immediately recognize the home and life to which she is entitled by birth.

As might be expected, racial attitudes which have since been recognized as offensive are expressed in the series. Blacks appear quite frequently, usually in the role of servants. They are consistently portrayed as stupid, silly, highly superstitious, and always eager to please the "white folks." For the most part, blacks are treated with a condescending affection. Lloyd's mother says of the family cook in *The Little Colonel's Christmas Vacation*, "Cindy is getting more fussy and exacting every year. . . . If she were not such a superior cook, I wouldn't put up with her whims, but in these days, when everybody is having so much trouble with

Frontispiece and title page for Johnston's autobiography. In chapter one she writes: "It has been a matter of interest to me to note that the [same] questions are asked again and again by my readers like an insistent refrain: 'How much is really true? What are their names in real life? . . .' I am offering this short biography, hoping that it will satisfy the curiosity of my correspondents. . . ."

servants, we'll have to humor her. She's a faithful old creature."

Occasionally, blacks serve as comic relief, as in *The Little Colonel: Maid of Honor* (1906). Soon after the formal wedding of Lloyd's cousin, two black servants marry. Their wedding is described as a source of amusement for Lloyd and other white guests who chuckle at the sight of the black people attempting to mimic aspects of the earlier wedding. These scenes are described in a matter-of-fact manner and the author offers no justifications or explanation for the characters' attitudes; these attitudes are displayed as common and acceptable.

In regard to general morals and values, Johnston employs tales with distinct symbols which are reiterated throughout the books. In *The Little Colonel's House Party*, the story is told of chiefs on a Samoan island who built a road in honor of Robert Louis Stevenson, whom they had named Tusitala, the Teller of Tales. The road was named the Road of Loving Hearts. Lloyd and her friends vow to devote themselves to building a "road of loving hearts" in the memories of others around them. They wear rings engraved with the name Tusitala to remind them of the importance of being kind and friendly. Another tale, in *The Little Colonel's*

Christmas Vacation, revolves around Edryn, a Knight of the Round Table whose motto is "keep tryst." Lloyd makes a rosary to which she adds a bead for each day in which she manages to keep tryst; of this string of beads she believes, "it did help when she could see every night a visible token that she had tried to live that day through unselfishly and well—that she had kept tryst with the duty of cheerfulness which we all owe the world." And as far as romance and marriage are concerned, the tale of Hildegarde, or "the three weavers," inspires the girls to form a club called "Order of Hildegarde." The various tales serve as connecting threads throughout the books and enable Johnston to make moral standards without putting the words in the mouths of characters. By offering the directives in the guise of pseudofolktales, she gives them a legitimate status without preaching or turning to religious tracts. Several of these tales were published separately and became popular in their own right. Order of Hildegarde clubs were formed across the United States, and Tusitala rings and Edryn rosaries became fads among young girls.

Johnston's plots are invariably based on a series of remarkable coincidences. In *The Little Colonel in Arizona* Lloyd cries out, "Isn't it queah how things happen!" and the reader can only agree. Everything works out; unexpected arrivals are timed perfectly to coincide with some agreeable circumstance, meetings seem almost predestined, and crises evolve into fortuitous happenings. The result is a somewhat artificial and contrived plot structure, yet the series of coincidences does enable events to occur and problems to be resolved neatly and, in so doing, facilitates the obligatory happy ending.

During the period in which she was writing the Little Colonel stories Johnston lived in Arizona, California, and Texas in an attempt to find a suitable climate for her ailing stepson. Following the death of the stepson, Johnston settled in Pewee Valley, Kentucky. She spent summers on Cape Cod, which became the setting for her later Georgina books.

Critics were generally kind to the Little Colonel books. In a 1913 article in *St. Nicholas* magazine, Margaret W. Vandercook wrote: "Lloyd is not just 'the Little Colonel'; she is the type of a beautiful, high-spirited, generous character toward which thousands of other girls aspire." A review in the *New York Times Book Review* (25 November 1905) stated: "There is a captivating quality about all these 'Little Colonel' books." Another review appearing earlier that same year in the *New York Times* (14 October 1905) was somewhat less enthusiastic but nonetheless recommended the books: "It is not easy to believe in quite so much virtue, but its chronicle is attractive, and Mrs. Johnston has the knack of suggesting helps to goodness of showing the bitterness of little sins, thus keeping the values of her picture of life fairly correct in spite of its roseate atmosphere."

Retrospective commentary, however, has been less favorable. In *Who's Who in Children's Books* (1975), Margery Fisher states: "Lloyd is a personality only when she is young enough to comment artlessly on her own faults. When she is old enough . . . to muse in girlish modesty about growing up, she loses any claim to join Jo March or Katy Carr in the memories of young readers. Surely a spice of mischief is needed if a heroine is to remain a favourite in a succession of books."

All of Johnston's books are out of print today. In terms of style they certainly would not stand up under the scrutinizing eyes of today's reviewers; contemporary mores would never permit the racism and role stereotyping; and children would most likely find the idealism and perpetual optimism boring. In her 1913 article in *St. Nicholas*, Vandercook suggested that "perhaps the 'mantle' of Louisa M. Alcott has fallen upon Annie Fellows Johnston; . . . they both seem to have written about girls and a kind of living that was real and not make-believe, and they both succeeded in attaining the first place among their readers. Miss Alcott belonged to those of us who were young twenty years ago; Mrs. Johnston belongs to those of us who are young now." Vandercook's remarks were less than prophetic. Alcott is still considered to have been a major writer for children; Johnston's stories are tied to culturally bound values and mores and have been unable to survive any social evolution.

References:

Dorothea Lawrance Mann, "The Author of the Little Colonel Series," *Publishers Weekly*, 120 (24 October 1931): 1925-1927;

Elizabeth Steele, "Mrs. Johnston's Little Colonel," in *Challenges in American Culture*, edited by Ray B. Brown and others (Bowling Green: Bowling Green Popular Press, 1970), pp. 217-223;

Margaret W. Vandercook, "Annie Fellows Johnston: The Beloved Writer of Books for Young People," *St. Nicholas*, 41 (December 1913): 129-130.

James Otis Kaler
(James Otis)

(19 March 1848-11 December 1912)

David L. Russell
Ferris State College

SELECTED BOOKS: *Toby Tyler; or, Ten Weeks with a Circus* (New York: Harper, 1881);

Clown's Protege (New York: Burt, 1883);

Mr. Stubbs's Brother; a Sequel to Toby Tyler (New York: Harper, 1883);

Tim and Tip; or, The Adventures of a Boy and a Dog (New York: Harper, 1883);

Left Behind; or, Ten Days a Newsboy (New York: Harper, 1884);

Raising the "Pearl" (New York: Harper, 1884);

Trapping in the Tropics (New York: Burt, 1884);

Silent Pete; or, The Stowaways (New York: Harper, 1886);

A Runaway Brig; or, An Accidental Cruise (New York: Burt, 1888);

The Castaways; or, On the Florida Reefs (New York: Burt, 1888);

Little Jo (Boston: Lothrop, 1888);

The Treasure Finders; A Boy's Adventures in Nicaragua (New York: Burt, 1889);

The Braganza Diamond (Philadelphia: Penn, 1891);

Jack the Hunchback; A Story of Adventure on the Coast of Maine (Boston: Burt, 1892);

Adventures of a Country Boy at the County Fair (Boston: Charles E. Brown & Co., 1893);

Jenny Wren's Boarding-house; A Story of Newsboy Life in New York (Boston: Estes & Lauriat, 1893);

Josiah in New York; or, A Coupon from the Fresh Air Fund (Boston: Bradley, 1893);

The Search for the Silver City; A Tale of Adventure in Yucatan (New York: Burt, 1893);

The Boys' Revolt; A Story of the Street Arabs of New York (Boston: Estes & Lauriat, 1894);

Chasing a Yacht; or, The Theft of the "Gem" (Philadelphia: Penn, 1894);

Jinny and His Partners (New York: Hurst, 1894);

Andy's Ward; or, The International Museum (Philadelphia: Penn, 1895);

The Boys of 1745 at the Capture of Louisbourg (Boston: Estes & Lauriat, 1895);

Ezra Jordan's Escape from the Massacre at Fort Loyall (Boston: Estes & Lauriat, 1895);

How Tommy Saved the Barn (New York & Boston: Crowell, 1895);

An Island Refuge; Casco Bay in 1676 (Boston: Estes & Lauriat, 1895);

Jerry's Family; A Story of a Street Waif of New York (Boston: Estes & Lauriat, 1895);

Neal, the Miller, a Son of Liberty (Boston: Estes & Lauriat, 1895);

With Lafayette at Yorktown; A Story of How Two Boys Joined the Continental Army (New York: Burt, 1895);

Wood Island Light; or, Ned Sanford's Refuge (New York: Hurst, 1895);

Admiral J. of Spurwink (Boston: Bradley, 1896);

The Boy Captain; or, From Forecastle to Cabin (Boston: Estes & Lauriat, 1896);

On Schedule Time (New York: Whittaker, 1896);

A Short Cruise (New York & Boston: Crowell, 1896);

Teddy and Carrots; Two Merchants of Newspaper Row (Boston: Estes & Lauriat, 1896);

Under the Liberty Tree; A Story of the "Boston Massacre" (Boston: Estes & Lauriat, 1896);

Wrecked on Spider Island; or, How Ned Rogers Found the Treasure (New York: Burt, 1896);

At the Siege of Quebec (Philadelphia: Penn, 1897);

The Signal Boys of '75; A Tale of Boston During the Siege (Boston: Estes & Lauriat, 1897);

With Washington at Monmouth; A Story of Three Philadelphia Boys (New York: Burt, 1897);

The Wreck of the "Circus" (New York & Boston: Crowell, 1897);

An Amateur Fireman (New York: Dutton, 1898);

The Boys of '98 (Boston: Estes, 1898);

The Capture of the "Laughing Mary"; A Story of Three New York Boys in 1776 (New York: Burt, 1898);

"The Charming Sally," Privateer Schooner of New York; A Tale of 1765 (Boston & New York: Houghton Mifflin, 1898);

Corporal 'Lige's Recruit; A Story of Crown Point and Ticonderoga (New York: Burt, 1898);

The Cruise of the "Comet"; The Story of a Privateer of

James Otis Kaler

1812, Sailing from Baltimore (Boston: Estes & Lauriat, 1898);

A Cruise with Paul Jones; A Story of Naval Warfare in 1778 (New York: Burt, 1898);

Dick in the Desert (New York & Boston: Crowell, 1898);

A District Messenger Boy and A Necktie Party (Boston: Lothrop, 1898);

Joel Harford (New York & Boston: Crowell, 1898);

Morgan, the Jersey Spy; A Story of the Siege of Yorktown in 1781 (New York: Burt, 1898);

The Navy Boys in New York Bay; A Story of Three Boys Who Took Command of the Schooner, "The Laughing Mary" (New York: Burt, 1898);

The Princess and Joe Potter (Boston: Estes & Lauriat, 1898);

Sarah Dillard's Ride; A Story of the Carolinas in 1780 (New York: Burt, 1898);

A Traitor's Escape; A Story of the Attempt to Seize Benedict Arnold after He Had Fled to New York (New York: Burt, 1898);

When Israel Putnam Served the King (Boston: Estes & Lauriat, 1898);

With Warren at Bunker Hill; A Story of the Siege of Boston (New York: Burt, 1898);

At the Siege of Havana; The Experience of Three Boys Serving under Israel Putnam in 1762 (New York: Burt, 1899);

Captain Tom, the Privateersman of the Armed Brig "Chausseur" (Boston: Estes, 1899);

Chased Through Norway; or, Two Million Dollars Missing (New York: Street & Smith, 1899);

Christmas at Deacon Hackett's; A Sequel to How Tommy Saved the Barn (New York & Boston: Crowell, 1899);

Down the Slope (New York: Werner, 1899);

The Life Savers; A Story of the United States Life-saving Service (New York: Dutton, 1899);

Messenger No. 48 (New York: Werner, 1899);

Off Santiago with Sampson (Boston: Estes, 1899);

Telegraph Tom's Venture (New York: Saalfield, 1899);

A Tory Plot; A Story of the Attempt to Kill General Washington in 1776 (New York: Burt, 1899);

Wheeling for Fortune (Philadelphia: McKay, 1899);

When Dewey Came to Manila; or, Among the Filipinos (Boston: Estes, 1899);

With Perry on Lake Erie; A Tale of 1812 (Boston: Wilde, 1899);

With the Swamp Fox; A Story of General Marion's Young Spies (New York: Burt, 1899);

The Armed Ship "America"; or, When We Sailed from Salem (Boston: Estes, 1900);

Aunt Hannah and Seth (New York: Crowell, 1900);

The Defense of Fort Henry; A Story of Wheeling Creek in 1777 (New York: Burt, 1900);

Fighting for the Empire; The Story of the War in South Africa (Boston: Estes, 1900);

Boston Boys of 1775; or, When We Besieged Boston (Boston: Estes, 1900);

Lobster Catchers; A Story of the Coast of Maine (New York: Dutton, 1900);

On the Kentucky Frontier; A Story of the Fighting Pioneers of the West (New York: Burt, 1900);

True Adventure Tales from American History in the Stirring Days of the Revolution (Boston: Page, 1900);

With Preble at Tripoli; A Story of "Old Ironsides" and the Tripolitan War (Boston & Chicago: Wilde, 1900);

Amos Dunkel, Oarsman; A Story of the Whale Boat Navy of 1776 (New York: Burt, 1901);

The Boy Spies with the Regulators; The Story of How the Boys Assisted the Carolina Patriots to Drive the British from That State (New York: Burt, 1901);

Found by the Circus (New York: Crowell, 1901);

Inland Waterways; or, The Cruise of the "Restless" (Philadelphia: McKay, 1901);

Larry Hudson's Ambition (Boston: Page, 1901);

"Our Uncle, the Major"; A Story of New York in 1765 (New York: Crowell, 1901);

The Story of Old Falmouth (New York: Crowell, 1901);

An Unprovoked Mutiny (New York: H. M. Caldwell, 1901);

When We Destroyed the Gaspee; A Story of Narragansett Bay in 1722 (Boston: Estes, 1901);

With Porter in the "Essex"; A Story of His Famous Cruise in Southern Waters During the War of 1812 (Boston & Chicago: Wilde, 1901);

With the Regulators; A Story of North Carolina in 1768 (New York: Burt, 1901);

The Cruise of the "Enterprise," Being a Story of the Struggle and Defeat of the French Privateering Expeditions Against the United States in 1779 (Boston & Chicago: Wilde, 1902);

How the Twins Captured a Hessian; A Story of Long Island in 1776 (New York: Crowell, 1902);

Reuben Green's Adventures at Yale (New York & London: Street & Smith, 1902);

The Story of Pemaquid (New York: Crowell, 1902);

The Treasure of Cocos Island; A Story of the Indian Ocean (New York: Burt, 1902);

Wan Lun and Dandy; The Story of a Chinese Boy and a Dog (New York: Burt, 1902);

Across the Delaware; A Boy's Story of the Battle of Trenton in 1777 (New York: Burt, 1903);

With Rodgers on the "President"; The Story of the Cruise Wherein the Flagship Fired the First Hostile Shot in the War with Great Britain for the Rights of American Seamen (Boston & Chicago: Wilde, 1903);

With the Treasure-hunters; A Story of the Florida Cays (Philadelphia & London: Lippincott, 1903);

At the Siege of Detroit; A Story of Two Ohio Boys in the War of 1812 (New York: Burt, 1904);

Defending the Island; A Story of Bar Harbor in 1758 (Boston: Estes, 1904);

Dorothy's Spy; A Story of the First "Fourth of July" Celebration (New York: Crowell, 1904);

The Minute Boys of the Green Mountains (Boston: Estes, 1904);

True Indian Tales from American History in the Stirring Days of the Early Colonists (Boston: L. C. Page, 1904);

The Minute Boys of the Mohawk Valley (Boston: Estes, 1905);

When Washington Served the King; A Boy's Story of Border Warfare in 1754 (New York: Burt, 1905);

Among the Fur Traders (New York: Crowell, 1906);

Joey at the Fair (New York: Crowell, 1906);

The Light Keepers; A Story of the United States Light-house Service (New York: Dutton, 1906);

The Minute Boys of the Wyoming Valley (Boston: Estes, 1906);

Billy Goat's Story, attributed to Kaler as Amy Prentice (New York: Burt, circa 1906);

Brown Owl's Story, attributed to Kaler as Amy Prentice (New York: Burt, circa 1906);

Plodding Turtle's Story, attributed to Kaler as Amy Prentice (New York: Burt, circa 1906);

Quacky Duck's Story, attributed to Kaler as Amy Prentice (New York: Burt, circa 1906);

Aboard the "Hylow" on Sable Island Bank (New York: Dutton, 1907);

Commodore Barney's Young Spies; A Boy's Story of the Burning of the City of Washington (New York: Burt, 1907);

The Minute Boys of South Carolina; A story of "How We Boys Aided Marion, the Swamp Fox" (Boston: Estes, 1907);

The Wreck of the "Ocean Queen"; A Story of the Sea (Boston: Page, 1907);

Afloat in Freedom's Cause; The Story of Two Boys in the War of 1812 (New York: Burt, 1908);

The Cruise of the "Phoebe"; A Story of Lobster Buying on the Eastern Coast (Boston: Estes, 1908);

The Minute Boys of Long Island; A Story of New York in 1776 (Boston: Estes, 1908);

Two Stowaways Aboard the "Ellen Maria" (New York: Crowell, 1908);

The Cruise of the "Pickering"; A Boy's Story of Privateering in 1780 (New York: Burt, 1909);

The Minute Boys of New York City (Boston: Estes, 1909);

"The Sarah Jane," Dicky Dalton, Captain; A Story of Tugboating in Portland Harbor (Boston: Estes, 1909);

Calvert of Maryland; A Story of Lord Baltimore's Colony (New York: American Book Company, 1910);

The Cruise of the "Sally D." (Philadelphia: Penn, 1910);

Geography of Maine (Portland: Eagle Press, 1910);

Mary of Plymouth; A Story of the Pilgrim Settlement (New York: American Book Company, 1910);

The Minute Boys of Boston (Boston: Estes, 1910);

Peter of Amsterdam; A Story of Old New York (New York: American Book Company, 1910);

Richard of Jamestown; A Story of the Virginia Colony (New York: American Book Company, 1910);

Roy Barton's Adventures on the Mexican Border (New York: Burt, 1910);

Ruth of Boston; A Story of the Massachusetts Bay Colony (New York: American Book Company, 1910);

Stephen of Philadelphia; A Story of Penn's Colony (New York: American Book Company, 1910);

The Wireless Station at Silver Fox Farm (New York: Crowell, 1910);

With Grant at Vicksburg; A Boy's Story of the Siege of Vicksburg (New York: Burt, 1910);

The Aeroplane at Silver Fox Farm (New York: Crowell, 1911);

Boy Scouts in the Maine Woods (New York: Crowell, 1911);

The Camp on Indian Island (Philadelphia: Penn, 1911);

The Minute Boys of Philadelphia (Boston: Estes, 1911);

Old Ben; The Friend of Toby Tyler and Mr. Stubbs' Brother (New York & London: Harper, 1911);

Ralph Gurney's Oil Speculation (New York: Burt, 1911);

With Sherman to the Sea; A Boy's Story of General Sherman's Famous March and Capture of Savannah (New York: Burt, 1911);

Antoine of Oregon; A Story of the Oregon Trail (New York: American Book Company, 1912);

Benjamin of Ohio; A Story of the Settlement of Marietta (New York: American Book Company, 1912);

Building an Airship at Silver Fox Farm (New York: Crowell, 1912);

Hannah of Kentucky; A Story of the Wilderness Road (New York: American Book Company, 1912);

The Minute Boys of Yorktown (Boston: Estes, 1912);

Seth of Colorado; A Story of the Settlement of Denver (New York: American Book Company, 1912);

"Wanted" and Other Stories (New York & London: Harper, 1912);

The Wreck of the "Princess" (Philadelphia: Penn, 1912);

Airship Cruising from Silver Fox Farm (New York: Crowell, 1913);

Boy Scouts in a Lumber Camp (New York: Crowell, 1913);

Martha of California; A Story of the California Trail (New York: American Book Company, 1913);

Philip of Texas; A Story of Sheep Raising in Texas (New York: American Book Company, 1913);

The Roaring Lions; or, The Famous Club of Ashbury (New York & London: Harper, 1913);

"Across the Range" and Other Stories (New York & London: Harper, 1914);

The Club at Crow's Corner (Philadelphia: Penn, 1915);

Tom Dexter Goes to School (Philadelphia: Penn, 1915).

OTHER: *The Story of American Heroism; Thrilling Narratives of Personal Adventures During the Great Civil War, as Told by the Medal Winners Role of Honor Men*, edited by Otis (New York: Werner, 1896);

The Life of John Paul Jones, Written from Original Letters and Manuscripts in the Possession of Relatives, and from the Collection Prepared by John Henry Shelburne. Together With Chevalier Jones' Own Account of the Campaign of the Liman, compiled and edited by Otis (New York: Burt, 1900).

James Otis Kaler, a popular and prolific writer of boys' adventure stories in the late nineteenth century, is remembered today as the author of *Toby Tyler; or, Ten Weeks with a Circus* (1881), a work which has gone through some thirty editions and remains in print. His other writings—numbering some one hundred and fifty—are largely forgotten, although many of them saw more than one printing in the author's lifetime. Aside from his authorship of *Toby Tyler*, he merits consideration because he so typified that late nineteenth-century spirit combining individualism, moralism, didacticism, and national pride.

Kaler, the son of James Otis and Maria Thompson Kaler, was born in Frankfort (now Winterport), Maine, on 19 March 1848. His father owned a summer hotel in Scarboro, and his childhood appears to have been happy, if uneventful. Writing seems to have been his calling and he was probably little more than thirteen when he went to Boston and found a job as a reporter with the *Boston Journal*. His paper sent him, when he was sixteen, to cover the Civil War—an assignment which undoubtedly instilled in him a sense of patriotism and a love of adventure, qualities which are pervasive in his later writings.

Though the chronology is hazy, his early experiences included a stint as a publicity man for a circus, which had a profound influence on his writing of *Toby Tyler*, and he spent some time in Philadelphia where he wrote syndicated sermons for a publishing house. These packaged sermons were preached from pulpits across the United States. He also worked for various newspapers in New York, as well as serving on the editorial staff of *Frank Leslie's Boys' and Girls' Weekly*. His connection with this magazine deserves some examination. Published between 1866 and 1884, the magazine gained a reputation for its sensationalized stories often with exotic settings and laced with Victorian moralism. It contained many serialized stories of poor young men achieving fame and fortune against overwhelming odds. If the magazine seldom exhibited quality, it was nevertheless extraordinarily popular, and it does not seem unreasonable to speculate that Kaler's own style may have been significantly influenced by his association with Frank Leslie, an entrepreneur of the first order. Indeed, much of Kaler's work bears the stamp of formulaic writing so often dictated by journals whose chief concern is increasing circulation. It was, in fact, in the magazines that Kaler's first great success (and his greatest success) appeared. *Toby Tyler; or, Ten Weeks with a Circus* was first serialized in *Harper's Young People* in 1880. Among the periodicals to which he contributed was *St. Nicholas*, in which his *Jenny Wren's Boarding-house* was serialized beginning in 1887, as was *Teddy and Carrots* in 1896.

Toby Tyler was immediately popular and was published in book form by Harper the year after its magazine appearance. Toby Tyler is a young boy from the fictional town of Guilford—a town which is said to be Kaler's boyhood home of Winterport, Maine. (There is, incidentally, a town by the name of Guilford in Maine, but it is inland whereas Toby Tyler's home is on the coast.) Actually, there is little in the setting of *Toby Tyler* that

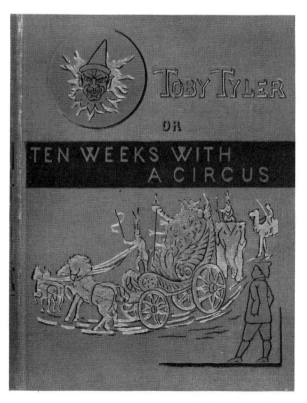

Front cover for Kaler's greatest commercial success, a novel loosely based on his experiences as a publicity man for a circus (Baldwin Library, University of Florida Libraries)

makes it distinctive and the location is of almost no importance. There is evidence that Kaler's own youthful experiences are recalled in the book. He had a childhood friend named Toby Thompson who made a great impression upon him, although there is no reason to suspect that this friend supplied any more than his first name for the novel. There is also mention, among Kaler's reminiscences, of someone named Steve Stubb who was locally famous for his root beer during the author's childhood. A Steve Stubbs is referred to in *Toby Tyler*—he never appears—and it is for him that Toby names his closest companion, a monkey. Toby remarks, "You look just like him, only he don't have quite so many whiskers." It is also possible that the characters of Toby's aunt and uncle, as well as others, were modeled on childhood acquaintances of the author. Kaler did not typically draw on his personal experiences for inspiration in his writing, and that may be regrettable, for *Toby Tyler* is unquestionably his best work and contains his only memorable characters.

The plot is simple. Toby, an orphan who lives with a couple he calls his aunt and uncle, although they are his foster parents and not related, is lured to the circus by an unscrupulous candy man. The boy realizes his mistake almost immediately and the romance of circus life quickly vanishes. The focus of the story becomes Toby's effort to save enough money to make his way back home to his aunt and uncle, whose essential goodness he now realizes.

It is worth dwelling on the matter of money for a moment. Kaler's young heroes are usually from families richer in love than in money and the prudent handling of meager finances is a continuing concern of these fellows. In *Adventures of a Country Boy at the County Fair* (1893), the potential conflict with the villains is virtually undermined by the phenomenal financial success of the hero, a simple country boy, in his entrepreneurial efforts during the course of the fair. In *Josiah in New York* (1893), there is a laborious accounting of young Josiah's expenditures during his stay in the big city. The common theme of these books is that of the simple youth coming by his money honestly, understanding its great importance, and therefore watching over it with great care if not always with success. Unlike the heroes of Horatio Alger, however, Kaler's boys do not generally soar to wealth and fame. The good life is the simple life, graced with honesty and hard work.

But to return to *Toby Tyler*, Toby's closest companion, the circus monkey Mr. Stubbs, is responsible for losing all Toby's hard-earned and carefully saved money, but not even this disaster can come between them. The fact that Toby actually steals Mr. Stubbs from the circus is not regarded as a criminal action by the author, which is difficult to understand except that Toby's intentions are good-hearted. Kaler introduces some interesting people who are attracted to Toby's ingenuous character (an attraction modern readers may not easily comprehend). Among his newfound friends are Mr. and Mrs. Treat, the circus thin man and fat lady, and there are also Old Ben, a kindly wagon driver, and little Ella, a child bareback rider whose shallow character is about as interesting as Toby's. With the blessings of his friends, Toby finally manages to escape the circus and the clutches of the wicked candy man. He takes with him Mr. Stubbs, who is subsequently killed by a hunter, mistaking him for a game animal. The death of Mr. Stubbs seems designed to reinforce Toby's lesson about the dire consequences of running away from home, and it also allows for some popular sentimentality. The grief-stricken Toby, cured of his wanderlust, finally returns home to a forgiving (and even repentant) uncle, who has longed for Toby as his own flesh and blood. The continuing interest in the book over the years undoubtedly has to do with its circus setting and circus characters, including Mr. Stubbs. (The fact that the sequel to *Toby Tyler* was called *Mr. Stubbs's Brother* suggests that the monkey was an extremely popular element in the original book.) The real interest in the book is in the adventures of Toby and not his character; Kaler does not write character studies. *Toby Tyler*, which has been recently republished, was exceedingly popular as late as the 1940s and 1950s, and in 1960, Walt Disney produced a motion picture version starring Kevin Corcoran.

Regarding *Toby Tyler's* further influence, this speculation is gingerly offered. For much of the first half of the twentieth century, there was a form of tent show popular chiefly in the Midwest, known as the Toby show. These shows featured a simple country boy named Toby, freckle-faced and red-headed, who continually outwitted the city slicker. Most of these shows were improvised farces relying on the talents of actors rather than on the ingenuity of the scripts. The idea seems to have been inspired or at least strongly influenced by the circus. While some studies have been made of these shows, they have failed to reveal the source of the name Toby, other than to say that it was a name commonly applied to a country boy. But consider the following description of the boy Toby Tyler at the beginning of the novel: "Toby was a very small boy,

with a round head covered with short red hair, a face as speckled as any turkey's egg, but thoroughly good-natured looking. . . . " It is difficult not to wonder if somewhere in someone's unconscious, Kaler's hero remained indelible and eventually gave his name to a whole new progeny of simple heroes.

Almost immediately after the success of *Toby Tyler*, Kaler produced its sequel, *Mr. Stubbs's Brother* (1883). Toby is a year older and enjoying a happy life with Uncle Daniel and Aunt Olive. To pass the long summer days, Toby and his friends decide to produce their own circus. At the same time, Toby befriends Abner, an orphan and a "cripple" (as if one affliction were not enough to evoke the reader's sentiment). The threads come together when, during the regular summer visit of Toby's old circus (and a happy reunion with his circus friends), Abner is seriously injured in an accident. His decline is steady and the boys' circus project is given a new purpose—Abner's entertainment. The race against time is felt as the boys rush to perfect their acts and prepare their exhibits before the summer's end and before Abner's expected death. Once again it is a monkey who foils the plot. Mr. Stubbs's Brother—a monkey given Toby by his circus friends during their visit and named for Toby's first monkey companion—manages to wreak havoc with the improvised circus, letting loose animals and tearing down the tent just before the grand opening. The loss is irreparable and following hard upon is Abner's demise. While Kaler does reintroduce his successful characters from the first book—the Treats, Old Ben, Little Ella—they have little to do but shower kindnesses upon Toby (who has not become much more interesting since the first book). Toby's young friends are no more fascinating than he is, and Abner's lengthy decline is more tedious than heartrending. There is no suspense, no character development, no conflict—unfortunately all typical of much of Kaler's writing.

Before considering the historical novels, which constitute the bulk of Kaler's writing, although not his best, it is useful to look at a work such as *Josiah in New York*, for it contains many elements typical of Kaler and his time. Subtitled *A Coupon from the Fresh Air Fund*, this work has as its theme the superiority of country living over that of the city. Josiah, a wholesome country boy, is invited to spend a vacation in the city with some young friends. His excitement soon dissipates as he encounters one misfortune after another—he meets hoodlums, heartless landladies, impoverished children, and, when his friends try their best

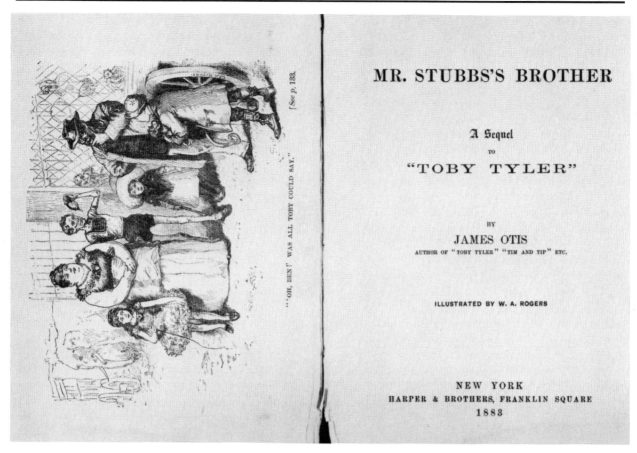

Frontispiece and title page for Kaler's novel in which Toby's circus friends pay him a visit and present him with a monkey whom he names Mr. Stubbs's Brother (Baldwin Library, University of Florida Libraries)

to show him a good time in the city, he seems determined to remain miserable and longs, with annoying persistence, for the country. His one happy experience in the city occurs when he sees the monkeys in the Central Park zoo (either Kaler himself had a special attachment to monkeys or he used them because of their appeal to children who read his books—or both). Readers are likely to tire of Josiah's harping on the city's faults and the country's virtues, and many will be perturbed by the boy's seeming ingratitude toward his friends' earnest efforts to entertain him. He eventually persuades his parents to take in a poor orphan girl, saving her from the greedy and villainous clutches of the city slickers. As for his other young friends from the city, they can hardly wait until their next opportunity to visit the country. The loose plot, the thin characterization, the lack of real conflict, and the moralizing are all typical of Kaler's fiction.

Perhaps as a result of his early experiences as a newspaper writer, Kaler developed an interest in travel adventures and historical fiction. He wrote tales of exotic places—the Yucatán, Nicaragua, the

Tropics—and had a strong preference for sea stories. Kaler's son fondly recalls his father telling stories to the neighborhood children about pirates and shipwrecks in which he himself figured as the rescuer. At one time Kaler purchased a steam yacht into which he was obliged to put nearly everything he had simply to make it seaworthy. In addition, he seems always to have had an interest in youth and in educating children. So it is not surprising that he should take the path of historical fiction, with particular emphasis on sea adventures. War stories were an overwhelming favorite with him—particularly those about the Revolutionary War and the War of 1812. He virtually ignored the Civil War, probably because he found it difficult to romanticize and unsuitable for his patriotic lessons. As with most of his writings, his historical novels remind readers that he once wrote sermons, although he is not reluctant to sensationalize his works with appropriate violence (a reminder that he also once worked for Frank Leslie). There is, nevertheless, considerably more bravado than bloodshed. In his historical fiction Kaler does not

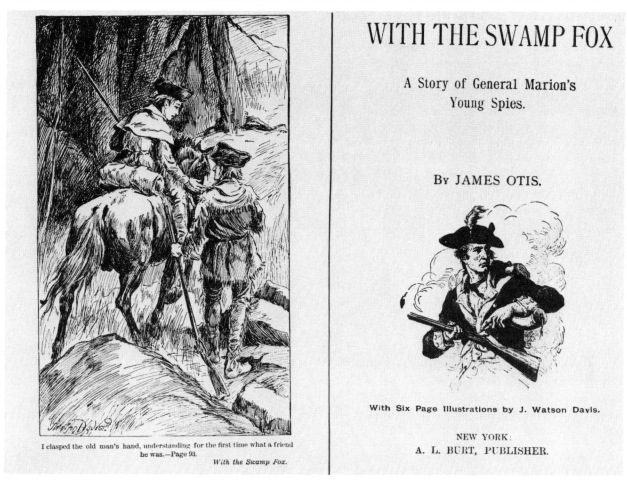

I clasped the old man's hand, understanding for the first time what a friend he was.—Page 93.

With the Swamp Fox.

WITH THE SWAMP FOX

A Story of General Marion's Young Spies.

By JAMES OTIS.

With Six Page Illustrations by J. Watson Davis.

NEW YORK:
A. L. BURT, PUBLISHER.

Frontispiece and title page for one of several historical novels by Kaler published in 1899 (Baldwin Library, University of Florida Libraries)

hesitate to include footnotes and even direct quotations from published histories. *With Perry on Lake Erie* (1899) is a fictional account of the events leading up to and including the Battle of Lake Erie during the War of 1812, and it is told in the manner of the popular "We Were There with . . . " series published by Grosset and Dunlap in the mid-twentieth century. It is a first-person narrative with footnotes included by the "Editor" and with a final commentary by the "Editor" who quotes at length from Benson J. Lossing's *Pictorial Field-Book of the War of 1812*. Even the boy narrator introduces quotations from Lossing's work. All this suggests that Kaler's purpose was more didactic than artistic.

Occasionally Kaler dabbled in something which more closely resembled history. His *The Life of John Paul Jones* (1900) is basically a compilation of quotations from letters and manuscripts recounting the important incidents of Jones's life. And he also edited *The Story of American Heroism*

(1896), some letters of Civil War Medal of Honor winners (a rare treatment of that conflict by Kaler). In *Mary of Plymouth* (1910) he employs a female central figure—also a rarity for Kaler—in a work which is a thinly disguised history of the Pilgrims' first year in America. By the last decade of his life, he was devoting all his writing energies to almost formulaic fiction designed to teach history to school children. But that was not all he was doing. Around 1898, Kaler returned to Maine and two important things happened to him. On 1 March 1898, he married his secretary, Amy Louella Scammon. And also in that year he was named superintendent of schools for the newly created town of South Portland, Maine, as well as for the nearby town of Cape Elizabeth. He seems to have had no special educational qualifications for the position, and the appointment may have been an honorific one. At any rate, the new job did not interfere with his writing. Indeed, his output steadily grew almost until the time of his death. He was increasingly in demand on the lecture circuit and spoke on a variety of topics—including himself. By all accounts, his marriage was exceedingly happy. His wife bore him two sons, Stephen and Otis, when he was over fifty years of age, and he greatly relished his role as father. He and his wife entertained frequently, and she often accompanied him on his travels to speaking engagements across the country. He seems to have been little concerned about money and lived modestly. Indeed, from external appearances his life was relatively free from hardship, which may explain why he was unable to project genuine conflict into his novels.

By and large his writings exhibit little variety in general subject matter and treatment, but about 1906, four books appeared which were entirely different from anything he had done before. *Billy Goat's Story*, *Brown Owl's Story*, *Plodding Turtle's Story*, and *Quacky Duck's Story* are short books illustrated by J. Watson Davis, obviously intended for much younger readers than Kaler was accustomed to writing for and published under a new pseudonym, Amy Prentice. It is by the authority of the James Otis Kaler Collection at the South Portland Public Library in Maine that this pseudonym is estab-

lished, although the *National Union Catalog* does not include it. These books may have been written specifically for his own children and the pseudonym suggests the strong influence of his wife—Amy—who, as his one-time secretary, might have been considered as something of an apprentice. This is all speculation, and the extent to which these works are Kaler's or to what degree his wife had a hand in them may never be known.

From the turn of the century on Kaler was producing from four to twelve new books a year, and as late as 1915, three years after his death, previously unpublished works were still appearing. He died, a popular and admired figure, following a short illness on 11 December 1912 in Portland.

Reference:

Larry Dale Clark, "Toby Shows: A Form of American Popular Theater," Ph.D. dissertation, University of Illinois, 1963.

Papers:

The James Otis Kaler Collection is at the South Portland Public Library, South Portland, Maine.

Harriet M. Lothrop
(Margaret Sidney)
(22 June 1844-2 August 1924)

Ruth K. MacDonald
New Mexico State University

BOOKS: *Tressy's Christmas*, by Sidney and others (Boston: Lothrop, 1880);

Five Little Peppers and How They Grew (Boston: Lothrop, 1881; London: Hodder & Stoughton, 1881);

Half Year at Broncton (Boston: Lothrop, 1881);

So as by Fire (Boston: Lothrop, 1881; London: Maxwell, 1883);

Ballad of the Lost Hare (Boston: Lothrop, 1882);

The Pettibone Name: A New England Story (Boston: Lothrop, 1882);

How They Went to Europe (Boston: Lothrop, 1884);

Ringing Words and Other Sketches (Boston: Lothrop, 1885);

On Easter Day (Boston: Lothrop, 1886);

The Golden West as Seen by the Ridgeway Club (Boston: Lothrop, 1886);

Hester, and Other New England Stories (Boston: Lothrop, 1886);

The Minute Man: A Ballad of "The Shot Heard Round the World" (Boston: Lothrop, 1886);

Two Modern Little Princes and Other Stories (Boston: Lothrop, 1886);

A New Departure for Girls (Boston: Lothrop, 1886);

Dilly and the Captain (Boston: Lothrop, 1887);

How Tony and Dorothy Made and Kept a Christian Home (Boston: Lothrop, 1888);

Old Concord: Her Highways and Byways (Boston: Lothrop, 1888);

St. George and the Dragon: A Story of Boy Life, and Kensington Junior (Boston: Lothrop, 1888);

The Little Red Shop (Boston: Lothrop, 1889);

Our Town: Dedicated to All Members of the Y.P.S.C.E. (Boston: Lothrop, 1889);

An Adirondack Cabin: A Family Story (Boston: Lothrop, 1890);

Five Little Peppers Midway (Boston: Lothrop, 1890; London: Unwin, 1909);

Rob: A Story for Boys (Boston: Lothrop, 1891);

Five Little Peppers Grown Up (Boston: Lothrop, 1892);

The Kaleidoscope, by Sidney and others (Boston: Lothrop, 1892);

Little Paul and the Frisbie School (Boston: Lothrop, 1893);

Whittier With the Children (Boston: Lothrop, 1893);

The Old Town Pump: A Story of East and West (Boston: Lothrop, 1895);

The Gingham Bag: The Tale of an Heirloom (Boston: Lothrop, 1896);

Phronsie Pepper: The Youngest of the Five Little Peppers (Boston: Lothrop, 1897);

A Little Maid of Concord Town: A Romance of the American Revolution (Boston: Lothrop, 1898);

The Stories Polly Pepper Told to the Five Little Peppers (Boston: Lothrop, 1899); republished as *Polly Pepper's Book* (New York: Grosset & Dunlap, 1947);

The Judges' Cave; Being a Romance of the New Haven Colony in the Days of the Regicides, 1661 (Boston: Lothrop, 1900);

The Adventures of Joel Pepper (Boston: Lothrop, 1900);

Five Little Peppers Abroad (Boston: Lothrop, 1902);

Sally: Mrs. Tubbs (Boston: Lothrop, 1903);

Five Little Peppers at School (Boston: Lothrop, 1903);

Five Little Peppers and Their Friends (Boston: Lothrop, 1904);

Ben Pepper (Boston: Lothrop, 1905);

Two Little Friends in Norway (Boston: Lothrop, Lee & Shepard, 1906);

Five Little Peppers in the Little Brown House (Boston: Lothrop, Lee & Shepard, 1907);

A Little Maid of Boston Town (Boston: Lothrop, Lee & Shepard, 1910);

Our Davie Pepper (Boston: Lothrop, Lee & Shepard, 1916).

OTHER: *Lullabies and Jingles,* edited by Sidney (Boston: Lothrop, 1893);

The Child's Day Book, with Helps Toward the Joy of Living and the Beautiful Heaven Above, edited by Sidney (Boston: Lothrop, 1893).

Harriet Mulford Stone Lothrop, who signed all of her works with the pseudonym Margaret Sidney, was the author of the Five Little Peppers series. The books concern the poor Pepper family with its five children, all of whom are happy in their poverty and rewarded eventually with wealth and a rich benefactor. Harriet Stone began writing of the Pepper family in short stories for *Wide Awake* monthly magazine for children in 1878. After the first two stories appeared, they were so popular that Stone was asked to write a year's worth of Pepper stories for the magazine. The stories were popular because of the obvious high spirits of the children while at play, for their optimism and hard work as well as moral rectitude in the face of temptation and nearly devastating poverty, and for the happiness of their home life.

Stone was born in New Haven, Connecticut, the daughter of architect Sidney Mason Stone and Harriet Mulford Stone. The family lived in luxury in the city of New Haven, where Stone was educated in private schools. The imagination which

Harriet M. Lothrop (Underwood & Underwood)

served her well as an author in adult life was cultivated in childhood by her avid reading and by trips which the family took to the country. On these trips she would search for a little brown house like the one she later created for the Peppers to live in and would imagine living there herself instead of in the confining elegance of the city houses which her father had built. She would imagine a family in the house and the happy times that they might have in the country. Her childhood daydreams eventually led to the series of vignettes about the Pepper family in their own little brown house in the mythical village of Badgertown.

Harriet Stone followed in the tradition of the American family story as established by Louisa May Alcott and Sarah Chauncy Woolsey (Susan Coolidge), but like Woolsey and unlike Alcott, she wrote for a young audience of both sexes. Life in the little brown house is particularly happy, and the family

is a close one; disruptions come from the outside, in the form of robbers or illness or accident rather than from internal squabbles. The Pepper children have no father; their mother must work at poorly paid jobs to support them. The children also help out as best they can, doing odd jobs and some of the housework. "To help mother" is the major theme of the first Pepper book and the others that followed it in the series. The mission keeps the children well behaved and hardworking; though they are occasionally despondent about their lack of money, they remember their purpose to be a credit to their mother and stick to their work with goodwill. The children are particularly adept at making do with what they have in order to celebrate holidays such as birthdays, Christmas, and Thanksgiving. When gifts from the outside do arrive, candy, food, or some other small donation from a friend, it is a cause for much celebration among

THE SURPRISE IS ALL THE DOCTOR COULD POSSIBLY ASK.

Illustration for Lothrop's Five Little Peppers and How They Grew *(Baldwin Library, University of Florida Libraries)*

the Peppers, and the gifts are all the more valuable for being so rare. The sequels follow the Peppers into their wealth at the benefit of an affluent friend who practically adopts them, but no matter how far the family travels, either socially or in distance from their origins, they recall their happy times in the little brown house and the virtues and discipline which their poverty has taught them.

The early Pepper stories attracted the attention of *Wide Awake*'s publisher Daniel Lothrop, whose avowed purpose was "to publish books which make for true, steadfast growth in right living." He was attracted to the optimism and moral fiber of the Pepper children and determined to know the woman behind the Margaret Sidney pseudonym. The two were married on 4 October 1881. Their daughter Margaret was born in 1885.

With Daniel Lothrop's encouragement, Harriet Lothrop filled out the background of the Peppers, assembled and revised the individual short stories to make them fit into a coherent story line, and published *Five Little Peppers and How They Grew* (1881) at her husband's publishing company. The "right living" of the Pepper family found a congenial place on the publisher Lothrop's list of books which prompted moral growth. The book was popular and has continued to be republished up to the present time. Children wrote to both the author and the publisher requesting further books of Pepper family adventures; the result was a series of twelve books, showing not only the further adventures of the Peppers while they are poor but also how the Pepper children grew up, established themselves in professions, and married.

Of all the Pepper books, the first one is the best; the others rework themes that are already enunciated in *Five Little Peppers and How They Grew*. The first book begins after the death of the Pepper children's father, who has left them and their mother no other inheritance besides the little brown house in which they live. The children are helpful to their hardworking mother and endure crises such as measles, injuries, and a temporarily missing baby sister with fortitude. They meet a rich young man who is vacationing in the neighborhood and who is immediately impressed by the warm affection between the Peppers. He himself is motherless, and his father is cold and uncaring about him. But the father, too, is taken with the Peppers when he meets them and invites them to live with him in his large, empty, elegant brown house in the city, which stands as a foil to the happiness and simplicity of the Peppers' home. Mrs. Pepper will not accept charity, and so will come only for a visit;

though she is poor, she is proud. But when Mr. King, the benefactor, hires her as a housekeeper, all objections are removed, and the Peppers stay permanently, calling Mr. King their grandfather and his son their brother. In the sequels, the Peppers are shown living in the large brown house, one which resembles the homes in which Lothrop lived and with which she was familiar. In spite of the romance of living in poverty in the country, Lothrop does not make the Peppers return to their former way of life; though she professed an idealized view of country life, she chose not to continue writing about it.

The story of *Five Little Peppers and How They Grew* is simply told with an earnestness that sometimes undercuts the spontaneous imaginative fancy of the children that makes them so attractive. Contemporary critics praised the book for its simplicity and for its unquestionable morality, but modern critics point to the lack of invention and the nearly perfect behavior of the children which makes them implausible. Poverty for them is almost blissful; Lothrop's portrayal of the condition of poverty is simpleminded in the sweetness of adversity that she finds in the family situation. In the sequels, the children continue their virtuous behavior, although they are not now poor and might now be inclined to fall into the ways of fashionable society. Their reminiscences of their early days in the later books are cloying and sentimental; the wealth with which they are rewarded is too fortuitous and equally as implausible as their goodness.

All the Pepper children establish themselves admirably in adult life. The girls marry well and have children, thus beginning a new bunch of little Peppers about whom stories will be told. The boys all enter worthy professions and make good. In the later books, such as *Phronsie Pepper* (1897) and *Five Little Peppers in the Little Brown House* (1907), the previously spontaneous Pepper children become staid and uninteresting, and it is clear that as Lothrop continued the series, her powers of invention failed, and she wrote more to satisfy readers who demanded to know how the Pepper children turned out than to gratify her own impulse to write.

Lothrop and her husband moved into Wayside, a historic house in Concord, Massachusetts, the former home of the Alcotts and the Nathaniel Hawthornes. The Lothrops took pains to restore the house and in the process became interested in the history of Concord and the preservation of the historic sites there. Lothrop wrote several children's novels and adult guidebooks about local history, all of which sold well because of her

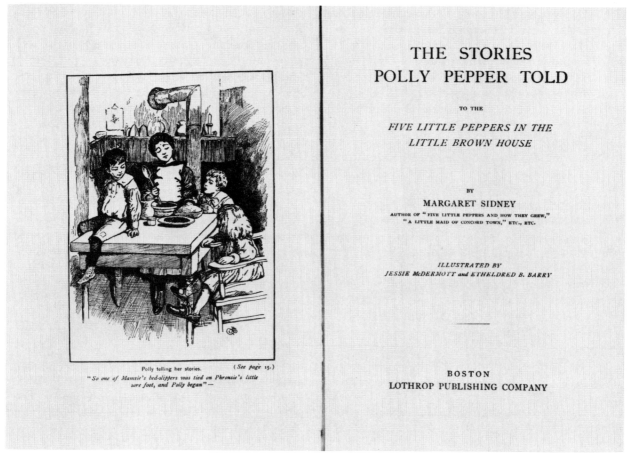

Frontispiece and title page for the fifth of twelve books about the Pepper children, published in 1899 (Baldwin Library, University of Florida Libraries)

established reputation as the Pepper family creator rather than from their independent literary merit. She also wrote other books for children, all of which concern good children who are frequently poor but hardworking. When her husband died in 1892, she managed his publishing company, selling it in 1894. In 1895, she founded the Concord chapter of the Daughters of the American Revolution. That same year she established the National Society of Children of the American Revolution in order that young people might learn the early history of America. Lothrop bought Orchard House, the building next to Wayside in which Louisa May Alcott wrote *Little Women* and in which the book is set. She held Orchard House for ten years until a nonprofit organization took over the maintenance and management of the building as a historic site.

Lothrop's works, especially the Pepper family stories, show the increasing sentimentality which the family story, especially when adapted for chil-

dren, took on. The idealization of the mother and of the deserving poor are evident here, and the continued demand for book after book in the Pepper series indicates the popular acceptance of such themes. Lothrop wrote, at least in the first Pepper book, for an audience of both sexes; in this way she broke the tradition of the family story written exclusively for girls. Certainly the wholesomeness of the Pepper tribe and their virtues in the face of adversity are still popular enough that *Five Little Peppers and How They Grew* continues to be read.

References:

Elizabeth Johnson, "Margaret Sidney vs. Harriet Lothrop," *Horn Book Magazine*, 47 (April 1971): 139-146, 313-320;

Margaret M. Lothrop, *The Wayside: Home of Authors* (Boston: American Book Company, 1940), pp. 153-187.

William Holmes McGuffey

(23 September 1800-4 May 1873)

Rebecca Lukens
Miami University

BOOKS: *The First Eclectic Reader* (Cincinnati: Truman & Smith, 1836);

The Second Eclectic Reader (Cincinnati: Truman & Smith, 1836);

The Third Eclectic Reader (Cincinnati: Truman & Smith, 1837);

The Fourth Eclectic Reader (Cincinnati: Truman & Smith, 1837);

The Eclectic Primer (Cincinnati: Truman & Smith, 1837).

William Holmes McGuffey, the second of eleven children of Alexander and Anna Holmes McGuffey, was born on 23 September 1800, on a farm near Washington, Pennsylvania. He became a teacher, professor, writer, and editor whose contribution to the field of children's literature lies not primarily in the creation of imaginative work but in the compiling of the McGuffey series of schoolbooks, the McGuffey Eclectic Readers. Some of what McGuffey included in the series was his own work; much of it was adapted from other sources, including other schoolbook series; other selections were by well-known writers or didactic verse written expressly for the series.

McGuffey's childhood from the age of two was spent near Youngstown, Ohio, in the hard life of rural America, the Northwest Territory of the pioneers. With his parents for his teachers, the boy read all that he could lay his hands on. He committed to memory many books of the Bible in their entirety and is said to have been able to recite from memory sermons he had heard only once. Like the stories about Abraham Lincoln, those about McGuffey include tales of reading by firelight as well as of long walks to borrow books from schoolmaster or preacher. As a youth McGuffey followed the custom of the time, becoming an itinerant who wandered over the Ohio territory. Many school districts claim McGuffey as one of those who stopped for a time in their communities, issued a call for pupils, and set up school.

One account of McGuffey's formal education has it that the Reverend Thomas Hughes, who ran the Old Stone Academy, overheard as he passed on horseback the impassioned prayers of Anna Holmes that her son be given an opportunity for further education. Hughes returned next morning to ask McGuffey's mother if there were any "likely" scholars around whom he might enroll. McGuffey became a student at the Old Stone Academy in Darlington, Pennsylvania, probably working for his tuition and maintenance by assisting in Reverend Hughes's garden, home, and church, rather than in the coal mines as most pupils did. For seventy-five cents a week he boarded at the academy and ate what the others did, an extremely simple diet.

Being turned down for a schoolmaster's job in Warren, Ohio, made McGuffey wish for more formal education. The two Yale graduates on the Board of Examiners who found McGuffey inadequately prepared did the young man a great service, because he then, in 1819, enrolled in Washington College, Washington, Pennsylvania. At Washington College he found in the Reverend Mr. Mylie an unusually good teacher, the perfect mentor for an eager and bright young man. Although McGuffey's A.B. degree is dated 26 September 1826, he had already been hired as a professor of ancient languages at Miami University, Oxford, Ohio, and had begun teaching late in the preceding year.

Less than fifteen months after joining the Miami University faculty, McGuffey, now almost twenty-seven, married Harriet Spinning, daughter of a Dayton judge. Stories of the romance, told by biographers in glowing and sentimental terms, report the necessity to court by letters addressed to the young woman's guardian, at that time, her brother. The couple circumvented the restrictions by underlining the initial of the middle name of Harriet's brother; thus McGuffey knew that his letters would go directly to her. To this marriage five children were born, two girls and three boys. Following the death of Harriet in 1850, McGuffey married Laura Howard, daughter of the dean of the School of Medicine at the University of Virginia. Their child, Anna, died at the age of four.

William Holmes McGuffey, early 1860s

During the Miami years, McGuffey was ordained a Presbyterian minister and preached in nearby communities. He argued with the Miami University president until he was permitted to teach courses in moral philosophy. During this time he also compiled the earliest of the Eclectic Readers for which he is famous. Truman and Smith, Cincinnati publishers, wished to produce a series of textbooks for the market in the opening West, composed at this time of Ohio, Kentucky, and Indiana, states newly added to the Union. Their first choice for writer of the textbooks was Catharine Beecher, daughter of Lyman Beecher and sister of Harriet Beecher Stowe, but since she was not interested in the education of young children, she declined. Driving a hard bargain with McGuffey, Truman and Smith committed him to compiling a series of four "graded readers" for royalties of ten percent up to one thousand dollars, at which point all profits belonged to the publishers. In 1836 the first two readers, graded not by class but by degree of reading difficulty, were on the market; *The Third Eclectic Reader* and *The Fourth Eclectic Reader* as well as the first *The Eclectic Primer* appeared soon thereafter in 1837. Harriet McGuffey is believed to have done the major part of the *Primer*.

In 1836, before the success of the Eclectic Readers (so named to show the breadth of the educational theory behind them) was certain, a new college was formed in Cincinnati and got off to a good start with McGuffey as its president. In 1839, when financial difficulties caused by the Panic of 1837 threatened to close Cincinnati College, McGuffey was persuaded to accept the presidency of Ohio University at Athens.

Despite another promising start, McGuffey soon found himself in difficult times again. Citizens of Athens who owned homes on the land granted to the university protested the increased assessments badly needed to maintain the university and the assessments were rescinded by the state legislature. Other difficulties kept the university from prospering, one of them the Calvinistic disciplinary measures of the stern new president. Another arose from McGuffey's efforts to save the young elms planted on the campus; he fenced in the campus, and fenced out the Athenian cows and pigs. Furor fostered by parents sent children into the streets to taunt the president with mudballs, and he responded by laying about him with a red leather horsewhip. One day in 1843, however, mud-covered and fed up with the animosity, he went home, told his wife to pack immediately, and left town. When he was well out of Athens, he wrote a letter of resignation.

Less colorful are the last years of McGuffey's life. For two years he taught at Woodward College in Cincinnati. Then, in 1845, he was appointed professor of moral philosophy at the University of Virginia, where he stayed until his death on 4 May 1873. Royalty payments from McGuffey's books had long since disappeared, but after the Civil War his publishers did show some gratitude in the form of Christmas donations of "choice smoked hams," contributions no doubt important to the welfare of the family. As a teacher, McGuffey was courteous and dignified, a man who tolerated no levity and spoke in perfectly modulated tones. According to Marcellus Green, McGuffey's student and a member of the University of Virginia class of 1872, McGuffey's learning was "profound" and "inexhaustible"; his teaching techniques were painstaking and highly successful.

McGuffey also participated in the activities of a group called the Western Literary Institute, founded in 1834. The Institute included leading proponents of state and national public education from all parts of the U.S. McGuffey, a leader among those who came from Ohio, Kentucky, Missouri, Indiana, Illinois, Louisiana, and Tennessee, was eloquent in his appeals for trained teachers, as well as for leisure time so that workers too might be educated.

Cincinnati was the intellectual headquarters of the new attitudes; of 385 printing presses in the West, 159 were in Ohio. The Ohio country at the time the first McGuffey Eclectic Readers were published was made up of about one hundred small towns plus the farms scattered about the valleys,

38 ECLECTIC SERIES.

LESSON XVI.

fụll lōad hĕav′y mid′dle hĕav′i er
slip wrŏng hănd′le brŏth′er de çēived′

A KIND BROTHER.

1. A boy was once sent from home to take a basket of things to his grandmother.

2. The basket was so full that it was very heavy. So his little brother went with him, to help carry the load.

SECOND READER. 39

3. They put a pole under the handle of the basket, and each then took hold of an end of the pole. In this way they could carry the basket very nicely.

4. Now the older boy thought, "My brother Tom does not know about this pole.

5. "If I slip the basket near him, his side will be heavy, and mine light; but if the basket is in the middle of the pole, it will be as heavy for me as it is for him.

6. "Tom does not know this as I do. But I will not do it. It would be wrong, and I will not do what is wrong."

7. Then he slipped the basket quite near his own end of the pole. His load was now heavier than that of his little brother.

8. Yet he was happy; for he felt that he had done right. Had he deceived his brother, he would not have felt at all happy.

112 ECLECTIC SERIES.

7. "He did come home. After all, he might still have been useful and happy, for his friends were willing to forgive the past. For a time, things went on well. He married a lovely woman, gave up his bad habits, and was doing well.

8. "But one thing, boys, ruined him forever. In the city, he had learned to take strong drink, and he said to me once, that when a man begins to drink, he never knows where it will end. 'Therefore,' said Tom, 'beware of the first drink!'

9. "It was not long before he began to follow his old habit. He knew the danger, but it seemed as if he could not resist his desire to drink. His poor mother soon died of grief and shame. His lovely wife followed her to the grave.

10. "He lost the respect of all, went on from bad to worse, and has long been a perfect sot. Last night, I had a letter from the city, stating that Tom Smith has been found guilty of stealing, and sent to the state-prison for ten years.

11. "There I suppose he will die, for he is now old. It is dreadful to think to what an end he has come. I could not but think,

THIRD READER. 113

as I read the letter, of what he said to me years ago, 'Beware of the first drink!'

12. "Ah, my dear boys, when old Uncle Philip is gone, remember that he told you

the story of Tom Smith, and said to you, 'Beware of the first drink!' 'The man who does this will never be a drunkard."

DEFINITIONS.—3. Hŏr′ri bly, *in a dreadful manner, terribly.* 4. Dē′çent, *modest, respectable.* 9. Re sĭst′, *withstand, overcome.* 10. Sŏt, *an habitual drunkard.* Guĭlt′y, *justly chargeable with a crime.*
3, 8.

Pages from 1879 revised editions of two McGuffey Eclectic Readers (Baldwin Library, University of Florida Libraries)

which added up to a population of about two million. Immigrants from Ireland, England, and Germany constituted about five hundred thousand inhabitants, the largest proportion of German origins. Truman and Smith saw that the foreign population was ripe for schoolbooks that spoke to their need to learn the language and spread the doctrine of personal and national growth and hard work. In tone and content the readers reflected the frontier spirit of the West. Eastern seaboard, Puritan ideas were diluted in this region, where children were less confined and less willing to read tales of the Day of Doom. Caught in the pioneering spirit of their parents, they wanted to read about moving onward and upward.

William Holmes McGuffey is responsible for the first four Eclectic Readers, although he is falsely given credit for work done by his younger brother Alexander, the compiler of *McGuffey's Rhetorical Guide* (1844; republished the same year as the *Fifth Eclectic Reader*), the major editor of the *McGuffey Eclectic Speller* (1846), and the one totally responsible for the *New Sixth Eclectic Reader* (1857). Alexander McGuffey, who concentrated his efforts on a thriving law practice, also taught English in a Cincinnati academy. Truman and Smith, by the time of the publication of the sixth reader, were eager to capitalize on William McGuffey's initial success; they managed by printing with a flourish Alexander's initial *A* to make it look like a *W* for William. In a huff, Alexander asked that his name not be given at all, and after a few years the name of William Holmes McGuffey appeared on the fifth and sixth Eclectic Readers. In some editions the publishers included the deceptive note that the author was "formerly a professor at Oxford." One biographer comments that as far as is known, Alexander was not even rewarded with choice smoked hams at Christmas.

The McGuffey Eclectic Readers have been both praised and criticized. Both attitudes seem justified. Obviously they filled the need of the time, but from a modern viewpoint they exhibit heavy didacticism, naive optimism, slippery hypocrisies, stern attitudes toward the young, division of the world into the good and the bad, and perpetuation of the least desirable Victorian attitudes. The white Protestant population was their readership; the books espoused such social movements as Temperance and ignored others, including slavery. Later Readers contained selections from the works of the best American writers, Washington Irving and Nathaniel Hawthorne among them, but also included the heavy-handed instruction of Ann

Alexander McGuffey, whose work on several McGuffey textbooks has been credited to his older brother William

Taylor, Maria Edgeworth, and Sarah Josepha Hale. The literary taste of the McGuffeys tended toward moralizers rather than artists, poetasters rather than poets.

The most significant concerns that the stories and verses deal with can be divided into three overlapping categories: social issues, moral issues, and religious beliefs. The stories, primarily for boys since McGuffey had little contact with girls in the classrooms of the day, show class-consciousness and antiurban sentiment; the kind farmer rescues the haughty nobleman who has fallen into the brook. The rich boy is eternally aware of his less fortunate countryman and wishes to give clothing, homes, land, and food to the poor.

Although heavenly reward is frequently promised, the good boy often gets an earthly reward within a matter of minutes, having to wait less time than did the heroes of McGuffey's contemporary Horatio Alger, Jr. At other times, punishment follows relentlessly behind misdeed, as in Aesop's fable about the boy who cried wolf. Since Truman and Smith had a good market for the Readers in the South, they wanted to avoid offending on the slavery issue. Indeed, McGuffey seems not to have had a firm view on the matter; his strongest references are to freeing a cageful of birds purchased by a wealthy man, an allegory discreet enough to keep from offending Southern readers. Pro-Union support seems clear in the story of "The Seven Sticks," the often told tale that demonstrates that the strength of a bonded group is greater than that of separate individuals.

Many subtle and not-so-subtle biases are evident in the Readers. While they praise education, they are anti-intellectual; lawyers, journalists, politicians, and gentlemen are all treated as superfluous. Hard work and a basic education for an agrarian society are often most praised. Victorian sex roles are constantly reinforced, not only by the nearly total absence of girls in the stories themselves but also by the subordinate roles of female characters when they do appear. In "The Greedy Girl," for example, gluttony serves to contrast with the sensibility of the bees, squirrels, and kittens. More than other stories, however, those of Washington Irving in the later Readers do dignify womanhood.

Moral issues are confronted throughout the Readers, too, sometimes in ways that seem to contemporary readers uncomfortably punitive. "The Lazy Schoolboy" is derisively laughed at for his indolence. In "The Little Chimney Sweep" the message is that by stealing small things, children become robbers. This short narrative about a boy who resists the temptation to steal a watch, lapses into a long harangue: the tale was apparently so heavily didactic that it was omitted in later editions. A negative example of consideration for others is given in "The Thoughtless Boys," a story of two boys who trip others by tying long grass across the path. A man who is running for a surgeon to bleed their own father falls and is injured, as once again, immediate consequences result from bad behavior. A moral issue contemporary readers may find offensively treated is the implied instruction to the poor to be content with poverty; its corollary, that the rich have an obligation to be benevolent, is only partially redemptive. The morals are many: A place for everything and everything in its place. The good and the honest will become rich and important. Speak the truth—as little George Washington did—and all will be well. Withholding love is just punishment for the bad child. Disobedience may bring on death by drowning. Truancy and trickery will lead to greater disobedience and a life of crime. Charity and personal industry reap rewards here and in heaven. Charity is better than envy, and gratitude has benefits. One may frighten one's friends to the point of mental derangement. And there are many more, equally strong.

Although God is often both felt and seen, religious issues are treated with caution; the Omniscient Eye appears in many selections. The religious emphasis, although surely Christian, seldom mentions Christ. Nature is evidence of the Creator's existence. But since the Readers' market was largely Protestant, a few anti-Catholic remarks did creep into the nonsectarian statements. Until 1857 a practice sentence in the teaching apparatus following one story read "He cannot tolerate a papist." Efforts were made to eliminate material of a "denominational character"; the selection entitled "The Character of Martin Luther," which included this statement, had been omitted by 1843: "The accounts of his [Luther's] death filled the Roman Catholic party with excessive as well as indecent joy." *The New England Primer* read by Eastern children told of the innately sinful nature of human beings condemned by original sin. McGuffey's Eclectic Readers, although highly didactic, at least occasionally depicted a God of benevolence who might even be one's friend.

The McGuffey Eclectic Readers remain interesting today primarily because of their historical impact and their reflection of American life and tastes in the nineteenth century. It has often been said that the influence of William Holmes McGuffey through his Readers was nearly as profound as that of the Bible. The 122,000,000 copies printed of the McGuffey Eclectic Readers helped form the moral, social, and literary attitudes of several generations and contributed much to the shaping of Middle America. The Readers, however, are still in use. According to a 1984 article in *Smithsonian* magazine there are "perhaps hundreds" of private and public schools that have recently adopted McGuffey's texts as part of their "response to a perceived erosion of quality in the American classroom."

References:

Stanley W. Lindberg, introduction to *The Annotated McGuffey: Selections from the McGuffey Eclectic Readers, 1836-1920* (New York: Van Nostrand Reinhold, 1976);

Harvey C. Minnich, *William Holmes McGuffey and His Readers* (New York: American Book Company, 1936);

Anna Marie Murphy and Cullen Murphy, "Onward, Upward with McGuffey and Those Readers," *Smithsonian*, 15 (November 1984): 182ff.;

Alice McGuffey Ruggles, *The Story of the McGuffeys* (New York: American Book Company, 1950);

John H. Westerhoff III, *McGuffey and His Readers* (New York: Abingdon, 1978).

Clement Clarke Moore
(15 July 1779-10 July 1863)

Marilyn F. Apseloff
Kent State University

BOOKS: *Observations Upon Certain Passages in Mr. Jefferson's Notes on Virginia, Which Appear to Have a Tendency to Subvert Religion and Establish a False Philosophy,* anonymous (New York, 1804);

An Inquiry into the Effects of Our Foreign Carrying Trade upon the Agriculture, Population, and Morals of the Country, as Columella (New York: Printed by D. & G. Bruce for E. Sargeant, 1806);

A Compendious Lexicon of the Hebrew Language, 2 volumes (New York: Printed & sold by Collins & Perkins, 1809);

A Sketch of Our Political Condition. Addressed to the Citizens of the United States, Without Distinction of Party, by A Citizen of New York (New York: Printed for Clement Clarke Moore, 1813);

A Plain Statement Addressed to the Proprietors of Real Estate in the City and County of New York, by A Landholder (New York: J. Eastburn, 1818);

Address Delivered Before the Alumni of Columbia College, on the 4th of May, 1825, in the Chapel of the College (New York: Bliss & White, 1825);

A Lecture Introductory to the Course of Hebrew Instruction in the General Theological Seminary of the Protestant Episcopal Church in the United States, Delivered in Christ's Church, New-York, on the Evening of November 14th, 1825 (New York: Swords, 1825);

Poems (New York: Bartlett & Welford, 1844);

A Visit from St. Nicholas (New York: Henry M. Onderdonk, 1848; London: Unwin, 1902);

George Castriot, Surnamed Scanderbeg, King of Albania (New York: D. Appleton/Philadelphia: G. S. Appleton, 1850).

OTHER: John Duer, *A New Translation with Notes,* of the Third Satire of Juvenal. To which are Added Miscellaneous Poems, Original and Translated (New York: Printed for E. Sargeant, 1806)—includes introduction, translation of Prometheus selection from Aeschylus, and poems by Moore;

Alexandre Henri Tessier, comp., *A Complete Treatise on Merinos and Other Sheep,* translated by Moore (New York, 1811);

Sermons by Benjamin Moore, D.D., 2 volumes, edited by Moore (New York, 1824);

Charles Fenno Hoffman, ed., *The New-York Book of Poetry* (New York: Dearborn, 1837)—includes poems by Moore.

Although Clement Clarke Moore wrote only one memorable poem for children, that narrative, "A Visit from St. Nicholas," has assured him of a secure place in the history of American letters. Moore wrote the poem for his own children and recited it to them on Christmas Eve 1822. After it was published anonymously the following year, it became increasingly popular, appearing in newspapers, school readers, other anthologies, and in many different single editions. It is still read today as a traditional part of the Christmas season in the United States and throughout the world.

Clement Clarke Moore was born in New York City, the son of the Reverend Benjamin Moore and Charity Clarke Moore. An only child, Clement was capably tutored at home by his father until he entered Columbia College; according to his biographer, Samuel White Patterson, he graduated in 1798 "at the head of his class, as his father had, thirty years earlier." In 1801 he earned his M.A. degree from Columbia; he was awarded an LL.D. in 1829. A very religious man, he gave a large portion of the land that he had inherited, part of his

Clement Clarke Moore

Chelsea estate and now called Chelsea Square, to the General Theological Seminary, where he was a professor of oriental and Greek literature from 1823 until he retired in 1850. At his retirement he purchased a house in Newport, Rhode Island, where he died on 10 July 1863.

During his lifetime Moore wrote on a variety of subjects. He produced a two-volume *A Compendious Lexicon of the Hebrew Language* (1809), a translation from the French of *A Complete Treatise on Merinos and Other Sheep* (1811), and the historical biography *George Castriot, Surnamed Scanderbeg, King of Albania* (1850). Throughout his life he also wrote poetry, which was published in the *Portfolio* and similar periodicals. *The New-York Book of Poetry* (1837), an anthology of works by New York poets, contained some written by Moore, including "A Visit from St. Nicholas," although "Anonymous" was still listed as the author. Not until 1844, when Moore's collection *Poems* was published, was "A Visit from St. Nicholas" acknowledged in print as having been written by Clement C. Moore, LL.D.

In 1813 Clement Moore married nineteen-year-old Catharine Elizabeth Taylor, with whom he eventually had nine children. There were various versions of how "A Visit from St. Nicholas" came to be written for the six Moore children who were born before Christmas 1822: perhaps the jingling harness of his sleigh that evening gave him his inspiration, or the description of St. Nicholas from Washington Irving's pseudonymous *History of New York* "by Diedrich Knickerbocker" (1809), or the anonymous poem "The Children's Friend" published the previous year describing "Old Santeclaus" who drives his reindeer "O'er chimney tops, and tracks of snow, To bring his yearly gift to you." Moore totally eliminated moralizing like that found in "The Children's Friend" (no harmful toys are left, such as cannons, swords, or rockets, and toys are left only for "good girls and boys" in the earlier poem), much to the delight of children ever since. Whatever the source of Moore's poem, apparently the physical model for St. Nicholas was a rotund Dutchman who lived nearby.

"A Visit from St. Nicholas" was written in rhyming anapests, a meter ideally suited to the subject. The vivid descriptions, especially of St. Nicholas and his reindeer, remain with the reader long after the poem has been read or heard. Here is sheer delight, for Moore was interested in entertaining his children, not in preaching to them. The eight tiny reindeer have been given names that trip on the tongue, but there is no listing of specific toys such as was included in "The Children's Friend," perhaps because Moore did not want to give his children any hints as to what gifts they would be receiving.

Since Clement Moore had written the narrative poem for his own family, he made no attempt to get it published. There are various reports about how the poem came to appear anonymously the following year in the *Troy* (N.Y.) *Sentinel.* Apparently the verses were transcribed by a houseguest who was either Miss Harriet Butler or a friend of hers; in either case, Miss Butler was most likely the person who sent the copy of the poem anonymously to the *Sentinel.* The editor, Orville L. Holley, published it on 23 December 1823, together with his praise of the poem and "his cordial thanks to whoever had sent him these Christmas verses." The poem was republished numerous times over the years, first in newspapers and other publications, and then in separate illustrated editions, the first of which appeared in 1848 with wood engravings by T. C. Boyd; the publisher was Henry M. Onderdonk of New York. Since that time dozens of editions have appeared; the poem has been translated all over the world and printed in braille and has inspired many illustrators and artists.

A visit from St. Nicholas

'Twas the night before Christmas, when all through
     the house
Not a creature was stirring, not even a mouse;
The stockings were hung by the chimney with care,
In hopes that St. Nicholas soon would be there;
The children were nestled all snug in their beds,
While visions of sugar-plums danced in their heads;
And Mamma in her 'kerchief, and I in my cap,
Had just settled our brains for a long winter's nap;
When out on the lawn there arose such a clatter,
I sprang from the bed to see what was the matter.
Away to the window I flew like a flash,
Tore open the shutters and threw up the sash.
The moon on the breast of the new-fallen snow
Gave the lustre of mid-day to objects below;
When, what to my wondering eyes should appear,
But a miniature sleigh, and eight tiny rein-deer,
With a little old driver, so lively and quick,
I knew in a moment it must be St. Nick.

Manuscript page published in the January 1875 issue of St. Nicholas *magazine*

Wood engraving by T. C. Boyd for the first separate publication of A Visit from St. Nicholas, *from a facsimile of the 1848 Onderdonk edition included in Arthur N. Hosking's* The Night Before Christmas, *1934 (Baldwin Library, University of Florida Libraries)*

Because the poem was published anonymously and became very popular, other people tried to claim authorship. The claimant taken most seriously was Major Henry Livingston, Jr., whose great-grandson spent many years trying to establish Major Livingston as the author. Livingston had also written verses for his children, but he made no written mention of "A Visit from St. Nicholas" during his lifetime, nor had his friends heard of his connection with the verses. They were said to have been published in a Poughkeepsie newspaper long before they appeared in the *Troy Sentinel,* but no copies of the paper containing the poem have ever turned up. Several magazine and newspaper articles appeared, especially during the 1940s, questioning the authorship, but scholars continue to give the credit to Clement Clarke Moore.

Biography:

Samuel White Patterson, *The Poet of Christmas Eve: A Life of Clement Clarke Moore* (New York: Morehouse-Gorham, 1956).

References:

Clarence Cook, "The Author of 'A Visit From St. Nicholas,' " *Century Magazine,* 55 (December 1897): 198-201;

Douglas Gilbert, "Not Even a Mouse Knows Who Wrote It," *New York World Telegram and The Sun,* 22 December 1944;

William S. Pelletreau, "The Visit of St. Nicholas: . . . With the Life of the Author," *Century Magazine* (December 1897);

Burton Rascoe, "Who Wrote 'The Night Before Christmas'?," *American Weekly* (21 December 1947).

Papers:

Collections of Moore's papers are at Harvard University's Houghton Library and the New York Public Library. The New York Historical Society has Moore's 1862 handwritten copy of "A Visit From St. Nicholas"; Moore's diary, begun in 1856, is at Low Library, Columbia University.

Kirk Munroe
(15 September 1850-16 June 1930)

Ken Donelson
Arizona State University

BOOKS: *Wakulla; A Story of Adventure in Florida* (New York: Harper, 1886);

The Flamingo Feather (New York: Harper, 1887; London: Nelson, 1888);

Derrick Sterling; A Story of the Mines (New York: Harper, 1888);

Chrystal, Jack & Co., and Delta Bixby; Two Stories (New York: Harper, 1889);

Dorymates; A Tale of the Fishing Banks (New York: Harper, 1889);

The Golden Days of '49; A Tale of the California Diggings (New York: Dodd, Mead, 1889; London: Allen, 1889);

Under Orders, The Story of a Young Reporter (New York: Putnam's, 1890; London, 1891);

Campmates; A Story of the Plains (New York: Harper, 1891; London, 1891);

Cab and Caboose; The Story of a Railroad Boy (New York: Putnam's, 1892);

Canoemates; A Story of the Florida Reef and Everglades (New York: Harper, 1892; London, 1892);

The Coral Ship; A Story of the Florida Reef (New York & London: Putnam's, 1893);

Raftmates; A Story of the Great River (New York: Harper, 1893; London, 1893);

The White Conquerors; A Tale of Toltec and Aztec (New York: Scribners, 1893; London: Blackie, 1893);

Big Cypress. The Story of an Everglade Homestead (Boston: Wilde, 1894; London, 1895);

The Fur-Seal's Tooth; A Story of Alaskan Adventure (New York: Harper, 1894; London: Arnold, 1895);

Snow-Shoes and Sledges; A Sequel to "The Fur-Seal's Tooth" (New York & London: Harper, 1895; London: Arnold, 1896);

At War With Pontiac; or The Totem of the Bear (New York: Scribners, 1895; London: Blackie, 1896);

Rick Dale; A Story of the Northwest Coast (New York: Harper, 1896; London: Arnold, 1896);

Through Swamp and Glade; A Tale of the Seminole War (New York: Scribners, 1896; London: Blackie, 1897);

The Ready Rangers; A Story of Boys, Boats, and Bicycles, Fire-buckets and Fun (Boston: Lothrop, 1897; London, 1897);

With Crockett and Bowie; or, Fighting for the Lone-star Flag; A Tale of Texas (New York: Scribners, 1897; London: Blackie, 1898);

The Painted Desert; A Story of Northern Arizona (New York: Harper, 1897; London: Osgood, 1897);

The Copper Princess; A Story of Lake Superior Mines (New York & London: Harper, 1898);

In Pirate Waters; A Tale of the American Navy (New York: Scribners, 1898; London: Blackie, 1899);

Midshipman Stuart; or, The Last Cruise of the "Essex"; A Tale of 1812 (New York: Scribners, 1899; London: 1899);

Shine Terrill, A Sea Island Ranger (Boston: Lothrop, 1899);

"Forward March"; A Tale of the Spanish-American War (New York & London: Harper, 1899);

Under the Great Bear (New York: Doubleday, Page, 1900; London: Cassell, 1900);

Brethren of the Coast; A Tale of the West Indies (New York: Scribners, 1900; London, 1900);

A Son of Sàtsuma; or, With Perry in Japan (New York: Scribners, 1901);

The Belt of Seven Totems; A Story of Massasoit (Philadelphia: Lippincott, 1901); republished as *Longfeather the Peacemaker, or The Belt of Seven Totems* (London: Newnes, 1901);

The Blue Dragon; A Tale of Recent Adventure in China (New York & London: Harper, 1904);

The Outcast Warrior; A Tale of the Red Frontier (New York: Appleton, 1905);

For the Mikado; or, A Japanese Middy in Action (New York & London: Harper, 1905);

In the Heart of the Everglades; Being the Story of the Adventures of Allan Lawton in the Early Homesteading Days of Florida and When the Seminole Indians Had No Legal Rights that the White Man Was Bound to Respect (Boston: Wilde, 1926).

PERIODICAL PUBLICATION: "The Adventure Book for Boys," *Bulletin of the American Library*

Association, 3 (September 1909): 267-269.

Kirk Munroe was the author of more than thirty factual and detailed adventure tales for boys. Many of his books are set in Florida, and the rest have wild and mysterious settings, including Alaska, California, Arizona, and Japan. Of writers prior to 1900, Munroe wrote the finest and most realistic, if somewhat moralistic, adventure books for boys. Although he was popular until the early 1900s, interest in his books faded undeservedly in subsequent years.

His life was full of adventure. Born not far from Prairie du Chien, Wisconsin, to Charles W. and Susan M. Hall Munroe, he was brought up in a frontier post at Fort Howard, Wisconsin. His family moved to Cambridge, Massachusetts, and there Munroe persuaded his parents to let him leave home when he was sixteen to return West to the frontier town of Kansas City. He worked with a surveying party on the Santa Fe Railroad for a year and then visited Colorado, Arizona, New Mexico, and Southern California. He fought Indians, was wounded, met Kit Carson, desperadoes, and soldiers, and then worked for a time with an engineering crew in California. He sailed to South America and crossed the continent before returning to Cambridge, where he enrolled at Harvard to study engineering. But wanderlust hit again, and a year later he was surveying for the Northern Pacific Railroad. He became friends with Buffalo Bill and Gen. George Custer before heading East to New York. Because he knew the Little Big Horn area, the *New York Sun* made him a special correspondent. He became assistant editor of the *New York Times* before becoming the first editor of *Harper's Young People* in 1879. Through *Harper's Young People* he met his first wife, Mary Barr, a contributor to the magazine. For three years, he worked closely with many writers, including James Otis Kaler, Howard Pyle, and William Dean Howells. In 1882 he explored by himself the Everglades area in a fourteen-foot canoe named the *Psyche* and became close friends with many Seminole Indians. In 1883 he moved permanently to Florida and began his first two books, *Wakulla* (1886) and *The Flamingo Feather* (1887), both about Seminoles. He founded the League of American Wheelmen (bicycle riders), whose membership reached more than 100,000. He stopped his writing when he was fifty-five to develop Florida real estate, particularly in Dade County. At the age of seventy-four he married his second wife, Mabel Stearns.

Munroe's novels are marked by careful research so smoothly integrated into the plot that boys rarely noticed the introduction of historical and geographical facts. Munroe cared deeply about the beliefs and ideals of whatever people he described. He had a genuine sympathy for the oppressed, particularly the Seminole Indians, which he expressed clearly for boy readers. Characterization was never his strong suit. Good characters and bad characters tended to remain much as they began, but his moral lessons were not lost on boys. Hard work, compassion, humility, endurance, and a bit of bravery will help young men advance in life, so Munroe taught. The lessons had been taught by Horatio Alger, but whereas Alger often preached, Munroe created characters whose lives offered more convincing lessons than all Alger's lectures and sermons. Munroe believed that he could best tell tales and instruct readers through adventure stories, for they complemented schoolwork and yet stimulated boys in a healthy way. In a talk to librarians, Munroe stated his ideas:

> [Through adventure stories, the boy] learns of what he may expect to encounter, of difficulties and how to overcome them, of successes and how to achieve them, of the

Kirk Munroe

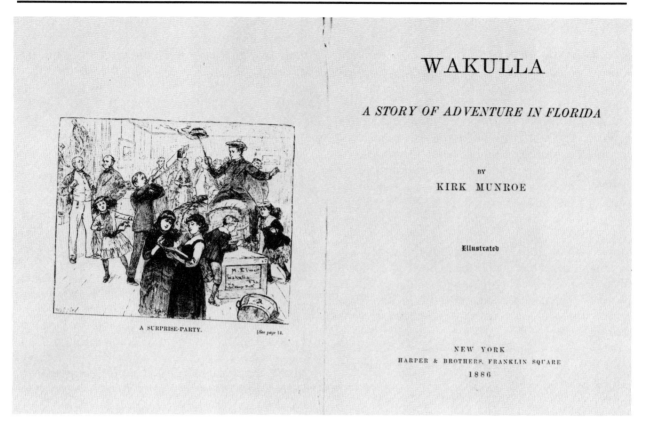

A SURPRISE-PARTY.   [*See page* 14.

WAKULLA

A STORY OF ADVENTURE IN FLORIDA

BY

KIRK MUNROE

Illustrated

NEW YORK
HARPER & BROTHERS, FRANKLIN SQUARE
1886

Frontispiece and title page for Munroe's first book about the Seminole Indians, with whom he lived while exploring the Florida Everglades in the early 1880s (Baldwin Library, University of Florida Libraries)

rewards of truth, honesty, bravery, and right living, and of the bitter penalties attached to their opposites.

The ideal "adventure" book for a normal boy should, then, combine a thrilling interest with sound instruction; for, unless it contains the former no boy will read it, and without the latter it had better be left unread. But its thrills must be those of possibilities, and its instruction must be absolutely reliable. . . .

Munroe's second and third books are probably his best. *The Flamingo Feather* is set in Florida. It is the story of young Réné de Veaux's passage from youth to manhood. In France in 1564, Réné's parents die in an epidemic, so he goes to live with his uncle who is bound for the New World with part of the French fleet. Réné has many adventures in Florida living with his Indian friend, Has-se, son of a chief. When some Indians revolt, the French settlers must survive the winter, and Réné and Has-se search for food. The rebellion is quelled just as the Spanish fleet arrives and attacks the settlement.

Réné is captured by a band of Indians who threaten to torture and kill him. In the nick of time, Has-se and other Indians arrive, and Réné is saved while Has-se dies rescuing his friend. Before his death, Has-se gives Réné the Indian sign of royalty, a flamingo feather, and asks Réné to be a son to the chief.

The book is spirited adventure, but Munroe never loses an opportunity to demonstrate that bravery, nobility, tenacity, and firmness of purpose are prerequisites to passage from boyhood to manhood. Although characters tend to be stereotyped and their dialogue sounds somewhat forced, they are nonetheless vividly portrayed. The novel could be criticized as escapist reading, but few contemporary books combine so much accurate information about Florida Indians with such dramatic action.

In *Derrick Sterling* (1888), the title character is called home from private school after his father dies. To support his mother, Derrick works in the Raven Brook Coal Mine. He befriends crippled Paul Evert and becomes an enemy to cruel and brutal Bill Tooley. The book describes fights, mine

"FAREWELL, TA-LAH-LO-KO!"

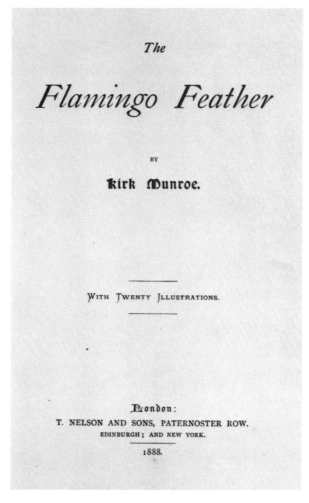

The

Flamingo Feather

BY

Kirk Munroe.

WITH TWENTY ILLUSTRATIONS.

London:
T. NELSON AND SONS, PATERNOSTER ROW.
EDINBURGH; AND NEW YORK.
1888.

Frontispiece and title page for the first British edition of Munroe's historical adventure novel about French settlers in the New World (Baldwin Library, University of Florida Libraries)

disasters, labor unrest, and other conflicts before a lawyer discovers that Derrick and his mother are heirs to property, and Derrick can leave the mine to return to school.

Action is varied and intense, sure to attract readers of the time. A pet mine rat which Derrick names Socrates and an extremely independent mule are intriguing characters. As with all Munroe's books, bad is bad and good is good, and never the twain will meet, but the constant action and the often effectively described situation of the miners propel readers onward. The novel exposes the harsh life of miners, and, although Munroe's pur-

pose is partially didactic, the novel has a Dickensian tone.

Two later books that remain of interest are *Under the Great Bear* (1900) and *For the Mikado* (1905). In the former, a young technical-school graduate finds employment with his guardian's mining company and is sent to Newfoundland to investigate future mines. Typical of Munroe's novels, the young man encounters many adventures and has numerous narrow escapes. The hero is never portrayed as a superman but rather as a person to whom strange adventures seem to happen. *For the Mikado* is about Takahaki, a Japanese midshipman at Annapolis, and his roommate and friend, Dunstar Casimir Brownleigh. "Taka" is called home at the outbreak of the Japanese-Russian War while Casimir becomes a war correspondent. Again, there are adventures galore and a wealth of information on Japanese life and culture.

Munroe was widely read by boys and almost always approved by critics, librarians, and teachers from the 1880s through the early 1900s. Then quietly, and unfortunately, his books declined in popularity. He wrote detailed, factual, realistic accounts of times, places, and incidents. Although his books were sometimes melodramatic, and didactic, they were neither sensational nor boring to young readers. He knew boys, and he knew what kinds of books they wanted and needed, and he gave them history amid exciting adventures. In the

1920s critic Hubert V. Coryell described the secret of Munroe's success: "The boy likes to learn things, he likes to read in books that not only tell him an exciting story, but also give him what he considers valuable information about things that he did not know before. This is probably one reason for the extreme popularity of the books of Kirk Munroe. Kirk Munroe almost always sets his story in some environment unfamiliar to the boy, but alluring to him because of its possibility of adventure."

Reference:

Hubert V. Coryell, "Getting the Boys to Read," *Good Housekeeping*, 77 (October 1923): 33, 208-213.

Peter Newell

(5 March 1862-15 January 1924)

Michael Patrick Hearn

BOOKS: *Topsys & Turvys* (New York: Century, 1893);

Topsys & Turvys, book two (New York: Century, 1894);

A Shadow Show (New York: Century, 1896);

Peter Newell's Pictures & Rhymes (New York & London: Harper, 1899);

The Hole Book (New York: Harper, 1908);

The Slant Book (New York: Harper, 1910);

The Rocket Book (New York: Harper, 1912).

PERIODICAL PUBLICATION: "*Alice's Adventures in Wonderland* from an Artist's Standpoint," *Harper's Monthly*, 103 (October 1901): 713-717.

During the Golden Age of American Illustration when work by such distinguished artists as Charles Dana Gibson, Howard Pyle, and Maxfield Parrish graced many of the nation's books and periodicals, one of the most original of the country's designers was Peter Newell. An illustrator of Mark Twain, Stephen Crane, and Lewis Carroll, Newell was famous for his gentle cartoons in rich, velvety flat tones which enlivened the Harper's family of

magazines—the *Monthly*, the *Weekly*, *Harper's Bazar*, *Harper's Young People*—and other national publications. However, perhaps his most enduring work was that for children: in particular *The Hole Book*, *The Slant Book*, and other novelty picture books which he both wrote and illustrated.

Peter Sheaf Hersey Newell was born on 5 March 1862, in the Midwest backwoods, the last of four children of George Frederick Newell, a wagon-maker, and Louisa N. Newell. "I broke out," he later recalled, "the same time as the Civil War did, in a crossroads in the country in MacDonough County, Illinois. The place hadn't any name, but its nickname was 'Gungiwam.' Our house was the only frame house in the place (the rest were log huts), and it was clapboarded with walnut." Even as a little boy, Newell showed a passion for drawing. He was known to draw on anything, the barn door, wagon wheels, the school blackboard. Evidently his parents encouraged his early interest in art, for while he was still in school, he entered a large oil painting, *The Good Samaritan*, in the annual Bushnell fair and won the blue ribbon.

However, on graduating from high school at age sixteen, the amateur artist was apprenticed in a local cigar factory. He stayed only three months. Fortunately a local entrepreneur took a personal interest in the boy's artistic reputation and found employment for his young protégé in a studio in nearby Jacksonville, Illinois. Here Newell made large crayon portraits by copying his subjects' photographs. Although uninspiring, this labor surely must have schooled the young artist in the subtleties of shading, modeling, and tonal progressions which served him well when he began to draw for the halftone process of the national magazines.

But Newell did not want to draw portraits. He wanted to be a cartoonist. Bored with his work in Jacksonville, he found the courage to submit a sketch to the editor of an Eastern magazine, *Harper's Bazar*. The reply was swift and confusing: while the note read, "No talent indicated," a check was enclosed. Encouraged by this paradoxical evaluation of his work, Newell set off for New York City in 1882 to seek his fortune.

He immediately enrolled at the Art Students League, but he barely survived a semester. Evidently he was restless with his studies. Once, when a waiter was brought in to pose for the sketch class, Newell's drawing aroused the most comment: he had drawn a dead cat on the waiter's tray. While at school, he continued to submit his drawings to the popular illustrated journals. "When I first began to draw for the magazines," he once told a reporter, "there were very few magazines that used pictures. There was *Harper's*, *Scribner's*, and *Godey's*—that was about all." Nevertheless, this young, largely self-taught artist succeeded in placing some of his comic designs with their editors. "When I was starting," Newell later admitted, "I cultivated not only my drawing, but my imagination. I tried to develop my power of conceiving humorous situations. . . . If an artist had an idea that caught the editor's fancy, he would receive more favorable attention than an artist who had nothing but a good drawing." Eventually Newell's cartoons began appearing regularly in the national periodicals, including the children's magazines *St. Nicholas* and *Harper's Young People* (later *Harper's Round Table*).

Newell earned his earliest recognition as an illustrator from his amusing pen-and-ink sketches. Magazine and book publishing was then replacing the old, laborious method of reproduction by wood engraving with the relatively cheaper and easier new process of photomechanical printing of illustrations. Unfortunately this new technology took some time to perfect, and in its early days, it did not allow for a variety of tone. Artists were required to work almost exclusively in line. Fortunately, be-

cause the camera as yet could not pick up the subtleties in gradation, errors could easily be corrected with white paint and then reworked in India ink. Another result of the limitations of this method of reproduction was artists too frequently employed several lines where only one was needed, and so these illustrations were often overwrought.

Newell, however, was drawn to the work of the masters. His early published sketches in line betray a great debt to the efforts of A. B. Frost and E. W. Kemble, two of the most popular and admired of American illustrators of their day. Newell learned as much from their subjects as from their clean, crisp pen-and-ink styles. Newell, too, became known for his cartoons of rural life, particularly Negro scenes; and consequently he, like Frost and Kemble, was erroneously thought to be a native of the South.

Encouraged by his initial success with the

Eastern magazines, Newell returned to Illinois and established his own illustration studio. Now confident of his chosen profession, Newell married his sweetheart Leona Dow Ashcroft on 5 February 1884. But Springfield did not prove to be the best place for an illustrator once he had a family to support, and so Newell became an itinerant artist who traveled through the Midwest and West, giving chalk talks when he could not get commissions for book and magazine work. In 1888, he and his family spent the summer in a tent, in Manitou, Colorado, not far from Colorado Springs. Life in the West was still rugged, and several homes near the Newells' were robbed. One morning while walking about the springs, the artist discovered a piece of zinc, covered with blood, in the road near his home. Worried for the safety of his wife and daughter, he went back to the tent and drew on a large piece of stiff paper the silhouettes of several fierce, rough-looking men. He then cut these out and arranged them along the side of the tent so that the light of the candle outlined them sharply against the canvas. Newell figured that anyone who passed by the tent would suspect by the shadows that it was inhabited by a band of formidable men and not by the gentle artist, his wife, and their little girl. Apparently this ruse succeeded in discouraging burglars, for the Newells, unlike their neighbors, were never bothered by the thieves.

Although he enjoyed the scenery of Manitou and the other places that he visited, Newell realized that if he were to continue as an illustrator he would have to return to New York. Since his last stay in the city, the publishing industry had begun to depend more and more on the halftone for book and magazine pictures. Although still limited to black and white, this new sensitive photomechanical process nevertheless was liberating to artists, for it gave them a wide range of tone for their designs. Many illustrators now turned from line to wash, and Newell followed the fashion.

One of his earliest experiments with the halftone was the little cartoon "Wild Flowers" (*Harper's Monthly,* August 1893), depicting a bug-eyed little girl being consoled by an elderly gentleman in a garden and accompanied by the following nonsense verse: " 'Of what are you afraid, my child?' inquired the kindly teacher./'Oh, sir, the flowers, they are wild!' replied the timid creature." This simple little design made Newell famous; and just like Gelett Burgess and his bit of nonsense "The Purple Cow," Newell could not avoid the great notoriety of "Wild Flowers." Its verse was widely quoted and memorized by his admirers, and Newell

never knew when he might meet up with one of them. "Not long ago," he told Joyce Kilmer in 1916, "I was to speak at a little dinner, and I admit that I was not very comfortable in my mind about it. A lady who sat near me watched me for a few moments and then wrote something on her menu, folded it up, and passed it on to me. I opened it and found my wild flower verse."

"Wild Flowers" was only the first of a series of little cartoons with comic verses which appeared sporadically in the back pages of *Harper's Monthly* and which eventually were collected as *Peter Newell's Pictures & Rhymes* (1899). This delightful volume proved to be as popular with children as with their parents. Newell possessed a gentle, innocent sense of humor like that of Edward Lear; and although he lacked the Englishman's ability as a poet, Newell nevertheless could make a clever turn of phrase, as in the following verse from his *Pictures & Rhymes:* "From Foxe's *Book of Martyrs,* Aunt Matilda slowly read, /'O, aunt, turn over a *new* leaf,' her youthful nephew said." And like the humor in Lear's limericks, the comedy in Newell's cartoons was as dependent upon the pictures as on the texts. However, Newell denied that he had ever seen or read Lear's *Book of Nonsense.*

In the halftone, Newell found the proper medium through which to express his particular kind of comedy. He was well aware of what the camera could and could not do; he knew its limitations and profited by them. Indeed, Newell was one of only a few artists of the period who did not sacrifice the distinctive character of their illustrations when transforming their styles from line to wash. Newell now simplified his compositions by containing the forms within bold outlines which in turn he filled in with richly varied flat tones. "I didn't do the first flat tones that were done in this country," he admitted. "Of course, the Japanese had done them before, and so had Boutet de Monvel." Also from the Japanese, Newell learned new forms of dramatic composition and the internal rhythms of intertwining curved lines and contrasting flat colors and patterns. From Oriental art, he learned to simplify to get the maximum effect desired; now his designs gained in strength as he dropped all superfluous detail, aware that the point of a cartoon must be immediately understood for it to have any impact. "Every man has his own individuality," he argued. "Some men have been influenced by other artists, but their personality must sooner or later appear in their work if they are to succeed." And succeed he did, in allowing his own personality to

WILD FLOWERS.

"Of what are you afraid, my child?" inquired the kindly teacher.
"Oh, sir, the flowers, they are wild," replied the timid creature.

A NEW-YEAR ANECDOTE

From Fox's *Book of Martyrs*, Aunt Matilda slowly read.
"O aunt, turn over a new leaf," her youthful nephew said.

Two of Newell's halftone cartoons, "Wild Flowers" as it appeared in Harper's Monthly, *August 1893, and "A New-Year Anecdote,"*
collected in Peter Newell's Pictures & Rhymes, *1899 (Baldwin Library, University of Florida Libraries)*

emerge through the flat, rhythmic style of his half-tone illustrations.

The deceptively simple, almost naive manner of his illustrations should not suggest that Newell was careless with their preparation. On the contrary, Newell labored on each design until it created just the effect that the artist intended. For each drawing, he made a careful preliminary sketch and then transferred this composition to a clean sheet of paper for the final version. He then finished the art with mixed media, sometimes reworking the drawing with pencil, India ink, crayon, wash, watercolor, and white paint for highlights. Many of his illustrations which were reproduced in black and white were originally done in full color. And so painstaking an artist was Newell that if a drawing did not come up to his standards, he did not hesitate to discard it and begin anew.

The Peter Newell manner had its admirers, but the original had no equal among its imitators. One of Newell's most ardent followers was the young Lyonel Feininger, the modern American painter. The future teacher at the famous Bauhaus in his early years as a professional illustrator contributed to *Harper's Young People* charming pictures for fairy tales, drawings which sported the flat tones and bounding outlines of Newell's work in the same periodical. Other artists were able to capture some of the technical grace of Newell's art, but none quite caught the distinctive comic spirit of Newell's famous cartoons.

Editors were drawn to Newell as much for his dependability as for his infectious good humor. He was given all kinds of texts to illustrate. Among the many books which he illustrated (many of which were originally serialized in magazines) were Mark Twain's *Following the Equator* (1897) and Stephen Crane's *Whilomville Stories* (1900). Perhaps his most famous book illustrations in his day were those for John Kendrick Bangs's *A House-Boat on the Styx* (1896) and its several sequels, and the success of these best-selling books was credited as much to the pictures as to their texts.

No matter what the commission, whether it be his own nonsense verses or Ivory Soap ads in the back pages of *St. Nicholas*, Newell was always conscientious in his labors. "An illustrator should be fully familiar with the story for which he is making the pictures," he believed. "I always read a story three or four times, so as to be thoroughly acquainted with it before I make any pictures for it. Accuracy in the representations of characters in fiction is an important part of an illustrator's equipment." Accuracy in small details was as important

to Newell as it was in the representation of characters. Newell was known to take considerable time to authenticate little points of costumes and settings for his illustrations. However, he never worked directly from the model. Instead, he relied on his own imagination and powers of invention. "It seems to me," he told Kilmer, "that an artist who is to make a success of illustrating must possess the qualities necessary for success on the stage. A successful illustrator must be able to reproduce characters and to produce the emotion present in the incident which he is depicting. All great illustrators have had this power—it is the only way in which an artist can give the text a correct interpretation. . . . He must be able to project himself into the scene he is drawing. He must identify himself with the characters of the situation. He must be able to induce the emotions which those characters are supposed to feel. . . . Many times I have found myself with my face distorted like those of the characters I was drawing." Indeed, many of his bug-eyed, spindly legged grotesques look much like the artist himself, a tall, gawky gentleman with bushy eyebrows, mustache, and abundant curly hair. "If an artist has this sort of imaginative power, this power of projecting himself into his work, and is a good draftsman," he concluded, "I think that he will be a successful illustrator."

Another reason for Newell's success in the field was that he was always working, for books, magazines, and newspapers. He knew well some of the problems created by unreasonable deadlines. He once admitted, "I have seen a few illustrations in which the artist has departed from the text—representing the hero of a story as smooth shaven when the author gave him a beard, for instance. But sometimes this is really not the artist's fault; it is the fault of the editor, who has given him an order for a lot of work to be done in a hurry, and has not given him sufficient time to read the story carefully." And Newell had no patience with the artist who did not diligently do his work. "I never could understand this bohemian business very well," he complained. "There are some writers and painters who do their work right along, like masons and carpenters. That's the way I do it. I don't see any reason why an artist shouldn't be an honest, hard-working citizen like anybody else. As a matter of fact, I am inclined to think that these people who sit around waiting for inspiration are lazy. The position that they take is nothing but a pose. If they got married and had responsibilities resting on them they'd speedily be cured. . . . Some of my best work has been done while I had a baby in my lap."

However, this hardworking father did find time to be with his own two girls and little boy. He became something of a local celebrity in Leonia, the New Jersey town named for Mrs. Newell; and he did all he could to contribute to the community. He served as a Sunday school superintendent and on the local boards of education and health; he was a founder and first president of the Men's Neighborhood Club of Leonia. He played the piano, flute, and cello, and sang in the church choir; he enjoyed fishing and tennis, but his particular passion was for chess. And what little spare time he had left, he spent carving little wooden figures. He was also a great favorite with the local boys and girls for his simple sleight of hand tricks, and all of them knew him as Uncle Peter.

The proud father was often inspired by his own children. Once, when he found one of them struggling with a picture book which was turned upside down, Newell decided to create a children's book which could be read at either angle. The two volumes of *Topsys & Turvys* (1893 and 1894) were the results. A child need only turn over this book of chromolithographed pictures to transform an elephant into an ostrich, a farmer into his pig, some ladies into butterflies, plates of ice cream into little boys. Hewell explained in the second volume: "This book is like a tumbler. It's thus that you begin it, But till it is inverted, there's always more within it." The concept of these books does seem simple enough, but surprisingly few other artists (notably Rex Whistler in *Oho!*, 1946; Hilary Knight in *Sylvia the Sloth*, 1969; and Gustave Verbeck in his early comic strip "The Upside-Downs of Lady Lovekins and Old Man Muffaroo") have attempted this clever and challenging form of picture storytelling. Newell followed his popular *Topsys & Turvys* with another ingenious picture book, *A Shadow Show* (1896), an obvious imitation of Charles Henry Bennett's *Shadows* (two volumes, 1857 and 1858). Like its Victorian prototype, *A Shadow Show* reveals the true nature of each of its subjects by the shape of its outline.

More than any other American illustrator of the day, Newell explored the possibilities of the form of the picture book. So inventive were his novelty books that this artist sometimes had to take out a patent rather than the usual copyright to protect his literary curiosities fully. In both *The Hole Book* (1908) and its sequel *The Rocket Book* (1912), a hole was actually cut through the pages to show the humorous consequences of, in the first volume, little Tom Potter's accidental shooting of his father's pistol and, in the second, naughty Fritz the janitor's boy's launching of a rocket which goes from the basement through the floors of an apartment building. Even more eccentric than this pair of "hole books" is *The Slant Book* (1910), trimmed on an angle to depict the adventures of a runaway baby carriage as it races down a steep hill. In each of these clever volumes, the silly two-color pictures are accompanied by doggerel which perhaps was not necessary, for the humor of each situation is so completely communicated in the illustration.

The most ambitious (and most controversial) of Newell's children's books were his editions of *Alice's Adventures in Wonderland* (1901), *Through the Looking Glass* (1902), and *The Hunting of the Snark* (1903). It is difficult to imagine Lewis Carroll's classic Alice books without the original illustrations by John Tenniel, but Harper and Brothers decided that the famous children's stories should be updated. It must have been an honor for Peter Newell to be chosen for this commission, but the artist was also prepared to defend the apparent audacity of his trying to replace Tenniel. "It may appear presumptuous . . . to portray what Alice means to me," Newell began his explanation in *Harper's Monthly* (October 1901). "But the kindness with which the public has received my other work, together with the encouragement of certain friends (to whom the inception of this undertaking is due) has inspired the hope in me that this more serious effort will not be altogether unwelcome." And seriously did Newell approach the project. "The dominant note in the character of Alice is childish purity and sweetness," the artist continued. "A sweet, childish spirit at home in the midst of mystery! . . . a little girl . . . with lessons to learn and duties to perform—a demure, quaint little girl, with a strict regard for the proprieties of life, and a delicate sense of consideration of the feelings of others. . . . And underlying all of this is that simple, sincere faith which seems to be the peculiar property of childhood, and which upon all occasions includes in her a respectable attitude, however absurd may be the situation."

Newell, however, in his pictures emphasized the absurdity, not the respectability, of Carroll's creations. Certainly Newell was somewhat restricted by Tenniel's original conceptions of the Mad Hatter, the March Hare, the Mock Turtle, the Cheshire Cat, and all the other odd personages; but the American brought them all vividly to life in his pictures. The books were crammed with full-page halftone plates, and Newell had the luxury of depicting incidents that Tenniel, firmly under Lewis Carroll's thumb, had not had the opportunity

*Front cover for one of Newell's children's books designed to be read right side up and upside down (Baldwin Library,
University of Florida Libraries)*

to illustrate; even the least important subject was
sympathetically treated by the new artist. Newell
argued that all of Carroll's absurd creatures were
"real characters on a common plane of humor, action, and interest," that *Alice's Adventures in Wonderland* was a play in which each subordinate actor
was excellent in his way as the lead. Only Newell's
Alice (based upon the artist's daughter Josephine)
disappoints; this dark-haired, rather plain, too mature child is not the ideal Alice.

Newell's *Alice* was not to everyone's taste, but
Harper and Brothers was pleased enough with the
new Carroll volumes to hire Newell to illustrate
Favorite Fairy Tales (1907). This project, in the same
elegant format as *Alice's Adventures in Wonderland*,
collected classic children's stories recommended by
such prominent public figures as Mark Twain,
Henry James, Howard Pyle, Grover Cleveland,
William Jennings Bryan, and Jane Addams. Al-

though the text did have errors (for example,
Charles Perrault is credited as the author of the
English fairy tales "Jack the Giant Killer" and "Jack
and the Beanstalk"), no such carelessness marred
the fine illustrations. Known primarily as a humorist, Newell on occasion had illustrated travesties
of nursery books; for example, Guy Wetmore Carryl's *Fables for the Frivolous* (1898) were elaborate
parodies of LaFontaine's work, his *Mother Goose for
Grown-Ups* (1900) take-offs of traditional nursery
rhymes. Newell, however, in interpreting such selections as "The Gastronomic Guile of Simple Simon" and "The Opportune Overthrow of Humpty
Dumpty," played it straight; his pictures of Simple
Simon and Humpty Dumpty in *Mother Goose for
Grown-Ups* were appropriate for any conventional
edition of Mother Goose rhymes. Likewise, in *Favorite Fairy Tales*, Newell successfully interpreted
the histories of such nursery celebrities as Aladdin,

The grocer boy was teasing Snip
    By pelting him with rice,
And keeping just beyond his reach—
    Which wasn't very nice.

Just then the bullet clipped the chain
    That held the pup, and—joy!
He fairly sprinted through the air,
    And nabbed that grocer boy!

Pages from The Hole Book, *one of Newell's experiments with picture-book form (Baldwin Library, University of Florida Libraries)*

Snow White and Rose Red, and Beauty and her Beast with uncommon grace and affection. The only disappointment with *Favorite Fairy Tales* is that, in restricting the artist to one picture a story, there are far fewer plates in this collection than in the earlier *Alice* books.

With the growth of the Sunday comic strip at the turn of the century, Newell, one of the country's most talented comic illustrators, tried his hand at the new form. In "The Naps of Polly Sleepyhead," which appeared in the *New York Sunday Herald*, beginning in 1906 Newell turned back to Lewis Carroll. Like Alice in Wonderland, Polly Sleepyhead went through marvelous adventures from which she awoke in the last frame. Newell's strip had already been anticipated by Winsor McCay's classic "Little Nemo in Slumberland," which had preceded "The Naps of Polly Sleepyhead" in the *Herald*'s Sunday funny papers. Although Newell's effort lacked the architectural extravagance of McCay's more famous dream series, "The Naps of Polly Sleepyhead" was beautifully drawn and possessed a simple, childlike humor, being perhaps too fragile to survive in the rough-and-tumble world of Buster

Brown and the Katzenjammer Kids. Newell's delightful strip lasted only about a year.

Since his death on 15 January 1924, in Little Neck, Long Island, Peter Newell has been largely forgotten. He now receives scant mention in the popular studies of American illustration and children's book artists. Perhaps his gentle slapstick now seems dated, while the anarchistic violence of the Katzenjammer Kids remains au courant. Nevertheless, Newell was an original, and his contribution to American illustration is inestimable. Fortunately a few of Newell's picture books have recently been republished, so new readers may find amusement in the charming wit of one of America's most inventive illustrators.

References:

Regina Armstrong, "The New Leaders in American Illustration," *Bookman*, 11 (June 1900): 334-341;

Mabel Hall Goltra, "Peter S. Newell, Cartoonist," *Illinois State Historical Society Journal*, 41 (June 1948): 134-145;

Philip Hofer, "Peter Newell's Pictures & Rhymes," *Colophon*, 5 (December 1934);

Joyce Kilmer, "Peter Newell Says Domesticity Helps Artists," *New York Times Sunday Magazine*, 17 September 1916;
Albert Lee, "Book Illustrators: Peter Newell," *Book Buyer* (July 1896);
C. B. Loomis, "Interesting People: Peter Newell," *American Magazine*, 72 (May 1911): 48-51.

George W. Peck

(28 September 1840-16 April 1916)

Ruth K. MacDonald
New Mexico State University

See also the Peck entry in *DLB 23, American Newspaper Journalists, 1873-1900.*

BOOKS: *Adventures of One Terence McGrant. A Brevet Irish Cousin of President Ulysses S. Grant* (New York: Lambert, 1871);
Peck's Fun: Being Extracts from the "La Crosse Sun" and "Peck's Sun," Milwaukee, compiled by V. W. Richardson (Milwaukee: Symes, Swain, 1879);
Peck's Sunshine: Being a Collection of Articles Written for Peck's Sun, Milwaukee, Wis., Generally Calculated to Throw Sunshine instead of Clouds on the Faces of Those Who Read Them (Chicago & St. Louis: Belford, Clarke, 1882);
Peck's Bad Boy and His Pa (Chicago: Belford, Clarke, 1883; London: Routledge, 1887);
Peck's Bad Boy, No. 2: The Grocery Man and Peck's Bad Boy (Chicago & New York: Belford, Clarke, 1883);
Mirth for the Million: Peck's Compendium of Fun, edited by "Elmo" (Thomas W. Handford) (Chicago: Belford, Clarke, 1883);
Peck's Boss Book (Chicago & New York: Belford, Clarke, 1884);
Will He Marry Her? A Domestic Drama for Home Reading (Chicago: Rhodes & McClure, 1885);
How Private Geo. W. Peck Put Down the Rebellion; or The Funny Experiences of a Raw Recruit (Chicago & New York: Belford, Clarke, 1887);
Peck's Irish Friend, Phelan Geoheagan (New York: Lovell, 1887);
The Prohibition Question: A Study of Its Results in Kentucky, Tennessee, Georgia, Oklahoma, Alabama, Louisiana, Texas, North Dakota and Maine (Milwaukee: Allied Printing, 1890);
Peck's Uncle Ike and the Red Headed Boy (Chicago: Belford, 1899);

Sunbeams: Humor, Sarcasm and Sense (New York: Hurst, 1900);
Peck's Red-Headed Boy (New York: Hurst, 1901);
Peck's Bad Boy Abroad (Chicago: Stanton, 1904);
Peck's Bad Boy with the Circus (Philadelphia: McKay, 1906);
Peck's Bad Boy with the Cowboys (Chicago: Stanton & Van Vliet, 1907);
Peck's Bad Boy in an Airship (Philadelphia: McKay, 1908).

George W. Peck

OTHER: *Wisconsin: Company Sketches of Counties, Towns, Events, Institutions, and Persons, Arranged in Cyclopedic Form,* edited by Peck (Madison: Western Historical Association, 1906).

George Wilbur Peck, a politician and journalist, is known primarily for his creation of the character Hennery, Peck's Bad Boy. Though the Bad Boy books were written for a popular audience, the readers of a weekly humor newspaper, they were read by children, and when Peck wrote *Peck's Uncle Ike and the Red Headed Boy* (1899), he acknowledged his juvenile readership in his dedication of the book to "bad boys who will later become pillars of society."

Born in Henderson, New York, to David B. and Alzina Peck, Peck moved to Cold Spring, Wisconsin, when he was three, and later to Whitewater, where he was educated in public schools. In 1855 he became a printer's devil on the *Whitewater Reg-*

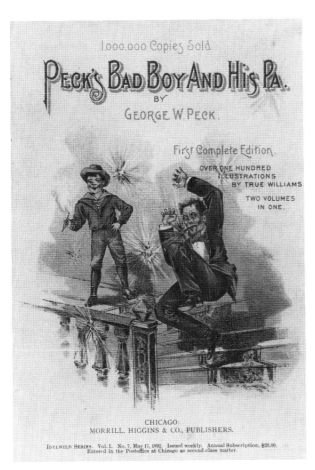

Front cover for an 1892 volume that includes Peck's Bad Boy and His Pa *and* Peck's Bad Boy, No. 2: The Grocery Man and Peck's Bad Boy *(Baldwin Library, University of Florida Libraries)*

ister, thus beginning a career in journalism which he pursued throughout his life. He was also an apprentice at other local newspapers, finally becoming a foreman for the *Watertown Republican.* In 1860 he purchased a half-interest in the *Jefferson County Republican,* just after his marriage in the same year to Francena Rowley, with whom he eventually had two sons. In 1863 he enlisted in the Fourth Wisconsin Cavalry, serving as private, sergeant, and finally second lieutenant until the unit disbanded in 1866. He returned to Ripon, Wisconsin, where he founded the *Ripon Representative,* in which his first humorous articles appeared. The articles, based roughly on his Civil War experiences, attracted the attention of former Wisconsin publisher Marcus M. Pomeroy, who invited Peck to be a columnist for his New York City newspaper, the *Democrat.*

In 1871 Peck returned to Wisconsin, having purchased Pomeroy's newspaper the *La Crosse Democrat;* with a partner he edited and published the *Democrat* for three years. In 1874 Peck founded the *La Crosse Sun,* a weekly which, after four difficult years, he moved to Milwaukee under the title *Peck's Sun.* In the *Sun* in 1882 the first Bad Boy stories appeared. In 1883 the first volume of the collected stories, *Peck's Bad Boy and His Pa,* was published followed by *Peck's Bad Boy, No. 2* in the same year. These were the most popular of Peck's works; his other Bad Boy books followed the same formula of a boy playing tricks on the stupid, hypocritical, deceitful grown-ups around him, especially his father.

Peck's stories about Hennery, the Bad Boy, are set in a Midwestern town. In one tale Hennery succeeds in burning his father by inserting matches into his shoes; in others he tricks his father into an assignation and then tips off his mother and embarrasses the family in front of their fellow parishioners at church. Hennery convinces any and all who will listen to go along with his preposterous schemes. He remains unashamed and unremorseful as he recounts his exploits to the local grocery man, who provides the appreciative audience for Hennery's embellished tales. As a Bad Boy, Hennery is more outrageous than his literary predecessors Tom Bailey, Tom Sawyer, or Huck Finn. The violence and sneakiness of his actions, the raucous obscenity of many of his jokes, and the racial and ethnic stereotypes that Peck presents in the stories no longer appeal to readers, nor would modern critics allow their appropriateness for children, but they were popular at the time. Perhaps these practical jokes were approved of not only

"I Am Going to Have Him Mended and Keep Him for a Souvenir," Said the Pussy Woman.

Illustration by Charles Lederer for the last of the Bad Boy books,
Peck's Bad Boy in an Airship *(Baldwin Library, University of Florida Libraries)*

because prankstering was in vogue at the time but also because Peck aimed them at popular targets: through Hennery he attacks social and political institutions, the sacred cows of the era, and he makes fun of ethnic groups, especially the Irish, who were accepted as inferiors and therefore considered just recipients of pranks.

Six collections of Bad Boy tales were published from 1899 to 1908. Uncle Ike and the boy have a battle of wits and stunts in *Peck's Uncle Ike and the Red Headed Boy* (1899); the stunts continue with other relatives and acquaintances in *Peck's Red-Headed Boy* (1901); the Bad Boy leaves home to explore the world in *Peck's Bad Boy Abroad* (1904), *Peck's Bad Boy with the Circus* (1906), *Peck's Bad Boy with the Cowboys* (1907), and *Peck's Bad Boy in an Airship* (1908). The books as a group are charac-

terized by Peck's use of vigorous, racy dialect and by his unfailing inventiveness in the creation of the Bad Boy's pranks. Hennery carries with him wherever he goes his irreverence for local custom and authority and his parochial conviction that the way things are done in Milwaukee is the clearly superior way. The later books were not as popular as the earlier ones. Peck seems to have lost some of the creativity and energy that went into the first two volumes, but the books made him financially comfortable throughout his life.

In 1908, the year of the last Bad Boy volume, Peck was one of the best known people in Wisconsin because of his appearances in print. He was elected mayor of Milwaukee in May; in November he was elected governor of the state by the widest plurality recorded to that date. His platform included opposition to the Bennett Law, which prohibited the teaching of foreign languages in schools. Many considered the law a result of Wisconsin xenophobia of Roman Catholic and Lutheran immigrants, who offered instruction in Latin or German in their schools. Though he made fun of such immigrants in his newspapers, Peck was not unsympathetic to them. He was reelected governor in 1892 but lost a third bid in 1894 and returned to writing. In 1904 he ran for governor a fourth time, but he was defeated by Robert M. LaFollette. Peck died in Milwaukee a famous and admired man.

Though Hennery would seem to the modern reader an anarchist of sorts, a juvenile delinquent running nearly out of control, he was perceived at the time as, above all, a free individual operating in a society where all behavior, so long as it was successful, was permissible, and where gentility, presumed authority, and sentimentality had no place. The influence of Peck's Bad Boy is most clearly seen in the Penrod stories of Booth Tarkington and in twentieth-century comic strips which require compactness and outrageousness of action to present single episodes. This kind of rough humor still appeals to children, and though it does not appear very frequently in their literature, it has been made available to them on television in cartoons and in such programs as *The Three Stooges*.

Reference:

E. F. Bleiler, Introduction to *Peck's Bad Boy and His Pa* (New York: Dover, 1958).

Howard Pyle

Jill P. May
Purdue University

BIRTH: Wilmington, Delaware, 5 March 1853, to William and Margaret Churchman Painter Pyle.

MARRIAGE: 12 April 1881 to Anne Poole; children: Sellers, Phoebe, Theodore, Howard, Eleanor, Godfrey, Wilfrid.

DEATH: Florence, Italy, 9 November 1911.

BOOKS: *The Merry Adventures of Robin Hood of Great Renown, in Nottinghamshire* (New York: Scribners, 1883; London: Low, 1883);

Within the Capes (New York: Scribners, 1885);

Pepper & Salt; or Seasoning for Young Folk (New York: Harper, 1885; London: Low, 1885);

The Rose of Paradise (New York: Harper, 1888);

The Wonder Clock; or, Four & Twenty Marvellous Tales, Being One for Each Hour of the Day, embellished with verses by Katharine Pyle (New York: Harper, 1888);

Otto of the Silver Hand (New York: Scribners, 1888; London: Low, 1888);

Men of Iron (New York: Harper, 1892; London: Osgood, McIlvaine, 1892);

A Modern Aladdin; or, The Wonderful Adventures of Oliver Munier (New York: Harper, 1892);

Twilight Land (New York: Harper, 1895; London: Osgood, McIlvaine, 1895);

The Story of Jack Ballister's Fortunes (New York: Century, 1895; London: Osgood, McIlvaine, 1896);

The Garden Behind the Moon (New York: Scribners, 1895; London: Lawrence & Bullen, 1895);

The Ghost of Captain Brand (Wilmington, Del.: Printed for Anne Poole Pyle, Thomas F. Bayard, Henry A. Dupont & J. Henry Harper by John Rogers, 1896);

A Catalogue of Drawings Illustrating the Life of Gen. Washington, and of Colonial Life (Philadelphia, 1897);

The Divinity of Labor. An Address Delivered At Commencement Exercises at Delaware College, June 16, 1897 (Wilmington, Del.: John M. Rogers Press, 1898);

The Price of Blood: An Extravaganza of New York Life in 1807 (Boston: Badger, 1899);

Rejected of Men: A Story of To-day (New York & London: Harper, 1903);

The Story of King Arthur and His Knights (New York: Scribners, 1903; London: Newnes, 1903);

The Story of the Champions of the Round Table (New York: Scribners, 1905; London: Newnes, 1905);

Stolen Treasure (New York & London: Harper, 1907);

The Story of Sir Launcelot and His Champions (New York: Scribners, 1907; London: Chapman & Hall, 1907);

The Ruby of Kishmoor (New York & London: Harper, 1908);

The Story of the Grail and the Passing of Arthur (New York: Scribners, 1910; London: Bickers, 1910).

OTHER: *The Buccaneers and Marooners of America*, edited with an introduction by Pyle (London: Unwin, 1891; New York: Macmillan, 1891);

School and Playground (Boston: Lothrop, 1891)—includes "Lambkin: Was He a Hero or a Prig" by Pyle;

Strange Stories of the Revolution (New York & London: Harper, 1907)—includes "Nancy Hansen's Project" by Pyle;

Shapes that Haunt the Dusk, edited by William Dean Howells and Henry Mills Alden (New York London: Harper, 1907)—includes "In Tenebras" by Pyle;

Adventures of Pirates and Sea-Rovers (New York & London: Harper, 1908)—includes "The Buccaneers—Wolves of the Spanish Main" and "The Fate of a Treasure Town" by Pyle;

The Book of Laughter, edited by Katherine N. Birdsall and George Haven Putnam (New York & London: Putnam's, 1911)—includes "Hans Gottenlieb, The Fiddler," "Robin Goodfellow and His Friend Bluetree," and "Drummer Fritz and His Exploits" by Pyle.

PERIODICAL PUBLICATIONS:

FICTION

"The Angel and the Child," *Harper's Magazine,* 100
    (May 1900): 830-834.

NONFICTION

"Chincoteague: The Island of Ponies," *Scribner's
    Monthly,* 13 (April 1877): 737-745;

"Old-Time Life in a Quaker Town," *Harper's New
    Monthly Magazine,* 62 (January 1881): 178-
    190;

"Chapbook Heroes," *Harper's Magazine,* 81 (June
    1890): 123-138;

"When I Was a Little Boy," *Woman's Home Com-
    panion,* 39 (April 1912): 5, 103.

Howard Pyle's innovative contributions to
children's literature are of paramount importance.
His name became synonymous with high artistic
standards in book format and in periodical illustration. He not only created graphics to complement children's stories; he also trained many of the

fine American artists whose works dominated the
American children's book field during the early
twentieth century. Pyle's understanding of classical
children's literature far surpassed that of most of
his contemporaries. An American who recreated
English legend, Pyle steeped himself in historic detail before beginning either his stories or his illustrations. As one critic commented, "Pyle was
exceptionally versatile, working with equal ease in
themes from folk tales, high Gothic romance, Colonial history . . . and children's fantasies, and was
in each genre, ultimately, a master of exquisite
mood and powerful design."

Born in Wilmington, Delaware, in 1853, Howard Pyle was of Quaker ancestry. Pyle's own childhood, in a community which supported abolition
of slaves and the Northern cause during the Civil
War, was peaceful. He attended the Friends' School
in Wilmington and later T. Clarkson Taylor's small
private school. Always surrounded by good literature with the best artwork available, Pyle learned
to appreciate the book's total format. He later con-
fessed, "In confidence, I still like the pictures in
books better than wall pictures." Since the Pyle family could not afford to send Pyle to Europe to study
art, he went to Philadelphia in 1869 to study with
an elderly Dutch gentleman, F. A. Van der Wielen.
Thus, Pyle, with his exclusively American training,
broke the tradition which dictated that artists study
abroad.

After almost three years of training with Van
der Wielen, Pyle returned home and worked with
his father in the family's leather business. He might
have remained in this business had he not traveled
to the Chincoteague Islands in 1876 and, consequently, written an illustrated story about the trip
which was accepted by *Scribner's Monthly.* One of
the magazine's owners, Roswell Smith, urged him
to come to New York City, and Pyle accepted the
challenge that launched his career as a graphic artist.

In 1877 illustrations and short tales by Pyle
appeared in *Harper's Weekly* and the juvenile magazine *St. Nicholas.* In 1878 *Harper's Weekly* published
his first full page illustration, *A Wreck in the Offing;*
another full page, which Pyle described as "my
'Carnival in Philadelphia'—during General Howe's
possession of the city," appeared in *Harper's New
Monthly Magazine* the same year. After taking evening classes at the Art Students League, Pyle returned to Wilmington, although he continued his
work with New York publishers. In April 1881, he
married Anne Poole, with whom he eventually had
seven children.

Pyle taught art to selected students and maintained a school at Chadds Ford until his death. He trained such illustrators as N. C. Wyeth, Frank Schoonover, and Jessie Willcox Smith. Each spoke fondly of his guidance, and each vividly recalled his personality. All seemed fond of him and equally admired his talent as teacher and as artist. More has been published concerning Pyle's art career than his literary efforts, but his books have become classics and are still found in most children's library collections. Even in his artistic endeavors Pyle insisted on creating a scene full of emotion and drama. As a teacher he required that his students write and illustrate stories. He rarely used models, but he avidly researched costumes and architectural styles for any period on which he based his illustrations. When discussing his technique Jessie Willcox Smith wrote:

> With Howard Pyle it was absolutely changed. There was your story and you knew your characters, and you imagined what they were doing, and in consequence you were bound to get the right composition because you lived these things. . . . It was simply that he was always mentally projected into his subject.

In 1933, twenty-two years after Pyle's death, Charles Scribner's Sons republished these books in the Howard Pyle Brandywine Edition. Each volume contained introductory remarks by some of Pyle's former art students. All described the man in glowing terms, but F. E. Schoonover's remarks were some of the most articulate. He wrote: "Certainly a sense of eternal obligation should ever possess the artists who were once his students and who are now working professionally, for Mr. Pyle gave everything for the advancement of the young artists. He gave not only his time and thought but quite often financial assistance. . . . Art seemed a very real thing then and we would all go back on our own pictures filled with a great wistful longing to do something worthwhile not only for ourselves but for the man who had such great faith in us."

Pyle's contribution to children's literature must be evaluated from two standpoints: his literary talents and his innovative, progressive attitude toward the graphic arts. Pyle created the total book when he wrote for children. He wrote the text, drew (or painted) his own illustrations, and even created his own calligraphy to explain the text or introduce the chapters. It is important to remember that prior to Pyle Americans considered

graphic artists less talented than those who worked on canvas and that American graphic art was considered crude or commercial in European circles. Pyle changed that attitude and developed such a far-reaching, though relatively small, group of followers that American children's books with carefully executed graphic art set the standard for Europeans in the early twentieth century. American illustrator Robert Lawson summed it up, saying, "Howard Pyle was to become more than a great illustrator; he was to become an American institution. . . . He was a one-man movement which would exert incalculable influence on the whole course of illustration in this country."

During his years in New York Pyle began to pursue the possibility of creating illustrations and tales for children based on the stories of Robin Hood. He hoped to sell them to *St. Nicholas* magazine to be published in serial. Later, when these stories were collected in book format and published as *The Merry Adventures of Robin Hood of Great Renown, in Nottinghamshire* (1883), they were able to stand together as a whole which contained all the excitement, fair battle, and bravery needed to make the book a classic. In fact, Pyle himself once commented that this was his book most apt to become a classic.

Pyle the Quaker had no qualms about writing high adventure. He began *The Merry Adventures of Robin Hood* with a preface which warned, "You who so plod amid serious things that you feel it shame to give yourself up even for a few short moments to mirth and joyousness in the land of Fancy; you who think that life hath nought to do with innocent laughter that can harm no one; these pages are not for you. Clap to the leaves and go no farther than this, for I tell you plainly that if you go farther you will be scandalized by seeing good, sober folks of real history so frisk and caper in gay colors and motley, that you would not know them but for the names tagged to them." In the same preface he says that this is not the land of fairy, but " 'Tis the land of Fancy, and is of that pleasant kind that, when you tire of it,—whisk!—you clap the leaves of this book together and 'tis gone. . . ."

Pyle based his renditions on Joseph Ritson's 1795 collection of Robin Hood ballads which had been engraved by Thomas Bewick. In Ritson's notes there is the comment that Robin Hood "is reported to have been wild and extravagant . . . insomuch that his inheritance being consumed or forfeited by his excesses, and his person outlawed for debt. . . ." Pyle changed these circumstances so that in his prologue Robin is outlawed due to two

Frontispiece and title page for Pyle's first book (Baldwin Library, University of Florida Libraries). According to Charles Abbott, Pyle considered The Merry Adventures of Robin Hood *"probably the only book of his which could in any sense be called a classic."*

acts committed when he was eighteen. Pyle takes care of Robin's youth to age twenty-four in less than five pages.

Pyle's book follows Robin Hood through his many adventures and shows Robin's encounters with the Sheriff of Nottingham. Most of the book is based on Robin's gathering of his band. Fair play and tricks abound, but toward the middle of the book, the tone changes, and events become more serious. Robin, however, remains a superhero capable of doing no harm except to those who deserve it.

Pyle's Robin Hood stories are a combination of legend, folk verse, and carefully constructed prose intertwined to create a literary classic which depicts English history in a manner understandable to children.

At times Pyle's use of language is an apt reflection of the historical period he portrays. Robin, for example, uses the term *Jew* to blaspheme, and when Pyle describes a scene between Robin Hood and those gathered at the butchers' banquet, the

lively conversation possesses a decidedly medieval flavor:

At last the dinner was ready to be served and the Sheriff bade Robin say grace, so Robin stood up and said: "Now Heaven bless us all and eke good meat and good sack within this house, and may all butchers be and remain as honest men as I am."

At this all laughed, the Sheriff loudest of all, for he said to himself, "Surely this is indeed some prodigal, and perchance I may empty his purse of some of the money that the fool throweth away so freely." Then he spake aloud to Robin, saying: "Thou art a jolly blade, and I love thee mightily;" and he smote Robin upon the shoulder.

Seldom is Pyle's prose too wordy or too contrived to lose the reader's attention. Yet, since it is a Quaker's interpretation of Old English, at times Pyle's wording seems cumbersome.

The book is impressive when evaluated as a

Venturesome · Boldness ·

A tailor came a-walking by,
The fire of courage in his eye.
"Where are you going, sir?" Said I.

"I slew a mouse
In our house,
Where other tailors live," said he,
"And not a Jack
Among the pack
Would dare to do the like; pardie!
Therefore, I'm going out to try
If there be greater men than I;
Or in the land
As bold a hand
At wielding brand as I, you see!"

The tailor came a-limping by
With woful face and clothes awry
And all his courage gone to pie.

"I met a knight
In armor bright,
And bade him stand and draw," said he
"He straightway did
As he was bid,
And treated me outrageously.
So I shall get me home again,
And probably shall there remain.
A little man,
Sir, always can
Be great with folk of less degree!"

Illustrated poem collected in Pyle's Pepper & Salt; or Seasoning for Young Folks

whole. Pyle's illustrations are rich in detail and impressive in line. Each full page illustration is bordered with details from nature and contains a caption carefully penned by Pyle. Several smaller illustrations and designs carry the mood of an era when England was less civilized, less populated, and more dominated by the church as well as the crown. As Elizabeth Nesbitt commented in her book *Howard Pyle* (1966), "No one can argue the truth of Joseph Pennell's remark, that Pyle created beautiful pictures of a country he had never seen."

Characterization in Pyle's book is also noteworthy. He introduces Robin Hood's band—Little John, Will Stutely, Will Scarlet, Friar Tuck, and Allan a Dale—in lengthy scenes designed to show that Robin was not always the master of all, but that fair play and respect brought these rogues together in congenial association. Pyle's Robin is a hero free of romantic involvement, and his rendition of the Robin Hood legend depicts a cheerful band of men joined together in brotherhood with a common love for honor, food, and sport. While they are the heroes, the sheriff in Pyle's version is not depicted as a villain. Rather, he is portrayed as a capitalistic human whose material desires and selfishness outweigh his spirit of humanity.

In the last chapter, Pyle writes: "Thus end the merry adventures of Robin Hood; for, in spite of his promise, it was many a year ere he saw Sherwood again. . . . Robin, through his great fame as an archer, became a favorite with the King, who, seeing how faithful and loyal he was, created him Earl of Huntingdon; so Robin followed the King to the wars, and found his time so full he had no chance to come back to Sherwood for even so much as a day. . . ." But the real end of Robin Hood is placed in the epilogue which contains the tale of Robin's death, caused by "his cousin, the Prioress of the Nunnery of Kirkless." Although Robin's death is solemnly portrayed, it is neither melodramatic nor morbid. The reader is reminded that Robin was forgiving and compassionate toward others, and that he was, in the end, a mortal hero.

Critics have solidly supported *The Merry Adventures of Robin Hood* as one of Pyle's strongest literary efforts. In the words of Charles Abbott, "Nothing that he did is so sure of a permanent place in the world of art and letters as the long series of books which began in 1883 with *The Merry Adventures of Robin Hood*. The text was only a retelling of the old stories . . . but to them he added a new reality, a definiteness, which so completely revivified their whole spirit that they could not fail to gain the ear of any normal child."

It is evident from Pyle's several references to King Arthur in *The Merry Adventures of Robin Hood* that he was already considering the possibilities of recreating Arthurian legends for children. His next book, however, was his first volume of literary fairy tales, published in 1885. Entitled *Pepper & Salt; or Seasoning for Young Folk*, this book contains original verse and illustrations as well as tales derived from Pyle's recollections of the folklore his mother read to him as a youth. Pyle combines the rambling style of oral folklore with an earthy vocabulary in his tales. In the words of John W. Vandercook, by recreating these stories, Pyle "rescued from the oblivion of yellowed, forgotten books old legends of central Europe and of early England, in which giants and fairies, ogres and strange small people of the woods were twice as real as mortal folk."

Pyle had begun writing the humorous poems contained in this volume of fairy tales in 1883 and had decorated them with pen-and-ink illustrations. The stories included in *Pepper & Salt* had been published one by one in *Harper's Young People* in 1885. Pyle probably always intended that the tales be gathered in book form and had simply tried to create a larger audience for the book by first publishing the stories in a popular children's periodical. When the stories and original verse were collected in book form, they were entirely compatible in mood.

Every one of these tales contains folk from the fairy or the underworld, and in every tale the humans get the best of these spirits. Pyle's humor is developed in his language and in his morals, but it would be much less effective without his illustrations. Although his settings might seem English, they contain a quaint mix of details from Dutch and American home life. Men and women alike wear clogs, windmills are depicted, and cats are seen lying cosily about in several home scenes.

Immediately after this first book of tales was published, Pyle's next series of fantasies began appearing in *Harper's Young People*. By 11 October 1887 twenty-six stories had appeared. All but two of the new tales were collected in *The Wonder Clock* (1888), which, like *Pepper & Salt*, has not been out of print since its original publication.

The Wonder Clock contains more sophisticated stories, but Pyle again relies on oral legend for his characters and plots. The book contains poems written for the volume by Pyle's sister Katharine. Although there are spirits and common folk in these tales, Pyle does not concentrate on these characters alone. Several stories contain personified animals, several involve kings and princesses, and a

One of Pyle's illustrations for "King Stork," first published in Harper's Young People *(November 1886) and collected in* The Wonder Clock *(1880)*

few contain princes. Most of the heroes are active young men with noble backgrounds.

What separates Pyle's tales from the oral folklore tradition is his use of conversations, of gentle asides to the reader, and his habit of summing up his stories with practical observations. In addition to format and overall tone, this collection differs from the earlier one in its characterizations. Pyle's men are plucky strivers. His women are not typical folklore heroines; they are clever, strong-minded young women who are outwardly beautiful and inwardly independent. These young heroines can help their heroes in adventures, but they can also cause problems. In "King Stork," for example, the young princess is in no hurry to marry and is willing to trick all the young men who seek her hand. When at last the drummer outwits the girl he is warned that "the princess is just as wicked as ever she was before, and if you do not keep your eyes open she will trip you up after all." He is advised to "hold tight to her and lay on the switch, no mat-

ter what happens, for that is the only way to save yourself and to save her." In the princess Pyle tries to depict both an intelligent heroine and one who will submit her life to the dominance of a male. Marriage, he seems to be saying, is best when the relationship is controlled by the husband. In fact, Pyle discouraged married women from the arts and trained only single females. In the words of one critic he is said to have supported the idea that "the average woman with ambitions loses them when she marries."

Pyle's writing had changed by the time he had completed *The Wonder Clock.* He was beginning to write more somber pieces with deeper meanings. He had moved from lighthearted, episodic prose to involved stories which could be interpreted in several ways. Although Pyle was still in the habit of speaking directly to the reader, he did it with less frequency, and his tone was less casual. Further, the focus of Pyle's portrayal of medieval times was shifting. With this shift came an overall change in format and in Pyle's illustrations. His two finest books are *The Merry Adventures of Robin Hood* and *Pepper & Salt*, esteemed as classics by critics. In his *Illustrating Children's Books* (1963), Henry C. Pitz wrote that "the earlier Pyle books were much finer examples of book design" and pointed out that they were "hearty and honest in their arrangement of type and pictures, free of false elegance, the work of a strong hand." They contained the elements found in many first endeavors; there were the experimentation and intensity that come with first trials. What Pyle lacked in literary expertise he counterbalanced with artistic innovation.

With *The Wonder Clock*, Pyle's format became standardized and therefore static. Each story had the same number of illustrations, each illustration was contained in a heavily lined square, and most of the titles had been illustrated with a rectangular pose of the main characters, creating a tableau effect. The freshness of page, the humor within the illustrations had disappeared. It was not to reappear in the books which Pyle later wrote and illustrated for children.

While the format had become standard, Pyle's treatment of legend and his writing style had not. At the end of 1888 *Otto of the Silver Hand* was published. It is another masterpiece which has continuously remained in print, but its greatness lies less in artistic format than in writing style.

Simply told in a strong narrative, this is the story of the darker side of the Middle Ages. In this short historical-fiction book Pyle recreates an era when powerful men governed harshly and were led to acts of greed, the sword, and vengeance. The book represents a divergence in Pyle's attitude toward the Middle Ages and the conditions of the common folk. Gone is the lust for life and the spirit of fair play which dominated his earlier children's books. In his foreword Pyle writes, "Poor little Otto's life was a stony and a thorny pathway, and it is well for all of us nowadays that we walk it in fancy and not in truth."

Pyle's story depicting the evils of war centers on a young lad's life, first in a monastery and later in his father's barony, on his loss of a hand due to his father's treachery, and on his eventual marriage to the daughter of his father's hated rival. For Pyle the marriage symbolizes the coming of a new order, for it brings together two youths who grew up in, but refused to accept, the barbaric society of ruthless killings, embracing instead the wise, peaceful teachings of the monks.

Although Pyle's theme and plot are noteworthy, it is his powerful use of description and of

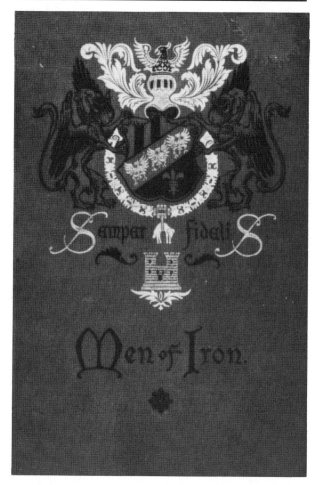

Front cover for Pyle's 1892 novel set in the time of Henry IV (Baldwin Library, University of Florida Libraries)

setting which makes the book exceptional. In this book the language is straightforward. Although Pyle does not attempt to reconstruct the language of the Middle Ages, he meticulously tries to portray the passions and the code of honor which ruled the medieval lords. He contrasts the nobility's way of life with the serenity of the religious orders. Certainly, the picture of the Middle Ages which Pyle presents is one-sided; yet, it is more realistic than his earlier heroic tales of Robin Hood. Death reigns, and people are ruled by a brutal system until Otto, through his marriage, breaks the brutality down, and Pyle ends: "The ruins of Drachenhausen were rebuilt, for the walls were there as sound as ever, though empty and gaping to the sky, but it was no longer the den of a robber baron, for beneath the scutcheon over the great gate was carved a new motto of the Vuelphs; a motto which the Emperor Rudolph himself had given: 'Manus argentea quam manus ferrea melior est.'"

In 1892 Pyle produced another book based on medieval life. *Men of Iron* is lengthier and less powerful in theme and style than *Otto of the Silver Hand*. Set in the time of Henry IV, this book deals with a young boy's training for knighthood and his eventual betrothal to a young maiden of proper lineage. Pyle's story concerns a family left without honor as a result of the plot against the life of Henry IV. Although the hero's father, Lord Gilbert Reginald Falworth, was not involved in the conspiracy, he sympathized with the rebels and was left in disgrace when the plot failed. Thus, his son Myles is trained as a squire with little hope of gaining courtly favor.

Pyle's story, set, unlike his earlier books, within courtly circles, depicts the fierceness and the brutality of the games and of the chivalry code. The heroes and villains are less clearly defined, and men of honor are shown to be proud and reckless

with their lives. The harshness of early training, the squires' bullying, and constant physical strife are all represented in this tale. Concerning this book Henry C. Pitz commented in *Howard Pyle: Writer, Illustrator, Founder of the Brandywine School* (1975): "Pyle's historical sense was extensive and thorough, yet it never conveyed a sense of mere accumulated facts. The knowledge seems to have been relived in his imagination long before words were found. His detailed story of young Myles's grueling years as a squire and his sudden leap into knighthood conveys a strong image of late medieval life."

The book's format lacks the verve of Pyle's earlier works. To illustrate this story, Pyle chose to use his own reproductions of oil paintings. Although carefully created, they lack the depth of expression or the crisp, fresh appearance contained in his black-and-white illustrations. Further,

Pyle at his studio, Wilmington, Delaware, circa 1900

since faces are not discernible, the illustrations do not strengthen the book's overall appeal. Quite possibly the book would have been better without the illustrations, but Pyle the artist could never have allowed this.

Pyle had steeped himself in historic lore and in background reading. He had carefully studied artists' reproductions of the European countryside, its peoples, and their dress. Since Pyle refused to use models for his illustrations, the places and the characters which he created were largely from his imagination. In 1889 Pyle sailed with his wife of eight years to Jamaica. Their two children were left in the United States with their grandmother; the couple enjoyed a brief vacation until they received a cablegram explaining that seven-year-old Sellers had died unexpectedly. By the time Pyle and his wife were able to return to Wilmington, the boy had been buried. To relieve his grief, Pyle wrote *The Garden Behind the Moon*, published in 1895. Abbott described it as "an exquisite, but perhaps too subtle, fairy-tale, treating allegorically of death and immortality."

This is a much more gentle book than Pyle's two medieval fictional tales. It has a fantasy plot concerning the boy David's journey behind the moon. While this story may seem a simple adventure tale, especially to very young children, its theme is the acceptance of death and it contains much of Pyle's philosophy concerning mankind, death, and reality. The land which Pyle creates in the moon garden is a wonderland: "behind the moon there lies the most wonderful, beautiful, never-to-be-forgotten garden that the mind can think of. In it live little children who play and romp, and laugh and sing, and are as merry and happy as the little white lambs in the green meadow in springtime." Pyle continues: "In it was the little boy whom I loved the best of all. He did not see me, but I saw him. . . . I was glad to see him, for he had gone out along the moon-path, and he had not come back again."

It is clear that though Pyle grieved over the death of his son, he did not believe that children should fear death. Thus, he reassures his young readers that the Moon-Angel's house is not "cold and awful" but "a calm, beautiful, lovely place, from the back-door of which you step into the other side of nowhere."

The book is written as if it were a casual conversation between the author and the reader, although Pyle does show some of the harshness of the real world. When David is looking down at the world from the moon house he sees a dead black woman and her live baby thrown overboard from a slave ship. Pyle writes: "It was very cool and pleasant down there at the bottom of the river. . . . Then somebody came walking along through the beds of long cool water grasses. It was the Moon-Angel. He came to where the black woman lay, and he took her by the hand. Then she arose and stood looking about her. The Moon-Angel picked up the baby and laid it in her arms. 'Come,' said he, 'we must be going.' "

Pyle rarely preached to his readers. When his stories contained strong themes the reader was given insight through adventure rather than through moralizing statements. In *The Garden Behind the Moon* Pyle occasionally lapses into moralistic statement, but such statements are always made in gentle tones of revelation, and they always contain hope. Thus, he finishes the scene of the woman and her child with these words: "Ah! Yes, little child. For there is as much joy and gladness over one poor black woman who enters into that place as there is over the whitest empress who ever walked the earth of Christendom."

It is interesting to note that by the 1890s Pyle was describing the freed slaves as black people rather than using the then-prominent term *negro*. Pyle's belief in the equality of all is also mirrored in the scene in which David meets the old woman who cleans the souls of men. The woman is explaining the creation story to David.

> "That was Adam and Eve," said David.
> "No;" said the old woman of the cliff; "it was Eve and Adam."
> "And what is the difference?," said David.
> "What is the difference when you say 'the light grows dim,' instead of saying 'the dim grows light?,' " said the old woman.

The Garden Behind the Moon is a beautifully written short fantasy, but it is not surprising that it has not remained in print. It lacks the battle scenes, high drama, and historical depth of Pyle's other books. Pyle's illustrations are once more in black and white, but they lack the crispness found in the artwork for his fairy-tale collections or his book about Robin Hood.

Pyle's last collection of original fairy tales, *Twilight Land*, was also published in 1895. This collection is neither as aesthetically pleasing nor as well written as the two earlier ones. Yet, the beginning of *Twilight Land* is as vivid as Pyle's introduction to Robin Hood's domain. He writes: "The earth and the air and the sky were all still, just as it is at

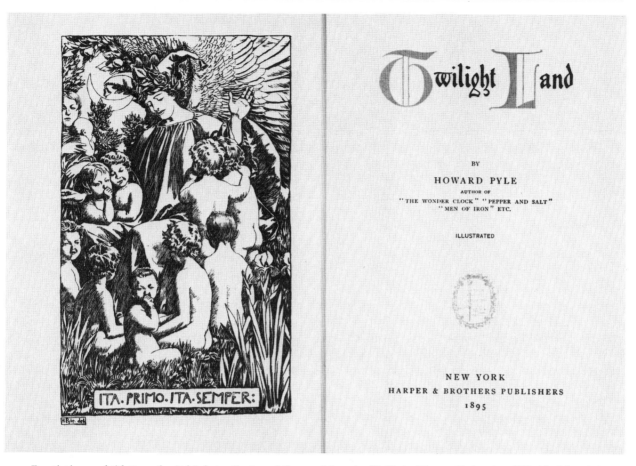

ITA·PRIMO·ITA·SEMPER:

Twilight Land

BY

HOWARD PYLE

AUTHOR OF

"THE WONDER CLOCK" "PEPPER AND SALT"
"MEN OF IRON" ETC.

ILLUSTRATED

NEW YORK
HARPER & BROTHERS PUBLISHERS
1895

Frontispiece and title page for Pyle's last collection of literary fairy tales (Baldwin Library, University of Florida Libraries)

twilight, and I heard them laughing and talking in the tap-room of the inn of the sign of Mother Goose—the clinking of the glasses, the rattling of knives and forks and plates and dishes. That was where I wished to go. So I went in. Mother Goose herself opened the door, and I was there." However, as a whole this collection cannot be considered important.

Eight years after *Twilight Land* Pyle produced the first of his books on King Arthur. Pyle's rendition of Arthurian legends is four books long and was published between 1903 and 1910. These books represent his last significant works in the field of children's literature.

Pyle's own introduction to the story of the Arthurian court had been through Sir Thomas Malory's *Morte d'Arthur*, which he had read during his youth. But as an adult he continued to study the legends and the times which had produced them. As Joseph Pennell wrote in his book *Modern Illustration* (1898), "Howard Pyle has brought all the resources of the past to aid him in the present, and is probably the most intelligent and able stu-

dent of the fifteenth century living today."

When Pyle began writing his story of King Arthur and his court, he abandoned the straightforward style he had adopted for his medieval novels, *Otto of the Silver Hand* and *Men of Iron,* and his fantasy, *The Garden Behind the Moon.* His prose is much heavier, and the author is less apt to speak directly to the reader. His style was not similar to Malory's but was his own conception of a formalized language pattern which he felt more closely fit the mood of medieval times. Pyle wrote his books about Arthur after he had studied the Welsh *Mabinogion* and Thomas Percy's eighteenth-century *Reliques of Ancient English Poetry.* It is certain that he also studied many other historic and mythic sources.

One of Pyle's restrictions was space. His knowledge of the Arthurian legend was extensive. He had studied German, English, and French sources. At one point he wrote: "I wish . . . I could write a half a dozen books instead of the three volumes . . . for in three books one can only touch upon a comparatively few of the . . : incidents of the Arthurian narrative. One can only take the direct thread, as it were, and string one's stories upon it. One can only narrate, and one must tell the direct narrative, treating it with as much original incident as possible." In the end Pyle did decide to write four volumes instead of three, so that he could offer a more complete retelling. Pyle's foreword in *The Story of King Arthur and His Knights* (1903) is written in a much simpler style than many of his earlier introductions. In it he says, "I believe that King Arthur was the most honorable, gentle Knight who ever lived in all the world." The foreword explains his rationale for recreating the Arthurian tale and is serious in tone.

Pyle divides *The Story of King Arthur and His Knights* into two parts. The first half deals with Arthur's winning of the crown, receiving the sword Excalibur from the Lady of the Lake, and marrying Lady Guinevere. Throughout this part of the book Pyle's depiction of Arthur is one of nobility; he is a powerful young ruler who uses force for right and who builds his kingdom's strength by aligning his enemies with him and by taking their sons to this castle to serve as knights. The idea of a knight errant's desire to seek adventure and to do battle in honor of a lady is aptly demonstrated, as is the noble attitude toward the code of honor.

The second half of the book tells of Merlin's death at the hands of Vivien, the disappearance of Sir Pellias from the land of mortals to the land of the fairies, and the marriage of Sir Gawaine to a fairy who turns mortal in order to remain with him.

Pyle moralizes more in his books of Arthurian tales than in any of his other writings for children. He seems intent on creating proverbs from his retellings, and at times he seems to treat the entire legend as a means to deliver platitudes. Thus, he writes, "it needs not that a man shall wear armor for to be a true knight, but only that he shall do his best endeavor with all patience and humility as it hath been ordained for him to do."

In 1905 *The Story of the Champions of the Round Table* was published. Divided into sections like *The Story of King Arthur and His Knights*, it deals with three knights of the Round Table, with the chivalric tenets of doing battle for a lady and looting castles overtaken for treasure, and with treachery and jealousy among rulers. Although Pyle points indirectly to the problems of the code of chivalry, the stories of knights errant and of battle do not show the negative sides of the Round Table. Instead, they portray a powerful group of warriors intent upon battle and gaining honor. All enemies of Arthur and of his knights are depicted as jealous, cruel

Title page for Pyle's second of four books about King Arthur's court. In a letter written while he was working with the Arthurian materials, Pyle complained that his progress was slow: "I wish to represent . . . all that is noble and high and great, and to omit, if possible, all that is cruel and mean and treacherous. Unfortunately the stories of chivalry seem to be very full . . . of meanness and of treachery . . . that discolor the very noblest of characters—such, even, as the character of King Arthur himself."

people, and their motives are shown to be selfish.

In the first part of the book Pyle does deal directly with the relationship between Launcelot and Guinevere, stating: "I am aware that there have been many scandalous things said concerning that friendship, but I do not choose to believe any such evil sayings. For there are always those who love to think and say evil things of others. Yet though it is not to be denied that Sir Launcelot never had for his lady any other dame than the Lady Guinevere, still no one hath ever said with truth that she regarded Sir Launcelot other than as her very dear friend. For Sir Launcelot always avouched with his knightly word, unto the last day of life, that the Lady Guinevere was noble and worthy in all ways, wherefore I choose to believe his knightly word and to hold that what he said was true." Pyle deals instead with the political intrigues of court, with the trickery of the fairy folk, and with the unrequited love of the knight for a lady from afar. By the time Pyle had completed retelling the legend in his four books, he had shown the darker side of chivalry. Both *The Story of Sir Launcelot and His Champions* (1907) and *The Story of the Grail and the Passing of Arthur* (1910) reflect this change.

Pyle's four books bring alive the days of chivalry more through narrative and dialogue than through character development. King Arthur remains strong, steady, and unblemished throughout. Queen Guinevere is portrayed as a beautiful woman full of folly and vanity, and Launcelot is seen as a man blinded by his adoration for another man's wife. The story is lengthy, yet it is fast paced, and its episodic adventures hold the reader's interest.

Reviewers generally greeted Pyle's versions of the Arthurian legends with favor. In 1905 the critic for the *Nation* wrote, "It is evident that this writer brings to his task wide knowledge and enthusiasm," and in 1907 the *Nation* called Pyle's *The Story of Sir Launcelot and His Champions* "Far superior to the average attempt." Nevertheless, those who have

Pyle with his wife Anne shortly before they went to Italy in November 1910

studied Pyle's work in detail have not deemed these books his best. As Charles Abbott commented in his biographical study, "as a whole, the books lack something of the compelling power of the earlier stories. They do not have the warmth and the fire of *Robin Hood* and *Men of Iron*." However, critics of Pyle's artwork have pointed to the Arthurian books as some of his finest. In Henry Pitz's estimation, the illustrations "rose to the level of their epic subject and included many of Pyle's finest conceptions."

Once Pyle had completed his Arthurian books he determined to travel abroad. He had studied reproduction of works by great Dutch and German masters, but he had never visited Europe or seen these works in their original formats. In 1910 he went to Italy and began reviewing these famous paintings. Their color and beauty amazed him. One critic commented that Pyle "had never, apparently, challenged or questioned the validity of the monochrome messages he had been receiving all of his life through wood engravings, heliotypes, photogravures, and process halftones." Just how Pyle would have used this knowledge gathered in Europe can never be known. While in Italy he was stricken by a severe attack of renal colic, and he died there in November 1911 at age fifty-eight.

Pyle's leadership in the field of children's literature has continually been acknowledged. In 1916 Pyle was described in a Michigan State literary publication as "our foremost American illustrator," with "sustained imagination and a certain charming quaintness eminently adapted to tales of fairyland or olden days." In a 1931 article for *Horn Book Magazine*, Oakley Thornton called Pyle's works for children "unfailing inspiration" to those studying illustration or literature and commented, "They gleam as guiding stars among the shadows of doubtful ways." And in a 1966 sketch for *The Illustrator in America, 1900-1960*, Harold Von Schmidt said that Pyle was "probably the greatest illustrator America has ever produced."

It is doubtful that Howard Pyle's classics will go out of print. To anyone engaged in the study of children's literature his books are landmarks, and, as such, essential reading.

References:

Charles Abbott, *Howard Pyle: A Chronicle* (New York: Harper & Row, 1923);

Brandywine River Museum, Chadds Ford, *The Brandywine Heritage: Howard Pyle, N. C. Wyeth, Andrew Wyeth, James Wyeth* (Greenwich, Conn.: New York Graphic Society, 1971);

Robert Lawson, "Howard Pyle and His Times," *Illustrators of Children's Books: 1744-1945*, edited by Bertha E. Mahoney, Louise Payson Latimer, and Beulah Folmsbee (Boston: Horn Book, 1947), pp. 105-122;

Willard Samuel Morse and Gertrude Brinkle, *Howard Pyle: A Record of His Illustrations and Writings* (Wilmington, Del.: Wilmington Society of the Fine Arts, 1975);

Elizabeth Nesbitt, *Howard Pyle* (New York: Walek, 1966);

Joseph Pennell, *Modern Illustration* (London: Bell, 1898);

Henry C. Pitz, *Howard Pyle: Writer, Illustrator, Founder of the Brandywine School* (New York: Clarkson N. Potter, 1975);

Pitz, *Illustrating Children's Books: History, Technique, Production* (New York: Watson-Guptill Publications, 1963);

Jessie Trimble, "The Founder of an American School of Art," *Outlook*, 85 (23 February 1907): 453-460;

John W. Vandercook, "Howard Pyle: Artist, Author, Founder of a School of Illustration," *Mentor* (June 1927): 1-14;

N. C. Wyeth, "Howard Pyle as I Knew Him," *Mentor* (June 1927): 15-17.

Papers:
There are collections of Pyle's papers at the Historical Society of Delaware, the Delaware Art Museum, and the libraries of Princeton University, the University of Texas at Austin, and the University of Virginia.

Louise-Clarke Pyrnelle
(19 June 1850-26 August 1907)

Susan E. Miller

BOOKS: *Diddie, Dumps, and Tot or Plantation Child-life* (New York: Harper, 1882);
Miss Li'l' Tweetty (New York & London: Harper, 1917).

Louise-Clarke Pyrnelle's works, once moderately popular, are now anachronistic. Both the author and her books are products of another era, a time far removed from the life experiences of today's children. It is doubtful that contemporary youthful readers would possess the ability to unravel the intertwined psychological and sociological conditions that gave rise to these stories. Without this understanding, the images presented in the books are degrading and misleading. While both stories are significant from anthropological and sociological perspectives, their worth as children's literature is overshadowed by the images they present. Nevertheless, Louise-Clarke Pyrnelle deserves a place among nineteenth-century children's writers, if not for the continued popularity of her work then for its historical relevance.

Louise Clarke was born on her father's plantation, Ittabena, near Uniontown, Alabama. Her father, Dr. Richard Clarke, a physician, was the son of a prominent Virginia family, and her mother, Elizabeth Carson Bates Clarke, was the daughter of a distinguished family from Alabama. Louise Clarke's childhood was spent on the plantation, where she was educated under the direction of private tutors. The defeat of the South in the Civil War, however, altered her family's situation. Dr. Clarke, who organized and served as captain of the Canebrake Rifle Guards, Company D, 4th Alabama Infantry Regiment during the war, lost his land and moved his family to Selma, Alabama. From 1865 through 1867, Clarke continued her education at Hammer Hall in Montgomery, later attending Mrs. Anna Randall Diehl's College of Education in Long Island, New York, and graduating from Professor McKay's Delsarte Academy in New York City. While in New York, she was offered an opportunity to act but chose to return to the South, where she began her teaching career as a governess. She later taught in public schools in Alabama,

Georgia, Florida, and Texas. In 1880, in Columbus, Georgia, she married John R. Pyrnelle of Brown's, Alabama. When her husband died in 1901, Louise-Clarke Pyrnelle moved from her home in Selma, Alabama, to Birmingham, where she died in 1907.

These events in Pyrnelle's life are reflected in her children's works. While she stated as her objective in writing *Diddie, Dumps, and Tot* (1882) and later *Miss Li'l' Tweetty* (1917) the desire to keep alive the stories and folkways of the Southern slaves, when the stories are viewed in relation to Pyrnelle's personal history, it is possible to get a feeling for the confusion, pain, and frustration that the fall of the South must have brought her as an adolescent child who had the supports of life pulled out from under her. Although she claims that the books were not written in defense of slavery, both *Diddie, Dumps, and Tot* and *Miss Li'l' Tweetty* present a positive view of plantation life.

It is understandable that Pyrnelle took this stance. Individuals heavily socialized into a culture, particularly one into which admission is restricted, are often blinded to the causes and consequences of their actions. This phenomenon is particularly evident in Pyrnelle's reaction to plantation life in the Old South. Through the selective eyes and memory of childhood, the author recalls a life which was idyllic for both the aristocracy and the slaves. In this version of reality, free slaves and poor whites represent the lowest and most unfortunate members of society. What is absent is an understanding of the economic and moral implications of this type of social stratification. Pyrnelle describes a system of marked contrasts and inequalities which, according to her perceptions, resulted in pleasure and security for all concerned. It is this viewpoint that makes her work significant from a sociological perspective but of questionable value as a source of children's entertainment or enlightenment.

In *Diddie, Dumps, and Tot*, the exploits of three daughters of a Southern planter are chronicled. The book takes its title from the nicknames of the three children: nine-year-old Diddie (Madeleine), five-year-old Dumps (Elinor), and three-year-old Tot (Eugenia). The girls' daily life on a Mississippi cotton plantation serves as a backdrop for the presentation of the folkways and stories typical of the pre-Civil War South. Although the book includes such folktales as "The Tar Baby," "Po' Nancy Jane O," and "How the Woodpecker's Head and the Robin's Breast Came to be Red" and describes such songs and games as "Monkey Motions," "Lipto," "De One I Like Bes'," and "Cotton-eyed Joe," the

real thrust of *Diddie, Dumps, and Tot* is its depiction of the interaction patterns between the social classes in the Old South and the beliefs and customs common to each group.

It is probable that contemporary children would enjoy the stories and songs in *Diddie, Dumps, and Tot*, but it is equally as improbable that they would understand the mechanisms behind the patterns of discrimination and self-effacement evident in this book. The explanation of the origin of black people and slavery is a case in point. Daddy Jake, the oldest slave on the plantation, tells how the fact that blacks are lazy resulted in their station in life: "Ef 'n de nigger hadn't ben so sleepy-headed, he'd er ben white, an' his hyar'd er ben straight des like yourn. Yer see, atter de Lord make 'im, den he lont him up 'gins de fence-corner in the sun fur to dry; an' no sooner wuz de Lord's back turnt, an' de sun 'gun ter come out kin'er hot, dan de nigger he 'gun ter nod, an'er little mo'n he wuz fas' ter sleep. Well wen de Lord sont atter 'im fur ter finish uv 'im up, de angel couldn't fin' 'im caze he didn't know de zack spot whar de Lord sot 'im; an' so he hollered an' called, an' de nigger he wuz 'sleep, an' he nuber hyeard 'im; so de angel tuck de white man, an' cyard him 'long, an' de Lord polished uv 'im off. Well, by'mby de nigger he waked up; but, dar now! he wuz bu'nt black, an' his hyar wuz all swuv'llt up right kinky. De Lord, seein, he wuz spilte, he didn't 'low fur ter finish 'im, an' wuz des 'bout'n ter thow 'im 'way, wen de white man axt fur 'im; so de Lord he finished 'im up des like he wuz, wid his skin black an' his hyar kunkt up, an' he gun 'im ter de white man, an' I see he's got 'im plum tell yit." This same self-image is evident in the reasoning of Jim, a young slave. When rejected by the girl he loves, he contemplates suicide: "an' ef 'n I didn't b'long ter nobody, I'd jump right inter dis creek an' drown myse'f. But I ain't got no right ter be killin' up marster's niggers dat way; I'm wuff er thousan' dollars, an' marster ain't got no thousan' dollars ter was'e in dis creek, long er dat lazy, shif'less, good-fur-nuffin' yaller nigger."

Diddie, Dumps, and Tot also brings out the tenuous position occupied by the slaves. While Mammy, the black slave, is ultimately responsible for the children, her power over them is limited. For example, when the children ask her to take them to see the encampment of the speculators (slave traders), Mammy refuses and tells Dumps that the Lord will pull her hair out for being disrespectful. Dumps retorts with, "You ain't none o' my mother. . . You're mos' black ez my shoes; an'

SANITARY MEASURES.

Illustration for Diddie, Dumps, and Tot, *written, according to Pyrnelle's preface, to keep "alive many of the old stories, legends, traditions, games, hymns, and superstitions of the Southern slaves."*

de Lord ain't er goin' ter pull all my hair off jes 'boutn you." Indignant, Mammy complains to the children's father, who calls Dumps in for questioning. When confronted, Dumps cries, "Mammy's ben er sa-a-as-sin me . . . an she said the Lord wuz goin' ter sen' an angel fur ter get my ha-air, an' she won't lem' me go-o-o ter see de spec-ec-ec-erlaters." Rather than siding with Mammy, Dumps's father agrees to take the children to the speculators' camp.

The book closes with a description of what happened to the family and the slaves after the Civil War. It is in this chapter that Pyrnelle's feelings come to the surface most clearly. The reader is told that the father died in glory for the South during the war, as did Diddie's young husband. The plantation burned to the ground; and with the freeing of the slaves, there was no money to rebuild it. Destroyed by the loss of her husband and home,

the children's mother went mad and was committed to the State Lunatic Asylum. Haunted by the sight of her young, dead husband, Diddie never remarried, preferring to devote her life to her son. The weight of caring for the children's invalid mother fell on the shoulders of Dumps, who as a consequence never married. The reader is told that only Tot escaped the trauma of the war, dying instead as a blameless child before the world she knew fell to ruin. A slight note of bitterness enters Pyrnelle's narration when she describes the slave Jim's life after the war: "He has been in Legislature, and spends his time making long and exciting speeches to the loyal leaguers against the Southern white, all unmindful of his happy childhood, and of the kind and generous master who strove in every way to render his bondage (for which that master was in no way to blame) a light and happy one."

The tone of defensiveness is more pronounced in *Diddie, Dumps, and Tot* than it is in *Miss Li'l' Tweetty*. This is not surprising given the publication dates of the two volumes. The first book was published in 1882 when the author was in her early thirties—the memories of the war and the changes it brought to her life were still vivid. That Pyrnelle was somewhat bitter is undeniable. For the child of an aristocratic Southern doctor to find herself without land or slaves, forced to teach school in order to make a living, life must have been difficult. In *Diddie, Dumps, and Tot* Pyrnelle makes clear the status of teachers in the pre-Civil War South. When Dumps asks whether Miss Carrie, the white tutor, is rich, Mammy replies: "She ain't no rich white folks . . . caze efn she wuz, she wouldn't be teachin' school for a livin', an' den ergin, efn she's so mighty rich, whar's her niggers?" The young author of *Diddie, Dumps, and Tot* must have felt robbed of her birthright.

By the time the second book was written at the close of her life, however, Pyrnelle seems to have gained some perspective on the events in her past or, at least, adjusted to the inevitable. The intensity of the writing style and the tone and imagery of *Miss Li'l' Tweetty* support this contention. The energy and emotion that infuse *Diddie, Dumps, and Tot* are absent in Pyrnelle's second children's book. This loss has both positive and negative consequences. On the positive side, *Miss Li'l' Tweetty* exhibits a less moralistic and patronizing tone than the earlier work. While the class distinctions are still evident, the derogations are less obvious and a sense of personal loss no longer haunts the story. As a result, *Miss Li'l' Tweetty* may be somewhat more effective as a contemporary children's story, although it still has some of the problems inherent in *Diddie, Dumps, and Tot*. However, the loss of vitality robs the book of much of its sociological and anthropological significance.

Unlike *Diddie, Dumps, and Tot, Miss Li'l' Tweetty* concentrates more upon the adventures of Li'l' Tweetty and her maid-in-training, Popsy, than it does upon the folkways and stories of the Southern slaves. In her first book, Pyrnelle used the children

as embodiments of the culture of the pre-Civil War South. In contrast, with a few notable exceptions such as the chapters concerned with the breaking of a voodoo curse, the emphasis on black cultural practices is missing in *Miss Li'l' Tweetty*. Instead, the reader's attention is directed toward the main events in the young white child's life.

The book is set on a plantation located along the Alabama River. Li'l' Tweetty (Mary) is the youngest child and only daughter of Dr. and Mrs. Weir. The major part of the book is devoted to two separate story lines: Li'l' Tweetty's attempt to secure the necessary materials to cure the voodoo curse afflicting her father's dearest slave, an adventure that nearly results in her death through drowning; and the flooding of the Alabama River. While this second book lacks the richness of culture found in *Diddie, Dumps, and Tot*, it does possess a depth of character development that is absent in the first book.

Part of the reason for the differences in the two books is undoubtedly the fact that Pyrnelle's life changed over the years. She taught school and lectured throughout the South, gaining some degree of recognition. Thus, whereas Pyrnelle seemed to draw upon some of her more painful memories in *Diddie, Dumps, and Tot*, by the time she wrote *Miss Li'l' Tweetty* she was able to temper her retrospections and concentrate on the characters and their values rather than simply upon the losses that resulted from the war. It is interesting to note that Pyrnelle does not even mention the war in *Miss Li'l' Tweetty*.

In summary, while *Diddie, Dumps, and Tot* and *Miss Li'l' Tweetty* lack wide contemporary appeal, they do possess a wealth of anthropological and sociological information and a degree of Southern innocence and charm that is characteristic of another era. For these reasons alone, both the books and their author deserve some attention.

Reference:

Sue Alice Sample, "A Study of Louise Clarke Pyrnelle," master's thesis, George Peabody College, 1930.

Laura E. Richards
(27 February 1850-14 January 1943)

Malcolm Usrey
Clemson University

SELECTED BOOKS: *Five Mice in a Mouse-Trap, by the Man in the Moon, Done in Vernacular, from the Lunacular* (Boston: Estes & Lauriat, 1880);

Little Tyrant (Boston: Estes & Lauriat, 1880);

Sketches and Scraps (Boston: Estes & Lauriat, 1881);

Our Baby's Favorite (Boston: Estes & Lauriat, 1881);

The Joyous Story of Toto (Boston: Roberts Brothers, 1885; London: Blackie, 1886);

Tell-Tale from Hill and Dale (Troy, N.Y.: Nims & Knight, 1886);

Kasper Kroak's Kaleidoscope, by Richards and Henry Baldwin (Troy, N.Y.: Nims & Knight, 1886);

Toto's Merry Winter (Boston: Roberts Brothers, 1887);

Queen Hildegarde (Boston: Estes & Lauriat, 1889; London: Gay & Bird, 1889);

In My Nursery (Boston: Roberts Brothers, 1890);

Captain January (Boston: Estes & Lauriat, 1891; London: Gay & Bird, 1891);

Hildegarde's Holiday: A Sequel to Queen Hildegarde (Boston: Estes & Lauriat, 1891; London: Gay & Bird, 1891);

Hildegarde's Home (Boston: Estes & Lauriat, 1892);

Glimpses of the French Court: Sketches from French History (Boston: Estes & Lauriat, 1893);

Melody (Boston: Estes & Lauriat, 1893; London: Gay & Bird, 1895);

Marie (Boston: Estes & Lauriat, 1894);

When I Was Your Age (Boston: Estes & Lauriat, 1894);

Narcissa; or, The Road to Rome. In Verona (Boston: Estes & Lauriat, 1894);

Five Minute Stories (Boston: Estes & Lauriat, 1895);

Hildegarde's Neighbors (Boston: Estes & Lauriat, 1895);

Jim of Hellas; or, In Durance Vile [and] Bethesda Pool (Boston: Estes & Lauriat, 1895);

Nautilus (Boston: Estes & Lauriat, 1895);

Isla Heron (Boston: Estes & Lauriat, 1896);

"Some Say" [and] Neighbors in Cyrus (Boston: Estes & Lauriat, 1896);

Hildegarde's Harvest (Boston: Estes & Lauriat, 1897);

Three Margarets (Boston: Estes & Lauriat, 1897);

Margaret Montfort (Boston: Estes, 1898);

Rosin the Beau (Boston: Estes & Lauriat, 1898);

Love and Rocks (Boston: Estes & Lauriat, 1898);

Sundown Songs (Boston: Little, Brown, 1899);

Chop-Chin and the Golden Dragon (Boston: Little, Brown, 1899);

The Golden-Breasted Kootoo (Boston: Little, Brown, 1899);

Peggy (Boston: Estes, 1899);

Quicksilver Sue (New York: Century, 1899);

For Tommy, and Other Stories (Boston: Estes, 1900);

Rita (Boston: Estes, 1900);

Fernley House (Boston: Estes, 1901);

Geoffrey Strong (Boston: Estes, 1901);

The Hurdy-Gurdy (Boston: Estes, 1902);

Mrs. Tree (Boston: Estes, 1902);

The Green Satin Gown (Boston: Estes, 1903);

More Five Minute Stories (Boston: Estes, 1903);

The Golden Windows: A Book of Fables for Young and Old (Boston: Little, Brown, 1903; London: Allenson, 1904);

The Merryweathers (Boston: Estes, 1904);

The Armstrongs (Boston: Estes, 1905);

Mrs. Tree's Will (Boston: Estes, 1906);

The Piccolo (Boston: Estes, 1906);

The Silver Crown: Another Book of Fables (Boston: Little, Brown, 1906; London: Allenson, 1906);

Grandmother: The Story of a Life That Was Never Lived (Boston: Estes, 1907);

The Pig Brother and Other Fables and Stories (Boston: Little, Brown, 1908);

The Wooing of Calvin Parks (Boston: Estes, 1908);

Florence Nightingale, The Angel of the Crimea (New York & London: Appleton, 1909);

Fairy Operettas (Boston: Little, Brown, 1916);

Pippin, A Wandering Flame (New York & London: Appleton, 1917);

Abigail Adams and Her Times (New York & London: Appleton, 1917);

A Daughter of Jehu (New York & London: Appleton, 1918);

Joan of Arc (New York & London: Appleton, 1919);

Honor Bright (Boston: Page, 1920);

In Blessed Cyrus (New York & London: Appleton, 1921);

The Squire (New York & London: Appleton, 1923);

Acting Charades (Boston: Walter H. Baker, 1924);

Seven Oriental Operettas (Boston: Walter H. Baker, 1924);

Honor Bright's New Adventure (Boston: Page, 1925);

Star Bright, A Sequel to Captain January (Boston: Page, 1927);

Laura Bridgman: The Story of an Opened Door (New York & London: Appleton, 1928);

Stepping Westward (New York & London: Appleton, 1931);

Tirra Lirra: Rhymes Old and New (Boston: Little, Brown, 1932; London: Harrap, 1933);

Merry-Go-Round: New Rhymes and Old (New York & London: Appleton-Century, 1935);

Samuel Gridley Howe (New York & London: Appleton-Century, 1935);

E. A. R. [Edwin Arlington Robinson] (Cambridge: Harvard University Press, 1936);

Harry in England (New York & London: Appleton-Century, 1937);

I Have a Song to Sing to You (New York & London: Appleton-Century, 1938);

The Hottentot, and Other Ditties, words and melodies by Richards, piano accompaniments by Twining Lynes (New York: Schirmer, 1939);

What Shall the Children Read? (New York & London: Appleton-Century, 1939).

"Up to Calvin's" (Boston: Estes, 1910);

A Happy Little Time (Boston: Estes, 1910);

The Naughty Comet and Other Fables and Stories (London: Allenson, 1910);

Two Noble Lives: Samuel Gridley Howe, Julia Ward Howe (Boston: Estes, 1911);

On Board the Mary Sands (Boston: Estes, 1911);

Jolly Jingles (Boston: Estes, 1912);

Miss Jimmy (Boston: Estes, 1913);

The Little Master (Boston: Estes, 1913; republished as *Our Little Feudal Cousin of Long Ago* (Boston: Page, 1922);

Three Minute Stories (Boston: Page, 1914);

Julia Ward Howe, 1819-1910, by Richards and Maude Howe Elliott, assisted by Florence Howe Hall (Boston: Houghton Mifflin, 1915);

The Pig Brother Play Book (Boston: Little, Brown, 1915);

Elizabeth Fry, The Angel of the Prisons (New York & London: Appleton, 1916);

Laura Elizabeth Howe Richards was a prolific writer of fiction and poetry for children and for adults. She wrote over ninety books, and one of her works for children, *Tirra Lirra: Rhymes Old and New*, remained in print for forty-eight years, a good record for a volume of verse. Richards has the distinction of being the first prominent American writer of nonsense verse for children, and until the past decade or so, the only woman to have written this kind of verse.

Richards's father, Samuel Gridley Howe, was principally an educator who worked with the blind, deaf, and mute. He was the main founder of the Perkins Institution and Massachusetts School for the Blind and the first person to teach a completely blind and deaf mute, Laura Bridgman, to communicate successfully with others. Laura Richards would eventually tell the story in her juvenile biography of Laura Bridgman (for whom Richards was named). Richards's mother, Julia Ward Howe, a poet and philosopher, is remembered as the author of "The Battle Hymn of the Republic."

Richards married Henry Richards, an architect, on 17 June 1871. The couple had five daughters and two sons; they lived in Boston until 1876, when they moved to Gardiner, Maine, where Henry Richards entered the family paper mill. The Richardses remained in Gardiner for the rest of their lives.

In her autobiography, *Stepping Westward* (1931), Laura Richards suggests that their lives were pleasant, almost enviably so, but there were difficulties even if Richards plays them down. Among their greatest difficulties, aside from the deaths of two of the children, was the burning of the pulp mill in 1893. Although they rebuilt the facility, it closed permanently in 1900. They then opened Camp Merryweather, a summer camp for boys on Lake Cobbosseecontee, one of their most successful ventures, which ran for more than thirty

years. It is evident that one of their problems was economic and that Laura Richards wrote, at least in part, to help out financially. After 1900, Camp Merryweather seems to have been their main source of income.

If Richards's autobiography has a failing, it is her extreme reluctance to reveal much about herself and even less about her own feelings; it is more of a record of her and her family's external lives, almost completely lacking the intimacy of really good autobiography. She tells very little about her own achievements or accomplishments. She does not mention, for example, that she and her sister won the Pulitzer Prize for Biography in 1917 for *Julia Ward Howe, 1819-1910* (1915); nor does she mention any of the philanthropic work she and her husband did for the town of Gardiner, such as helping to establish a public high school, working to bring public health nurses to the area, or striving to stop abusive child labor practices.

Richards's first published work appeared in 1880, *Five Mice in a Mouse-Trap*, the first of about forty-five works of fiction she would write for children. The most popular book she wrote for children was *Captain January*, published in 1891, and according to her autobiography, it was still her

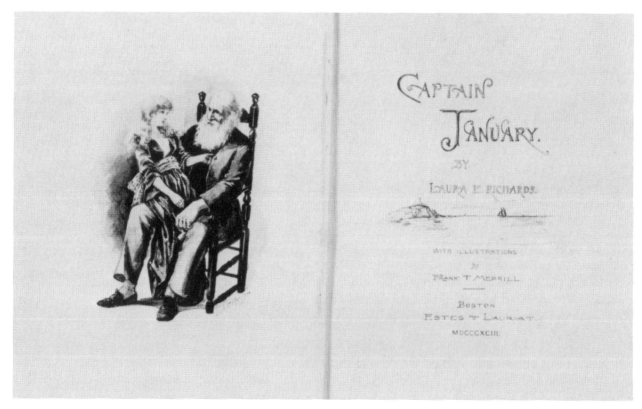

Frontispiece and title page for an 1893 edition of Richards's best-selling children's book (Baldwin Library, University of Florida Libraries)

best-selling book in 1931 even though it had been one of the most difficult for which to find a publisher. Richards recalled she had sent it "to every reputable publisher, . . . in this country, and to several in England. No one would have it." A lachrymose and sentimental novel, it tells how Captain Januarius Judkins, an eighty-year-old retired seaman and keeper of a lighthouse on an island off the coast of Maine, had rescued an infant child ten years earlier. During a terrific storm he had found the child lashed to a spar with her drowned mother; there was no clue to the child's identity, so he named her Star Bright and reared her with great love and tenderness and taught her how to read and write from the plays of Shakespeare and the King James Bible. When Star is about ten, the time of the story, her aunt, coming near the island on an excursion boat, happens to see her and recognizes her as her dead sister's child; and though Mrs. Morton wants Star to live with her, Star refuses, insisting that she remain with "Daddy Captain," which she does until he dies. There is little in the book that would appeal to children today except its sentimentality as it has no conflict to speak of, but it perhaps appealed to earlier generations because Star Bright is an outspoken little dragon when it is necessary; she says things to her foster father and to her newly discovered aunt that children of the time were not permitted to say to any older person. And it may have appealed because it lacked the didacticism prevalent in many books for children of the time. Its sequel, *Star Bright*, published thirty-six years after *Captain January*, has sixteen-year-old Star living with her aunt and cousin after having been for several years in a school for girls. The speech of Star is one of the most interesting aspects of the book, for she often speaks in direct quotations from Shakespeare and the Bible, most frequently from Shakespeare. This aberration may have caused children, and surely adults, to admire the book, the character of Star, and the ingeniousness of the author, but it merely amuses now. Another remarkable aspect of the book is the use of numerous coincidences to advance the plot (as in *Captain January*). The second book, however, has more tension than the first because Richards is attempting to get her homesick heroine back to the lighthouse island; and, though it takes Star several years, she succeeds thanks to a series of rather improbable coincidences. If these two books indicate the kinds of fiction Richards wrote for children, it is perhaps just as well that all of her fiction for children is out of print.

Tirra Lirra: Rhymes Old and New first appeared

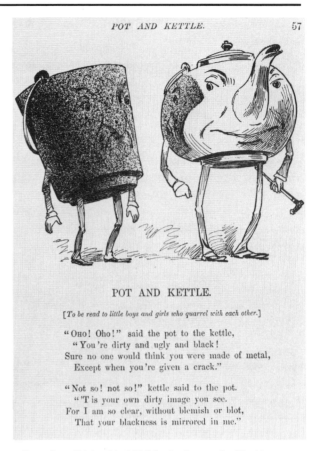

Page from Richards's 1890 book of verse, In My Nursery *(Baldwin Library, University of Florida Libraries)*

in 1932 and was republished with an introduction by May Hill Arbuthnot in 1955. Taken from periodicals and earlier books of poetry and including some new previously unpublished poems, *Tirra Lirra* is a diverse collection of nonsense poetry, some not very good, but most excellent. It is not clear from her autobiography just when Richards began writing poetry, but her "Hurdy Gurdy," as she called her gift for nonsense verse, "was usually ready at my call," and she often wrote her poems with her pad resting on the backs of her babies as she bounced them on her knees.

Tirra Lirra is one of the best books of nonsense verse for children because of several qualities, including absurd incongruities, exaggerated rhythms, and Richards's use of sound. Readers are surprised to find a shark singing blithely and merrily from a housetop in "The Shark" and a woman falling in love with a man because she likes the back of his head in "Nonsense Verses." In "The Uncle of Cato Theophilus Jones," Richards uses rhythm as well as exaggerated alliteration, consonance, and assonance to advantage:

> The uncle of Cato Theophilus Jones,
> He sang to his lute in tumultuous tones,
> "Oh twanklety twinklety twanklety twee,
> The young Georgiana is lovely to see!"

Richards also caricatures rhyme, both end and internal, to enhance the nonsense. In "The Unfortunate Grocer," "grocer" and "No sir!" are end rhymes; in "The Buffalo," Richards pairs "Buffalo" with "snuffle, oh!" Internal rhyme Richards uses often; one of the best examples is in "The Seven Little Tigers and the Aged Cook":

> They were feeling rather cross, for they had n't any sauce
> To eat with their pudding or their pie;
> So they rumpled up their hair, in a spasm of despair,
> And vowed that the aged cook should die.

Nonsense poetry without onomatopoeia would hardly be nonsense, and Richards uses it and a staccato rhythm to create the delightfully nonsensical mood of "The Song of the Corn Popper":

> Pip! pop! flippety flop!
> Here am I, all ready to pop.
> Girls and boys, the fire burns clear;
> Gather about the chimney here.
> Big ones, little ones, all in a row.
> Hop away, pop away! here we go!

Richards's most outrageous use of rhythm to heighten nonsense is in "The Orang-Outang," a tour de force of walloping grace:

> Orang-outang-tang,
> Oring-outing-ting,
> He set himself up to king-outing-ting.
>   He called up the Gibbons
>   And decked them with ribbons,
> And vowed he would teach them to sing-outing-ting.

One of her babies surely must have needed considerable bouncing the day she wrote "The Orang-Outang."

A few of the poems are pure nonsense and create delightful absurdities. The pig and Uncle Jehoshaphat in "My Uncle Jehoshaphat" love each other and have a race in the lake to see which can swim better; one swims up and one swims down, so they both win the prize and then ride into "town on the brindled calf." In "He and His Family," there is a kangaroo whose father is a whale, whose mother is a shark, and whose uncles and bride are all other kinds of fish.

Tirra Lirra has several narrative nonsense poems equal to, if not better than, some of Edward Lear's. "The Gargoyle and the Griffin" tells how a Gargoyle and a Griffin, while searching in China for Confucius, found a Gorgon playing an organ and "stood staring"

> With their goggle-eyes a-glaring,
> Till the Gorgon chanced to look at them; and then—
>   alas, the day!
> . . . .
> Not for long they made their moan there;
> There were both turned into stone there.

The evil Baron Ponderoso envies the peasant Roderigo his pheasant, Ferdinando, in "Roderigo and Ferdinando," and Ponderoso steals the golden pheasant only to be constantly jabbed by a starling, which is the pheasant metamorphosed.

Both Edward Lear and Lewis Carroll made extensive use of made-up words. Richards, too, coins names of beings and places: "a Wallachian Hospodar" rides about in the rain searching for a rhyme for his name; she has a Crumpet Cat and a Muffin Bird living on the coast of "High Barbaree"; and there are families called "the Rummy-jums" and "the Viddipocks." In the Alps, a brigand and an actor hunt a "Gnoodle," surely as rare a beast as Carroll's "frumious Bandersnatch" or "Jabberwock." And then there are Timothy Tiggs and Tomothy Toggs, who "got stuck in the bogothybogs." Even though Richards does not use invented words as frequently as Carroll and Lear, her coinages are equally good and nonsensical. In "Spots and Stripes," an ocelot puts his safety in "jeopard" because his spots are of the wrong kind. In "Good Advice," readers are advised not to be "brusque and bunctionary."

One of the noteworthy aspects of many of Richards's poems is violence. A mockingbird causes a frog to break its neck; a Hottentot gets eaten by a lioness; skinny little Mrs. Snipkin hits Mrs. Wobblechin with her "little pipkin," causing her to tumble out the window. An Arab hangs his niece and her sweetheart because the niece stole the Arab's "choicest scarab"; and a little cossack on the River Don is pulled in by the fish and drowns. Violence also appears in the poetry of Lear, Carroll, and Hilaire Belloc, which indicates that Richards was familiar with this tradition in nonsense poetry. Perhaps violence served as a kind of comic relief for

Richards (right) with her mother, Julia Ward Howe, her daughter Julia Ward Shaw, and her grandson Henry Shaw

poets who consciously or unconsciously revolted against the saccharine and overly pious, didactic poetry most often written for children. Or, perhaps the realization that the pious poetry of the nineteenth century rarely had any excitement called forth violence to rectify that lack.

Richards's poetry is often made richer by her use of poetic arabesques. A pig has an "impudent quirk" in its tail; there are "the prawns and the shrimps, with their curls and their crimps"; and "every man's blood up on end it stood,/And their hair ran cold in their veins." There is "the lolloping lizard" who had "a piteous pain in his gizzard"; and "The Wizard of Wogg With his Glimmering Glog," which, according to a footnote, is "A magical instrument, little in use to-day."

Richards seems to have been familiar with the cautionary verses of Hilaire Belloc because some of her poems are reminiscent of his. As in Belloc's poetry, in Richards's evildoers often get their comeuppance. In "Roderigo and Ferdinando," Ponderoso is punished for stealing; in "Forty Little Ducklings," an Ancient Gander tells the young

ducks that the river is very near, though it is not, and when they finally return, the first thing they do after they recover from their trek is "to peck the Ancient Gander, till he ran away and hid." A camel in "A Brief Ballad of Araby" causes so much trouble that "They wished to find relief of him,/ And so they made corned beef of him,/And ate him then and there." This kind of didacticism, if it can be called that, is so ridiculous that perhaps only the most sensitive—or guilt-ridden—reader would notice the lessons.

Richards's reputation rests on her nonsense poetry for children, not on her fiction. *Tirra Lirra* is a remarkably refreshing book of nonsense, some of the best written by an American. Her verses are as accomplished as, if somewhat derivative of, those of Edward Lear and Lewis Carroll, though in some ways Richards's work recalls poems by Hilaire Belloc. Mrs. Richards has been called the Queen of Nonsense Verse, and though the title may not convey fully her merit as a nonsense poet for children, it is a title she earned and still deserves.

Reference:
Ruth Hill Viguers, "Laura E. Richards, Joyous Companion," *Horn Book Magazine*, 32 (April 1956): 87-97; 32 (June 1956): 163-167; 32 (October 1956): 376-388, 467-478.

Papers:
There are small collections of Richards's papers at the Colby College Library, Waterville, Maine, and the Gardiner (Maine) Public Library.

Horace E. Scudder
(16 October 1838-11 January 1902)

Mark Irwin West
University of North Carolina at Charlotte

SELECTED BOOKS: *Seven Little People and Their Friends* (New York: A. D. F. Randolf, 1862);

Dream Children (Cambridge, Mass.: Sever & Francis, 1864);

Stories from My Attic (New York: Hurd & Houghton, 1869);

Doings of the Bodley Family in Town and Country (New York: Hurd & Houghton, 1875);

The Dwellers in Five-Sisters' Court (New York: Hurd & Houghton, 1876);

The Bodleys Telling Stories (New York: Hurd & Houghton, 1878);

The Bodleys on Wheels (Boston: Houghton Osgood, 1879);

The Bodleys Afoot (Boston: Houghton Osgood, 1880);

Mr. Bodley Abroad (Boston: Houghton Mifflin, 1880);

Stories and Romances (Boston: Houghton Mifflin, 1880);

Boston Town (Boston: Houghton Mifflin, 1881);

The Bodley Grandchildren and Their Journey in Holland (Boston: Houghton Mifflin, 1882);

Noah Webster (Boston: Houghton Mifflin, 1882);

The English Bodley Family (Boston: Houghton Mifflin, 1884);

A History of the United States of America, Preceded by a Narrative of the Discovery and Settlement of North America and of the Events Which Led to the Independence of the Thirteen English Colonies, for the Use of Schools and Academies (Philadelphia: J. H. Butler/Boston: W. Ware, 1884);

The Viking Bodleys (Boston: Houghton Mifflin, 1885);

Men and Letters: Essays in Characterization and Criticism (Boston & New York: Houghton Mifflin, 1887);

Portraits and Biographical Sketches of Twenty American Authors (Boston & New York: Houghton Mifflin, 1887);

Literature in School: An Address and Two Essays (Boston & New York: Houghton Mifflin, 1888);

George Washington: An Historical Biography (Boston

& New York: Houghton Mifflin, 1889);

A Short History of the United States of America, for the Use of Beginners (New York: Taintor/Boston: W. Ware, 1890);

The Riverside Primer and Reader, by Scudder, J. F. Hall, and C. F. Newkink (Boston: Houghton Mifflin, 1893);

Childhood in Literature and Art (Boston & New York: Houghton Mifflin, 1894);

Henry Oscar Houghton: A Biographical Outline (Cambridge, Mass.: Houghton Mifflin, 1897);

A History of the United States of America, With an Introduction Narrating the Discovery and Settlement of North America (New York & Chicago: Sheldon, 1897);

James Russell Lowell: A Biography (Boston & New York: Houghton Mifflin, 1901).

OTHER: *The Children's Book: A Collection of the Best and Most Famous Stories and Poems in the English Language,* edited by Scudder (Boston: Houghton Mifflin, 1881);

The Book of Fables, Chiefly from Aesop, edited by Scudder (Boston: Houghton Mifflin, 1882);

The Book of Folk Stories, retold by Scudder (Boston: Houghton Mifflin, 1887);

Fables and Folk Stories (Boston: Houghton Mifflin, 1890); republished as *The Book of Fables and Folk Stories* (Boston: Houghton Mifflin, 1906);

The Book of Legends Told Over Again, retold by Scudder (Boston: Houghton Mifflin, 1890).

Scudder's first published story about the Bodley family, which appeared in the juvenile magazine he edited from 1867 to 1870 (Baldwin Library, University of Florida Libraries)

Although Horace E. Scudder wrote numerous books for children, he had a more profound impact on American children's literature as an editor and critic than he did as an author. Through his editorial work on the *Riverside Magazine for Young People* and the *Riverside Literature Series for Young People,* he attempted to provide children with high quality literature. He believed that children's literature should be the subject of serious literary criticism. This attitude is reflected not only in his magazine articles and reviews of children's books but also in his pioneering treatise, *Childhood in Literature and Art.*

Horace Elisha Scudder was born in Boston, Massachusetts. Being the last of seven children, he seldom lacked company during his early years. His parents, Charles Scudder, a successful merchant, and Sarah Lathrop Coit Scudder, were both native New Englanders. Charles Scudder, who served as a deacon in the Union Church, exerted a strong religious influence on his children. Horace Scudder attended Roxbury and Boston Latin schools before

entering Williams College. While in college, he devoted himself to classical studies and to editing the *Williams Quarterly.* He graduated in 1858 at the age of twenty.

Shortly after his graduation, Scudder moved to New York, where he worked for three years as a teacher of private pupils. It was during this period that he became an admirer of Hans Christian Andersen. In 1861 he published an article about Andersen's work in the *National Quarterly Review.* Using Andersen's fairy tales as his model, he began writing fanciful children's stories. These stories first appeared in newspapers, but in 1862 Scudder decided to bring together seven of his favorite stories for publication as a book. He entitled this collection *Seven Little People and Their Friends.* The book received a lengthy and very positive review from the *Atlantic Monthly.* Encouraged by the success of his first book, Scudder produced a second collection of children's stories under the title of *Dream Children* in 1864.

With the death of his father, Scudder returned to Boston where, in 1866, he met Henry O. Houghton of the Hurd and Houghton publishing firm. The two quickly became close friends, and Scudder began working for Houghton as an editorial assistant. Houghton, however, had bigger plans for Scudder. He decided to launch a children's magazine, and he asked Scudder to head it. Thus, in 1867 Scudder became the editor of the *Riverside Magazine for Young People*. One of his first acts as editor was to contact Andersen and ask him if he would be willing to contribute stories to the new magazine. Andersen agreed, and over the course of the magazine's brief existence, he contributed seventeen stories, ten of which had not been published before. Scudder also secured contributions from Jacob Abbott, Mary Mapes Dodge, Edward Everett Hale, Helen Hunt Jackson, Sarah Orne Jewett, Frank R. Stockton, and many other talented writers. The magazine's illustrators were of equal stature. The art work of John La Farge, Thomas Nast, Winslow Homer, E. B. Bensell, and H. L. Stephens regularly appeared in the magazine. However, Scudder's editorials were the magazine's most unusual feature. These editorials were aimed at parents and dealt with children's reading. They contained some of the first serious criticism of children's literature published in America. Scudder continued to edit the *Riverside Magazine* until 1870 when it was forced to cease publication because of financial problems.

The year before the *Riverside Magazine* folded, Scudder produced his third children's book, *Stories from My Attic* (1869). The book's contents resemble those of a magazine. It includes a few stories, a discussion of William Blake's art, and some biographical, historical, and travel sketches. One of the stories, "The Neighbors," is particularly appealing. It features two cats who talk to each other while sitting on the edges of their respective masters' roofs.

During the early 1870s, Scudder's contributions to children's literature were minimal. On 30 October 1873 he married Grace Owen, and they settled into a home in Cambridge, Massachusetts. Shortly thereafter they had twin daughters. He continued his association with Hurd and Houghton, and in 1875 he was named its literary adviser, a position he retained when the firm was later reorganized into Houghton, Mifflin and Company.

From 1875 to 1885 Scudder produced a series of eight children's books about the adventures of

the Bodley family. He first introduced this New England family in a story that appeared in the *Riverside Magazine* in 1867. The first book of the series, *Doings of the Bodley Family in Town and Country* (1875), is set in the late 1840s, and as Scudder admitted in a letter, it is in part a reminiscence of his own boyhood. The book deals with the experiences of the family as they move from Boston to Roxbury. In the second book, *The Bodleys Telling Stories* (1878), Scudder has his characters relate stories from American history. This volume also contains an account of the family's journey to Cape Cod. *The Bodleys on Wheels* (1879) and *The Bodleys Afoot* (1880) are both about the family's travels through New England. In *Mr. Bodley Abroad* (1880), Scudder provides his readers with a glimpse of Europe as seen through the eyes of Mr. Bodley. In the final three books of the series, *The Bodley Grandchildren and Their Journey in Holland* (1882), *The English Bodley Family* (1884), and *The Viking Bodleys* (1885), the Bodley grandchildren are the main characters. The Bodley books were quite popular, and other authors soon began to write similar travel stories for children.

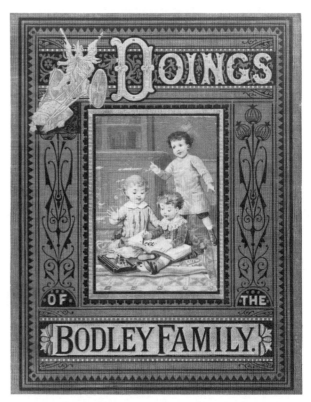

Front cover for an 1878 edition of Scudder's first collection of Bodley tales, set in late-1840s New England (Baldwin Library, University of Florida Libraries)

Scudder's long-standing belief in the value of fanciful children's literature led him to edit several collections of nursery classics for Houghton, Mifflin and Company. The most notable of these anthologies is *The Children's Book,* published in 1881. Scudder included fables, fairy tales, Andersen's stories, nursery rhymes, and Greek myths in this one-volume library. He also edited *The Book of Fables, Chiefly from Aesop* (1882), *The Book of Folk Stories* (1887), *Fables and Folk Stories* (1890), and *The Book of Legends* (1890).

Scudder was dissatisfied with the readers that were used in public schools. In his opinion, the people who edited these textbooks had "lost their sense of literature as a fine art, and looked upon it as only an exercise in elocution and the vehicle for knowledge." It particularly bothered him that children were only provided with fragments of great books and poems. He believed that children should read works of literature in their entirety, and to this end he created the Riverside Literature Series for Young People. The books in this series were designed primarily for use in schools. They were inexpensive and small enough to fit inside a child's pockets. Among the over two hundred books listed in the series were works by Coleridge, Defoe, Dickens, Hawthorne, Longfellow, Shakespeare, and many other literary giants. Also included in the series was Scudder's critically acclaimed biography *George Washington: An Historical Biography,* published in 1889.

In 1882 Scudder was invited to deliver a series of lectures at the Lowell Institute. He chose as his theme the portrayal of children in Western literature and art. A revised version of these lectures was published in 1894 under the title of *Childhood in Literature and Art.* The book is Scudder's most original piece of scholarship. In addition to providing valuable insights into the treatment of childhood in Western literature, it includes a thoughtful analysis of American children's literature and an excellent introduction to Hans Christian Andersen.

Though Scudder's literary career revolved around children, he also had a significant impact on adult literature. He wrote several adult books, including *The Dwellers in Five-Sisters' Court* (1876), *Stories and Romances* (1880), *Noah Webster* (1882), and *James Russell Lowell: A Biography* (1901). From 1890 to 1898 he served as editor of the *Atlantic Monthly.* However, he is best remembered for his Bodley books and his untiring efforts to provide children with outstanding literature.

Letters:

Waldemar Westergaard, ed., *The Andersen-Scudder Letters: Hans Christian Andersen's Correspondence with Horace Elisha Scudder* (Berkeley & Los Angeles: University of California Press, 1949).

References:

Alexander V. G. Allen, "Horace E. Scudder: An Appreciation," *Atlantic Monthly,* 91 (April 1903): 549-560;

Jean Hersholt, "The Two Never Met," *Saturday Review of Literature,* 29 (21 December 1946): 18-19;

Alice M. Jordan, *From Rollo to Tom Sawyer* (Boston: Horn Book, 1948), pp. 113-122.

Lydia Huntley Sigourney
(1 September 1791-10 June 1865)

Carol Gay
Youngstown State University

See also the Sigourney entry in *DLB 1, The American Renaissance in New England.*

SELECTED BOOKS: *Moral Pieces, in Prose and Verse* (Hartford, Conn.: Sheldon & Godwin, 1815);

Traits of the Aborigines of America, anonymous (Cambridge, Mass.: Hilliard & Metcalf, 1822);

Sketch of Connecticut, Forty Years Since, anonymous (Hartford, Conn.: Oliver D. Cooke, 1824);

Poems (Boston: S. G. Goodrich/Hartford, Conn.: H. & F. J. Huntington, 1827);

Female Biography; Containing Sketches of the Life and Character of Twelve American Women, anonymous (Philadelphia: American Sunday-School Union, 1829);

Evening Readings in History: Comprising Portions of the History of Assyria, Egypt, Tyre, Syria, Persia, and the Sacred Scriptures; With Questions, Arranged for the Use of the Young, and of Family Circles, anonymous (Springfield, Mass.: G. & C. Merriam, 1833; London, 1834);

Letters to Young Ladies, anonymous (Hartford, Conn.: Printed by P. Canfield, 1833; London: Simpkin, Marshall, 1835; revised, Hartford, Conn.: William Watson, 1835; enlarged, New York: Harper, 1837; enlarged again, London: Jackson & Walford/Edinburgh: Innes, 1841; New York: Harper, 1842);

How to Be Happy. Written for the Children of Some Young Friends, anonymous (Hartford, Conn.: D. F. Robinson, 1833);

Biography of Pious Persons; Abridged for Youth, anonymous, two volumes (Springfield, Mass.: G. & C. Merriam, 1833);

The Farmer and the Soldier. A Tale, as L. H. S. (Hartford, Conn.: Printed by J. Hubbard Wells, 1833);

A Report of the Hartford Female Beneficent Society (Hartford, Conn.: Printed by Hanmer & Comstock, 1833);

Sketches (Philadelphia: Key & Biddle, 1834; London: Rich, 1834);

Poetry for Children (Hartford, Conn.: Robinson & Pratt, 1834); enlarged as *Poems for Children* (Hartford, Conn.: Canfield & Robins, 1836);

Poems (Philadelphia: Key & Biddle, 1834; enlarged, Philadelphia: Key & Biddle, 1836);

Lays From the West, collected and arranged by Joseph Belcher (London: Ward, 1834);

Tales and Essays for Children (Hartford, Conn.: F. J. Huntington, 1835);

Memoir of Margaret and Henrietta Flower, anonymous (Boston: Perkins, Marvin/Philadelphia: Henry Perkins, 1835);

Zinzedorff, and Other Poems (New York: Leavitt,

322

Lord/Boston: Crocker & Brewster, 1835);

History of Marcus Aurelius, Emperor of Rome (Hartford, Conn.: Belknap & Hammersley, 1836);

Olive Buds (Hartford, Conn.: William Watson, 1836);

The Girl's Reading-Book, in Prose and Poetry (New York: J. Orville Taylor, 1838; revised, New York: J. Orville Taylor, 1839); republished as *The Book for Girls, Consisting of Original Articles in Prose and Poetry* (New York: Turner & Hayden, 1844);

Letters to Mothers (Hartford, Conn.: Printed by Hudson & Skinner, 1838; London: Wiley & Putnam, 1839; enlarged, New York: Harper, 1839);

Select Poems (Philadelphia: Frederick W. Greenough, 1838);

The Boy's Reading-Book, in Prose and Poetry (New York: J. Orville Taylor, 1839); revised and enlarged as *The Boy's Book* (New York: Turner, Hughes & Hayden, 1843);

Memoir of Mary Anne Hooker, Author of "The Life of David," Etc. Etc. Etc. Written for The American Sunday-School Union, and Revised by the Committee of Publication, anonymous (Philadelphia: American Sunday-School Union, 1840);

Pocahontas, and Other Poems (London: Robert Tyas, 1841; republished with differing contents, New York: Harper, 1841);

Poems, Religious and Elegiac (London: Robert Tyas, 1841); republished in part in *Pocahontas, and Other Poems* (New York: Harper, 1841);

Pleasant Memories of Pleasant Lands (Boston: James Munroe, 1842; London: Tilt & Bogue, 1843; enlarged, Boston: James Munroe, 1844; revised and enlarged again, Boston & Cambridge: James Munroe, 1856);

The Pictorial Reader, Consisting of Original Articles for the Instruction of Young Children (New York: Turner & Hayden, 1844); republished as *The Child's Book, Consisting of Original Articles, in Prose and Poetry* (New York: Turner & Hayden, 1844);

Scenes in My Native Land (Boston: James Munroe, 1845; London: Wiley & Putnam, 1845);

Poetry for Seamen (Boston: James Munroe, 1845); enlarged as *Poems for the Sea* (Hartford, Conn.: H. S. Parsons, 1850); republished as *The Sea and the Sailor* (Hartford, Conn.: F. A. Brown, 1857);

The Voice of Flowers (Hartford, Conn.: H. S. Parsons, 1846);

Myrtis, With Other Etchings and Sketchings (New York: Harper, 1846);

The Weeping Willow (Hartford, Conn.: H. S. Parsons, 1847);

Water-Drops (New York & Pittsburgh: Robert Carter, 1848);

Illustrated Poems . . . With Designs by Felix O. C. Darley, Engraved by American Artists (Philadelphia: Carey & Hart, 1849);

Whisper to a Bride (Hartford, Conn.: H. S. Parsons, 1850; enlarged, Hartford, Conn.: Wm. Jas. Hamersley, 1851);

Letters to My Pupils: With Narrative and Biographical Sketches (New York: Robert Carter, 1851);

Examples of Life and Death (New York: Scribners, 1851);

Olive Leaves (New York: Robert Carter, 1852; London: Delf, 1852);

The Faded Hope (New York: Robert Carter, 1853); republished as *Faded Hopes* (London: Nisbet, 1853);

Memoir of Mrs. Harriet Newell Cook (New York: Robert Carter, 1853);

The Western Home, and Other Poems (Philadelphia: Parry & McMillan, 1854);

Past Meridian (New York: Appleton/Boston: Jewett, 1854; London: Hall, 1855; enlarged, Hartford, Conn.: F. A. Brown, 1856; revised and enlarged again, Hartford, Conn.: Brown & Gross, 1864);

Sayings for the Little Ones and Poems for Their Mothers (Buffalo: Phinney/New York: Ivison & Phinney, 1855);

Examples from the Eighteenth and Nineteenth Centuries, first series (New York: Scribners, 1857);

Lucy Howard's Journal (New York: Harper, 1858; London: Low, 1858);

The Daily Counsellor (Boston: Brown & Gross, 1859);

Gleanings (Hartford, Conn.: Brown & Gross, 1860);

The Man of Uz, and Other Poems (Hartford, Conn.: Williams, Wiley & Waterman, 1862);

Letters of Life (New York: Appleton, 1866).

Lydia Howard Huntley Sigourney, "the sweet singer of Hartford," was with little doubt the most popular poet of the nineteenth century. Her work, which included volumes of prose and poetry and innumerable periodical contributions, appealed particularly to young women and their mothers. The twentieth century, however, has either ignored her or treated her with contempt, at times tempered with condescension. Her poetry and prose are so imbued with all the worst traits of nineteenth-century sentimentality, religiosity, and morbidity that few have been able to discuss her work with any degree of objectivity, at least until the 1970s.

Born the only daughter of a gardener, Ezekiel Huntley, and his second wife, Zerviah Wentworth Huntley, she was often in the home of her father's employer, a wealthy and aged widow, Mrs. Daniel Lathrop. Mrs. Lathrop, evidently drawn by the child's intelligence and pliant good nature, kept Lydia Huntley with her often during her last years, relying on her increasingly until her death when Lydia was fourteen. The years spent at the side of Mrs. Lathrop, reading aloud from the books the elderly woman wanted to hear—Edward Young's poem *Night Thoughts*, for instance, and other such funereal works popular at the time—undoubtedly had a lasting impact on the young girl. "The cream of all my happiness was a loving intercourse with venerable age," she wrote in her autobiographical *Letters of Life* (1866). The precocious child was encouraged to read not only by the Widow Lathrop but also by her mother, who provided her with Ann Radcliffe's *The Mysteries of Udolpho* and prodded her to write a novel when she was eight. To this support was added that of the Wadsworth family of Hartford, grateful relatives of Mrs. Lathrop who aided Lydia Huntley throughout her life.

When she was twenty, having read widely and prepared herself by a stay in Hartford with the Wadsworths brushing up on such areas of feminine education as art and needlework, she opened a school of her own in Norwich with a close friend, Nancy Maria Hyde. She intended to help support her parents and to become independent, and this she did. After two years, she closed the Norwich school, and, encouraged by the Wadsworths, moved to Hartford and opened a school there. This time Huntley decided to ignore the particularly feminine branches of learning in order to concentrate on such subjects as reading, arithmetic, rhetoric, natural and moral philosophy, and history. Although she conducted the school for only four years, its impact upon her students can perhaps be judged by the fact that for forty-five years after its closing students were still holding school reunions.

In 1815 Daniel Wadsworth raised subscriptions for her first published work, wrote the introduction for it, and helped her see it through the press. Discussing *Moral Pieces, in Prose and Verse* (1815), the critic for the *North American Review* described its author as "a most deserving and interesting young woman" who had managed to free "herself from the humblest penury, and still found leisure at a very early age, to compose this volume." This book gave evidence of Sigourney's fluent and facile skill, her predilection for the sentimental, the historical, and the moralistic, and her fondness for the extremely popular graveyard school of poetry.

In 1819 she married Charles Sigourney, a widower with three children who was a prosperous hardware merchant in Hartford. She continued to write but now she had her work published anonymously since her husband had strong objections to women achieving public notice. She threw her energies into raising his children, designing and decorating the house he built for her, and eventually raising her own children with him. The Sigourneys had five children, three of whom died at birth. Mary, born in 1827, and Andrew, born in 1831, survived.

Lydia Sigourney was active in philanthropic work, producing poetry and occasional pieces and contributing regularly to at least twenty periodicals to raise funds for charities and causes that she espoused. By the early 1830s, she was publishing prodigiously; from 1832 to 1834 at least ten books appeared, among them the extremely popular *Letters to Young Ladies*. For a while, the incentive for this outpouring was to provide money for household extras, for her aging parents, and for the char-

Sigourney's husband Charles, whom she married in 1819

ities she supported; but it became increasingly clear in the late 1820s and early 1830s that her husband's financial situation was not as secure as it had been. By 1832 his prosperity had vanished, and from this point on, it was Lydia Sigourney's income as a writer that provided for the household. In 1833, ignoring her husband's objections, she began publishing under her own name. By 1839 the family had recovered economically because of Lydia Sigourney's business acumen and literary success.

Throughout her life Sigourney had an intense drive to attain financial security, undoubtedly nurtured by the genteel poverty of her youth and by the jarring realization that her husband was unable to fulfill the role of provider, as society had led her to expect. This important facet of her character at times led her into practices that were questioned even at the height of her popularity. She curried the favor, for instance, of the celebrated and famous by keeping track of birthdays and anniversaries and sending little gifts and complimentary notes, thereby cultivating, if possible, some sort of acquaintanceship. She was overly eager to rush into print correspondence she had frequently elicited by such methods, correspondence that the writers assumed would be private. One well-publicized incident during her lifetime was her ill-considered inclusion in *Pleasant Memories of Pleasant Lands* (1842) of a personal letter from the wife of

Robert Southey revealing his mental disintegration. The letter implied an intimate friendship when, in fact, none existed. Sigourney allowed her name to appear as an editor of *Godey's Lady's Book* for a handsome sum but evidently had no compunctions about accepting money from its rival *Ladies Companion*, even though what Godey had in mind was the exclusive right to her name. She seems to have practiced quite successfully a variety of techniques for putting her name before the public in order to capture the mass reading market, which she helped to create. Through her success, she was a pioneer and role model for the professional woman writer of her century.

The nineteenth century, however, did not admire either a skillful business woman or a successful writer. It was necessary for Sigourney to maintain the conventional role of the female, and there is no evidence that she did not fill it willingly and well, though there is evidence of a rocky relationship with Charles Sigourney. It was pointed out, for instance, in John S. Hart's *The Female Prose Writers of America*, published in 1852, that she "sacrificed no womanly or household duty, no office of friendship or benevolence for the society of the muses. That she is able to perform so much in so many varied departments of literature and social obligation, is owing to her diligence. She acquired in early life that lesson—simple, homely, but invalu-

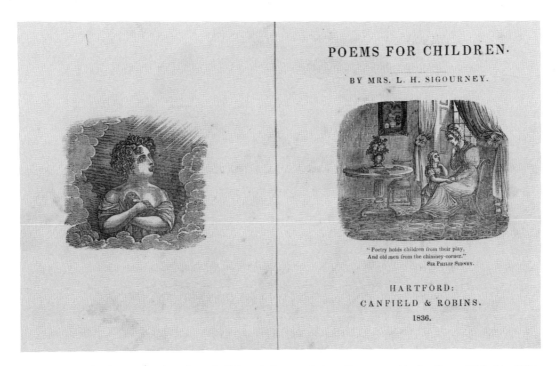

*Frontispiece and title page for the enlarged edition of Sigourney's juvenile poetry collection first published in 1834
(Baldwin Library, University of Florida Libraries)*

Letter to Sigourney from Edgar Allan Poe asking her to contribute to Graham's Magazine *(Connecticut Historical Society)*

able—to make the most of passing time." This she did without a doubt, because her contemporary reputation rested not only upon her prodigious literary output, but also, and almost equally, upon her ability to expend countless hours on good works and charitable deeds and to respond to demands made upon her by her audience by maintaining a voluminous correspondence with readers. Her readers admired her works, and they also respected her deeds (or most of them).

Her success can be accounted for because she was able to project an image of herself as the ideal nineteenth-century woman. Her readers saw a prolific writer able to deal with the romantic, sentimental, pious subjects they wanted to read about in a style that appealed to them with its profusion of such euphonious and euphemistic phrases as " 'neath the billows," "curls of gold," "rich velvet of the curtaining banks." The Lydia Sigourney they saw was a good wife who declared that "Woman should keep in her own sphere and not attempt to fill men's place," a superlative mother who responded in real life and in her poetry to the needs of her children and to the needs of mothers who knew grief and loss through the death of their children, and they saw a woman who, while denying a woman's right to financial independence, was able to achieve it. At what cost, they would never know; it is doubtful if Lydia Sigourney ever knew. At any rate, she built a contemporary reputation that even Edgar Allan Poe, an astute and at times an acrimonious critic, hesitated to attack too harshly, his most biting complaint (and one which Sigourney never forgave him) being that her work was overly derivative. However, he, like others, was driven by her popularity to plead for a monthly contribution to his periodical, *Graham's Magazine*, for which he assured her she would be paid a sum "at least as liberal as that of any publisher in America." By 1849 her reputation was secure and on a level with Longfellow's and Bryant's; that year her *Illustrated Poems* was published in an elegant series that also included their works.

Although most critics tend to ascribe Lydia Sigourney's appeal to the multitudes of young adolescent girls and women who read her books, to her ability to cater to the tastes of a mass reading market, there are a few qualities in her work that can perhaps earn her a more secure place in posterity. Gordon Haight, her sole biographer, comments condescendingly in *Mrs. Sigourney: The Sweet Singer of Hartford* (1930) that "More often than not it was the *woman* rather than the *authoress* that wrote her poems." Perhaps, however, this is more of a

strength than a weakness. Emily Watts, in *The Poetry of American Women From 1632 to 1945*, observes that the pressures which forced Sigourney into the excessive output of her most popular years indeed make her poetry "padded, pedantic, and prudish" but that her early poems show promise and her greatest poetic skill. Sigourney's anonymity at the beginning of her career allowed her to experiment freely with topic and theme, and Watts believes that an analysis of these early works can furnish an objective evaluation of Sigourney's strengths as a poet. For Watts, the 1834 collection of her work, entitled simply *Poems*, "represents her best poetry." In these poems can be found what might be termed her unique contribution to American poetry, her attempt "to deal honestly and in fairly real terms with the emotions, frustrations, and tragedies of the deaths of real children and their real mothers." Sigourney does this in different, more realistic terms from the graveyard school that influenced her so much.

In ascribing to, and serving, willingly or unwillingly, as the representative of the nineteenth century's prescription that a woman's identity came not from any professional function but solely from her role as wife and mother, and primarily the latter, Sigourney was faced with the tragic problem of so many of her sisters: how to cope with the extraordinarily high death rate of their children. If the only role that women could perform was that of mother, how then could they deal with the stunning fact of failure when their offspring did not survive? Having experienced the deaths of three of her children at birth and later the death of her nineteen-year-old son, she was able to strike a deep and authentic note of despair and failure in her death poems, a chord different from Bryant's in "Thanatopsis" and Whitman's in "Out of the Cradle Endlessly Rocking" and perhaps, in Watts's view, not struck again until Robert Frost's "Home Burial." The American quality of these poems, their democratic drift that everyone—even the very least, the child and the woman—is equal in the face of death, and her repeated insistence on "the significance of the family," further add, in Watts's view, stature to Sigourney's place in American poetry.

Lydia Huntley Sigourney outlived her husband Charles by eleven years. She died on 10 June 1865 in Hartford, Connecticut, beloved and respected as a poet and as a woman.

Biography:
Gordon S. Haight, *Mrs. Sigourney: The Sweet Singer*

of Hartford (New Haven: Yale University Press, 1930).

References:

John S. Hart, *The Female Prose Writers of America* (Philadelphia: E. H. Butler, 1852), pp. 76-83;

Emily Watts, *The Poetry of American Women from 1632 to 1945* (Austin: University of Texas Press, 1977);

A. D. Wood, "Mrs. Sigourney and the Sensibility of the Inner Space," *New England Quarterly*, 45 (June 1972): 163-181.

Papers:

Major collections of Lydia Howard Sigourney's correspondence are at the Connecticut Historical Society and the Yale University Library.

Charles Asbury Stephens

(21 October 1844?-22 September 1931)

Motley Deakin
University of Florida

SELECTED BOOKS: *Camping Out: As Recorded by "Kit"* (Boston: Osgood, 1872; London: Trübner, 1872);

Left on Labrador, or the Cruise of the Schooner-Yacht "Curlew." As Recorded by "Wash" (Boston: Osgood, 1872; London: Trübner, 1872);

Off to the Geysers, or the Young Yachters in Iceland. As Recorded by "Wade" (Boston: Osgood, 1872; London: Trübner, 1872);

Lynx-Hunting. By the Author of Camping Out (Boston: Osgood, 1873; London: Trübner, 1873);

Fox-Hunting, as Recorded by Raed (Boston: Osgood, 1873; London: Trübner, 1873);

On the Amazons; or, The Cruise of "The Rambler." As Recorded by Wash (Boston: Osgood, 1873; London: Trübner, 1874);

The Young Moose Hunters: A Backwoods-boy's Story (Boston: Shepard, 1874; London: Partridge, 1892);

The Knockabout Club in the Woods: The Adventures of Six Young Men in the Wilds of Maine and Canada (Boston: Estes & Lauriat, 1882); republished as *Adventures of Six Young Men in the Wilds of Maine and Canada; or the Knockabout Club* (London: Dean, 1884);

The Knockabout Club Alongshore: The Adventures of a Party of Young Men on a Trip from Boston to the Land of the Midnight Sun (Boston: Estes & Lauriat, 1882);

The Knockabout Club in the Tropics: The Adventures of a Party of Young Men in New Mexico, Mexico, and Central America (Boston: Estes & Lauriat, 1883);

Living Matter: Its Cycle of Growth and Decline in Animal Organisms (Norway Lake, Maine: The Laboratory Company, 1888);

Pluri-Cellular Man. Whence and what is the intellect, or "soul"? What becomes of the Soul? Is it possible to save the soul? from the Biological Standpoint (Norway Lake, Maine: The Laboratory Company, 1892);

Long Life: The Occasional Review of an Investigation of the Intimate Causes of Old-Aging and Organic Death, with a View to their Alleviation and Removal (Norway Lake, Maine: The Laboratory Company, 1896);

Natural Salvation. The message of science. Outlining of the first principles of immortal life on earth (Norway Lake, Maine: The Laboratory Company, 1903);

The Ark of 1803. A Story of Louisiana Purchase Times (New York: Barnes, 1904);

Pioneer Boys Afloat on the Mississippi. A Story of Louisiana Purchase Times (New York: Barnes, 1907);

When Life Was Young at the Old Farm in Maine (Norway Lake, Maine: Old Squire's Bookstore, 1912);

A Great Year of Our Lives at the Old Squire's (Boston: Youth's Companion, 1912);

Salvation by Science (Boston: Colonial Press, 1913);

Immortal Life. How it will be achieved (Boston: Colonial Press, 1920);

A Busy Year at the Old Squire's (Boston: Youth's Companion, 1922);

Molly's Baby. A Little Heroine of the Sea (Boston: Youth's Companion, 1924);

Haps and Mishaps at the Old Farm (Boston: Perry Mason, 1925);

Stories of My Home Folks (Boston: Perry Mason, 1926);

Katahdin Camps (Boston & New York: Houghton Mifflin, 1928);

My Folks in Maine (Norway, Maine: Old Squire's Bookstore, 1934);

A Wildwood Romance (Norway, Maine: Old Squire's Bookstore, 1935).

The significance of Charles Asbury Stephens as a writer of children's literature is tied to his long, successful association with the popular periodical *Youth's Companion,* whose phenomenal increase in circulation to a peak of five hundred thousand copies in 1890 he helped achieve. He was prolific, writing some three thousand short stories and sketches and about two hundred fifty serials, many of them under a variety of pseudonyms, of which the best known probably was Charles Adams. Some of his work was reprinted in book form.

Most of his writing for children can be classified into two categories, travel stories and reminiscences of his childhood. His work, particularly his travel stories, contains a strong pedagogical element, even to the point that educating readers at times becomes the primary emphasis. Convinced that children preferred stories which they believed to be real, Stephens cultivated that characteristic in his writing, making his presentation as factual and circumstantial as he could. His stories often read like freshly remembered records of his own experience. The value of his work lies more in his liveliness of presentation and in the wealth of factual information he gives his readers than it does in its literary quality, which often is marred by evidence of its hasty composition. At its best, his work captures, simply and vividly, life as Stephens knew it in late-nineteenth-century New England.

Stephens, the only child of Simon and Harriet N. Upton Stevens, was born in Norway, Maine, and spent his childhood there. The year of his birth, though sometimes given as 1847, was probably 1844. His ancestors, from whom he adopted the spelling of his surname, had helped found the community and lived there for several generations. The experiences of his childhood, as he recorded them in over two hundred sketches and stories, appear to be typical of that time and place. They record

From a July 1907 issue of Youth's Companion, *the magazine with which Stephens was associated for over sixty years*

how he worked on the farm and in the timber. They tell how he hiked and camped, hunted and fished in what was still mostly a wilderness. His educational experiences also appear in these sketches. He went to school when money and time made it possible, first to District School No. 11, then to the Norway Liberal Institute, and finally to Bowdoin College. While in college he paid all his expenses; he completed the curriculum in two years, graduating in 1869 at the top of his class.

In his book of reminiscences, *Stories of My Home Folks* (1926), Stephens describes how, as "a youth just emerging from his teens," he first met Daniel Ford, publisher of *Youth's Companion.* With the encouragement of Elijah Kellogg, a professor at Bowdoin, Stephens had already had a few items published, a serial entitled "Guess" in *Ballou's Monthly Magazine* and some short articles in *Our Flag of Boston,* but he was uncertain about trying to make a career of writing until he sold his first two stories to Ford for fourteen dollars. This success at *Youth's Companion* began his long association with the periodical and encouraged him shortly thereafter (April 1871) to marry Christine Stevens, his second cousin. They had two daughters.

THE

KNOCKABOUT CLUB

IN THE WOODS.

*THE ADVENTURES OF SIX YOUNG MEN IN THE WILDS
OF MAINE AND CANADA.*

BY

C. A. STEPHENS,

AUTHOR OF "CAMPING OUT," "LEFT ON LABRADOR," "FOX HUNTING," "ON THE AMAZONS,"
"THE YOUNG MOOSE HUNTERS," ETC.

FULLY ILLUSTRATED.

BOSTON:
ESTES AND LAURIAT.
1882.

Frontispiece and title page for the first Knockabout Club adventure (Baldwin Library, University of Florida Libraries). The three Knockabout Club books and the five Camping Out titles were fictionalized reports of Stephens's travels as a writer for Youth's Companion.

Stephens enjoyed traveling. Soon after he began working for *Youth's Companion* he journeyed to Washington, D.C., and Mt. Vernon with the understanding that he write a report of his experiences for publication in the magazine. The success of this effort led to twenty years of travel over much of North and Central America, to the West Indies and Europe, most of which he reported in *Youth's Companion* and then later assembled in part in two series of books, the Camping Out series, published from 1872 to 1874 (*Camping Out: As Recorded by "Kit"; Left on Labrador, or the Cruise of the Schooner-Yacht "Curlew." As Recorded by "Wash"; Off to the Geysers, or the Young Yachters in Iceland. As Recorded by "Wade"; Lynx-Hunting. By the Author of Camping Out; Fox-Hunting, as Recorded by Raed; On the Amazons; or, The Cruise of "The Rambler." As Recorded by Wash*), and the Knockabout Club series, published in 1882 and 1883 (*The Knockabout Club in the Woods; The*

Knockabout Club Alongshore; The Knockabout Club in the Tropics).

In several of these books he promoted his idea of a traveling college, which he envisioned as a group of young men on board a ship journeying to some unusual place and there studying its characteristics and history. The characters Stephens used in these stories are thinly disguised presentations of himself and some of his close associates; he is Kit, his cousin Verril Addison is Wash, and two other friends are Wade and Raed. Structurally, these books consist of a series of incidents loosely held together by this group of characters. As they travel, each of the characters has his special interest (geology or botany, for example) which it is his responsibility to study. He must then inform his companions of what he has learned, and thus the function of the traveling college is fulfilled.

The other large component of Stephens's

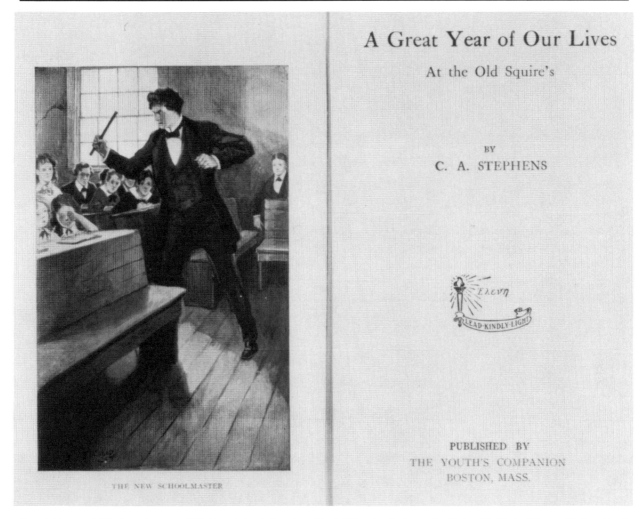

A Great Year of Our Lives

At the Old Squire's

BY

C. A. STEPHENS

PUBLISHED BY
THE YOUTH'S COMPANION
BOSTON, MASS.

THE NEW SCHOOLMASTER

Frontispiece and title page for one of Stephens's books based on his childhood experiences in Maine (Baldwin Library, University of Florida Libraries)

writing for children, his stories about his childhood experiences in Maine, were assembled into books which, in form, are similar to the travel books. A group of young people engages in loosely related activities characteristic of their age and circumstances, and often their endeavors are illustrative of some moral principle. These books constitute the Old Squire series, which originally included three books: *When Life Was Young at the Old Farm in Maine* (1912), *A Great Year of Our Lives at the Old Squire's* (1912), and *A Busy Year at the Old Squire's* (1922). *Molly's Baby. A Little Heroine of the Sea* (1924) was added when the original series titles were republished.

In 1884 Stephens was encouraged by Ford to enroll in Boston University for the purpose of obtaining his doctor's degree in medicine. Ford asked

Stephens to do this because he wanted a member on the staff of *Youth's Companion* who could report medical items factually and accurately. Stephens attended medical school and graduated in 1887 while at the same time maintaining an active relationship with the magazine. Biology had always been an interest of his, and earlier he had done some research into the causes of old age, particularly as they related to cells. With his studies completed, he turned more actively to research, building a laboratory near his old home in Norway, Maine. He developed a theory that life could be prolonged by renewing the biogen, a hypothetical protein molecule thought to be essential for such basic biological processes as assimilation and disassimilation. From 1888 to 1920, he wrote a series of books on his theory and research. Terms such as "long life," "natural salvation," "immortal life," all taken from the titles of his books, reflect the nature of his interest.

During this same period he wrote most of his reminiscences of his youth. His wife died in 1911. In December 1912 he married Minnie Scalar Plummer, a native of the nearby community of South Paris and famous as an opera singer. Stephens continued to work and write until he died in 1931. From 1934 to 1936 a memorial edition of his work was published.

Bibliography:

Louise Harris, *A Comprehensive Bibliography of C. A. Stephens* (Providence: C. A. Stephens Collection, Brown University, 1965).

Reference:

Louise Hams, *None but the Best* (Providence: C. A. Stephens Collection, Brown University, 1966).

Papers:

The C. A. Stephens Collection is at Brown University.

Frank R. Stockton
(5 April 1834-20 April 1902)

Jill P. May
Purdue University

BOOKS: *A Northern Voice for the Dissolution of the Union of the United States of America* (N.p., 1860);

Ting-a-ling (New York: Hurd & Houghton, 1870; London: Ward & Downey, 1889);

Round-about Rambles in Lands of Fact and Fancy (New York: Scribner, Armstrong, 1872);

The Home: Where It Should Be and What To Put In It, by Stockton and Marian Stockton (New York: Putnam's, 1873);

What Might Have Been Expected (New York: Dodd, Mead, 1874; London: Routledge, 1874);

Tales Out of School (New York: Scribner, Armstrong, 1876);

Rudder Grange (New York: Scribners, 1879; London: Hamilton, 1883; revised, New York: Scribners, 1879);

A Jolly Fellowship (New York: Scribners, 1880; London: Kegan Paul, 1880);

The Floating Prince and Other Fairy Tales (New York: Scribners, 1881; London: Ward & Downey, 1889);

The Lady, or the Tiger? And Other Stories (New York: Scribners, 1884; London: Hamilton, 1884);

The Story of Viteau (New York: Scribners, 1884; London: Low, 1884);

The Late Mrs. Null (New York: Scribners, 1886; London: Low, 1886);

The Christmas Wreck and Other Stories (New York: Scribners, 1886);

The Casting Away of Mrs. Lecks and Mrs. Aleshine (New York: Century, 1886; London: Low, 1886);

The Bee-Man of Orn and Other Fanciful Tales (New York: Scribners, 1887; London: Low, 1888);

The Hundredth Man (New York: Century, 1887; London: Low, 1887);

The Dusantes. A Sequel to "The Casting Away of Mrs.

Lecks and Mrs. Aleshine" (New York: Century, 1888; London: Low, 1888);

Amos Kilbright: His Adscititious Experiences, with Other Stories (New York: Scribners, 1888; London: Unwin, 1888);

The Great War Syndicate (London: Longmans Green, 1889; New York: Collier, 1889);

Personally Conducted (New York: Scribners, 1889; London: Low, 1889);

The Stories of the Three Burglars (New York: Dodd, Mead, 1889; London: Low, 1890);

Ardis Claverden (New York: Dodd, Mead, 1890; London: Low, 1890);

The Cosmic Bean; or, The Great Show in Kobol-Land (London: Black & White Publishing, 1891);

The Rudder Grangers Abroad and Other Stories (New York: Scribners, 1891; London: Low, 1891);

The Squirrel Inn (New York: Century, 1891; London: Low, 1891);

The House of Martha (Boston & New York: Houghton Mifflin, 1891; London: Osgood, McIlvaine, 1891);

The Clocks of Rondaine and Other Stories (New York: Scribners, 1892; London: Low, 1892);

The Watchmaker's Wife and Other Stories (New York: Scribners, 1893);

Pomona's Travels (New York: Scribners, 1894; London: Cassell, 1894);

The Adventures of Captain Horn (New York: Scribners, 1895; London: Cassell, 1895);

Mrs. Cliff's Yacht (New York: Scribners, 1896; London: Cassell, 1896);

Captain Chap or The Rolling Stones (London: Nummo, 1896; Philadelphia: Lippincott, 1897);

A Story-Teller's Pack (New York: Scribners, 1897; London: Cassell, 1897);

The Great Stone of Sardis. A Novel (New York & London: Harper, 1898);

The Girl at Cobhurst (New York: Scribners, 1898; London: Cassell, 1898);

The Buccaneers and Pirates of Our Coasts (New York & London: Macmillan, 1898);

The Associate Hermits (New York & London: Harper, 1899);

The Vizier of the Two-Horned Alexander (New York: Century, 1899);

The Young Master of Hyson Hall (Philadelphia: Lippincott, 1900; London: Chatto, 1900);

Afield and Afloat (New York: Scribners, 1900; London: Cassell, 1900);

A Bicycle of Cathay. A Novel (New York & London: Harper, 1900; London: Harper, 1900);

Kate Bonnet. The Romance of a Pirate's Daughter (New

Frank R. Stockton

York: Appleton, 1902; London: Cassell, 1902);

John Gayther's Garden and the Stories Told Therein (New York: Scribners, 1902; London: Cassell, 1902);

The Captain's Toll-gate (New York: Appleton, 1903; London: Cassell, 1903);

The Lost Dryad (Riverside, Conn.: Printed at Hillacre for the United Workers of Greenwich, 1912);

The Poor Count's Christmas (New York: Stokes, 1927).

Frank R. Stockton is best remembered as the author of the short story "The Lady, or the Tiger?," but he is also acknowledged as an American humorist and the first associate editor of prestigious children's publication *St. Nicholas,* whose work for the magazine helped to establish its high standards. Although Stockton is a minor children's author and is not read extensively by modern youngsters, some of his short fantasy stories have remained in print.

Born in Philadelphia on 5 April 1834, Francis Richard Stockton was the third son of William Smith Stockton and his second wife, Emily Drean Stockton. Since their first two children had died in infancy, he was the eldest living child. Stockton was a slight, frail boy who was born with one leg shorter than the other. His physical activities were limited during his youth, so he began creating lengthy stories. Often these tales were developed in his imagination for several days before he began to put them on paper. He later wrote that these early tales "were constructed according to my own ideas. I caused the fanciful creatures who inhabited the world of fairy-land to act, as far as possible for them to do so, as if they were inhabitants of the real world. . . . I obliged these creatures to infuse into their extraordinary actions a certain leaven of common sense."

Stockton attended Central High School, a small boys' school. While he was a student there, he won a prize for a short story in a contest sponsored by the *Boys' and Girls' Journal*. In February 1852 he graduated from Central High and began working as a wood engraver's apprentice. Although Stockton was working as an engraver, he continued to create short stories and began submitting them for publication. In 1855 his first story appeared in the *American Courier, A Family Newspaper*. Entitled "The Slight Mistake," it is a fast-paced romance concerning a young girl's apparent duplicity and eventual engagement to the story's hero. Four years later his second story, "Kate," was published in the *Southern Literary Messenger*. Although his writing career was more challenging to him than his work as an engraver, he could not afford to devote his efforts totally to fiction until he was twenty-six years old. He married Mary Ann Edwards Tuttle, a young woman whom his mother had employed to teach in her private school, in April 1860, and shortly thereafter he began writing a story entitled "A Story of Champaigne," which was serialized in the *Southern Literary Messenger* in 1861. Stockton's awareness of the bitterness and anger that Southerners were feeling toward Northern intervention in the matter of slavery led him to rationalize that the Southern states should be allowed to secede from the Union—a viewpoint he supported in a privately published pamphlet entitled *A Northern Voice for the Dissolution of the Union of the United States of America* (1860). Shortly after it was printed, Fort Sumter fell and Stockton withdrew his pamphlet.

Stockton's first children's story, "Ting-a-ling," appeared in the *Riverside Magazine* during November and December of 1867. Ting-a-ling resembles Thumbelina in size, but he is a resourceful elf whose best friend is a giant. Together they help humans solve their problems. With this work Stockton established his fairy-tale formula. The action

is fast paced, and though most of the story demonstrates the importance of being optimistic and helping others, Stockton's primary goal is to entertain rather than to teach. In 1870 *Ting-a-ling* was published as a book.

In 1868 Stockton had become an editorial assistant to Mary Mapes Dodge on the new children's magazine *Hearth and Home*, a position which led to his appointment as Dodge's assistant editor on *St. Nicholas* in 1873. His second book was published in 1872. Entitled *Round-about Rambles in Lands of Fact and Fancy*, it is a curious combination of short stories and essays which deal with scientific information concerning nature. It is written in a condescending tone which is not characteristic of Stockton's other juvenile works.

At *St. Nicholas* Stockton's editorial life took on new speed. Although he was assistant editor, he was in the office more often than Mary Mapes Dodge and at times was forced to write materials for the journal. Some of these stories were pub-

Title page for Stockton's first book for children, the story of an elf and a giant who work together to help humans solve their problems (Baldwin Library, University of Florida Libraries)

lished under the pseudonyms Paul Fort and John Lewes. As Paul Fort he wrote stories in French and German and invited readers to send translations to the editorial offices. Some of the articles which he wrote were expository; most were never published after their appearances in the periodical.

In 1874 a short version of one of Stockton's best adult fiction books, *Rudder Grange,* appeared in *Scribner's Magazine.* This work, written in Stockton's whimsical style, tells the story of a couple who take in a servant named Pomona. A hapless, cheerful girl who constantly creates chaos in the house, Pomona is a typical Stockton character. She is both disarming and comical. Although Pomona is a humorous figure, Stockton never presents her as a stereotype or caricature. His low-key tone offsets the wild antics of his characters, making absurdities seem like everyday occurrences. *Rudder Grange* was published in book form in 1879. It was so successful with readers that Stockton wrote two sequels, *The Rudder Grangers Abroad* (1891) and *Pomona's Travels* (1894).

In 1876 Stockton produced another collection of children's stories, *Tales Out of School,* which, like the earlier *Round-about Rambles,* included several short whimsical pieces mixed with some informative narratives. Stockton's editorial responsibilities at *St. Nicholas* were heavy; his work schedule also included his own writing of book manuscripts. Never a strong man, Stockton began to experience painful eye problems, until, in 1876, he became unable to continue writing and reading. He was never able to return fully to his work as an editor, and his disability hampered his work as a fiction writer. However, he began dictating his stories, working them out in his imagination. Royalties from *Rudder Grange* and its sequels and income from his steady contributions to *St. Nicholas* enabled him to begin traveling widely.

In 1881 Stockton produced *The Floating Prince and Other Fairy Tales,* a collection of several humorous stories previously published in *St. Nicholas.* In 1882 *Century Magazine* published his most famous short story, "The Lady, or the Tiger?" It had originally been written to be read before a literary society to which he belonged, and it caused so much discussion that Stockton decided to submit it for publication. This slight story deals with a young woman whose father, the ruler of the kingdom, is determined to punish her lover after he finds out about their relationship. In an arena the young man is faced with two doors, one of which he must open. Behind one stands a beautiful maiden; behind the other is a hungry tiger. The princess sig-

nals that he should open the door on the right. The suspense is built around the idea that love can destroy as well as redeem one. Stockton himself presents no answer to the dilemma. The entire story is a puzzle concerning morality. After Stockton received hundreds of queries about the ultimate decision, he finally released the following statement: "If you decide which it was—the lady, or the tiger/ you find out what kind of a person you are yourself."

Immediately after the publication of this immensely popular story, Stockton suffered a crisis. After so intriguing a story, publishers were reticent to publish Stockton stories which they deemed below the standard of "The Lady, or the Tiger?" When the Stocktons returned from a European tour in 1884, Frank Stockton was in ill health. His recovery was slow and his time to write more restricted. His slow pace and his travels to Virginia helped Stockton regain his health until he was able to write stories and letters and to read for short intervals.

During the next few years Stockton produced one of his best humorous adult novels, *The Casting Away of Mrs. Lecks and Mrs. Aleshine* (1886), and created the literary fairy tales on which his reputation as a children's writer is based. These tales, originally published in *St. Nicholas,* were collected in *The Bee-Man of Orn and Other Fanciful Tales* (1887).

In 1884 Stockton's "The Queen's Museum" appeared in *St. Nicholas.* The story's main character is a queen who collects rare buttonholes and who insists that all of her subjects visit the museum where she displays them or go to prison. Other characters are a stranger who shows the queen the error in her ways, a hermit's pupil, and a robber captain. The entire plot follows the stranger's journey to find objects of interest to the kingdom's people and his plan to rob the queen of her buttonhole collection. Although the plot is entertaining, it is Stockton's droll wit which makes this story classic. By the end of the story the pupil and the robber captain have exchanged roles. Stockton writes: " 'I am tired,' the Captain said, 'of a robber's life. I have stolen so much that I cannot use what I have. I take no further interest in accumulating spoils. The quiet of a hermit's life attracts me; and, if you like, we will change places. I will become the pupil of your old master, and you shall be the captain of my band.' " The stranger has by now married the queen. When he learns that the pupil has become a robber, he strikes a bargain: the pupil will only rob robbers. Thus, "The first place they robbed was their own cave, and as they all had excellent

ST. NICHOLAS.

VOL. II.   APRIL, 1875.   NO. 6.

CINDERELLA.

BY FRANK R. STOCKTON.

SHE did not live in the days of fairies and giants, when pumpkins could be changed into chariots, and rats and mice to prancing steeds and liveried footmen.

But it did not matter much. She sat by the great fire-place in the kitchen and dreamed day-dreams about fairy-land and its beautiful sights and wonderful transformations, and when she took off her wooden shoes and warmed her little bare foot by the blaze on the hearth, she sometimes dreamed of a glass slipper, and a Prince, with long white waving plumes, to try it on. And it always fitted her. Of course, if it had not, there would have been no sense in dreaming about it.

She was a little French girl, and she lived in an old farm-house, where they burned brushwood under the great iron pot that hung in the fire-place, and where the great mantel-piece, so high up that she had to stand on a chair to reach it, was crowded with curious old pitchers and glasses and plates and jugs that nobody used, and where the carved doors, and, indeed, almost everything about the place but the people who lived there, looked nearly old enough to have come down from fairy days.

There, before the fire, with the two heads on the ends of the andirons for company, she would sit for hours and dream day-dreams. The two heads on the andirons were so very attentive and still that they seemed as if they were listening to what she was thinking, and, although the backs of their heads must have been very hot, they never interrupted her.

She wished she *had* lived in the old days and had had a fairy godmother. Old Mère Christine was her godmother, and a very good and kind one

she was too, but she had no magic wand and could not change her red bodice and woolen skirt into beautiful silken robes, nor could she make a splendid chariot out of a pumpkin. The only thing at all magical that she could do was to turn flour and butter into delicious little cakes, and a rolling-pin was all the wand she had.

Her two sisters, too, were not so very cross, and they did not make her do all the work. Lizette was married, and had her baby to attend to, but she was nearly always busy at something about the house; and Julie was very industrious.

And as to the Prince, she had never seen him at all.

So she had to dream about all the bad things as well as the good things that happened to the real Cinderella, so long, long ago.

She was sitting before the fire one day, watching the fire to keep it lively under the pot, and thinking about the days when there were kind fairies and goblins to make fires for good little girls and to hang up magical pots, out of which they might scoop anything good to eat that they might fancy; and so she gradually got to thinking about her favorite old story of Cinderella.

She sat like her beloved heroine in the castle kitchen, and in her mind she saw her cruel sisters pass down the grand staircase, dressed in their rich silks and satins, and proudly get into their coaches and drive away to the parties and balls, in which their hearts delighted.

She saw her wicked stepmother as she shook her fist at her, whenever she dared venture to look out at that dismal ashy kitchen, where everything seemed as if the cooking were always just over, and

VOL. II.—22.

From a tale by Stockton which appeared in St. Nicholas *nearly two years after the magazine began publication with Stockton as assistant editor (Baldwin Library, University of Florida Libraries)*

memories, they knew from whom the various goods had been stolen, and everything was put in its proper order. The ex-pupil then led his band against the other dens of robbers in the kingdom, and his movements were conducted with such dash and vigor that the various hordes scattered in every direction, while their treasures in their dens were returned to the owners, or, if these could not be found, were given to the poor." Stockton's technique of delivering his moral in a simple statement is aptly demonstrated in this story when the stranger tells the queen, "we cannot make other people like a thing simply because we like ourselves."

In 1885 Stockton's "Old Pipes and the Dryad" appeared in *St. Nicholas.* Slower paced than "The Queen's Museum," "Old Pipes and the Dryad" deals with old age and eternal youth. An old man's rejuvenation through the acts of a beautiful dryad is less humorous in tone, more pastoral in setting. In this short fantasy the twist-of-fate device Stock-

ton liked so much to use points to nature's final control over all. After Old Pipes and his mother have each grown younger by twenty years, the Dryad returns to her tree certain that Old Pipes will return in the spring to let her out. Stockton ends his story: "The Dryad was not mistaken when she trusted in the piper. When the warm days came again, he went to the oak tree to let her out. But to his sorrow and surprise he found the great tree lying upon the ground. A winter storm had blown it down, and it lay with its trunk shattered and split. And what became of the Dryad, no one ever knew."

"The Griffin and the Minor Canon," another 1885 contribution to *St. Nicholas,* is a lengthier story. It contains the ironic humor found in "The Queen's Museum" and the careful characterization found in "Old Pipes and the Dryad." Like these two stories, it does have a moral lesson. Although this time it is more pronounced, Stockton's didacticism is never heavy-handed. In fact, the youthful reader might not pick up Stockton's irony concerning the organized church, religious practices, and human nature.

The Griffin, upon hearing that his image carved in stone adorns the town church, decides that he will travel to the church and view the work. When he arrives in the town all, save a gentle Minor Canon, refuse to meet with the Griffin. The Minor Canon is fearful of the Griffin, but he is also aware of his duty toward the townspeople, a group who cares little about religion or the well-being of others. An unusual friendship begins between the Griffin and the Minor Canon. At first the Griffin's interest in the church is in his carved image, but gradually he shifts his interest to the Minor Canon, and at last he begins following the young priest about as he performs his church duties.

When the villagers perceive that the Griffin has no intention of leaving, the wealthy and powerful flee, leaving the town to the working class and the poor. At first the common people seem able to return to their duties, but as the equinox grows near they remember that soon the Griffin will need to eat. These selfish people determine that the Minor Canon must leave so that the Griffin will follow him.

The Griffin, however, does not follow the Minor Canon. Instead he remains behind and assumes his friend's duties. When the townspeople finally approach the Griffin and suggest that they will prepare an excellent banquet for him, or at the most allow him to eat the orphans, the Griffin replies, "From what I have seen of the people in this town, I do not think I could relish anything which was prepared by them. They appear to be all cowards, and therefore mean and selfish. As for eating one of them, old or young, I could not think of it for a moment. In fact, there was only one creature in the whole place for whom I could have had any appetite and that is the Minor Canon, who has gone away. He was brave and good and honest, and I think I should have relished him." In the end the Griffin brings the Minor Canon back to the town and returns to his own home where he "gradually declined and died." This portrayal of mankind's drive for self-preservation is much more caustic than those in the earlier two fantasies. In "The Griffin and the Minor Canon" Stockton points to society as a morally weak group unable to see the virtuous man in its midst.

Stockton's dislike for deceitful people and his appreciation for the quiet, gentle man who is out of step with society is often found in his short children's fantasies. Many of his most memorable characters are sensible people who try to follow the dictates of society only to discover that society is misguided. Usually Stockton's main characters are able to find contentment within the very society which caused them anxiety. Typically, the Minor Canon returns home and continues to serve those people who drove him out of the village.

Three additional tales—"The Bee-Man of Orn," "Prince Hassak's March," and "The Banished King"—also published in *St. Nicholas* during the 1880s, round out Stockton's most significant writings for children. Concerning Stockton's fairy tales, his wife once wrote, "Children like the stories, but the deeper meaning underlying them all was beyond the grasp of a child's mind. These stories Mr. Stockton took great pleasure in writing, and always regarded them as some of his best work. . . ."

Critics tend to agree with Stockton's view. His biographer Martin I. J. Griffin commented in 1939, "This group of short 'fanciful tales,' as Stockton called them, were written at a time when Stockton was reaching the zenith of his powers. . . . They represent a phase of Stockton's work which made contributions to the literature of the world. They are timeless . . . in their simplicity, . . . their amazing complexity, in their humanity, and in their hu-

Stockton in 1896

mor, a rich addition to our American literature, and to the gentle wisdom of the world."

Stockton's contemporaries held both the author and his writing in high regard. In 1901 one critic wrote, "The supreme quality which Mr. Stockton possesses . . . is his inventiveness. He is an Edison amongst the patient students and gropers after the dramatic truths of human life. . . . The persons in these stories are usually matter of fact in their manner, but the springs which work the characters are often marvels of ingenuity." Another contemporary stated, "It was impossible to be with him and not feel an affectionate regard for him. He was direct, humorous, often gay in his subdued way; but one always felt a certain tenderness toward him."

In 1899 Stockton bought a home in the Shenandoah Valley of Virginia. There he settled and began gardening. Concerning his last years, Mrs. Stockton wrote, "Truly life was never sweeter to him than at its end, and the world was never brighter to him than when he shut his eyes upon it." Stockton died on 20 April 1902. Among students of children's literature, his reputation remains as a creator of narratives about common heroes who flourish within society because of their natural goodness.

Biographies:

Biographical Sketch, in Stockton's *The Captain's Toll-gate, with A Memorial Sketch by Mrs. Stockton* (New York: Appleton, 1903);

Martin I. J. Griffin, *Frank R. Stockton: A Critical Biography* (Philadelphia: University of Pennsylvania Press, 1939).

References:

William Chislette, Jr., *Moderns and Near-Moderns: Essays on Henry James, Stockton, Shaw, and Others* (New York: Grafton Press, 1928);

W. D. Howells, "Mr. Stockton and All His Works," *Book Buyer*, 20 (February 1900): 19-21;

Hamilton W. Mabie, "Frank R. Stockton," *Book Buyer*, 24 (June 1902): 355-357.

Papers:

There is a collection of Stockton's papers at the Clifton Waller Barrett Library, University of Virginia.

Harriet Beecher Stowe
(14 June 1811-1 July 1896)

Millicent Lenz
State University of New York at Albany

See also the Stowe entries in *DLB 1, The American Renaissance in New England,* and *DLB 12, American Realists and Naturalists.*

*SELECTED BOOKS: *Primary Geography for Children on an Improved Plan,* by Stowe and Catharine Beecher (Cincinnati: Corey, Webster & Fairbank, 1833);

Prize Tale: A New England Sketch (Lowell, Mass.: Gilman, 1834);

The Mayflower; or, Sketches of Scenes and Characters among the Descendants of the Pilgrims (New York: Harper, 1843); enlarged as *The Mayflower and Miscellaneous Writings* (Boston: Phillips, Sampson, 1855);

---

* This list omits British editions for books first published in the United States.

Uncle Tom's Cabin; or, Life Among the Lowly, 2 volumes (Boston: Jewett/Cleveland: Jewett, Proctor & Worthington, 1852);

Uncle Sam's Emancipation; Earthly Care, a Heavenly Discipline; and Other Sketches (Philadelphia: Hazard, 1853);

Sunny Memories of Foreign Lands, 2 volumes (Boston: Phillips, Sampson/New York: Derby, 1854);

The Christian Slave. A Drama Founded on a Portion of Uncle Tom's Cabin (Boston: Phillips, Sampson, 1855);

Dred; A Tale of the Great Dismal Swamp, 2 volumes (Boston: Phillips, Sampson, 1856); republished as *Nina Gordon: A Tale of the Great Dismal Swamp,* 2 volumes (Boston: Ticknor & Fields, 1866);

Our Charley, and What to Do With Him (Boston: Phillips, Sampson, 1858);

(Boston: Ticknor & Fields, 1862);

The Minister's Wooing (New York: Derby & Jackson, 1859);

The Pearl of Orr's Island: A Story of the Coast of Maine

Agnes of Sorrento (Boston: Ticknor & Fields, 1862);

A Reply to "The Affectionate and Christian Address of Many Thousands of Women of Great Britain and Ireland to Their Sisters, the Women of the United States of America" (London: Low, 1863);

House and Home Papers, as Christopher Crowfield (Boston: Ticknor & Fields, 1865);

Little Foxes, as Crowfield (Boston: Ticknor & Fields, 1866);

Religious Poems (Boston: Ticknor & Fields, 1867);

Stories About Our Dogs (Edinburgh: Nimmo, 1867);

The Daisy's First Winter, and Other Stories (Boston: Fields, Osgood, 1867); republished with differing contents as *Queer Little Folks* (London: Nelson, 1886);

Queer Little People (Boston: Ticknor & Fields, 1867);

The Chimney-Corner, as Crowfield (Boston: Ticknor & Fields, 1868);

Men of Our Times; or, Leading Patriots of the Day (Hartford, Conn.: Hartford Publishing Company/New York: Denison, 1868); republished as *The Lives and Deeds of Our Self-Made Men* (Hartford, Conn.: Worthington, Dustin, 1872);

Oldtown Folks (Boston: Fields, Osgood, 1869);

The American Woman's Home, by Stowe and Catharine Beecher (New York & Boston: Ford, 1869); revised and enlarged as *The New Housekeeper's Manual* (New York: Ford, 1874);

Lady Byron Vindicated. A History of the Byron Controversy, from Its Beginning in 1816 to the Present Time (Boston: Fields, Osgood, 1870);

Little Pussy Willow (Boston: Fields, Osgood, 1870);

My Wife and I; or, Harry Henderson's History (New York: Ford, 1871)

Pink and White Tyranny. A Society Novel (Boston: Roberts, 1871);

Six of One by Half a Dozen of the Other. An Every Day Novel, by Stowe, Edward Everett Hale, Lucretia Peabody Hale, and others (Boston: Roberts Brothers, 1872);

Sam Lawson's Oldtown Fireside Stories (Boston: Osgood, 1872);

Palmetto-Leaves (Boston: Osgood, 1873);

Woman in Sacred History (New York: Fords, Howard & Hulbert, 1873); republished as *Bible Heroines* (New York: Fords, Howard & Hulbert, 1878);

Betty's Bright Idea. Also Deacon Pitkin's Farm, and The First Christmas of New England (New York: National Temperance Society & Publishing House, 1875);

We and Our Neighbors; or, The Records of an Unfashionable Street (New York: Ford, 1875);

Footsteps of the Master (New York: Ford, 1877);

Poganuc People: Their Loves and Lives (New York: Fords, Howard & Hulbert, 1878);

A Dog's Mission; or, The Story of the Old Avery House and Other Stories (New York: Fords, Howard & Hulbert, 1880).

Collection: *The Writings of Harriet Beecher Stowe*, 16 volumes (Boston & New York: Houghton Mifflin, 1896).

OTHER: "Nelly's Heroics," in *Nelly's Heroics, with Other Heroic Stories* (Boston: Lothrop, 1883).

Harriet Beecher Stowe's greatest fame derives from the impact of *Uncle Tom's Cabin* upon readers of all ages. Its characters, Uncle Tom, Little Eva, Topsy, and Simon Legree, have assumed mythological dimensions in the folk imagination of the world. The author clearly conceived of the novel as suitable for a family audience including young children. Her books written specifically for children have suffered relative obscurity. If literary historians mention them at all, it is condescendingly. In *Harriet Beecher Stowe* (1963) John R. Adams remarks of her "children's stories" that they "can be disregarded without serious consequences, except as they add a touch of fantasy not exhibited elsewhere in her works: for the most part they contain the same ideas as her books for adults, with much the same expression." However, because *Uncle Tom's Cabin* is one of the few works by an American woman writer of her time still read today, and because she was one of the most influential women of the Victorian age, her works merit more attention than they have received for their significance in the history of children's literature.

Born in Litchfield, Connecticut, Harriet Beecher was the seventh child of Lyman and Roxanna Foote Beecher. Her older siblings were, in order of birth, Catharine (eleven years her senior), William, Edward, Mary, George, the "first" Harriet

Catharine Beecher, who received credit as co-author of the 1833 Primary Geography for Children, *even though her younger sister Harriet had done all of the writing*

(who died in infancy in 1808); following Harriet were Henry Ward, her favorite brother, and Charles, the last child of Roxanna Foote Beecher, who died in 1816. Janet A. Emig in "The Flower in the Cleft: The Writings of Harriet Beecher Stowe" (1963) recommends two chapters contributed by Stowe to the autobiography of Lyman Beecher (1863)—Chapter 46, "Filial Recollections," and Chapter 69, "Early Remembrances"—for insight into the psychological link between her early life experiences and the themes of her writings. Her father could not know, when he lamented Harriet's sex at the time of her birth, that this child would, in the words of Forrest Wilson, grow up to "outpreach her father and all her gifted brothers combined" and indeed become "a major prophetess."

The Beechers' household included two Negro bond servants who had been brought from Long Island as children and Aunt Esther Beecher, Lyman Beecher's half-sister, a spinster who was the prototype of Ophelia in *Uncle Tom's Cabin*. Esther Beecher was a talented storyteller and amateur naturalist, whose stories about small beasts, told to cheer the children in their illnesses, are reflected in Harriet Beecher Stowe's tales for the young. It was Esther Beecher who introduced her niece to the poetry of Lord Byron. The girl retained beautiful memories of her deceased mother, who presided over the household in spirit. The sketch she wrote of "Aunt Mary" (collected in *The Mayflower*, 1843) reflects her mother, just as it reflects an actual Aunt Mary, Roxanna Beecher's sister, whose experience as the wife of a Jamaican plantation owner provided Harriet Beecher's introduction to the horror of African slavery.

After the death of her mother Harriet Beecher was taken to live with her Aunt Harriet Foote at Nutplains, near Guilford, Connecticut. During her year there, the child came under the dual influences of her aunt's Episcopal faith and the romantic tales of her aunt's seafaring brother, Samuel Foote. In 1817 Lyman Beecher married again. Harriet reportedly expressed her childish resentment of her new stepmother, Harriet Porter, by telling her, "Because you have come and married my pa, when I am big enough I mean to go and marry your pa." Despite this challenge from the precocious stepchild, the new stepmother reveals in her letters that she saw and appreciated the girl's exceptional qualities: at six and one-half, Harriet Beecher was a fluent reader, with twenty-seven hymns and two long chapters of the Bible committed to memory. In a family letter, the child at eight is described as an "odd" little girl, a phrase that later became part of the working title for the highly autobiographical *Poganuc People* (1878)—"Early Days of an Odd Little Girl."

At eight (though the usual age was twelve) Harriet Beecher enrolled at Miss Sarah Pierce's school in Litchfield. The world she inhabited was not child-centered: the only toy she remembered having was a wooden doll carved by a village craftsman, and, except for one or two of Maria Edgeworth's stories, there were no "juvenile" books available. Yet Harriet Beecher discovered the pleasure of literature, for her father allowed her the run of his library. She recalled how his reading of the Declaration of Independence inspired her with heroic fervor "to do something, I knew not what: to fight for my country, or to make some declaration on my own account." Dolly Cushing of *Poganuc People* reflects Harriet Beecher's own youthful love of Bible stories and Bunyan's *Pilgrim's Progress* as well as her weariness of Presbyterian austerity and her attraction to the rich, sensuous spirituality of the Episcopal Christmas service. Dolly's imagination is nurtured on the Arabian Nights and Cotton Mather's *Magnalia Christi Americana*. At Miss Pierce's school, the girl Harriet was encouraged in her writing efforts by a revered teacher, John Brace. With her schoolgirl friends she came under the spell of the Byron cult. At twelve she won a prize for her essay "Can the Immortality of the Soul be Proved by the Light of Nature?"—an exceptional piece even for an odd little girl steeped in the idiom of evangelism.

Harriet Beecher's youth was not without trauma. She suffered a near-fatal bout with scarlet fever (which took the life of her half-brother, Frederick, the first of Harriet Porter Beecher's four children by Lyman Beecher); and she experienced vicariously the suffering of her oldest sister, Catharine, over the loss of her fiancé, Alexander Metcalf Fisher, in an accident at sea. (The ill-starred romance was fictionalized in Stowe's *The Minister's Wooing*, 1859.) The impact of this tragedy on the religious attitudes of the Beecher family was drastic. Catharine Beecher began to doubt the validity of a God who could withhold His grace from her beloved (by Calvinist beliefs, Fisher was accounted eternally lost, for his diary testified to his lack of a "conversion" experience). In his will, he left Catharine his library and the sum of $2,000. The books she shipped to the Litchfield parsonage, where Lyman Beecher fell under the spell of *Ivanhoe*, lifted his ban on novel reading, and let his children discover the riches of Scott. With the money, Cathar-

ine Beecher opened a school, the Hartford Female Academy, where Harriet continued her education in the fall of 1824.

When she had turned thirteen the previous summer, there had occurred the first landmark in Harriet Beecher's spiritual life, her conversion, reflected in Dolly Cushing's conversion in *Poganuc People*. In the novel Dr. Cushing's sermon on "Jesus as the soul-friend offered to every human being" moves Dolly to an ecstatic, joyful trust in a loving God. Dr. Beecher's sermon that had similarly moved his daughter was oddly enough inspired by the death of Lord Byron, whom Lyman Beecher viewed as an example of a noble soul forever lost. Catharine Beecher questioned the validity of her sister's "easy" conversion and declared she was "afraid that there might be something wrong in the case of a lamb that had come into the fold without first being chased all over the lot by the shepherd. . . ."

At the Academy Harriet Beecher formed a lifelong friendship with Georgiana May (later the Mrs. Sukes to whom Beecher wrote many important letters), studied Latin, and yearned to become a poet. In 1825 she surreptitiously began a drama, "Cleon," whose main character, a Greek lord residing at Nero's court, embraces Christianity only after much searching and doubting. Besides reflecting his creator's own spiritual struggles, Cleon is a prototype of such Byronic figures as Augustine St. Clare. In *The Rungless Ladder: Harriet Beecher Stowe and New England Puritanism* (1954), Charles Foster observes: "Harriet in imagination did what her father . . . could not do in reality: she converted Byron." The drama was cut short when Catharine Beecher insisted that her sister turn from such frivolity to the study of Joseph Butler's *The Analogy of Religion, Natural and Revealed, to the Constitution and Course of Nature.*

Harriet Beecher's adolescent emotional vicissitudes were exacerbated when the Congregationalist minister in Hartford (where she joined the church in 1825), thinking she lacked sufficient conviction of sin, urged her to attend to her "deceitfulness of heart." Thereby he launched her upon years of spiritual self-torture. Lyman Beecher was now in Boston, where he had moved in 1826 to become minister of the Hanover Street church. In a letter to him Catharine revealed that Harriet had expressed the desire to "die young . . . rather than live . . . a trouble to everyone."

By 1829 Harriet had become a full-time teacher at Catharine's school, now thriving and incorporated with the Hartford Female Seminary.

Yet she still had no beau, in a day when an unwed girl of twenty was considered a confirmed old maid. Her loneliness and melancholia found expression in a letter to her brother Edward in February of 1829: "I believe that there never was a person more dependent on the good and evil opinions of those around than I am. This desire to be loved forms . . . the great motive for all my actions." The summer of the same year was, however, a spiritual turning point, for in July she could report to Edward that she had achieved a faith in Christ as a revelation of God's mercy and compassion—"just such a God as I need." Later she wrote to Georgiana May her conviction that love was the basis of all existence—"the all in all of mind."

In 1832 Dr. Beecher became president of the newly founded Lane Theological Seminary in Cincinnati. Catharine Beecher, transplanted to Cincinnati, founded the Western Female Institute with her sister as one of the teachers. Before leaving for the West, Harriet Beecher had vowed to Georgiana May her determination to give up the "pernicious" habit of meditation and mix in society as other people did. But in her new surroundings she found it difficult to translate her resolve into action.

Her first book, *Primary Geography for Children on an Improved Plan*, was brought out in Cincinnati in 1833. Though Harriet Beecher had done all of the writing, she shared credit with her sister Catharine. Soon after it was published Harriet wrote Georgiana May, telling her of Bishop John B. Purcell's visit to the school, his praise of "my poor little geography," and his thanks for "the unprejudiced manner in which I handled the Catholic question in it." John R. Adams quotes a brief review of this book which appeared in *Western Monthly*, June 1833: "This is a very capital little book. The authoresses are accomplished young ladies, who have made the tuition of youth their study and business for several years, and who unite to a competent knowledge of the subject, an intimate acquaintance with the best modes of teaching children. Writing books for children is one of the most difficult, and surely one of the most useful branches of authorship. We most cordially recommend this, as a successful effort in this noble field."

Not much later, she complained to Georgiana May of the tedium and triviality of her teaching duties and contrasted her dull existence with "the life of Madame de Staël and 'Corinne.'" In America, she felt, the "rigid" forms of society and "constant habits of self-government" inhibited the desire for a full and passionate life. Her first published story, "Isabelle and Her Sister Kate, and

Their Cousin," signed May, appeared in the *Western Monthly* in February of 1834, two months prior to the publication of her prizewinning "A New England Sketch" (*Western Monthly*, April 1834), usually considered her initial appearance in print. "A New England Sketch" was reprinted in the *Cincinnati Chronicle*, 3 May 1834. It appeared as "Uncle Tim" in *The Mayflower* and as "Uncle Lot" in *The Mayflower and Miscellaneous Writings* (1855). It was published separately as *Prize Tale: A New England Sketch* (1834). These successes gave her heightened spirits and a new belief in her own abilities.

She was influenced at this time by the social-literary circle sponsored by her uncle Samuel Foote, the Semi-Colon Club (named by a circuitous reasoning process from the Spanish for Columbus, *Colón*). It is possible that she heard the 1837-1838 lectures of Alexander Kinmont, a Swedenborgian philosopher who preached a radical theory: he maintained that the evolving American culture needed the contributions of warmth and gentleness from blacks and women in order to balance the aggressiveness of male Anglo-Saxons. Whether or not influenced by Kinmont, Harriet Beecher began to develop more positive feelings about education and a conviction that American culture sorely needed a stronger element of feminine nurturance; she wrote to Georgiana May: "teaching will never be rightly done till it passes into *female* hands," for men, however knowledgeable, lack the "patience, long-suffering, and gentleness necessary to superintend the formation of character." Societal prejudice must be overcome to find those rare women with "original, planning minds."

When Henry Ward Beecher graduated from Amherst in June of 1834, Harriet traveled East for the occasion, viewing Niagara Falls on the way. While in the East she learned of the untimely death of her Cincinnati friend Eliza Tyler Stowe, the wife of Lane Theological Seminary's Professor Calvin E. Stowe. Harriet Beecher's sympathy for the childless widower ripened into love, and after a short engagement, she married Stowe in January of 1836. Later in life in a letter to Mrs. Eliza Lee Cabot Follen (author of *The Well-Spent Hour*, a juvenile classic Harriet read to her own children), she described her husband as "a man rich in Greek and Hebrew, Latin and Arabic, and, alas! rich in nothing else." In September of the same year, while Calvin Stowe was abroad, Harriet gave birth to her first children, the twins Eliza Tyler and Harriet Beecher. Five other children would follow—Henry Ellis in 1838, Frederick William in 1840, Georgiana May in 1843, Samuel Charles in 1848 (who died in

Calvin Stowe, who married Harriet Beecher in January 1836

infancy in 1849), and Charles Edward, her biographer and the only one of her sons to survive her, in 1850.

As a new wife and mother, Stowe felt torn between domestic cares and the desire to write. Several years after her marriage she wrote to Mary Dutton that she had earned enough from her writing to add a hired girl to the kitchen and a governess to the nursery, in order to have about three hours a day to devote to writing. She added, "if you see my name coming out everywhere, you may be sure of one thing—that I do it for *the pay.*" With time for reflection and writing, she proceeded to publish *The Mayflower.* Kathryn Kish Sklar relates how Catharine collected the tales, prepared them for publication, and wrote an introduction, as well as possibly intervening with Harper to arrange for publication of the work. The collection contains two stories which were later included in volume sixteen of Stowe's collected works, *Stories and Sketches for the Young* (1896)—"Christmas; or the Good Fairy" and "Little Fred, the Canal Boy." "Christmas" is a moralistic tale of a rich, jaded young lady, weary of trying to please wealthy friends, who becomes a

Lady Bountiful to the poor. Hardly attuned to the tastes of children, it is, however, typical of the sentimental realism of the day. Similarly, "Little Fred" depends for its effect on the domestic pathos of a boy orphaned at an early age, who falls under evil influences but is redeemed by memories of his mother and sister and the efforts of an urban minister. The tale rushes to an unconvincing close as though the author had grown weary of it herself.

Nevertheless, the impetus that *The Mayflower* lent to Stowe's writing career was immense; she began to realize that she might profit from being a "literary lady." Her husband appreciated her success and encouraged her, advising her to sign her works Harriet Beecher Stowe, as it "is a name euphonious, flowing, and full of meaning." Events in the wider world were further shaping her destiny as a writer. The controversy between abolitionist and proslavery factions was growing in intensity, and Stowe observed scenes which she would later turn into episodes in *Uncle Tom's Cabin.* In the famous letter to Mrs. Follen, she compared her grief at her infant son Charley's death in 1849 with "what a poor slave mother may feel when her child is torn away from her"; she added that she had prayed that "this crushing of my own heart might enable me to work out some great good to others. . . ."

In 1850 Calvin Stowe was appointed to the Collins Professorship of Natural and Revealed Religion at Bowdoin College, Brunswick, Maine. Harriet and three of the children moved there in April of 1850, while Calvin Stowe remained to finish his duties at Lane Theological Seminary before bringing the remaining two children to New England. The year 1850 also saw the passage of the Fugitive Slave Act, which spurred Isabella Porter Jones Beecher, Edward Beecher's wife, to write to Harriet Stowe, "Now Hattie, if I could use a pen as you can, I would write something that would make this whole nation feel what a cursed thing slavery is." The effect on Stowe is legendary: after reading the letter to her children, she rose to her feet and vowed "I *will* write something, I will if I live."

At communion in February of 1851 at the First Parish Church in Brunswick, Stowe had a vision of an old slave, a gentle Christian man, being flogged to death yet praying for forgiveness for his torturers. She wrote this scene—which became the final scene of *Uncle Tom's Cabin*—and read it to her children, who reportedly wept. On 15 May 1851 a notice appeared in the *National Era* of a new story by Mrs. H. B. Stowe entitled "Uncle Tom's Cabin; or, The Man That Was a Thing." Beginning on 5 June 1851 the story was serialized with a new sub-

Uncle Tom

The cabin of Uncle Tom was a small log building close adjoining to "the house" — as the negro always *par excellence* designates the masters dwelling. In front it had a neat garden patch where strawberries, raspberries & a variety of fruits & vegetables flourished under careful tending — down. The whole front of the dwelling was covered with a large scarlet bignonia & a native multiflora rose which entwisting & interlacing left scarce a vestage of the building to be seen & in the spring was redundant with its clusters of roses & in summer so bear brilliant with the scarlet tubes of the bignonia. Various gay, brilliant annuals such as marigolds four o'clocks & petunias found here and there a thrifty corner to vegetate unfold their glories & were the delight & pride of aunt Chloe's heart

Let us enter the dwelling — The evening meal at "the house" is over & Aunt Chloe who presides over its preparation as head cook has left to inferior officers in the kitchen the business of clearing away & washing dishes & come out into her own snug territory to "get her old man's supper" & therefore doubt not that it is her you see by the fire place presiding with anxious interest

Page from the manuscript of Uncle Tom's Cabin *(Forrest Wilson,* Crusader in Crinoline: The Life of Harriet Beecher Stowe, *1941)*

title, "Life Among the Lowly." *Uncle Tom's Cabin* ran until 1 April 1852, much longer than the editor had anticipated. The first edition of the book appeared on 20 March 1852, before the serial had been completed. Twenty thousand copies sold in the first three weeks, and sales figures continued to mount. Within a year, the book had run through 120 printings, or 300,000 copies sold, and Stowe had earned royalties beyond her wildest hopes: $10,000 in the first four months alone (she had hoped the novel might bring her enough for a silk dress). The book brought accolades as well from such eminent writers as Henry Wadsworth Longfellow and John Greenleaf Whittier. Before long the "incendiary" book had been translated into many languages and was known worldwide.

In 1852, when Calvin Stowe was appointed professor of sacred literature at Andover Theological Seminary, the Stowes took up residence in Massachusetts, where they continued to live until they moved to Hartford in 1863. On their 1853 trip to Europe they were received with great acclaim; Harriet Stowe's meeting with the widowed Lady Byron began a friendship which led to her later writing of *Lady Byron Vindicated* (1870). Adaptations of *Uncle Tom's Cabin* had begun to appear. A note in *Pictures and Stories from Uncle Tom's Cabin*, published in 1853, proclaims, "This little work is designed to adapt Mrs. Stowe's touching narrative to the understanding of the youngest readers and to foster in their hearts a generous sympathy for the wronged Negro Race of America." The words to "Little Eva's Song" were contributed by John Greenleaf Whittier.

Although there were many adaptations of Stowe's novel, it is evident that she thought the book in its original version suitable for children. She read it to her own children as she wrote it and shared the first Little Eva episode with her class of schoolchildren in September 1851. Perhaps the most compelling evidence that she saw her audience as including children is her appeal to "youthful readers" gathered in their "pleasant family circles" in the final installment in the *National Era*: "Dear children, you will soon be men and women, and I hope that you will learn from this story always to remember and pity the poor and oppressed. When you grow up, show your pity by doing all you can for them. Never, if you can help it, let a colored child be shut out from school or treated with neglect or contempt on account of his color. Remember the sweet example of little Eva.... Then, when you grow up, I hope the foolish and unchristian prejudice against people merely on ac-

count of their complexion will be done away with."

In Forrest Wilson's estimation, the appeal of *Uncle Tom's Cabin* for young readers derives from its naiveté, its "essential simplicity," and "passions as fundamental and universal as an epic." Further, its imagery is highly visual, its scenes dramatic. In a letter to the editor of the *National Era* Stowe stressed her wish to create "pictures," to "paint" the evils of slavery so vividly that all would be moved to reject it. Henry James remarked on the visual quality of the novel in *A Small Boy and Others* (1913), asserting that it was "for an immense number of people, much less a book than a state of vision." Leslie Fiedler points out in *Love and Death in the American Novel* (revised edition, 1966) how the dramatic version simplified the book in the "folk mind." He adds that the book is in fact complex, yet American readers have "chosen to preserve only the child's book"—granting only Uncle Tom and Topsy and Little Eva "archetypal stature."

In Stowe's own estimation she was an instrument of divine power, asserting that "the Lord himself wrote it." Although she belonged to an age of sentimental piety, she transcended its limitations when she addressed the issue of slavery and made her characters struggle with cosmic forces. George Sand, reviewing the French edition, wrote: "Mrs. Stowe is all instinct; it is the very reason she appears to some not to have talent; ... she has genius as humanity feels the need of genius,—the genius of goodness, not that of the man of letters, but that of the saint." The essential nature of *Uncle Tom's Cabin*, Sand continued, is "domestic and of the family.... Mothers, young girls, little children, servants can read, yet 'superior man' can't disdain them." "Children ... are the true heroes of Mrs. Stowe's work."

To understand *Uncle Tom's Cabin* and much of Stowe's other work it is useful to bear in mind her views on childhood and its corollary motherhood. She clearly concurred with the sentimentalist view of the child's nature; in the essay "Children" she maintains that "*the world*" makes "of the all-believing child, the sneering sceptic; of the beautiful and modest, the shameless and abandoned." This view of the child's nature harmonizes with the ideas in Horace Bushnell's *Christian Nurture* (1861) and Catharine Beecher's *Religious Training of Children in the School, the Family and the Church* (1864), as well as with Emerson's belief in the natural virtues of the young. Yet Stowe was frank and realistic enough to write on another occasion that whereas the first child is always a poem to its mother, those that follow are "unsentimental prose." Edmund

Charles Wagenknecht, who includes a chapter entitled "The Mother" in his 1965 book on Stowe, quotes a passage from her papers that suggests a virtually sacramental view of motherhood: "In thinking how all my life and strength and almost my separate consciousness passed away from me into my children and how they seem to depend on me from day to day for sympathy, I seemed to understand what Christ meant when he spoke of himself as being made bread and giving his flesh and blood as the vital food for his own."

Of her seven children, she lost four during her lifetime: Samuel Charles died in infancy; Henry, in his college days, drowned in the Connecticut River, July 1859; Frederick disappeared after struggling with alcoholism and the consequences of a wound sustained in the Civil War; and finally Georgiana died after years of nervous illness in 1887. Whereas grief over Charley increased her sympathy with slave mothers, the loss of Henry, as Forrest Wilson reports, made her "ready to curse God and die." Frederick's disappearance must have weighed heavily upon her, for in her senility she is said to have embraced a stranger on the street in Hartford, thinking him to be her long-lost son. Georgiana's death followed hard upon that of Henry Ward Beecher, her favorite brother.

Stowe's experiences as a woman and mother are reflected throughout her writing. She does not question the sentimental assumptions about women and motherhood; her novels and essays show that she believed women to be the "spiritual guides" of children and men. The chapter on "The Natural and the Spiritual" in *The Pearl of Orr's Island* (1862) expresses her view that predominantly spiritual persons, such as artists, poets, and seers, have traits commonly associated with women. Stowe also subscribes to the Platonic concept of the "man-woman," cited in her description of Esther in *Oldtown Folks* (1869): "Plato says somewhere that the only perfect human thinker and philosopher who will ever arise will be the MAN-WOMAN, or a human being who unites perfectly the nature of the two sexes." The perfect androgyne unites the male logic and intellect with the female "heart" and "moral perceptions." In Esther these elements are imperfectly fused, and she suffers in consequence the rebellion of heart against head. It seems Stowe felt considerable empathy for Esther's predicament.

In their 1972 volume of feminist criticism, *O Those Extraordinary Women!*, Seon Manley and Susan Belcher have speculated that the genesis of *Uncle Tom's Cabin* was the "breakdown of family life as witnessed by her own marriage" and that the book was "in part a retreat from Calvin Stowe." This perspective on her marital situation seems distorted, however, and Adams may be closer to the truth when he says that *Uncle Tom's Cabin* was Stowe's "declaration of independence, her revolution and her emancipation proclamation," not from her marriage, but from debts, personal sorrows, and family difficulties. If she did not say no to many of the primary ideals of her age, she did say no emphatically to its most corrupt institution, slavery, and scathingly criticized the church to the degree that it tolerated such dehumanization and exploitation. Wagenknecht points to "her courageous rejection of the barbarous theology on which she was reared, her amazing lack of prudery, her ability to face the human condition without blinking." The radical nature of her achievement in *Uncle Tom's Cabin* is expressed in the best-known anecdote about Stowe. In November 1862 she traveled to Washington, D.C., to visit her son Frederick, then in the infantry. There she met President Lincoln, who, as family tradition maintains, called her "the little lady who made this big war."

Black reaction to Stowe's achievement has gone full circle, from Paul Laurence Dunbar's adulatory sonnet in *Century Magazine*, November 1898, through James Baldwin's rejection of "Uncle Tomism," to the view expressed by Jessie M. Birtha in "The Portrayal of the Black in Children's Literature," included in Donnarae MacCann and Gloria Woodard's *The Black American in Books for Children* (1972). According to Birtha, whereas *Little Black Sambo* and *Epaminondas* should be relegated to the historical collection for their value to adults in tracing the development of children's literature, *Uncle Tom's Cabin* "may be considered from a somewhat different viewpoint," and children should be encouraged to evaluate it in the light of the time in which it was written. The omission of *Uncle Tom's Cabin* from *Children's Catalog*, as Dorothy M. Broderick notes in *Image of the Black American in Children's Literature* (1973), resulted from the editorial opinion that the book had already been analyzed ad infinitum as adult literature. This omission should in no way diminish its importance as a classic for young readers.

Three years after the success of *Uncle Tom's Cabin*, a volume entitled *First Geography for Children* (1855) and based upon the geography of 1833 made its appearance. Though it has been generally agreed that Stowe wrote the *Primary Geography* of 1833 (and Catharine Beecher simply lent her name to it), the authorship of the 1855 work is uncertain.

It may have been the work of Catharine Beecher, attributed to Stowe to stimulate sales, but according to at least one contemporary of Stowe, Stowe "busied herself " writing it in "leisure hours."

Our Charley, and What to Do With Him, published in 1858, opens with an essay admonishing parents to give their children attention at an early age while they are still malleable. The stories which follow are meant for mothers to share with their youngsters. "Take Care of the Hook" is a cautionary tale about a fish who fails to obey his mother; "A Talk about Birds" is a lesson on kindness to God's creatures; "The Nest in the Orchard" demonstrates Stowe's talent as an observer of nature, as well as incorporating a lesson on the horror of shooting birds; and "The Happy Child" is a sentimentalized character sketch of a boy faithfully enduring a fatal affliction. *Stories About Our Dogs* (1867) views animals as "a sacred trust" from God; "Aunt Esther's Rules" urges the humane killing of unwanted kittens, and "Sir Walter Scott and His

Dogs" is a eulogy of the affection both Scott and Lord Byron felt for "man's best friend." The title story of *The Daisy's First Winter, and Other Stories* (1867) is a religious fable of death (winter) and renewal; the wise tree, Daisy's mentor, explains that " 'the Good Shepherd never loses a seed, never a root, never a flower: they will all come again.' "

In October of 1865, with the story "Hum, Son of Buz," Stowe began to contribute to *Our Young Folks.* For several years thereafter, a story or sketch by her appeared in each issue. In October of 1873 *Our Young Folks* was absorbed by *St. Nicholas.* Though she never received much for these contributions, she enjoyed writing for young people, and eventually she produced four profitable juvenile books. After *The Daisy's First Winter* came *Queer Little People* (1867), *Little Pussy Willow* (1870), and *A Dog's Mission* (1880).

Queer Little People contains animal fables as well as several realistic stories. "The Hen That Hatched Ducks" provides the humor of incongru-

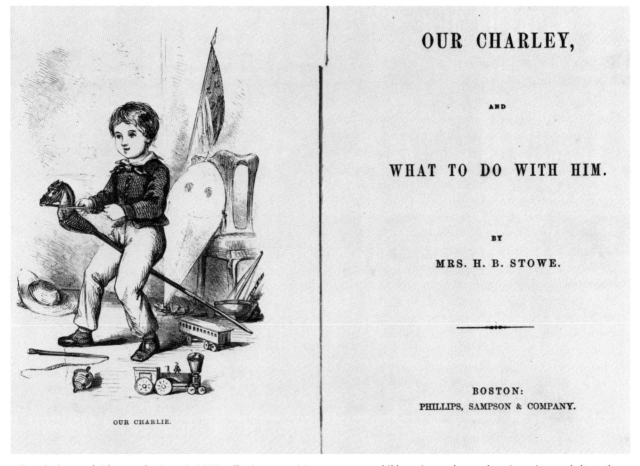

OUR CHARLIE.

OUR CHARLEY,

AND

WHAT TO DO WITH HIM.

BY

MRS. H. B. STOWE.

BOSTON:
PHILLIPS, SAMPSON & COMPANY.

Frontispiece and title page for Stowe's 1858 collection comprising an essay on child rearing and several stories written to help mothers entertain and instruct their youngsters (Baldwin Library, University of Florida Libraries)

Stowe, 1884

ity plus wordplay in such names as "Mrs. Feathertop"—a flighty young thing who surprises all the old hens by becoming an excellent mother. In other stories of the collection, Stowe pokes gentle fun at the human foible of pride and works out a conflict between the claims of education versus those of natural endowments. "The History of Tip-Top" is another cautionary tale, a warning not to succumb to evil temptations; "The Nutcrackers of Nutcracker Lodge" satirizes the "artistic temperament" through the character of Featherhead, who, according to his doting mother, "has such fine feelings so much above those of the common crowd"—but is sadly humbled owing to his overweening pride. "Mother Magpie's Mischief" is a fable satirizing those who meddle with natural propensities: Bullfrog makes a fool of himself when at Magpie's instigation he tries to sing like Tommy Oriole. "Our Country Neighbors" is realistic, treating the notion of the "food chain" that encompasses all of nature, whereby all creatures feed upon others and are finally devoured themselves. "Little Whiskey" mixes the realistic and the fanciful, teaching the moral "don't steal." "Miss Katy-Did and

Miss Cricket" is a heavy-handed allegory intended to show the folly of prejudice against those of a different color. "The Minister's Watermelons" is perhaps the most interesting piece in the group, a realistic tale about Bill Somers, an upright young man who is spellbound by the worldly wise Byronesque El Vinton but is reformed in time to retain his place in the good graces of Lucy, the minister's virtuous daughter. "Little Captain Trott" appeared first in the *Atlantic Monthly* for March 1869; it is a sentimentalized sketch of a mischievous but charming boy, somewhat reminiscent of "Little Charley." "Lulu's Pupil" is a playful Spitz dog, Muff, portrayed in loving detail, who succeeds in training people to live with him.

Little Pussy Willow, as Adams describes it, is "an extended fable expounding the difference between the wholesome life of a country child and the pampered existence of a vain daughter of wealth." The contrast between the natural, humble, industrious country child and the rich, artificial, sickly city girl is in the tradition of Thomas Day's *The History of Sandford and Merton* (1783, 1786, 1789). The theme is summed up thus: "Now the greatest trouble about girls and women is, not that they think too much of outside beauty, but that they do not think enough of inside beauty." In *Little Pussy Willow* the author creates one of her comical figures in the shrewd but tenderhearted Dr. Hardhack.

A Dog's Mission centers upon Miss Zarviah Avery, a recluse who is humanized by the dog Trip. But it is the little girl, Blue Eyes, who completes Miss Avery's redemption. Adams has called this "by imitation a tribute to *Silas Marner*."

Nelly's Heroics, with Other Heroic Stories (1883), a volume attributed to Stowe in Margaret Holbrook Hildreth's 1976 bibliography, appeared in at least two editions with differing contents. Hildreth lists the fifteen stories in the copy at the Stowe-Day Memorial Library. A copy held by the University of Texas at Austin, with identical titles, publisher, and date, contains nine stories, only four of which are common to both books, and attributes all but the title story to other authors. Stowe's story, "Nelly's Heroics," treats the conflict between Nelly's dreams of daring deeds and the dull, duty-bound "heroics" to which she is limited by her age and sex. Nelly, having learned that heroic people are those who "do the duty that lies next to them," grows up to be "a strong good woman" in a world where values are clearly drawn.

It remains for literary critics to assess fully Stowe's importance in the history of children's lit-

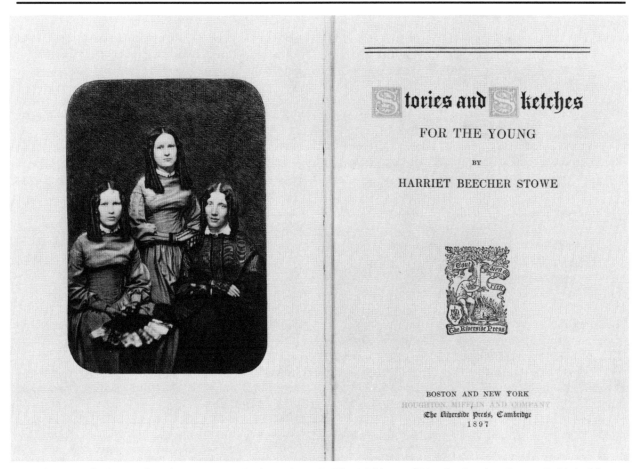

Frontispiece and title page for a later printing of volume sixteen in The Writings of Harriet Beecher Stowe *(Baldwin Library, University of Florida Libraries). Stowe is pictured on the frontispiece with her twin daughters, Harriet (seated) and Eliza.*

erature. In *The Innocent Eye: Childhood in Mark Twain's Imagination* (1961), Albert Stone has noted that she is one of those nineteenth-century writers—including Dickens, Hawthorne, Jacob Abbott, Thomas Bailey Aldrich, and Louisa May Alcott—who "created models and prototypes for stories about children." In the introductory note to volume sixteen of Stowe's collected writings, *Stories and Sketches for the Young,* Stowe is described as a domestic woman irresistibly drawn to portray children and to write stories for them. She was, moreover, "so acutely sensible of the world of nature, loving its flowers, trees, and all animate and inanimate objects" that her mind seized upon this material when she came to write for the young. Her writings resist categorizing; she "was naturally a companion for young and old, without too nice a calculation of adaptation to either class"—an assessment with which it is difficult to disagree.

Janet A. Emig lists the flaws of her writing style: "a very imperfect sense of architectonics," the

resorting to *deus ex machina,* shifts in point of view, a style "as flowery as a funeral home," and evidences of "haste, over-facility and fatigue." Yet Emig also recognizes that if the "measure of the importance of a writer is the size of the world he chooses to people, Mrs. Stowe must be considered a major writer." The test of time seems to have validated the judgment of James Russell Lowell, who, in his review of *The Minister's Wooing,* attributed Stowe's power to her gift for going instinctively to the "organic elements of human nature."

Her novelistic gifts—the powers of dramatization, visualization, and mythmaking—are of a high order in her best works. Critics have suggested a tension in Stowe's philosophy between the view of life as ultimately spiritual tragedy (an ironic perspective shared with Byron) and her strongly romantic preservation (particularly in her works specifically for the young) of her own childhood view of the world: that life is a pilgrimage fraught with pitfalls, but the faithful pilgrim will at last gain paradise. Where Stowe allows these two perspectives to come into dialogue—as in *Uncle Tom's Cabin*—she gives us her finest and richest art.

Letters:

Life of Harriet Beecher Stowe Compiled from Her Letters and Journals, edited by Charles Edward Stowe (Boston: Houghton Mifflin, 1889);

Life and Letters of Harriet Beecher Stowe, edited by Annie A. Fields (Boston: Houghton Mifflin, 1897).

Bibliographies:

Margaret Holbrook Hildreth, *Harriet Beecher Stowe: A Bibliography* (Hamden, Conn.: Archon Books, 1976);

Jean Ashton, *Harriet Beecher Stowe: A Reference Guide* (Boston: G. K. Hall, 1977).

Biographies:

Charles Edward Stowe and L. B. Stowe, *Harriet Beecher Stowe, The Story of Her Life* (Boston: Houghton Mifflin, 1911);

Forrest Wilson, *Crusader in Crinoline: The Life of Harriet Beecher Stowe* (Philadelphia: Lippincott, 1941);

Noel B. Gerson, *Harriet Beecher Stowe: A Biography* (New York: Praeger, 1976).

References:

John R. Adams, *Harriet Beecher Stowe* (New York: Twayne, 1963);

Elizabeth Ammons, ed., *Critical Essays on Harriet Beecher Stowe* (Boston: G. K. Hall, 1980);

Alice C. Crozier, *The Novels of Harriet Beecher Stowe* (New York: Oxford University Press, 1969);

Paul John Eakin, *The New England Girl: Cultural Ideals in Hawthorne, Stowe, Howells, and James* (Athens: University of Georgia Press, 1976);

Janet A. Emig, "The Flower in the Cleft: The Writings of Harriet Beecher Stowe," *Bulletin of the Historical and Philosophical Society of Ohio,* 21 (October 1963): 222-238;

Charles Foster, *The Rungless Ladder: Harriet Beecher Stowe and New England Puritanism* (Durham: Duke University Press, 1954);

Gayle Kimball, *The Religious Ideas of Harriet Beecher Stowe: Her Gospel of Womanhood* (New York: Edwin Mellen, 1982);

Kathryn Kish Sklar, *Catharine Beecher: A Study in American Domesticity* (New Haven: Yale University Press, 1973);

Albert E. Stone, *The Innocent Eye: Childhood in Mark Twain's Imagination* (New Haven: Yale University Press, 1961);

Stowe-Day Memorial Library, *The Papers of Harriet Beecher Stowe* (Hartford, Conn.: Stowe-Day Foundation, 1977);

Edward Charles Wagenknecht, *Harriet Beecher Stowe: The Known and the Unknown* (New York: Oxford University Press, 1965).

Papers:

Stowe's papers are in the Beecher-Stowe Collection at Schlesinger Library, Radcliffe College, Harvard University, and at the Stowe-Day Memorial Library, Hartford, Connecticut.

Edward Stratemeyer
(4 October 1862-10 May 1930)

Mary-Agnes Taylor
Southwest Texas State University

SELECTED BOOKS: The Last Cruise of the Spitfire; or, Luke Foster's Strange Voyage (New York: Merriam, 1894);

Richard Dare's Venture; or, Striking Out for Himself (New York: Merriam, 1894);

Reuben Stone's Discovery; or, The Young Miller of Torrent Bend (New York: Merriam, 1895);

By Pluck, not Luck; or, Dan Granbury's Struggle to Rise, as Arthur M. Winfield (New York: Allison, 1897);

Fighting for his Own; or, The Fortunes of a Young Artist (New York: Allison, 1897);

Gun and Sled; or, The Young Hunters of Snow-top Island, as Captain Ralph Bonehill (New York: Allison, 1897);

Leo the Circus Boy; or, Life under the Great White Canvas, as Captain Ralph Bonehill (New York: Allison, 1897);

The Missing Tin Box; or, The Stolen Railroad Bonds, as Arthur M. Winfield (New York: Allison, 1897);

The Rival Bicyclists; or, Fun and Adventure on the Wheel, as Captain Ralph Bonehill (Chicago: Donohue, 1897);

Schooldays of Fred Harley; or, Rivals for All Honors, as Arthur M. Winfield (New York: Allison, 1897);

Shorthand Tom; or, The Exploits of a Young Reporter (New York: Allison, 1897);

The Young Oarsman of Lakeview, as Captain Ralph Bonehill (New York: Allison, 1897);

The Minute Boys of Lexington (Boston: Estes & Lauriat, 1898);

Under Dewey at Manila; or, The War Fortunes of a Castaway (Boston: Lee & Shepard, 1898);

A Young Volunteer in Cuba; or, Fighting for the Single Star (Boston: Lee & Shepard, 1898);

Fighting in Cuban Waters; or, Under Schley on the Brooklyn (Boston: Lee & Shepard, 1899);

The Minute Boys of Bunker Hill (Boston: Estes, 1899);

Off for Hawaii; or, The Mystery of a Great Volcano, as

Captain Ralph Bonehill (New York: Mershon, 1899);

Oliver Bright's Search; or, The Mystery of a Mine (Boston: Lee & Shepard, 1899);

The Rover Boys at School; or, The Cadets of Putnam Hall, as Arthur M. Winfield (New York: Mershon, 1899);

The Rover Boys in the Jungle; or, Stirring Adventures in Africa, as Arthur M. Winfield (New York: Mershon, 1899);

The Rover Boys on the Ocean; or, A Chase for a Fortune, as Arthur M. Winfield (New York: Mershon, 1899);

A Sailor Boy with Dewey; or, Afloat in the Philippines, as Captain Ralph Bonehill (New York: Mershon, 1899);

To Alaska for Gold; or, The Fortune Hunters of the Yukon (Boston: Lee & Shepard, 1899);

Under Otis in the Philippines; or, A Young Officer in the Tropics (Boston: Lee & Shepard, 1899);

When Santiago Fell; or, The War Adventures of Two Chums, as Ralph Bonehill (New York: Mershon, 1899);

Between Boer and Briton; or, Two Boys' Adventures in South Africa (Boston: Lee & Shepard, 1900);

For the Liberty of Texas, as Captain Ralph Bonehill (Boston: Estes, 1900);

The Campaign of the Jungle; or, Under Lawton through Luzon (Boston: Lee & Shepard, 1900);

On to Pekin; or, Old Glory in China (Boston: Lee & Shepard, 1900);

The Rover Boys out West; or, The Search for a Lost Mine, as Arthur M. Winfield (New York: Mershon, 1900);

True to Himself; or, Roger Strong's Struggle for Place (Boston: Lee & Shepard, 1900);

The Young Bandmaster; or, Concert Stage and Battlefield, as Captain Ralph Bonehill (New York: Mershon, 1900);

Young Hunters in Porto Rico; or, The Search for a Lost Treasure, as Captain Ralph Bonehill (Chicago & New York: Donohue, 1900);

American Boys' Life of William McKinley (Boston: Lee & Shepard, 1901);

---

* This list omits British editions.

351

Edward Stratemeyer

Boys of the Fort; or, A Young Captain's Pluck, as Captain Ralph Bonehill (New York: Mershon, 1901);

The Putnam Hall Cadets; or, Good Times in School and Out (New York: Mershon, 1901);

The Rover Boys on the Great Lakes; or, The Secret of the Island Cave, as Arthur M. Winfield (New York: Mershon, 1901);

Three Young Ranchmen; or, Daring Adventures in the Great West, as Captain Ralph Bonehill (Akron & New York: Saalfield, 1901);

Under MacArthur in Luzon; or, Last Battles in the Philippines (Boston: Lee & Shepard, 1901);

With Taylor on the Rio Grande, as Captain Ralph Bonehill (Boston: Estes, 1901);

With Washington in the West; or, A Soldier Boy's Battles in the Wilderness (Boston: Lee & Shepard, 1901);

A Young Inventor's Pluck; or, The Mystery of the Willington Legacy, as Arthur M. Winfield (Akron & New York: Saalfield, 1901);

Bob, the Photographer; or, A Hero in Spite of Himself, as Arthur M. Winfield (New York: Wessels, 1902);

The Boyland Boomer; or, Dick Arbuckle's Adventures in Oklahoma, as Captain Ralph Bonehill (Akron & New York: Saalfield, 1902);

Larry Barlow's Ambition; or, The Adventures of a Young Fireman, as Arthur M. Winfield (Akron & New York: Saalfield, 1902);

Lost in the Land of Ice; or, Daring Adventures Around the South Pole, as Captain Ralph Bonehill (New York: Wessels, 1902);

Lost on the Orinoco; or, American Boys in Venezuela (Boston: Lee & Shepard, 1902);

Marching on Niagara; or, The Soldier Boys of the Old Frontier (Boston: Lee & Shepard, 1902);

Mark Dale's Stage Venture; or, Bound to Be an Actor, as Arthur M. Winfield (New York & London: Street & Smith, 1902);

Neka, the Boy Conjurer; or, A Mystery of the Stage, as Captain Ralph Bonehill (Philadelphia: Street & Smith, 1902);

The Rover Boys in the Mountains; or, A Hunt for Fun and Fortune, as Arthur M. Winfield (New York: Mershon, 1902);

Tour of the Zero Club; or, Adventures Amid Ice and Snow, as Captain Ralph Bonehill (New York & London: Street & Smith, 1902);

Under Scott in Mexico, as Captain Ralph Bonehill (Boston: Estes, 1902);

With Custer in the Black Hills; or, A Young Scout Among the Indians, as Captain Ralph Bonehill (New York: Mershon, 1902);

The Young Bank Clerk; or, Mark Vincent's Strange Discovery, as Arthur M. Winfield (New York & London: Street & Smith, 1902);

The Young Bridge Tender; or, Ralph Nelson's Upward Struggle, as Arthur M. Winfield (New York & London: Street & Smith, 1902);

The Young Volcano Explorers; or, American Boys in the West Indies (Boston: Lee & Shepard, 1902);

At the Fall of Montreal; or, A Soldier Boy's Final Victory (Boston: Lee & Shepard, 1903);

Bound to be an Electrician; or, Franklin Bell's Success (Boston: Lee & Shepard, 1903);

Joe the Surveyor; or, The Value of the Lost Claim (Boston: Lee & Shepard, 1903);

The Rover Boys on Land and Sea; or, The Crusoes of Seven Islands, as Arthur M. Winfield (New York: Mershon, 1903);

Two Young Lumbermen; or, From Maine to Oregon for Fortune (Boston: Lee & Shepard, 1903);

With Boone on the Frontier; or, The Pioneer Boys of Old Kentucky, as Captain Ralph Bonehill (New York: Mershon, 1903);

The Young Auctioneer; or, The Polishing of a Rolling Stone (Boston: Lee & Shepard, 1903);

American Boys' Life of Theodore Roosevelt (Boston: Lee & Shepard, 1904; enlarged, Boston: Lothrop, Lee & Shepard, 1906);

The Island Camp; or, The Young Hunters of Lakeport, as Captain Ralph Bonehill (New York: Barnes, 1904); republished as *The Gun Club Boys of Lakeport; or, The Island Camp,* as Stratemeyer (Boston: Lothrop, Lee & Shepard, 1908);

Larry the Wanderer; or, The Rise of a Nobody (Boston: Lee & Shepard, 1904);

On the Trail of Pontiac; or, the Pioneer Boys of the Ohio (Boston: Lee & Shepard, 1904);

Pioneer Boys of the Great Northwest; or, With Lewis and Clark across the Rockies (New York: Mershon, 1904);

The Rover Boys in Camp; or, The Rivals of Pine Island, as Arthur M. Winfield (New York: Mershon, 1904);

Under the Mikado's Flag; or, Young Soldiers of Fortune (Boston: Lothrop, Lee & Shepard, 1904);

Young Explorers of the Amazon; or, American Boys in Brazil (Boston: Lee & Shepard, 1904);

At the Fall of Port Arthur; or, A Young American in the Japanese Navy (Boston: Lee & Shepard, 1905);

Dave Porter at Oak Hall; or, The Schooldays of An American Boy (Boston: Lee & Shepard, 1905);

The Fort in the Wilderness; or, The Soldier Boys of the Indian Trails (Boston: Lee & Shepard, 1905);

The Rover Boys on the River; or, The Search for the Missing Houseboat, as Arthur M. Winfield (New York: Stitt, 1905);

The Winning Run; or, The Baseball Boys of Lakeport, as Captain Ralph Bonehill (New York: Barnes, 1905);

Dave Porter in the South Seas; or, The Strange Cruise of the Stormy Petrel (Boston: Lothrop, Lee & Shepard, 1906);

Four Boy Hunters; or, The Outing of the Gun Club, as Captain Ralph Bonehill (New York: Cupples & Leon, 1906);

Pioneer Boys of the Gold Fields; or, The Nugget Hunters of '49, as Captain Ralph Bonehill (New York: Stitt, 1906);

The Putnam Hall Rivals; or, Fun and Sport Afloat and Ashore, as Arthur M. Winfield (New York: Mershon, 1906);

The Rover Boys on the Plains; or, The Mystery of Red Rock Ranch, as Arthur M. Winfield (New York: Mershon, 1906);

Trail and Trading Post; or, The Young Hunters of the Ohio (Boston: Lothrop, Lee & Shepard, 1906);

Under Togo for Japan; or, Three Young Americans on Land and Sea (Boston: Lothrop, Lee & Shepard, 1906);

Dave Porter's Return to School; or, Winning the Medal of Honor (Boston: Lothrop, Lee & Shepard, 1907);

Defending His Flag; or, A Boy in Blue and a Boy in Gray (Boston: Lothrop, Lee & Shepard, 1907);

Guns and Snowshoes; or, The Winter Outing of the Young Hunters (New York: Cupples & Leon, 1907);

The Rover Boys in Southern Waters; or, The Deserted Steam Yacht, as Arthur M. Winfield (New York: Mershon, 1907);

Treasure Seekers of the Andes; or, American Boys in Peru (Boston: Lothrop, Lee & Shepard, 1907);

The Boat Club Boys of Lakeport; or, The Water Champions (Boston: Lothrop, Lee & Shepard, 1908);

Dave Porter in the Far North; or, The Pluck of an American Schoolboy (Boston: Lothrop, Lee & Shepard, 1908);

The Putnam Hall Champions; or, Bound to Win Out, as Arthur M. Winfield (New York: Grosset & Dunlap, 1908);

The Rover Boys on the Farm; or, The Last Days at Putnam Hall (New York: Grosset & Dunlap, 1908);

Young Hunters of the Lake; or, Out with Rod and Gun, as Captain Ralph Bonehill (New York: Cupples & Leon, 1908);

Dave Porter and his Classmates; or, For the Honor of Oak Hall (Boston: Lothrop, Lee & Shepard, 1909);

First at the North Pole; or, Two Boys in the Arctic Circle (Boston: Lothrop, Lee & Shepard, 1909);

The Football Boys of Lakeport; or, More Goals than One (Boston: Lothrop, Lee & Shepard, 1909);

The Putnam Hall Rebellion; or, The Rival Runaways, as Arthur M. Winfield (New York: Grosset & Dunlap, 1909);

The Rover Boys on Treasure Isle; or, The Strange Cruise of the Steam Yacht, as Arthur M. Winfield (New

York: Grosset & Dunlap, 1909);

The Automobile Boys of Lakeport; or, A Run for Fun and Fame (Boston: Lothrop, Lee & Shepard, 1910);

Dave Porter at Star Ranch; or, The Cowboy's Secret (Boston: Lothrop, Lee & Shepard, 1910);

Out with Gun and Camera; or, The Boy Hunters in the Mountains, as Captain Ralph Bonehill (New York: Cupples & Leon, 1910);

The Putnam Hall Encampment; or, The Secret of the Old Mill, as Arthur M. Winfield (New York: Grosset & Dunlap, 1910);

The Rover Boys at College; or, The Right Road and the Wrong, as Arthur M. Winfield (New York: Grosset & Dunlap, 1910);

Chased across the Pampas; or, American Boys in Argentina and Homeward Bound (Boston: Lothrop, Lee & Shepard, 1911);

Dave Porter and His Rivals; or, The Chums and Foes of Oak Hall (Boston: Lothrop, Lee & Shepard, 1911);

The Putnam Hall Mystery; or, The School Chums' Strange Discovery, as Arthur M. Winfield (New York: Grosset & Dunlap, 1911);

The Rover Boys Down East; or, The Struggle for the Stanhope Fortune, as Arthur M. Winfield (New York: Grosset & Dunlap, 1911);

The Aircraft Boys of Lakeport; or, Rivals of the Clouds (Boston: Lothrop, Lee & Shepard, 1912);

Dave Porter on Cave Island; or, A Schoolboy's Mysterious Mission (Boston: Lothrop, Lee & Shepard, 1912);

The Rover Boys in the Air; or, From College Campus to the Clouds, as Arthur M. Winfield (New York: Grosset & Dunlap, 1912);

Dave Porter and the Runaways; or, Last Days at Oak Hall (Boston: Lothrop, Lee & Shepard, 1913);

The Rover Boys in New York; or, Saving their Father's Honor, as Arthur M. Winfield (New York: Grosset & Dunlap, 1913);

Dave Porter in the Gold Fields; or, The Search for the Landslide Mine (Boston: Lothrop, Lee & Shepard, 1914);

The Rover Boys in Alaska; or, Lost in the Fields of Ice, as Arthur M. Winfield (New York: Grosset & Dunlap, 1914);

Dave Porter at Bear Camp; or, The Wild Man of Mirror Lake (Boston: Lothrop, Lee & Shepard, 1915);

The Rover Boys in Business; or, The Search for the Missing Bonds, as Arthur M. Winfield (New York: Grosset & Dunlap, 1915);

Dave Porter and his Double; or, The Disappearance of the Basswood Fortune (Boston: Lothrop, Lee & Shepard, 1916);

The Rover Boys on a Tour; or, Last Days at Brill College, as Arthur M. Winfield (New York: Grosset & Dunlap, 1916);

Dave Porter's Great Search; or, The Perils of a Young Civil Engineer (Boston: Lothrop, Lee & Shepard, 1917);

The Rover Boys at Colby Hall; or, The Struggles of the Young Cadets, as Arthur M. Winfield (New York: Grosset & Dunlap, 1917);

Dave Porter Under Fire; or, A Young Army Engineer in France (Boston: Lothrop, Lee & Shepard, 1918);

The Rover Boys on Snowshoe Island; or, The Old Lumberman's Treasure Box, as Arthur M. Winfield (New York: Grosset & Dunlap, 1918);

Dave Porter's War Honors; or, At the Front with the Fighting Engineers (Boston: Lothrop, Lee & Shepard, 1919);

The Rover Boys Under Canvas; or, The Mystery of the Wrecked Submarine, as Arthur M. Winfield (New York: Grosset & Dunlap, 1919);

The Rover Boys on a Hunt; or, The Mysterious House in the Woods, as Arthur M. Winfield (New York: Grosset & Dunlap, 1920);

The Rover Boys in the Land of Luck; or, Stirring Adventures in the Oil Fields, as Arthur M. Winfield (New York: Grosset & Dunlap, 1921);

The Rover Boys at Big Horn Ranch; or, The Cowboys' Double Round-up, as Arthur M. Winfield (New York: Grosset & Dunlap, 1922);

The Rover Boys at Big Bear Lake; or, The Camps of the Rival Cadets, as Arthur M. Winfield (New York: Grosset & Dunlap, 1923);

The Rover Boys Shipwrecked; or, A Thrilling Hunt for Pirates' Gold, as Arthur M. Winfield (New York: Grosset & Dunlap, 1924);

The Rover Boys on Sunset Trail; or, The Old Miner's Mysterious Message, as Arthur M. Winfield (New York: Grosset & Dunlap, 1925);

The Rover Boys Winning a Fortune; or, Strenuous Days Afloat and Ashore, as Arthur M. Winfield (New York: Grossett & Dunlap, 1926).

OTHER: William Taylor Adams (Oliver Optic), *An Undivided Union,* completed by Stratemeyer (Boston: Lee & Shepard, 1899);

Horatio Alger, Jr., *Out for Business or Robert Frost's Strange Career,* completed by Stratemeyer as Arthur M. Winfield (New York: Mershon, 1900);

Alger, *Falling in With Fortune or The Experiences of a Young Secretary,* completed by Stratemeyer as Arthur M. Winfield (New York: Mershon, 1900);

Alger, *Young Captain Jack or The Son of a Soldier,* completed by Stratemeyer as Arthur M. Winfield (New York: Mershon, 1901);

Alger, *Nelson the Newsboy or Afloat in New York,* completed by Stratemeyer as Arthur M. Winfield (New York: Mershon, 1901);

Alger, *Lost at Sea or Robert Roscoe's Strange Cruise,* completed by Stratemeyer (Rahway, N.J. & New York: Mershon, 1904);

Alger, *Jerry, the Backwoods Boy or The Parkhurst Treasure,* completed by Stratemeyer (New York: Mershon, 1904);

Alger, *The Young Book Agent or, Frank Hardy's Road to Success,* completed by Stratemeyer (New York: Stitt, 1905);

Alger, *From Farm to Fortune or, Nat Nason's Strange Experience,* completed by Stratemeyer (New York: Stitt, 1905);

Alger, *Joe the Hotel Boy or Winning Out by Pluck,* completed by Stratemeyer (New York: Cupples & Leon, 1906);

Alger, *Randy of the River or The Adventures of a Young Deckhand,* completed by Stratemeyer (New York: Chatterton-Peck, 1906);

Alger, *Ben Logan's Triumph or The Boys of Boxwood Academy,* completed by Stratemeyer (New York: Cupples & Leon, 1908).

In terms of prolificacy, no author in the history of children's literature can approach the output of Edward Stratemeyer. Added to his own works, there are hundreds of series books whose plots he outlined for a highly secret, constantly changing corps of ghostwriters using house names that still remain the property of the Stratemeyer Syndicate. Available documentation attests that between the years of 1886 and 1930, Edward Stratemeyer published 150 titles that were exclusively his own and that he also masterminded a literary machine which produced some 700 titles published under more than sixty-five pseudonyms and translated into a dozen languages. In 1926, the American Library Association sponsored a survey of juvenile reading preferences, querying 36,000 children in thirty-four different cities about their favorite books; ninety-eight percent of these children responded with a Stratemeyer title. Although the syndicate's series list has greatly shrunk since World War II, figures indicate that the Stratemeyer Syndicate still sells about 6,000,000 books each year and that it has well-laid plans to carry on at that rate.

Curiously, little is known about Stratemeyer's private life. He was born in Elizabeth, New Jersey, on 4 October 1862. His father, a middle-class German immigrant, migrated to California during the era of the Gold Rush but later returned to New Jersey to settle the estate of a deceased brother. Thus, young Edward Stratemeyer spent his boyhood in Elizabeth where he read with a passion the works of Horatio Alger, Jr., and William Taylor Adams (Oliver Optic). The dime novel was in its heyday, and its plots were gloriously compatible with the American dream. Unlike some of the super heroes he would later create, Stratemeyer did not attend preparatory school or college, but quite like all of his leading characters, he grew up indoctrinated with the Alger-Adams dogma which proclaimed that clean living and hard work brought just rewards. He married Magdalene Baker Van Camp, and of that union two daughters were born: Harriet and Edna. Upon Stratemeyer's death, 10 May 1930, his children carried on not only the syndicate he had founded, but also the stern code of secrecy to which he adhered. After a

Cover for one of Alger's posthumously published novels completed by Stratemeyer from the author's notes

frustrated attempt to find out something about the private life of Stratemeyer, the staff writers for the April 1934 *Fortune Magazine* reported the daughters were amazed at their efforts to pry. What, the new overseers of the syndicate wanted to know, would their clients think if they discovered that their revered gallery of juvenile authors was nothing but a waxworks invented by Stratemeyer? Furthermore, they felt so strongly about maintaining the illusion that, in spite of their great veneration of him, they refused to authorize any of the attempts that were then being made to write this biography. This position of secrecy was held to so firmly that once, during Stratemeyer's life, when a reader insisted upon some information about May Hollis Barton, a publisher's assistant created an entirely fabulous biography, never letting on that the "she" was in reality a kindly, stocky, nearsighted "he."

In marked contrast to the sketchy information about Stratemeyer's private life, literally reams of information can be amassed about his professional life. His writing career began in 1886 while he was working at his brother Maurice Stratemeyer's tobacco shop in Elizabeth, New Jersey. Reports are that during a slow time at the store, he tore off a sheet of brown wrapping paper and began to write *Victor Horton's Idea*, an eighteen-thousand-word serial which he sent to the Philadelphia weekly for boys, *Golden Days*. A letter of acceptance, which included a check for $75.00, encouraged him to write more. His next effort, again for *Golden Days*, was titled *Captain Bob's Secret; or, The Treasures of Bass Island*. Under his own name and as Ralph Hamilton, he wrote serials for *Golden Days* from 1890 to 1895.

The bulk of Stratemeyer's literary apprenticeship was served in writing and editing for periodicals. Contributions to Frank Munsey's *Golden Argosy* caught the attention of Street and Smith publishers who, in 1893, offered him the editorship of *Good News*. His stories built the magazine's circulation to more than 200,000. In 1895, he edited Street and Smith's *Young Sports of America*, later entitled *Young People of America*, and in 1896 he added the editorship of *Bright Days*. During this time, he was advancing his penchant for pen names. Many of the dime novels that he wrote for Log Cabin Library were signed Ralph Bonehill or Allan Chapman and he used the female pseudonym Julia Edwards for his women's serials in the *New York Weekly*. Probably the greatest advantage of his association with Street and Smith, however, was his exposure to the literary idols of the time—Frank

Dey, creator of dime novel detective hero Nick Carter; Upton Sinclair, who wrote the True Blue series as Ensign Clark Fitch, USN; prolific dime novelist Edward S. Ellis; William Taylor Adams; and Horatio Alger himself. When Alger and Adams died, Stratemeyer was chosen to complete their unfinished works. He edited two Optic novels and completed *An Undivided Union* (1899), the final volume in Adams's Blue and Gray—On Land series. From notes and outlines he finished eleven books in the Rise of Life series under Alger's name. Meanwhile, he had not neglected his own creations. By the end of 1897, he had six series and sixteen hardcover books in print, but it was in 1898 that his big breakthrough came.

Stratemeyer had written a book about two boys on a battleship and submitted it to Lothrop, Lee and Shepard. A short time thereafter, the press announced Admiral Dewey's victory at Manila Bay. Almost immediately Stratemeyer received a letter of acceptance from the publishers with the request that he revise the manuscript to parallel Dewey's victory. Thus teenaged Larry Russell and his pals were transferred to the scene of the Pacific Fleet, and *Under Dewey at Manila; or, The War Fortunes of a Castaway* (1898) became volume one of the Old Glory series. The book went through multiple printings, and its characters were ubiquitous in sequels, charging up San Juan Hill, serving under Commodore Schley aboard the *Brooklyn*, returning to the Philippines with General Otis, riding into Santa Cruz with Major General Lawton, and finally serving on General MacArthur's staff in Luzon.

Recognizing the popular appeal of war and patriotism, Stratemeyer dashed off in addition to the six Old Glory titles (1898-1901), two Minute Boys books (1898-1899); four in the Soldiers of Fortune series (1900-1906); three on the Mexican War (1900-1902); and six which formed the Colonial series (1901-1906). These early books are important in two respects: they are crammed with well-researched facts and they make use of some literary techniques that mark virtually all of the author's later works.

From the very beginning of his writing career Stratemeyer had the voice of a storyteller, speaking personally to the reader, and that *I-you* tone was a note that sounded regardless of title or pen name. He spoke directly to his reader first in the preface of the book and then periodically in the text. Routinely, the preface of volume one carried the good news of more books to come, although two or three volumes were often published simultaneously to see if a series was going to succeed. The preface of

Frontispieces and title pages from two of Stratemeyer's series. Volume one of the Old Glory series (top) was the author's first commercial success; Stratemeyer's biography of Roosevelt was the second and final book in the American Boys' Biographical series, which also included the Life of William McKinley, *published in 1901 (Baldwin Library, University of Florida Libraries).*

all books beyond volume one carried the message that this book was "a complete story in itself"; however, there were others the reader would surely not want to miss. Brief summaries of the other volumes followed. In case a reader skipped the preface, the same message was slipped into the text of the story in several places. For example in *On the Trail of Pontiac; or, The Pioneer Boys of the Ohio* (volume four of the Colonial series, 1904), the author neatly inserts on page four, "This was at the time that George Washington, the future President of our country, was a young surveyor, and in the first volume of this series, entitled 'With Washington in the West,' I related how Dave fell in with Washington and became his assistant, and how, later on, Dave became a soldier to march under Washington during the disastrous Braddock campaign against Fort Duquesne." Page five mentions volume two, *Marching on Niagara* (1902), and gives the particulars of volume three, *At the Fall of Montreal* (1903). In both books the heroes, Dave Morris and his cousin Henry, fight bravely to defeat the French and in the fourth volume are now ready to move with their elders in the peaceful reestablishment of a family trading post. But trouble lurks in the persons of the powerful Indian chief, Pontiac, and a disgruntled Frenchman: "I shall show them that, though France is beaten, Jean Bevoir still lives. . . . The trading-post on the Kinotah with its beautiful lands, shall be mine—the Morrises shall never possess it!"

Fast-paced battle scenes pepper the historical books, but the scenes are reported in a straightforward, objective fashion with no attempt to exploit gory details. The works are replete with clichés, and although the following examples are from *On the Trail of Pontiac*, they can be found again and again in other books. "The Indians are on the warpath and they mean business." No matter how threatening a life-and-death situation, the characters are repeatedly described as "in a pickle." They take to the wilderness as "ducks take to water," but, nevertheless, often find themselves "striking their heads against a stone wall." Still, "no two ways about it," the culprits are bound to be apprehended and will "turn over a new leaf."

Stratemeyer's, and the syndicate's, choices of antagonists offer clues about existing attitudes toward various ethnic groups. Just as feelings toward Jews would filter through later in the Tom Swift series, the Colonial series reflects feelings toward the French and the Indians. Although he includes a token number of good Indians in *On the Trail of Pontiac*, his general attitude is suggested by young Henry Morris's report that "Sam Barringford says we won't have any real peace until the redskins have had one whipping they won't forget as long as they live." Sam is a man who knows the situation; he has lived among the natives since he was six years old.

Though some of the stylistic devices of the early books may be faulted by the modern reader, it should be noted that at the time of their publication the books received high praise from well-respected sources. But the astute businessman in Stratemeyer did not let the praise mislead him. War stories and even the Alger rags-to-riches themes were becoming dated. He needed fresher ideas with which the new generation of teens could identify. Although he had no such schooling himself, he outlined several series about upper-middle-class students. The fifteen-volume Dave Porter series (1905-1919), the six-title Lakeport series (1904-1912), and the six Putnam Hall books (1901-1911) enjoyed wide readership, but their success was modest compared with Stratemeyer's favorite of all series: the Rover Boys series for Young Americans (1899-1926).

It is believed that the pen name for the Rovers and the Putnam Hall books—Arthur M. Winfield—was suggested by Stratemeyer's mother. The Arthur was simply for author; the M. he hoped would represent the sale of a million copies; and Winfield was literally for winning the field. His hopes were more than fulfilled. Between the publication of the first three volumes late in 1899 and the publication of the last volume in 1926, sales ran somewhere between five and six millions of copies. In all there were thirty volumes in the series. The first twenty dealt with the adventures of the three brothers, Dick, Tom, and Sam and the last ten with their respective children. The tone and the nature of the series is reflected in the introduction, which in volume one reads:

> MY DEAR BOYS: "The Rover Boys at School" has been written that those of you who have never put in a term or more at an American military academy for boys may gain some insight into the workings of such an institution.
>
> While Putnam Hall is not the real name of the particular place of learning I had in mind while penning this tale for your amusement and instruction, there is really such a school, and dear Captain Putnam is a living person, as are also the lively, wide-awake, fun-loving Rover brothers, Dick, Tom, and Sam, and their schoolfellows, Larry, Fred, and Frank. The same can be said, to a certain degree, of the bully Dan Baxter, and his

toady, the sneak commonly known as "Mumps."

The present story is complete in itself, but it is written as the first of a series, to be followed by "The Rover Boys in the Jungle," in both of which volumes we will again meet many of our former characters.

Trusting that this tale will find as much favor in your hands as have my previous stories, I remain,

Affectionately and sincerely yours,
Arthur M. Winfield

Possibly motivated by his fondness for the Rovers, he began, toward the end of the series, to sign his introductions Edward Stratemeyer instead of Arthur M. Winfield, a revelation which he assiduously forbade the parade of ghostwriters that populated the syndicate he established shortly after his creation of The Bobbsey Twins series.

The popularity of the Bobbsey Twins books, the first of which was published in 1904, probably convinced Stratemeyer that no one writer could keep pace with prodigious literary visions he entertained. In 1906 he established the Stratemeyer Syndicate. His practice was to outline plots and mail these to fledgling writers who were sworn to secrecy and paid from $50.00 to $250.00 per book. Regardless of future sales, all rights to both pen names and book royalties belonged to the syndicate—a condition of considerable significance in view of the fact that the Bobbsey Twins is one of the series that continued publication after World War II and which to date has sold, according to various estimates, from thirty to fifty million copies.

After formation of the syndicate, it becomes more difficult to say which books Stratemeyer actually wrote, but it is reasonably certain that he masterminded and edited all the volumes produced before his death. A parade of series filled the time between the Bobbsey Twins, begun in 1904, and another of his greats—the Tom Swift series. In 1910 Stratemeyer directed his assistant, Howard Garis, to drop other work and begin the scientific research necessary for the Swift series. The first volume, *Tom Swift and His Motor-Cycle*, appeared later that year. Hero Tom Swift, a virtuous Anglo-Saxon boy who never attended college, is a mechanical genius unhampered by a lack of money and blessed with an imagination that deals easily with motorcycles, airplanes, speedboats, photo telephones, war tanks, and other ingenious devices. He was patterned after Stratemeyer's idol, Henry Ford, and many of his inventions later came into being. In fact, only twice

in the thirty-eight-book series did Tom attempt to realize ideas that were not workable then or in the future. These were a process for using lightning to make artificial diamonds and the creation of a silent airplane engine. There is one major invention featured with each book. Always there is a thrilling chase and a villain trying to steal or ruin Tom's work. In fact, this series, published under the pseudonym Victor Appleton, contains a catalogue of some of the most wicked villains ever created for juvenile fiction. In addition to the murderous Jew, Greenbaum, there are, as Arthur Prager puts it in "Bless My Collar Button, If It Isn't Tom Swift!" (1976),

felons of every stamp: arsonists, bushwhackers, kidnappers, bank robbers, and even a molester who tried to force his attentions on Mary. In the first few books, before Tom had hit his stride, the nemesis was bully Andy Foger, a boy about Tom's age. The grown-up heavies came later. In the war there were German spies, and afterward there were unscrupulous business competitors.

By manipulating the villains, Stratemeyer was able to work off some of his own prejudices. Tycoons in fancy clothes were usually swindlers. Foreigners were to be avoided or mistrusted.

Other common prejudices of the time are evident in nonvillainous characters. These are usually slapstick, eye-rolling blacks such as Tom's faithful servant, Rad, and Dinah, the Bobbseys' cook. Over the years, these characters were changed in later printings to meet the social demands of the time. Most secondary characters became less ethnically stereotyped; however, the slapstick actions, the low comedy puns, and the cliff-hangers remained. Although some recent critics judge the Tom Swift books to be Stratemeyer's best work, some of his contemporaries took a radically different view.

James E. West, Chief Scout Executive for the Boy Scouts of America, considered the mass-produced series books an exploitation of juvenile taste and a danger to character development. Thus, in moral defense of his young charges, he organized the Library Commission of the Boy Scouts of America. Franklin K. Mathiews, chief librarian of the BSA, presented publishers with an approved Boy Scout list of books which did not include the Stratemeyer Syndicate's Boy Scout series. The mystery, murder, and arson in these books Mathiews considered very unscoutlike, and in 1914 he wrote for the *Outlook* an emotionally charged diatribe entitled "Blowing Out the Boys' Brains." Stratemeyer's sales dropped, but he countered with his own approved list. With his near monopoly threatened, he altered his approach; future series would tone down danger, thrills, and violence.

It is impossible to say whether the criticism or praise of the series books should be directed specifically toward Stratemeyer or toward his writers. Gradually, more and more material surfaces about the ghostwriters, as they or researchers seek to bypass the old oaths of silence.

John T. Dizer in his *Tom Swift® & Company, "Boys' Books" by Stratemeyer and Others* (1982) says that Stratemeyer usually made a point of writing at least one book in each series. Dizer further reports that "Tom's name came from an 1894 Stratemeyer Serial, *Shorthand Tom*. Howard Garis . . . did much contract writing for Stratemeyer and apparently was involved in about thirty-six of the

forty books in the original Tom Swift Series." Dizer deplores the controversy "over who actually wrote the Motor Boys and Tom Swift": "Stratemeyer personally read and edited all his books and then issued them under one of his many house names. There is no question that Howard Garis [and many others] wrote for Stratemeyer. . . . However, it should be remembered that these books were written under contract to Stratemeyer, based on characters and plots developed by him; the format and even the main situations were his." The *National Union Catalog, Pre-1956 Imprints* offers no clarification on the problem of authorship. The entry for the Tom Swift series reads "see Victor Appleton, pseudonym" and lists Appleton titles separately. Similarly, the Bobbsey Twins entry refers the reader to "Laura Lee Hope, pseudonym," under which the titles are listed. One point, it seems, can be made with certainty; until his death, Stratemeyer

Covers from two Stratemeyer Syndicate series. The Tom Swift series, created by Stratemeyer in 1910, ran to forty volumes. At left, the half-way mark: volume twenty, published in 1917 (Thomas Cooper Library, University of South Carolina). The Tom Swift, Jr., series (thirty-third and final volume at right), chronicling the adventures of Tom's son, was published from 1954 to 1971.

was in firm control of the syndicate and its writers, and he most certainly did not allow negative criticism to erode his empire.

By 1927, Stratemeyer had regained his place as ruling champion of the juvenile audience; however, he was as yet to create two detective series that would outsell all previous listings except the Bobbsey Twins. These were the Nancy Drew and the Hardy Boys books. Again, in these series it is uncertain who wrote which titles.

In January 1969, Arthur Prager's *Saturday Review* article "The Secret of Nancy Drew" attributed authorship of the Nancy Drew series to Harriet Stratemeyer Adams, Andrew Svenson, and four anonymous ghostwriters, all writing under the name of Carolyn Keene. The article drew a personal response from Mrs. Adams, as Prager reports in his 1971 book, *Rascals at Large:* "Mrs. Adams pointed out that my remark about Nancy being written by her, Mr. Svenson, and four anonymous ghostwriters was incorrect. Although the Syndicate uses contract writers for some of its series, she does all the Nancys herself, and has done so since the death of her father, the late Edward Stratemeyer, who was Nancy's creator, and who wrote the first three books of the series."

For the Hardy Boys Stratemeyer received a different sort of credit. All of this series was written by Leslie McFarlane, a shade who wrote and told all in his 1976 autobiography, *The Ghost of the Hardy Boys.* Under the pen name of Frank W. Dixon, McFarlane had produced other books for the syndicate, but he believed that they were inferior works. He decided that he would give his best to the Hardy Boys. When no notice or praise came for his extra effort, he was disappointed. He rationalized that Stratemeyer considered the books his own and not McFarlane's. McFarlane contented himself with the implied compliment of receiving assignments beyond the first three "breeders," but he had not the slightest notion that by half a century later the series would have run to sixty volumes and he would have written the first twenty. The pay remained at the fixed price—$150.00 per book. Faithfully, McFarlane sent in the manuscripts; he put the finished books on a special shelf and never bothered to reread them. Rather oddly he recalls,

> It was not until sometime in the 1940s, as a matter of fact, that I had discovered that Franklin W. Dixon and the Hardy Boys were conjurable names. One day my son had come into the workroom, which had never been

exalted into a "study," and pointed to the bookcase with its shelf of Hardy Boys originals. "Why do you keep these books, Dad? Did you read them when you were a kid?" "Read them? I wrote them." And then, because it doesn't do to deceive any youngster, "At least, I wrote the words."

In any evaluation of Stratemeyer's literary contribution, one must admit that ever since the days of the Mathiews attack, verbal battles have raged over the value of syndicated books. In the spring 1974 issue of the *Journal of Popular Culture,* Peter Soderbergh has detailed the interesting history of opinions which have fluctuated madly from 1914 through 1974. Clearly, no one can claim that the books are great literature, but, equally clearly, no one can deny that they have provided great entertainment and have been among the most popular and enduring contributions to the world of juvenile books. In a 1978 article in *Children's Literature,* Ken Donelson has presented an impressive list of short writings that give isolated glimpses of Edward Stratemeyer, and in *Tom Swift®& Company,* John Dizer offers extensive bibliographies of Stratemeyer's works, but a definitive biography of this American pied piper of print remains to be written.

References:

John T. Dizer, *Tom Swift®& Company: "Boys' Books" by Stratemeyer and Others* (Jefferson, N.C.: McFarland, 1982);

Ken Donelson, "Nancy, Tom, and Assorted Friends in the Stratemeyer Syndicate Then and Now," *Children's Literature,* 7 (1978): 17-44;

"For Indeed It was He," *Fortune Magazine,* 9 (April 1934): 86-89, 193-194, 204-209; republished in *Only Connect: Readings on Children's Literature,* edited by Sheila Egoff and others (New York: Oxford University Press, 1969), pp. 41-61;

Leslie McFarlane, *The Ghost of the Hardy Boys* (New York: Two Continents, 1976);

Arthur Prager, "Bless My Collar Button, If It Isn't Tom Swift!," *American Heritage,* 28 (December 1976): 65-75;

Prager, "Edward Stratemeyer and his Book Machine," *Saturday Review,* 54 (10 July 1971): 15-17, 52-53;

Prager, *Rascals at Large, or, The Clue in the Old Nostalgia* (Garden City: Doubleday, 1971);

Prager, "The Secret of Nancy Drew," *Saturday Review,* 52 (25 January 1969): 18-19, 34;

Peter Soderbergh, "The Stratemeyer Strain: Educators and the Juvenile Series Book, 1900-
1974," *Journal of Popular Culture*, 7 (Spring 1974): 864-872.

Susan Bogert Warner
(Elizabeth Wetherell)
(11 July 1819-17 March 1885)

Ruth K. MacDonald
New Mexico State University

See also the Warner entry in *DLB 3, Antebellum Writers in New York and the South.*

SELECTED BOOKS: *The Wide, Wide World* (2 volumes, New York: Putnam's, 1850; 1 volume, London: Nisbet, 1852);

Queechy, 2 volumes (New York: Putnam's, 1852; London: Nisbet, 1852);

American Female Patriotism: A Prize Essay (New York: Fletcher, 1852);

The Law and the Testimony (New York: Carter, 1853; London: Nisbet, 1853);

Carl Krinken: His Christmas Stocking, by Warner and Anna Warner (New York: Putnam's, 1853); republished as *The Christmas Stocking* (London: Nisbet, 1853);

The Hills of Shatemuc, 2 volumes (New York: Appleton, 1856; London, 1856);

Say and Seal, 2 volumes, by Warner and Anna Warner (Philadelphia: Lippincott, 1860; London, 1860);

The Old Helmet, 2 volumes (New York: Carter, 1863; London: Nisbet, 1863)

Melbourne House, 2 volumes (New York: Carter, 1864; London, 1864);

Walks from Eden (New York: Carter, 1865; London, 1866);

The House of Israel (London, 1866; New York: Carter, 1867);

Daisy, 2 volumes (Philadelphia: Lippincott, 1869; London: Nisbet, 1868, 1869);

Daisy in the Field (New York: Carter, 1869; London: Nisbet, 1869);

The Broken Walls of Jerusalem and the Rebuilding of Them (New York: Carter, 1870; London: Nisbet, 1879);

"What She Could" (New York: Carter, 1870; London: Nisbet, 1870);

The House in Town (New York: Carter, 1870; London: Nisbet, 1871);

Opportunities (New York: Carter, 1871); republished with *"What She Could"* (London: Nisbet, 1880);

Lessons on the Standard Bearers of the Old Testament (New York: Randolph, 1872; London, 1872);

Susan Bogert Warner

Trading (London: Nisbet, 1872; New York: Carter, 1873);

The Little Camp on Eagle Hill (New York: Carter, 1873; London: Nisbet, 1874);

Sceptres and Crowns (London: Nisbet, 1874; New York: Carter, 1875);

Willow Brook (New York: Carter, 1874; London: Nisbet, 1874);

Bread and Oranges (New York: Carter, 1875; London: 1875);

The Flag of Truce (New York: Carter, 1875; London, 1875);

Wych Hazel, by Warner and Anna Warner (New York: Putnam's, 1876; London: Nisbet, 1876);

The Gold of Chickaree, by Warner and Anna Warner (New York: Putnam's, 1876; London: Nisbet, 1876);

The Rapids of Niagara (New York: Carter, 1876);

Pine Needles (New York: Carter, 1877; London: Nisbet, 1877);

Diana (New York: Putnam's, 1877; London: Nisbet, 1877);

The Kingdom of Judah (New York: Carter, 1878; London: Nisbet, 1878);

My Desire (New York: Carter, 1879; London: Nisbet, 1879);

The End of a Coil (New York: Carter, 1880; London: Nisbet, 1880);

The Letter of Credit (New York: Carter, 1881; London: Nisbet, 1881);

Nobody (New York: Carter, 1882; London: Nisbet, 1882);

Stephen, M.D. (New York: Carter, 1883; London: Nisbet, 1883);

A Red Wallflower (New York: Carter, 1884; London: Nisbet, 1884);

Daisy Plains (New York: Carter, 1885; London: Nisbet, 1885).

Susan Bogert Warner (pseudonym Elizabeth Wetherell) was the author of over thirty novels. Although she did not intend her works for a juvenile audience, her first two novels, *The Wide, Wide World* (1850) and *Queechy* (1852), both feature an adolescent girl as the main character and were widely read by adolescent girls of the time. These domestic novels established Warner's reputation as a writer of wide popularity and appeal. The two enjoyed an unprecedented publishing success; in fact, *The Wide, Wide World* has been called the first American best-seller by several literary historians. In subsequent novels, most of a highly religious and moral nature, Warner followed the formula

that she had established in her first two books.

Warner was the elder of two daughters born to Henry Whiting Warner and Anna Marsh Bartlett Warner. Her parents were respected members of New York City society, and it was in an atmosphere of graciousness and wealth that Susan Warner and her sister Anna grew up. The family steadily rose in wealth and social standing, due to Mr. Warner's real estate investments. In the Panic of 1837, Henry Warner lost his fortune. His family, including his sister who had replaced his wife as head of the household at Anna Warner's death in 1828, was forced to retire to Constitution Island on the Hudson River, an isolated farm site which Mr. Warner had originally purchased to develop into a country estate; however, the house and grounds remained unimproved throughout the Warner sisters' lives. It was this turn in the family's fortune that led Susan Warner and her sister Anna to writing. As the 1840s progressed, the family sank deeper into poverty. In 1848 her aunt suggested that Susan Warner write a book and sell it. The result was Warner's first and most popular novel, *The Wide, Wide World.*

All of Warner's novels, as well as those of her

Warner's sister and frequent collaborator, Anna Bartlett Warner

sister Anna, deal with the genteel society the two had known during their family's prosperous period and with the evangelical Protestantism which they both professed. Susan Warner's novels also feature her extremely well-developed talent for enumerating the details of northern New England farm life and society. Though the novels' local color is their most interesting feature for twentieth-century critics, it was the religious fervor that impressed contemporary readers. Warner's novels are all frankly didactic about the emotional brand of Protestantism which she practiced. Her idealized characters, who are mostly female, all study the Bible in order to determine God's will and then submit themselves totally to His plan. In the Warner hierarchy of characters, the aristocrats are identified not only by their good breeding but also by the source and inspiration for those manners—a belief in God which commands a quiet self-assurance and concern for God's other creatures. If these aristocratic heroines are poverty-stricken, it is only a temporary state of affairs, ordained by God to test their faithfulness and make them strong; by the end of the novels, they will receive their just earthly rewards.

The Wide, Wide World was popular with mid-nineteenth-century girls because its heroine, Ellen Montgomery, was one of their own, with emotions and in domestic situations with which they could identify. Like Warner's father, Ellen's has suffered reverses of fortune which have strapped the formerly wealthy family. While her parents go abroad, both for her mother's health and for her father's financial recovery, Ellen is forced to abandon the comfortable city life she has known and go to an isolated farm owned by her aunt, Fortune Emerson. The townspeople call the aunt Miss Fortune, an intentional pun on Warner's part, for that is what she is to Ellen. Aunt Fortune does not sympathize with Ellen's desire for fine clothing or for religious or educational training. She has no tolerance for Ellen's fastidiousness, nor will she minister to Ellen's needs for affection or understanding. The novel is a study of Ellen's growth, both in the religious submission which her mother has encouraged her to practice and in her ability to take care of herself by performing domestic labor and by becoming emotionally self-sufficient.

In the course of the novel, Ellen's parents die, thus abandoning her to the "wide, wide world" of the title, but she finds succor in the home of the Humphreys, the local minister and his two adult children, John and Alice. As a test of her faithful submission to her superiors, the Humphreys en-

courage Ellen to submit to her aunt with a good will rather than to antagonize her. They also encourage her desire for knowledge, especially in ladylike accomplishments such as sketching, mastering French, sewing, and making tea. John and Alice are extremely idealized characters, with none of the faults of the more realistic characters such as Fortune Emerson, but their function is not novelistic realism, but rather the presentation, according to Warner's didactic scheme, of the ideal Christian life, combining faith and good breeding. It is not surprising that Alice Humphreys dies, since she is too good for the world. It is also not surprising that at the end of the novel Warner leads the reader to believe that Ellen and John will eventually marry, for John is the only man in the novel refined and faithful enough for the reformed and improved Ellen.

Opposed to the Humphreys are the local farm folk, including Fortune Emerson. While they are drawn with verisimilitude which gives them a vitality that the Humphreys and even Ellen lack, in the scheme of the novel they and their way of life are condemned as uncouth and unworthy of Ellen and her higher aspirations. The dialogue and narration in the country scenes are immediate and even humorous at times. The life on the farm teaches Ellen to take care of herself by doing the household chores, as is usual for heroines in domestic fiction, and acquiring enough independence to run the farm when the need arises. But it is clear that Warner considers this sort of life too hard, both physically and mentally, for a soul as sensitive as Ellen. While the twentieth-century critic may find the farm life more interesting than the more passive and sterile intellectual life of the Humphreys because of the energy with which Warner describes it, she and her readers would have found its quaintness and crudity distasteful.

Sometimes the country life is brutal. The "wide, wide world" has no concern for Ellen's feelings or for the physical exhaustion that living on a farm brings her. There is no one besides Alice and John Humphreys who acts on Ellen's behalf to protect her from Aunt Fortune, although there are a few other characters who comfort her in her plight without offering any concrete help. *The Wide, Wide World* may be a domestic novel, but the happy domestic life is not represented. Ellen's only hope is to be rescued from the world by marriage to John, which guarantees her moral and spiritual development and indicates her superiority to that world.

Modern critics have complained about Ellen's tearfulness and the lack of plot development and

Engraved title page from one of the more than eight hundred editions of Warner's first novel

way of coping with powerlessness as well as with moral conscience.

Though the book was a huge success, selling thousands of copies and going through many printings in both England and America, its commercial success did not do much to help the Warner family's poverty. Both Susan and her sister Anna saw their writing as a way to turn a quick profit; they therefore sold the copyrights to their publishers and never received any royalties. Though their books were published in England as well as in the United States, British copyright laws did not guarantee that foreign authors would see any of the profits. Money was constantly needed in spite of their books' successes, and the sisters were always at work on projects to supply their needs.

Susan Warner's second book, *Queechy*, deals more directly with the society which snubbed her family when their fortune was lost. Its heroine, Fleda Ringgan, is an orphan like Ellen Montgom-

In high glee, then, Fleda climbed to her seat in the little wagon, and her Grandfather with some difficulty mounted to his place beside her.—p. 2, vol. i.

Frontispiece for an 1859 edition of Queechy *(Baldwin Library, University of Florida Libraries). With this edition there were twenty-one thousand copies of Warner's second novel in print.*

realistic characterization, while praising Warner's skill as a local colorist. To criticize the novel in this way is not to understand Warner's purpose or her audience's tastes. Warner set out to write a religious story that illustrated her Christian faith and Ellen's spiritual growth rather than to write a novel of literary artistry; therefore, criticism of Warner's technique does not apply, nor does such an approach reveal the sources of the book's popularity. Warner's audience and critics contemporary with her approved of the fervent, emotional, antiintellectual quality of the religion she presents; they also identified with the mortification Ellen suffers in her poverty, with the powerlessness she experiences at the hands of her guardian, and with the satisfaction granted their fantasies by the gentle and faithful John's promise of marriage at the book's end. Ellen's decision to comply and conform with Aunt Fortune rather than to destroy herself by stubborn defiance or self-abnegating submission is a practical

ery, but before she is forced to take care of herself by running a farm in the country village from which the book takes its name, she has a few years when her aunt and uncle treat her to the advantages of education, wealth, and social grace in Paris. By the time that financial reverses force her and her family to the country, Fleda is a teenager with a taste for the finer things in life, much as Susan Warner was at the time of her father's real estate failures. Fleda is already a moral and religious paragon, made of the rarified stuff of angels, and therefore in no need of spiritual improvement as Ellen Montgomery was. Her faith is not tested so much as her endurance; she has the assurance that in the afterlife she will be rewarded for her suffering, but she must first tax her physical strength by farming and her domestic ingenuity by keeping house in order that her family not starve or suffer social ignominy. She is also a spiritual mentor for the man she eventually marries. He is an English aristocrat who finally takes Fleda to his English country estate and protects her from the squalor and brutality of country life as well as the maliciousness of city life. But first she must convert him to Christianity. She is a little girl when she first meets him, and he a young man, but by the time she is old enough to marry him, he has become a thoroughly evangelical Christian, wealthy but socially aloof, a leader of men but not one of them himself.

Since Warner based her novel on the society which she knew before her father's financial failure, by the time of the book's publication the habits of fashionable society had changed enough that the fashions were clearly out of style. The Warner family was no longer privy to the goings-on in society. In the novel anachronism and also the deep embarrassment Warner felt when her finances no longer permitted her to remain stylish and her former friends abandoned her are evident. Her religion gave her, as it does Fleda, a sense of personal worth and a mechanism for transcending the mundane vicissitudes of life. Contemporary critics were quick to point to the book's inaccuracies, but they also applauded the morality and social distinctions which the book presents. Though Fleda falls from social grace with her uncle's loss of wealth, she remains an aristocrat in spirit through her breeding and good manners, a condition which Warner suggests is a direct result of her religious faith. Her marriage to the fantastically wealthy English gentleman who can take her away from the discomfort and displeasure she has known may be unrealistic, but its acceptance by the book's audi-ence clearly indicates the interest that Warner's readers had in the traditional forms of aristocracy.

The popularity of *The Wide, Wide World* and *Queechy* can be gauged in several ways. Sales of the two books totaled 104,000 in the first three years after the first book's publication. Several fictional heroines, including Jo March of Louisa May Alcott's *Little Women* (1868-1869) and Katy Carr of Sarah Chauncy Woolsey's *What Katy Did* (1873) are described as reading *The Wide, Wide World*. Encouraged by her success and spurred on by financial need and evangelical zeal, Warner continued to write until her death in 1885, though her public gradually tired of her standard themes, characters, and settings. Of note among her later books are *The Hills of Shatemuc* (1856), interesting more for her use of biographical information about her father than for its literary value; *Melbourne House* (1864) and its sequels, the two-volume *Daisy* (1868, 1869) and *Daisy in the Field* (1869), which are forerunners, both in characterization of the heroine and in use of a Southern setting, of Martha Finley's Elsie Dinsmore series; and *Say and Seal* (1860), an early collaboration of Susan and Anna Warner which shows unusual insight into the social stratification found in the New England in which the book is set. Though these and other books by Warner attracted little critical attention at the time, they sold well enough for her publisher to keep printing her books and producing new ones.

Though Susan Warner has had little continuing influence on children's literature, her popularity and her formula for successful books—the poor, afflicted, teenaged heroine in situations which tax her domestic skills and her evangelical piety—suggested to other women writers that this kind of domestic fiction might be profitable. Warner's works have attracted little modern attention even from critics of adult literature and what comment there is has been adverse for lack of understanding of Warner's didactic rather than literary intent. But her popularity in her own time indicates her readers' preference for the domestic and evangelical subjects with which she dealt.

Letters:

Olivia E. Phelps Stokes, *Letters and Memories of Susan and Anna Bartlett Warner* (New York: Putnam's, 1925).

Bibliography:

Dorothy Hurlbut Sanderson, *They Wrote for a Living: A Bibliography of the Works of Susan Bogert Warner and Anna Bartlett Warner* (West Point,

N.Y.: Constitution Island Association, 1976).

Biography:

Anna Warner, *Susan Warner ("Elizabeth Wetherell")* (New York: Putnam's, 1909).

References:

Mabel Baker, *The Warner Family and the Warner Books* (West Point, N.Y.: Constitution Island Association, 1971);

Nina Baym, *Woman's Fiction; A Guide to Novels by and about Women in America, 1820-1870* (Ithaca

& London: Cornell University Press, 1978), pp. 150-165;

Edward Halsey Foster, *Susan and Anna Warner* (Boston: Twayne, 1978);

Alice M. Jordan, "Susan Warner and Her Wide, Wide World," *Horn Book Magazine*, 10 (September 1934): 287-293;

Grace Overmyer, "Hudson River Bluestockings— The Warner Sisters of Constitution Island," *New York History*, 40 (April 1959): 137-158;

Henry Nash Smith, "The Scribbling Women and the Cosmic Success Story," *Critical Inquiry*, 1 (September 1974): 47-70.

Noah Webster

(16 October 1758-28 May 1843)

Carol Billman

See also the Webster entries in *DLB 1, The American Renaissance in New England,* and *DLB 37, American Writers of the Early Republic.*

SELECTED BOOKS: A Grammatical Institute, of the English Language, Comprising, an Easy, Concise, and Systematic Method of Education, Designed for the Use of English Schools in America. In Three Parts. Part I. Containing, a New and Accurate Standard of Pronunciation (Hartford: Printed by Hudson & Goodwin for the author, 1783);

A Grammatical Institute of the English Language, Comprising, An Easy, Concise, and Systematic Method of Education, Designed for the Use of English Schools in America. In Three Parts. Part II. Containing a Plain and Comprehensive Grammar . . . (Hartford: Printed by Hudson & Goodwin for the author, 1784);

A Grammatical Institute of the English Language; Comprising an Easy, Concise and Systematic Method of Education; Designed for the Use of Schools in America. In Three Parts. Part III: Containing the Necessary Rules of Reading and Speaking, and a Variety of Essays . . . (Hartford: Printed by Barlow & Babcock for the author, 1785);

*Webster's textbooks were frequently revised and abridged. Only significant editions are included in this list.

Sketches of American Policy. Under the Following Heads: I. Theory of Government. II. Governments on the Eastern Continent. III. American States; or the Principles of the American Constitutions Contrasted with Those of European States. IV. Plan of Policy for Improving the Advantages and Perpetuating the Union of the American States (Hartford: Printed by Hudson & Goodwin, 1785);

The American Spelling Book . . . (Philadelphia: Young & M'Culloch, 1787; revised edition, Philadelphia: Published by Jacob Johnson & Co., 1804);

An American Selection of Lessons in Reading and Speaking. Calculated to Improve the Minds and Refine the Tastes of Youth. . . . Being the Third Part of A Grammatical Institute of the English Language . . . , Greatly Enlarged (Philadelphia: Printed & sold by Young & M'Culloch, 1787; revised edition, New Haven: From Sidney's Press for I. Beers & Co. and I. Cooke & Co., 1804);

An Examination into the Leading Principles of the Federal Constitution Proposed by the Late Convention Held at Philadelphia. With Answers to the Principle Objections That Have Been Raised Against the System (Philadelphia: Printed & sold by Prichard & Hall, 1787);

An Introduction to English Grammar; Being an Abridgement of the Second Part of the Grammatical Insti-

tute (Philadelphia: Printed by W. Young, 1788);

Dissertations on the English Language; With Notes, Historical and Critical. To Which Is Added, By Way of Appendix, An Essay on a Reformed Mode of Spelling, with Dr. Franklin's Arguments on that Subject (Boston: Printed by Isaiah Thomas & Co. for the author, 1789);

Attention! or, New Thoughts on a Serious Subject; Being an Enquiry into the Excise Laws of Connecticut . . . (Hartford: Printed & sold by Hudson & Goodwin, 1789);

The Little Reader's Assistant . . . (Hartford: Printed by Elisha Babcock, 1790);

A Collection of Essays and Fugitive Writings. On Moral, Historical, Political and Literary Subjects (Boston: Printed by I. Thomas & E. T. Andrews for the author, 1790);

The Prompter; or A Commentary on Common Sayings and Subjects, Which Are Full of Common Sense, the Best Sense in the World . . . (Hartford: Printed by Hudson & Goodwin, 1791);

Effects of Slavery, on Morals and Industry (Hartford: Printed by Hudson & Goodwin, 1793);

The Revolution in France, Considered in Respect to Its Progress and Effects (New York: Printed & published by George Bunce & Co., 1794);

Noah Webster, 1833 portrait by James Herring

A Letter to the Governors, Instructors and Trustees of the Universities, and Other Seminaries of Learning, in the United States, on the Errors of English Grammars (New York: Printed by George F. Hopkins for the author, 1798);

An Oration Pronounced before the Citizens of New-Haven on the Anniversary of the Independence of the United States, July 4th 1798 . . . (New Haven: Printed by T. & S. Green, 1798);

A Brief History of Epidemic and Pestilential Diseases; With the Principal Phenomena of the Physical World, Which Precede and Accompany Them, and Observations Deduced from the Facts Stated, 2 volumes (Hartford: Printed by Hudson & Goodwin, 1799; London: Printed for G. G. & J. Robinson, 1800);

Ten Letters to Dr. Joseph Priestly, in Answer to His Letters to the Inhabitants of Northumberland (New Haven: Printed by Read & Morse, 1800);

A Rod for the Fool's Back (New Haven?, 1800);

A Letter to General Hamilton, Occasioned by His Letter to President Adams (New York?, 1800);

Miscellaneous Papers on Political and Commercial Subjects . . . (New York: Printed by E. Belden & Co., 1802);

Elements of Useful Knowledge. Volume I. Containing a Historical and Geographical Account of the United States: For the Use of Schools (Hartford: Printed & sold by Hudson & Goodwin, 1802);

An Oration Pronounced before the Citizens of New Haven, on the Anniversary of the Declaration of Independence; July, 1802 . . . (New Haven: Printed by William W. Morse, 1802);

An Address to the Citizens of Connecticut (New Haven: Printed by J. Walter, 1803);

Elements of Useful Knowledge. Volume II. Containing a Historical and Geographical Account of the United States: For the Use of Schools (New Haven: From Sidney's Press for the author, 1804);

Elements of Useful Knowledge. Vol. III. Containing a Historical and Geographical Account of the Empires and States in Europe, Asia and Africa, with Their Colonies. To Which Is Added, a Brief Description of New Holland, and the Principal Islands in the Pacific and Indian Oceans. For the Use of Schools (New Haven: Printed by O. Steele & Co. and published by Bronson, Walter & Co., 1806);

A Compendious Dictionary of the English Language (New Haven: From Sidney's Press, 1806);

A Dictionary of the English Language; Compiled for the Use of Common Schools in the United States (New Haven: From Sidney's Press for John & David

West in Boston, Brisban & Brannan in New
York, Lincoln & Gleason and Oliver D. Cooke
in Hartford, and I. Cooke & Co. in New Haven, 1807);

*A Philosophical and Practical Grammar of the English
Language* (New Haven: Printed by Oliver &
Steele for Brisban & Brannan, 1807);

*A Letter to Dr. David Ramsay, of Charleston, (S.C.)
Respecting the Errors in Johnson's Dictionary, and
Other Lexicons* (New Haven: Printed by Oliver
Steele & Co., 1807);

*The Peculiar Doctrines of the Gospel, Explained and
Defended* (New York: J. Seymour, 1809);

*History of Animals; Being the Fourth Volume of Elements
of Useful Knowledge. For the Use of Schools, and
Young Persons of Both Sexes* (New Haven:
Printed by Walter & Steele and published &
sold by Howe & Deforest and Walter & Steele,
1812);

*An Oration Pronounced before the Knox and Warren
Branches of the Washington Benevolent Society, at
Amherst, on the Celebration of the Anniversary of
the Declaration of Independence, July 4, 1814*
(Northampton: Printed by William Butler,
1814);

*A Letter to the Honorable John Pickering, on the Subject
of his Vocabulary; or, Collection of Words and
Phrases, Supposed to Be Peculiar to the United
States of America* (Boston: Printed by T. W.
White and published by West & Richardson,
1817);

*An Address, Delivered before the Hampshire, Franklin
and Hampden Agricultural Society, at Their Annual Meeting in Northampton, Oct. 14, 1818*
(Northampton: Printed by Thomas W. Shepard & Co., 1818);

*A Plea for a Miserable World. I. An Address Delivered
at the Laying of the Corner Stone of the Building
Erecting for the Charity Institution in Amherst,
Massachusetts, August 9, 1820, by Noah Webster,
Esq. II. A Sermon Delivered on the Same Occasion,
by Rev. Daniel A Clark, Pastor of the First Church
and Society in Amherst. III. A Brief Account of the
Origin of the Institution* (Boston: Printed by
Ezra Lincoln, 1820);

*Letters to a Young Gentleman Commencing His Education: To Which is Subjoined a Brief History of
the United States* (New Haven: Printed by S.
Converse and sold by Howe & Spalding,
1823);

An American Dictionary of the English Language . . . ,
2 volumes (New Haven: Printed by Hezekiah
Howe/New York: Published by S. Converse,
1828); republished as *A Dictionary of the English Language*, 12 parts (London: Printed for
Black, Young & Young, 1830-1832);

*The Elementary Spelling Book; Being an Improvement
on the American Spelling Book* (New York:
Printed by A. Chandler & published by J. P.
Haven & R. Lockwood, 1829);

*A Dictionary of the English Language; Abridged from
the American Dictionary . . .* (New York: White,
Gallaher & White, 1830);

Biography for the Use of Schools (New Haven: Printed
by Hezekiah Howe, 1830);

An Improved Grammar of the English Language (New
Haven: Published & sold by Hezekiah Howe,
1831);

*History of the United States; to Which Is Prefixed a Brief
Historical Account of Our English Ancestors, from
the Dispersion of Babel, to Their Migration to
America; and of the Conquest of South America,
by the Spaniards* (New Haven: Printed by Baldwin & Treadway and published by Durrie &
Peck, 1832; revised edition, Cincinnati: Published by Corey, Fairbank & Webster, 1835);

Value of the Bible, and Excellence of the Christian Religion: For the Use of Families and Schools (New
Haven: Published by Durrie & Peck, 1834);

*A Brief View 1. Of Errors and Obscurities in the Common
Version of the Scriptures; Addressed to Bible Societies, Clergymen and Other Friends of Religion.
2. Of Errors and Defects in Class-Books Used in
Seminaries of Learning; Including Dictionaries
and Grammars of the English, French, Greek and
Latin Languages; Addressed to Instructors of
Youth, and Students, with a Few Hints to Statesmen, Members of Congress, and Heads of Departments. To Which Is Added, 3. A Few Plagiarisms,
Showing the Way in Which Books May Be Made,
by Those Who Use Borrowed Capital* (New Haven, 1834?);

Instructive and Entertaining Lessons for Youth . . .
(New Haven: Published by S. Babcock and
Durrie & Peck, 1835);

*The Teacher; A Supplement to the Elementary Spelling
Book* (New Haven: Published by S. Babcock,
1836);

*A Letter to the Hon. Daniel Webster, on the Political
Affairs of the United States*, as Marcellus (Philadelphia: Printed by J. Crissy, 1837);

*Mistakes and Corrections. 1. Improprieties in the Common Version of the Scriptures; With Specimens of
Amended Language in Webster's Edition of the Bible. 2. Explanations of Prepositions, in English,
and Other Languages. These Constitute a Very Difficult Part of Philology. 3. Errors in English Grammars. 4. Mistakes in the Hebrew Lexicon of*

Gesenius, and In Some Derivations of Dr. Horwitz. 5. Errors in Butter's Scholar's Companion and in Town's Analysis. 6. Errors in Richardson's Dictionary (New Haven: Printed by B. L. Hamlen, 1837);

Appeal to Americans . . . , as Sidney (New York?, 1838?);

Observations on Language, and on the Errors of Class-Books; Addressed to the Members of the New York Lyceum. Also, Observations on Commerce, Addressed to the Members of the Mercantile Library Association, in New York (New Haven: Printed by S. Babcock, 1839);

A Manual of Useful Studies: For the Instruction of Young Persons of Both Sexes, in Families and Schools (New Haven: Printed & published by S. Babcock, 1839);

A Collection of Papers on Political, Literary and Moral Subjects (Boston: Tappan & Dennett/Philadelphia: Smith & Peck, 1843).

OTHER: *The New-England Primer, "Amended and Improved . . . ,"* edited by Webster (New York: Printed by J. Patterson, 1789);

John Winthrop, *A Journal of the Transactions and Occurrences in the Settlement of Massachusetts and the Other New-England Colonies, from the Year 1630 to 1644,* edited by Webster (Hartford: Printed by Elisha Babcock, 1790);

A Collection of Papers on the Subject of Bilious Fevers, Prevalent in the United States for a Few Years Past, edited by Webster (New York: Printed by Hopkins, Webb & Co., 1796);

The Holy Bible, Containing the Old and New Testaments, in the Common Version. With Amendments of the Language by Noah Webster, LL.D. (New Haven: Published by Durrie & Peck, 1833).

The man whose name is used generically to mean dictionary contributed not only his famous *An American Dictionary of the English Language* (1828) toward the education of young Americans in the early days of the republic but also a series of textbooks on subjects from history and geography to astronomy, medicine, and, of course, spelling and grammar. While his name has not been forgotten, his achievements as the first important lexicographer in the United States have over the last century and a half received only mixed reviews. But his impact on Americans' understanding of their language and, more broadly, their attitudes toward education cannot be denied. In his person and through his pedagogical writings Noah Webster set firmly in place in the minds of generations of Americans the image of the authoritarian schoolmaster.

Born outside Hartford, Connecticut, on 16 October 1758, Webster was the son of Noah Webster, a Calvinist farmer, and Mercy Steele Webster. Even in his youth, Webster was a zealous person. As Horace E. Scudder noted in his 1881 biography, "it was at once his fortune and his misfortune to pass his life contemporaneously with the birth and adolescence of a great nation, and to feel the passion of the hour." Webster belonged to a state guard regiment that marched to Saratoga but saw no action. After graduation from Yale in 1778, he took a position as a schoolteacher and began to read law in his spare time. Observing firsthand the disrepair of the American educational system, he started to think of what he could do for the ailing but lucrative textbook business. Webster passed the bar examinations in 1781 but never established a practice and returned to his educational enterprises. Soon began the flurry of writing that would occupy him throughout his long life. The range of subjects he addressed in print illustrates how indefatigable and how self-confident he was. Educator, political essayist, editor of the *American Magazine,* founder of Amherst College, lobbyist, chronicler of epidemic diseases, lexicographer, grammarian, and experimental scientist, Webster actively sought in his life and his writing "to whip vice and folly out of the country," as Thomas Pyles put it in *Words and Ways of American English* (1952). One of his last projects was an Americanized and prudishly whitewashed version of the King James Bible (1833). Busy to the end of his life, at eighty he mortgaged his home to publish the second edition of his *American Dictionary,* and in 1841 he delivered a long address at Hartford on the two hundredth anniversary of the founding of Connecticut. At his death on 28 May 1843, he said: "I have struggled with many difficulties. Some I have been able to overcome, and by some I have been overcome. I have made many mistakes, but I love my country, and have labored for the youth of my country, and I trust no precept of mine has taught any dear youth to sin."

In 1783 Webster published his renowned speller as the first part of three in *A Grammatical Institute, of the English Language.* The spelling book, known popularly as the "Blue-Backed Speller" because of its paper covers, was revised and retitled *The American Spelling Book* in 1787. Another thorough revision, *The Elementary Spelling Book,* was published in 1829. It is estimated that the book has sold up to 1,000,000 copies, though Webster did

FABLE I.—*Of the* BOY *that ftole* APPLES.

Illustration first used in a 1789 edition of The American Spelling Book *to accompany Webster's fable "Of the Boy That Stole Apples" (American Antiquarian Society)*

not realize the profit he might have from the many editions; a good businessman he was not. In his preface to the first edition of the speller the author clearly indicates that patriotism and language are yoked in his thinking. One purpose in the speller, he says, is to familiarize children with the spelling of American names, but "To diffuse an uniformity and purity of language in America—to destroy the provincial prejudices that originate in the trifling differences of dialect and produce reciprocal ridicule—to promote the interest of literature and the harmony of the United States, is the most ardent wish of the author; and it is his highest ambition to deserve the approbation and encouragement of his countrymen." While one of Webster's major causes is manifested in this statement, the desire for a "Federal English," or national standard, a chief means he proposed for effecting that standard—spelling reform—is interestingly not an issue in the speller. It is noteworthy that Noah Webster, so opposed to the notion of British au-

thority in matters of the language, was not at all hesitant to dictate rules and criteria for determining the *correct* national standard he advocated.

In some editions of the speller Webster prescribes morals and manners through the fables and essays he includes, as indicated by such titles as "Of Charity," "Of Avarice," "Of Industry," and perhaps the most famous, "Of the Boy That Stole Apples." In "The Description of a Bad Boy," Webster concludes emphatically: "In short he neglects every thing that he should learn, and minds nothing but play or mischief by which means he becomes, as he grows up, a confirmed blockhead, incapable of any thing but wickedness or folly, despised by all men of sense and virtue, and generally dies a beggar."

Parts two (a grammar, published in 1784) and three (a reader, published in 1785) of *A Grammatical Institute* present similar injunctions and maxims. In the preface to the last volume, in fact, the schoolmaster admits that his purpose in the collection has been "to refine and establish our language, to fa-

KNOWLEDGE and FAME are gain'd not by surprise;
He that would win, must LABOR for the prize:
'Tis thus the youth, from lisping A, B, C,
Attains, at length, a Master's high degree.

Frontispiece by Alexander Anderson that for the first time appeared in the revised 1819 edition of The American Spelling Book *published by John Holbrook (New York Public Library, Astor, Lenox and Tilden Foundations). According to Webster's bibliographer, Emily Ellsworth Ford Skeel, "The four lines of verse below the picture have not been found elsewhere despite search and inquiry; Webster may have written them himself."*

cilitate the acquisition of grammatical knowledge, and diffuse the principles of virtue and patriotism." This last aim accounts for the "Address to the Ladies" and "An Address to Young Gentlemen" included at the end of the reader and in which Webster takes it upon himself to coach his young readers in, among other things, choosing a marriage partner. It should, however, be noted that the Connecticut teacher was not unrelentingly dogmatic or moralistic in the texts he prepared for school children. His edition of *The New-England Primer*, "Amended and Improved" (1789), for exam-

ple, substitutes for the couplet "In Adam's Fall/We sinned all" the unassuming "A Was an Apple-pie made by the cook."

In 1789 Webster published *Dissertations on the English Language*, which included his most radical proposals for the reform of the language. Dedicated to Benjamin Franklin, the work again connects linguistic and national unity: "We have therefore the fairest opportunity of establishing a national language, and of giving it uniformity and perspicuity, in North America. . . . The minds of the Americans are roused by the events of a revolution; the necessity of organizing the political body and of forming constitutions of government that shall secure freedom and property, has called all the faculties of mind into exertion; and the danger of losing the benefits of independence, has disposed every man to embrace any scheme that shall tend, in its future operation, to reconcile the people of America to each other, and weaken the prejudices which oppose a cordial union." *Reezon*, as Webster would have had the word spelled, could be used to ascertain, most particularly, the spelling standard. By 1806, when Webster published his first dictionary, he had modified his position on spelling reform. While he still deplored the irregularities of English orthography, he now recognized that cultural change and usage—and thus pronunciation—dictate language change, not legislated written forms. Still, some of the spellings promoted by Webster in *A Compendious Dictionary of the English Language* have become common usage: the dropping of *k* in such words as *musick* and *physick;* the use of *-er* for the British *-re* in *meter* and *center;* the use of *-or* for *-our* in *color* and *favor.*

Even as he prepared his first dictionary, Webster was thinking ahead to a more ambitious lexicographical work; in the preface to *A Compendious Dictionary* he proclaimed, "With these extensive views of this subject, have I entered upon the plan of compiling, for my fellow citizens, a dictionary which shall exhibit a far more correct state of the language than any work of this kind. In the mean time, this compend is offered to the public, as a convenient manual." In 1828 the two-volume *An American Dictionary of the English Language* appeared. This work shows Webster's continued reliance on Samuel Johnson's *Dictionary of the English Language* (1755) but also contains several original features—for example, extended definitions; thousands of new entries, many American words and technical terms; illustrative quotations taken from sources other than English writers. It is in this third matter that the word *American* in the title of the dictionary is justified, for by this time Webster was even less adamant regarding the issue of linguistic independence for America.

During and after the preparation of his second dictionary, Webster published several new textbooks, including the three volumes of *Elements of Useful Knowledge* (1802-1806), *Letters to a Young Gentleman Commencing His Education* (1823), *Biography for the Use of Schools* (1830), *History of the United States* (1832), and *A Manual of Useful Studies* (1839). In these there is the same patriotic and moral fervor rampant in his first text, *A Grammatical Institute*. In the preface to volume one of *Elements of Useful Knowledge*, he writes that the "mode of employing natural philosophy in the service of religion and piety, has been practiced by the ablest authors and best men in all ages—it furnishes powerful aids to that firm belief in the being and providence of

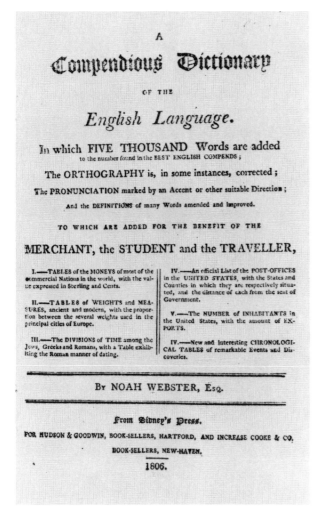

Title page for Webster's first dictionary (New York Public Library, Astor, Lenox and Tilden Foundations)

God...." And the *Biography* incorporates short sketches of Biblical figures and American pioneers and statesmen alongside those of classical authors and European writers and scholars.

Scholarly reaction to and interpretation of Noah Webster's lexicography have not been so sanguine as Webster's own pronouncements about his contribution; in fact, shortly after Webster's death, the famous "war of the dictionaries" between the camp of Webster's followers and that of his former collaborator Joseph E. Worcester questioned Webster's authority. His ignorance of the important work of contemporary historical-comparative philologists in Europe is glaring; it renders his etymologies idiosyncratic and useless and leads to his outdated acceptance of the Biblical theory about the origin of language. A lesser sin is his Yankee regionalism that continually undermines his calls for a *national* language: one of his definitions for *sauce* in the 1828 dictionary reads, "In New England, culinary vegetables and roots eaten with flesh. This application of the word falls in nearly with the definition.... *Sauce* consisting of stewed apples, is a great article in some parts of New England; but cranberries make the most delicious sauce."

His gift for definition, however, is generally acknowledged as is his real part in raising the linguistic confidence of the young country and setting the prevailing prescriptive attitudes Americans still have about grammar. His influence on the schooling of American children is similar. At Webster's birth Benjamin Harris's *New England Primer* was virtually the only available "native" textbook; Webster's pioneering work in the readers, geographies, and histories would be followed throughout the century by the efforts of William Holmes McGuffey, Charles Goodrich, Samuel Griswold Goodrich (Peter Parley), Edward Eggleston, and Edward Everett Hale. And through his texts Webster began establishing the national heritage in the minds of American children, a task that was continued by Jacob Abbott, Horatio Alger, Jr., and other writers of children's fiction in the 1800s.

Letters:
Letters of Noah Webster, edited by Harry R. Warfel (New York: Library Publishers, 1953).

Bibliography:
Emily E. Ford Skeel, comp., *A Bibliography of the Writings of Noah Webster*, edited by Edwin H. Carpenter, Jr. (New York: New York Public Library, 1958).

Biographies:

Horace E. Scudder, *Noah Webster* (Boston: Houghton Mifflin, 1881);

Emily E. Ford, *Notes on the Life of Noah Webster* (New York: Privately printed, 1912);

Ervin C. Shoemaker, *Noah Webster: Pioneer of Learning* (New York: Columbia University Press, 1936);

Harry R. Warfel, *Noah Webster: Schoolmaster to America* (New York: Macmillan, 1936);

Richard M. Rollins, *The Long Journey of Noah Webster* (Philadelphia: University of Pennsylvania Press, 1980).

References:

Joseph H. Friend, *The Development of American Lexicography 1798-1864* (The Hague: Mouton, 1967);

Thomas Pyles, *Words and Ways of American English* (New York: Random House, 1952);

Ronald A. Wells, *Dictionaries and the Authoritarian Tradition* (The Hague: Mouton, 1973).

Papers:

Webster's papers are at the New York Public Library and the Sterling Memorial Library at Yale University.

Mason Locke Weems
(11 October 1759-23 May 1825)

Carol Billman

See also the Weems entries in *DLB 30, American Historians, 1607-1865,* and *DLB 37, American Writers of the Early Republic.*

SELECTED BOOKS: *The Philanthropist; or, A Good Twelve Cents Worth of Political Love Powder* (N.p., 1799);

A History of the Life and Death, Virtues, and Exploits of General George Washington, anonymous (George-Town, S.C.: Printed for the Rev.M. L. Weems by Green & English, 1800); enlarged as *The Life of George Washington, with Curious Anecdotes, Equally Honourable to Himself, and Exemplary to His Young Countrymen* (Philadelphia: Printed for the author by R. Cochran, 1808); republished as *A History of the Life and Death, Virtues and Exploits of General George Washington, with Curious Anecdotes, Equally Honourable to Himself and Exemplary to His Young Countrymen* (Philadelphia & London: Lippincott, 1918);

The True Patriot: or, An Oration, on the Beauties and Beatitudes of a Republic; and the Abominations and Desolations of Despotism . . . (Philadelphia: Printed by William W. Woodward for the author, 1802);

God's Revenge against Murder; or, The Drowned Wife of Stephens Creek. A Tragedy (Augusta, Ga.:

Printed by Hobby & Bunce, 1807);

The Life of Gen. Francis Marion in the Revolutionary War, against the British and Tories in South-Carolina and Georgia (Philadelphia: Mathew Carey, 1809);

The Devil in Petticoats, or God's Revenge against Husband Killing, Exemplified in the Awful History of Mrs. Rebecca Cotton (Augusta: Printed by Daniel Starnes, 1810); revised as *The Bad Wife's Looking Glass; or, God's Revenge against Cruelty to Husbands. Exemplified in the Awful History of the Beautiful but Depraved Mrs. Rebecca Cotton, who Most Inhumanly Murdered Her Husband . . .* (Charleston: Printed for the author, 1823);

God's Revenge against Gambling. Exemplified in the Miserable Lives and Untimely Deaths of a Number of Persons of Both Sexes, Who Had Sacrificed their Health, Wealth, and Honor at the Gaming Tables . . . (Augusta: Hobby & Bunce, 1810);

God's Revenge against Drunkenness; or, The New Drunkard's Looking Glass . . . (Philadelphia, 1812); revised as *The Drunkard's Looking-Glass, Reflecting a Faithful Likeness of the Drunkard in Sundry Very Interesting Attitudes; With Lively Representations of the Many Strange Capers Which He Cuts at Different Stages of His Disease* (Philadelphia?, 1813);

God's Revenge against Adultery, Awfully Exemplified in

the Following Cases of American Crim. Con. I. The
Accomplished Dr. Theodore Wilson, (Delaware,)
who for Seducing Mrs. Nancy Wiley, Had His
Brains Blown Out by Her Husband. II. The Ele-
gant James Oneale, Esq. (North Carolina,) who for
Seducing the Beautiful Miss Matilda Lestrange,
Was Killed by Her Brother (Baltimore: Printed
by Ralph W. Pomeroy, 1815);

The Life of Dr. Benjamin Franklin, written Chiefly by
Himself . . . (Baltimore: Printed by Ralph W.
Pomeroy, 1815); enlarged as *The Life of Ben-*
jamin Franklin, with Many Choice Anecdotes and
Admirable Sayings of this Great Man (Philadel-
phia: Mathew Carey, 1818);

God's Revenge against Duelling; or, The Duellists Look-
ing Glass . . . (Georgetown: Published by E.
Weems for the author, 1820; revised, Philadelphia: Printed by J. Bioren for the author,
1821);

The Life of William Penn, the Settler of Pennsylvania,
the Founder of Philadelphia, and One of the First
Law Givers (Philadelphia: H. C. Carey & I.
Lea, 1822).

Mason L Weems

When Mason Locke Weems published his no-
torious biography of George Washington at the
turn of the nineteenth century, he signaled the na-
tionalistic spirit of a new country working to record—and embellish, if need be—a heritage that
would unite Americans. In his 1947 study of best-
sellers, Frank Luther Mott names Benjamin Franklin's *Autobiography* and Weems's *The Life of George
Washington* the most popular pieces of historical
reading in the early days of the United States. Daniel J. Boorstin has called Weems's work "perhaps
the most widely read, most influential book ever
written about American history." In terms of
American children's literature, Weems set in place
the hagiographical approach to life writing that
would be the rule in biography written for children
throughout the 1800s. Strongly moralistic as well,
Weems's life of the first president reads like the
historical counterpart of a Horatio Alger tale: a
story of the dramatic and deserved rise of a virtuous lad, liberally punctuated with edifying comments by the narrator to his reader.

Weems was born in Anne Arundel County,
Maryland, on 11 October 1759. He was the nineteenth child of David Weems, a Scottish farmer,
and his second wife, Esther Hill Weems. His own
life record, especially the early years, includes gaps
that have sometimes been filled by conjecture not
unlike the fictional interpolations in his biographical writing. It has, for example, been suggested that

he was a doctor in the Royal Navy at the beginning
of the Revolutionary War; this guess stems from
the likelihood that from 1773 to 1776 Weems was
a medical student in London and possibly Edinburgh as well. This celebrator of the American experience did, in fact, spend several of the war years
on the other side of the Atlantic. He was one of
the few Americans ordained by the Archbishop of
Canterbury, in 1784, for Anglican ministry in the
United States. Despite the fact that the title page
for the sixth edition of Weems's biography of
Washington proclaims the author "formerly Rector
of Mount-Vernon Parish," a nonexistent post, the
minister had by 1792 given up the life of a cleric
tied to a local parish in order to sell his ideas on
morality, patriotism, and religion on the road.

A curious blend of preacher, entrepreneur,
bookseller and publisher, and musician (he played
his fiddle publicly), Weems enjoyed a long career
as an itinerant purveyor of American culture. Initially he traveled on foot and later in a wagon,

covering the mid-Atlantic region from his home in Maryland. He met through his work Frances Ewell, the daughter of an affluent Virginian. They were married in July 1795 and eventually had ten children. On the road Weems sold his own books and those of Mathew Carey and C. P. Wayne of Philadelphia. His active correspondence with the former, with whom he had a thirty-year association, is a rich source for understanding what he intended in his writing. His popular success with the life of Washington notwithstanding, Weems remained a traveling bookman until his death in Beaufort, South Carolina, on 23 May 1825.

In addition to the major and minor biographies, Parson Weems produced throughout his long traveling career a multitude of didactic pamphlets definitely not for the "young countrymen" he had in mind when he wrote the life of Washington. Weems produced tracts advocating matrimony and declaiming against the breaking of the Ten Commandments or against such lesser misdeeds as drunkenness, gambling, and dueling. Like the biography, these pamphlets were best-sellers, certainly due in part to his active promotion of their contents to those along his route. According to Harold Kellock in *Parson Weems of the Cherry-Tree* (1928), Weems never missed the chance to speak out against drunkenness in particular: "When the book-peddling business was slack, he would not infrequently enter a grog-shop, give a lively imitation of a toper in successive stages of drunkenness, and wind up by selling his tract to the astonished and amused onlookers, possibly supplementing the written work with a brief admonition toward the temperate life."

In 1799 Weems published a pamphlet dedicated to George Washington entitled *The Philanthropist; or, A Good Twelve Cents Worth of Political Love Powder*. The next year he produced a pamphlet which contained the first version of his life of Washington. Another apocryphal story concerning Weems's life and work is that this biography was based on a funeral sermon preached by the parson/author upon the occasion of Washington's death in 1799. But letters to Mathew Carey demonstrate that Weems was already contemplating the biography as early as 1797, conceiving of it from the outset as a popular and profitable work. Six months before Washington's death, he wrote Carey: "I have nearly ready for the press a piece christen^d 'The Beauties of Washington.' Tis artfully drawn up, enliven^d with anecdotes, and in my humble opinion, marvellously fitted, '*ad captandum—gustum populi Americani ! ! !*'"

The first edition was eighty pages in length and entitled *A History of the Life and Death, Virtues, and Exploits of General George Washington*. By 1808, when the sixth edition was published, the work had burgeoned into a book of over 200 pages retitled *The Life of George Washington, with Curious Anecdotes, Equally Honourable to Himself, and Exemplary to His Young Countrymen*. The publishing history is lengthy: by 1825, the year Weems died, a twenty-ninth "edition" had appeared, and over eighty printings had been issued by 1927, the year of the last one. Unfortunately for Weems, he early on sold the copyright of the work to Carey for approximately one thousand dollars.

As Weems openly exclaimed in his letter to Carey, his *Life of Washington* was "enliven^d with anecdotes," particularly concerning the boyhood of the father of the country. Weems's purpose was to present the private as well as the public figure. At the outset of later editions of the life he announced:

> Private life is always *real* life. . . .
> Of these private deeds of Washington very little has been said. In most of the elegant orations pronounced to his praise, you see nothing of Washington below *the clouds*— nothing of Washington the *dutiful son*—the affectionate brother—the cheerful schoolboy—the diligent surveyor—the neat draftsman—the laborious farmer—and widow's husband—the orphan's father—the poor man's friend. No! this is not the Washington you see; 'tis only Washington the HERO, and the Demigod. . . . Washington the *sun beam* in council, or the *storm* in war.

He was, no doubt, thinking of the unpopular, official five-volume life published from 1804 to 1807 by Chief Justice John Marshall, which Weems had tried unsuccessfully to sell. Its flaws were many: overly formal and overly long, turgid in style, it has been called a "white elephant," a "Mausoleum," "the publishing catastrophe of its age." Weems's work was by comparison brief, amusing, and easily committed to memory with its anecdotal narratives. It was, in short, perfectly suited to the popular clamor for Washingtoniana.

The life begins with a hortatory first chapter that concludes: "For who among us can hope that his son shall ever be called, like Washington, to direct the storm of war, or to ravish the ears of deeply listening Senates? To be constantly placing him then, before our children, in this high character, what is it but like springing in the clouds a golden Phoenix, which no mortal calibre can ever

Handbill written by Weems announcing the sale of John Marshall's biography of Washington, published by C. P. Wayne of Philadelphia
(Wilson Library, University of North Carolina at Chapel Hill)

hope to reach? . . . Oh, no! give us his *private virtues!* In *these*, every youth is interested, because in these every youth may become a Washington—a Washington in piety and patriotism,—in industry and honour—and consequently a Washington, in what alone deserves the name, SELF ESTEEM and UNIVERSAL RESPECT."

Eleven chapters devoted to presenting the life chronologically follow, including two on his childhood and youth, a subject to which Marshall had given only a page in the second volume of his work. Weems's biography ends with four chapters that underscore the exemplary character of his subject: his religious faith, his benevolence, his industry, and his patriotism. In chapter fifteen on industry is found the biographer's strongest declaration of the humble origins from which Washington lifted himself through persistence and hard work; readers are told that "his whole inheritance was but a small tract of poor land in Stafford county, and a few negroes," but that "he resolved to make up the deficiency by dint of industry and economy." Thus Weems's life from start to finish makes it clear that Washington's triumph was a case of virtue rewarded.

The Life of Washington contains such primary material as "Washington's Last Words To the People of the United States" (September 1796) and excerpts from his correspondence, but it also bears the mark of Weems's storytelling ability. The death of Washington, for example, is treated in high melodramatic style, a mode of presentation that would become conventional in nineteenth-century American biography. The fictionalized vignettes the biographer is best known for, however, concern the early years of Washington: the hatchet and cherry tree drama; the story of the cabbage seeds planted by George's father to spell the boy's name;

the parable George's father tells about the apple seed that bears fruit; and the account of Mary Washington's prophetic dream just before her son was born. This last anecdote illustrates well Weems's practice of drawing moral conclusions from his narrative. In this instance, in fact, Weems provides an allegorical gloss for the mother's dream of a new house and a fire that is extinguished by her son: "This, though certainly a very curious dream, needs no Daniel to interpret it; especially if we take Mrs. Washington's *new house,* for the young Colony Government—the fire on its east side, for the North's civil war—the gourd which Washington first employed, for the American 3 and 6 months inlistments—the old man with his cap and iron rod [who helped extinguish the blaze], for Doctor Franklin—. . . and the new roof proposed by Washington, for a staunch honest Republic—

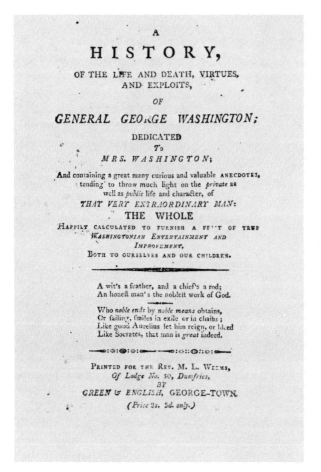

Title page for the first edition of Weems's biography of Washington (John Carter Brown Library, Brown University). In a 1799 letter to Mathew Carey, Weems described his work-in-progress as "artfully drawn up, enliven'd with anecdotes, and in my humble opinion, marvellously fitted, 'ad captandum—gustum populi Americani!!!' "

that *'equal government,'* which, by guarding alike the welfare of all, ought by all to be so heartily beloved as to *endure for ever.*" This story elsewhere illustrates Weems's colloquial and dramatic style; his use of dialogue, especially, goes far in explaining the popularity of his life of Washington over those stiffer works like Marshall's. When his mother first calls to George for help, for example, the future president answers boyishly: "High! Ma! what makes you call so angry! 'an't I a good boy—don't I always run to you soon as I hear you call?"

Although Weems's place in history rests firmly on his life of Washington, he wrote three other biographies during his career, one of Francis Marion (1809), one of Benjamin Franklin (1815), and one of William Penn (1822). Eager to capitalize on the popularity of his *Life of Washington,* Weems peddled the Washington, Marion, and Franklin biographies as a set. The connection between the lives of Marion and Washington is underscored in the biography of the former, which excepting the work on Washington was easily Weems's best-received publication. General Francis "Swamp Fox" Marion, after whom Weems had named his own second child, begins with this epigraph: "On Vernon's Chief why lavish all our lays;/Come, honest Muse, and sing great Marion's praise." The history of this "Washington of the South" concludes with a belabored comparison: "And if any higher praise of Marion were necessary, it is to be found in the very remarkable resemblance between him and the great Washington. They both came forward, volunteers in the service of their country; they both learned the military art in the hard and hazardous schools of Indian warfare; they were both such true soldiers in *vigilance,* that no enemy could ever surprise them; and so equal in *undaunted valor,* that nothing could ever dishearten them: while as to the still nobler virtues of patience, disinterestedness, self-government, severity to themselves and generosity to their enemies, it is difficult to determine whether Marion or Washington most deserve our admiration. . . ."

The life of Marion is significantly different from the work on Washington in that it is a collaborative venture: the story of Marion as told, in first person narration, by his own lieutenant and friend, Peter Horry. Horry, unable to set down his recollections in writing, took the material to Weems. An interesting correspondence between the two reveals Weems's intentions and methods in writing biography. He wrote Horry on 3 August 1808: "I beg you to indulge no fears that Marion will ever die, while I can say or write anything to immortalize him. . . . I hope in three weeks to have it all chiselled out in the rough cast. It will then take me another three weeks to polish and color it in a style that will, I hope, sometimes excite a smile and sometimes call forth a tear." Horry, however, was not at all pleased with the liberties Weems took; in 1809 he wrote to his collaborator,

> Nor have the public received the real history of General Marion. *You have carved and mutilated it with so many* erroneous statements, that your embellishments, observations and remarks must necessarily be erroneous as proceeding from false grounds. *Most certainly 'tis not MY history,* but *YOUR* romance.

Peter Horry's assessment of Weems's work was echoed throughout the nineteenth century by those biographers and historians who reconsidered the subject on which the parson had stamped his mark indelibly. A century after his death William Roscoe Thayer and Rupert Hughes, following the example set a generation earlier by Henry Cabot Lodge, were still attacking Weems and his flourishes. Unhistorical, sanctimonious, ludicrously elevated in its narrative style—Weems's biographical writing was at times all of these things. But neither Weems nor his most famous biography can be quietly dismissed, as the historians' disclaimers make clear. His major work reflects and was reflected in much children's literature of its era. By 1800, for example, the American spirit embodied by Weems had manifested itself even in the long-established *New England Primer*, in which the couplet "Whales in the Sea/God's voice obey" was replaced by "By Washington/Great deeds were done." Weems's cherry tree anecdote was picked up by William Holmes McGuffey in some editions of his Eclectic Readers. The 1832 *Life of George Washington* copyrighted by Samuel Griswold Goodrich and Morrison Heady's *The Farmer Boy, and How He Became Commander-in-Chief* (1864), among other works, incorporate Weemsian vignettes, usually without disclosure of sources and with further embellishment. Even in 1895, Elbridge Brooks in his *The True Story of George Washington* discusses and ultimately de-

bunks the hatchet and cherry tree episode. More broadly, Weems established an approach toward biography that was followed throughout the century.

Finally, Weems the man is an important part of the popular culture and literary history of America. He has been variously described as the "Livy of the Common People," part P. T. Barnum/part Horatio Alger, a con man, a harmless trickster, a "one-man market-research enterprise." He is also an early representative of the many authoritative, often ordained men who spoke through their moralized fiction and fictionalized history confidently and emphatically to nineteenth-century American children, teaching them the value of American ingenuity and perseverance.

Letters:
Volumes 2 and 3 of *Mason Locke Weems: His Works and Ways*, 3 volumes, edited by Emily Ellsworth Ford Skeel (New York: Privately printed, 1929).

Bibliography:
Volume 1 of *Mason Locke Weems: His Works and Ways*, 3 volumes, edited by Emily Ellsworth Ford Skeel (New York: Privately printed, 1929).

References:
Daniel J. Boorstin, *The Americans: The National Experience* (New York: Random House, 1965);
William A. Bryan, *George Washington in American Literature 1775-1865* (New York: Columbia University Press, 1952);
Harold Kellock, *Parson Weems of the Cherry-Tree* (New York & London: Century, 1928);
Lewis Leary, *The Book-Peddling Parson: An Account of the Life and Works of Mason Locke Weems* (Chapel Hill, N.C.: Algonquin Books, 1984);
Frank Luther Mott, *Golden Multitudes: The Story of the Best Sellers in the United States* (New York: Bowker, 1947);
Lawrence C. Wroth, *Parson Weems: A Biographical and Critical Study* (Baltimore: Eichelberger Book Company, 1911).

Kate Douglas Wiggin

(28 September 1856-24 August 1923)

Anita Moss
University of North Carolina at Charlotte

SELECTED BOOKS: *The Story of Patsy: A Reminiscence* (San Francisco: C. A. Murdock, 1883; revised and enlarged, Boston: Houghton Mifflin, 1889; London: Gay & Bird, 1889);

The Birds' Christmas Carol (San Francisco: C. A. Murdock, 1887; London: Gay & Bird, 1891);

A Summer in a Cañon: A California Story (Boston & New York: Houghton Mifflin, 1889);

The Story Hour: A Book for the Home and Kindergarten, by Wiggin and Nora Archibald Smith (Boston & New York: Houghton Mifflin, 1890);

Timothy's Quest: A Story for Anybody, Old or Young (Boston & New York: Houghton Mifflin, 1890; London: Gay & Bird, 1893);

Children's Rights: A Book of Nursery Logic (Boston & New York: Houghton Mifflin, 1892; London: Gay & Bird, 1892);

Polly Oliver's Problem: A Story for Girls (Boston & New York: Houghton Mifflin, 1893; London: Gay & Bird, 1894);

A Cathedral Courtship and Penelope's English Experiences (Boston & New York: Houghton Mifflin, 1893; London: Gay & Bird, 1893);

Froebel's Gifts, by Wiggin and Smith (Boston: Houghton Mifflin, 1895);

The Village Watch-Tower (Boston & New York: Houghton Mifflin, 1895; London: Gay & Bird, 1895);

Froebel's Occupations, by Wiggin and Smith (Boston: Houghton Mifflin, 1896);

Kindergarten Principles and Practice, by Wiggin and Smith (Boston: Houghton Mifflin, 1896);

Marm Lisa (Boston & New York: Houghton Mifflin, 1896; London: Gay & Bird, 1896);

Nine Love Songs and a Carol (Boston: Houghton Mifflin, 1896);

Penelope's Experiences in Scotland (London: Gay & Bird, 1898); republished as *Penelope's Progress* (Boston & New York: Houghton Mifflin, 1898);

Penelope's English Experiences (New York: Houghton Mifflin, 1900; London: Gay & Bird, 1901);

Penelope's Irish Experiences (Boston & New York: Houghton Mifflin, 1901; London: Gay & Bird, 1901);

The Diary of a Goose Girl (Boston & New York: Houghton Mifflin, 1902; London: Gay & Bird, 1902);

Half-a-dozen Housekeepers (Philadelphia: H. Altemus, 1903; London: Kelly, 1903);

Rebecca of Sunnybrook Farm (Boston & New York: Houghton Mifflin, 1903; London: Gay & Bird, 1907);

The Affair at the Inn, by Wiggin and others (Boston & New York: Houghton Mifflin, 1904);

A Village Stradivarius (London: Gay & Bird, 1904);

Rose o' the River (Boston & New York: Houghton Mifflin, 1905; London: Constable, 1905);

Finding a Home (Boston & New York: Houghton Mifflin, 1907);

The Old Peabody Pew: A Christmas Romance of an Old Country Church (Boston & New York: Houghton Mifflin, 1907; London: A. Constable, 1907);

New Chronicles of Rebecca (Boston: Houghton Mifflin, 1907; London: Hodder & Stoughton, 1912);

Susanna and Sue (Boston & New York: Houghton Mifflin, 1909; London: Hodder & Stoughton, 1909);

Mother Carey's Chickens (Boston & New York: Houghton Mifflin, 1911; London: Hodder & Stoughton, 1911);

Robinetta, by Wiggin and others (Boston & New York: Houghton Mifflin, 1911; London: Gay & Hancock, 1911);

A Child's Journey with Dickens (Boston and New York: Houghton Mifflin, 1912; London: Hodder & Stoughton, 1912);

The Story of Waitstill Baxter (Boston & New York: Houghton Mifflin, 1913; London: Hodder & Stoughton, 1913);

The Birds' Christmas Carol: Dramatic Version, by Wiggin and Helen Ingersoll (Boston & New York: Houghton Mifflin, 1914);

Bluebeard: A Musical Fantasy (New York & London: Harper, 1914);

Kate Douglas Wiggin

The Girl and the Kingdom: Learning to Teach (Los Angeles: Privately printed, 1915);

Penelope's Postscripts: Switzerland, Venice, Wales, Devon, Home (Boston & New York: Houghton Mifflin, 1915; London: Hodder & Stoughton, 1915);

The Romance of a Christmas Card (Boston & New York: Houghton Mifflin, 1916; London: Hodder & Stoughton, 1916);

Ladies in Waiting (Boston & New York: Houghton Mifflin, 1919; London: Hodder & Stoughton, 1919);

My Garden of Memory: An Autobiography (Boston & New York: Houghton Mifflin, 1923; London: Hodder & Stoughton, 1924);

The Quilt of Happiness (Boston: Houghton Mifflin, 1923);

Creeping Jenny and Other New England Stories (Boston & New York: Houghton Mifflin, 1924);

Love by Express: A Novel of California (Buxton, Maine: Privately printed by the Dorcas Society, 1924);

A Thorn in the Flesh: A Monologue (Boston: Badger, 1925);

The Spirit of Christmas (Boston & New York: Houghton Mifflin, 1927);

A Thanksgiving Retrospect; or, Simplicity of Life in Old New England (Boston & New York: Houghton Mifflin, 1928).

Collection: *The Writings of Kate Douglas Wiggin*, 9 volumes (Boston & New York: Houghton Mifflin, 1917).

OTHER: *Kindergarten Chimes: A Collection of Songs and Games Composed and Arranged for Kindergarten*, edited by Wiggin (Boston: Oliver Ditson, 1885; revised and enlarged, Boston: Oliver Ditson, 1887);

The Kindergarten, edited by Wiggin (New York: Harper, 1893);

Golden Numbers: Poems for Children and Young People, edited by Wiggin and Nora Archibald Smith (Boston: Houghton Mifflin, 1902);

The Posy Ring: Verses and Poems for the Youngest Children, edited by Wiggin and Smith (Boston: Houghton Mifflin, 1903); republished as *Poems Every Child Should Know* (New York: Doubleday, Doran, 1942);

The Fairy Ring, edited by Wiggin and Smith (New York: McClure, Phillips, 1906); republished as *Fairy Stories Every Child Should Know* (New York: Doubleday, Doran, 1942);

Baby's Friend and Nursery Heroes and Heroines, edited by Wiggin and Smith (Garden City: Doubleday, Page, 1907);

Magic Casements: A Second Fairy Book, edited by Wiggin and Smith (New York: McClure, 1907);

Pinafore Palace: A Book of Rhymes for the Nursery, edited by Wiggin and Smith (New York: McClure, 1907);

Tales of Laughter: A Third Fairy Book, edited by Wiggin and Smith (New York: McClure, 1908);

Tales of Wonder: A Fourth Fairy Book, edited by Wiggin and Smith (New York: Doubleday, Page, 1909);

The Talking Beasts: A Book of Fable Wisdom, edited by Wiggin and Smith (Garden City: Doubleday, Page, 1911);

A Book of Dorcas Dishes: Family Recipes by the Dorcas Society of Hollis and Buxton, edited by Wiggin (Cambridge, Mass.: Privately printed, 1911);

An Hour with the Fairies, edited by Wiggin and Smith (Garden City: Doubleday, Page, 1911);

Jane Porter, *The Scottish Chiefs*, edited by Wiggin and Smith (New York: Scribners, 1921);

Baby's Plays and Journeys, edited by Wiggin and Smith (Garden City: Doubleday, Page, 1923);

Nursery Nonsense, edited by Wiggin and Smith (Garden City: Doubleday, Page, 1923);

Palace Bedtime, edited by Wiggin and Smith (Garden City: Doubleday, Page, 1923);

Twilight Stories: More Tales for the Story Hour, edited by Wiggin and Smith (Boston & New York: Houghton Mifflin, 1925).

Kate Douglas Wiggin, who is remembered for her achievement in writing children's books and popular sentimental novels for adults, for helping to establish the first free kindergarten west of the Rockies, and for spending many years in the training of kindergarten teachers, was born in Philadelphia, 28 September 1856. Her mother, Helen Elizabeth Dyer Smith, was descended from the Knights and the Dyers, who had lived several generations in Maine. Her father, Robert Noah Smith, who was born in Providence, Rhode Island, held a bachelor's degree from Brown University and a law degree from Harvard University. A brilliant and promising lawyer, he was practicing successfully in Philadelphia when his daughters, Kate and Nora, were born. Robert Smith died suddenly on a business trip when Kate was three. Although she lost her father at such an early age, she later indicated that his qualities of mind and spirit were an abiding presence in her life and career.

Shortly after her husband's death, Mrs. Smith took her two daughters to Portland, Maine, where Kate attended dame school and revealed a promising musical talent. After their mother's marriage to a distant cousin, Dr. Albion Bradbury, the two Smith girls moved to a pleasant rural home, an idyllic pastoral setting, in Hollis, Maine. This comfortable dwelling was only a short distance from the house which later became Quillcote, the author's home in later years and the place where she wrote many of her books.

In this green, shady spot, near the Saco River, Kate and Nora Smith enjoyed the garden, caves, ponds, seesaws, the shelters for play and imaginative experience in which the young Kate Smith practiced her future role of teacher by conducting a singing school for frogs. The girls also busied themselves with piano lessons, household chores, and voracious reading. In the autumn Kate Smith gloried in the brilliant fall colors and the making of cider from tart New England apples. In the winters she participated in snowball fights and coasting downhill and long evenings popping corn and roasting apples before the fire. The prospective woman of letters began practicing her craft at the age of ten by keeping a daily journal. Though she denied that the diary revealed much talent, it is full of the humor and the vivid description characteristic of her mature writing.

Throughout her life, Kate Douglas Wiggin was an avid reader. In childhood she read magazines which interested her parents—*Harper's Magazine, Littell's Living Age*—and the family's favorite books, which included *Robinson Crusoe, The Lamplighter, Typee, Uncle Tom's Cabin*, and the Bible. She read books written primarily for adults with the exception of Jacob Abbott's Rollo books and those by Maria Edgeworth and Letitia Barbauld. The literary hero of the family, however, and the writer whose influence upon Wiggin was perhaps most profound was Charles Dickens. She named her yellow dog Pip; the canary, the lamb, the cow, all the creatures on the farm were named for Dickens's characters, and her sled was called the Artful Dodger. According to Nora Smith, one of her sister's most memorable childhood experiences was traveling on the same train with the famous novelist. She sat beside him and discussed his works knowledgeably.

Kate Douglas Smith's education began in the dame school at Portland, Maine. Her stepfather, a Bowdoin graduate, also conducted lessons for the children at home. For a few terms she attended the district school in Hollis and, for a few weeks, the brick school in Buxton. At age thirteen, Kate Smith became a boarding pupil at Gorham Female Seminary, eight miles from Hollis. Here she formed a close friendship with her Latin teacher, Mary Smith, who became the model for Rebecca's beloved teacher in *Rebecca of Sunnybrook Farm* (1903). At Gorham Female Seminary Kate won the Gold Medal for Elocution and prizes for French and English (but not composition). She attended the senior class in the grammar school and the freshman class in high school at Gorham. The following winter she studied at Morison Academy and came under the influence of the Baptist minister Dr. Richard Fuller, her spiritual mentor.

Although Kate Smith was soon to leave Maine and go to California, Maine's local color—its characters, values, and vivid dialect—were deeply embedded in her imagination. Later Maine became the setting for her most important literary achievements, and she returned finally to make Hollis her permanent home.

In 1873, when Kate Smith was seventeen, her stepfather moved his family to Santa Barbara, California, for the sake of his health. Kate Smith followed after finishing school and became extremely popular among the young people of Santa Barbara. Her vivacious personality, her accomplishments in music, dancing, and theater, as well as her generous, lively spirit won her friends wherever she went throughout her life. In California she became friends with well-known singer Annie Louise Cary and made the acquaintance of many theater people.

Such social pleasantry ended abruptly in 1876 when Dr. Bradbury died. He had put his entire fortune and that of his wife into land speculation. Bradbury's unwise investments left his wife, his two stepdaughters, and a twelve-year-old son in desperate economic circumstances. To earn a living the two girls immediately went to work. Nora Smith, who had just completed her work at Santa Barbara College, gave French and Spanish lessons. Kate Smith quickly learned to play the organ and became an organist at church services. She also launched her literary career by writing a story based on her experiences at Gorham Female Seminary entitled "Half a Dozen Housekeepers." In the fall of 1876, to the delight of the entire family, *St. Nicholas* magazine accepted the story and sent her a check for $150. This initial success sent Kate Smith scurrying back to her desk to write, only to find that she had nothing else to say. She did manage to complete "Katherine D. Smith," an account of the exploits of a group of New England girls. The piece appeared in three installments of *St. Nicholas* in 1878. In this sketch Kate Smith created two of her most famous characters—Rebecca's crusty Aunt Miranda and gentle Aunt Jane, who were to reappear as the memorable aunts of the Brick House in *Rebecca of Sunnybrook Farm.* At this stage of her life, however, Kate Smith was unready for full-fledged authorship. Her career took an exciting turn when she met Mrs. Carolina M. Severance, whom she later called her "fairy godmother."

In the early summer of 1877, Severance, often called the Mother of Women's Clubs, came from Boston to Santa Barbara. Kate Smith struck up an immediate, warm friendship with the progressive Severance, who advocated dietary and dress reform, universal suffrage, and the economic independence of women. Her most profound interest, however, was in progressive educational programs. Severance interested Kate Smith in the kindergarten method, which had been introduced into New England by Elizabeth Peabody and Horace Mann. The method had grown out of the educational theory of Friedrich Froebel (1782-1852), a German educator who had founded the first kindergarten in 1837. At the time Severance had moved to California, Marie Kraus-Boelté, a pupil of Frau Froebel, had also established a kindergarten in New York. Froebel believed that children

learned by doing things; that instruction could take place through active and amusing play. The effect upon Kate Douglas Smith was immediate and powerful.

A few months after Smith had met Severance, Emma Marwedel, a trainer of kindergarten teachers in Washington, D.C., came to Los Angeles to establish a training school. Kate's family mortgaged more property (the last they had) to secure the one hundred dollars needed for tuition, while Severance generously allowed Kate to be a guest in her home during her course of study at the school. After a year of intensive training and practical experience, Kate Douglas Smith graduated from the training school and set up a small kindergarten, the Swallow's Nest. In the summer of 1878 Felix Adler, celebrated preacher, teacher, lecturer, and author, came to San Francisco to gather support for the first free kindergarten west of the Rocky Mountains. Kate Douglas Smith was chosen to be its first teacher. The Silver Street Kindergarten in San Francisco became famous because of the arduous dedication of the young Smith. During her tenure as kindergarten teacher, she was privileged to study in the summer of 1879 with the New England sages Elizabeth Peabody and Bronson Alcott. During the same summer she also met Ralph Waldo Emerson, Margaret Fuller, and many other famous members of the Concord School of Philosophy.

The dedicated young teacher continued her efforts until December 1881, when she married a childhood friend, Samuel Bradley Wiggin, a young lawyer from Boston who had moved to San Francisco to practice law. Upon her marriage, Kate Douglas Wiggin left the kindergarten in the hands of her sister, who had already acquired extensive teaching experience. Even after her marriage, Wiggin continued to conduct and to supervise the training school for kindergarten teachers.

Though she moved to New York with her husband in 1885, Wiggin's active efforts on behalf of kindergartens continued throughout her life. She returned to San Francisco each spring to present final lectures, to administer examinations, and to participate in graduation. She also toured the United States, visiting kindergartens in Chicago, Detroit, St. Louis, Washington, Philadelphia, New York, and Boston. In September 1889, while his wife was in California working in the training school, Samuel Wiggin died suddenly in New York. Exhausted from her tireless efforts, Kate Douglas Wiggin was forced to take a much less active part in kindergarten work after 1889. In helping to establish the first free kindergarten west of the Rockies and in training dozens of teachers who moved into many different parts of the United States, Wiggin exerted a permanent influence on American education. At the end of her life she reaffirmed her commitment to teaching, noting that she believed that nature had intended for her to teach rather than to write.

Wiggin's kindergarten work was, however, the reason for her return to authorship. In 1881 she wrote *The Story of Patsy* in order to raise money for the Silver Street Kindergarten. The author herself denied that the book, privately printed in 1883, possessed much literary merit. In 1889 Wiggin revised and expanded the story, which was published by Houghton Mifflin the same year. *The Story of Patsy* is written from the point of view of a weary kindergarten teacher, a character modeled on Wiggin herself. The teacher, Miss Kate, emerges as a wise tutor much in the manner of Rousseau's ideal described in his treatise on education, *Émile* (1762).

She settles disputes through the benign use of reason. She gently persuades her pupils to behave on grounds of reason, rather than from fear of punishment. The central character of the story, Patsy, has suffered from brutal abuse. His drunken father had thrown him down two flights of stairs when Patsy was an infant, an incident which had left the child grotesquely deformed. Much like Dickens's Tiny Tim, Patsy cheerfully accepts his suffering and brightens the lives of Miss Kate and the other children. In the touching deathbed scene, Miss Kate lifts the child into her arms and sings him the kindergarten hymn "Father, we thank thee for the night." *The Story of Patsy* clearly belongs to the tradition of the moral tale with its stereotyped characters and its excessive didacticism. At the same time the story gives the reader some insight into the actual social ambience in which the kindergarten flourished. It was an oasis in the midst of poverty, disease, ignorance, and ethnic conflict. While Wiggin's portrayal of Patsy is undoubtedly too sen-

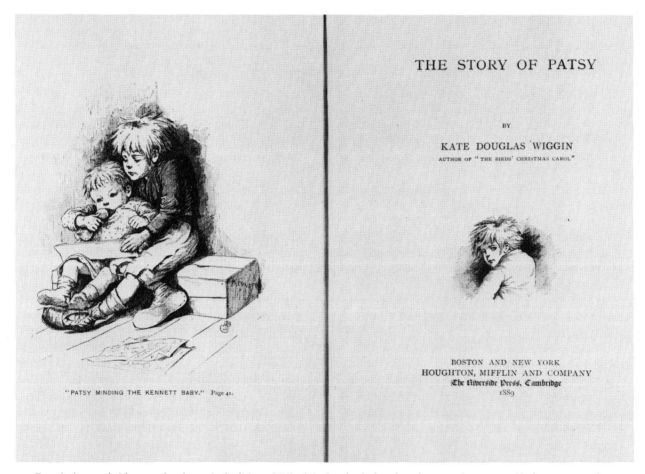

"PATSY MINDING THE KENNETT BABY." Page 41.

THE STORY OF PATSY

BY

KATE DOUGLAS WIGGIN
AUTHOR OF "THE BIRDS' CHRISTMAS CAROL"

BOSTON AND NEW YORK
HOUGHTON, MIFFLIN AND COMPANY
The Riverside Press, Cambridge
1889

Frontispiece and title page for the revised edition of Wiggin's first book, based on her experiences as a kindergarten teacher (Baldwin Library, University of Florida Libraries)

timental by modern standards, the frequent deaths of children gave Wiggin much pain during her years of teaching.

In 1887 Wiggin produced *The Birds' Christmas Carol* also in order to replenish the treasury of the Silver Street Kindergarten. According to Nora Smith in *Kate Douglas Wiggin as Her Sister Knew Her* (1925), *The Birds' Christmas Carol* was an immediate and lasting success in England and America; it sold 750,000 copies and was translated into German, Swedish, and Japanese. The book also became a favorite selection for dramatic presentation. Nora Smith indicates that hundreds of babies were named Carol in honor of the book's heroine and that Carol Clubs appeared from Maine to California.

Wiggin was steeped in the writings of William Wordsworth and Charles Dickens, and the depiction of childhood in her books owes much to these two literary giants. At her sentimental worst, Wig-

Wiggin, probably in the late 1870s

gin writes about saintly, sickly children who resemble Dickens's little Nell or Paul Dombey. After melting the icy hearts of wicked adults, they die gracefully and beautifully. At her best, Wiggin creates such lively children as Rebecca of *Rebecca of Sunnybrook Farm* or Nancy of *Mother Carey's Chickens* (1911), who have imagination, intelligence, and active, healthy bodies.

In *The Birds' Christmas Carol* the narrative begins early on Christmas morning with the Bird family, which had just been blessed by the birth of a lovely baby girl. When Mrs. Bird hears joyous Christmas carols from the church next door, she names the child Carol, as a token of the child's holy birthday. This blessed child becomes beautiful, good, but physically weak. Carol spends most of her time in bed. The excessively sweet sentimentality of the tale is balanced to some degree by the homely humor of the neighboring Ruggles family. Their mother scrubs them within an inch of their lives and instructs them in table manners as they prepare for Christmas dinner with Carol. After cheerfully presiding over the Christmas feast and handing out presents to the Ruggles children, Carol quietly dies in her bed listening to Christmas hymns. This tale highlights the child's capacity to redeem the adult community and to liberate beauty in the lives of others through goodness and purity.

The success of *The Story of Patsy* and *The Birds' Christmas Carol* enabled Wiggin to travel and to rest in the years immediately following her husband's death. She eventually met and became friends with such literary figures as William Dean Howells, Mark Twain, Henry James, John Masefield, Lady Gregory, and many others. Writing became her central occupation, and her public eagerly awaited publication of her literary creations. Late in 1890 Houghton Mifflin published *Timothy's Quest* and *The Story Hour*, a group of stories which Wiggin and Nora Smith had used in their kindergarten classes. In the spring of 1891, Wiggin visited Buxton, Maine, rented rooms in an old-fashioned white house, and wrote *Polly Oliver's Problem* (1893). *Timothy's Quest* achieved enormous popularity in Great Britain. A favorite of Wiggin's, the work was later produced in film.

Like Wiggin's first two books, *Timothy's Quest* is thoroughly sentimental. Despite its excessive sentimentality and its obvious debts to Dickens's *The Old Curiosity Shop*, the tale is charming to modern readers. In this book Wiggin begins to depict her native Maine, to draw upon its rustic characters and humor, traits which would be developed fully in Wiggin's best work. In this tale two orphaned chil-

Front wrapper for Wiggin's 1887 Christmas story written to raise money for San Francisco's Silver Street Kindergarten (Collection of Pauline and Howard Behrman)

dren, Timothy, an eight-year-old boy, Gay, Timothy's beautiful two-year-old sister, and their dog Rags have lived precariously with Flossy, a slovenly drunken woman who receives money from an unknown source to keep the children. When Flossy dies, Timothy learns that the neighbors intend to place him and Gay in an orphans' asylum. Timothy runs away with Gay and Rags, determined to find a good home. The tired children and the bedraggled dog arrive at last in the home of a selfish spinster, Miss Avilda Cummins, and her companion, Samanthy Ann. Eventually the beauty and goodness of Timothy and Gay melt the hard heart of Miss "Vilda," who gives them a true home at last.

Timothy's Quest belongs to the tradition of sentimental nineteenth-century fiction. Like Frances Hodgson Burnett's *Little Lord Fauntleroy* (1886), *Timothy's Quest* is a Cinderella story in which the stepmother figure (Miss Vilda) has a heart of gold. Much of the sentimentality of the book is relieved by the humorous and vivid descriptions of Maine's

eccentric characters. The people of Pleasant River are warmhearted and generous beneath their homely dialect and their crabbed exteriors. These stern, hardworking, abstemious, thrifty, churchgoing folk find it difficult to express emotion, but they exhibit admirable virtues and values—compassion, self-effacing generosity, loyalty, and a staunch devotion to duty. Jabe Slocum, Avilda Cummins, and Samanthy Ann Ripley are amusing and memorable characters who anticipate those who appear in Wiggin's classic work, *Rebecca of Sunnybrook Farm*. Wiggin makes a notable contribution to regional American fiction in *Timothy's Quest*, then, for the book marks the first time that a realistic portrayal of inland rural life in Maine had appeared.

During this period Wiggin also wrote *A Summer in a Cañon* (1889), a work which she considered of lesser quality than most of her other books. The work is the somewhat monotonous, episodic account of the summer that several well-bred boys and girls spend in a cañon in California. The structure, plot, and characterization of the book are flawed, though Wiggin was able to use several of the work's characters successfully a few years later in *Polly Oliver's Problem.*

Set in Santa Barbara and San Francisco, *Polly Oliver's Problem* centers on two essential problems of its spirited sixteen-year-old heroine. First, Polly must care for her invalid mother and free herself from the troublesome boarders whom her mother was forced to take in after the death of her husband. After her mother's death, Polly's problem is to find a life of her own. While not generally regarded as one of Wiggin's best books, the novel is strengthened by vivid characterization, by insights into the California of Wiggin's girlhood, by convincing dialogue, and by a coherent plot. The book was well received at the time of its publication, though it is little known today.

A significant period in Wiggin's literary development began on 24 May 1890 when she and two friends sailed from New York on the North German liner *Ems,* to tour England and the Continent. This trip was the first of many such voyages abroad. Wiggin made careful, vivid notes on her travels, which later provided material for her popular travel books, including *A Cathedral Courtship* (1893), *Penelope's Experiences in Scotland* (1898), *Penelope's English Experiences* (1900), and *Penelope's Irish Experiences* (1901). According to Nora Smith, the Penelope stories especially were popular both in the United States and abroad.

A Cathedral Courtship tells the sentimental story of a young American girl's experience of touring the English cathedrals with her aunt, a New England spinster. In her diary she confides her growing attraction to John Quincey Copley, a young architect from Boston. Katharine and John fall in love and eventually become engaged. Though the tale is little more than a charming entertainment, the characters do reveal the biases, manners, and mores of well-bred young people. The Penelope stories reveal the young heroine's witty observations and present a genuine sense of European characters. Though seldom read today, these books helped to make Kate Douglas Wiggin enormously popular abroad, where she was welcomed into aristocratic homes and literary circles. These books based on Wiggin's travels made her, according to the *Spectator,* "one of the most successful of the ambassadors between America and Great Britain."

From 1890 to 1894, Wiggin traveled widely and wrote prolifically. She earned additional, needed money for herself, her mother, and sister

Wiggin (seated) with her sister Nora Archibald Smith, 1897

through extensive public readings. Wiggin's demanding schedule and the difficult circumstances under which she often traveled eventually strained her nerves and physical health. Afflicted with intensely painful headaches, she frequently found it necessary to retreat and to recover. In 1892 she suffered a total collapse and was admitted to a private hospital for treatment.

In 1893 Wiggin's mother and sister joined her in Chicago, where the World's Fair was exciting the imaginations of Americans. After their experience at the fair, the three women decided to spend the summer in Hollis, Maine, the childhood home of the two sisters. The family found rooms in the home of Mrs. Jane Akers, where Wiggin was able to complete several reviews and short pieces for the *Atlantic Monthly,* including "The Fore-Room Rug" (1894), which became a favorite selection for Wiggin's public readings. This peaceful and productive summer, Wiggin writes in her autobiography, *My Garden of Memory* (1923), was a time of rest, growth, and happiness. When the nearby Carll House became vacant, Wiggin leased it and became the temporary proprietor of "ten acres of hayfield, the most beautiful maples and elms in the village, and a defunct apple orchard."

Wiggin soon became active in the civic life of Hollis. Her public reading for the minister's salary fund in the old Tory Hill Meeting House at Buxton Lower Corner was the first of many such appearances in the years to come. Later she purchased the property Quillcote and spent many happy hours writing under a big apple tree in the orchard.

In 1894, after seeing another group of teachers through graduation at the training school in San Francisco, Wiggin prepared for another voyage to England. On this trip she met and fell in love with George Christopher Riggs, an American importer of linens who was widely read and widely traveled. Before the *Britannic* had reached her destination, Riggs had proposed, and Wiggin had accepted. Upon their return to the United States, Riggs visited Hollis and received a warm reception into the family. The wedding took place in All Souls' Church in New York, 30 March 1895.

After her marriage to George Riggs, Wiggin's life settled into a stable and happy pattern. Each year the couple spent three months of the spring in Europe, the summer at Quillcote, and the winter months in New York. She continued to acquire new friends at home and abroad. At home she and her husband enjoyed books, music, theater, and travel, as well as an active social and civic life. In England Wiggin participated in such groups as the Royal Literary Fund, the Women Writers' Society, the Whitefriars' Club, and the Authors' Society. In sum, her life with Riggs was full and rich, and despite serious bouts of illness, she continued to write prolifically from the time of her second marriage until the outbreak of World War I.

Wiggin spent a total of fifteen seasons in England. In addition to *A Cathedral Courtship* and the early Penelope stories, she produced two works of life in England—*Robinetta* (1911) and *Penelope's Postscripts* (1915). *Robinetta* was written in collaboration with Mary and Jane Findlater and Charlotte Stewart and first published serially as "The Admiral's Niece" in the *Woman's Home Companion*, from November 1910 to March 1911. The book was published by Houghton Mifflin in February 1911. A pleasant romance, *Robinetta* details the attempts of rivals Mark Lavendar and Carnaby de Tracy to win the hand of Robinetta, who is carefully guarded by her unpleasant aunt, Mrs. de Tracy. *Penelope's Postscripts* describes Penelope's further adventurous travels in Switzerland, Venice, Wales, and Devon and includes a pleasant account of her happy and serene married life in New England. The volume contains autobiographical details, since it is based on Wiggin's own travels.

The summers at Quillcote provided the peaceful environment and time Wiggin needed for her writing, though oddly enough she did not write her masterpiece there. Late in 1903, Wiggin was in a New York hospital recovering from an illness when she experienced a vivid waking dream. She envisioned a stagecoach bumping along a dusty country road, its only passenger a little, dark-eyed girl with braided dark hair. Although she was too weak and ill to write, Wiggin named the character Rebecca Rowena Randall. During her convalescent stay at Pinehurst, North Carolina, Wiggin began work on the book and completed it at a sanitarium in Dansville, New York.

The seeds of *Rebecca of Sunnybrook Farm* had appeared much earlier in 1877 in Wiggin's story "Half a Dozen Housekeepers." The setting, Hollis, Maine, the personality of Rebecca, her relatives, friends, and teachers, the vivid Maine dialect, details of domestic and school life, the pain of debt and insufficient income—all of these features issue from Wiggin's own experiences.

The most memorable and durable aspect of Wiggin's masterpiece is the character of Rebecca herself. Full of life, intelligence, imagination, and exhibiting a close affinity with nature, Rebecca embodies the Wordsworthian ideal of childhood. Indeed, Wiggin makes the Wordsworthian influence explicit by quoting his poetry in the epigraph and by entitling the first chapter "We Are Seven."

The reader encounters Rebecca first on her stagecoach ride from Sunnybrook farm to the Brick House in Riverboro, Maine. Rebecca recounts her past history and her plans for the future to Jeremiah Cobb, the driver who becomes one of Rebecca's closest friends in Riverboro. Rebecca's aunts, known as the Sawyer sisters in Riverboro, live in the sturdy home of their girlhood and practice New England virtues—thrift, piety, sobriety. Although Aunt Jane is gentle and loving, she is dominated by the stern, iron-willed Aunt Miranda, who offers Rebecca only close-handed and grudging hospitality, a surfeit of criticism, rules, and regulations.

Rebecca herself is a pastoral child. Free-spirited, carefree, impulsive, generous, and imaginative, she writes poetry and describes her love for the natural beauties of Sunnybrook Farm—its chattering brook and young green trees. Romances and other stories provide Rebecca with most of her ideas about life. In the first chapter of the novel, she compares her experiences to fairy tales, alluding specifically to "Cinderella," "The Enchanted

Quillcote, Wiggin's home in Hollis, Maine

Frog," and others. Later in the novel, while trying to sell soap to raise money for a poor family, Rebecca meets her generous benefactor, whom she calls Mr. Aladdin. Still later in her development, Rebecca compares her life to that of Maggie Tulliver in George Eliot's *The Mill on the Floss*.

Throughout the novel, Rebecca's mother, brothers, and sisters remain shadowy figures. The reader learns that her father, Lorenzo de Medici Randall, had been a charming and talented, but thoroughly ineffectual, man who had fathered seven children and then died, leaving the burden of rearing them to his wife, Aurelia. Aunt Miranda despises the Randall strain in Rebecca, who looks and talks much like her father. A central conflict and an important dimension of the book is the tension between the spirited Rebecca and the taciturn Aunt Miranda, whose stormy relationship is made a bit easier by the placid Aunt Jane. Gradually, however, Rebecca makes her way into the selfish, materialistic spinster's heart. At last Rebecca

finishes school, returns home to care for her ailing mother, and inherits the Brick House when Aunt Miranda dies.

Wiggin's classic for children, *Rebecca of Sunnybrook Farm*, is a felicitous mixture of romance and realism. Through goodness, industry, and imagination, the young heroine rises from relative poverty to comparative wealth. Yet Rebecca's happiness is tempered with grim realities—debts, the necessities of duty, labor, and self-sacrifice. Wiggin clearly endorses the traditional value of hard work, the importance of property, and the need for duty and piety. Family and community are prominent institutions in the novel. The book also reveals a strong New England emphasis upon education, yet Rebecca's education functions not as an ornament and accomplishment for herself but in order that she may serve her family and community more effectively. Rebecca achieves finally what her parents had failed to achieve—to establish

REBECCA

Of Sunnybrook Farm

BY
KATE DOUGLAS WIGGIN

BOSTON AND NEW YORK
HOUGHTON, MIFFLIN AND COMPANY
The Riverside Press, Cambridge
1903

Title page for Wiggin's best-known book, inspired by a vivid waking dream she experienced while recovering from an illness

a home and a secure place in the community for herself and the rest of the family.

When *Rebecca of Sunnybrook Farm* was published in 1903, prominent literary figures from all over the world paid Wiggin tribute. Mark Twain called the book "beautiful and moving and satisfying." Wiggin also received letters of tribute from Frances Hodgson Burnett, Mary Mapes Dodge, Thomas Bailey Aldrich, Sarah Orne Jewett, Jack London, and many others. The book was not only the best but also the most popular of Wiggin's works. Because of Rebecca's engaging character, the book's convincing dialogue, and coherent structure, the work may be read with pleasure by contemporary children. In this book Wiggin vividly reveals the child's experience, not the adult's nostalgic view of what childhood should be. This feature significantly sets *Rebecca of Sunnybrook Farm* apart from Wiggin's many sentimental novels.

New Chronicles of Rebecca (1907) includes eleven complete episodes from Rebecca's life which

did not appear in the earlier volume. Six of these sketches appeared in *Scribner's Magazine,* August-December 1906 and January-March 1907, before the book was published by Houghton Mifflin in 1907. While the structure of *New Chronicles of Rebecca* is not as satisfying as that of *Rebecca of Sunnybrook Farm,* characterization, depictions of setting, use of dialogue, and descriptions of action and setting are all strong. The book includes several adventures in which Rebecca's best friend, Emma Jane Perkins, and Rebecca participate, and the volume ends with Emma Jane's engagement to Abijah Flagg and Rebecca's growing awareness of Adam Ladd's love for her. Rebecca is keenly aware that Emma Jane's marriage marks a passage into the responsibilities of adulthood. For a time at least, Rebecca must make her way alone.

From March to May 1905 Wiggin's love story, *Rose o' the River,* appeared in *Century Magazine;* it was published as a book by Houghton Mifflin later that year. Lovely Rose must choose between her virtuous fiancé Steve Waterman and the vain Claude Merrill, a salesman from Boston. In jealousy Steve breaks off the engagement; Rose becomes disillusioned with Claude just in time to save herself from an unfortunate match. Except for Rose's Grandfather "Old Kennebec" Wiley, who delights the reader with legendary tales of adventures on the Kennebec River, the characterizations of this work are stereotyped.

In 1909 Houghton Mifflin published *Susanna and Sue,* one of Wiggin's most unusual works. Though not notable for its literary quality, the book reveals the author's interest in the Shakers. As a child she had visited a Shaker community. In *Susanna and Sue* Wiggin tells the story of a thirty-year-old mother, who, abandoned by her husband, lives with the Shakers, healing her bruised heart and spirit in the serene, if austere, atmosphere of their village at Alfred, Maine. At last Susanna realizes that her first duty is to her family. Returning home, she finds that her husband has returned and has reformed his life. The couple resolve to abide in their home together. Although plot and characterizations of this story are implausible, the book presents some interesting perceptions concerning the Shaker way of life.

Mother Carey's Chickens, the most widely read of Wiggin's books other than *Rebecca of Sunnybrook Farm* and *The Birds' Christmas Carol,* was written during the summer of 1909 and appeared serially in the *Ladies' Home Journal,* November 1910 through April 1911. Houghton Mifflin published it in 1911, the same year that *Robinetta* appeared. Well received upon publication, *Mother Carey's Chickens* continued to be popular for many years after the author's death. This warm story of family loyalty is a lively and interesting narrative, though the book is scarcely known today. The family's problems begin when Mrs. Carey's husband, a sea captain, suddenly dies, leaving her to care for her four children (Mother Carey's chickens). The family must exist on a tiny income grudgingly augmented by a spinster relative, Cousin Anne, whose character closely resembles that of Aunt Miranda in *Rebecca of Sunnybrook Farm*. The plot of the novel revolves around the Careys' attempts to make a new home from the "yellow house," a house which the father had once admired while picnicking with the family.

Mother Carey and her flock soon become favorites in the tiny Maine community. Nancy, the oldest Carey child, has imagination and initiative which bring joy to her family and community. She writes stories, as Wiggin did herself, to help earn money for the family. She also becomes friends with the absent landlord, an ambassador in Germany, and through him meets her future husband. The title of the book comes from Charles Kingsley's classic for children, *The Water-Babies* (1863); the lost petrels, which Kingsley refers to as "Mother Carey's chickens," find their way to a safe home and harbor in a fairy-tale ending of good fortune and domestic bliss, just as Wiggin's family is safely settled at last. Indeed, the structure and the characterizations of the entire novel closely resemble those of a fairy tale. Death, loss, and poverty threaten the well-being of an entire family, when the good, innocent, imaginative, and beautiful heroine, Nancy, exerts her efforts and wins a "godfather's" beneficence and support.

World War I interrupted the pleasant routine of Wiggin's life, separating her from beloved friends in England and Europe. She wrote little during the war, perhaps because her happy optimistic heroines and fairy-tale endings seemed incongruent with the cataclysmic death and destruction of the time. Nevertheless, she remained active during these years and spent much of her time at Quillcote in Hollis, Maine, where she was president of the local Red Cross. During this period she continued to adapt her books for the theater and to work tirelessly on behalf of kindergartens and children's hospitals.

One of the most famous and beloved dramatizations of Wiggin's works was that of the 1907 novel *The Old Peabody Pew*. According to Nora Smith, *The Old Peabody Pew* grew out of a cleaning campaign conducted in the Old Tory Hill Meeting House by the members of the Dorcas Society of Hollis and Buxton, Maine, to which both Wiggin and her sister belonged. The sisters noticed that one of their friends of the Dorcas Society was scrubbing a pew which belonged to a long-absent neighbor. This incident inspired Kate to write the love story of Nancy Wentworth, an attractive thirty-five-year-old spinster who volunteers to clean the Old Peabody Pew for Justin Peabody, a young man who had traveled to Detroit ten years earlier, promising to return and to marry Nancy as soon as his luck had changed. When Justin receives a letter from Mrs. Burbank, asking for a donation toward the upkeep of the pew, he is encouraged to return. Shortly before Christmas, Justin returns, and the faithful lovers are reunited in a touching scene. The novel is chiefly a tale of unrelieved sentimentality. Pious, solemn virtue is unremittingly rewarded. Only Miss Lobelia Brewster, a sassy and sharp-tongued spinster who detests men and argues that women would make more reliable carpenters and painters, introduces a humorous touch into an otherwise trite melodrama.

Nora Smith indicates that this sentimental romance won immediate popularity. A letter from Buenos Aires, Argentina, in 1915, describes the success with which the tale had been adapted for a church play in that city, an idea which inspired a dramatic version of the work, published in the *Ladies' Home Journal* in 1917. The first of many performances of *The Old Peabody Pew* took place on 16 August 1916 at the old Tory Hill Meeting House in Buxton. Nora Smith wrote that in the United States in 1924 alone, the play was presented in seventy-four towns in nineteen states, figures which attest to the power with which Wiggin addressed her contemporary audience.

While Kate Douglas Wiggin was aware of the profound social changes wrought by World War I, she continued to write the same kind of stories after the war and to look to the past, rather than to the future, for inspiration. She was treated as a prominent woman of letters, honored by the New York Kindergarten Association for her years of service, and invited by the *San Francisco Examiner*, as one of the six most distinguished women in the world, to attend the Panama Pacific International Exposition.

Wiggin's work continued to be widely popular. Houghton Mifflin published a handsome nine-volume edition of *The Writings of Kate Douglas Wiggin* in 1917 and brought out a new edition of *Polly Oliver's Problem*. In addition to preparing numerous

Cast for a Buenos Aires production of The Old Peabody Pew. *In an August 1915 letter to Wiggin, Jennie E. Howard, a retired American teacher living in Buenos Aires, reported that her ladies' club had dramatized Wiggin's 1907 novel "in a simple way." Howard's letter encouraged Wiggin to write a dramatic version of her own, which was first performed in Buxton, Maine, in August 1916.*

short stories and reviews, Wiggin was hard at work on her autobiography, *My Garden of Memory,* during the years 1919 to 1922. By the fall she had completed much of the work. Wiggin was at this time intensely aware that her health was rapidly failing and that time was short. Her energy had quickly declined, and her headaches had become more frequent and more severe.

In the early months of 1923, Wiggin's husband George Riggs lived in the South because of illness, while Wiggin and her sister devoted themselves entirely to the autobiography. Despite her declining health, Wiggin had nearly completed the manuscript when she sailed for England with her husband in April. During this voyage she became seriously ill but recovered briefly and worked feverishly once more. Early in August she sent the final chapters to Nora Smith at Quillcote. With relief Wiggin received Nora's cable, approving the chapters. She died on 24 August 1923 at a nursing home at Harrow-on-the-Hill.

The body of Kate Douglas Wiggin was cre-

mated in accordance with her wishes. Riggs returned to Quillcote with the ashes, whereupon a service was conducted by the Reverend Roderick Stebbins, a friend of Wiggin's from California. After the service Riggs scattered the ashes, as his wife had wished, into the foaming rapids of the Saco River. Later, behind the Old Tory Hill Meeting House Riggs placed in memory of Kate Douglas Wiggin a plain Celtic cross of Vermont marble, inscribed with Hans Christian Andersen's line from the tale of the Flax with which Wiggin had ended her autobiography, "The song is never ended."

During her long and productive writing career, Kate Douglas Wiggin earned the acclaim of her contemporaries as well as of young readers. Although few of her sentimental works appeal to modern audiences, *Rebecca of Sunnybrook Farm* remains a classic of American children's literature. Other works, particularly *Timothy's Quest, The New Chronicles of Rebecca,* and *Mother Carey's Chickens,* deserve to be read more than they are, and Wiggin deserves continuing admiration for her many contributions to the education and enjoyment of young children.

Biography:
Nora Archibald Smith, *Kate Douglas Wiggin as Her Sister Knew Her* (Boston & New York: Houghton Mifflin, 1925).

References:
Helen Frances Benner, *Kate Douglas Wiggin's Country of Childhood* (Orono, Maine: University of Maine Studies, 1956);
Edna Boutwell, "Kate Douglas Wiggin: The Lady with the Golden Key," in *The Hewins Lectures*, edited by Siri Andrews (Boston: Horn Book, 1963).

Augusta Jane Evans Wilson

(8 May 1835-9 May 1909)

Ken Donelson
Arizona State University

BOOKS: *Inez: A Tale of the Alamo,* anonymous (New York: Harper, 1855; London: Nicholson, 1883);
Beulah (New York: Derby & Jackson, 1859; London: Knight, 1860);
Macaria; or, Altars of Sacrifice (Richmond: West & Johnson, 1863; London: Saunders, 1864);
St. Elmo (New York: Carleton, 1867; London: Simpkin, 1883);
Vashti; or, Until Death Us Do Part (New York: Carleton, 1869; London: Nicholson, 1883);
Infelice (New York: Carleton, 1875; London: Nicholson, 1883);
At the Mercy of Tiberius (New York: Dillingham, 1887; London: Low, 1887);
A Speckled Bird (New York: Dillingham, 1902; London: Hutchinson, 1902);
Devota (New York: Dillingham, 1907; London: Unwin, 1907).

Once highly regarded by the general public, particularly girls and women, and disliked intensely by many literary critics, Augusta Jane Evans Wilson's books have not worn well, but they unquestionably represent the domestic novels of the time. Her best-known book, *St. Elmo* (1867), may well have been the most popular.

Nathaniel Hawthorne bitterly opposed the popular domestic novels. In 1855 he wrote his publisher, "America is now wholly given over to a d--d mob of scribbling women, and I should have no chance of success while the public taste is occupied with their trash—and should be ashamed of myself if I did succeed. What is the mystery of these innumerable editions of [Maria Susanna Cummins's] the 'Lamplighter,' and other books neither better nor worse?—Worse they could not be, and better they need not be, when they sell by the 100,000." The domestic novel, the best-selling literature from 1850 through the 1870s, began with Susan Warner (who wrote under the pseudonym of Elizabeth Wetherell) and *The Wide, Wide World* in 1850. Far better written than any of the novels that followed, *The Wide, Wide World* preached morality, woman's submission to man, the religion of the heart and the Bible, the glories of suffering, and the virtues of cultural, social, and political conservatism. Domestic novels typically featured a young girl, usually orphaned and placed in the home of a relative or another benefactor, who met a dark and handsome young man with shadows in his past, a man untrustworthy but inevitably redeemable and worth loving.

Wilson did not subscribe to all the tenets of the domestic novel. She believed that women must be subservient to their husbands, but she believed with equal fervor that women had a duty to use their minds to control their lives. Although she used most of the trappings of the domestic novel, Wilson offered readers her particular brand of mid-nineteenth-century feminism. Women and girls by the thousands eagerly read her books.

Wilson's popularity is somewhat of a mystery to modern readers. Her sentimental novels are incredibly long; her paragraphs and sentences are lengthy. Her writing is convoluted and often difficult to follow, in part because of her immense vocabulary. Whether that vocabulary was functional or simply intended to impress readers has been controversial ever since publication of her first book. But the vocabulary gave readers, possibly especially young girls, the distinct impression that while they were being entertained, they were receiving an education as well.

Perhaps Wilson was popular because she asked questions that other women were asking, particularly about religion. Questions about marriage, love, responsibility, skepticism, Darwinism, philosophy, women's duties, and women's rights ran through her books. Although her characters had little relationship to reality, these stereotypes excited contemporary enthusiasm.

She was a Southerner who believed that the Southern way of life, including slavery, was inherently superior to that of any other civilization. Born the oldest in a family of eight in Columbus, Georgia, she was educated almost exclusively at home by her mother, Sarah Skrine Howard Evans, who inculcated in her a love of books. Early in her childhood, her father, Matthew Ryan Evans, moved the family to Texas, first to Galveston, then to Houston, and finally to San Antonio, where she was enraptured by the Alamo and the legends surrounding it. In 1849 the family removed to Alabama. At fifteen, Wilson began writing *Inez* (1855), a sentimental, moralistic, and virulently anti-Catholic novel.

Wilson presented *Inez* as a present to her father in 1854. Although the book is filled with empty rhetoric and the evil machinations of a villainous Jesuit priest, there is a certain power in Wilson's first novel. Encouraged by friends, in 1859 she produced her second novel, *Beulah,* which, as the first of her questioning books, deals with reli-

Augusta Jane Evans Wilson, 1902

gious doubt. Beulah is beloved of Dr. Guy Hartwell, her guardian. His love is unrequited, so in typical domestic-novel fashion he leaves, not to return for five years. She studies, struggles with her reading, her beliefs, and her questions, and finally, she is once again the Christian she had been. Dr. Hartwell returns from the Orient in time to propose marriage, and they marry, he presumably now ready to guide her to Eternal Life. The novel is little more than another domestic novel save for the crisis of faith Beulah undergoes. She reads Poe, De Quincey, Emerson, Carlyle, Goethe, German transcendentalists, Locke, Descartes, Hume, Spinoza, and more, much, much more. But the reading troubles her and her religion is toppled until she realizes that faith is far greater than questioning, and she accepts and returns to her original state. The book sold 22,000 copies in the first nine months.

Wilson ardently supported the secessionist cause, and her third novel, *Macaria; or, Altars of Sacrifice*, was dedicated "To the Brave Soldiers of the Southern Army" when it was published in 1863. Printed by a Richmond, Virginia, firm on crude wrapping paper and bound in boards covered with wallpaper, the book is a manifesto about Southern bravery and the Southern cause. Union General George Henry Thomas so opposed the book that he pronounced it dangerous contraband and banned all copies among his troops. The first part of the book attempts to refute the charges made by Harriet Beecher Stowe in *Uncle Tom's Cabin* by presenting an idealized picture of the South; the last 120 pages make clear Wilson's love of the Southern cause and her hatred of Northern abolitionism.

St. Elmo, her fourth novel and by far her best-selling and most famous book, is an almost perfect example of the domestic novel. Edna Earl, orphaned daughter of a blacksmith, is rescued from a train wreck by Mrs. Murray, the snobbish widow of a wealthy planter. Mrs. Murray determines to raise Edna as her own daughter, and pastor Allan Hammond is put in charge of Edna's education. St. Elmo Murray, Mrs. Murray's son, is indulgent, arrogant, and proud; his shadowy past includes a duel and a reputation as a vile seducer of women. St. Elmo takes one look at the pure Edna, falls in love, is scorned, and immediately goes away for four years. By the time he returns, Edna has studied Greek, Latin, Sanskrit, Chaldee, Hebrew, and Arabic. She abhors St. Elmo as she did before. She has become a novelist, and although critics attack her book, she perseveres, as Wilson did, despite critical disapproval. St. Elmo continues his court-

1890 portrait of Lorenzo Madison Wilson by Nicola Marschall (Collection of Dr. and Mrs. M. Wilson Gaillard). Wilson was sixty years old when he married Augusta Jane Evans in 1868.

ship and is consistently rejected. Finally, St. Elmo sees the light, becomes a Christian and then a minister, and wins Edna, who renounces her writing as a duty owed to her husband.

St. Elmo's publisher boasted that one million people had read the novel within four months of publication, and it certainly was one of three best-selling novels of the nineteenth-century (exceeded in sales only by *Uncle Tom's Cabin* and Lew Wallace's *Ben-Hur*), and it was still a highly popular novel as late as 1893. It was twice filmed, in 1914 and in 1923, the latter production featuring John Gilbert as St. Elmo and Bessie Love as Edna Earl. Thirteen towns were established as, or rechristened, St. Elmo; a girls' school, several Southern plantations, steamboats, and hotels also took the name. St. Elmo punch and St. Elmo cigars appeared on the market. And no one has any idea how many children, born in the 1860s and 1870s, had Wilson to credit for their first name.

Wilson's vocabulary, always immense, flowered profusely in *St. Elmo*. In one paragraph that ran to 108 lines of print, Wilson uses the words below to describe St. Elmo's rooms:

> *bizarrerie* . . . a villa of Parthenope . . . Lucanian Sybaris . . . Oval ormolu tables . . . buhl chairs . . . marquetrie cabinets . . . intaglios . . . Abraxoids . . . Mnesarchus . . . Samian lapidary . . . ring of Polycrates . . . verd-antique table . . . uncial letters . . . some ruined Laura in the Nitrian desert . . . St. Macarius . . . Kyrie eleison, Christe eleison . . . amphorae . . . Falernian . . . Herculaneum . . . some luxurious triclinium in the days of Titus . . . Nebuchadnezzar's diary . . . sombre mysteries of Rosicrucianism . . . Elzevir Terence . . . a curious Birman book . . . black rhyta from Chiusi . . . cylix . . . A grayhaired Cimbrian Prophetess . . . architrave of the Cave Temple at Elephanta . . . that miracle of Saracenic architecture, the Taj Mahal at Agra . . . this mimic tomb of Noor-Mahal. . . .

Charles Henry Webb produced a parody eight months after *St. Elmo*'s publication, *St. Twel-mo; or, The Cuneiform Cyclopedist of Chattanooga* (1867), which argued that one explanation for the dullness and slowness of the original book was that Edna had swallowed an unabridged dictionary when she was a child.

In December 1868 the author of *St. Elmo* married Lorenzo Madison Wilson, a rich Mobile businessman. She was thereafter the mistress of a large home, but she continued to write. Her later books sold well, but they added little to her reputation after *St. Elmo*. Although she continued to oppose women's suffrage, arguing, as she had in *St. Elmo*, that a woman's place was in the home, she insisted in all her novels that every woman was obligated to use her talents and abilities to the utmost.

Today Wilson's books can be found in secondhand bookstores but rarely on home bookshelves.

Critics paid as little attention to her as possible, though when a new Wilson book appeared, they attacked it. Wilson, however, generally ignored her critics. She knew that readers liked her, and she knew their interests. Few novelists, before or after Wilson, have been as popular.

Biography:
William Perry Fidler, *Augusta Evans Wilson, 1835-1909* (University, Ala.: University of Alabama Press, 1951).

References:
William W. Brewton, "St. Elmo and St. Twelvemo," *Saturday Review of Literature*, 5 (22 June 1929): 1123-1124;

Earnest Elmo Calkins, "Named for a Bestseller," *Saturday Review of Literature*, 21 (16 December 1939): 3-4, 14, 16-17;

Esther Jane Carrier, *Fiction in Public Libraries, 1876-1900* (New York: Scarecrow Press, 1965), pp. 287-290;

Alexander Cowie, *The Rise of the American Novel* (New York: American Book Co., 1948), pp. 430-434;

J. C. Derby, *Fifty Years Among Authors, Books and Publishers* (New York: Carleton, 1884), pp. 389-399;

Mary Forrest (Julia Deane Freeman), *Women of the South Distinguished in Literature* (New York: Richardson, 1865), pp. 328-353;

Jay B. Hubbell, *The Southern American Literature, 1607-1900* (Durham: Duke University Press, 1954), pp. 610-616;

Arthur Bartlett Maurice, " 'Best Sellers' of Yesterday," *Bookman*, 31 (March 1910): 35-42;

Barbara Welter, *Dimity Convictions: The American Woman in the Nineteenth Century* (Athens: Ohio University Press, 1976), pp. 105-111.

Sarah Chauncy Woolsey
(Susan Coolidge)
(29 January 1835-9 April 1905)

Ruth K. MacDonald
New Mexico State University

SELECTED BOOKS: *The New-Year's Bargain* (Boston: Roberts Brothers, 1872; London: Warne, 1872);
What Katy Did (Boston: Roberts Brothers, 1873; London: Warne, Lock & Tyler, 1873);
What Katy Did at School (Boston: Roberts Brothers, 1874; London: Warne, Lock & Tyler, 1874);
Mischief's Thanksgiving, and Other Stories (Boston: Roberts Brothers, 1874; London: Routledge, 1875);
Nine Little Goslings (Boston: Roberts Brothers, 1875);
For Summer Afternoons (Boston: Roberts Brothers, 1876);
Eyebright. A Story (Boston: Roberts Brothers, 1879; London: Routledge, 1879);
Verses (Boston: Roberts Brothers, 1880);
Crosspatch, and Other Stories. Adapted from the Myths of Mother Goose (Boston: Roberts Brothers, 1881; London: Bogue, 1881);
A Guernsey Lily; or, How the Feud Was Healed; A Story for Girls and Boys (Boston: Roberts Brothers, 1881);
A Round Dozen (Boston: Roberts Brothers, 1883);
A Little Country Girl (Boston: Roberts Brothers, 1885);
What Katy Did Next (Boston: Roberts Brothers, 1886; London: Ward, Lock, 1887);
A Short History of the City of Philadelphia from its Foundation to the Present Time (Boston: Roberts Brothers, 1887);
Clover (Boston: Roberts Brothers, 1888);
Just Sixteen (Boston: Roberts Brothers, 1889);
A Few More Verses (Boston: Roberts Brothers, 1889);
In the High Valley. Being the Fifth and Last Volume of the Katy Did Series (Boston: Roberts Brothers, 1890);
Rhymes and Ballads for Girls and Boys (Boston: Roberts Brothers, 1892);
The Barberry Bush, and Eight Other Stories about Girls for Girls (Boston: Roberts Brothers, 1893);
Not Quite Eighteen (Boston: Roberts Brothers, 1894);

An Old Convent School in Paris, and Other Papers (Boston: Roberts Brothers, 1895);
Curly Locks (Boston: Little, Brown, 1899);
The Rule of Three (Philadelphia: Henry Altemus, 1904);
A Sheaf of Stories (Boston: Little, Brown, 1906);
Last Verses (Boston: Little, Brown, 1906).

OTHER: *The Diary and Letters of Frances Burney, Madame d'Arblay*, revised and edited by Woolsey (Boston: Roberts Brothers, 1880);
The Letters of Jane Austen, Selected from the Compilation of Her Great Nephew Edward, Lord Bradbourne, edited by Woolsey (Boston: Roberts Brothers, 1892).

Sarah Chauncy Woolsey (pseudonym Susan Coolidge) was the author of many novels and short stories for children, but she is known chiefly for the Katy series of five books, published between 1873 and 1890. The Katy books center on the title character, Katy, a lively and mischievous young girl, the eldest of a family of five whose mother has died. Katy means well and fully intends to be a mother to her younger siblings, but in the first volume of the series she strays from her original purpose because of her childish thoughtlessness. The books trace not only Katy's maturation, but also that of her sisters and brothers. The first book of the series is definitely the best, but throughout Woolsey shows an ear for the chatter of children at play and a keen sense of the waywardness of basically good children into various forms of naughtiness.

Woolsey was born in Cleveland, Ohio, to the highly educated family of John Mumford and Jane Andrews Woolsey, who were related to several presidents of Yale University. She was educated in private schools in Cleveland and, in her teens, at Mrs. Hubbard's Boarding School in Hanover, New Hampshire. She showed herself to be an exceptional student, especially in history and literature. In 1855 the Woolsey family moved to New Haven,

397

Sarah Chauncy Woolsey

Connecticut. With a characteristic purposiveness, Woolsey devoted her time during the Civil War to hospital work and organizing a nursing staff. The family remained in New Haven until 1870, when they spent two years in Europe following the death of Mr. Woolsey. On their return, they moved to Newport, Rhode Island, where Woolsey spent the remainder of her life.

Though Woolsey had shown a propensity to write and had produced short stories and poems in her youth, her first appearance in print did not occur until 1872, with *The New-Year's Bargain*, a book for girls that, like her later works, bore the pseudonym Susan Coolidge. It is possible that she decided to begin writing for publication at this time because of her father's death and a consequent need to help support her family. *What Katy Did*, the first Katy book, was published in 1873 by Roberts Brothers, Louisa May Alcott's publisher, for whom Woolsey was a consulting editor. Woolsey, all of whose works appeared under the imprints of Roberts Brothers and their successors Little, Brown, was advertised and widely held to be another Alcott, in that she wrote wholesome domestic fiction directed primarily, though not exclusively, at girls,

which showed real children of both sexes with both faults and attractive liveliness. Though Katy Carr is the main character of *What Katy Did*, she is not the only character who is well developed. Woolsey portrays an entire family of five equally attractive children, as well as a next-door-neighbor girl who is frequently present for the Carr family activities. The story is somewhat autobiographical, set in a house much like the Woolseys' in Cleveland, with a family configuration of siblings much like that of the Woolseys, though Mrs. Woolsey did not die as Mrs. Carr has. Woolsey is adept at recalling the sometimes frenzied quality of children's games as well as their sincere contrition when the games go awry and an adult must intervene. Though Woolsey tames Katy's wild ways by giving her a back injury that confines her to bed for several years to reconsider her childish and thoughtless ways, she does not kill Katy's spirit of playfulness, which continues into the sequels. Katy may be the main focus of the story, but Woolsey has developed the characters of Katy's brothers well enough so that boys might also be interested in the book, a ploy Alcott used to widen her readership as well.

The second Katy book appeared in 1874. *What Katy Did at School*, a book more clearly of interest to an audience of girls, is also based on Woolsey's own experiences, this time at boarding school in Hanover. Katy is now called Miss Carr as befits her newfound dignity at age sixteen; she and her younger sister Clover are sent to school for a year so that they may avoid becoming prematurely aged by the care and concerns of running the Carr household. In this book Katy is a much improved, more thoughtful, much better behaved girl than she was in the earlier volume, but she is still the leader of her mates in games and plans that befit children who are nearly, but not quite, adults. At school the Carr sisters make the acquaintances of several characters who reappear in later books.

The third Katy book did not appear until 1886. In the intervening period Woolsey wrote many short stories for children which appeared in *St. Nicholas;* she compiled several collections of her short stories and poems for children, including *Eyebright* (1879) and *The Barberry Bush* (1893), made several trips to Europe, and traveled with Helen Hunt Jackson through the western United States. *What Katy Did Next* brings Katy to a Europe familiar to Woolsey, where Katy sees the sights and shows what a good, resourceful young woman she is. At the end of the book she is engaged to Ned Worthington (his worthiness is implied by his name), a young naval officer who is the brother of her trav-

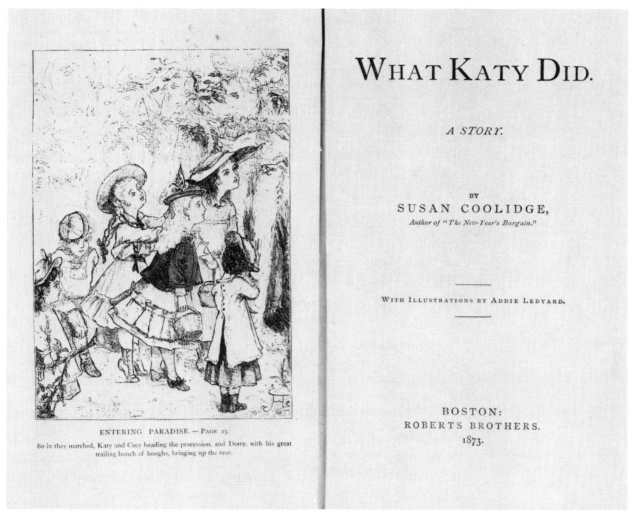

WHAT KATY DID.

A STORY.

BY
SUSAN COOLIDGE,
Author of "The New-Year's Bargain."

WITH ILLUSTRATIONS BY ADDIE LEDYARD.

BOSTON:
ROBERTS BROTHERS.
1873.

ENTERING PARADISE. — PAGE 23.

So in they marched, Katy and Cecy heading the procession, and Dorry, with his great
trailing bunch of boughs, bringing up the rear.

*Frontispiece and title page for Woolsey's book introducing the Carr children—Katy and her four sisters and brothers—as they adjust
to their mother's recent death (Baldwin Library, University of Florida Libraries)*

eling companion. Though the book might easily have degenerated into a travelogue, it does not. The incidents are still lively, though the character of Katy is much toned down in a way that might disappoint the readers of the earlier novels. By the end of the novel, she seems all too matronly, too concerned with motherhood and utterly divorced from her childhood pranks, to satisfy Katy's earlier followers, though the promise of a fairy-tale marriage and a happily-ever-after ending must have satisfied many others. Woolsey may have unconsciously shifted the later books to an older audience, though the logotype used in the Katy series continued to lure younger readers into reading them.

The last two Katy books shift their focus away from Katy to other members of the Carr family. At the beginning of *Clover* (1888), Katy's wedding

to Ned takes place, and she is only fleetingly visible in the rest of the series, although there are frequent references to her by her various siblings. It would seem that Woolsey lost interest in the prim young wife that Katy becomes and that she found few possibilities for such a presence in her story line. Interest in Clover, Katy's younger sister and the title character, takes over; she becomes a nurse to her younger brother Phil and takes him to Colorado to convalesce from an unspecified debilitating illness. There she sees the countryside, which Woolsey knew from her travels with Helen Hunt Jackson, is wooed by the local young men, and finally meets and marries an English gentleman who has adopted the life of a rancher. By the end of the fifth book in the series, *In the High Valley* (1890), all the remaining Carr sisters and brothers are married to worthy partners, most of whom they meet

These girls were Clover and Elsie Carr. — PAGE 7.

Frontispiece by Jessie McDermot for What Katy Did Next, *Woolsey's 1886 book based on her travels in Europe (Baldwin Library, University of Florida Libraries)*

in Colorado, and the family, with the exception of one brother who chooses to remain in the family homestead with his new English wife, has moved to Colorado. That there should be so many worthy partners of English origin in Colorado is evidence of a certain snobbery and unrealistic plotting on Woolsey's part; and her ravings over the beauty of the landscape through various mouthpieces in the two books become tiresome. Finally, the match-making and travelogue impulses overwhelm Woolsey's powers of invention; the books mostly trace the movements of various Carr family members cross-country. The happy valley in Colorado be-

comes a kind of paradise for all the Carrs, and the ending of the series is too pat and too exotic and unlikely in setting to be believable.

Woolsey's books for adults, including editions of the diary and letters of Fanney Burney (1880) and the correspondence of Jane Austen (1892), as well as her *A Short History of the City of Philadelphia* (1887), attest to the high literary and scholarly standards set by her family, which she carried on in spite of her lack of direct connection with university life. Her volumes of poetry, though hardly of the first order, reveal an acquaintance with the traditions of English and American verse ranging far beyond that fostered by the polite, superficial education generally deemed appropriate for ladies of her time. Her willingness to travel, and her ensuing voluminous writings about those travels, show an inquiring mind, eager to see the world and experience as much of it as possible. Her praise of Colorado at the end of the Katy books is typical of her lack of parochial fear about the world in general and her ability to appreciate the strange as well as the familiar.

Woolsey's greatest achievement in writing for children is *What Katy Did;* there she produces a family story for children younger than the adolescents that Alcott's *Little Women* portrays. Like Alcott, Woolsey tames her children, but unlike Alcott's characters, Woolsey's are more impulsive, more intractable, less overwhelmed by guilt when they fail. The overriding religious concern of Alcott's books is not present in the Katy books. Woolsey's skill at producing young characters who are lively, ingenious in their play, and basically good although limited by some faults is particularly important for its influence on such fictional characters as the heroines of Kate Douglas Wiggin's *Rebecca of Sunnybrook Farm* (1903) and Lucy Maud Montgomery's *Anne of Green Gables* (1908). Her influence on the family story may be observed in Harriet M. Lothrop's Five Little Peppers series.

Reference:

Frances C. Darling, "Susan Coolidge; 1835-1905," *Horn Book Magazine*, 35 (June 1959): 232-245.

Checklist for Further Reading

This bibliography focuses on studies that deal with eighteenth- and nineteenth-century American children's literature. Important general studies and critical works that have become standards in the study of children's literature have been included as well. Although major journals in the field of children's literature have been omitted from this checklist, they are valuable sources of further information on many of the authors covered in this volume. Among the best known and most useful periodicals are: Children's Literature Association *Quarterly; Children's Literature,* the annual journal of the Children's Literature Division of the Modern Language Association; *Children's Literature in Education; Horn Book Magazine;* and *Phaedrus: An International Journal of Children's Literature Research.* Articles from these journals have not been included in this bibliography, but several articles from journals outside the field of children's literature have been included when their importance to the topic equals that of monographic literature. Additional articles of this type may be identified in general and subject periodical indexes under headings related to children's literature.

Also of interest to students of eighteenth- and nineteenth-century American children's literature are *Children's Literature Abstracts,* no. 1- , May 1973- (Birmingham, England: International Federation of Library Associations, Sub-section on Library Work with Children); Virginia Haviland's *Children's Literature: A Guide to Reference Sources* (Washington, D.C.: Library of Congress, 1966) and its supplements; Suzanne Rahn's *Children's Literature: An Annotated Bibliography of the History and Criticism* (New York: Garland Publishing, 1981); and Elva S. Smith's *The History of Children's Literature: A Syllabus with Selected Bibliographies,* second edition, revised and enlarged by Margaret Hodges and Susan Steinfirst (Chicago: American Library Association, 1980).

AMERICAN BACKGROUNDS: HISTORICAL AND CRITICAL STUDIES

Attebery, Brian. *The Fantasy Tradition in American Literature: From Irving to Le Guin.* Bloomington: Indiana University Press, 1980.

Bingham, Jane, and Grayce Scholt. *Fifteen Centuries of Children's Literature: An Annotated Chronology of British and American Works in Historical Context.* Westport, Conn.: Greenwood Press, 1980.

Davis, Glenn. *Childhood and History in America.* New York: Psychohistory Press, 1976.

Halsey, Rosalie V. *Forgotten Books of the American Nursery; A History of the Development of the American Story-book.* Boston: Charles E. Goodspeed, 1911; republished, Detroit: Singing Tree, 1969.

Haviland, Virginia, and Margaret N. Coughlan. *Yankee Doodle's Literary Sampler of Prose, Poetry and Pictures.* New York: Crowell, 1974.

Jordan, Alice M. *From Rollo to Tom Sawyer and Other Papers.* Boston: Horn Book, 1948.

Kelly, R. Gordon. "American Children's Literature: An Historiographical Review." *American Literary Realism,* 6 (Spring 1973): 89-107.

Kiefer, Monica. *American Children Through Their Books, 1770-1835.* Philadelphia: University of Pennsylvania Press, 1948; republished, 1970.

Lystad, Mary. *From Dr. Mather to Dr. Seuss: 200 Years of American Books for Children.* Boston: G. K. Hall, 1980.

MacLeod, Anne Scott. *A Moral Tale: Children's Fiction and American Culture 1820-1860.* Hamden, Conn.: Archon Books, 1975.

Meigs, Cornelia L., and others. *A Critical History of Children's Literature: A Survey of Children's Books in English.* Revised ed. New York: Macmillan, 1969.

Thwaite, Mary F. *From Primer to Pleasure in Reading: An Introduction to the History of Children's Books in England from the Invention of Printing to 1914, with an Outline of Some Developments in Other Countries.* 2nd ed. London: Library Association, 1972; Boston: Horn Book, 1972.

Townsend, John Rowe. *Written for Children: An Outline of English Children's Literature.* Philadelphia: Lippincott, 1983.

CRITICAL STUDIES

Altstetter, M. F. "Early American Magazines for Children." *Peabody Journal of Education,* 19 (November 1941): 131-136.

Andrews, Siri, ed. *The Hewins Lectures, 1947-1962.* Boston: Horn Book, 1963.

Ashton, John. *Chap-Books of the Eighteenth Century.* London: Chatto & Windus, 1882; republished, New York: Kelley, 1968.

Barnes, Walter. *The Children's Poets: Analyses and Appraisals of the Greatest English and American Poets for Children.* Yonkers-on-Hudson: World, 1924.

Barry, Florence V. *A Century of Children's Books.* New York: Doran, 1923.

Broderick, Dorothy. *Image of the Black in Children's Fiction.* New York: Bowker, 1973.

Carpenter, Charles. *History of American Schoolbooks.* Philadelphia: University of Pennsylvania Press, 1963.

Carpenter, Humphrey, and Mari Prichard. *The Oxford Companion to Children's Literature.* New York: Oxford University Press, 1984.

Darling, Richard L. *The Rise of Children's Book Reviewing in America, 1865-1881.* New York: Bowker, 1968.

Duff, Annis. *"Longer Flight": A Family Grows Up with Books.* New York: Viking, 1955.

Egoff, Sheila, G. T. Stubbs, and L. F. Ashley, eds. *Only Connect: Readings on Children's Literature.* 2nd ed. New York: Oxford University Press, 1980.

Ellis, Alec. *A History of Children's Reading and Literature.* Oxford & New York: Pergamon Press, 1968.

Folmsbee, Beulah. *A Little History of the Horn Book.* Boston: Horn Book, 1942.

Fraser, James H., ed. *Society and Children's Literature.* Boston: Godine, in association with the American Library Association, 1978.

Fryatt, Norma R., ed. *A Horn Book Sampler on Children's Books and Reading: Selected from Twenty-five Years of Horn Book Magazine, 1924-1948.* Boston: Horn Book, 1959.

Gillespie, Margaret C. *Literature for Children: History and Trends.* Dubuque, Iowa: Brown, 1970.

Grey, J. E. "Historical Study of Children's Books." *History of Education Society Bulletin,* 7 (September 1971): 23-31.

Haviland, Virginia, ed. *Children and Literature: Views and Reviews.* Glenview, Ill.: Scott, Foresman, 1973.

Haviland. *The Travelogue Storybook of the Nineteenth Century.* Boston: Horn Book, 1950.

Hazard, Paul. *Books, Children and Men.* Translated by Marguerite Mitchell. 4th ed. Boston: Horn Book, 1960.

Hewins, Caroline M. *A Mid-Century Child and Her Books.* New York: Macmillan, 1926; republished, Detroit: Singing Tree, 1969.

Johnson, Clifton. *Old-time Schools and Schoolbooks.* New York: Macmillan, 1904; republished, New York: Dover, 1963.

Kelly, R. Gordon. *Mother Was a Lady: Self and Society in Selected American Children's Periodicals, 1865-1890.* Westport, Conn.: Greenwood Press, 1974.

Kolmer, E. "The McGuffey Readers: Exponents of American Classical Liberalism." *Journal of General Education,* 27 (Winter 1976): 309-316.

Livermore, George. *The Origin, History and Character of the New England Primer. Being a Series of Articles Contributed to "The Cambridge Chronicle."* New York: Heartman, 1915.

Mahony, Bertha E., and Elinor Whitney. *Realms of Gold in Children's Books.* Garden City: Doubleday, Doran, 1929.

Moore, Anne Carroll. *My Roads to Childhood: Views and Reviews of Children's Books.* Boston: Horn Book, 1961.

Rayward, W. Boyd. "What Shall They Read? A Historical Perspective." *Wilson Library Bulletin,* 51 (October 1976): 146-153.

Richardson, Selma K., ed. *Research About Nineteenth-Century Children and Books: Portrait Studies.* Monograph No. 17. Urbana: University of Illinois, Graduate School of Library Science, 1980.

Robinson, Evelyn R., ed. *Readings About Children's Literature.* New York: McKay, 1966.

Shaffer, Ellen. "The Children's Books of the American Sunday-School Union." *American Book Collector,* 17 (October 1966): 21-28.

Smith, Lillian H. *The Unreluctant Years.* Chicago: American Library Association, 1953.

Tucker, Nicholas. *The Child and the Book: A Psychological and Literary Exploration.* Cambridge & New York: Cambridge University Press, 1981.

Weiss, Harry B. *A Book About Chapbooks: The People's Literature of Bygone Times.* Trenton, N.J., 1942; republished, Hatboro, Pa.: Folklore Association, 1969.

Wishy, Bernard. *The Child and the Republic: The Dawn of Modern American Child Nurture.* Philadelphia: University of Pennsylvania Press, 1967.

Yolen, Jane. *Touch Magic: Fantasy, Faerie and Folklore in the Literature of Childhood.* New York: Philomel Books, 1981.

BIBLIOGRAPHIES, COLLECTIONS, AND CATALOGUES

American Antiquarian Society. *Exhibit of American Children's Books Printed Before 1800.* Worcester, Mass.: American Antiquarian Society, 1928.

Blanck, Jacob N. *Peter Parley to Penrod: A Bibliographical Description of the Best-Loved American Juvenile Books.* Cambridge, Mass.: Research Classics, 1961.

Bobbitt, Mary R. *A Bibliography of Etiquette Books Published in America Before 1900.* New York: New York Public Library, 1947.

Davidson, Gustav. *First Editions in American Juvenilia and Problems in Their Identification.* Chicago: Normandie House, 1939.

de Vries, Leonard. *Flowers of Delight; Culled . . . from the Osborne Collection of Early Children's Books. An Agreeable Garland of Prose and Poetry for the Instruction and Amusement of Little Masters and Misses and Their Distinguished Parents.* New York: Pantheon, 1965.

Erisman, Fred. "American Regional Juvenile Literature, 1870-1910: An Annotated Bibliography." *American Literary Realism,* 6 (Spring 1973): 109-122.

Field, Carolyn W., ed. *Special Collections in Children's Literature.* Revised ed. Chicago: American Library Association, 1982.

Neuburg, Victor E. *Chapbooks: A Guide to Reference Material on English, Scottish and American Chapbook Literature of the Eighteenth and Nineteenth Centuries.* 2nd ed. London: Woburn Press, 1972.

Nietz, John A. *Old Textbooks: Spelling, Grammar, Reading, Arithmetic, Geography, American History, Civil Government, Physiology, Penmanship, Art, Music, as Taught in the Common Schools from Colonial Days to 1900.* Pittsburgh: University of Pittsburgh Press, 1961.

Pierpont Morgan Library. *Early Children's Books and Their Illustration.* Boston: Godine, 1975.

Quayle, Eric. *The Collector's Book of Children's Books.* New York: Potter, 1971.

Rosenbach, Abraham S. W. *Books and Bidders; The Adventures of a Bibliophile.* Boston: Little, Brown, 1927.

Rosenbach. *Early American Children's Books with Bibliographical Descriptions of the Books in His Private Collection.* Portland, Maine: Southworth Press, 1933; republished, New York: Kraus, 1966.

St. John, Judith. *The Osborne Collection of Early Children's Books, 1476-1910: A Catalogue.* 2 vols. Toronto: Toronto Public Library, 1958, 1975.

Targ, William, ed. *Bibliophile in the Nursery.* Cleveland & New York: World, 1957.

Welch, d'Alte A. *A Bibliography of American Children's Books Printed Prior to 1821.* Worcester, Mass.: American Antiquarian Society, 1972.

PROFILES: PUBLISHERS AND ILLUSTRATORS

Abbott, Jacob. *The Harper Establishment, or, How the Story Books Are Made.* New York: Harper, 1855.

Bland, David. *A History of Book Illustration.* 2nd ed. Berkeley: University of California Press, 1969.

Gaine, Hugh. *The Journals of Hugh Gaine, Printer.* Edited by Paul Leicester Ford. 2 vols. New York: Dodd, Mead, 1902; republished, New York: Arno, 1970.

Hamilton, Sinclair. *Early American Book Illustrators and Wood Engravers, 1670-1870; A Catalogue of a Collection of American Books, Illustrated for the Most Part with Woodcuts and Wood Engravings, in the Princeton Library.* Princeton: Princeton University Press, 1968.

Johannsen, Albert. *The House of Beadle and Adams and Its Dime and Nickel Novels, the Story of a Vanished Literature.* 2 vols. Norman: University of Oklahoma Press, 1950.

Marble, Annie Russell. *From 'Prentice to Patron: The Life Story of Isaiah Thomas.* New York: Appleton, 1935.

Meyer, Susan E. *A Treasury of the Great Children's Book Illustrators.* New York: Abrams, 1983.

Miller, Bertha (Mahony), Louise P. Latimer, and Beulah Folmsbee, comps. *Illustrators of Children's Books, 1774-1945.* Boston: Horn Book, 1947.

Muir, Percival H. *Victorian Illustrated Books.* New York: Praeger, 1971.

Pitz, Henry C., ed. *A Treasury of American Book Illustration.* New York: American Studio Books and Watson-Guptill Publications, 1947.

Shipton, Clifford K. *Isaiah Thomas, Printer, Patriot and Philanthropist, 1749-1831.* Rochester, New York: Leo Hart, 1948.

Weiss, Harry Bischoff. *The Printers and Publishers of Children's Books in New York City, 1698-1830.* New York: New York Public Library, 1948.

Whalley, Joyce Irene. *Cobwebs to Catch Flies: Illustrated Books for the Nursery and Schoolroom, 1700-1900.* Berkeley: University of California Press, 1975.

Contributors

Marilyn F. Apseloff .... *Kent State University*
Norma Bagnall ....*Missouri Western State College*
Carol Billman ....*Kemblesville, Pennsylvania*
Phyllis Bixler ....*Kansas State University*
Paul Eugen Camp .... *University of South Florida*
Motley Deakin ....*University of Florida*
J. B. Dobkin... *University of South Florida*
Carol A. Doll .... *University of South Carolina*
Ken Donelson...*Arizona State University*
Carol Gay...*Youngstown State University*
David L. Greene .... *Piedmont College*
Michael Patrick Hearn ....*New York, New York*
Edward J. Jennerich... *Virginia Intermont College*
Marilyn H. Karrenbrock .... *University of Tennessee*
Marilyn Kaye ....*St. John's University*
Hugh T. Keenan ....*Georgia State University*
Millicent Lenz..*State University of New York at Albany*
Rebecca Lukens..*Miami University*
Ruth K. MacDonald .... *New Mexico State University*
Jill P. May ....*Purdue University*
Susan E. Miller .... *Orlando, Florida*
Anita Moss...*University of North Carolina at Charlotte*
Taimi M. Ranta ....*Illinois State University*
David L. Russell ....*Ferris State College*
M. Sarah Smedman...*University of North Carolina at Charlotte*
Charlotte Spivack .... *University of Massachusetts*
Douglas Street ....*Texas A & M University*
Mary-Agnes Taylor ....*Southwest Texas State University*
Malcolm Usrey .... *Clemson University*
Mark Irwin West ....*University of North Carolina at Charlotte*
Virginia L. Wolf .... *University of Wisconsin-Stout*

Cumulative Index

Dictionary of Literary Biography, Volumes 1-42
Dictionary of Literary Biography Yearbook, 1980-1984
Dictionary of Literary Biography Documentary Series, Volumes 1-4

Cumulative Index

DLB before number: *Dictionary of Literary Biography*, Volumes 1-42
Y before number: *Dictionary of Literary Biography Yearbook*, 1980-1984
DS before number: *Dictionary of Literary Biography Documentary Series*, Volumes 1-4

A

M

N

O

P

S

U

V